SPORT IN AMERICAN CULTURE

From Ali to X-Games

SPORT IN AMERICAN CULTURE

From Ali to X-Games

JOYCE D. DUNCAN

A B C · C L I O

Santa Barbara, California   Denver, Colorado   Oxford, England

Library of Congress Cataloging-in-Publication Data

Duncan, Joyce, 1946–
    Sport in American culture : from Ali to X-games / Joyce D. Duncan.
        p. cm.
    Includes bibliographical references and index.
    ISBN 1-57607-024-7 (hardback : alk. paper) — ISBN 1-85109-559-4 (eBook)
    1. Sports—Sociological aspects—United States—Encyclopedias. I. Title.

    GV706.2.D86 2004
    306.4'83'0973—dc22

                                                          2004017583

08   07   06   05   04   10 9 8 7 6 5 4 3 2 1

This book is also available on the World Wide Web as an eBook.
Visit abc-clio.com for details.

ABC-CLIO, Inc.
130 Cremona Drive, P.O. Box 1911
Santa Barbara, California 93116-1911

This book is printed on acid-free paper.
Manufactured in the United States of America

Contents

Preface, **xi**
Introduction, **xiii**

Sport in American Culture
From Ali to X-Games

Preface

From Canada to Latin America and throughout the fifty states, sport is everywhere. It permeates our language, our conversation and our literature; it consumes the evening news; it bedecks our apparel; it accounts for our leisure time; it accounts for our popular culture and creates material culture; it provides us with heroes for the long haul and for the short term; it offers us national icons and national disgraces; it gives hope and false hope to our children; it boosts our national economy as it depletes our own. In short, sport in the Americas is more than a metaphor for life; it is life.

The Encyclopedia of Sport in American Culture reflects the myriad ways in which sport is as necessary as the fine arts to the cultural air we breathe. Although there are many works on the market that incorporate facts, statistics, how-to's, and biographies of sport figures, this work is unique in that the emphasis is on the cultural impact that sport has had on American culture. The word "sport," rather than "sports," was selected purposely to connote the inclusion of more than those games played for public performance and for financial gain.

Topics were selected by the editorial board (with a few suggested by writers along the way) to reflect that unbreakable tie between our cultural world and the world of sport. The editors realize that the list is not now, and probably never could be, complete. The sport world, like life, is constantly changing; new heroes appear and others fall overnight. We hope that the selection is broad enough that each reader will find some

person or topic of interest and that readers will forgive any oversights on our parts. It is our hope that the topics reflect an overview of the industry, the cultural connections between sport and society, and some of the major players making those connections.

The Encyclopedia of Sport in American Culture is a work essential to sport researchers, academics, students, and sport fans. It has been compiled by scholars, professionals, and sport enthusiasts from all over the world and edited by a board involved in sport literature, sport history, and popular culture. Its emphasis is on the process whereby sport has created billion-dollar industries and millionaire superstars; has had an impact on television, literature, and film; and has invented role models, created heroes, and bolstered national pride. There is no area of culture in the Americas that has not been touched in some way by the adoration of athletes and athletics.

This work includes standard biographical information on sport heroes but hones those biographies to emphasize the individual cultural impact of each person selected. It includes the customary divisions addressing individual sports, but it demonstrates how each of those sports has changed the way Americans think about society. It addresses such phenomena as the billion-dollar athletic apparel industry, particularly the monies garnered through the sales of sneakers; the way sport has become big business; the importance of sport statistics as an educational tool; the way sport has affected gender and racial views; and how it has helped define national identity. In addition to these expected categories, the work also addresses such unusual areas of cultural impact as Wheaties, Hula-Hoops, fetishes, comic books, music, and religion. The bottom-line question the editors have used as a guideline in the creation of this work is this: why do Americans who have no intention of running pay $80 for running shoes?

Obviously, a work of this scope requires a variety of thanks to those who made it possible. Not the least of those is a hearty thank-you to the inventors of the Internet, since this work is essentially a product of that technology. Writers were "interviewed" and contracted through e-mail, an undertaking that those in publishing admitted was unique when this process began. Much

thanks goes to ABC-CLIO and Alicia Merritt for long-suffering faith, to the editorial board for mentoring and encouragement, and to the contributors for diligence, for meeting deadlines, and for fine work. On a personal note, I would also like to thank Don Johnson, Lyle Olsen, and Jack Higgs of the Sport Literature Association, without whom my education in sport and life would be less well rounded; to Tim Morris, Jeff Segrave, and Richard Olsen for going above and beyond; and to Jerry Nave and Teresa Brooks-Taylor for the moral support furnished by listening to my periodic whimpering.

We hope you enjoy the result.

—*Joyce Duncan*

Introduction

Sport as Cultural Artifact

To define sport as cultural artifact is to assert that sport somehow reflects the larger culture in unique and important ways. This encyclopedia is a tribute to the insights derived from such a perspective. Those studying sport as cultural artifact move beyond describing how a sport is played or how it meets the requirements of a specific definition. Instead, they analyze how particular features of the sport, such as rules and equipment, give insight into the larger culture. Often these insights focus on the ideals and core values of a culture or subculture. In elaborating on sport as cultural artifact, it is important to define what is meant by both terms.

Culture can be viewed as the total system of meanings within which groups of people live their lives. It is sometimes called a "web of meaning." For instance, clothing has the practical function of keeping one safe from cold or direct sun. But clothing is also symbolic—it has meaning beyond its function. Clothing often reflects moral codes on such issues as nudity and promiscuity, and it often indicates the wearer's social or economic standing. It might give insight into religious beliefs or aspects of the wearer's personality. Clothing choices are influenced by, and are often indicative of, the culture in which the wearer lives.

Culture is conveyed through signs—things that stand for other things. Some signs are nonverbal or visual, such as when a referee signals the penalty for a personal foul in basketball. Some signs are spoken or written words called symbols, such as the word "football" or the *K*'s that hang from a stadium when a top pitcher is striking out batters.

There are also signs, rich in meaning, called artifacts. When referring to cultural artifacts, there is a natural tendency to think of archeology. That reference is important but incomplete. The act of trying to decipher what a culture was like based on pots, tools, and scattered documents has much in common with analyzing various sports by examining the equipment used and a rule book. Cultural artifacts can be very recent and diverse. They can give insight into the current culture, not just a culture of the past. Most cultural scholars take a broad definition of "artifact."

In *Rhetoric in Popular Culture,* Barry Brummett argues that artifacts are the material signs of abstract groups. "Football fans," for instance, is an abstract group. Fans of the Green Bay Packers and of other teams are unique subgroups of football fans. But how can one spot a Green Bay Packer fan? What clothing, activities, and paraphernalia would be the material, physical, and observable evidence identifying that group or a football fan in general? Perhaps the person is wearing a Green Bay Packer football jersey featuring the number of a favored player. Perhaps he or she is wearing the famous wedge of cheese, a highly symbolic head ornament. Packer fans may take part in tailgating before the game if they are fortunate enough to attend the game, or they may invite other fans to their homes to watch the game. The foods served may become "traditional" and symbolically tied to the event. As the game proceeds, fans at home or in the stands may engage in behaviors they feel will influence the outcome of the game. Altering one's dress to invoke a change in momentum—such as wearing rally caps—is but one example of the symbolic dimensions of fan behavior that reflect cultural ideals. The belief that the intensity of fan commitment can change the outcome of a game is not rational or logical. But, for many, face painting and chanting are tied to the cultural value that effort can overcome "fate." This can be traced back to the Puritan work ethic that is part of U.S. myth and culture.

Various areas of sport can be interpreted as cultural artifacts, including media coverage, sport figures, specific sporting events, and the games themselves. Scholars have examined sport coverage by the media by comparing *Sports Illustrated*'s depictions of women athletes and men athletes. Others have scrutinized coverage for racial bias and for the ways core U.S. values are celebrated. Sometimes scholars treat a significant sport figure as an artifact. Muhammad Ali, for example, is not just a person; he is also a symbol of cultural ideals because he is an Olympic gold medal winner and professional champion and because he is highly individualistic. He was controversial because of his decision to convert to Islam and because he was often outspoken about issues of race and politics and boisterous in his interviews. To answer the question of why Ali was chosen to be the final torchbearer of the Atlanta Olympics, one must look beyond the private citizen who was good at boxing. One must consider the fact that he is a material sign or symbol of what it means to be a member of several abstract groups: American, black American, athlete, activist, and others.

Sporting events can also be considered as cultural artifacts. Michael Real, writing in the *Journal of Communication*, is one of many scholars who have examined specific events in terms of the way they reflect core U.S. values. His analysis of the Super Bowl as mythic spectacle demonstrates how various features of the event itself and the media coverage of the event embody core U.S. values. Clear heroes are defined with the broad-cast, which includes a collective or communal dimension. Typically, the Super Bowl is viewed with friends and transformed into a social event. Other analysts have examined less obvious events, such as minor league baseball games, Little League games, and even para-sport events, such as the National Basketball Association (NBA) draft.

Finally, sport itself may be examined as cultural artifact. Allen Guttmann in *From Ritual to Record: The Nature of Modern Sports* has made insightful connections between the characteristics of baseball and football and their association with America's agrarian and industrial cultures. For example, baseball is played in a field and does not use a clock. The sport emphasizes individual play punctuated by moments of cooperative action. This reflects values central to an agrarian or rural lifestyle. Football is far more collective. There are huddles between each play, and each person has a far more specialized task than in baseball. In addition, the clock plays a central role in the playing of the game. These features reflect the nation's shift from an agrarian culture to an industrial one.

Sport is central to every culture, and certain sports have gained universal appeal while others have strong ties to particular cultures. The various ways in which fans, players, and media engage a particular sport can often be quite revealing about the larger culture from which they come.

—*Richard K. Olsen, Jr.*
Department of Communication Studies
University of North Carolina at Wilmington

For further reading:

Brummett, Barry. 1994. *Rhetoric in Popular Culture.* New York: St. Martin's Press.

Guttmann, Allen. 1978. *From Ritual to Record: The Nature of Modern Sports.* New York: Columbia University Press.

Novak, Michael. 1985. "American Sports, American Virtues." In *American Sport Culture: The Humanistic Dimensions,* edited by Wiley L. Umphlett, 34–49. Cranbury, NJ: Associated University Presses.

Real, Michael. 1975. "Superbowl: Mythic Spectacle." *Journal of Communication* 25: 31–43.

AARON, HENRY "HANK" LOUIS
(1934–)

As the first to surpass Babe Ruth's major league record of 714 home runs, Hank Aaron, longtime outfielder for the Milwaukee, later Atlanta, Braves, became not only baseball's home-run king but also a symbol of the excellence that black athletes achieved while struggling for integration. The soft-spoken son of a Mobile, Alabama, shipyard worker, Hank Aaron was an unlikely spokesman for civil rights, but his skill as a long-ball hitter yielded him spectacular opportunities to promote equal rights throughout his career. One of eight children, he learned to hit homemade baseballs, fashioned from discarded golf balls wrapped in nylon hose. In 1952, as major league baseball was beginning to integrate, Aaron, at age eighteen, signed his first professional contract with the Indianapolis Clowns of the Negro Leagues. He and Ernie Banks were the last two superstar players to emigrate from the Negro Leagues, joining the likes of Jackie Robinson, Larry Doby, Satchel Paige, Willie Mays, Roy Campanella, and Monte Irvin.

Not long after Aaron signed with the Milwaukee Braves, he experienced his first civil rights challenge, the integration of the South Atlantic (Sally) League. The Sally League was a Class A League in the heart of the South with a fifty-year tradition of excluding black players. Aaron and four other African American players broke the league color line in 1953, to the dismay of segregationists. He and the other black players endured death threats, rock throwing, and racial epithets in addition to the traditional indignities of segregation: having to lodge and eat at separate establishments, to drink from separate water fountains, to use separate showers, and to suffer constant surveillance and abuse.

Even after he was added to the Milwaukee Braves roster in 1954 and led Milwaukee to a World Series title in 1957, Aaron was forced to lodge at segregated facilities during the Braves' spring training in Bradenton, Florida. In 1961, he and other black players protested their separate accommodations to the Braves' management, who ultimately agreed to find integrated lodgings for all their players. In 1966, he spoke even more forcefully about race in a *Jet* magazine cover story entitled "Henry Aaron Blasts Racism in Baseball."

The integration of the Sally League and of the Braves' training facilities and Aaron's occasional statements about race in the 1960s were only premonitions of the struggles he would endure during the 1973 and 1974 baseball seasons, when he

> *Although Hank Aaron broke Babe Ruth's home-run record, acclaim was not forthcoming. On the contrary, he was the target of racial slurs and death threats, and many considered it a travesty that a black man would even attempt to unseat the great Babe Ruth.*

Hank Aaron holds up the ball that broke Babe Ruth's home-run record April 8, 1974. In the fourth inning, Aaron hit the ball over the wall for the 715th record-breaking home run off Dodger pitcher Al Downing. With Aaron is his personal bodyguard, Calvin Wardlow.
(BETTMANN/CORBIS)

approached and surpassed Babe Ruth's home-run record. His pursuit of the record attracted widespread media coverage and massive public attention. He received some 930,000 pieces of mail during 1973 and early 1974, including many hundreds of letters containing racial slurs. Because he received death threats during the home-run chase, he was constantly escorted by an Atlanta police officer, and the Federal Bureau of Investigation looked into a plot to kidnap his daughter, who was then in college. When he hit the record-smashing homer, number 715, off Al Downing of the Los Angeles Dodgers on the rainy night of

April 8, 1974, Aaron's first words were "Thank God, it's over."

After retirement, Aaron lived in Atlanta, where he served as a senior vice president and special assistant to Braves president Stan Kasten. He was also a vice president and board member of Turner Broadcasting.

—*Jeff Powers-Beck*

See also: Banks, Ernest "Ernie"; Negro Baseball Leagues; Robinson, Jack Roosevelt "Jackie"; Ruth, George Herman "Babe," Jr.

For further reading:
Rennert, Richard Scott. 1993. *Baseball Great Henry Aaron.* New York: Chelsea House.

ABDUL-JABBAR, KAREEM
(1947–)

Born Ferdinand Lewis Alcindor Jr. on April 16, 1947, Kareem Abdul-Jabbar is among the greatest centers and overall players in collegiate and professional basketball. When he retired in 1989, no National Basketball Association (NBA) player held as many individual or team records, including most points scored and most games played. As a college player and as a professional, the former New Yorker helped the city of Los Angeles sustain its winning tradition from the late 1960s through the 1980s as both the University of California, Los Angeles (UCLA) Bruins and the Los Angeles Lakers won a string of championships. Although often regarded as the elder statesman—or "old man," according to some younger players—Abdul-Jabbar was instrumental in shaping the modern version of the NBA, both on and off the court.

Known for his strict regimen and discipline, the seven-foot-two center brought grace, agility, and versatility to the game, distancing himself from the more plodding, slow-footed players in the NBA's early years. His signature shot, the "skyhook," was nearly impossible to defend against due to his height and agility. When the Lakers added point guard Earvin "Magic" Johnson to the roster in 1979, the duo created an up-tempo, showy style of playing, dubbed "showtime," a performance that fans now expect from the modern NBA.

Throughout his career, Kareem Abdul-Jabbar used his time away from basketball to make bold and often controversial political statements. He authored four books that deliberately and consciously challenged the stereotype that black male athletes were less than intelligent. Furthermore, the former Laker produced and starred in a number of films and television shows, many of which represented him and the African American community in a positive and authoritative manner.

—*La'Tonya Rease Miles*

See also: Basketball; National Basketball Association

For further reading:

Abdul-Jabbar, Kareem. 1990. *Kareem*. New York: Warner Books.

———. 2000. *A Season on the Reservation: My Sojourn with the White Mountain Apache*. New York: William Morrow.

Abdul-Jabbar, Kareem, and Peter Knobler. 1993. *Giant Steps: The Autobiography of Kareem Abdul-Jabbar*. New York: Bantam.

ACADEMIC SKEPTICISM OF SPORT

Although some faculty members support college athletics, there are many who are concerned about the increasing commercialization of and emphasis on intercollegiate sports on campus. Certainly, there is a great deal of resentment when faculty members compare their incomes to those of coaches, even at small schools, or when honors students realize that their scholarships do not include the same perks, including free meals, as the athletic scholarships of many of their classmates. There is, in fact, much skepticism regarding the performance of star athletes in the class-

room. Faculty members share stories of telephone calls from coaches asking them to extend "courtesy" to team members so they will not lose their eligibility to compete. Such skepticism is increased when nonathletes on campus note that various tutorial services and computer labs exist for "athletes only" to help them pass their exams.

The general skepticism arises over the role of athletics on campus and the true purpose of colleges and universities. To most academics, it seems obvious that, at best, athletics should be an adjunct to the overall goal of transmitting knowledge, skills, and perhaps even wisdom from one generation to another. There may be arguments over whose knowledge, skills, and wisdom are to be transmitted and even over what constitutes those desired ends; however, most academics do not consider sport as one of the components that indicates the essential function of an institution of higher learning.

Academics also tend to be increasingly concerned about the use of sport as a means of student recruitment. The "bread and circuses" atmosphere smacks of commercialism and the corporate ideal of giving customers what they want, whereas education has generally sought to give students what they need to master essential disciplines.

Interestingly, academic skepticism of sport finds a reflection in a wider arena. The public increasingly views professional athletes as wealthy and selfish or as violating cultural and legal norms with increasing impunity. In fact, a survey by *Sports Media Challenge* found that 70 percent of professional sport teams and 70 percent of collegiate athletic programs had experienced a crisis related to athletes' mistakes off the playing field in the year preceding the survey (http://www.sports mediachallenge.com/ 1998). There is even doubt regarding the good deeds of athletes since the Giving Back Fund, a consulting group established in 1997 to help athletes manage their foundations, has helped some athletes seek redemption through giving money in meaningful ways.

The ruling by the National Collegiate Athletic Association (NCAA) that athletes could hold part-time employment aroused much suspicion that they were getting more than the allowed amount. Furthermore, when the NCAA allowed these jobs to be administered by athletic boosters, even coaches of Division I teams were upset. It was feared that there would be insufficient policing to enforce the $2,000-per-year limit on what athletes could earn in addition to a full scholarship.

The issue of boosters further fuels skepticism of college athletics. Boosters are typically suspected of finding ways around NCAA recruiting and scholarship regulations. Such benefits to athletes as no-show jobs, under-the-table payments, free trips and meals, and even cars have all been linked to boosters. Each new piece of evidence of favoritism for athletes adds to academics' cynicism toward intercollegiate sport. They note that boosters, including generous alumni, tend to give more money for athletic facilities than for campus libraries, leading them to question whether the tail is wagging the dog instead of vice versa.

—*Frank A. Salamone*

See also: Altruism and Activism

For further reading:

Erardi, John. 1998. "Jobs-for-Athletes Decision Draws Skepticism." *Cincinnati Enquirer,* April 23.

Krupa, Greg. 1998. "Fund Helps Athletes Win at the Game of Charity." *Boston Globe,* August 9.

Sports Media Challenge. 1998. http://www.sports mediachallenge.com/. Accessed July 2004.

ACADEMICS AND SPORT

Since the Greeks decreed the value of a sound mind in a sound body, there has been an uneasy relationship between academics and athletics. The ideal of the scholar-athlete exists in fiction far more than in everyday scholastic life. Although there have undeniably been athletes who excelled on the field and in the classroom, like the Rhodes scholar and for-mer U.S. senator Bill Bradley, on high school and college campuses, sporting and academic pursuits are more often in opposition than in alignment. The relationship is often ambivalent at best.

> *National Collegiate Athletic Association records clearly indicate that known and legitimate student aid to athletes tops $100 million per year.*

A coach who demands academic excellence from his or her athletes continues to be newsworthy. The Associated Press, for example, thought the story of a Richmond, California, high school coach who benched players who were falling behind academically merited national distribution. (Locke, 1999) More typical, however, are cases of preferential treatment—extra tutoring, courtesy passing grades, and other favors—given to student-athletes. Many colleges have openly noted the value of a winning team to overall recruitment. Winning teams bring new students to campus, and admissions officers routinely use team success as a promotional feature. Thus administrators and alumni, as well as many faculty members, are often willing to tolerate substandard performance from star athletes for the "good of the whole."

The National Collegiate Athletic Association (NCAA) attempts to ensure that the proper relationship is maintained between athletics and academics at member institutions. The association was inaugurated in response to the many injuries sustained by college football players attempting the flying wedge, the major offensive play in football in 1905. Because some of those injuries resulted in death, many colleges eliminated football from their athletic program, and there were serious efforts to abolish the game from intercollegiate competition. Only intervention by President Theodore Roosevelt saved the game. He called representatives of thirteen institutions to a conference, and from that gathering the Intercollegiate Athletic Association of the United States (IAAUS) was born. The IAAUS was the forerunner of the present NCAA, which was founded in 1910.

In 1921, the NCAA organized its first national championship, the National Collegiate Track and Field Championships. The association grew along with college athletics, but abuses grew as well. After World War II, the NCAA set up a "sanity code" that was supposed to curb the egregious abuses in recruiting and offering financial aid to student-athletes. In 1952, the group established a national headquarters in Kansas City, Missouri, and began regulating television coverage of college sport. Since then, the NCAA has created three competitive divisions for intercollegiate athletics, adding one for women in 1980, and strengthened enforcement policies.

The Internet is also becoming an invaluable aid to colleges for finding new athletes and to athletes for locating schools that match their abilities. A number of Internet services specialize in matching student-athletes to institutions of higher education. NCAA records clearly indicate that known and legitimate student aid to athletes tops $100 million per year. ("NCAA," 2000) However, the percentage of athletes who receive scholarships and graduate is far below the number of those graduating on academic scholarship.

The prevalence and influence of sport in U.S. society is immense. It begins early in life. Similarly, pressure on schools to accommodate students who do not meet academic standards also begins at an early age. That pressure often comes from parents, who argue that children should not be punished for low academic standing and that participation in sport will help keep student-athletes in school and will lead to better grades. It is also pointed out that athletics can enable poor students to get into college so that they can, perhaps, make it into professional leagues or make contacts leading to future employment.

For many alumni, athletics serve as a means of staying in contact with their alma mater, and they provide an emotional tie that relieves the tedium of the humdrum, everyday world. Donations thus follow victories and successful seasons. Many Americans judge colleges and universities by the success of their teams rather than by the quality of their research or instruction. The corruption and educational failure that frequently accompany college athletics programs is often viewed as part of the price paid for a well-rounded college experience.

—*Frank A. Salamone*

See also: Academic Skepticism of Sport

For further reading:

Funk, Gary D. 1991. *Major Violation: The Unbalanced Priorities in Athletics and Academics.* Champaign, IL: Leisure Press.

Lapchick, Richard. E. 1987. *On the Mark: Putting the Student Back in Student-Athlete.* Lexington, MA: Lexington Books.

Locke, Michelle. 1999. "Coach Benches Winning Basketball Team for Poor Grades." Associated Press, Jan 9, np.

"NCAA Group to Vote on Cutting Summer Recruiting and Scholarship Limits." 2000. Associated Press, April 9, np.

Zimblast, Andrew W. 1999. *Unpaid Professionals: Commercialism and Conflict in Big-Time College Sports.* Princeton: Princeton University Press.

ADOLESCENT SPORT NOVELS

For more than a century, sport novels for teenagers have provided young readers with books ranging from tales of game action to literary coming-of-age stories. Sport novels for teenagers were popular long before writers of serious adult fiction turned their attention to sport. One of the earliest adolescent sport novels, Charles M. Sheldon's *Captains of the Orient Baseball Nine*, appeared in 1882. It was followed by a flood of sport books by pulp writers, such as Gilbert Patten, Edward Stratemeyer, Ralph Henry Barbour, and William Heyliger, from the turn of the century to the early 1940s. Early instances of sport novels focused on game-related events, with play-by-play sport action making up a significant part of their texts.

Sport novels have continued to find an audience among teenage readers. Authors such as Thomas Dygard, Matt Christopher, and Dean Hughes have written sport novels that appeal to young persons who enjoy reading about athletic competition and games. Christopher's and Hughes's novels appeared as series books, thus capitalizing on the late-twentieth-century juvenile and young-adult marketing trends.

Many of John Tunis's works for adolescents, including *All American* (1942), foreshadowed a new variety of sport novels for teenagers: stories that used sport as a background setting for larger social conflicts. The sport novels of Robert Lipsyte, Bruce Brooks, Chris Crutcher, Will Weaver, and others are a kind of athletic Bildungsroman and are less concerned with sport action than they are with an athlete-protagonist moving from adolescence to maturity. Some of these novels have broad appeal; one of them, Brooks's *The Moves Make the Man* (1984), was a 1985 Newbury Honor Book. The genre generally tends to focus on male readers, especially on reluctant readers.

The passage of Title IX created more opportunities for female athletes and a corresponding increase in the potential audience for sport novels for adolescent women. Though still heavily outnumbered by sport novels for young men, the works in this genre with women protagonists or about women's sport have gained ground since R. R. Knudson's *Zanballer* (1972), a novel about an athletic high school girl, first appeared. *In Lane Three, Alex Archer* (1989), by Tessa Duder, is a noteworthy and well-written example of an athletic Bildungsroman with a female protagonist.

—*Chris Crowe*

See also: Literature, Sport in; Merriwell, Frank

For further reading:
Brooks, Bruce. 1984. *The Moves Make the Man: A Novel*. New York: Harper & Row.
———. 1993. *Boys Will Be*. New York: Henry Holt.
Crutcher, Chris. 1995. *Ironman: A Novel*. New York: Greenwillow Books.
Lipsyte, Robert. 2003. *The Contender*. New York: HarperCollins.

AEROBICS, AS EXERCISE

Based on cardiovascular activity, aerobics spawned the fitness craze. Kenneth H. Cooper, an Air Force surgeon, coined the term "aerobics" in a book by that title published in 1968. Cooper viewed aerobic activity as the cornerstone of physical fitness, and he devised a cardiovascular fitness test based on the ability to run a mile and a half in twelve minutes, a skill borrowed from military training. Soundly endorsed by the medical community of the 1970s, the program contributed to the popularity of running during the decade.

Inspired by Cooper's work, Jacki Sorenson, a dancer turned fitness expert, is credited with inventing aerobic dancing for armed forces television in 1968. Another pioneer, Judi Sheppard Missett, began teaching classes in 1969 and created Jazzercise, a form of aerobic dance combining jazz and cardiovascular activity. By the 1980s, the term "aerobics" had become synonymous with a particular form of cardiovascular exercise combining traditional calisthenics with popular dance styles in a class-based format geared toward people who are not customarily involved in athletic endeavor, primarily women.

By 1972, aerobic dance had its own professional association for instructors, the International Dance Exercise Association (IDEA). Aerobics became a national trend in the 1980s with the growth of the fitness video market, which actress Jane Fonda popularized with her first tape in 1982. By 1990, aerobics was beginning to diversify into a plethora of specialized forms tailored to different exercise regimens, such as low-impact aerobics, circuit training, plyometrics, step aerobics, water aerobics, boxing, and sliding. Yet by the mid-1990s, fitness professionals were reporting declining attendance in aerobics classes due to increasing levels of boredom among physically fit women, who began looking to other sports and to more-intensive workout routines, such as weight lifting and running, to keep themselves in shape.

—*Stephanie Dyer*

See also: Fitness Marketing and Magazines

For further reading:

Cooper, Kenneth H. 1985. *The Aerobics Program for Total Well-Being.* New York: Bantam.

ALI, MUHAMMAD (1942–)

Former heavyweight boxing champion Muhammad Ali remains one of the most recognized figures in sport, both for his accomplishments in the ring and for his influence on the civil rights and antiwar movements of the 1960s. Self-described as "the greatest," Muhammad Ali probably did more to popularize boxing than anyone in the history of the sport. Born Cassius Marcellus Clay Jr. in Louisville, Kentucky, he took up boxing when he was twelve to seek revenge for his bicycle having been stolen.

Cassius Clay first gained national prominence by winning a gold medal in the 1960 Olympics. The following year, he turned professional and built up an impressive string of victories. Clay received growing media attention, not only because of his boxing talent but also because of his uncanny ability to predict the exact round in which he would knock out his opponent. In addition, the young heavyweight contender routinely made those predictions in poetic form, a flamboyance that quickly earned him the media nickname the "Louisville Lip."

Finally, in 1964, Clay earned a match with heavyweight champion Sonny Liston. Although Clay began as the underdog, he was crowned the new champion when Liston could not answer the bell for the seventh round. The day after the fight, Clay announced that he had adopted the Muslim faith and changed his name to Muhammad Ali. Referring to Clay as his "slave name," Muhammad Ali moved to the forefront of the emerging black pride movement of the 1960s. However, his decision to join the Nation of Islam angered many white American fans who viewed the group as militant and antiwhite.

Muhammad Ali remained one of the most controversial public figures during the turbulent period of civil unrest. While Ali defended his title several times between 1964 and 1967, the United States became further embroiled in the Vietnam War. Once again, Ali generated headlines beyond the sport pages when, citing his religious beliefs, he refused to be inducted into the armed forces. As a result, he was convicted of violating federal law and stripped of the heavyweight title. With his boxing license suspended for over three years, Ali became a popular speaker on the college lecture circuit and a leading figure in the growing antiwar movement. Ali's objection to the draft on religious grounds eventually made its way to the U.S. Supreme Court, which reversed his conviction in 1971.

Ali resumed his boxing career, but in March 1971, he lost in his first attempt to regain the championship. His opponent in the match was Joe Frazier, who had claimed the vacated title in 1968. The Frazier fight was the first of three legendary battles between the two men. Ali won the next two encounters with Frazier; however, by the time of their second match, Frazier had already lost the championship title to George Foreman.

Having crushed all of his opponents almost effortlessly, Foreman was seen as invincible, and Muhammad Ali was thought to have no realistic chance of dethroning the champion when the two fought in Kinshasa, Zaire, in 1974. Despite

> *Referring to Clay as his "slave name," Muhammad Ali moved to the forefront of the emerging black pride movement of the 1960s. However, his decision to join the Nation of Islam angered many white American fans who viewed the group as militant and antiwhite.*

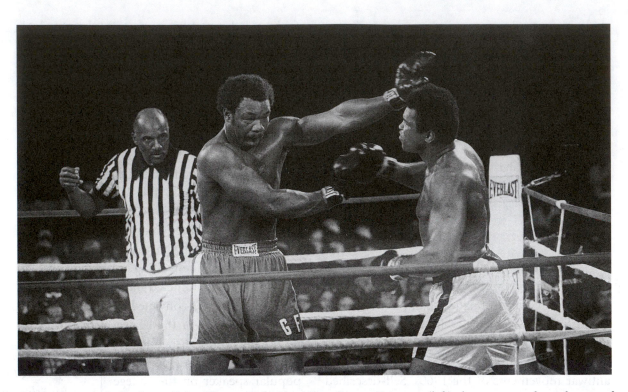

October 29, 1974. Kinshasa, Zaire. Heavyweight champion George Foreman (left) throws a punch to the eye of Muhammad Ali during their title bout. This shot twisted Ali's face but not his direction. He went on to regain his title by a kayo in the 8th round.
(BETTMANN/CORBIS)

the odds, however, Ali shocked the sport world with a spectacular eighth-round knockout of Foreman. The fight, dubbed the "Rumble in the Jungle," would later be immortalized in the Academy Award–winning documentary *When We Were Kings* (1997). By the late 1970s, many considered Ali to have the most recognized face in the world.

Another memorable encounter with Frazier, in 1975, was dubbed the "Thrilla in Manila." The fight was stopped in the fourteenth round, and Ali emerged victorious. In 1978, Ali lost to and then regained the title from Leon Spinks, making Ali the first heavyweight to win the world championship three times.

After consecutive losses to Larry Holmes and Trevor Berbick, Ali retired from the ring in 1981. He had begun to show signs of slowed speech and deteriorating motor skills and was diagnosed with Parkinson's disease. With medication and treatment, he became a frequent spokesperson for the disability and helped lobby Congress for funding to treat Parkinson's. In July 1996, Ali captivated the nation once again as he lit the inaugural flame for the Olympic Games in Atlanta, Georgia, and in 2001, he was portrayed by summer blockbuster star Will Smith in the film, *Ali.*

—*Thomas C. Reynolds*

See also: Boxing; Foreman, George Edward; Frazier, Joe

For further reading:
Goldstein, Alan. 2001. *Muhammad Ali: The Eyewitness Story of a Boxing Legend.* Toronto: Metro Books.
Remnick, David. 1998. *King of the World: Muhammad Ali and the Rise of an American Hero.* New York: Random House.

ALL-AMERICAN GIRLS PROFESSIONAL BASEBALL LEAGUE

By giving women an opportunity to participate in a sport that had previously been an all-male domain, the All-American Girls Professional Baseball League (AAGPBL) broke the traditional stereotypes surrounding women and sport. During World War II, baseball faced many challenges. Star players, such as Joe DiMaggio, entered the armed forces to serve their country, leaving their clubs with empty slots on their rosters. President Franklin Delano Roosevelt, however, believed that baseball played a key role in bolstering the country's morale. Thus, in 1943, he issued his "Green Light Letter" authorizing the continuation of the World Series, even while the Office of Defense curtailed individual travel to conserve oil for war use.

In the same year, Chicago Cubs owner Philip Wrigley founded a unique league that helped keep baseball alive. His players could not be drafted because they were women, the new recruits of the All-American Girls Professional Baseball League. Nearly seven hundred women played in the AAGPBL for more than a dozen professional teams, mainly representing midwestern cities. However, the women came from all over the United States and Canada and even from Cuba. Most were scouted while taking part in women's softball leagues at all levels of play.

As the women moved from softball to baseball, they learned to pitch a progressively smaller ball, first sidearm and, eventually, overhand, and to run progressively longer distances between bases until they had adapted to baseball's rules. However, the one thing that never matched the men's game was the uniform. The AAGPBL players wore tunics and short skirts. Although the uniforms were not practical, they created the definitively feminine image the owners wanted. During the war, women entered the workforce as a temporary solution to labor shortages, but they were still portrayed in the standard image of homemakers who only happened to work in factories. Baseball followed the same pattern, with the women wearing feminine uniforms and receiving charm-school training.

Players attended charm school to be taught to behave like ladies. They were shown how to walk, how to dress, how to wear makeup, and how to talk to the press. Consequently, newspaper articles often contained more about the players' personal appearance and family life than about their playing skill. The clubs also hired chaperones to keep the women in line and assumed responsibility for the players when they were not on the field.

Women who played baseball in the All-American Girls Professional Baseball League were required to attend charm school and to be constantly chaperoned when they were on the road.

The first season of the new league opened with four clubs, representing Kenosha, Wisconsin; Racine, Wisconsin; Rockford, Illinois; and South Bend, Indiana. Team names reflected the feminine image as well, with monikers such as the Daisies (Fort Wayne, Indiana), the Belles (Racine), the Millerettes (Minneapolis, Minnesota), and the Peaches (Rockford). Racine won the first championship but surrendered the crown to the new Milwaukee, Wisconsin, club in 1944. Minneapolis joined the league in 1944, though by 1945, both new clubs had moved on, to Fort Wayne and Grand Rapids, Michigan, respectively. By 1948, the league reached ten franchises, its highest number; however, only one season later, a slow decline had begun and eventually led to the league's demise at the end of the 1954 season.

By the mid-1950s, the United States had returned to the image of a traditional household, with a mom at home raising the kids and a dad out working to provide for his family. Professional women baseball players did not fit this image; thus, attendance at games fell and recruiting players became difficult. In addition, major league baseball players returned from the war, and a second league no longer seemed necessary. The advent of televised games also hurt smaller leagues because people could watch the best players from their homes and did not need to go out to the local park.

Highlights and statistics from the women's league can be found in a wing dedicated to women in baseball at the National Baseball Hall of Fame in Cooperstown, New York. In 1992, the little-remembered league captured the public imagination through the film *A League of Their Own*. The efforts of Hollywood brought the players and events of that era to the attention of many who had not even known they existed, contributing to women's history as well as to sport history.

—*Leslie Heaphy*

See also: Baseball

For further reading:
Browne, Lois. 1993. *Girls of Summer: The Real Story of the All-American Girls Professional Baseball League.* New York: HarperCollins.
Macy, Sue. 1995. *A Whole New Ball Game: The Story of the All-American Girls Professional Baseball League.* New York: Puffin.

ALLEN, MEL (1914–1996)

One of the first recognizable voices in sport, Mel Allen was the radio and television personality of the New York Yankees from 1946 to 1964, and to baseball fans across the United States, his booming baritone, sweetened with an Alabama drawl, became a symbol of baseball's dominant team, as well as a symbol of the sport. A native of Birmingham, Alabama, Allen joined CBS as a staff announcer in 1937, a year after earning his law degree from the University of Alabama. During his years as the "Voice of the Yankees," New York won sixteen American League pennants and eleven World Series titles, and Allen became the nation's most famous baseball broadcaster. He covered twenty World Series and twenty All-Star

games for NBC, broadcast dozens of important events, and narrated sport highlights for Fox Movietone Newsreels, one of the primary sources of news for the pretelevision generation.

Adding to the sport lexicon, Allen was an unabashed Yankee rooter, and his signature phrase "How about that!" was recognized from coast to coast. One of television's most effective pitchmen, Allen described Yankee home runs as "Ballentine blasts" or "White Owl whoppers," alluding to commercial products of the era. Consequently, in 1960, the National Association of Direct Selling Companies named him Salesman of the Year. From 1954 to 1964, his partner in the Yankee broadcast booth was Red Barber, whose relaxed delivery provided a perfect counterpoint to Allen's enthusiastic style.

After the 1964 season, the Yankee dynasty began to fade, and Allen was fired. His high-energy style, the Yankees feared, was dated and inappropriate for the increasingly polished sport television industry. From 1977 until his death, Allen narrated *This Week in Baseball,* a syndicated highlights program that set the tone for the national fascination with televised sport commentary. In 1978, he and Barber shared the initial Ford Frick Award for broadcasting excellence awarded by the Baseball Hall of Fame.

—*Tim Ashwell*

See also: Television, Impact on Sport

For further reading:
Smith, Curt. 1995. *The Storytellers: From Mel Allen to Bob Costas; Sixty Years of Baseball Tales from the Broadcast Booth.* New York: Macmillan

ALTRUISM AND ACTIVISM

To accrue tax breaks for escalating salaries and to feel the personal gratification of "giving something back," many athletes have established foundations and clinics to aid charitable causes.

Others have used the fame they acquired through sport activities to campaign for various causes, from racial and gender equality to AIDS research.

By the end of the twentieth century, supporting private charities had become such a commonplace activity for many professional athletes that a consulting group, the Giving Back Fund, was established to help athletes manage their foundations. Since the institution in 1977 of the Dave Winfield Foundation, the first known charitable foundation created by a sport star, organizations have drawn enormous profits from the involvement of athletes. Athletes are natural drawing cards for events, and having a star's name associated with a cause made that cause seem more viable.

The majority of these foundations raised money to help children, often at-risk inner-city residents of the communities with which professional teams were affiliated. Yankee star Dave Winfield, the prototype for athletes involved in such community-service work, raised money by staging softball games for charity. Through his foundation, Winfield helped thousands of area youngsters find summer jobs. Golfing dynamo Tiger Woods sponsored golf clinics for children in major cities across the country; Cincinnati Bengals' tight end Tony McGee supported an off-season football camp for inner-city children; Florence Griffith Joyner coached children on behalf of the youth foundation bearing her name; the Michael Jordan Foundation raised $1 million for children in need and provided grants and services to philanthropic organizations; and boxing promoter Don King funded a national literacy program for grade school children.

Many of these foundations exhibited extraordinary success. Golfer Chi Chi Rodriquez purchased an aging golf course and started a private school for troubled kids. The school used golf as a teaching tool, and the children in the school demonstrated marked improvement in their reading, writing, and math skills. Hockey star Cam Neely, after the death of his parents from cancer, raised money for cancer research and founded Neely House, a residential facility for families of cancer victims being treated in Boston Hospital. Dan Marino of the Miami Dolphins created Touchdown for Tots, donating $500 for each touchdown pass he threw, and raising more than $700,000 in matching corporate funds to meet the educational, physical, and emotional needs of children in the Miami community. Baltimore Orioles' Cal Ripkin Jr. began the Ripkin Learning Center, an adult literacy program.

Other athletes have used their fame as a platform from which to demonstrate advocacy for a particular cause. Best-known for these espousals was Jackie Robinson, who broke the color line in professional baseball and shared his victories with the National Association for the Advancement of Colored People (NAACP) and the Urban League. Through a variety of media events—such as the "Battle of the Sexes" between tennis diva Billie Jean King and Bobby Riggs—King and others used fame as a vehicle to underscore the athletic acumen of women and to encourage the equal treatment of women athletes. More recently, Olympic diver Greg Louganis served as an advocate for gay rights and was instrumental in working with Pets Are Wonderful Support/Los Angeles (PAWS/LA), an organization that helps persons with AIDS care for their pets. And tennis champion Arthur Ashe, who contracted AIDS through a blood transfusion, was given a leadership award for his efforts in educating the public about safe sex and AIDS awareness.

—*Joyce Duncan*

See also: Ashe, Arthur Robert, Jr.; "Battle of the Sexes"; Jordan, Michael; Robinson, Jack Roosevelt "Jackie"

For further reading:

"Athletes, Agents and Image." 1998. *The Grantsmanship Center (TGCI) Magazine,* Winter. http://www.tgci.com (accessed July 12, 2003).

Perskie, Joe. 1998. "Shaky Foundations." *Sport* (Nov.) 89: 98-103.

AMATEUR ATHLETIC ACT

Clashes between competing amateur sport organizations in the United States negatively affected the success of U.S. athletes in international competitions, particularly in relation to athletes from the countries of the former Soviet Union and other eastern European nations. In response, Congress passed the Amateur Athletic Act in 1978. The act created stricter and more direct lines of governance of individual amateur sports in order to settle the endless disputes and to increase U.S. athletes' successes in international competitions.

Throughout the twentieth century, there were power clashes between amateur sport organizations like the Amateur Athletic Union of the United States (AAU) and the National Collegiate Athletic Association (NCAA). The governing bodies of amateur sport had developed informally without direct sanction from the U.S. government and thus often had overlapping jurisdictions. These battles led to disorganization, which hurt the performance of U.S. athletes in such important international competitions as the Olympics and the Pan-American Games.

The political importance of international sport competitions increased greatly during the cold war between the United States and the Soviet Union. Both countries exploited athletic success in events like the Olympics to demonstrate the superiority of their own economic and political systems. In 1972, the U.S. Olympic team suffered a number of embarrassing organizational mishaps and in consequence garnered a relatively poor medal count compared to its Soviet counterpart. Cold war prerogatives encouraged President Gerald Ford to initiate a presidential study group, the President's Commission on Olympic Sports (PCOS), to recommend changes in the overlapping and contentious structure of U.S. amateur sports' governance, which many blamed for the general disorganization of amateur sport and the lack of success in the 1972 Olympics. A generally unsatisfactory showing during the 1976 Olympics encouraged ongoing investigation.

Based on the recommendations of the PCOS, Congress passed the Amateur Athletic Act in 1978. The act eliminated organizational squabbling by granting the U.S. Olympic Committee (USOC) explicit control in overseeing an individual, single-purpose governing body, the national governing body (NGB), for each specific amateur sport. Multisport governing groups, like the Amateur Athletic Union (AAU), were to be eliminated. This created more clearly defined and more direct responsibility for each sport and eliminated disruptive jurisdictional arguments.

In addition, the act covered a number of other important issues. It required a large increase in athlete representation in the individual NGBs. It also addressed the financing of amateur sport, national and regional athletic-training facilities, promotion, athletes' rights, and public participation. As a result of the Amateur Athletic Act, the AAU, which had been declining in stature anyway, altered its focus to youth development and recreation programs. It also created a more explicit role for the U.S. government in legitimizing organizations governing amateur sport.

—*Joseph M. Turrini*

See also: Amateur Athletic Union; International Olympic Committee; Olympic Games

For further reading:
Lovesey, Peter. 1979. *The Official Centenary History of the Amateur Athletic Association.* Enfield, England: Guinness Superlatives.

AMATEUR ATHLETIC UNION

The Amateur Athletic Union (AAU) of the United States established a strict and exclusionary policy of amateurism and controlled U.S. participation in the Olympic Games and other elite amateur athletic competitions before restricting its focus to youth development and recreation. The New

The biggest upset of the National Amateur Athletic Union Junior Track and Field Meet in Chicago (1933) came when Jimmy Johnson of Illinois defeated Jesse Owens of Cleveland in the 100-meter finals of the National Amateur Athletic Union Junior Championships Meet at Soldier Field in Chicago. Two weeks before Owens had tied the world record—9.4 in the 100-yard dash.
(BETTMANN/CORBIS)

York Athletic Club formed the AAU in 1888 as a nonprofit, private organization to regulate amateur sport. The AAU's primary goal was to establish and maintain a strict amateur ethic based on that found in the British Athletic Association. The AAU's initial support of amateurism was an attempt to maintain the social exclusivity of the upper-class clubs that formed the founding organization and sponsored amateur athletic competitions.

Based on the AAU's position as the dominant amateur sport organization in the United States, the group organized U.S. participation in all Olympic events between the initiation of the modern games in 1896 and 1921. In addition, the AAU continued to participate with other amateur organizations in the selection of those Olympic teams after 1921.

Because the AAU initially came into being informally as a private organization and not one sanctioned by the government, the group's control of many individual sports was challenged throughout the twentieth century. Consequently, the AAU lost power over many amateur sports, as leaders in those sports formed associations that governed their individual sport and that were not under the multisport AAU umbrella. The AAU maintained charge over its most important sport, track and field, until 1978, when Congress passed the Amateur Athletic Act. The AAU continued to exist after the Amateur Athletic Act was enforced, but its focus became much more limited, concentrating on youth-development programs and recreation as opposed to elite international athletics.

—*Joseph M. Turrini*

See also: International Olympic Committee; Olympic Games

For further reading:

Flath, Arnold William. 1964. *A History of Relations between the National Collegiate Athletic Association and the Amateur Athletic Union of the United States (1905–1963)*. Champaign, IL: Stipes.

AMATEURISM

Although connotatively associated with unskilled participation, amateurism, the nineteenth-century ethic of gentlemen, has had a major influence on sport. Since the 1872 decision to disqualify watermen who made their living on the water and who entered the Schuylkill Regatta, sport organizations have generally defined amateur athletes as persons who play for the sake of the sport, team, or community without prospect of financial gain. This unusual notion of amateurism evolved from British sporting tradition.

Originally, amateurism comes from the Latin word *amator*, "lover," and in the Roman Empire, *amateur* was used to denote athletes in the Olympics who did not capitalize on their fame. In the modern era, "amateur" was first used in eighteenth-century England to distinguish gentlemen pugilists and horsemen who did not receive side bets or prizes. By the mid-nineteenth century, middle- and upper-class Britons, who socialized through a network of exclusive clubs, came to interpret professionalism or remuneration for sport as incompatible with their class. Hence, amateurs were more than simply lovers of sport; they were elitists who excluded the working classes.

Americans also developed a version of amateurism. When the Knickerbocker Club in New York initiated modern organized baseball, it defined membership on the basis of class, admitting to the club only doctors, lawyers, clerks, and businessmen and stipulating that only gentlemen could play. Furthermore, the rules forbade ungentlemanly, obscene, or ill-mannered behavior. Belatedly, as the new sport spread and the number of paying spectators increased, teams began hiring players, and professionalism was accepted by the National Association of Baseball Players in 1869.

The decades that followed witnessed the spread of amateurism. In addition to the Schuylkill episode, amateurism was established in track-and-field events by the Amateur Athletic Union (AAU), formed in 1888. Coupled with such organizational developments was the growth of Muscular Christianity, closely associated with the Young Men's Christian Association (YMCA) and the Young Women's Christian Association (YWCA). James Naismith, the YMCA instructor who invented basketball, considered his game the perfect winter activity to tame workers, or what he termed the "unruly class."

This trend was combined with the growing physical education movement led by advocates such as Edward Hitchcock of Amherst College. Consequently, college athletics, particularly intercollegiate baseball and football, began a period of rapid growth. The exclusivity of higher education and the gentlemanly ethic perpetuated amateurism into the twentieth century. The National Collegiate Athletic Association (NCAA; 1910) protected the amateur ethic by prohibiting colleges from offering inducements to or recruiting athletes, barring ineligible or professional athletes from competing in college athletics, and prohibiting improper and unsportsmanlike conduct. Individuals, such as golfer Bobby Jones (1902–1971), epitomized amateurism in their gentlemanly aversion to money and scrupulous obedience of rules.

As spectatorship increased and control of intercollegiate sports came under the sway of school administrators, however, amateurism was steadily undermined. During the 1960s, Ohio State University sold out its 85,000-seat stadium for every home football game. With vastly increased gate and television revenues, intercollegiate athletics placed a premium on winning. The results were scholarships—in effect, salaries—for student-athletes, highly paid coaches, and marketing. During the 1980s, beginning with the legalization of trust funds for track-and-field competitors, professional athletes were allowed to compete in many Olympic sports. True amateurism was relegated largely to the less popular and less profitable sports.

—*Neal R. McCrillis*

See also: Amateur Athletic Union; Muscular Christianity; Olympic Games

For further reading:

Allison, Lincoln. 2001. *Amateurism in Sport: An Analysis and a Defense.* Portland, OR: Frank Cass.

National Collegiate Athletic Association. 1999. "Division I Legislation Summary by Category: Amateurism." http://www.ncaa.org/databases/legislation/1999/99summarya.html.

Sack, Allen L., and Ellen J. Staurowsky. 1998. *College Athletes for Hire: The Evolution and Legacy of the NCAA's Amateur Myth.* Westport, CT: Praeger.

AMERICAN BASKETBALL ASSOCIATION

Although short-lived, the American Basketball Association (ABA) changed the way basketball was viewed by the United States viewing public. By forming an alternative professional basketball league that stressed a wide-open and fast-paced game, a three-point shot, and a slam-dunk contest, the maverick American Basketball Association (ABA) spearheaded the style of professional basketball mass-marketed by the National Basketball Association (NBA) to U.S. and international adults and youth in the 1980s and 1990s.

The ABA was launched in 1967 with eleven teams. It was promoted by businessmen who wanted to bring professional basketball franchises to U.S. cities to which the NBA had yet to expand. In 1976, after the league disbanded for financial reasons, four of its teams—the San Antonio Spurs, the New York Nets, the Denver Nuggets, and the Indiana Pacers—were successful enough to join the NBA.

Throughout its short tenure, the ABA faced constant financial instability. The lack of a national television contract severely limited the appeal of the league outside the second-tier cities that held franchises, and attendance at games was generally sparse. As a result, the league tried a variety of promotions to draw fans to the seats of their small and often-cold arenas. The use of a multicolored red, white, and blue basketball was designed to draw younger fans to the league as well as to appeal to audiences watching the games in color on local television. Gimmicks such as slam-dunk competitions were employed to showcase ABA players and to attract fans. A three-point shot was instituted to help make the games more exciting and to allow for higher scoring.

What made the ABA unique, however, was the style of basketball practiced by a host of flamboyant players. Players such as Julius "Dr. J." Erving, George Gervin, and Connie Hawkins created a fast-paced, wide-open, high-scoring brand of basketball that was more fan oriented than the slower-paced, more-disciplined style of the NBA. Teams did not hesitate to recruit or draft any player who would enhance their popularity. They often competed with NBA teams for college draftees and displayed no qualms about drafting undergraduates or even, as in the case of Moses Malone, recent high school graduates. When the league folded, many ABA stars joined NBA teams and made an immediate impact on the game with their high-flying style. In fact, ten of the twenty-nine players in the first NBA All-Star game after the ABA disbanded were former ABA players.

In 1996, the NBA honored the twentieth anniversary of the ABA's disbanding. Much of the ABA's entertaining style of basketball, promotional gimmicks such as the slam-dunk contest, and rules, including the three-point shot, had been adopted by the NBA in the 1980s to resuscitate professional basketball and to transform the league into one of the most watched and most successfully marketed spectator sports in the United States. The modern NBA, with its Hollywood-type glamour, personalities, and promotions, reflects the legacy of the defunct ABA, and much of its appeal to youth, especially to urban youth familiar with a "playground" style of basketball, is owed to that league.

—*John Fea*

See also: Basketball; National Basketball Association

For further reading:

Pluto, Terry. 1990. *Loose Balls: The Short, Wild Life of the American Basketball Association.* New York: Simon and Schuster.

THE AMERICAN GLADIATORS

The American Gladiators (TAG) was originally an ABC program. The series debuted in 1989 and ran until 1997. The show pitted civilian contenders against appropriately named Gladiators, including Nitro, Hawk, Gemini, and Dallas. The contests designed specifically for the show included such favorites as Assault, Breakthrough and Conquer, Powerball, the Wall, Whiplash, and Joust competitions. The games were modified as the series matured to emphasize a variety of athletic attributes beyond brute strength.

The reactions to *TAG* were predictably mixed. Some critics argued that *TAG* had more in common with tacky kitsch than with sport. Others referred to it as "crash TV," and *Sports Illustrated* even suggested that participation in *TAG* by two top collegiate running backs qualified as a sign that the apocalypse was upon us. However, *TAG* doubled in popularity in its first two years and rose to a top-five position. In addition, it boasted significant participation by celebrity athletes, including Seth Joyner, Tony Dorsett, Danny Manning, and host, Joe Theismann.

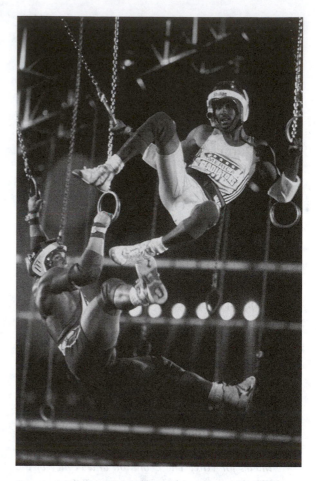

Some critics argued that American Gladiators *had more in common with tacky kitsch than with sport. February 1, 1993.*

(ROB BROWN/CORBIS SYGMA)

In an age of oversized GI Joe action figures and video games that framed each clash as epic, the popularity of the Gladiators was clear. They were video figures come to life. With bright, easily identifiable costumes, phenomenal physiques, names that suggested special powers, and dramatic verbal and physical posturing, their characters were unambiguous and entertaining. Some parents even viewed the Gladiators as positive role models because they were not involved with drugs, they ate healthy foods, and they took care of their bodies. The concept of Gladiators as role models spawned a variety of cross-marketing efforts, including video games, action figures, and vitamins.

In addition to the televised series, there was a live dinner theater spectacle in Orlando, Florida. The 1,600-seat theater opened in December 1995 and charged patrons $34.95 each to enjoy live battles while consuming healthy meals that featured chicken and salad. To maintain interest, there were a variety of categories of contestants: Hard Hats, Top Jocks, Top Cops, and Military, among others. Unfortunately, this was not enough to sustain interest, and the project closed in 1997.

Although the live version of the show failed, the formula for success on television proved to be quite versatile, and versions ran in the United Kingdom, Australia, South Africa, Russia, Finland, and Germany at one time or another. U.S. television was quick to produce a variety of similar programs. Although the ensuing shows did not always use the formula central to *TAG*, that show's popularity fostered close imitation in other programs, including *Blade Warriors, Sand Blast,* and *Gladiators 2000.* Although most critics have defined *Gladiators* as having been produced solely for television, the idea originated with ironworkers in Erie, Pennsylvania, according to an article in *Entertainment Weekly.* The popularity of that community competition, originally designed as a fund-raiser, prompted one of the promoters, Johnny Ferraro, to take the idea to television.

The popularity of *TAG* can be examined from a number of perspectives. Some analysts suggest that the David-versus-Goliath-type clash explained the show's appeal, which was enhanced by the view of professional bodybuilders as machines that invoked the age-old theme of man versus machine. In addition, the backgrounds of the contestants often revealed a class struggle that is basic to the American mythology, and the format of the show allowed these themes to be visually portrayed in dynamic ways. As recently as 2000, Tribune Entertainment and MGM Television were reconsidering the show for syndication in the United States.

—*Richard K. Olsen Jr.*

See also: Bollea, Terry Gene "Hulk Hogan"; Television, Impact on Sport; World Wrestling Federation

For further reading:

Jacobs, A. J. 1995. "Battle of the Flexes." *Entertainment Weekly,* February 17, 47.

Rinehart, Robert. 1994. "Sport as Kitsch: A Case Study of *The American Gladiators.*" *Journal of Popular Culture* 28: 25–34.

Simpson, J. C. 1991. "Real-Life Davids vs. Goliaths." *Time,* October 21, 102–104.

AMERICA'S CUP

The America's Cup race, until recently an American-dominated race and social gathering, has become an internationally televised event celebrating the yachting community's grandest spectacle. The America's Cup was named for the first race, which was held off Great Britain in 1851 and won by the U.S. boat *America.* It has always been a race for privately wealthy yachtsmen and yachtswomen, bolstered by freighter loads of corporate sponsorship. The Cup, an "ugly mug" or "Auld Mug," is the pinnacle of formula racing on the high seas.

Over the decades, the design of the boats has slowly changed, incorporating the famed 12-meter sloop from 1956 to 1987, until the *Stars and Stripes* catamaran won in 1988. Notable skippers have included Sir Thomas Lipton, the founder of the Lipton Tea Company; media mogul Ted Turner, who is known as "Captain Outrageous"; and perennial skipper Dennis Connor, who has more wins than any other America's Cup pilot. The race is run only when a challenge has been issued, and competitors are eliminated through an expensive, grueling "race-off" until only two boats—defender and challenger—match skill, luck, and design. The defender is from the current championship country and is not necessarily the same "team" from year to year.

Any number of boats may enter the elimination races. Aided by on-board cameras, split screens, satellite transmissions, and computer graphics, a growing worldwide television audience can watch the on-deck crew while simultaneously enjoying a traditional bird's-eye view.

—*Charles Moore*

See also: Television, Impact on Sport

For further reading:
Shaw, David. 2002. *America's Victory: The Heroic Story of a Team of Ordinary Americans, and How They Won the Greatest Yacht Race Ever.* New York: Free Press.

ANGELL, ROGER (1926–)

Beginning in 1962, Roger Angell chronicled major league baseball for *The New Yorker* magazine and penned a series of best-selling books, reporting baseball from a fan's perspective, becoming an important and popular voice for the game and allowing fans to feel as if they were part of the activity. Angell began writing about baseball as a commentator, but rather than presenting a journalistic reporting of games, he conspicuously took a fan's perspective. He openly pulled for personal favorites, especially the New York Mets and the Boston Red Sox, and he wrote more extensively about them than about other teams. These reports were collected into five exceptionally popular baseball books.

Angell's first baseball collection, *The Summer Game* (1972), chronicled a fan's witnessing the phenomenal development of the New York Mets from a first-year expansion team, and one of the worst teams in baseball history, to World Series champions in only seven years. The writer's later books often reported his fictitious fan's reaction to various cultural and sport changes involving baseball. His second collection of reports, *Five Seasons* (1977), narrated the 1972–1977 baseball

seasons, recorded the varied fortunes of the Mets and the Red Sox, acknowledged the social and financial changes that free agency brought to the game, and foresaw the expansion of baseball's postseason and interleague play.

Late Innings (1983), Angell's account of the 1978–1981 baseball seasons, detailed baseball's work stoppages and the opening of locker rooms to women reporters. *Season Ticket* (1988), which covered 1982–1987, recorded the fall of the Red Sox in 1986 and a detailed account of the Oakland Athletics' attempts to succeed. *Once More around the Park* (1991) chronicled the late 1980s, and *Baseball* (1984) and *A Baseball Century: The History of the National League* (1987) presented extended popular histories of the game.

—*Daniel T. Durbin*

See also: Baseball; Sport Journalism

For further reading:
Kettmann, Steve, ed. 2003. *Game Time: A Baseball Companion.* New York: Harcourt.

APPAREL, IN SPORT

If it were possible to select only one thing that makes a statement about the cultural impact of sport on North American society, that one thing would be apparel. During the last three decades of the twentieth century, athletic apparel changed from the drab white gym socks and grubby tennies of the 1950s and 1960s to clothes that make a fashion statement. Athletic apparel became an essential component for every well-stocked wardrobe. Those who actually participated in sport—either as amateurs or as professionals—could dress the part and purge the wallet, paying big bucks to look good at the local gym or for peer support on the hard court or the open field.

In the middle years of the century, dressing for running was a simple task of throwing on oversized sweats and a pair of Keds. By the end of the century, the apparel industry would have us believe that the same weekend athlete could not leave home without satin running shorts and a matching jacket with an easily identified logo; color-coordinated socks, gloves, and sweatband; and shoes that were specially designed for a particular form of endeavor—and that retailed for a

> *If it were possible to select only one thing that makes a statement about the cultural impact of sport on North American society, that one thing would be apparel. Finding a clothes closet in the United States or Canada or the Latin countries— or, indeed, much of the world—that does not contain a portion of this $10-billion-a-year industry is a rarity.*

hefty price. Whether marathoner or middle-aged, overweight stockbroker, clothes made the man or woman and created a mystique of athletic prowess, an illusion well worth the money. Advertising moguls pushed the revealed and subliminal message that it was impossible to participate well in any athletic endeavor without being appropriately garbed and geared.

Professional sport teams, always alert to ways to win a chunk of the U.S. dollar, cashed in on the trend, as casual wear adopted the symbols and colors of favored teams. By the 1990s, merchandising of clothing and products was essential to professional sport to cover players' substantial salaries. Apparel firms were required to pay sport leagues an official "licensing" fee to use sport images. The firms were making money by riding the tide of audience appeal, and fearing they could be fined and ordered to stop production for using such images without permission, they complied. For the teams, clever marketing often compensated for lagging sales, and many teams increased revenues by changing logos or colors to gain more money from loyal fans who altered their attire to reflect the new look.

Generating income from logo-decorated clothing is not only the province of professional, national, or international sports; it trickles down to the college and high school levels as well, with teens and young people scrambling to purchase T-shirts, jackets, gloves, sweatbands, socks, and even underwear bearing the symbol of their alma mater or favorite regional or home team. If those teams win championship games, the region explodes with their colors, and the apparel stores cannot force the safe door closed.

Although football, basketball, and baseball control the majority of the logo apparel market, they are not the only sports that push adherence to dress codes. Tennis players, golfers, racquetball enthusiasts, weight lifters, and other sport aficionados feel the pressure to deck themselves in the finery of the professionals, to seek the newest, the best, and even the most recently autographed selection of athletic sartorial splendor.

—*Joyce Duncan*

See also: Marketing of Sport; Sneakers

For further reading:

MarketResearch.com. 2001. *MarketLooks: The Women's Athletic Apparel Market.* Ebooks. http://market research.com.

ARCHERY

In contemporary society, the ancient practice of using a bow and arrow in hunting, in warfare, or for sport revolves around medieval men in tights or Olympians. Although archery's origins date to as early as the Aurignacian period, some 25,000 years before the modern era, the earliest people known to practice archery were the ancient Egyptians, who used the skill to hunt as well as to fight the Persians. Archery's mythic foundations began with fourteenth-century Swiss marksman William Tell. Legend holds that Tell was commanded by an Austrian governor to shoot an apple from his own son's head with a bow and

Mrs. Jennette Baise of Plainfield, New Jersey. The 1934 champ is pictured as she won the Woman's Archery match at the New Jersey State Championships in Lincoln Park. She shot 719 points. September 6, 1937. (BETTMANN/CORBIS)

arrow. Later that century, ballads spread throughout England about the valiant bandit Robin Hood, who also wielded a bow and arrow and was acclaimed for stealing from the rich and giving to the poor. The actor Errol Flynn later made the character legendary on the silver screen.

As a sport, archery became popular in England in the seventeenth century and later in the United States with the creation of the United Bowmen of Philadelphia in 1828. It first appeared as an Olympic event in 1900 and was an event again in 1904, 1908, and 1920, but it was discontinued due to confusion over the rules.

Readmitted into the Olympic competition in 1972 with a set of standard international regulations, archery grew in popularity. It was not until the Atlanta games in 1996, however, when American Justin Huish won gold medals in the men's individual and team competitions, that the sport came to be widely noticed in the United States. The young Californian became a celebrity, sporting dark glasses, long hair, and an earring. A media darling, Huish brought a new popularity to the ancient sport.

—*Amy Bass*

See also: Olympic Games

For further reading:
U.S. Olympic Committee. 1997. *A Basic Guide to Archery* (An Official U.S. Olympic Committee Sports Series). Irvine, CA: Griffin Publishing.

ARÊTE

Inextricably linked to the athletics of the ancient Greek world and loaded with a plethora of meanings, the Greek word *arête* has come to denote the quest for all-around excellence and perfection through sport. The Greeks used the term primarily to describe men, but it was, on occasion, also applied to women, horses, and even city-states. Not translatable into a simple, one-word equivalent in modern U.S. English, *arête* connotes a variety of concepts, including excellence, skill, pride, goodness, valor, nobility, and virtue. Consequently, although the word is difficult to define and apply precisely, at the core of *arête* are the notions of ephemeral excellence and transient triumph. To some extent, *arête* resided in every ancient Greek, yet at the same time, it was a goal to be sought or an ideal to be attained, whether in athletics, politics, economics, art, military combat, or daily life. *Arête,* coupled with the concept of *aidos,* which connoted courage, respect, honesty, fair play, and a sense of propriety, spoke to the ancient Greek ideal of completeness—the whole human.

To modern scholars, *arête* has come to represent an artificial distinction by which the study of athletics is divorced from the study of the other aspects of the ancient world. Consequently, although in antiquity *arête* was not restricted to the characterizations of athletes, in the modern era, *arête* has endowed ancient athletics with an aura of the quest for perfection, a quest transcendent of the more mundane affairs of politics, business, and welfare.

A concept embraced and celebrated by Pierre de Coubertin, the founder of the modern Olympic Games, as a component of his ideology of Olympianism, *arête* denotes the quest for all-around excellence and perfection through athletic participation.

—*Jeffrey O. Segrave*

See also: Coubertin, Baron Pierre de; Olympic Games

For further reading:

Miller, Stephen G. 1991. *Arete: Greek Sports from Ancient Sources.* Berkeley and Los Angeles: University of California Press.

ARMSTRONG, LANCE (1971–)

It may be impossible to measure the level of impact that Lance Armstrong has had on the cycling world, on the care and treatment of cancer, and on American culture in general. What is seen is the interest he has created in cycling for United States fans. Competitive cycling was considered a European sport and relatively few Americans followed the events before the Lance Armstrong era. Although some did show interest during the period of Greg Lemond's success, it was not close to the level of interest produced by the success and compelling personal story of Lance Armstrong. In response to his popularity, the Outdoor Life Network (OLN) broadcast the entire twenty-one stages of the Tour de France. They also aired a thirty-minute special immediately following their daily broadcast of the Tour de France, "The Lance Armstrong Chronicles," where he was referred to as an athlete, an actor, and an innovator. It is difficult to predict the long-term impact that Lance

Armstrong will have on American cycling, but many agree that the impact will be significant.

Armstrong was born September 18, 1971, and raised in Plano, Texas. He won the Iron Kids Triathlon at age 13 and became a professional triathlete at the age of 16. By his senior year in high school, however, Armstrong changed his athletic focus from triathlete to cyclist and qualified to train with the U.S. Olympic developmental team in Colorado Springs, Colorado. After graduation from high school, he turned his attention to cycling on a full-time basis.

In 1991 he became the U.S. National Amateur Champion and competed in the 1992 Olympic games in Barcelona. Following the Barcelona Olympics, the cyclist entered his first professional race, the 1992 Classico San Sebastian. In 1993 Armstrong gained ten titles, including the U.S. PRO Championship and the Thrift Drug Triple Crown, becoming the youngest ever world champion. In the same year, he won his first stage victory in the Tour De France. His racing team, Team Motorola, became the first U.S. team to be ranked in the top five worldwide. During this time, he developed a growing fan base and began to receive media attention.

Over the next three years, Armstrong became the number-one ranked cyclist in the world and the first American to win the Classico San Sebastian in 1995. He also continued to have success winning stages at the Tour De France and he originated the Lance Armstrong Junior Olympic Race Series in 1995 as a way to give back to the sport of cycling. He was named the Velo News American Male Cyclist of the Year for 1995.

In addition to becoming the first person to recapture the Tour Du Pont, he became the first American to win the Belgian spring classic Fleche Wallone in 1996 and competed as a member of the 1996 U.S. Olympic Team in Atlanta. At the peak of his success, in October of 1996, pain forced him to stop cycling. Tests revealed that he had advanced testicular cancer and that the cancer had spread to his stomach, lungs, and brain.

US Postal team rider Lance Armstrong celebrates on the podium after winning the Tour de France 2003 cycling race (July 27, 2003). Armstrong won the 100th anniversary Tour de France, and became the fifth five-time winner of the tour along with Jacques Anquetil of France, Eddy Merckx of Belgium, Bernard Hinault of France, and Miguel Indurain of Spain.

(REUTERS/CORBIS)

Armstrong underwent three surgeries, two to remove the malignant testicle and one to remove the cancer from his brain. The prognosis for recovery was less than 50 percent. In addition to the surgeries, he began an aggressive and relatively new form of chemotherapy called "VIP," a cocktail of chemicals: Ifosfamide, Etoposide, and Platinol. The aggressive treatment proved successful and he began training and riding again only five months after his diagnosis.

Despite the physical and emotional hardships, Armstrong maintains that cancer was an unexpected gift and "the best thing that ever happened to me" (Armstrong 2000, 3). He claims that can-

cer helped him to mature and establish new priorities. Within months of his diagnosis, he founded the Lance Armstrong Foundation, an international nonprofit foundation to benefit cancer research, to promote cancer awareness and the importance of early detection, and to help people manage and survive cancer. Through the foundation and his status as a world-class athlete and celebrity, he has become a well-known spokesperson for cancer awareness.

In May 1998, Armstrong returned to U.S. cycling by winning the Sprint 56k Criterium in Austin, Texas. The event marked the beginning of what could be called the greatest comeback in sports history as he joined the United States Post Office (USPS) pro cycling team. The cyclist won the 1998 Tour de Luxemburg, the Rheinland-Pfalz Rundfarht in Germany, and the Cascade Classic in Oregon. He finished the 1998 season with a fourth place finish at the World Championships in Holland. In addition to his racing successes, he provided his foundation with over $300,000 for research.

In 1999 Armstrong won his first Tour de France, the race he has referred to as the super bowl of the sport. Unlike three-time American winner Greg Lemond, who was on a French team when he won the tour, Armstrong took the honors on an American team, team USPS. Winning the Tour de France was not only considered a victory for him and team USPS but for cancer survivors around the world. Armstrong ended the year by competing in three professional mountain biking races and by welcoming his son Luke into the world on October 12.

While training for the Tour de France in 2000, Armstrong had an accident, exploding a tire on a 45 mph descent and crashing head first into a stone retaining wall. Fortunately, he did not suffer any serious injuries and went on to win the tour. While preparing for the 2000 Olympics in Sydney, he was hit by a car and fractured his C-7 vertebra. In spite of his injury, he competed in the Olympics and came away with a bronze medal in the time trial.

Armstrong entered the 2001 Tour de France as the favorite to win. He overcame challenges from other riders and bad weather conditions to win his third consecutive tour. Following his victory, Lance prepared for the birth of his twin daughters, Isabelle Rose and Grace Elizabeth. His cycling focus and the focus of team USPS turned to the 2002 Tour de France.

In 2002, Armstrong was performing at his peak. He won his fourth consecutive Tour de France. He was recognized as Sports Illustrated "Sportsman of the Year" and as the Associated Press's "Male Athlete of the Year" (www.laf.org 2004). Athletic success and media acclaim allowed him to continue to be an effective spokesperson for cancer research on a national and international stage.

In his fifth straight victory in the 2003 Tour de France, he tied and shared the honors with Spaniard Miguel Indurain. Although the 2003 tour is considered the hardest fought of his Tour de France victories, Armstrong broke the record in 2004 and become the only man to win a sixth consecutive Tour de France. Following the Tour de France, he plans to participate on the U.S. Olympic team at the 2004 games in Athens.

In 2000 Armstrong's autobiography *It's Not About the Bike: My Journey Back to Life* became a *New York Times* best seller. The book is an honest look at facing and overcoming cancer. His story is inspirational and the stage he commands as perhaps the greatest cyclist of all time has created the opportunity for significant exposure and the opportunity to get out his message. His work through the Lance Armstrong Foundation continues to have a real and lasting impact on the research, early detection, and treatment of cancer.

—*Craig Riordan*

See Also: Athletes as Symbolic Heroes; Bicycling

For further reading:

Armstrong, Lance, with Sally Jenkins. 2000. *It's Not About the Bike: My Journey Back to Life.* New York: Berkley Books.

Gutman, Bill. 2003. *Lance Armstrong: A Biography.* New York: Simon Spotlight Entertainment.

Specter, Michael. 2002. "The Long Ride." *The New Yorker Magazine,* July 15, 48–58.

www.laf.org, Lance Armstrong Foundation Website. Accessed June 2004.

www.lancearmstrong.com, Lance Armstrong Official Website. Accessed June 2004.

ARMY-NAVY RIVALRY

Extending for more than a century, the Army-Navy rivalry in college football has become, for many observers, a contest that exemplifies both self-sacrificing military virtue and pure amateur athletics in an arena increasingly dominated by commercial and professional interests.

When West Point cadet Dennis Michie challenged the U.S. Naval Academy to a football game in 1890, the two service academies not only began a rivalry that continues but also precipitated the evolution of a new sport. Brawling in the stands and injury, even death, on the field marked the early years of football, including those games played at the academies. After an admiral and a general reportedly came to blows at the 1893 Army-Navy game and subsequently resorted to a duel, President Grover Cleveland curtailed the game, which did not resume until 1899. The game was canceled again in 1909 after Army athlete Gene Byrne was killed in a game against Harvard University; he was the fourteenth player nationwide to die that year.

Despite these setbacks and tragedies, the sport and the rivalry evolved and prospered. Following a two-year hiatus during World War I, the Army-Navy game benefited from the growing popularity of sport in general. The game, however, was not yet of national standing. The game was suspended again during the 1928–1929 season when the two academies could not agree on rules for player eligibility. The contest resumed in 1930 and has never again been interrupted.

During and after World War II, the Army-Navy game became the most important contest in col-

Navy players celebrate on the field after winning the 103rd Army-Navy football game at Giants Stadium in East Rutherford, New Jersey (December 7, 2002). The final score was 58 to 12.
(REUTERS/CORBIS)

lege football. Army won the national championship three straight times (in 1944, 1945, and 1946) and was undefeated in five of the six seasons from 1944 to 1949. Army's Felix "Doc" Blanchard and Glenn Davis, the legendary "Mr. Inside" and "Mr. Outside," respectively, consecutively won the Heisman Trophy in 1945 and 1946. The game remained nationally important through the 1960s with the Heisman being awarded to Army's Pete Dawkins (1958) and to Navy's Joseph Bellino (1960) and Roger Staubach (1963). In 1967, Army received an invitation to the Sugar Bowl but was forced to decline because

the unpopularity of the ongoing Vietnam War made security uncertain. Neither team has received a major bowl invitation since.

During the Vietnam War, the military virtues that had helped popularize the Army-Navy game became divisive. Of greater long-term importance to the quality of the rivalry, however, was the rise of professional football. In the 1960s, professional football finally became financially successful. Although at one time a military career paid comparably to a career in professional sport, the disparity in salaries soon became marked. Since the academies' obligatory postgraduation military service made a professional football career unlikely, the institutions could no longer attract the game's most talented players.

Though the game has lost its importance in college rankings, the Army-Navy rivalry retains a large and loyal following and is always broadcast on national television. With the recovery in popularity of military service, the Army-Navy football game has become an example of dedication not to monetary rewards but to self-effacing sportsmanship by those who, while opponents on the playing field, may soon become comrades on the battlefield.

—*Daniel W. Stewart*

See also: Football

For further reading:

Feinstein, John. 1997. *A Civil War, Army vs. Navy: A Year inside College Football's Purest Rivalry.* Boston: Little, Brown.

Gill, Wesley F. 1985. *Uncommon Valor: The Army-Navy Football Rivalry.* Champaign, IL: Human Kinetics Publishers.

ARTISTS OF SPORT

Throughout U.S. history, artists in all disciplines have documented a wide variety of sporting scenes, depicted individual and team sporting events, and commemorated athletic heroes. As a result, sport was elevated to the highest form of artistic endeavor, and simultaneously, sport was portrayed as part of normal, everyday life.

Sport imagery has gradually been integrated into the daily lives of Americans. The earliest examples of sport artistry in the United States originated in the form of equestrian paintings that were extremely popular during the late eighteenth century. During the mid-1800s, these paintings gave way to a variety of other sporting or hunting scenes, which included many animals from dogs to foxes and hares. One of the notable artists of the period was Edward Troye (1808–1874), who

is considered the foremost U.S. sport painter of the nineteenth century and who specialized in portraits of horses and racing scenes in the British style.

By the end of the 1800s, another painter had emerged on the sport horizon. U.S. realist painter Thomas Eakins (1844–1916) created a series of works during the 1870s reflecting rowing and sculling along the Schuylkill River. The detail in his art is so remarkable that the exact location of the landscape can be documented, a feature that made Eakins's works truly unique for his era. He also created paintings of swimmers and boxers. In addition to painting, Eakins was a stop-action photography enthusiast and followed the work of Eadweard Muybridge (1830–1904), who studied the anatomy and movement of the human body during various forms of physical activity. Eakins's photographic efforts achieved the same level of craftsmanship and detail, and he was one of the first artists to create paintings fashioned from the photographs he had taken.

An outstanding contemporary of Troye and Eakins was Winslow Homer (1836–1910), who was skilled in the arts of painting, lithography, illustration, and watercolor. His primary contribution to the budding genre of sport-related art was naturalistic scenes of the sea and fishing along with documentation of family outings, such as children at play, riding horseback, and playing croquet. His fluid, almost-impressionistic style helped create works that were both dramatic and powerful. Homer was also a regular illustrator for *Harper's Weekly* and reached a greater American audience due to his magazine exposure.

Frederic Remington (1861–1909), from the same era, is considered one of the foremost painters and sculptors in the United States. Armed with only a few years of formal artistic training, Remington traveled west to document an era that was rapidly vanishing due to settlement and technological progress. He was drawn to the rough life of the emerging breed of cowboy and to the diminishing existence of Native Americans in western society. From these experiences, he created wonderful bronze sculptures of cowboys and horses in motion. His paintings and illustrations had an impressionistic quality that exemplified the carefree spirit and beauty of the wide-open spaces of the western United States. As an illustrator, he created numerous works related to metropolitan sport, football, and horse racing that were featured with short stories he wrote and published.

Another major artist in the genre was George Bellows (1882–1925), who as a child displayed equal talents for drawing and for athletics. Bellows played a variety of sports and, as a young man, participated in semiprofessional baseball during the summer of 1904. He sold several of his drawings that year to earn money to pursue his career as an artist. His most notable works capture the essence of the sleazy underworld associated with the illegal "prizefighting clubs" of the early 1900s. His radical style eventually gave way to masterfully composed and organized life studies of the sport world he loved.

In a simpler, more innocent way, artist Norman Rockwell (1894–1978) brought art into the homes of a vast majority of Americans. As a realistic painter, Rockwell depicted scenes of true Americana in the narrative genre of such nineteenth-century artists as William Sydney Mount and Winslow Homer. As an illustrator for the *Saturday Evening Post* from 1916 to 1963, Rockwell's view of everyday life, including the prevalence of sport, permeated U.S. culture.

With the popular advent of photography, sport shots were plastered from coast to coast in a variety of newspapers and magazines. Photographic journalists captured events from around the world and brought them home to Americans. Among the most notable of these photographers are Richard Clarkson (1932–), Neil Leifer (1942–), and John Zimmerman (1929–2002). One of those photographers in constant demand is Annie Liebovitz (1949–), who creates theatrical images of well-known sport personalities and who has photographed many Olympic athletes.

Although photography brought a deluge of sport images into homes, mainstream U.S. artists are applying their techniques and skill to create masterpieces of U.S. culture. The most popular of contemporary American sport painters is LeRoy Neiman (1927–). Neiman has been described as an American impressionist and is known primarily as a colorist. His paintings and serigraphs seem to explode with color and dramatic excitement. Neiman served as the official artist for five Olympiads and created works related to basketball, boxing, billiards, cycling, golf, hockey, gymnastics, and swimming.

There are literally hundreds of other artists who captured the essence of beauty in motion and the rush of excitement in sport. Regardless of their fame or obscurity, they all have one thing in common: they create memorable images that reflect U.S. popular culture.

—*Stephen Allan Patrick*

See also: Neiman, LeRoy; Olympic Games; Rockwell, Norman

For further reading:
Davis, Ron. 1988. "Olympics Gallery." *Runner's World*, October, 46–51.
Higgs, Robert J. 1982. *Sports: A Reference Guide.* Westport, CT: Greenwood Press.
"Playful Paintings." 1994. *The Economist*, April 30, 76–78.

ASHE, ARTHUR ROBERT, JR.
(1943–1993)

The first African American male to achieve greatness on the tennis court, Arthur Ashe became one of the most popular and highly respected sport figures of the late twentieth century. Born and raised in Richmond, Virginia, Ashe first gained fame in 1961 by desegregating and winning the U.S. interscholastic tournament. Four years later, as a University of California, Los Angeles, senior, he won the national intercollegiate singles tennis championship, and in 1968, he rose to number one in the national rankings after winning both the U.S. Amateur and the U.S. Open titles. During an eleven-year professional career, the tennis player won thirty-three singles titles, including the Australian Open in 1970 and Wimbledon in 1975. A member of ten Davis Cup teams, he also served as U.S. Davis Cup captain from 1981 to 1985.

In 1972, Ashe helped found the Association of Tennis Professionals, of which he later served as president. Throughout the early years of open tennis, he was an important symbol of integrity and enlightened leadership and a role model for young African Americans. In addition, his intelligence, poise, and grace under pressure made him an immensely popular figure whose appeal transcended race and athletic accomplishment. The author of an acclaimed multivolume study of African American athletes, *Hard Road to Glory* (1988), he also coauthored, with Princeton professor Arnold Rampersad, a best-selling memoir aptly titled *Days of Grace* (1993). Ashe contracted AIDS from a 1988 blood transfusion, and when he died in 1993, the entire nation mourned his passing.

—*Raymond Arsenault*

See also: Altruism and Activism; Civil Rights and Sport

For further reading:

Quackenbush, Robert M. 1994. *Arthur Ashe and His Match with History.* New York: Simon and Schuster.

ATHLETE

An athlete is a person who takes part in competitive (against others or himself) sport. An athlete typically possesses either the natural prerequisites or the developed ability for athletic competition, including strength, speed, coordination, agility, and endurance. Though athletes have historically been associated with performance, the modern athlete has taken on an incredibly diverse and broad range of attributes, ranging from role model to cultural or national icon to economic entity.

The earliest evidence of athletics comes from Sumeria, where, archeologists have determined, wrestling took place approximately five thousand years ago. Although wrestling probably evolved as a survival skill, the concept of athlete emerges when participants train and practice to engage in the activity for sport, competition, or entertainment.

The Olympic Games, which began around 776 B.C. in Greece, represent the first gathering for the expressed purpose of demonstrating athletic skill in celebrated contests, primarily track and field, with defined and honored winners or outstanding athletes. With the advent of the modern Olympic Games in A.D. 1896, an international forum was established wherein athletes could compete in measured contests and develop a variety of other characteristics that would redefine the athlete in the twentieth century. The modern athlete is a finely tuned competitor but also a cultural icon, a hero, a role model, a patriot, a businessperson, a member of the socioeconomic elite, and an internationally recognized personality.

In the late twentieth century, for example, probably no person better exemplified the multiple roles of the athlete than professional basketball player Michael Jordan. Recognized as perhaps the greatest athlete ever to play his sport, Jordan was equally notable for his marketability. He endorsed a wide-ranging variety of products, from athletic shoes to automobiles to underwear. His face, even in silhouette, was among the most recognized images in the world, and children around the globe labeled him as their hero.

Other athletes, such as Muhammad Ali, used their international recognition to address social and political issues well beyond the parameters of athletic performance. This lofty status and consequent behavior, both positive and negative, caused athletes to be scrutinized as much for their off-field activities as for their performance in their respective sports. Whether amateur or professional, the modern athlete is expected to serve as a role model who demonstrates such positive cultural values as teamwork and community service.

If in their private lives they fail to meet those expectations, athletes quickly fall from grace. Endorsements are refused or taken away, and the ensuing media blitz quickly demolishes the pedestal they stand on. Thus, at the beginning of the twenty-first century, the definition of an athlete includes attitudinal, behavioral, and societal criteria in addition to the traditional prerequisite physical ability.

—*Sean C. Madden*

See also: Athletes as Symbolic Heroes; Jordan, Michael; Olympic Games

For further reading:

Deford, Frank. 2002. *The Heart of a Champion: Celebrating the Spirit and Character of America's Sports Heroes.* Chanhassen, MN: NorthWord Books.

Ireland, Mary, and Aurelia Nattiv, eds. 2003. *The Female Athlete.* Philadelphia: W. B. Saunders.

Jones, Charlie, and Frank Deford, eds. 1997. *What Makes Winners Win: Thoughts and Reflections from Successful Athletes.* Secaucus, NJ: Birch Lane Press.

ATHLETES, ABOVE THE LAW

In addition to being enamored with the on-field triumphs of professional athletes, Americans are also fascinated with the off-field exploits of sport heroes. The U.S. media ensures not only that the statistics of favored players are accessible but also that the reader is privy to the troubles athletes face in their personal lives. During 1995, in the United States, for example, newspaper articles covered 350 intercollegiate and professional athletes, nearly all men, who were implicated in 252 crimes and faced criminal charges. Criminal assault cases outnumbered any other type of offense, and most of the assault cases involved women as victims. Drug possession and drug use were the next most frequently mentioned charges.

When athletes are implicated in criminal acts or arrested, the incidents may not result in the jail or prison time that ordinary citizens involved in comparable situations might expect. In more-

mundane cases, popular athletes may be processed quickly through the court system. For example, when gifted baseball player Barry Bonds appeared in county court in 1994 to petition to have his family support payments reduced, the judge granted his request and subsequently asked for Bonds's autograph. It is this type of incident that has led people, in settings as varied as dinner tables, barber shops, taverns, or talk-radio shows, to speculate that athletes receive preferential treatment from the criminal justice system.

Of 217 collegiate or professional athletes accused of felony sexual violence between 1986 and 1995, 79 percent were arrested and 54 percent were indicted; however, only 31 percent were successfully prosecuted. This low figure does not necessarily demonstrate that law enforcement officials are doing a poor job of policing sport stars; instead, it may reflect the reluctance on the part of juries to convict popular athletes (Benedict 1997, 79–80).

In addition, high-profile athletes can afford to spend large sums of money to settle cases out of court and thus may avoid prosecution and jail time. Before Mike Tyson's trial for rape began, the victim, Desiree Washington, was offered $1 million to drop the charges and settle the case privately. Although Washington declined this offer, other victims may accept, thus helping wealthy athletes escape criminal prosecution. Furthermore, when athletes are required to appear in court, court dates may be delayed several months to allow players to continue to participate in their athletic endeavors. And since athletes often benefit from access to high-priced attorneys and legal-defense teams, it is reasonable to suggest that they have unusual advantages when dealing with the judicial system.

Therefore, while it may be too strong a generalization to say that athletes are above the law, it appears to be true that athletes profit from their high status when they encounter different phases of the criminal justice system. Many criminal violations by college athletes go unreported to the police or to the press. A study of campus police records and internal judicial affairs documents from thirty National Collegiate Athletic Association (NCAA) Division I institutions that had basketball and football teams revealed that crimes against women were far less likely than others to be reported to police—particularly when the perpetrator was an athlete (Benedict 1997, 64).

Although this subject has generated enormous interest in the United States, it is a topic that requires much more systematic research. More facts need to be uncovered about the different phases of the criminal justice process; for instance, how do jurors perceive athletes, how do officers treat athletes, and how do judges handle cases involving athletes? Gender discrimination also requires investigation; that is, do certain athletes receive preferential treatment because they are men who come into contact with a disproportionately male criminal justice system? When these types of questions are properly investigated and answered, one can properly conclude whether or not athletes are actually above the law.

—*Todd Schoepflin*

See also: Simpson, Orenthal James "O. J."; Tyson, Mike

For further reading:

Benedict, Jeff. 1997. *Public Heroes, Private Felons.* Boston: Northeastern University Press.
Coakley, Jay. 1998. *Sport in Society: Issues and Controversies.* 6th ed. New York: McGraw-Hill.

ATHLETES AS ACTORS

Having excelled in one public venue, some athletes attempt to capitalize on their established celebrity to forge a career in acting. Athletic celebrities have been the stuff of product marketing for decades. In the twentieth century, the athlete-as-spokesperson phenomenon resulted in putting these men and women onto radio and television and into the movies. The step from filmed celebrity as product endorser to filmed celebrity as performer was short and seemingly inevitable.

Modern collegiate and professional athletes attempt to use their sport-acquired popularity as an entree into the world of acting. Far greater numbers attempt this cultural crossover, however, than succeed. Those who prove the most successful eventually develop public personas based solely on their acting skills, while the majority remain notable as athletes who happen to act. Luminaries from all corners of the athletic world who have made one or both of these adjustments include college football star Burt Reynolds; professional football players Jim Brown, Alex Karras, "Broadway" Joe Namath, and O. J. Simpson; baseball players Chuck Conners, Bert Convey, and Joe Garagiola; basketball superstars Michael Jordan and Dennis Rodman; and Olympic favorites Johnny Weissmuller, Bruce Jenner, and Cathy Rigby.

Those athletes have achieved levels of success as actors beyond guest appearances on television situation comedies. Many, in fact, are far better known as actors than they were originally as athletes, despite having been relatively successful in their individual sport. On the other hand, situation comedies have proven a popular first step for many aspiring actor-athletes, following closely behind commercials, talk shows, and game shows. The accessibility of roles in situation comedies may be attributable, in part, to the fact that this forum often allows the athletes to "play themselves" in guest shots. Unfortunately, these appearances seldom have anything to do with serious acting and often do little to contradict the stereotype of the "dumb jock." Many athletes who succeed in establishing careers as performers never escape their history in athletics and are often cast in similar roles, like former gymnast Cathy Rigby flitting about the stage as the athletic Peter Pan or Michael Jordan playing hoops with cartoon characters in the movie *Space Jam.* An unusual extension of this category includes individuals such as André the Giant, Mr. T and Hulk Hogan, who remained figures of questionable ability as actors but who continued to appear regularly nonetheless.

Olympic champion Johnny Weissmuller as Tarzan and Johnny Sheffield as his foster son in MGM's 1941 movie Tarzan's Secret Treasure.

(Underwood & Underwood/Corbis)

The athlete-as-actor cultural crossover displays a disproportionate overrepresentation of white men, reflecting the historic gender imbalance seen in athletics.

—*David Maslow*

See also: Cartoons and Sport; Film and Sport; Jordan, Michael; Rodman, Dennis

For further reading:

Hill, Raymond. 1975. *O.J. Simpson.* New York: Random House.

Issacs, Stan. 1970. *Jim Brown: The Golden Year, 1964.* Englewood Cliffs, NJ: Prentice Hall.

Kriegel, Mark. 2004. *Namath: A biography.* NY: Viking, 2004.

ATHLETES AS SYMBOLIC HEROES

Because of sport's dramatic and entertaining nature, its capacity for direct confrontation, and its popularity and visibility, athletes have often been viewed as symbolic heroes for larger cultural issues. The capacity for dramatic action and individual will within a team context has historically drawn passionate responses from the public. As sport has become more organized and commercialized, athletic heroes have played significant social roles as exemplars of the character and ideals of their fan base.

In the late nineteenth century, as the United States became more urban, industrial, and modern, sport was the province of men, and its greatest heroes embodied a rugged, masculine ethic. The bellicose, hard-drinking boxing champion John L. Sullivan and the fiery Chicago White Stockings manager Cap Anson typified an aggressive individuality that most of their admirers found sorely lacking in their own increasingly regimented lives. The Chicago White Stockings was the original name of the Chicago Cubs around 1900. The name for the American league franchise was "borrowed" from his previous rivals by team owner, Charles Comiskey.

Ty Cobb of the Detroit Tigers, one of baseball's greatest players of the early twentieth century, incorporated many of these same aggressively masculine values; he feuded with umpires, slid into bases with spikes raised, and verbally baited opponents. Yet Cobb incorporated these residual values with the emergent ethic of the self-made man. Like the hero in a Horatio Alger novel, Cobb was celebrated for succeeding through hard work, rational thought, and plucky individualism. Thus, Cobb embodied the principles of an age of production.

Babe Ruth, on the other hand, symbolized the age of consumption. Ruth, the New York Yankees' legendary slugger of the 1920s, did not calculate and scheme like Cobb; rather, he swung his bat as hard as he could and hit long, dramatic home runs. Like an overgrown child, Ruth was determined to eat and drink enormous amounts, sleep with hundreds of women, buy and discard clothes at will, and play baseball simply because it was fun. More than any other figure, Ruth symbolized the glamour, frenzy, and indiscriminate consumption of the Roaring Twenties.

Ethnic, gender, and racial groups have also traditionally identified with one of their own succeeding in the sport world. Jewish fans particularly idolized Jewish baseball players like Detroit Tigers' Hank Greenberg and Los Angeles Dodgers' Sandy Koufax, and Italian Americans tended to cheer the loudest for the graceful New York Yankee Joe DiMaggio. Women athletes, from the versatile Babe Didrikson Zaharias of the 1920s to recent tennis stars Chris Evert and Martina Navratilova, have provided inspiration for generations of women. Black athletes like boxer Joe Louis and sprinter Jesse Owens served as dignified role models for a generation of African Americans in the decades preceding racial integration and as U.S. heroes for their symbolic victories over German athletes during Adolf Hitler's ascension to power.

In the modern era, two athletes in particular have used their athletic success to transcend the sporting world and effect social change. Black baseball pioneer and Brooklyn Dodger Jackie Robinson earned legions of admirers for his self-control in the face of prejudice. Robinson became an outspoken advocate for racial integration and black economic development. In addition to Robinson, boxer Muhammad Ali's conversion to the Nation of Islam and his refusal to enter the Vietnam War made him the most visible expression of black nationalism in the 1960s.

Despite the increasingly corporate nature of sport, athletes continue to symbolize the qualities associated with historical eras or groups of people. Indeed, without heroes, sport would cease to have any resonance in society.

—*Aram Goudsouzian*

See also: Ali, Muhammad; Robinson, Jack Roosevelt "Jackie"; Ruth, George Herman "Babe," Jr.; Sullivan, John L.

For further reading:
Vanderwerken, David L., and Spencer K. Wertz. 1985. *Sport Inside Out*. Fort Worth: Texas Christian University Press.

ATLANTIC CITY, NEW JERSEY

In the early twentieth century, Atlantic City, New Jersey, was a popular resort offering a variety of commercial athletic spectacles to its visitors, but it became best known as the home of the Miss America Pageant, as the East Coast version of Las Vegas, and as the model for the game of Monopoly.

Atlantic City was founded in 1854 and soon became a popular resort for swimming, sailing, and fishing. In the late nineteenth century, local entrepreneurs built huge amusement piers where tourists danced, roller-skated, and watched concerts and basketball games. In the 1920s, Steel Pier became famous for its Water Circus, featuring high divers, human cannonballs, and speedboat and water-skiing acts. The famous High-Diving Horse, ridden by a young woman in a bathing suit, leaped off a forty-foot platform into a pool of water. Animals that imitated human athletes were popular at Steel Pier, which in the 1930s also featured boxing cats and Rex, the water-skiing Wonder Dog. The Water Circus remained popular into the early 1960s.

Pier owners seeking tourist attention frequently hired sport celebrities to appear in the city. In 1933, for example, 7,500 fans watched heavyweight champion Primo Carnero fight JoJo the Boxing Kangaroo at Steel Pier. Swimming star Gertrude Ederle performed at the resort shortly after swimming the English Channel in 1926. During the Depression era, endurance events such as dance marathons, including a contest at the Million Dollar Pier that lasted from May 26 to October 19, 1932, captured tourists' attention. Alvin "Shipwreck" Kelly broke his own record by sitting on a flagpole over Steel Pier for fifty days in the summer of 1930.

Atlantic City offered more traditional sporting events for those who did not enjoy the carnival atmosphere of the piers. The Bacharach Giants, a Negro League baseball team active from 1916 to 1934, was popular with African Americans employed in the local resort industry, but it was ignored by the predominantly white tourists. The city's enormous convention center, completed in 1929, functioned as an early indoor sport arena. It seated 40,000 spectators for boxing or wrestling matches or 25,000 spectators for hockey games featuring the semipro Atlantic City Seagulls. Convention Hall staged indoor football games starting in 1930, decades before the construction of the Astrodome in Houston, Texas. In keeping with the predominance of noncompetitive athletic spectacles in the resort, after 1941, the convention center also served as the summer home of the Ice Capades.

In 1935, inspired by memories of vacations in Atlantic City, Charles Darrow sold the patent for a board game called Monopoly to Parker Brothers. Players of the best-selling game bought and sold properties named after the city's streets and railroads. The city and the game became so inter-

Steel Pier in Atlantic City became famous for its Water Circus, featuring high divers, human cannonballs, and speed-boat and water-skiing acts (August 1899).
(BETTMANN/CORBIS)

twined in the national imagination that, in 1973, protests prevented the local government from changing the names of Mediterranean Avenue and Baltic Avenue, the least expensive Monopoly properties.

After the 1950s, changing travel patterns meant that fewer people visited Atlantic City. To most Americans, the resort became familiar primarily as the home of the Miss America Pageant. Local boosters, hoping to encourage visitors to stay at the resort after Labor Day, staged the first pageant in September 1921. Although the pageant was not exactly a sporting event, it was a competition based to some extent on physical characteristics,

and the local preliminaries that led to its national championship followed a pattern common in amateur athletics. Although the early pageant was primarily a beauty contest, organizers added a talent competition and began awarding scholarships to the winners in the 1940s. It was first televised, live from the convention center, in 1954, and watching the televised pageant became an annual ritual for millions of people who had never been to Atlantic City.

Although Miss America remained a U.S. icon, Atlantic City itself faced ruin as declining tourism destroyed its economic base. Since Prohibition, visitors had been betting on horse races and playing craps and roulette in the illegal back rooms of local night clubs. In the 1970s, local politicians argued that only legalized gambling could revitalize the resort, and Merv Griffin's Resorts International became the first legal casino on the East Coast in 1978. Employees were solicited from Nevada's industry and were cautiously screened to weed out possible affiliation with organized crime.

A casino building boom revitalized the Boardwalk in the 1970s and 1980s. Always a part of Atlantic City's mystique, spectacle continued to be an important part of local entertainment, with casinos such as the Trump Taj Mahal and Bally's Wild West competing for tourist dollars with fanciful buildings and elaborate decorations. Legalized gambling attracted regional tourism to Atlantic City, but it has not restored it to its earlier position as one of the country's leading resorts.

—*Debbie Ann Doyle*

See also: Gambling; Swimming

For further reading:

Funnell, Charles E. 1975. *By the Beautiful Sea: The Rise and High Times of That Great American Resort, Atlantic City.* New Brunswick, NJ: Rutgers University Press.

AUDIENCE RITUALS

To be part of an audience for a sporting event or to follow the trials and triumphs of an athlete or team is to engage in a ritual process. The universal function of ritual is to confirm a sense of shared experience and an underlying cultural order through a ceremonial symbolic performance. Although the audience member's role in ritual performances can be passive, as in casual television watching, one of the reasons for watching a sporting event is to register and share in a connection to one's cultural environment and in an implied sense of community through a staged rite. Sport audiences share vicariously in the mythic resonance of the athlete's heroic journey through various obstacles.

Ritual is a means of performing the fundamentally human practice of imposing meaning on life. The depth of meaning a sporting event carries depends on the weight of the emotional or material investment of the audience member. Sport audiences have many choices in the amount of their investment. To flip through sport channels as a fleeting escape from one's worries is a minimal investment; consequently, the possible rewards in terms of meaning are minimal. However, the more serious fan who buys season tickets, braves parking and weather, and makes pilgrimages to championships derives enormous meaning from audience rituals. In addition, gambling is perhaps the most direct material way to invest in a deep connection to a sporting event—bettors' fortunes rise and fall according to the seriousness of the risk they have taken and the outcome of the event.

The Super Bowl may be the single largest annual audience ritual. The most watched television programs are Super Bowls, and global audiences may number over 130 million. Super Bowl parties have become a U.S. institution, drawing both serious fans and many who do not usually care about football but who simply wish to be included in what they recognize as a widely shared ceremonial experience. Audiences proceed from the solemnity of the national anthem to the unveiling of the latest million-dollar commercials to the often one-sided action on the field to the Hollywood-style halftime show to the presentation of the world-championship trophy. The Super Bowl stages the reliable symbolic and narrative structure, heroic archetypes, and community celebration of a cultural form that rituals have provided throughout human history.

Sport events are a classic example of what Daniel Boorstin calls pseudo events, artificially preconceived dramas like awards ceremonies, political elections, and press conferences that are actually performances reported as news. Sport provides nightly newscasts with material that can be prepared in advance, regardless of the outcome of the events. The show-business superficiality and corruption of the sport world can be easily criticized, and sport audiences are often held in disdain for investing a part of their identities in such a world and for wasting their time by passively consuming escapist entertainment. These criticisms, however valid, do not alter the fact that contemporary sport provides its audiences with the ritual function of enacted mythology, with symbolic meaning, and with a sense of participation in community that have been the foundation of human experience since ancient times.

—*Geoffrey Rubinstein*

See also: Gambling; Mythology of Sport; Television, Impact on Sport

For further reading:
Boorstin, Daniel J. 1983. *The Discoverers.* New York: Random House.

AUTOMOBILE RACING

During every weekend of summer in every state, automobile racing on dirt tracks or on concrete super speedways continues, having long outgrown its humble beginnings. In the United States, automobile racing evolved to massive tracks and noisy horsepower equal to the macho masculinity of the country. From its beginning as a diversion for moonshine-runners, automobile racing has become a big-league, worldwide blood sport, selling thrills, spills, and mud in the face while vying for television money and against local noise-pollution and blue laws.

Fans of automobile racing and the drivers who participate in the sport have a love-hate relationship. The fans want their favorite to win, but they also attend the races in the hopes of seeing collisions and mayhem. Major automobile racing is one of the most evident displays of Yankee mechanical precision, and any shade-tree mechanic can get a start, given enough luck, ingenuity, the right car, and fearlessness.

Racetracks are modern temples. Drivers are gods. Owners are saints. Promoters are visionaries. Racing families are dynasties. And the U.S. public acknowledges these facts through the ritual of merchandising—a fortune is shelled out of the collective U.S. purse each year, not only for expensive, premium seating at racing events but also for the tons of memorabilia, T-shirts, mugs, posters, and pennants featuring the likenesses of those gods and dynasties. In automobile racing, goddesses are rare.

Fans cheer and celebrate the victories of their favorites, and the favorites are rewarded with a checkered flag, an enormous purse, and media coverage.

As in any professional sport, the few well-known stars overshadow the tens of thousands of unknowns and never-will-be's. Along with professionals at all levels, there are legions of amateurs who hold no illusions of ever becoming pros; they just want to have fun. Rabid fans flock to the concessions operated by local churches and volunteer fire departments to buy the merchandise and drink the sodas. In the stands, they criticize the "other guy" and swoon at the mere mention of their favorite's latest four-wheeled feat.

Race courses are commodities. Tracks are bought, closed, opened, enshrined, and even forgotten, leaving behind acres of scrubland. The vastness of the Indianapolis 500 Raceway, for example, is awe inspiring from the inside during May and July but not much use the rest of the year, except possibly as a golf course. As an economic boon, the total impact of automobile racing is incalculable. In the big leagues, the sport is white and male. In the amateur ranks, most notably the Sports Car Club of America, diversity exists on paper. Ultimately, money gets a driver into the sport, and money keeps him there. Automobile racing is not a place for the poor or the unemployed. Beyond a car and garage, the basic team needs a trailer, tools, spare parts, tires, gas,

In 1957, this three-car crash occurred on the north turn of the 125-mile race for modified stock cars. The event was one of the many during the NASCAR Speed Week races which drew crowds of over 40,000 people. Top drivers of U.S. and Canada competed on the famous beach and road course.
(BETTMANN/CORBIS)

and food. There are volumes published on how to be an amateur racer on someone else's budget.

Automobile racing has been the subject of movies, songs, folklore, and business acumen. Its vertical integration reaches into a majority of businesses and communities, pitching everything from cornflakes to mufflers.

—*Charles Moore*

See also: National Association for Stock Car Auto Racing

For further reading:

Keyser, Michael, and Brian Redman. 1999. *The Speed Merchants: The Drivers, the Cars, the Tracks; A Journey through the World of Motor Racing: 1969–1972.* Cambridge, MA: Bentley Publishing.

BANKS, ERNEST "ERNIE"
(1931–)

In Chicago, a city marked by deep racial divisions, Ernie Banks, who broke into the major leagues just six years after Jackie Robinson integrated baseball, became known as "Mr. Cub" and earned the love and respect of fans, regardless of their racial or ethnic backgrounds. Banks was the first African American to play for the Chicago Cubs. He joined the major league team late in the 1953 season, straight from the Kansas City Monarchs of the Negro American League, and he immediately established himself as the Cubs' regular shortstop and rising star. The tall, slim, right-handed hitter had surprising power. In 1955, his second full season, he became the first shortstop in the history of the majors to hit forty home runs in a single season, ending that season with forty-four home runs. He followed that season with four more years in which he hit over forty home runs, between 1957 and 1960, as well as earning Most Valuable Player Awards in 1958 and 1959. In 1959, he also established a record for shortstops with a .985 fielding percentage. Banks moved to first base in 1962, and he remained a productive hitter until near the end of his career.

Banks retired in 1971 with a nineteen-year total of 512 home runs. He spent his entire career with the Cubs, a team mired in mediocrity during most his tenure with them, and he never had the oppor-

Chicago Cubs shortstop and 1959 MVP winner Ernie Banks posed with members of the Long Island City Boys' Club in Queens, New York. Banks was on a speaking tour at Boys' Clubs across the country.
(Bettmann/Corbis)

tunity to play in a World Series. He was as much beloved for his unceasing enthusiasm for the game as he was for his hitting prowess. He often expressed the wish that he could play a doubleheader, rather than a single game. "Mr. Cub" was inducted into the Baseball Hall of Fame in 1977.

—*Edward J. Rielly*

See also: Negro Baseball Leagues; Robinson, Jack Roosevelt "Jackie"

For further reading:

May, Julian. 1973. *Ernie Banks, Home Run Slugger.* Mankato, MN: Crestwood House.

BASEBALL

A distinct U.S. adaptation of English tag sports, the model for all other professional U.S. team sports, and the oldest and most successful U.S. athletic export to other cultures, baseball is simply "the national pastime."

Origins of Baseball

For many years, a widely believed myth held that Abner Doubleday invented baseball near Cooperstown, New York, in the 1830s. This origin myth has great cultural resonance. A Civil War hero, Doubleday was seen as forging a new nation in war and binding that nation together in peace through his creation of a national pastime.

The myth is nonsense, however. Doubleday was not even living in Cooperstown when he was supposed to have invented baseball. But Cooperstown, as the site of the National Baseball Hall of Fame and Museum, has parlayed the fabrication into a tourist industry. The meanings of the myth are significant for U.S. cultural nationalism. The main proponents of the Doubleday/Cooperstown origin myth, including Albert Spalding, wanted to see baseball as uniquely American, without a connection to rounders or cricket, its close British cousins. The intensity of belief in the origin myth reflects a deep U.S. distrust of acknowledging English origins and influences.

Despite the resistance of believers in the Doubleday myth, it is clear that U.S. baseball developed from the game of rounders. Rounders, like cricket, one o'cat, and other games, arrived in America along with English settlers. All these games are similar, involving running to the safety of a base before being tagged with a ball. Baseball evolved from such sports and cricket in the 1820s and 1830s in the United States. Some early baseball clubs were made up of cricketers looking for novelty.

Many see baseball as the pastoral sport in U.S. culture. Its lawns and its agrarian rhythm, set by the cycles of alternate play rather than by a clock, mark it as a country sport. This is only a fantasy about the game, however. Originally, baseball was an urban sport, the recreation of tradesmen and skilled laborers in early-nineteenth-century New York City.

The symbolic impact of baseball on U.S. culture is therefore that of a little piece of idealized countryside transported into the middle of the city. The game has great stability. Unlike football and basketball, baseball has remained the same for well over a century, not only in its basic rules but also in its style of play. Baseball fans of every generation find in their contemporary game an ideal package for nostalgia, a nostalgia they relate to "country things."

Work and Play

The first professional baseball leagues were founded in the 1870s, almost fifty years before the National Football League and well before even the invention of basketball. Baseball became a business before most modern U.S. sports had reached their current form of play. However, since the earliest days, baseball fans have decried commercialism in the game, and baseball is filled

> *For many years, the widely believed myth was that Abner Doubleday invented baseball near Cooperstown, New York, in the 1830s, binding the nation together in peace through his creation of a national pastime. The myth is nonsense, however. Doubleday was not even living in Cooperstown when he was supposed to have invented baseball.*

with conflicts about the appropriate relation of play to work.

Professional baseball players have formed unions and mounted job actions throughout the history of the sport. The strength of labor organization in the game has varied in ways that parallel the general culture's attitude toward labor activism. Union activity was strongest in the 1880s and 1890s, again in the 1910s, and increasingly from the late 1960s through the 1990s. In between, players were pitted against one another by tough competition for jobs within the game and by the infamous "reserve clause," a section of player contracts that bound a player to one team indefinitely. U.S. Supreme Court decisions that exempted baseball from antitrust laws preserved the sport as a peculiar model of work in U.S. culture by protecting the reserve clause.

Cultural attitudes toward work in the sport, however, changed with the political times. Working-class fans saw early labor movements and individual player holdouts as heroic. Since the 1970s, however, effective labor organizing has meant that players earn salaries in the millions of dollars. To protect the system of free agency that led to these salaries, the players went on an extended strike in 1994–1995. This strike was terribly unpopular with fans, who saw the players' demands as unjustified during an era of waning labor activism in the wider culture.

Importing People, Exporting Culture

Baseball has been a route into U.S. culture for generations of immigrants. In the nineteenth century, Irish immigrants learned about U.S. culture and joined its social institutions, preeminently through baseball. In later decades, Italian, Polish, and Jewish newcomers to the large cities played and watched ball games as they were assimilating into U.S. culture. The segregation of the sport from the earliest times ensured that white immigrants could melt into all-white teams, reinforcing racial barriers in U.S. cities.

In the later twentieth century, the sport was also popular among Latin American and Asian American immigrants. In these cases, though, baseball had done its work abroad before the arrival of these later waves of immigration. As the power of the United States spread across the globe in the early twentieth century, baseball followed the flag and the commercial interests of U.S. companies. One can trace the sphere of U.S. imperial interest simply by listing those nations where baseball became naturalized as a national pastime: Japan, Korea, Taiwan, the Philippines, Mexico, Cuba, the Dominican Republic, Puerto Rico, and Venezuela. Strong relations between the U.S. game and its exported versions were maintained by frequent tours of college teams and star professionals. During the winter seasons, American stars, both black and white, filled the ranks of teams in Latin America.

Myth and Language

U.S. English is filled with expressions drawn from baseball. Most Americans know that coming "out of left field" is to do or say something unexpected. To "get to first base" is to have initial success, often in a sexual sense. And "playing hardball" has become more a metaphor for business toughness than a literal phrase for the game itself.

Baseball has so woven itself into U.S. culture that twentieth-century life and language were unthinkable without it. Great events from the sport's history took on symbolic significance. The 1919 "Black Sox" scandal, in which members of the Chicago White Sox conspired to throw the World Series, is a great example of betrayal in U.S. history, epitomized by the child who supposedly asked conspirator Joe Jackson to "say it ain't so, Joe." Babe Ruth is the classic U.S. overreaching hero, the Paul Bunyan of sport. Jackie Robinson stands for the courage of the whole civil rights movement, Lou Gehrig for dignity in the face of death, and Leo Durocher for the unprincipled desire to win at any cost, because "nice guys finish last."

The sport has moved beyond symbol into the realm of myth. Baseball is the source of a rich

The New York Yankees take on the Minnesota Twins on opening day in 1988 at Yankee Stadium. (DUOMO/CORBIS)

mythic literature, including novels like Bernard Malamud's *The Natural* (1952), Eric Rolfe Greenberg's *The Celebrant: A Novel* (1986), and Robert Coover's *The Universal Baseball Association, Inc., J. Henry Waugh, Prop.* (1968). In addition, the journey of the batter/runner around the bases has been seen as the mythic journey of theorist Joseph Campbell's archetypal heroes.

The game's numbers fascinate Americans. Both the statistics in which its records are expressed and its internal structure of number—nine players, nine innings, three strikes—have deep symbolic resonance. And as the archetypal game that fathers play with sons, baseball has deep significance for gender in the United States, particularly as women gaze at and enjoy watching men play and also as women themselves play baseball and take on roles traditionally associated with men.

—*Tim Morris*

See also: Language of Sport; National Baseball Hall of Fame; Negro Baseball Leagues; Supreme Court Decisions

For further reading:

Alexander, Charles. 1991. *Our Game: An American Baseball History.* New York: Holt.

Goldstein, Warren. 1989. *Playing for Keeps: A History of Early Baseball.* Ithaca, NY: Cornell University Press.

Seymour, Harold. 1990. *Baseball: The People's Game.* New York: Oxford University Press.

BASEBALL, MINOR LEAGUES

Minor league baseball is a symbol of the so-called golden era when the game and the United States seemed pure and innocent, but, simultaneously, the minors were interwoven into the fabric of the mass consumer culture of the late twentieth century. Nostalgia for a simpler time, chasing a dream to the big leagues, a connection with one's youth, and Main Street small-town America explain the lure of minor league baseball.

The minors developed during the last several decades of the nineteenth century as numerous leagues struggled for major league status. In 1901, the National Association of Professional Baseball Leagues (NAPBL) was formed as an umbrella organization for minor league teams, after which the minors flourished. Small-town newspapers promoted their games, and teams became symbols of civic pride, as competition between rival communities linked towns, both culturally and socially, to a region.

By the mid-1930s, many leagues had dissolved, but the Depression actually fostered a resurgence of interest in the minors as Americans sought escape from hard times in inexpensive entertainment. Toward the end of the decade, team owners built many small, intimate new ballparks with odd configurations and lights. Attendance increased as fans went to the games after work, when the heat of the summer day had lessened somewhat. These new venues, and the broadcast of the games by over four hundred local radio stations, developed a close relationship between fans and teams. By 1949, a record 59 leagues, 464 teams, and 10,000 players drew nearly 42 million fans.

During the 1950s, a rapidly expanding mass popular culture drew attention away from the minors. Television and air conditioning brought people indoors to watch major league games. During that decade, other distractions, such as rock 'n' roll, shopping malls, suburban backyard barbecues, and Technicolor movies, drew the attention of the U.S. consumer. In addition, interstate highways made it easier for fans to go to major league games. As the population shifted westward, major league franchises followed, encroaching on minor league markets. By 1956,

attendance had fallen over 50 percent, and 240 teams went out of business.

Many Americans, during the political and social upheaval of the latter part of the twentieth century, lost faith in government officials and community leaders. In parallel fashion, baseball fans became equally disillusioned with the major league version of the game, which had come to be dominated by inaccessible millionaire players and greedy owners who appeared more concerned with money, television contracts, and product endorsements than with playing a game or fulfilling a childhood dream. The battles over free agency, particularly the 1994 strike and loss of the World Series—along with high ticket prices, drug use and gambling by players, congested traffic on the way to large and sterile multisport stadium complexes, and artificial turf— diminished the integrity of the majors. In contrast, innovative minor league owners and promoters showcased the minors as a grassroots game that echoed the virtues of America's past. They built quaint ballparks that re-created an era in which families and communities could gather socially, creating a nostalgic sense of place, away from the modern, fast-paced life of the late twentieth century. Several movies, such as *Bull Durham* (1988), *The Natural* (1984), and, in particular, *Field of Dreams* (1989), reflected those themes. In 1991, the NAPBL, in partnership with Major League Baseball Properties, authorized the licensed international marketing of minor league team caps and clothing merchandise. Paradoxically, while the minors became the symbol of a past golden era in the United States, they became, at the same time, a full participant in the mass consumer culture of U.S. society.

—*Stephen W. Charry*

See also: Athletes, as Symbolic Heroes; Baseball; Baseball Films; Television, Impact on Sport

For further reading:

Davis, Hank. 1997. *Small-Town Heroes: Images of Minor League Baseball.* Iowa City: University of Iowa Press.

BASEBALL FILMS

A staple of comedy and melodrama in the 1940s, the Hollywood baseball film changed with the film industry, offering psychological realism in the 1950s through the 1970s, then magical realism in the 1980s and 1990s. Film reflects U.S. culture through the prism of baseball but rarely portrays the sport itself with much accuracy.

Silent films sometimes featured baseball stars as themselves. It was common for sport stars of the 1910s to tour in vaudeville in the off-season. Early baseball films were extensions of these vaudeville acts. Baseball comedy was a staple of both live and animated shorts in the 1930s and 1940s. In early films, baseball was a common frame of reference for gags and light melodrama. All classes and ages were assumed to be able to relate to the sport; indeed, it exposed certain gender barriers that were exploitable for humor, as in the opening number of *Damn Yankees* (1958), where wives bemoan their husbands' attachment to baseball.

The Pride of the Yankees (1942) was a watershed in Hollywood's representation of the game. Despite its roots in star vaudeville (Babe Ruth plays himself in this biopic about Lou Gehrig), *The Pride of the Yankees* tries to be a tragedy. Sam Wood's film casts Gary Cooper as the doomed Gehrig, aligning the baseball star with the western and war heroes that Cooper had played in other movies. This film spawned some lesser imitations (James Stewart as Monty Stratton in *The Stratton Story* [1949]; Ronald Reagan as Grover Cleveland Alexander in *The Winning Team* [1952]) and some *much*-lesser imitations (William Bendix in *The Babe Ruth Story* [1948]). All these films were intent on making their protagonists into semi-tragic heroes.

Whimsy also figures in baseball films from this period, including *It Happens Every Spring* and *Take Me Out to the Ballgame* (both 1949) and *Angels in the Outfield* (1951). *It Happens Every Spring* vividly shows class concerns. A professor, Ray Milland, uses science to become an unbeat-able pitcher. But he is ashamed of his skill and tries to hide it from his peers, his colleagues, and his girlfriend. Paul Douglas, as his catcher, stands for the untutored element of society that Milland's character must keep away from his genteel connections.

Later films point to a grittier approach in Hollywood. *Fear Strikes Out* (1957) and *Bang the Drum Slowly* (1973) present the dark side of baseball heroism during an era when Westerns, war films, and spy pictures also gave viewers anti-heroes and ambivalent endings. In *Fear Strikes Out*, Anthony Perkins plays real-life major league player Jimmy Piersall. As in other biopics, the hero struggles against disabilities, but in this case, the disabilities are mental illness and a dysfunctional family. The model is less *The Stratton Story* than *Rebel Without a Cause*. In *Bang the Drum Slowly*, from a novel by Mark Harris, Robert De Niro plays a dying ballplayer—not as a Gehrig-like hero but as a limited, fearful, ordinary man.

The erosion of film censorship in the 1970s did not lead, oddly enough, to foul-mouthed, raunchy baseball movies. The most exaggerated of baseball pictures was perhaps *The Bad News Bears* (1976), featuring Walter Matthau as a profane, irresponsible coach of a youth baseball team. But Hollywood did not choose baseball films to launch the kind of assault on puritanism that characterized such other 1970s films as *Shampoo* (1975), *Network* (1976), or *Apocalypse Now* (1979). Exempt from iconoclasm, baseball resurfaced in film after the re-romanticizing of the movies by directors Steven Spielberg and George Lucas in the late 1970s and early 1980s.

Key to the revival of baseball films in the Reagan presidential era was *The Natural* (1984), starring Robert Redford as Roy Hobbs. An antihero in Bernard Malamud's 1952 novel, Hobbs became, in Redford's portrayal, a magical-realist hero who succeeds where his textual original failed. The film seemed to capture the longing of Americans of the 1980s for a more stirring, if less realistic, view of the past.

Bull Durham (1988) and *Field of Dreams* (1989), both starring Kevin Costner, used baseball as a vehicle for magical realism. Mainly a romantic comedy, *Bull Durham* had a metaphysical edge, with Susan Sarandon musing on the religion of baseball. *Field of Dreams* transformed W. P. Kinsella's novel *Shoeless Joe* into an uncomplicated fantasy, celebrating the corn-fed values of family, farm, and good clean fun in a field.

The early 1990s saw films that capitalized on the sentimental magic of *Field of Dreams*. *Angels in the Outfield* was remade in 1994, turning the gentle spiritual presences of the 1951 film into action figures and cranking up the melodrama. Tommy Lee Jones played Ty Cobb in the florid biopic *Cobb* (1995); John Goodman made a more plausible but even larger than life Babe Ruth in *The Babe* (1992). And fantasy was more oriented toward families in films like *Rookie of the Year* (1993) and *Three Wishes* (1995).

The most culturally significant 1990s baseball film, however, had no fantastic elements. *A League of Their Own* (1992), directed by Penny Marshall, was mild in its feminism and conventional in its bushers-make-good plot. But the setting—professional baseball played by women in the 1940s—was unprecedented. The achievements of women ballplayers, obscure before the film's release, quickly gained general currency in U.S. culture. *A League of Their Own* managed to mix nostalgia for a simpler time with a spirited critique of the values of a simpler time. It struck a chord with viewers of both sexes.

Documentary film about baseball has generally had less cultural impact than fictional films. Newsreels brought baseball to the attention of the huge film-going audiences of the 1920s through the 1950s. The quasi-documentary style of films like *The Jackie Robinson Story* (1950)—in which Robinson played himself in a biopic—melts into fiction. The most significant documentary on baseball came late in the twentieth century: Ken Burns's massive *Baseball* (1994) was shown on public television in nine parts, or "innings." As never before, U.S. intellectuals and high-middle-brow audiences had, in one of their favorite media, justification for a sophisticated view of baseball. Appearances in the film by noted academics like Shelby Foote and Doris Kearns Goodwin made them celebrities and confirmed both their cultural authority and the social cachet of baseball.

—*Tim Morris*

See also: Gehrig, Lou; Kinsella, William P.; Malamud, Bernard; Ruth, George Herman "Babe," Jr.

For further reading:

DiPiero, Thomas. 1997. "Angels in the (Out)Field of Vision." *Camera Obscura* 40–41 (May): 200–225.

Grella, George. 1997. "The Baseball Moment in American Film." *Aethlon* 14, no. 2 (Spring): 7–16.

McGimpsey, David. 2000. *Imagining Baseball: America's Pastime and Popular Culture.* Bloomington: Indiana University Press.

BASEBALL STRIKES

Labor unrest has been a feature of baseball since the sport became professional in the 1860s. As highly visible features of the U.S. labor scene, quarrels between baseball management and labor have become a standard of U.S. attitudes toward labor organization.

Early labor action in baseball did not take the form of strikes. Disputes between players and clubs in the 1870s, the first decade of organized professional baseball, usually ended in a player jumping his contract. The free-labor market tightened in the 1880s, however, with the introduction by management of the "reserve clause" that bound a player to one team indefinitely. To challenge owners, nineteenth-century players tended to form wildcat leagues: the Union Association of 1884 and the Player's League of 1890. Both leagues were short-lived, and never again would players move to create their own alternative workplace.

The fans at Yankee Stadium have their say about the baseball strike. Negotiatiors were to meet in still another effort to settle the owner-player differences (August 4, 1985).
(BETTMANN/CORBIS)

In the first two decades of the twentieth century, the capital required to organize cooperative leagues was out of players' reach. In this respect, baseball followed a traditional cultural pattern of proceeding from artisan production toward a fully capitalized workplace. A special status for baseball was clinched in 1922 when the U.S. Supreme Court ruled that major league baseball was exempt from antitrust laws; since 1922, no rival entrepreneurs have established new leagues, as has happened in other major team sports.

Although labor unrest flourished in nineteenth-century baseball, the sport remained largely exempt from labor action during the years 1890–1965. In May 1912, Detroit Tigers players went on a wildcat strike in support of a suspended Ty Cobb, but the action was short-lived. During the 1918 World Series, a group of Boston Red Sox players, represented by Harry Hooper, threatened to sit out a game unless they were given a fairer share of the gate proceeds; again, the affair was transitory, and the threat was never carried out. Significantly, in light of later public contempt for striking players, Hooper earned the public's respect and emerged from the 1918 dispute with great dignity.

Even as the Depression culminated in the auto-industry strikes of the late 1930s, baseball seemed a placid, paternalistic workplace. Players, bound by unbreakable contracts, accepted individual annual salaries based mostly on owners' dictates, a situation that persisted for several decades.

In 1965, the previously weak players' union hired Marvin Miller, a professional organizer. Collective bargaining finally became a reality. The key issue was, and remains, free agency—the principle that a baseball player is as free as any other worker to sell his labor. Where most unions have bargained for job security and predictable pay increases based on seniority or job grade, baseball players have, somewhat paradoxically, insisted on an unfettered labor market. To this end, players struck briefly at the start of the 1972 season and again in 1981, 1985, and 1994–1995. Only a few games were missed in 1972 and 1985, but the 1981 strike canceled the middle of the season, and the 1994 action wiped out the World Series.

The cultural impact of these baseball strikes shifted significantly from the 1970s to the 1990s. The first free-agent ballplayers were popular heroes. In 1969, Curt Flood, the first player to challenge the reserve clause, became an emblem of integrity. Early free agents in the 1970s, like Andy Messersmith and Catfish Hunter, were celebrated as entrepreneurial free spirits. With their long hair or lavish mustaches, these early free agents seemed a throwback to nineteenth-century contract jumpers.

Such popularity was brief. Free agency drove up player salaries. Although fans of the early 1970s could empathize with a $10,000-a-year player who was suddenly earning six figures, they began to be less complacent about million-dollar players who were suddenly being handed multi-million-dollar contracts. The 1981 baseball strike shared headlines with the air-traffic controllers' strike of the same year. Although the air-traffic controllers' union was broken by the antilabor stand of President Ronald Reagan, baseball players achieved their demands. U.S. workers were ambivalent about the air-traffic controllers' strike; most applauded Reagan's firmness, but others were hostile toward the supervisors and other "replacement workers" who took the controllers' jobs. When the by-now affluent ballplayers won their strike demands, public opinion compared them to the much less well-off controllers and began to turn against the players.

The 1985 strike was momentary. By 1994, how-ever, player salaries had climbed toward an *average* rate of a million dollars a year. Owners, by contrast, seemed to have modest demands: greater parity, stability for "small-market" franchises, and restraint on high spending. After the cancellation of the World Series, the winter passed without progress. Owners prepared to start 1995 with "replacement players." Such a strategy had worked for National Football League (NFL) owners in 1987 when players went on strike. But the more highly individual nature of baseball limited the appeal of replacement teams. In the end, no replacement games were officially played, as owners caved in once more to player demands in the spring of 1995.

The negative public reaction to the 1994–1995 strike was unprecedented. Replacement players shone as hard-working dreamers, not picket-line-crossing scabs. Players were seen as betraying the traditions of the sport for a bagful of money from owners and fans. By the mid-1990s, large-scale job actions in the United States were nearly extinct. Union membership among the general population was dropping, spurred by a demographic shift in population toward right-to-work states in the Sunbelt and by the decline of traditional industries. People looked at the players and saw not workers but rich celebrities.

As the twentieth century ended, baseball faced the certainty of more labor unrest in the early twenty-first century. Meanwhile, ballplayer salaries continue to rise. Not even Sammy Sosa proved exempt from fans' scorn when he demanded a better contract in the summer of 2000. The next baseball strike—or the threat of one—will once again test Americans' fundamental values about labor and collective bargaining.

—*Tim Morris*

See also: Big Business, Sport as; Home-Run Race of 1998; Supreme Court Decisions

For further reading:
Helyar, John. 1994. *Lords of the Realm: The Real History of Baseball.* New York: Villard.

Miller, Marvin. 1992. *A Whole Different Ball Game: The Inside Story of Baseball's New Deal*. New York: Simon and Schuster.

Zingg, Paul J. 1993. *Harry Hooper: An American Baseball Life*. Urbana: University of Illinois Press.

BASKETBALL

From its humble beginnings as a game that involved throwing a soccer ball into a peach basket, basketball has become one of the world's most popular sports. Its style and attitude reflect the dominant influence of African American culture, an influence that has not only reshaped the way the game is played but internationalized its appeal.

From Peach Baskets to the National Basketball Association

Although considered a quintessentially U.S. game, basketball was, in fact, developed by a Canadian. In 1891, James Naismith, a thirty-year-old native of Almonte, Ontario, was working as a physical education instructor for the International Young Men's Christian Association (YMCA) Training School in Springfield, Massachusetts. During one particularly severe winter, Naismith wanted to invent an indoor team game that would be more physically and mentally invigorating than simple calisthenics and gymnastics. Initially and unsuccessfully, he attempted to bring football, soccer, and lacrosse inside, only to find that the roughness of those games was not what he had envisioned in an indoor sport. Armed with a soccer ball, Naismith searched for something, preferably boxes, that would function as goals. The building superintendent offered him the use of two peach baskets, and Naismith had them nailed to the lower rails of the balcony at both ends of the gym. After quickly scribbling down the game's thirteen rules and changing the name from "box ball" to "basketball," Naismith was ready to introduce the new game.

Basketball made its debut in Springfield, Massachusetts, on January 15, 1892. Within months, the game was being played at YMCAs throughout New England and New York. Later that year, basketball spread to the West Coast, and the sport's first intercollegiate game took place in 1895 when the Minneapolis State School of Agriculture defeated Hamline University, 9–3. The game barely resembled basketball as it is played today; those early teams consisted of nine men, who could pass the ball but could not dribble or move with it. Further complicating both teams' efforts to score was the goaltender who guarded each basket.

Professional basketball began not long after the sport's collegiate debut. Although the first professional game took place in 1896 in Trenton, New Jersey, the first professional basketball league was not formed until 1898. After the 1903 collapse of the National League, as it was called, professional basketball went through a series of regional leagues that included the Eastern League, the Central League, the Massachusetts League, and the Hudson River League. The games were free-wheeling and often violent, fouls were infrequently called, and players had to be concerned not only with the rough play of their opponents but also with that of overzealous fans. The game's popularity was growing, however, and by the early 1920s, a league championship series drew crowds in excess of ten thousand. Still, basketball's popularity was regionally circumscribed; the game, with only a few exceptions, had not developed a national audience.

In 1946, the Basketball Association of America (BAA) was inaugurated. Organized as a way to fill arena seats between hockey games, the eleven-team league, despite having more publicity and playing in larger venues, had much less talent than its rival, the National Basketball League (NBL), which had been in operation since the late 1930s. The NBL's star player was six-foot-eleven George Mikan of the Minneapolis Lakers. Mikan was the game's first dominating center. Recognizing the impact a player such as Mikan could have on a league, BAA commissioner Maurice Podoloff convinced the Minneapolis Lakers, as well as the NBL's other financially sound franchises in Fort Wayne and Indianapolis, to join the BAA. The NBL, reduced to small-market teams in places like Sheboygan, Wisconsin, and Waterloo, Iowa, could no longer compete with the BAA, which, in 1949, renamed itself the National Basketball Association (NBA), thus beginning the modern age of professional basketball.

Basketball in Black and White

Nelson George has written that the early history of basketball was the "by-product of a very rational, very rigid, very white world of values and institutions" (1992, 15). From 1895 to 1920, only eight African American men played on white college varsity teams, most notably Paul Robeson, who played at Rutgers from 1915 to 1918. In 1916, five of the nation's best-known black universities joined to form the Central Interscholastic Athletic Association (CIAA). In Atlanta, Georgia, Morehouse College and several other southern black universities formed the Southwest Athletic Conference (SWAC). The impact of these conferences on black participation in basketball was enormous. In the 1920s and 1930s, black basketball powerhouses began to emerge at colleges such as Morgan State in Baltimore, Maryland; Virginia Union in Richmond; and Xavier in New Orleans, Louisiana.

Race was an issue in the professional ranks as well. The early leagues were all white and resisted, or were hostile to, the idea of integrated play. In the 1920s and 1930s, the Harlem Renaissance, also known as "the Rens," an all-black team with black ownership and management, won over two thousand games. Basketball's most famous all-black team began playing during this period under the name of the Savoy Big Five. In 1926, the team was purchased by white entrepreneur Abe Saperstein. The team changed its name numerous times, eventually settling on the Harlem Globetrotters.

From the Globetrotter's inception until the late 1950s, talented black players who wanted a career in basketball, most significantly University of Kansas star and future NBA Hall of Famer Wilt Chamberlain, played for the Globetrotters, despite the fact that the Globetrotters did as much clowning as playing.

In 1950, the NBA color line was broken when the Boston Celtics drafted Chuck Cooper. Slowly, the game was changing. The introduction of the 24-second shot clock in 1954 sped up the action and, suddenly, basketball went from being a bruising, slow-paced, half-court game to one that accented full-court running and passing. African Americans brought to the game a liberating, improvisational style of play that had been developed at the all-black colleges and, perhaps more important, in urban school yards.

A New Game

As basketball became faster and more intense, the sport's popularity increased dramatically, though it still lagged behind baseball and football. Helping the game considerably was the merger of the NBA with the short-lived but tremendously exciting American Basketball Association (ABA) in 1976. The ABA infused the NBA with some of the most vigorous basketball talent to come along in years: David "Skywalker" Thompson, George "the Ice Man" Gervin, Artis "the A-Train" Gilmore, and, most spectacularly, Julius "Dr. J." Erving. With this influx of talent came a change in basketball attitude and ideology. Clearly, the game had attained a panache demonstrated by excessively baggy shorts, elaborately designed sneakers, tattoos, and the "anti-Afro," the shaved head.

Still, for all its dazzling talent, basketball continued to run a poor third in viewership and status to football and baseball. Although major television networks did cover basketball, some play-off games were broadcast on taped delay rather than live. Not helping the sport's public image were a series of drug arrests and gambling investigations in the NBA and college recruiting violations in the mid-1970s. Nearly all the professional franchises were losing money, and the negative press led many to believe that the game was fundamentally corrupt. This situation changed dramatically with the success of the National Collegiate Athletic Association (NCAA) men's tournament, the entry of Earvin "Magic" Johnson and Larry Bird into the pro ranks, and the naming of David Stern as NBA commissioner. A consummate businessman, Stern was able to clean up the game, work amicably with the players' union, negotiate better television contracts, and package and sell the NBA as the best sport entertainment on the planet with an accent on youth appeal. At times the promotion was garish, but it worked, and less than a decade after Stern took over, basketball was more popular and generating more money. Despite its troubled early racial history, basketball became a sport whose playing ranks were dominated by African Americans and whose coaches and general managers increasingly included persons of color. In the late 1960s, Boston Celtics center Bill Russell became the game's first black head coach, and in the early 1970s, Wayne Embry became its first black general manager. In the college game, high-profile programs, such as those of the University of Oklahoma and the University of Kentucky, hired black coaches. Basketball exhibited a more progressive spirit than professional football, which named its first black head coach in 1989.

As the men's professional game gained popularity during the late 1980s with the ascendancy of Michael Jordan to "greatest player ever" status and as the men's NCAA championship game became one of the most watched televised sport events in the world, basketball moved into the global marketplace. Women players, having few options to play professionally after college, formed two professional leagues, the American Basketball League (ABL) and the Women's National Basketball Association (WNBA). Women also joined the ranks of NBA's referees.

—*John Dougan*

See also: Basketball Hall of Fame; Johnson, Earvin "Magic," Jr.

For further reading:
George, Nelson. 1992. *Elevating the Game: Black Men and Basketball.* New York: HarperCollins.
Halberstam, David. 1981. *The Breaks of the Game.* New York: Knopf.
Jares, Joseph. 1971. *Basketball: The American Game.* Chicago: Follett.
Peterson, Robert. 1990. *Cages to Jump Shots: Pro Basketball's Early Years.* New York: Oxford University Press.

BASKETBALL HALL OF FAME

The Basketball Hall of Fame is unique in its celebration of basketball as a game with U.S. roots and global popularity. Although its focus is on the accomplishments of the best players in the National Basketball Association (NBA), the Hall of Fame honors the impact made by players and coaches, both men and women, from around the world.

The origins of the Basketball Hall of Fame go back to 1941, when the game's founder, James Naismith, began raising funds to build a facility on the campus of Springfield College in Massachusetts to honor the world's greatest players. Despite initial enthusiasm for the project, fundraising efforts were put on hold after Naismith's death in 1943. College officials pursued the idea as a fitting memorial to the founder but postponed the endeavor until after World War II. Revival of the project began in 1949 under the guidance of Springfield College basketball coach Edward Hickock, and ten years later, the Hall of Fame inducted its first members, starting with, appropriately, James Naismith.

Groundbreaking for the Hall of Fame building took place in 1961, and the facility opened to the public in 1968 as the Naismith Memorial Basketball Hall of Fame. In less than a decade, the Hall of Fame outgrew its modest space. In addition, it was difficult to find on the Springfield College campus. In 1978, a proposal was initiated to relocate the Hall of Fame in the city's downtown business district, and in 1985, the new three-level, state-of-the-art, hands-on, multimedia Basketball Hall of Fame opened its doors.

In keeping with Naismith's original philosophy, the Hall of Fame celebrates basketball as a global game. Although the overwhelming majority of inductees are from the ranks of the NBA, the Hall of Fame has consistently included the best foreign players and coaches, both men and women, among its ranks. As the international popularity of basketball has skyrocketed, so too has the Hall of Fame, which, since the opening of the new facility, has drawn in excess of two million visitors.

—*John Dougan*

See also: Basketball

For further reading:

Hoops Heroes: The Basketball Hall of Fame. London: Checkerbee Publishing, 2001.

Padwe, Sandy. 1970. *Basketball's Hall of Fame.* Englewood Cliffs, NJ: Prentice-Hall.

Billie Jean King returns the ball to Bobby Riggs during the first set of their $100,000 "Battle of the Sexes" at the Astrodome (September 20, 1973).
(BETTMANN/CORBIS)

"BATTLE OF THE SEXES"

Billie Jean King's victory over Bobby Riggs in the tennis match labeled the "Battle of the Sexes" dispelled the perception promoted by Riggs and others that women could not compete, physically or emotionally, in athletic contests against men. Thus, the competition became another milepost in the women's liberation movement as well as a major event in the commercialization of sport.

The genesis of the match was a 1971 challenge by fifty-three-year-old Bobby Riggs, a consummate tennis hustler and gambler. Riggs scoffed at the demands of the U.S. Lawn Tennis Association Women's Tour that prize money for women on the pro tennis circuit should equal men's purses, claiming that he could beat any woman player and that the women's game was too dull to deserve equal prize money. Riggs had won three titles at Wimbledon in 1939 and two U.S. Open Men's Championships, in 1939 and 1941. Riggs's challenge in 1971 was aimed at Billie Jean King, the acknowledged leader of the effort of women's tennis to end prize-money inequities.

King had begun her campaign the previous year after winning the Italian Tennis Championship and receiving $600, whereas the male victor was awarded $3,500. King called for a boycott of the Pacific Southwest Championship, where the women's winning share was $1,500, compared to the $12,500 purse for men. When the U.S. Lawn Tennis Association resisted these demands,

King, late in 1970, with Gladys Heldman and others, organized the Virginia Slims Circuit for Women, financed by the Philip Morris Corporation. Within three years, twenty-two cities had hosted events, paying out a total of $775,000 in prize money for women's tennis; by comparison, in the same period, men had played in twenty-four venues for a total of $1,280,000. In 1973, the U.S. Open became the first major tournament to equalize prize money, with each winner receiving $25,000. This campaign, among the several feminist movements of the day, meant that some athletes, like King, became feminists, while some feminists came to appreciate the role of athletics within the movement.

Meanwhile, Riggs, whose challenge to King was rejected in 1973, found a willing opponent in Margaret Court, a thirty-year-old Australian ace and winner of three Wimbledon and five U.S. Open Championships. Played on Mother's Day in a San Diego–area country club, the match lasted less than an hour, with Riggs victorious at 6–2, 6–1. Using a combination of lobs, drop volleys, and angled spin shots, Riggs easily broke Court's rhythm and concentration. Calling his victory a vindication of his boastful prediction, Riggs renewed his challenge to King and happily adopted the mantle of "Male Chauvinist Pig." For King, Court's defeat meant that a match with Riggs was inevitable.

On July 11, details of the "Battle of the Sexes" were revealed. Each contestant was promised $100,000 in ancillary rights and an extra $100,000 would go to the winner. The fifty-five-year-old Riggs, favored at 8–5 in Las Vegas betting pools, dubbed his match with the twenty-nine-year-old King "the Libber versus the Lobber," and he looked forward to his "ultimate hustle."

King's preparation for the match, following her July victory at Wimbledon, was businesslike, with traditional media appointments and practice sessions. Riggs and his entourage, on the other hand, gloried in the limelight, appearing in exhibitions wearing a red-checkered gingham minidress, white riding hood, and flower sleeves, holding news conferences at every opportunity and promoting various products, including a regimen of vitamin pills that he insisted kept him fit. Riggs stressed the emotional strain of the match and questioned King's ability as a woman to withstand the pressure of representing the women's liberation movement. His role as favorite with the oddsmakers extended to 5–2.

As the contest approached, the money involved represented a new level of sport's commercialization. Over thirty nations were on a worldwide television feed. The Houston Astrodome bid $300,000 to become the event site, and its printed event program contained over $100,000 worth of ads. Live gate receipts were expected to be $450,000. ABC television paid $750,000 for the television rights. In all, commercial sponsors invested over $2 million in the event.

The "Battle of the Sexes" was over in two hours and four minutes with King victorious 6–4, 6–3, 6–3. Described as "shocking" by *Sports Illustrated* and "crushing" by the *New York Times,* King's triumph left no doubt as to her superiority. Dictating the match's tempo, King attacked Riggs's softball deliveries, varied the pace of her ground strokes, moved Riggs from corner to corner, and controlled him at the net and from the baseline. Characterizing the match as the "culmination" of her nineteen-year career, King proved that women could compete in and survive athletic pressure situations.

—David Bernstein

See also: Big Business, Sport as

For further reading:

LeCompte, Tom. 2003. *The Last Sure Thing: The Life and Times of Bobby Riggs.* Skunkworks Publishing.

Weinberg, Robert, and Billie Jean King. 2002. *Tennis: Winning the Mental Game.* Robert Weinberg, Inc.

BEAR BAITING

One of the earliest sporting contests in colonial America, bear baiting reflected the harshness of the period and featured spectacles of animals versus animals. The American colonies were rough places for early settlers. An ocean away from the "civilized world" of Europe, colonists were forced to start over in the wilds of New England. Most of their time was spent on the basics of survival, including clearing land, building communities, hunting, fishing, and farming.

Leisure time was a commodity that was not often found. When it was, usually on holidays, residents enjoyed a wide assortment of folk games. Some of these games were traditions brought over from England. Others, however, were events created in and symbolic of the new environment, reflecting the harshness of survival in the New World. Shooting events, horse racing, and boating were skills developed in the everyday lives of the colonists. Other events, often referred to as blood sport, featured animals as the main source of entertainment. Bear baiting, along with cockfighting and gander pulling were some of the most popular events. (The neck of a gander was greased, and then the bird was hung head down from a projecting limb. The horseman who could ride by at full speed and pull off the gander's head won both the contest and the gander. ["Paintings from the Life of Abraham Lincoln." http://www. wedevelopsolutions.com/Ransom/Illpaintings .htm. Accessed May, 2003.])

Bears, one of the largest and most ferocious of the predators encountered by the early settlers, were captured and tied to a stake or otherwise detained. Another animal, often a bull or a dog, would then be set as an opponent for the bear. Nature, usually terrifying to the settlers, could now be used for entertainment. Wagering would take place on the eventual outcome of the battle. There are also recorded instances of humans challenging the bears, with the bears usually being further handicapped to better the odds of the human.

—*Robert S. Brown*

See also: Blood Sport; Cockfighting

For further reading:

MacInnes, I. 2003. "Mastiffs and Spaniels: Gender and Nation in the English Dog." *Textual Practice* 17 (March): 21–41.

BERRA, LAWRENCE PETER "YOGI" (1925–)

Yogi Berra is best remembered for his long career and for his contributions to baseball lore of such classic comments as "you can see a lot by observing" and "it's déjà vu all over again," an expression popularized as slang near the end of the twentieth century. He was born Lawrence Peter Berra in St. Louis, Missouri, the son of Italian immigrants, Pietro and Paulina Berra.

Yogi, whose boyhood nickname came from his alleged resemblance to a Hindu fakir or yogi, was an outstanding athlete in several sports as a child. Leaving school at age fourteen, he worked in a shoe factory but attracted the attention of major league scouts while he was playing sandlot baseball. In 1943, Berra signed with the New York Yankees' minor league team (the Norfolk Tars, Yankee's Class B Piedmont League) in Norfolk, Virginia. He is credited with driving in twenty-three runs in one game while in this league.

After combat service in the U.S. Navy from 1943 to 1946, Berra became a star catcher and clutch hitter for the Yankees from 1946 to 1963, and he won the American League's Most Valuable Player Award three times. With his cheerful, steady leadership, the short, stocky catcher helped the Yankees win fourteen pennants and ten World Series championships. Berra's .285 batting average, 1,430 runs batted in, and 358 home runs led to his election to the Baseball Hall of Fame in 1972. He held the record for playing in the most World Series (fourteen) and in the most World Series Games (seventy-five) and for the most World Series hits (seventy-one). He also played in fifteen All-Star games during his impressive career.

Berra was the manager of the Yankees in 1964

and again from 1984 to 1985. He served as player/coach for the National League New York Mets and was the Mets manager from 1972 to 1975. He ended his career as manager of the Houston Astros from 1986 to 1992, becoming one of the few managers to win pennants in both the American and National Leagues.

—*Peter C. Holloran*

See also: Baseball; Baseball, Minor Leagues

For further reading:

Pepe, Phil. 1974. *The Wit and Wisdom of Yogi Berra.* New York: Hawthorne Books.

BICYCLING

The social impact of bicycling is that of increasingly innovative technology, political action, and personal liberation. The automotive and aviation industries were also significantly enriched through the inventions and the development of manufacturing techniques pioneered by the bicycle industry.

The 1890s, known as the Gay Nineties, were days of liberation and celebration. The bicycle was the latest fad and a popular form of transportation during the period. When the modern bicycle with chain drive, pneumatic tires, and brakes was developed, the average person could ride to the countryside for the day. For women, this was an especially liberating time. Bicycles designed for women were introduced by W. E. Smith in 1887, and Mrs. Smith publicly demonstrated one when she rode down Pennsylvania Avenue. Subsequently, bicycling also changed women's fashion. The apparel of Amelia Bloomer in 1851 became popular with the women cyclists of the day, and the nickname "bloomers" was attached to the clothing. In addition, women on bicycles discredited the notion that women could not participate in strenuous activity.

It was undoubtedly the bicycle craze of the 1890s that caused more people than ever to question the role of women in athletics. Their participation was no longer confined to the privacy of clubs; they came out onto the roadways for everyone to see. Susan B. Anthony, for example, believed that cycling did more to emancipate women than anything else in the world.

By the 1990s, bicycling was entrenched as a form of transportation and of recreation and as a competitive sport. Millions of riders spend billions of dollars on equipment, clothing, accessories, and vacations to promote the sport.

—*Trip Bowers*

See also: Women Bicyclists

For further reading:

Bulger, Margery A. 1982. "American Sportswomen in the 19th Century." *Journal of Popular Culture* 16: 190–191.

Judson, Arthur. 1956. *Riding High: The Story of the Bicycle.* New York: E. P. Dutton.

Willard, Frances E. 1991. *How I Learned to Ride the Bicycle: Reflections of an Influential 19th Century Woman.* Reprint. Sunnyvale, CA: Fair Oaks.

BIG BUSINESS, SPORT AS

By the end of the twentieth century, organized sport, driven by necessity and by greed, had become big business, an industry as organized as any other in the United States. With escalating player salaries and skyrocketing prices for media rights, money was the essential ingredient for success in sport, an ironic state given that money was once considered a corrupter of the purity of athletic competition.

Of primary importance in producing escalating player salaries and prices for media rights was the creation of winning teams and the achievement of championship seasons. To try to guarantee winning, teams and leagues paid exorbitant salaries and put together extravagant packages of incentives to lure and to keep the best players in the game. With the advent of this new player clout, attorneys, accountants, entrepreneurs, and salesmen became as integral to organized sport as the players for whom they secured salaries of six figures and up. A portion of those funds had to be covered through higher ticket prices for fans, who were also encouraged to purchase "loyalty" merchandise displaying their favorite team's colors or logo. The balance of the funds was assured through the sale of celebrity-endorsed products displayed during the competitions and through television coverage of athletic events.

According to *The Economist,* Rupert Murdock, purportedly the most powerful media mogul in the world and the owner of the Los Angeles Dodgers, stated sport overpowers all other programming as the incentive for persons to subscribe to cable television. The network stations and their advertisers are well aware of this preference and of the competition from cable channels, particularly the powerhouse networks of ESPN and ESPN2.

Bidding wars among the networks have raised the costs of broadcast rights to unprecedented amounts that increase annually as the popularity of televised sport grows. Rights to broadcast the world soccer games from 1990 to 1998, for example, were purchased for $344 million, but it has been estimated that the event has cost $2.2 billion for subsequent coverage from 1999 to 2004. The National Football League was expected to net between $17.6 billion and $18 billion over the eight years preceding 2006 (*The Economist* 347, 14–18).

The big-business phenomenon has even intruded on the Olympic Games, the last bastion of the amateur athlete. In addition to the money tourists spend on merchandise—from key chains to T-shirts—bearing the iconic, joined-circle logo, extraordinary amounts of money go to Olympic organizers from the broadcast rights to the events for an estimated 37 billion viewers. In 1948, the British Broadcasting Company (BBC) paid the International Olympic Committee (IOC) a paltry $30,000 for the rights to televise the event. Those

fees had risen to $895 million for the 1996 Atlanta games and to $1.3 billion for the 2000 games in Sydney, Australia.

—Joyce Duncan

See also: Apparel, in Sport; Marketing of Sport; Olympic Games

For further reading:
Armstong, Stephen. 1996. "The Olympics: Who'll Win Sponsors' Gold?" *Campaign,* July 12, 26–29.

Benner, Bill. 2002. "Big-Time Sports: Big Business, Small Minds." *Indianapolis Business Journal* July 15, 23: 18.

"The Paymasters." 1998. *The Economist* 347, June 6, 14–18.

Wood, Robin. 2000. "Sports Merchandise Big Business for Small Teams." *Capital District Business Review,* June 5, 1.

BILLIARDS AND POOL

In 1998, it was estimated that over 44.5 million Americans had played billiards at least once (Krakowka 1998, 59). Billiards is a broad term for a variety of games such as snooker, carom, and pocket billiards or "pool" that involve a cloth topped table with cushioned rails and pockets, a cue stick, and hard balls. The balls were originally made of ivory but are now created from a variety of synthetic resins. Those who play more than twenty-five times a year outnumber participants in all other sports but basketball. Many proponents of billiards have suggested the game will continue to be a significant part of the sporting life in the United States. Despite its popularity, billiards is destined to inhabit the margins of sport and of U.S. culture. It is simultaneously "high class" and "low class" and is often symbolic of being on "the wrong side of town." There is even some controversy over whether it is a sport at all, putting it on the margins of sporting behavior as well.

The seductive glamour and the sometimes-seedy reality of billiards are explored most directly

Willie Hoppe, former world's champion at 18.2 billiards, tries to win the three-cushion title from Bob Cannefax. Hoppe is shown here holding a bridge for Bob Cannefax at the Strand Billiard Academy in New York City, where Cannefax and Hoppe are playing their three-cushion match in blocks (ca. 1935).
(HULTON-DEUTSCH COLLECTION/CORBIS)

in the films *The Hustler* (1961) and *The Color of Money* (1986). It is important, however, to remember that the cultural richness of billiards can symbolize many things. Billiards tables are frequently used symbolically in television and film. A billiards table in a private dwelling is often an indication of wealth and a desire for competitive leisure. The negotiation in the film *Indecent Proposal* (1993) between characters played by Robert Redford, a millionaire, and Woody Harrelson, the financially desperate husband of the woman Redford's character offers to pay to have sex with, occurs during a game of pocket billiards. The game on the table energizes and visualizes the

verbal negotiation taking place. This symbolism of wealth is easily achieved, since billiards tables can cost more than $30,000.

Taken out of the private dwelling, pool halls are often used by filmmakers as a sign of being down and out. In *Bull Durham* (1988), the pool hall is where Kevin Costner's character realizes that his baseball-playing days are behind him. Even the classic musical *The Music Man* (1957) makes reference to pool halls as a source of trouble: "Trouble with a capital 'T'. And that rhymes with 'P' and that stands for pool!" Used in these ways, the pool hall functions as a synecdoche, a type of metaphor or symbol in which the part represents the whole. Thus, the pool hall is often a synecdoche for the "bad side of town."

The connections between pool and science are also rich. In the film *Little Man Tate* (1991), the lead character's mathematical and scientific prowess manifest in an immediate ability to play pool well. Other connections have been more formal, and several academic journals offer studies involving motion, energy, and the like and use the billiards table as a "laboratory." Again, the marginal and complex nature of pool presents itself: pool is considered a game learned by the less educated who use it to gamble, yet pool is also used by physicists to explore complex theories of motion and energy.

The history of pool is full of colorful characters with colorful nicknames—further illustrating the ambiguous identity of pool. The stories and characters add to the attraction of pool as a subculture and as a symbol of the variety of American culture.

—*Richard K. Olsen Jr.*

See also: Film and Sport; Wanderone, Rudolph, Jr. "Minnesota Fats"

For further reading:

Byrne, Robert. 1987. *Byrne's Standard Book of Pool and Billiards.* San Diego, CA: Harcourt Brace Jovanovich.

Krakowka, Lisa. 1998. "Pool Parties." *American Demographics* 20: 59.

Rushin, Steve. 1993. "Willie Mosconi." *Sports Illustrated,* September 27, 44.

BIRD, LARRY (1956–)

Larry Bird's talent and tenacity, matched by that of his archrival, Magic Johnson, and masterfully marketed by Commissioner David Stern, revived the National Basketball Association (NBA) during the 1980s. Both Bird and Johnson redefined athletic stardom and the mass marketing that accompanied celebrity.

Larry Bird honed his skills in the heartland of hoop hysteria: the Hoosier state of Indiana. After an unhappy stint at Indiana University, Bird transferred to Indiana State University, where his all-round game led the basketball program to national prominence. However, in 1979, the team lost its record of no defeats in the National Collegiate Athletic Association (NCAA) to the Michigan State Spartans led by Magic Johnson, and the rivalry began.

Drafted by the Boston Celtics, Bird entered the NBA at a time of dwindling attendance and plummeting television ratings. Pundits proposed many explanations, the most alarming of which was the estrangement of a predominantly white audience from an increasingly black sport. Thus, Bird became the basketball equivalent of the "Great White Hope."

Bird fit the role perfectly. With the Celtics, he led some of the whitest teams in the league to championships in 1981, 1984, and 1986. To his fans, Bird's physical shortcomings, including slowness, were more than offset by his court genius. The contrasting stereotypes of the physically gifted black athlete and smart white player exploded during the 1987 Eastern Division finals when African American Isaiah Thomas, another Laker rival, insinuated that Bird's stardom owed more to race than to talent.

Grounded by age and injury, Bird retired in 1992, but not before winning an Olympic gold medal with the Dream Team. After several years as a special assistant to the Celtic organization, the personification of Celtic pride, Larry Bird, returned home in 1997 to coach the Indiana Pacers.

—*David L. Richards*

See also: Basketball; Johnson, Earvin "Magic," Jr.; National Basketball Association

For further reading:

Bird, Larry, Pat Riley, and Jackie Macmullan. 2000. *Bird Watching: On Playing and Coaching the Game I Love.* New York: Warner Books.

BLACK SOX SCANDAL

Marking a loss of innocence for many fans of organized sport, the so-called Black Sox scandal, in which several prominent Chicago White Sox ballplayers allegedly conspired with gamblers to throw the 1919 World Series to the Cincinnati Reds, is the most infamous sport scandal in U.S. history and has become entrenched in the collective memory and popular imagination. Due to the scandalous darkening of the sport, the popular press began referring to the White Sox as the Black Sox, giving birth to the legend.

Baseball's Darkest Hour

From the beginning, the Black Sox scandal was clouded by uncertainty, which may have contributed to its allure as a public spectacle. Confusion reigned as to who did or did not play to the best of his ability during the series, who had accepted money from gamblers, and who knew what and when. What is certain is that in early October 1919, the White Sox, led by outfielder Shoeless Joe Jackson and pitcher Eddie Cicotte, were favored to beat the Reds in the World Series, but they lost, five games to three. Many Chicagoans, perhaps especially White Sox team owner Charles Comiskey and manager Kid Gleason, were bitterly disappointed by the Sox' poor play. Often brilliant during the regular season, Cicotte and Lefty Williams were unusually erratic on the pitching mound. First baseman Chick Gandil, who organized much of the plot, shortstop Swede Risberg, and center fielder Hap Felsch were less than stellar. Jackson and third baseman Buck Weaver, however, were impressive: Jackson had a World Series–record twelve hits, including the only

Marking a loss of innocence for many fans of organized sport, the Black Sox scandal, in which several prominent Chicago White Sox ballplayers allegedly conspired with gamblers to throw the 1919 World Series to the Cincinnati Reds, is the most infamous sport scandal in U.S. history.

home run during the series, and a .375 batting average, and Weaver hit and fielded well.

A little less than a year later—after the publication of damning newspaper articles and as rumors of wrongdoing slowly began to percolate—Cicotte, Williams, and Jackson testified before a Cook County grand jury about the fixed World Series. Cicotte and Williams confessed that they had conspired with gamblers to lose the series; Jackson explained that he had known of the scam and had unwillingly accepted bribe money but that he had played to win. It is an apocryphal story but, apparently, Jackson was confronted by a disillusioned street urchin on the steps of the courthouse after his testimony: "Say it ain't so, Joe," the youngster begged. To which Jackson reportedly replied, "Yes, kid, I'm afraid it is."

All told, eight ballplayers—including Weaver, who persistently denied being involved in the scheme—were implicated in the imbroglio. The news sent shock waves of disbelief and righteous indignation across the country. Although eventually acquitted of conspiracy charges, the eight implicated men were, nevertheless, banished from the game by the baseball commissioner, Judge Kennesaw Mountain Landis. Landis had been hired by nervous team owners in November of 1920 to lend moral authority, stability, and the appearance of integrity to the game.

In retrospect, the Black Sox scandal happened for a variety of reasons. There had been a long history of association among baseball players and gamblers; fixed games, though not necessarily common, were nothing new. With few exceptions, the bosses of the game ignored or inadequately punished such malfeasance. Moral laxity and lack of leadership fostered conditions in which game fixing could continue. In addition, exceedingly poor labor-management relations had plagued professional baseball for decades. Many major leaguers at the time felt they were exploited by their employers, partly due to the reserve clause, first instituted in 1879, that bound players to the same team indefinitely. This situation engendered

Team photograph of the Chicago White Sox, the team that was involved in the Chicago Black Sox scandal (September 18, 1919).
(BETTMANN/CORBIS)

a sense of powerlessness and bitterness on the part of some ballplayers. Added to those conditions, the 1919 White Sox were split by tremendous internal dissension: one faction, made up almost entirely of poorly educated working-class men from rural communities, barely spoke to their teammates and harbored deep enmity toward Charles Comiskey, their employer. Taken together, these social conditions and an unfortunate alliance of dishonest ballplayers and gamblers contributed to the Big Fix.

An Enduring Social Drama

Rife with symbolic possibilities, the Black Sox scandal remains in the U.S. consciousness for myriad reasons. Obviously, it stands as a moment of betrayal, of disillusionment, and of lost innocence. Because many people remain intrigued by

the mystery surrounding the occurrence, the Black Sox scandal has been frequently interpreted. Numerous journalists, poets, playwrights, novelists, historians, and filmmakers have reconstructed the scandal and put it to various uses. One can feel the anguish of the banished ballplayers in Nelson Algren's prose poem "The Swede Was a Hard Guy" (1942), can hear clear echoes of the affair in Bernard Malamud's *The Natural* (1952), can witness Joe Jackson's resurrection in W. P. Kinsella's *Shoeless Joe* (1982), the novel interpreted by Phil Alden Robinson for the film *Field of Dreams* (1989), can consider competing versions of the event in Harry Stein's *Hoopla* (1983), and can contemplate the scandal's complex morality in *Eight Men Out* (1988), John Sayles's movie adaptation of Eliot Asinof's highly respected history of the event. Collectively, these and other narratives illustrate the Black Sox scandal's remarkable endurance as a U.S. social drama, even as it recedes further into the past.

—*Daniel A. Nathan*

See also: Baseball; Kinsella, William P.

For further reading:

Asinof, Eliot. 1963. *Eight Men Out: The Black Sox and the 1919 World Series.* New York: Henry Holt.

Candelaria, Cordelia. 1989. *Seeking the Perfect Game: Baseball in American Literature.* Westport, CT: Greenwood Press.

Frommer, Harvey. 1992. *Shoeless Joe and Ragtime Baseball.* Dallas, TX: Taylor Publishing.

Grella, George. 1975. "Baseball and the American Dream." *Massachusetts Review* 16, no. 3 (Summer): 550–567.

Messenger, Christian. 1991. "Expansion Draft: Baseball Fiction of the 1980s." In *The Achievement of American Sport Literature: A Critical Appraisal,* edited by Wiley L. Umphlett. Cranbury, NJ: Associated University Presses, 62–79.

Voigt, David Q. 1976. "The Chicago Black Sox and the Myth of Baseball's Single Sin." In *America through Baseball.* Chicago: Nelson-Hall, 65–76.

BLACKOUTS, TELEVISION

Conceived as a means of protecting the business interests of sport promoters, television blackouts are a hotly contested political issue and the subject of frequent litigation reflecting the nation's passion for sport. Sport promoters enjoy the revenue and publicity generated by television coverage, but they also worry that fans will choose to stay home and watch a game on television rather than buy a ticket to the event. Consequently, in 1952, the National Football League (NFL) established a league-wide ban on television broadcasts of home games, a regulation that was upheld by the courts through challenges both by the U.S. Department of Justice and by football fans. As professional football became increasingly popular in the 1960s, agitation against the policy increased, and loyal fans, who could not obtain tickets to local games, often traveled miles to visit friends who could pull in fuzzy transmissions of the game from out-of-town stations.

In 1973, Congress passed antiblackout legislation that barred the NFL from blocking home telecasts of games that were sold out seventy-two hours in advance. Dubbed "the Redskin Rule" because it allowed congressional staffers to watch the sold-out games of the Washington Redskins, the antiblackout legislation expired in 1975 but has remained NFL policy because the league feared new and more-restrictive government regulation.

Although sport promoters are legally entitled to televise or not to televise their events, the nation's love of sport television made blackout rules an attractive target for politicians. Since sport leagues rely on government for favorable tax rules and for stadium funding, they became increasingly wary of alienating voting fans and their representatives.

—*Tim Ashwell*

See also: Television, Impact on Sport

For further reading:

"Sports Blackouts Sought." 1990. *Television Digest,* September 10, 8.

Walker, Sam. 2001. "The People vs. NFL." *Wall Street Journal,* October 5.

BLOOD SPORT

A majority of sport is potentially bloody, but only a few can be classified as blood sport—sport in which victory is achieved specifically through the mangling, and often the death, of an opponent. Blood sport involves an animal, usually a bear, a bull, a dog, or a gamecock. Sport involving the latter two animals, in spite of illegality and moral outcry, flourishes in the United States. The persons who train and fight gamecocks and dogs and those who attend the matches as spectators do so for a variety of reasons. The sport and consequent camaraderie—particularly male bonding, although the sport has no sexist parameters—and the gambling, the potential of untold wealth, are the primary drawing cards.

Blood sport is not new. It dates from antiquity. References to both cockfighting and dogfighting can be traced to oral ancient Babylonian history, and cockfighters, especially, take great pride in calling their trade "the oldest sport in the world." The earliest recorded cockfight dates from 517 B.C. in China, and it is likely that gamecocks entered North America on Columbus's second voyage in 1493. Many of those involved in cockfighting point to the involvement in the sport of the nation's founding fathers, specifically George Washington and Thomas Jefferson.

Both "cockers" and "pitmen" put forth large sums of money and an incredible amount of time in caring for and preparing their animals for the ring. The cost of a strong but untried pit bull pup can begin at $500 and go up to thousands of dollars. A single fighting cock is worth $100 or so, and a dozen eggs often fetch as much as $25. In addition, trainers must purchase gaffs (the razor-sharp metal spurs attached to the birds' legs, costing $70) for cockfighting, tie-out cords, sparring muffs, cat mills (a treadmill device with a caged, and thus uncatchable, cat attached, used to train fighting dogs), powders, vaccines, saws, shears, worm pills, cables, chains, food, and entry fees.

There is more information on record about cockfighting than there is about dogfighting, perhaps due to cockfighting being more common and more accepted, while dogfighting is less public. People don't mind seeing a chicken killed, but it becomes especially cruel when a puppy is involved. Pitmen, as dog handlers are called, state that it is the confusion between a pit bull, bred to fight, and a house dog that causes the greatest amount of public consternation. They contend that it is crueler not to allow the dogs to fight because it is their nature to do so. In the late 1990s, the fine for merely being a spectator at a dogfight was around $10,000, whereas the fine for participating in a cockfight was only $2,500. Dogfighting is a felony nationwide, whereas cockfighting carries only misdemeanor charges in most states and is a legalized sport in four. The amendments to the Animal Welfare Act of 1976 declared blood sport illegal, but in most areas, particularly in the rural parts of the South and the Southwest, cockers and pitmen are unafraid of the law. The major fear of those who practice blood sport is an attack by members of an area humane society or animal rights group.

Although the two sports have some things in common, there is one major difference. Although pit dogs are normally removed from the fray bloody but alive, fighting cocks are required to achieve victory by killing their opponent. This rule has less to do with the nature of the breed in the pit than it does with the nature of the humans in the stands. It is believed that betting might be considered fixed or prearranged if a wounded bird is removed during the fight.

Attendance at blood sport events is a family affair. Men, women, teenagers, and small children are allowed as long as they pay the admission fee, approximately ten dollars. Thus, the sport is retained and passed on to the next generation through the most traditional method available. Over half of cockfighters and a majority of dogfighters reside in the U.S. Southeast or Southwest, and the sport is particularly popular among Cajuns, Mississippi Delta blacks, Mexican Americans, and rural whites.

—*Joyce Duncan*

See also: Bear Baiting; Cockfighting

For further reading:

Dundes, Alan. 1994. *The Cockfight: A Casebook.* Madison: University of Wisconsin Press.
Stratton, Richard F. 1983. *The World of the American Pit Bull Terrier.* Neptune City, NJ: TFH.

BLOOMER GIRLS

Developed in the late nineteenth century, so-called Bloomer girl teams gave women the chance to play baseball. Although baseball of the time was primarily a man's sport, a number of colleges, such as Vassar and Smith, fielded women's teams. For other women wanting to play baseball, the only option was the Bloomer teams. Many of these early squads had two men on the team, often the pitcher and catcher, but the other members were women. The cultural significance of the Bloomer teams was that they served as an entrée for women into public participation in sport during a time when many felt women were physically inferior and should have no interests outside the home.

Bloomer girls teams appeared across the country. The name, used in Chicago, New York, and other locales, was tied to suffragette Amelia Jenks Bloomer and not to the pants that also bore her name. The teams played all comers as they barnstormed across the country. One night, their opponent might be an amateur club, and the next night's opponent might be semiprofessional. Many promoters brought in men to round out the games. Male players were called "toppers" for the curly feminine wigs they wore atop their own hair.

Some of the best-known teams played throughout the 1880s and into the early twentieth century. The *Boston Herald* carried an account of a 1903 game that starred Maud Nelson, one of the most famous of the women players, renowned for her hitting, fielding, and pitching. The Chicago Bloomer girls were covered by newspapers in Cincinnati, New York, Boston, and Chicago as they traveled the country. These early teams helped lay the foundation for the later development of the All-American Girls Professional Baseball League of the 1940s and 1950s. Though none of the teams were permanent, the Bloomer girls showed it was possible for women to play baseball, until then considered a man's sport.

—*Leslie Heaphy*

See also: All-American Girls Professional Baseball League; Children in Sport: Girls in "Boys' Sports".

For further reading:

Berlage, Gai. 1994. *Women in Baseball*. Westport, CT: Praeger.
Gregorich, Barbara. 1993. *Women at Play*. New York: Harcourt, Brace.

BOLLEA, TERRY GENE "HULK HOGAN" (1953–)

With a larger-than-life physique and unlimited charisma, professional wrestler Hulk Hogan became one of the most recognizable sport figures in the world during the 1980s. A native of Florida, Hulk Hogan, born Terry Gene Bollea, was a mediocre wrestler even by professional standards. Although he was freakishly large, he seemed destined to spend his career in small promotions as the stereotypical villain. In 1983, however, Hogan's fortunes changed dramatically.

Hogan assumed the persona of "good guy" in the American Wrestling Association and was an immediate hit with the fans. His new popularity, combined with an appearance in the film *Rocky III* (1982), made him a natural choice to be the champion of the expanding World Wrestling Federation.

Hulk Hogan was a wrestling promoter's dream. People were captivated by the six-foot-five, three-hundred-pound brawler and intrigued by his twenty-four-inch arms, dubbed "the pythons." By 1985, "Hulkamania" was synonymous with wrestling, and thousands of people who had never followed the sport before became die-hard "Hulkamaniacs."

Hogan had the ability to control the emotions of the crowd better than most of his contemporaries, and that charisma gave him huge crossover appeal. He was a regular guest on television talk shows, had a short-lived cartoon series, and starred in a number of B movies. In addition, his image could be seen in commercials for a variety of products such as Right Guard deodorant. By the late 1980s, he was one of the most recognized sport personalities in the world.

Following the steroid scandals of the early 1990s that tainted many of the wrestling stars, Hulk Hogan returned to the airways on *World Championship Wrestling*. The long-time hero rejuvenated his career by becoming a villain once more.

—*Kenneth Phillips*

See also: Steroids; Wagner, "Gorgeous George" Raymond; Wrestling, Professional

For further reading:

Hogan, Hulk. 2002. *Hollywood Hulk Hogan*. New York: Pocket Star.

Hunter, Matt. 2000. *The Story of the Wrestler They Call "Hollywood" Hulk Hogan*. Philadelphia: Chelsea House.

BOONE AND CROCKETT CLUB

Founded in 1887 by Theodore Roosevelt, the Boone and Crockett Club was one of the earliest conservation groups to function on a national level. It remains a significant force in North American wildlife research and big-game management.

Named in honor of the frontiersmen Daniel Boone and Davy Crockett, the Boone and Crockett Club was founded "to promote manly sport with the rifle," to encourage travel and exploration in wild and unknown lands, to work for the conservation of North American wildlife, especially big game, and to further legislation for those purposes. Its charter limits regular membership to 150 individuals, all of whom must be big-game hunters who are concerned with the protection of wildlife and wildlife habitat.

Although the club is best known as a record-keeping institution for trophy hunters, it has also been, from its inception, an advocacy organization for hunting ethics; its members are required to hunt in "fair chase," a term that implies a respectful relationship between humans, animals, and the land they share. Many members—including George Bird Grinnell, Gifford Pinchot, Aldo Leopold, and Jay "Ding" Darling—have been prominent conservationists, and their influence has helped the club bring about the enactment of game laws and laws for the protection of the redwoods and the establishment of Yellowstone and Denali National Parks.

The Boone and Crockett Club also maintains a chair in wildlife biology and conservation at the University of Montana, manages a six-thousand-acre demonstration ranch on the Rocky Mountain front range, administers a grants-in-aid program, and publishes *Records of North American Big Game* and the quarterly magazine *Fair Chase*.

—*Daniel J. Philippon*

See also: Outdoor Clubs

For further reading:

Roosevelt, Theodore, and George Bird Grinnell, eds. [1897] 1988. *Trail and Camp-Fire: The Book of the Boone and Crockett Club*. New York: Forest and Stream Publishing Company, 1897. Reprint, Missoula, MT: Boone and Crockett Club.

BOSTON MARATHON

Transformed from a small, elite regional event during its first decades into a competitive, participatory fitness celebration, the Boston Marathon has gained both national and international significance. Through the growth of participatory running in the United States beginning in the 1960s, marathoning in general and the Boston Marathon in particular have gained prominence and respect.

Organized by the upper-class Boston Athletic Association (BAA), the first Boston Marathon was held in 1897; it is the oldest continuously offered race in the United States. The BAA was part of a general trend associated with the creation of amateur track and field run by elite social athletic clubs in the last thirty years of the nineteenth century. Although the marathon events were controlled by the socially elite, the participants were

Timothy Cherigat of Kenya crosses the finish line to win the men's division of the 108th Boston Marathon with a time of 2:10:37. The 2004 Boston Marathon was run with temperatures in the 80-degree Fahrenheit range, adding an extra challenge for all the runners and giving the runners from warmer climates an advantage.
(JIM BOURG/REUTERS/CORBIS)

mostly from the working classes and were often immigrants during the marathon's first fifty years. Race participation grew modestly, occasionally reaching as many as two hundred runners, but the real growth was reflected in the number of spectators who lined the course, eventually reaching hundreds of thousands.

In the 1950s, the international significance of the Boston Marathon increased. Top runners from foreign countries dominated the activity, which continued to attract around two hundred starters annually. During the same time, college-educated U.S. participants with middle-class backgrounds gravitated toward the competition. Until 1972, the race was officially closed to participation by women; nonetheless, one woman, Roberta Gibb, finished unofficially in 1966. The following year Katherine Switzer competed officially as K. Switzer.

Beginning in the 1960s, participation in the event grew dramatically. Although the BAA limited the size of the field by requiring participants to qualify, the number of runners regularly exceeded five thousand. In 1986, race officials enlisted John Hancock Financial Services as a sponsor and abandoned its outdated amateur standing by offering prize money as well as appearance fees. This reestablished the Boston Marathon as one of the elite international marathons.

—*Joseph M. Turrini*

See also: Marketing of Sport; Running

For further reading:

Rodgers, Bill, and Tom Derderian. 2003. *The Boston Marathon: A Century of Blood, Sweat, and Cheers.* Chicago: Triumph Books.

BOUTON, JIM (1939–)

Pitcher Jim Bouton's groundbreaking, tell-all memoir of his 1969 season with the expansion team the Seattle Pilots, *Ball Four* (1970), is a watershed work for the demythologizing of professional baseball and the creation of the sport exposé. Bouton's major league career spanned nine seasons, from 1962–1970. During that time, he played for the New York Yankees, the Seattle Pilots, and the Houston Astros. Bouton's experience with each of these teams is chronicled in *Ball Four,* but the primary focus of the book is his 1969 comeback from an arm injury as a knuckleball pitcher with the first-year Seattle team.

Bouton's diary-like account of the Seattle season was the first book of its kind to betray the owner-player-sportswriter conspiracy of silence surrounding the inner workings of baseball. Bouton's bold, insightful, and often hysterically funny descriptions of owners' tyrannical manipulations, managers' cutthroat decisions, and ballplayers' adolescent antics conveyed his belief that "we are all better off looking across at someone, rather than up" (Bouton 2003). Though Bouton was denounced by owners, players, and managers alike for the book's apparent destruction of baseball's heroes and of the sport's wholesome image, his startling truth telling won widespread acclaim from the general public, not only for its revelations but also for its eminent readability. One of *Ball Four's* unintended side effects, however, was

that it also opened the door to a new genre of "kiss-and-tell" sport books that competed to reach new heights of sensationalism. As a testament to *Ball Four's* continuing appeal, the twentieth-anniversary edition included chapters entitled "Ball Five" (ten years later) and "Ball Six" (twenty years later), which continued to follow the lives of many of Bouton's teammates and traced the book's powerful multigenerational attraction.

—*Mark W. Evans*

See also: Big Business, Sport as

For further reading:

Bouton, Jim. 2003. *Foul Ball: My Life and Hard Times Trying to Save an Old Ballpark.* North Egremont, MA: Bulldog Publishing.

BOWLING

Originating in ancient Egypt, modern bowling has become a major U.S. sport. In 1996, for example, bowling drew 82 million participants of both genders and all races, income levels, and physical abilities. In modern U.S. bowling, the participant rolls a ball underhand at ten, fifteen-inch-tall pins set in a triangular formation, sixty feet from the bowler. It was played in seventeenth-century America by Dutch colonists, who used nine pins. The early game was played primarily as a lawn sport, but it was outlawed in many states around 1841 because it was the subject of extensive gambling. To evade the law, wealthy advocates moved the sport inside, building lanes in their mansions and adding a tenth pin to differentiate the game from its outdoors predecessor.

By the late nineteenth century, several attempts to standardize rules and equipment had failed. However, in 1895, organizers in New York City formed the American Bowling Congress, which would become the sanctioning body a hundred years later for more than 4.5 million registered amateur bowlers.

Bowling fans watch the American Bowling Congress tournament in 1905.
(CORBIS)

During World War II, bowling's permanence in U.S. culture was cemented when the military built 4,500 lanes on its bases and bowling centers exceeded 5,000 nationwide. Bowling was a demonstration sport in the 1983 Pan-American Games and an exhibition sport in the 1988 Olympics.

"Pin boys," hired to set up pins and return bowling balls to the participants, became a part of bowling culture, but by the mid-1960s, they were replaced with automated pinsetters. Automated, computerized scoring soon followed.

Organized and "open" recreational bowling takes place in every state, at every level—youth, junior, adult, senior citizen, amateur, collegiate, professional, and physically challenged. Organized bowling includes leagues and tournaments for individuals, doubles, mixed-gender doubles, and male, female, and mixed teams, usually made up of three to five members. In 1995, the National Bowling Stadium opened in Reno, Nevada, where the American Bowling Congress hosted its national tournament for more than 91,000 participants.

—*Harry Amana*

See also: Pan-American Games

For further reading:

Krakowka, Lisa. 1998. "Bowling Throws a Strike." *American Demographics,* July.

Krebs, Paula M. 2001. "I Bowl, Therefore I Am." *Chronicle of Higher Education,* June 22, B21.

BOXING

A brutal and often controversial sport, boxing is the vehicle by which many generations of impoverished Americans sought to achieve wealth and fame despite the ever-present risk of exploitation and physical injury. The origins of boxing in the United States date to the American colonial period, when the sport was a favorite pastime of the British aristocracy. Boxing did not gain any broad popularity in the United States, however, until the late 1800s. Prior to that, prizefighting had met with opposition both from the religious community, who found it immoral, and from most state legislatures. As a result, boxing competitions were often held in secluded locations to avoid raids by the police.

This situation changed with the crowning of John L. Sullivan as heavyweight champion in 1882. Known as "the Boston Strongboy," Sullivan was considered boxing's first "world champion," since he defeated challengers from both the United States and England. He was the first truly to capture the public imagination, and the national media that had condemned the sport only a few years earlier were soon trumpeting the athletic feats of the "Great John L." Sullivan reigned as champion during the so-called bare-knuckles era of boxing. Contestants did not wear gloves and often engaged in "fights to the finish," with no set time limits.

The first champion of the modern era was James J. Corbett, who defeated Sullivan in 1892. The match was the first heavyweight championship bout conducted under Queensbury rules with boxers wearing gloves and fighting for a set number of three-minute rounds. By minimizing some of the apparent violence, the changes reduced some of the public criticism that surrounded the game.

Boxing as Upward Mobility

Both Sullivan and Corbett were Irish immigrants, and they represented the first in a long line of fighters who turned to boxing in order to escape poverty and discrimination. Boxing's most accomplished participants came from those groups who found themselves denied full access to the American dream. Jewish Americans during the 1920s and 1930s, Italian Americans in the 1940s and 1950s, and African Americans throughout much of the 1900s used boxing as the first step toward economic success and social acceptance. Boxing thus embodied the imagery of the industrial era, when it was felt that a rugged individual, through hard work and self-determination, could overcome the obstacles before him.

Those obstacles were greater for some boxers than for others. Although African Americans were among the earliest participants in the sport, no black was permitted to challenge the heavyweight champion until 1908, when Jack Johnson dethroned Tommy Burns to win the title. Faced with political and public opposition to the idea of a black heavyweight champion, Burns and Johnson were forced to fight in Australia. After Johnson lost the title in 1915, no black fighter received a shot at the championship until twenty-two years later, when Joe Louis became the longest-reigning champion in boxing history.

The Heavyweights

Boxing's unique blend of individual perseverance and human tragedy has made it a popular backdrop for Hollywood films. The lives of Jim Corbett and Jack Johnson were each made into movies, as were the exploits of former middleweight champion Jake LaMotta in the Academy Award–winning film *Raging Bull* (1981). Most Hollywood depictions of boxing, however,

> *Boxing did not gain any broad popularity in the United States until the late 1800s. Prior to that, prizefighting had met with opposition both from the religious community, who found it immoral, and from most state legislatures. As a result, boxing competitions were often held in secluded locations to avoid raids by the police.*

have revolved around heavyweights. Although there are several weight classes, the heavyweight division has always been the most visible and compelling.

Not surprisingly, competition for the heavyweight championship title has often carried with it much larger social and political implications. In the late 1930s, Adolf Hitler cheered German heavyweight Max Schmeling's victories as evidence of Aryan supremacy. Consequently, Joe Louis's knockout of Schmeling in 1938, which was followed by his service in the U.S. Army during World War II, was a huge source of U.S. pride. Of all the celebrated champions in boxing, however, none has had a greater effect on U.S. culture than Muhammad Ali. Whether for his role in the civil rights movement or his opposition to the Vietnam War, Ali's notoriety far exceeded his undeniable greatness as a boxer.

Despite its glorious moments, boxing's relationship with U.S. society has been both turbulent and controversial. In particular, the fight game has often been associated with organized crime, leading to both real and perceived instances of fight fixing. Insufficient regulation and unscrupulous management, furthermore, have led to frequent exploitation of boxers. More recently, the brutal nature of the sport has led to renewed calls for its abolition, especially among members of the medical profession. It is not unusual for several boxers to die in any given year as a result of injuries sustained in the ring.

Still, boxing endures. For all its flaws, few events can match the public spectacle and human drama of a championship fight between two of the world's best boxers.

—*Thomas C. Reynolds*

See also: Ali, Muhammad; Big Business, Sport as; Film and Sport

For further reading:
Sammons, Jeffrey T. 1990. *Beyond the Ring: The Role of Boxing in American Society.* Urbana: University of Illinois Press.

"BOYS OF SUMMER"

Immortalized in Roger Kahn's 1972 best seller, *The Boys of Summer,* the Brooklyn Dodgers of 1947 to 1957 were a team that perennially lost the World Series but made history as the first racially integrated franchise in major league baseball.

The saga of the "boys of summer" began in 1947 when Jackie Robinson became the first African American to play in the major leagues. Daily, facing threats of strikes from fellow major leaguers and racial epithets from fans, Robinson persevered and changed the game of baseball forever.

Between 1947 and 1957, Robinson and the Brooklyn Dodgers went to the World Series six times. They won only once, in 1955. Nonetheless, their fans loved the Dodgers as a team that represented the diversity of the United States and the challenge of racial integration. The Dodgers brought together African Americans like Robinson, Roy Campanella, and Joe Black, Southerners like Pee Wee Reese and Preacher Roe, Italian Americans like Carl Furillo, and Jews like Sandy Koufax. The Dodgers, or "dem Bums," as they were affectionately called, were heroes to Brooklyn's ethnically diverse working classes.

The "boys of summer" saga ended in 1957 when Walter O'Malley announced he was taking the Dodgers away from Ebbets Field in Brooklyn and moving them to Los Angeles, where he could build a new stadium without the political entanglements he found in New York. The Dodgers' move was notable for several reasons: it was a brutal blow to the cultural identity of Brooklynites, a sign that the entire nation was looking westward for its postwar future, and a lesson that, even in baseball, money was still the dominant force.

—*Michael A. Lerner*

See also: Baseball; Robinson, Jack Roosevelt "Jackie"

For further reading:
Prince, Carl E. 1996. *Brooklyn's Dodgers: The Bums, the Borough, and the Best of Baseball, 1947–1957.* New York: Oxford University Press.

BRYANT, PAUL "BEAR"
(1913–1983)

Due to his gridiron success and powerful personal presence, Paul "Bear" Bryant personified the quintessential college football coach for many fans. The son of a sharecropper from Moro Bottom, Arkansas, Paul Bryant earned an early reputation for tenacity in addition to the nickname he gained by wrestling a bear in a theatre in nearby Fordyce at the age of twelve. That energy, tough-mindedness, and rural upbringing took him to the University of Alabama, where he played four years on a football scholarship. After graduation, he turned to coaching and began his legendary career.

Bryant served as head coach at the University of Kentucky, the University of Maryland at College Park, Texas A&M University, and, ultimately, at his alma mater, the University of Alabama. Under his leadership, Crimson Tide football became synonymous with success. In twenty-five years at Alabama, Bryant led his teams to six national titles, thirteen Southeastern Conference championships, and twenty-four consecutive bowl games. His disciplined, strict, and often harsh training regimen was employed to illustrate his philosophy of coaching, building men as well as winning teams.

The demanding coach served as a model for others in his field, and in many ways, he helped ease racial tension in the South by embracing integration. He was one of the first white southern coaches actively to recruit black talent, leading others to follow suit.

Bear Bryant died a month after leading the Crimson Tide to a victory in the 1982 Liberty Bowl. The over half a million fans who lined the procession route from Tuscaloosa to Birmingham were testament to his popularity, and his obituaries in the *New York Times, The New Yorker,* and other national publications indicated his important and lasting influence on U.S. sport and culture.

—*Richard D. Starnes*

See also: Discrimination, Racial, in Sport; Football

For further reading:

Dent, Jim. 1999. *The Junction Boys: How Ten Days in Hell with Bear Bryant Forged a Championship Team.* New York: St. Martin's Press.

BULLFIGHTING

Bullfighting, an ancient contest pitting man against bull in a fight to the death, enjoys widespread popularity in Spain and, to a lesser extent, in the Spanish-speaking regions of the Americas. The sport, known also as *corrida de toros,* existed at least by the twelfth century and reached its peak of popularity from the seventeenth to the twentieth centuries. The bullfight pits the matador, or torero, in the bullring, or *plaza de toros,* against a bull bred and trained to be aggressive. The matador faces the bull with a sword and a muleta, a red cloth attached to a wooden staff.

Before the matador attempts to kill the bull, picadors on horseback stab the animal with lances in order to weaken the animal's shoulder muscles and cause its head to droop, offering the matador a target between the bull's shoulders. Banderilleros then stick two-foot-long darts into the bull, exciting its rage.

Finally, the matador faces the bull head-to-head, and after inciting the bull to make several passes around his body, he attempts the kill. The occupation of matador is highly dangerous and requires considerable skill. The objective is not merely to kill the bull but to do so with grace and aesthetic refinement, moving as close to the bull as possible without being gored.

The most famous account of bullfighting is Ernest Hemingway's *Death in the Afternoon* (1932). To Hemingway, bullfighting became a metaphor for life, for an individual courageously facing an adversary even while knowing that ultimately it would defeat him. Others see bullfighting as a sport or a great spectacle, and it

The traditional running of the bulls, which fascinated among others, Ernest Hemingway, in Pamplona, Spain. Six fighting bulls thunder down the street in this famous bullfighting city; youths display their courage by running in front of them (July 12, 1969).
(BETTMANN/CORBIS)

remains a tourist attraction for those vacationing in Central and South American countries. Still others view it as a cruel and bloodthirsty exercise in injury and death—for humans, bulls, and horses.

—*Edward J. Rielly*

See also: Blood Sport; Hemingway, Ernest

For further reading:
Sherwood, Lyn A., and Barnaby Conrad. 2001. *Yankees in the Afternoon: An Illustrated History of American Bullfighting.* Jefferson, NC: McFarland.

BULLS, RUNNING THE

Running the bulls has long been a part of the annual Festival of San Fermin in Pamplona, Spain, and a way for participants to demonstrate their courage and their daring, although some would say their recklessness. Made famous worldwide by its depiction in Ernest Hemingway's novel, *The Sun Also Rises* (1926), the running of the bulls occurs during the annual two-week Festival of San Fermin, held in July. At eight o'clock each morning of the bullfights, bulls are run through city streets to the bullring, where they are held in pens until the evening.

Several hundred people, most of them men and many of them Americans, run ahead of the bulls through streets barricaded at intersections to prevent both the bulls and the runners from quitting the race. The objective is to outrun the bulls to the arena and, of course, to avoid injury. The bulls become as frightened as the humans at the noise and the activity, and the more frightened they become, the more dangerous they prove to be to their rivals in the race.

The most dangerous bull is one that has become separated from the others. It is then likely to start flailing about and to attack anyone who may have fallen among the shoving crowd of runners. It is not unusual for individuals to be trampled or gored by the bulls or to be injured by other runners. Deaths, however, are uncommon. Since 1920, about a dozen runners have been killed. The threat of injury or death does not seem to deter new participants.

For some American men, running the bulls, an act romanticized in film and fiction, appears to be the ultimate feat of masculinity. Some of these runners arrived inspired by Hollywood or by their reading of Hemingway, who himself never actually ran with the bulls.

—*Edward J. Rielly*

See also: Bullfighting; Hemingway, Ernest

For further reading:

Gray, Gary. 2001. *Running with the Bulls: Fiestas, Corridas, Toreros, and an American's Adventure in Pamplona.* Guilford, CT: Lyons Press.

BUNGEE JUMPING

Bungee (sometimes spelled bungy or bungi) jumping is the practice of jumping, dropping, or being released into the air while attached to elasticized cords, and it is not a sport in the strictest sense. A sport requires a certain level of competition, athleticism, and/or play, and dangling by one foot from a giant rubber band does not necessarily qualify in either area. Although it may be a vehicle of athletic competition, incorporating acrobatic stunts, flips, and twists resembling those in springboard diving, bungee jumping is best known and most widely promoted as an outlet for thrill seekers. The specifics are variable—the launching pad can be a bridge, a tower, a crane, a skyscraper, a hot air balloon, or even a helicopter—but the objective always revolves around risk, fear, and the production of an "adrenaline rush." Indeed, although safety and strict regulation have become primary concerns, bungee jumping remains unforgiving in the sense that one small slip-up—a broken or dangling cord, a misfit harness, an error in measurement—is likely to be fatal. Bungee jumping as a fad typifies the U.S. passion for danger, seen also in extreme sport and reality television prevalent in the late twentieth century

Bungee jumping adopts the name of the elastic bungee cords used as tie-downs on bicycles or cars. Originally developed for military use, the cords employed for human suspension are much longer and stronger and often consist of bundles of cords. These are fixed to a harness that, in turn, is strapped onto the torso or the ankles. The jumper, from high enough not to crash into whatever surface lies below, plunges, rebounds, and then drops and bounces again and again until coming to a halt. Bungee cords typically stretch two to four times their original length, and the jumper experiences weightlessness followed by pressure of 1.2 to 3.5 Gs.

Although the origins of bungee jumping are unconvincingly traced to native customs among Pacific islanders, who are said to dive from heights while attached to vines, the form using modern equipment probably began among members of England's Oxford Dangerous Sports Club. That group dangled off a bridge in Bristol in 1979 and later bungeed off the Golden Gate Bridge and the bridge over Colorado's Royal Gorge. Their antics inspired daredevils in New Zealand, Australia, France, and the United States, and the business of selling the bungee experience was born. Bungee reached its height of popularity in the United States in the early 1990s, as some two hundred companies across the country charged approximately fifty dollars per plummet at amusement parks, state fairs, and other sites.

Largely in response to concerns of state regulators and the insurance industry, the U.S. Bungee Association was formed in 1990 to develop organized and coherent guidelines for the activity. States adopted legislation to address safety concerns, covering site approval, testing of equipment, procedures, licensing, and insurance. Some states outlawed headfirst diving with ankle harnesses, "catapulting" or prestretching a jumper's rope, collective jumps, or takeoffs from anything but a fixed platform. Others banned bungee jumping altogether. By the mid-1990s, government inspectors had shut down many of the bungee outfits, and regulation tamed the action that remained. Bridge jumping remains a gener-ally illegal but occasionally renegade variant.

Some of the earliest companies to offer bungee jumping are concentrated in northern California and the West and have diversified, sponsoring performance teams and contracting for advertising, movie stunts, and exhibitions. Supervised jumping has proven extremely safe, with only occasional grisly accidents, usually attributed to errors by maverick jumpers. Bungee continues worldwide in both sanctioned commercial forms and surreptitiously. Aficionados promote the sensory excitement and fear of the fall, while critics consider leaping to possible death a perplexingly pointless endeavor.

—*Judy Polumbaum*

See also: Extreme Sports

For further reading:

Menz, Paul G. 1993. "The Physics of Bungee Jumping." *The Physics Teacher,* 31 (November): 483–488.
Thigpen, David E. 1991. "Bungee Jumping Comes of Age." *Time,* April 15.

C

CAMP, WALTER (1859–1925)

Walter Camp, designated the "Father of American Football," created the All-America team, and the term "All-American" has since become part of the national vernacular. A native of Connecticut, Camp attended Yale University in 1876, beginning a lifelong relationship with the school. While at Yale, he played football and eventually served as coach-adviser, helping to develop the game into a distinctly American amalgamation of rugby and soccer.

Camp attended every football rules conference from 1877, when he was an undergraduate, to his death in 1925, and he is responsible for such innovations as the eleven-man team. Prior to the eleven-man team, the number of players varied. During Camp's day it was not uncommon to see fifteen-man teams. The first game ever played featured twenty-five men on each side. He also invented the line of scrimmage, definitive possession, the "gridiron" marking of the field, and the present point system. Camp's best-known contribution was his collaboration with Caspar Whitney and *Collier's* magazine to select a team of outstanding college football players. Annually, the selected group was recognized as the All-America team, and the team members were called All-Americans. Each year, some of Camp's nominees were on the winning team, sometimes making up the whole team.

Although Camp was one of football's greatest innovators, he guarded the game like a fiefdom and opposed later additions, most notably the forward pass, as unnecessary. Many felt the game had passed Camp by, but after his death in 1925, the Rules Conference cemented his status as "Father of American Football." His staunch opposition to the forward pass was soon lost in the memory of his other accomplishments.

—*Kurt Edward Kemper*

See also: Football

For further reading:
Powell, Harford Willing Hare. [1926] 1970. *Walter Camp, the Father of American Football.* Reprint, Freeport, NY: Books for Libraries Press.

CAMPANELLA, ROY (1921–1993)

As opposed to many athletes who were vocal advocates of racial equality, Roy Campanella, the first black catcher in major league baseball, helped integrate the game through his stellar play and gentlemanly demeanor. Born in 1921 in Philadelphia to a black mother and an Italian father, Campanella played professional baseball as catcher for the Baltimore Elite Giants of the Negro National League at fifteen years old. During the next eight years, he worked with various Negro League teams as well as with leagues in Mexico and South America.

Roy Campanella of the Dodgers is shown at Ebbets Field (Brooklyn, 1951).
(Bettmann/Corbis)

Early in 1946, Campanella signed a contract with the major league Brooklyn Dodgers, who assigned him to the minor leagues for seasoning. After only two years in the minors, Campanella made his major league debut, joining Jackie Robinson on the Dodgers roster. Unlike Robinson, however, Campanella had no desire to be a pioneer or a spokesperson for his race; instead, he let his play on the field speak for him as he became the finest catcher in the National League. Due to his reticence, he received a certain amount of criticism during his career for not being vocal enough about racial issues. Others, such as Robinson, who were actively seeking racial equality, not only in sport but also in society in general, considered Campanella's quiet demeanor and jovial attitude a subject for derision.

An automobile accident in 1958 ended Campanella's baseball career and left him quadriplegic. After the accident, he operated a business and did some community relations work for the Los Angeles Dodgers. He was elected to the National Baseball Hall of Fame in 1969.

—*Jeffrey S. Obermeyer*

See also: National Baseball Hall of Fame; Negro Baseball Leagues; Robinson, Jack Roosevelt "Jackie"

For further reading:

Campanella, Roy, and Jules Tygiel. 1995. *It's Good to Be Alive.* Lincoln: University of Nebraska Press.

exclusively Canadian during the 1996 season. The teams in the Western Division are the British Columbia Lions, the Edmonton Eskimos, the Saskatchewan Roughriders, and the Calgary Stampeders. The teams in the Eastern Division are the Hamilton Tiger-Cats, the Winnipeg Blue-bombers, the Toronto Argonauts, and the Montreal Alouettes. From 1954 to 1986, these teams played continuously as the Canadian Football Council. Each team predates the existence of the league, with most being outgrowths of amateur rugby teams.

The most significant difference between CFL rules and National Football League (NFL) rules is that a team must make a first down in three attempts, rather than four. In addition, the CFL field is much larger than the NFL field: 110 yards long by 65 yards wide. Goal posts are positioned on the goal line, and the end zone is 20 yards long. Each team uses twelve players, rather than the eleven allowed in the NFL; those players are drawn from a roster of thirty-seven, twenty of whom must be Canadian.

—*Dale Jacobs*

See also: Football

For further reading:

Goodman, Jeffrey. 1982. *Huddling Up: The Inside Story of the Canadian Football League.* Don Mills, ON: Fitzhenry and Whiteside.

CANADIAN FOOTBALL LEAGUE

Although Canadians primarily follow hockey, with a nod to baseball, they have also developed an affinity for football. The Canadian Football League (CFL) is distinctly Canadian, differing from U.S. professional football in its rules and traditions. Formed in 1958, the CFL is made up of eight teams in two divisions. After making a short foray into U.S. markets, such as Baltimore, Maryland; Shreveport, Louisiana; Sacramento, California; and Las Vegas, Nevada, the CFL became

CANADIAN WRITERS OF SPORT LITERATURE

As in U.S. literature about sport, Canadian literature of all genres contains vibrant representations and reflections on the nature and place of sport in Canadians' lives and culture. Roch LaCarriere's *The Hockey Sweater* is one of Canada's most famous children's stories. It is a tale about a young boy from Ste. Justine, Quebec, who mistakenly receives a Toronto Maple Leaf sweater, instead of the Montreal Canadiens sweater he requested. Although a children's tale, the story is ultimately about the tension between French and English Canada and about the love of hockey throughout the country. Another popular children's book, Michael Arvaarluk Kusugak's *Baseball Bats for Christmas,* hinges on Canada's cultural diversity. An isolated Inuit community receives a shipment of Christmas trees, but, being unfamiliar with that particular tradition, the children think the trees, when stripped of their branches, are baseball bats. In both stories, sport is not simply recreation but an important cultural practice.

W. O. Mitchell's *The Black Bonspiel of Wullie MacCrimmon* is a play about a curler who challenges the devil to a single match. Using curling, a sport most avidly played in the Canadian prairies, the work explores and pokes fun at religion, ethnicity, and regionalism in Canada. Rick Salutin's *Les Canadiens,* much like LaCarriere's children's story, employs hockey, specifically the Montreal Canadiens, to represent Quebec's identity and its struggles with English Canada. The play begins on the Plains of Abraham, where the English defeated the French in 1759, and ends in 1976, when the Parti Québécois was elected to govern Quebec. These two plays dramatize Canadian political and religious history acted out through sport. Kenneth Brown's *Life after Hockey* is a one-man drama on in-line skates that illustrates the extent to which hockey is a religion in Canada.

Hockey is the inspiration for a significant body of Canadian poetry, from individual poems like Al Purdy's "Hockey Players" and "Homage to Ree-Shard" to entire collections about the sport, like John B. Lee's *Hockey Player Sonnets* and Richard Harrison's *Hero of the Play.* George Bowering is Canada's unofficial baseball poet, and poets like Raymond Souster and Erin Moure have written on a variety of sports. Canadian poetry of sport employs many of the same conventions as U.S. writing: celebrations of the hero and the antihero and portraits of games and places.

Canadian novelists who have made a single sport the focus of their work have frequently drawn on baseball rather than hockey, perhaps lending support to the idea that baseball is the sport of novelists. W. P. Kinsella's *Shoeless Joe* (the basis for the film *Field of Dreams*), his *Iowa Baseball Confederacy,* and Paul Quarrington's *Home Game* head the list of famous Canadian novels about baseball. Quarrington, on the other hand, has also written two novels about hockey players, *King Leary* and *Logan in Overtime.*

Canadian novelists present scenes that include sport as a central image or metaphor, as Robert Kroetsch did in his use of rodeos to illustrate the difficulty of "riding" language in *The Words of My Roaring* and in his use of hockey to illustrate the precarious act of balancing control and chaos in *What the Crow Said,* and as Margaret Atwood did in referring to Canadians' love of baseball as a sign of U.S. infiltration into Canadian life in *Surfacing* (1987).

Canadian nonfiction about sport turns the focus back to hockey, as authors try to establish ways in which the sport defines Canada. Former Montreal Canadien goalie Ken Dryden wrote about his experiences in hockey in *The Game* and provided an analysis of the role of hockey in the Canadian psyche in *The Home Game.* Radio personality Peter Gzowski described the importance of hockey to Canada in *The Game of Our Lives,* and Doug Beardsley drew on personal experience and cultural events to define Canada as a *Country on Ice.* Although baseball fiction is as prominent in Canada as is the fiction relating to hockey, no sport can unseat the central position of hockey when trying to define Canadian identity.

—*Kevin Brooks*

See also: Hockey; Literature, Sport in

For further reading:

Beardsley, Doug, ed. 1989. *The Rocket, the Flower, the Hammer and Me: A Hockey Fiction Reader.* Vancouver, BC: Polestar.

Brooks, Kevin, and Sean Brooks, eds. 1996. *Thru the Smoky End Boards: Canadian Poetry about Sports and Games.* Vancouver, BC: Polestar.

Humber, William, and John St. James, eds. 1996. *All I Thought about Was Baseball: Writings on a Canadian Pastime.* Toronto: University of Toronto Press.

CANDLESTICK PARK

The birth, growth, name change, and demise of Candlestick Park in the short span of forty years reflects the changing patterns of U.S. migration and the corporate transformation of U.S. sport. Candlestick Park was built in 1960 to house the San Francisco Giants professional baseball team, newly relocated from the historic Polo Grounds of New York. This 43,000-seat open-air stadium became one of the first sport symbols of the westward migration of Americans, a migration that accelerated after World War II. Enlarged to 62,000 seats in 1971, the stadium also became home to professional football's San Francisco 49ers.

Named for the jagged rocks and trees of the surrounding landscape, rising from the tidelands like giant candlesticks, the park is widely known for its chilly, swirling winds and consequent zany ball flights. Considering the park's location, it is also miraculous that the park incurred only minor damage from the great earthquake that rocked the San Francisco Bay area during the 1989 World Series.

Affectionately known by ESPN sportscasters and fans alike as the "Stick," Candlestick Park hosted numerous football play-off games leading to the 49ers' five Super Bowl championships (as well as the last concert by the Beatles in 1966). In 1995, the park's name was officially changed to 3Com Park, reflecting a controversial corporate sponsorship by a Silicon Valley–based computer software company.

—*John Paul Ryan*

See also: Baseball; ESPN; Football

For further reading:

"Candlestick Reborn." 2002. *Multinational Monitor,* September, 4.

Fimrite, Ron. 1999. "Good Riddance: Few Will Mourn When the Last Baseball Game Is Played at Candlestick Park." *Sports Illustrated,* October 4, R4+.

CARD GAMES

Card games are endemic in U.S. culture. They range from old maid and go fish for young children, to gin, bridge, and canasta games played at adult social clubs and tournaments, to innumerable games of poker played in friendly Friday-night sessions in kitchens and basements, to high-stakes blackjack tables at grand casinos.

The Oxford Guide to Card Games lists hundreds of games played with a deck of cards. The makeup of that deck depends on the nature of the game. The deck most common in the United States consists of fifty-two cards—thirteen cards in each of four suits—plus two jokers. Variations exist for such popular card games as bridge, hearts, pinochle, euchre, and canasta, but all are originally based on the traditional deck of fifty-two.

U.S. culture's fascination with card games revolves around the pleasure or profit that one or more persons obtain from playing the game. However, most cardplayers also have some awareness of the long tradition of "reading" one's future in a deck of cards and of the ultimate connection of a regular deck to the more mystically oriented tarot deck. Thus, the spirit at the heart of gambling in and on card games may be this sense of "seeing" into the future. Another connection that is also part of the cultural appeal of cards are the tricks that can entertain bored sitting-room guests or dazzle audiences when performed by sleight-of-hand artists and magicians.

The card games most readily associated with sport are variations of poker and blackjack. Superstitions, maneuvers, and tricks often refer to infamous or ill-fated historical games (such as the "dead man's hand," a pair of black aces and a pair of black eights, with the fifth card unknown, said to be the hand Wild Bill Hickok was holding when

People from around the United States and from other countries gather yearly at the Horseshoe Casino to play in the month-long World Series of Poker tournament, where the winner can pocket over $1 million (2001).
(DAVID BUTOW/CORBIS)

he was shot from behind); to cities or regions such as Chicago, the Bronx, Kansas City, Las Vegas, Texas, or the Old Wild West; or to the mythology of con men, cheaters, and oddsmakers.

Another cultural phenomenon related to card games is the wealth of words, terms, and expressions that have entered the U.S. vocabulary, from street lingo to business parlance. "Ace in the hole," "wild card," "raise the stakes," "up the ante," "trump card," "bluffing," "call his bluff," "throw in one's chips," "fold," and "shark" or "sharpster" are just a few of the terms directly gleaned from card games. As with many other popular sports, Americans have appropriated the language of card games to describe life situations beyond the realm of the card table.

—John Slack

See also: Language of Sport; Las Vegas, Nevada

For further reading:

Hargrave, Catherine Perry. 1966. *A History of Playing Cards and a Bibliography of Cards and Gaming.* New York: Dover.

Partlett, David. 1990. *The Oxford Guide to Card Games.* Oxford and New York: Oxford University Press.

CARNIVALS

Although traditionally the word "carnival" refers to an animated public celebration that, if practiced according to Christian tradition, comes just before the observance of Lent and represents one of the most deeply rooted social rituals in Western culture; in North America, however, the word can generally refer to any type of traveling amusement show that features rides, various games of chance, and other entertainments, usually accompanied by a host of food vendors. Modern carnivals reflect a long tradition of spectacle and sport historically available in traveling shows from the 1800s of P. T. Barnum, who popularized feats of strength and freakishness, to Buffalo Bill Cody, who added rodeo-type acts of bravado. Carnivals have in common a carefree mood and are sites of popular recreation and sport. Different from a circus (before you ask, Barnum's was not initially considered a circus, but a freak show), where public entertainment takes place within the bounds of a structured amphitheater of some kind, carnivals include a menagerie of activities and sideshows where the public can elect to become active participants in games of chance or skill. Associated with carnivals are various tests of physical prowess and amusement rides, such as the Ferris wheel, which debuted in 1893 at the World's Columbian Exposition in Chicago.

More specifically, however, Carnival—or Mardi Gras, as the ritual is named in the United States—can have more-seasonal and Christian connotations. Carnival began in medieval Europe as an urban and courtly reaction to Lenten rules that imposed restrictions on meat eating, marriage, and sex. Gradually, the tradition spread to the Americas, where today Carnival is eagerly anticipated in a number of places, including, most notably, Rio de Janeiro, Havana, where it is a three-week celebration, Veracruz, and New Orleans.

Carnival involves a process of role reversal usually signifying some sort of rebellion against established linguistic, cultural, artistic, religious, social, or political values. Often this involves various acts of clowning and gaudy mischief making. The celebration usually includes the naming of "kings" and "queens," wild dancing, and colorful parades. In New Orleans, Carnival/Mardi Gras is a social celebration rich in cultural significance because it

represents the coming together of African, French, Spanish, and Anglo-American traditions.

—*Andrew G. Wood*

See also: Latino Athletes

For further reading:
Powell, Tom. 2003. "Midways on Road Most of Year." *Amusement Business,* June 30, 15.

CARTOONS AND SPORT

For the most part, when U.S. animated cartoons feature sport, they focus on neither athletic prowess nor inspired gamesmanship; the competition provides a theme or background for tangentially related adventure. Hanna-Barbera, once the dominant animation studio for U.S. television, plundered basic plots from live-action theatrical releases, for example, mining *Those Daring Young Men in Their Jaunty Jalopies* and *Those Magnificent Men in Their Flying Machines* to develop *Wacky Races* for their characters. In addition, their *Animalympics* series adapted the Olympic Games so that Yogi Bear, Magilla Gorilla, and the rest of the characters could experience other sport-themed comic misadventures.

The studio acquired the rights to animate the Harlem Globetrotters, making them "guest stars" on such programs as *The Scooby-Doo Mysteries* and briefly giving them their own series. Still, sport remains peripheral in these programs, reduced to having a Globetrotter's trick shots foil a bad guy's escape. The translation of the Globetrotters to Saturday morning cartoons indicates the negligible importance of sport to television animation and is, perhaps, a poignant reminder of the blurring between athletic competition and other fantasy-based entertainment.

American theatrical animated short features by such major studios as Disney and Warner Brothers, on the other hand, have traditionally emphasized differences between the everyman hero and the athletically adept. The Disney shorts make Mickey Mouse, Donald Duck, and especially Goofy the butt of the joke, and comedy derives from their uncoordinated attempts to master the basics of game play. The feistier Warner Brothers short features, however, tend to present athletes as elitist bullies that mistakenly, and later regrettably, assume their physical prowess gives them rightful dominance over the wilier, physically unassuming characters such as Bugs Bunny and Daffy Duck.

Both Disney's and Warner Brothers' formulas have worked consistently as long as the protagonists have not been true athletes. However, Warner Brothers tampered with this mix in producing *Space Jam* (1996), an outgrowth of over-hyped corporate fandom and marketing frenzy. In this feature-length live-action/animated combo, Michael Jordan joins a basketball team made up of Looney Tunes characters, following the absurd premise that the bullying athletes from space will halt their evil plans if defeated in a game. The film received a frigid response from critics and only lukewarm consumer interest in merchandising, which may prevent similar projects.

—*Thomas Alan Holmes*

See also: Comics and Sport; Popular Culture and Sport

For further reading:
Connellan, Tom. 1997. *Inside the Magic Kingdom: Seven Keys to Disney's Success.* Austin, TX: Bard Press.
Sennett, Ted. 1989. *Art of Hanna-Barbera: Fifty Years of Creativity.* New York: Viking Press.

"CASEY AT THE BAT"

Although its origin was disputed for many years, the poem "Casey at the Bat: A Ballad of the Republic, Sung in the Year 1888" was written by Ernest L. Thayer and was first published by the *San Francisco Examiner* on June 3, 1888. Its tale of an overconfident hitter who strikes out, loses the ball game, and disappoints an entire town has inspired hundreds of variant poems, numerous songs, artwork, reenactments, and even an opera.

> *Though the identity of the author was no longer disputed after 1938, the name of the real Casey in "Casey at the Bat" has always been an area of controversy.*

The fascination of "Casey at the Bat" derives partly from the mystery surrounding its origin, the identity of Casey, and the location of his team's hometown, Mudville, and partly from its distinctively American theme of the individual struggling against great adversity. Confusion over the origin of the poem arose because Thayer signed the poem with his usual pseudonym, "Phin." The poem gained national exposure and fame after the actor De Wolf Hopper made reciting the verse a regular feature of his traveling performances in 1892. Though the identity of the author was no longer disputed after 1938, the name of the real Casey has always been an area of controversy. One suggestion is the 1880s baseball hero Mike "King" Kelly, whose athletic feats were recorded in the song "Slide Kelly, Slide." Other nominees are John Patrick Parnell Cahill, Daniel Maurice Casey, O. Robinson Casey, and Dennis Patrick Casey, all ballplayers from the late nineteenth century.

Thayer stated that the poem was not based on fact, but speculations on the identity of the true Mudville have included Stockton, California; Mudville, Kansas; Boston, and Philadelphia. Perhaps the geographical diversity of these locations reflects the transcendent nature of the theme of the poem, the individual's struggle against adversity, both a feature of baseball and of the American ideal. However, the poem itself approaches the theme with a hint of parody: The hero's overconfidence, a quality that initially charms the crowds who have come to see him, harms his team's record and disappoints his fans when he watches two perfectly good pitches go by and then strikes out on a third. Casey fails the Mudville nine and his supporters while doing exactly what they want him to do, heightening the drama and enlarging his reputation and the spectacle of his performance. Variant poems have explored the theme from the perspectives of the pitcher or of Casey's family members and have developed versions that show Casey's redeeming himself, Casey's later exploits, and other permutations. Eugene C. Murdock's *Mighty Casey: All-American* (1984) includes approximately seventy-five examples of variants on the poem as well as a description of the 1953 one-act opera *The Mighty Casey*, written by William Shuman and Jeremy Gury. In "Casey at the Bat" and its many artistic progeny, the paradox of the individual's struggle and success versus sacrifice for the group plays itself out daily in the game of baseball, in its literature, and in many other works of sport literature.

—*Kathleen Sullivan Porter*

See also: Fan Behavior; Popular Culture and Sport; Sport Literature, as Discipline

For further reading:

Gardner, Martin, ed. 1995. *The Annotated "Casey at the Bat": A Collection of Ballads about the Mighty Casey.* New York: Dover.

CHEERLEADING

Although many do not consider cheerleading a sport, it has all the earmarks of an athletic endeavor: entrance into the lineup is competitive, and routines are physically grueling. In an era when cheerleaders have been involved in media-exploitive stories—from relatively minor incidents such as being penalized for slipping laxatives to the other team's squad and using abusive language directed at their opponents to the rather bizarre case of the Texas parent who participated in a murder-for-hire scheme to guarantee her daughter's place in the cheerleading lineup—this nonsport has gained more attention than many on-field athletic confrontations.

In the latter part of the twentieth century, a pretty face and good vocal projection were not as important for a cheerleader as gymnastic ability coupled with no fear of falling. One of the popular routines of the era was the "bat swing," wherein two young men on the second tier of a pyramid project a young woman upward by her ankles and flip her into the air.

At the high school level, cheerleaders compete annually for national titles against some five thousand teams from around the country. For college cheerleaders, professional full-time coaches and scholarships are offered. In addition, formal cheerleading schools for younger children—at a cost of over twenty dollars an hour for lessons—have become increasingly popular.

If a cheerleader has enough talent, he or she can audition for "professional" squads attached to professional sport teams, such as the Dallas Cowboys or the Los Angeles Raiders. From a field of over five hundred competitors, the Raiders select only forty-eight for their cheering team. Appearance is important in the choice, but the ability to dance well is usually the deciding criterion. There is no quota placed on age, race, height, or hair color.

Although cheerleading may seem to be a glamorous but essentially unfruitful profession and although it has been criticized for objectifying women, cheerleading is often an entrée into other fields. Cheerleaders are offered personal appearances, radio and television exposure, and photographic work. For many, cheerleading has been a launching pad into the entertainment industry, as exemplified by entertainer Paula Abdul, actress Teri Hatcher of *Lois and Clark* fame, and choreographer Diane Alexander, who created the dance routines for several Janet Jackson videos.

Approximately 10 percent of cheerleaders at all levels are men, and cheerleading generates millions of dollars annually in costume and pom-pom marketing.

—*Joyce Duncan*

See also: Football; Popular Culture and Sport

For further reading:
Adams, Natalie Guice, and Pamela Jean Bettis. 2003. *Cheerleader! An American Icon.* New York: Palgrave Macmillan.

CHILDREN IN SPORT: COMPETITION AND SOCIALIZATION

Sport provides children with an outlet for competition, thereby giving them the opportunity to compare their abilities with those of others and socializing them into certain patterns of behavior. Children under the age of eight often have no concept of competition. These youngsters play for the pure enjoyment of the game and the company of friends. It is not unusual for them to complete a game without knowing or caring who won. They do not compare their abilities to those of their playmates. Instead, they are concerned simply with the outcome of their own efforts, for example, how far they can throw the ball or how many baskets they can shoot.

As children mature, however, they begin to notice the abilities of others in relation to their own. Introducing competition into sport changes the approach; winning becomes important, and

Little League baseball players in dugout. Competition may damage children. Once the focus shifts from play to winning and to evaluating athleticism, sport participation can create stress.
(PATRIK GIARDINO/CORBIS)

achievement is valued as contributing to the cooperative team effort. Competition also provides an objective measurement of an individual child's ability in comparison with others, quantifiable through game scores and statistics. Individual performances can thus be contrasted and evaluated.

> *In organized sport, such as Little League baseball, competition may damage children. Once the focus shifts from play to winning and to evaluating athleticism, sport participation can create stress. Sometimes, parents unintentionally invite the harmful aspects of competition by expecting their own child to excel, while simultaneously disparaging opposing players and other children.*

In organized sport, such as Little League baseball, competition may damage children. Once the focus shifts from play to winning and to evaluating athleticism, sport participation can create stress. Sometimes, parents unintentionally invite the harmful aspects of competition by expecting their own child to excel while simultaneously disparaging opposing players and other children. Sport also socializes children by teaching them, in an enjoyable way, a number of positive behaviors. Children develop skills and abilities, encounter the work ethic, learn respect for others, discover the concept of individual responsibility, develop cooperation and teamwork, learn to defer to others when appropriate, begin to understand racial and ethnic differences, and appreciate the value of sacrifice and modesty.

—*Debra Dagavarian-Bonar*

See also: Children in Sport: Girls in "Boys' Sports"; Parental Involvement

For further reading:
Bigelow, Bob, Tom Moroney, and Linda Hall. 2001. *Just Let the Kids Play: How to Stop Other Adults from Ruining Your Child's Fun and Success in Youth Sports.* Deerfield Beach, FL: Health Communications.
Sheehy, Harry, Danny Peary, and Joe Torre. 2002. *Raising a Team Player: Teaching Kids Lasting Values on the Field, on the Court and on the Bench.* North Adams, MA: Storey Books.

CHILDREN IN SPORT: GIRLS IN "BOYS' SPORTS"

Although the line between girls' and boys' sport has blurred since Title IX was passed in 1972, girls still have difficulty in participating in contact sports, like football, wrestling, cricket, and ice hockey, and traditionally all-male sports, such as baseball, due to opposition, sometimes subtle, from male teammates, coaches, fans, and parents.

Since Title IX, girls have participated in boys' sports in two ways: by becoming members of coeducational teams or by forming all-girl teams. Contact sports, like football, wrestling, and cricket, however, often become coeducational because fewer people are interested in forming all-girl teams. In addition, the safety concerns of male team members, coaches, fans, and parents may limit those who are willing or able to participate. Questions about whether girls should play, the effect of their participation on boys, the male coaches' response to girls, fan concern about the girls' ability to help the team win, and the parents' influence and perception of the girls' participation burdens girls in their decision to play. Proponents argue for the simple enjoyment of the play, the competition, the exercise, and the social interaction. Arguments against girls' participation focus on safety and harassment by male teammates.

Girls are successful on their own teams. In the late 1990s, more than 250 girls' and women's teams were registered with USA Hockey, ice hockey's national governing body. In 1997, Tara Mounsey was the first girl to become the New Hampshire Player of the Year. The 1998 Winter

Olympics in Nagano, Japan, premiered women's ice hockey as a medal event. Internationally, girls play Australian-rules football in Australia and New Zealand and cricket in the Caribbean, and girls' football teams are now forming in the United States.

Although baseball has been less successful in integrating Little League or in establishing girls-only teams, the Reviving Baseball in Inner-cities program (RBI) has taught baseball to approximately 76,000 girls and boys.

—*Kathleen Sullivan Porter*

See also: All-American Girls Professional Baseball League; "Battle of the Sexes"; Title IX

For further reading:

Salter, David. 1996. *Crashing the Old Boy's Network: The Tragedies and Triumphs of Girls and Women in Sports.* Westport, CT: Praeger.

CHILDREN IN SPORT: NECESSITY OF PLAY

Play is at the heart of how children form their identities and their relationships to the culture around them. It is in playing and only in playing, child psychologist Donald Winnicott explains, that the individual child or adult is able to be creative and to use the whole personality, and it is only in being creative that the individual discovers the self. Children develop through imaginative engagement with the world around them. They acquire language skills by playful experimentation with the words they hear. They develop social skills by modeling behaviors to which they are exposed in make-believe games and dramas. They bring these skills into an increasingly complex arena of cultural play that includes the arts and ritual and competitive practices, like sport. Winnicott identifies play and compliance as the two broad categories of human activity, suggesting that imaginative play is the arena in which humans feel life to be worth living.

The importance of play in child development reflects and reenacts its importance in the development of the human species. One viable theory of cultural evolution is proposed in Johan Huizinga's *Homo Ludens,* which suggests that play, rather than toolmaking or other "serious" orientations toward progress, is the most fundamental element in how humans form cultures.

—*Geoffrey Rubinstein*

See also: Children in Sport, Competition and Socialization

For further reading:

Andersonn, Christopher, and Barbara Andersonn. 2000. *Will You Still Love Me If I Don't Win? A Guide for Parents of Young Athletes.* Dallas, TX: Taylor Publishing.

Burnett, Darrell J. 2001. *It's Just a Game! Youth, Sports, and Self-Esteem: A Guide for Parents.* iUniverse.com.

Huizinga, Johan. 1970. *Homo Ludens: A Study of the Play Element in Culture.* London: Maurice Temple Smith Ltd.

Winnicott, Donald. 1957. *The Child and the Outside World.* London: Tavistock Publications.

CIVIL RIGHTS AND SPORT

By demanding equal treatment in athletics, as well as in other areas of society, African Americans demonstrated their unwillingness to accept injustice in any form. As African Americans began migrating northward and westward after the turn of the twentieth century, they found greater economic opportunities than in the South, but they still had relatively limited opportunities when compared to the white majority. These exclusionary policies included athletics, where many blacks found success but primarily in segregated contests and venues. In athletics, African Americans initially demonstrated their abilities in hopes of gaining wider acceptance in society. However, as the confrontational phase of the civil rights movement evolved, blacks began to use sport as a platform to demand their just place in society.

Although interracial boxing matches always garnered public attention, it was not until 1936 that white Americans took positive notice of a black athlete. Jesse Owens, a student at Ohio State University, was poised to take center stage at the Nazi-orchestrated Berlin Olympics. Americans reveled in Owens's four-gold-medal performance and his rebuke of Nazi racial attitudes. When Owens returned to Ohio State, however, he did so as a custodian and never received a degree. Owens's experience highlighted the inequity of U.S. sporting contests. No professional sport fielded integrated teams, and with the exception of some northern and western colleges, few integrated athletic opportunities were presented to U.S. blacks. When the Brooklyn Dodgers signed Jackie Robinson in 1947, it was a landmark event for civil rights, both on and off the field. Prior to Robinson's breakthrough, Kenny Washington and Woody Strode, teammates of Robinson's at the University of California, Los Angeles (UCLA), joined the National Football League (NFL) in 1945, breaking the color barrier in that league; while Don Barksdale, also of UCLA, joined the National Basketball Association (NBA) in 1949. All of this occurred at the same time that the civil rights movement was assuming a more activist stance in the courts and was beginning to exercise what many would later term "direct action."

As criticism of the South's Jim Crow policies mounted, supporters of the civil rights movement found that sport, and U.S. obsession with it, proved an ideal platform upon which to rail against racial injustice. In the late 1950s, southern proponents of Jim Crow began backing down from earlier refusals to play against integrated teams. At almost exactly the same moment, teams, supported by their fans, from outside the South began refusing to play segregated teams. Publicized events such as UCLA's refusal to play Alabama in the 1962 Rose Bowl and the defeat of all-white Kentucky by integrated Texas Western

University (now Texas–El Paso) in the 1966 basketball national championship game put the refusal to suit up with and against blacks in a harsh light. Although Jim Crow suffered its final legal defeat in the mid-1960s, refusal to integrate southern athletic institutions persisted, with the University of Texas winning college football's last all-white national championship as late as 1970.

As the civil rights movement in general took a more militant and confrontational stance, so did the struggle for justice in and through athletics. Heavyweight champion Cassius Clay, later Muhammad Ali, surprised and divided the sport world when he refused conscription into the U.S. military and opposed U.S. efforts in the Vietnam War. Ali's subsequent loss of his title galvanized not only those in the civil rights movement but also those opposed to the war. Protests, boycotts, and sit-ins at sporting events, increasingly covered by television, served as effective weapons in the struggle for integrated seating, open admissions policies, and general fair treatment.

The 1968 Mexico City Summer Olympic Games was the backdrop of the most direct challenge to the racial sporting status quo when black athletes, led by San Jose State professor Harry Edwards, called for a boycott of the games to protest what many black athletes felt was nothing more than white Americans' use of the black athlete as a sporting spectacle. Athletes such as Lew Alcindor, later Kareem Abdul-Jabbar, refused to attend the games at all, while Tommie Smith and John Carlos, gold and bronze medalists in the 200-meter race, shocked the world when they stood atop the medal stand during the national anthem with their heads bowed and their black-gloved fists raised in the black power salute. As the confrontational phase of the civil rights movement subsided, athletes such as Arthur Ashe continued to use their prominent public exposure in the 1970s and early 1980s to protest racial injustice both in the United States and in South Africa. Activists replaced their outrage over segregated participation with their contempt for the disparity of blacks in positions of coaching, management, and ownership in sport.

—*Kurt Edward Kemper*

See also: Discrimination, Racial, in Sport; Mexico City Summer Olympic Games, 1968

For further reading:

Bass, Amy. 2002. *Not the Triumph but the Struggle: The 1968 Olympics and the Making of the Black Athlete.* Minneapolis: University of Minnesota Press.

Coombs, Karen Mueller. 1997. *Jackie Robinson: Baseball's Civil Rights Legend.* Springfield, NJ: Enslow.

ties across the United States, and he became one of the few baseball players to be honored with a commemorative postage stamp. Baseball's Roberto Clemente Award is given annually to the game's most distinguished humanitarian of the year.

—*Tim Morris*

See also: Latino Athletes; Latino Sport; Valenzuela, Fernando

For further reading:

Wagenheim, Kal. 2001. *Clemente!* Foreword by Wilfrid Sheed. Chicago: Olmstead Press.

CLEMENTE, ROBERTO
(1934–1972)

As a role model for many ballplayers and fans and a national hero in his native Puerto Rico, Roberto Clemente combined brilliant baseball play with distinguished humanitarian work off the field. As a player, Clemente was typical of a great natural talent who struggled against injuries. Significant in baseball history for his playing achievements alone, including three thousand base hits, he was unfortunately tagged with an unjustified reputation for moodiness, which became a negative stereotype of Latin ballplayers.

Clemente's cultural impact, however, came from being the outstanding Puerto Rican star among the ballplayers who broke into the major leagues during the integration of the 1940s and 1950s and for using his star status to further charitable work. Born the son of a cane laborer, Clemente grew up in poverty. As a baseball star, he worked every winter in Puerto Rico to raise money for underprivileged children, an effort that culminated, after his death, in the founding of San Juan Sports City, a community center for the poor.

Clemente was killed in a plane crash while delivering supplies to victims of the 1972 earthquake in Nicaragua. He was elected to the National Baseball Hall of Fame, schools and other facilities were named after him in Puerto Rican communi-

COCKFIGHTING

A blood sport involving two gamecocks in a battle to the death, held as single matches or in multiple single match tournaments called derbies, cockfighting has generated tremendous protest and legislation; however, game breeders and handlers legally pursue the sport in six states (Arizona, Louisiana, Missouri, New Mexico, Oklahoma, and Virginia) and throughout the world.

A cockfight is held in a ring between two birds whose feet have been fitted with gaffs, like needles or knives, and which are separated by handlers when they become entangled. The winning bird earns prize money by killing or mortally wounding the other bird, and it is this inherent violence that has generated questions about the legitimacy of cockfighting as a sport.

Practitioners contend that gamecocks instinctively fight to defend their territories and that breeding and training is a natural outgrowth of their innate abilities. The opposition argues that handlers entice the birds to fight and that the sport is cruel and should be banned. Those opposed to cockfighting receive much publicity and funding from organizations such as the Humane Society of the United States and the American Society for the Prevention of Cruelty to Animals. The activism of these groups has resulted in legislation banning cockfighting; however, breeders, who raise and

NCAA Football 2003, Michigan vs. Ohio State. Michigan freshman Diana Schorry, 18, is lifted by Michigan fans, after Michigan scored with 7:55 left in the fourth quarter to go ahead 35 to 21.
(DAVID BERGMAN/CORBIS)

train the birds, and handlers still practice the sport. Recently, women have become breeders and handlers in regular and powder-puff derbies. The cultural impact of cockfighting throughout the world is represented in a collection of writings about the sport edited by Alan Dundes, *The Cockfight: A Casebook* (1994), as well as in a variety of references in other works of literature.

—*Kathleen Sullivan Porter*

See also: Blood Sport

For further reading:
Dundes, Alan. 1994. *The Cockfight: A Casebook.* Madison: University of Wisconsin Press.

COLLEGE FOOTBALL

College football fills stadiums during the fall, attracts a broad national television audience, and continues to exhibit all the tradition, pageantry, and passion of amateur athletics. Now governed by the National Collegiate Athletic Association (NCAA), college football originated in the eastern part of the United States in the late 1800s. The game, largely derived from rugby, was developed by early coaches such as Glenn Scobey "Pop" Warner, Amos Alonzo Stagg, and John Heisman and evolved over the years into what has become modern college football.

In each region of the United States, college football exhibits a distinctive nature and evokes a unique reaction from its fans. However, nowhere is the sport more loved and fervently followed than in the Deep South, where it is often followed with almost-religious fervor. Having relatively few professional football teams and traditions during the early days of organized sport, the South embraced college football, and many southern college teams regularly drew crowds of more than eighty thousand fans to their stadiums. Modern fans and alumni in many areas of the country arrive days before a game and camp out on college campuses. There, they engage in what is popularly known as tailgating, a cultural phenomenon also connected to automobile racing and professional sport teams. Usually conducted in parking lots adjacent to college campuses, tailgating entails outdoor grilling, picnicking, visiting old friends, and reliving memories of college days and the team's past games.

Great rivalries stretching back more than a century, including Michigan versus Ohio State, Auburn versus Alabama, and Army versus Navy, exist in college football. These rivalries are generational, as parents pass on to their children the love of a school and a team and the fierce desire to defeat their bitter rival for another year. Many of the games are surrounded with lore stretching back to the nineteenth century, traditions that evoke deep passions and annual excitement in students, fans, and supporters year after year.

The top division of college football, alone among all NCAA sports, stages no play-off to determine a national champion. The championship is decided by wire-service polls of coaches and sportswriters after the season ends and after the postseason bowl games have been played. This system sometimes results in the crowning of multiple champions in a single season, a situation that usually leads to spirited arguments during the off-season among journalists, commentators, and fans.

Even though the sport has reached high levels of success and popularity, it continues to wrestle with problems. For years, the NCAA sought to reconcile the amateur nature of the sport with the vast sums of money its players generate for the schools. The problem of unscrupulous sport agents and boosters secretly paying players led to numerous college programs being placed on probation or being otherwise penalized. Officials also fear that college football has evolved into a farm system for professional football, often at the expense of the educa-tion of the athletes. Even so, the sport continues to grow and flourish across the United States, attracting fine athletes and new fans each year.

—*Van Plexico*

See also: Television, Impact on Sport

For further reading:

Hayes, Matt. 2003. "The Heat Is On—and Off." *Sporting News,* June 30, 56–58.
King, Kelley. 2003. "Inside College Football." *Sports Illustrated,* March 31, 46.

COLLEGE FOOTBALL ASSOCIATION

In an attempt to redefine the management of college football, the College Football Association (CFA) indirectly helped increase television coverage of the game and influenced the number of bowl games played annually. Formed in the late 1970s by the most prominent college football programs, the CFA was in response to the so-called "Robin Hood" proposals that called for limitations on scholarships and revenue sharing. Consisting of sixty-one of college football's major programs, the CFA attempted to gain greater control over television revenues and bowl games from the rest of the National Collegiate Athletic Association (NCAA). As a special-interest group, the CFA argued that it was unfair for small schools to vote on how much television revenue the schools that earned it should receive. Because of its ratings pull with television networks, the CFA helped institute a restructuring of the NCAA in which the largest programs, classified as Division I-A, based on such things as colleges' seating capacity in stadiums and undergraduate enrollment, gained exclusive discretionary power over their television contracts and the nature of college football.

By far, the CFA's main concern was authority over and distribution of television revenue. Because its membership included the largest football programs, and therefore the ones most attractive to television, the CFA, after a series of court decisions, successfully wrested control over contracts from the NCAA. The success of the CFA proved to be its undoing, however, when the University of Notre Dame broke away in 1990 to sign its own agreement with NBC, thereby opening the way for smaller conferences and bowl games and, ironically, other CFA members to negotiate their own television contracts as well. The proliferation of such independent negotiation drove the CFA to extinction by the late 1990s, but not before fans could see games on no less than nine different broadcast and cable channels on any given fall Saturday. The increased exposure gave birth to smaller bowl games, like the Las Vegas and Alamo Bowls, and sparked the massive conference realignment of the 1990s.

—*Kurt Edward Kemper*

See also: ESPN; Television, Impact on Sport

For further reading:

Lederman, Douglas. 1990. "College Football Association, at Annual Meeting, Rejects Some Reforms Proposed by NCAA and Attacks the NFL for Interfering with Students." *Chronicle of Higher Education,* June 13, 44.

Maisel, Ivan. 1993. "The CFA Is Having a Devil of a Time." *Sporting News,* June 14, 44.

Watterson, John Sayle. 2000. *College Football: History, Spectacle, Controversy.* Baltimore: Johns Hopkins University Press.

COMICS AND SPORT

The presentation of sport in U.S. comic strips and comic books tends to fall into three main categories: products intended to exploit the devotion of fans, biographical or how-to material to motivate and instruct both fans and amateur athletes, and pithy commentary regarding sport's influence on society at large. Sport comic books, usually sold as collectibles to fans who ordinarily do not read comics, tend to offer the most egregious example of marketing exploitation. Historically,

various comics publishers, such as Charlton and Dell, featured a limited number of sport-themed titles; however, these titles never gained the popularity of comics based on superheroes or licensed movie and television characters. It was rare that a sport-themed comic book lasted more than a few issues; one that did was Street & Smith's *Sports Comics,* which began with a biography of Lou Gehrig and was later titled *True Sports Picture Stories* and was published from 1940 to 1949.

This fact has not discouraged some newer companies; in the early 1990s, for example, a few small independent comics publishers attempted to gain a toehold in the highly competitive comics market by adding sport-themed titles to their rosters. Vortex Comics produced *The Legends of NASCAR;* covers featuring embossed mock autographs, holographic images, and individually imprinted serial numbers hid the flaccid script and wooden illustrations inside. Revolutionary Comics also offered a small number of biographic comics that featured important baseball heroes such as Babe Ruth and Ty Cobb. Aircel Comics even produced an "adult" baseball-themed comic, *Hardball.* None of these companies, however, met with much success. DC Comics and Marvel Comics, the two largest comics publishers in the United States, only rarely publish sport-themed comics. In the mid-1970s, DC's Superman climbed into the ring with Muhammad Ali for the *All-New Collector's Edition,* volume 7, #C-58, in an exercise of mutual admiration and canny marketing. Superman is defeated by Ali. Marvel Comics attempted to boost sales during a failing comic-book market by producing such specialty titles as *The Dallas Cowboys and Spider-Man* (1983); Marvel also produced *NFL Superpro,* a short-lived series featuring the questionable sportsmanship of preternaturally powered mutants in competition with normal human athletes. Although non-sport comic books might occasionally feature a sport-themed story—the quintessential example is the footraces between DC Comics' Superman and the Flash to determine which is "the fastest man alive"—most publishers and editors recognize the negligible appeal of presenting athletic competition in comic-book form when the likely consumer base can just as easily find a game to watch on cable television or play a simulation on a computer or electronic gaming system. In fact, it appears that most U.S. comic-book readers have little interest in sport-themed comic books. In the late 1990s, the premier wholesale source of comics in the United States, Diamond Distribution, offered only a handful of sport-related comic books among the 750–1,000 monthly titles in its catalog. This situation means that most sport-related comic books become collector's items bought by speculators who will not read them, fearing some slight damage to the book will diminish its perceived future market value.

Comic strips, on the other hand, reach their readers through newspapers' subscriptions to feature syndicates; thus, strips must inform and entertain to attract readers. Comic strips and single-panel features that present real-life athletes tend to do so with a great deal of reverence, bordering on scarcely contained awe. *Play Better Golf with Jack Nicklaus* and *Stan Smith's Tennis Class,* for example, rely so heavily on the identification of the sport figures that the strips are otherwise anonymous. The adventures of fictional characters, however, tend to offer a mixed response to the importance of sport. Occasionally the protagonist of a strip is an athlete; however, his or her adventures, like those of Ham Fisher's *Joe Palooka,* most often take place outside of athletic competition. The economics of newspaper production by the 1980s and 1990s ruled out the presentation of games in daily strips, and the need for increased advertising space reduced most daily strips to a maximum of three or four small panels. A newspaper may cut as much as one-third of a Sunday color strip in order to cram more features into a limited number of pages. As a result, comic strips are more likely to comment on sport than to depict it.

The most widely syndicated sport-themed comic strip in the United States, *Tank McNamara* by Jeff Millar and Bill Hinds, regularly satirizes the extravagances of professional sport, and it often enjoys a place in the sport section rather than on the comics page. Like nonsport comic strips, *Tank McNamara* challenges readers' priorities when it comes to their interest in sport. In *Doonesbury,* for example, G. B. Trudeau presents B. D., a character so consumed with his identity as a football player that he never removes his helmet. More often, however, comic-strip protagonists do not consider themselves athletes; they look at sport from the outside. Still, no one has a greater love of baseball than Charlie Brown in Charles Schulz's *Peanuts;* he will stand on the mound of a flooded field and refuse to accept the fact that the game has been rained out. On the other hand, no one has a greater suspicion of coerced conformity and misplaced priorities in organized sport than Calvin of Bill Watterson's *Calvin & Hobbes.* Whether as a major theme or a temporary subject, sport evokes a wide range of response in U.S. comic strips.

—*Thomas Alan Holmes*

See also: Cartoons and Sport

For further reading:

Mankoff, Robert, and Michael Crawford. 2003. *The New Yorker Book of Baseball Cartoons.* Princeton: Bloomberg Press.

Wallace, Joseph, ed. 1994. *The Baseball Anthology: 125 Years of Stories, Poems, Articles, Photographs, Drawings, Interviews, Cartoons and Other Memorabilia.* Foreword by Sparky Anderson. New York: Abrams.

COMMUNITIES, IMPACT OF SPORT ON

The impact of sport on communities reflects the history of the infiltration of sport into the center of commerce, politics, and culture of the modern state. Prior to the late nineteenth century, sport was essentially an element of an aristocratic life. Although sport, or games, have been prevalent at all class levels in society for several centuries, participation in sport generally required the kind of

> *Sport is an activity that takes one out of the ordinary definitions of space and time. Sport transforms city street corners into verdant pastures and hours and minutes into innings and outs. It frees spectator and player from ordinary utilitarian duties and ordinary definitions and transports them into a different world where life is not serious, by ordinary standards, but instead is more intensely lived.*

leisure time that was available only to those living a gentlemanly existence. The talents needed to participate were highly cultivated. With the professionalization of sport in the late nineteenth century, however, a new intermediate chapter in the history of sport was created.

Early professional sport teams developed natural civic rivalries between communities. Plutocrats, members of the civic elite, owned those professional teams, not to make money—though occasionally the teams did make money—but rather as part of a civic and gentlemanly way of life. This era ended during the 1960s, even though the remnants of past times persist.

The 1970s began with the gradual and progressive integration of organized sport, especially professional sport, with other aspects of the economy and culture. Television was a prime force behind this involvement, providing the exposure conducive to favorable publicity. A major league team, like a convention center and a symphony orchestra, became a source of civic pride and a symbol that a community had achieved major city status.

By financing and building modern sport stadiums, local politicians and civic elites used sport to rejuvenate cities, inflate real estate values, promote commerce, and generate revenue. Although few modern stadiums ever bring in amounts even approaching as much revenue as promoters predict, the real benefits of a new stadium to a city are often indirect and psychological. To many people, a gleaming modern sport stadium is a sign that a city has a progressive and dynamic leadership and can provide its citizenry and visitors with the high-quality entertainment normally associated with major cities. In reality, the motives of stadium promoters are frequently self-serving. Through taxation, part of the cost of providing this high-quality entertainment is frequently assumed by many community residents who have little or no interest in sport.

Television can stimulate the building of stadiums by providing civic "dreamers" around the country with frequent images of modern sport structures. Aspiring civic promoters know that if their community can build a modern sport facility, their chances of reaping favorable national publicity improve tremendously. Television, however, may also serve as a deterrent to the construction of stadiums. Even though civic backers may anticipate few problems in stimulating attendance, a city may have difficulty attracting a franchise for some sports if it is located in a weak television market.

> *Sport allows spectators to watch, without blinking, the odd behavior of oddly dressed people. In sport, one sees the origins of culture: the creation, for no utilitarian reason, of a separate symbolic world peopled by mythic figures—pirates and Vikings, heroes and villains.*

For individuals, sport, like play, can be viewed as an end in itself. It is an activity that takes one out of the ordinary definitions of space and time. Sport transforms city street corners into verdant pastures and hours and minutes into innings and outs. It frees spectator and player from ordinary utilitarian duties and ordinary definitions and transports them into a different world where life is not serious, by ordinary standards, but instead is more intensely lived. Sport allows spectators to watch, without blinking, the odd behavior of oddly dressed people.

In sport, one sees the origins of culture: the creation, for no utilitarian reason, of a separate symbolic world peopled by mythic figures (pirates and Vikings, heroes and villains); intensely dramatic and conclusive; lived, like a religious service or a symphony, according to transformed space and transfigured time; creating unique social groupings (fans) filled with arcane lore (statistics) and marked off from others who do not live in the world of football, baseball, and other sports.

—*Donald E. Parente*

See also: Economics of Sport; Metaphor, Sport as, for Life; Television, Impact on Sport

For further reading:
Gratton, Chris, and Ian Henry, eds. 2001. *Sport in the City.* New York: Routledge.
Krauss, Rebecca S. 2003. *Minor League Baseball: Community Building through Hometown Sports.* New York: Hayworth Press.

THE COMPLEAT ANGLER

The Compleat Angler, written by Izaak Walton, the "father" or "patron saint" of fishing, not only provides instructions for angling but also presents an imaginative pastoral world. It has helped shape the U.S. conception of fishing, environmental conservation, and the pastoral.

First printed in 1653, *The Compleat Angler* underwent five editions. To the fifth edition in 1676, Walton's friend Charles Cotton added, among other things, instructions on fly-fishing. *The Compleat Angler* was the first fishing book to provide a complete pastoral picture of angling as a way of life. It consists primarily of a dialogue

between a fisherman and other characters, including shepherds and milkmaids, who not only discuss ways of preparing bait and catching fish but also sing songs and exchange bits of fishing history and lore.

The Compleat Angler has undergone nearly five hundred editions; it is one of the most reprinted books in the English language and has been continuously in print since 1750. A yearning for escape from urbanization in the nineteenth-century United States led to the production of the first and many subsequent U.S. editions of the work, which created a simultaneous rise in the popularity of recreational fishing. Most angling literature written in English since the seventeenth century is in some way indebted to Walton's work: Norman Maclean's *A River Runs Through It* (1976) is a recent example.

The Compleat Angler also influenced twentieth-century conservationist movements. In 1922, a group of Chicago sportsmen formed the Izaak Walton League. Named for Walton because of his conservationist stance, the organization's goal is to combat water pollution and environmental abuses.

—*Anne E. McIlhaney*

See also: Fishing, Fly and Bait; Women and Fishing

For further reading:
Bevan, Jonquil. 1988. *Izaak Walton's "The Compleat Angler": The Art of Recreation.* New York: St. Martin's Press.
Browning, Mark. 1988. *Haunted by Waters: Fly Fishing in North American Literature.* Athens: Ohio University Press.
Cooper, John R. 1968. *The Art of "The Compleat Angler."* Durham, NC: Duke University Press.

COMPUTERS AND SPORT

Since the invention of the personal computer (PC), computers have helped make sport a central focus of U.S. culture: helping analyze and enhance performance; connecting the fans to the steady flow of scores, gossip, and other information; and allowing fans to reenact sport fantasies through video games.

Computers were relatively ignored in sport until the 1980s, when the media's appetite for information highlighted the possibilities of being able to retrieve information more rapidly, particularly in baseball, with its traditional dependence on statistics. Baltimore Orioles manager Earl Weaver, for example, commissioned a college student to prepare reports on how each of his batters fared against each opposing pitcher and on how his pitchers fared against opposing batters. His superior access to data was one of many factors that helped him produce a string of pennant winners.

In 1997–1998, St. Louis Cardinals manager Tony La Russa, then the lifetime leader in wins among active managers, commissioned a custom computer program to analyze batter and pitcher tendencies through millions of different combinations of factors. The system ties statistical data to videotapes of batters' and pitchers' performances so that individual at bats can not only be analyzed but also called up on a video screen for players and coaches to review.

This use of video to display and analyze performance is likewise familiar to television viewers, who can see high-resolution, slow-motion replays while commentators point out minute variances in style and mechanics. Children then go to the playground and try to repeat the same detailed motions as they play. Whereas video games draw children away from the playground, this technology encourages them to return.

In the 1990s, "motion-capture" technology became one of the analysis tools. In this technique, sensors are placed on an athlete's body and the movement of every major joint and bone is "captured" in three dimensions by the computer. This allows an on-screen synthetic computer figure to reenact an athlete's movements exactly. The technology is used, especially in track and field, golf, and baseball, to isolate problems. It was used

as a key element in the superrealistic sport video games and computer games of the 1990s.

The preoccupation with sport in U.S. culture is fostered by the twenty-four-hour flow of information broadcast through computers. Home satellite decoding systems are microprocessor based, as are the sport pagers that allow fans to see the score and situation in any game at any moment.

Computer sport games are big business, building the fan base, enhancing the celebrity of major stars, and redirecting some outside play to inside joystick jockeying. The first playable computer simulation was a model of the 1954 baseball season written by student Don Daglow at Pomona College in 1971 on a PDP-10 mainframe computer.

Video games have exerted more cultural influence than PC simulations in the twenty years the electronic games have been available. PCs reside in the den or home office, whereas video games are played on the television set as part of an entertainment area in the living room. PCs are bought for working at home; video games are bought for entertainment. Computers are often off-limits to children, who thrive and outperform their parents on video games. Thus, PC games emphasize strategy for adults, whereas video games focus on reenacting, for younger audiences, the fantasy of being a star athlete.

—*Don L. Daglow*

See also: Video Arcades; Video Games

For further reading:
Jasper, James. 1985. *More Basic Betting: Programming to Win.* New York: St. Martin's Press.
Sullivan, Donald. 1984. *Winning by Computer.* Hollywood, CA: Gambling Times.

CONNORS, JAMES SCOTT "JIMMY" (1952–)

With his flamboyant personality, his aggressive style on and off the court, and his unusual two-handed forehand, James Scott "Jimmy" Connors, one of the sport's first "bad boys," helped transform professional tennis from a polite and gentlemanly activity for the wealthy to an intensely competitive and entertaining spectator sport with nationwide appeal.

Raised in Belleville, Illinois, Connors began playing tennis at the age of two under the tutelage of his mother, Gloria, who became a regular attendee at all of her son's early matches. After winning the National Collegiate Athletic Association (NCAA) tennis championship in 1971, Connors turned professional and began a storied career that would earn him 125 singles titles, eight Grand Slam titles, and the number-one ranking in the tennis world for 159 straight weeks from 1974 to 1978.

Connors's gritty style, public temper, and hostile on-court fits of rage, including the regular smashing of his rackets, increased the popularity of tennis in the 1970s and 1980s. His much-publicized engagement to women's tennis star Chris Evert, though later broken, further raised his celebrity status and brought additional exposure to the sport. In addition, he regularly defied the tennis establishment by refusing to play for the U.S. Davis Cup team or to participate in the World Championship Tennis Circuit.

The star's exciting, fist-pumping displays of on-court emotion had one last hurrah in the 1991 U.S. Open, a tournament he had won five times. At the age of thirty-nine and unseeded, Connors shocked the tennis world and won the hearts of all tennis fans by advancing to the semifinals before losing to Jim Courier. After retirement, Connors became an active participant, and part founder, of the Nuveen Over-35 Tennis Tour.

—*John Fea*

See also: Evert, Christine Marie

For further reading:
Batson, Larry. 1975. *Jimmy Connors.* Mankato, MN: Creative Education.

COOVER, ROBERT (1932–)

Robert Coover's *Universal Baseball Association, Inc., J. Henry Waugh, Prop.* (1968), generally acclaimed as one of the best baseball novels, anticipated the popularity of sophisticated board and computer games on sport-related themes in the last quarter of the twentieth century.

A writer of novels, short stories, poetry, and plays, Coover was born in Charles City, Iowa, in 1932. He graduated from Indiana University in 1953. His first novel, *The Origin of the Brunists* (1966), won the William Faulkner Award, and *The Public Burning* (1977) was nominated for the National Book Award.

Coover's significance for sport in U.S. culture rests primarily on his second novel, *The Universal Baseball Association,* the comically serious story of J. Henry Waugh, creator of a complex dice baseball game. Waugh painstakingly records the statistics of every game and invests his imagined players with names, personalities, and life histories. It is a game in which almost anything can happen, including the death of Waugh's favorite player.

Publication of the novel prompted many readers to write to Coover, amazed that someone else seemed to share their passion for parlor baseball. Coover shared their surprise. Yet he insisted that his novel was not written for baseball buffs. *The Universal Baseball Association* was less a book about board games than it was a symbol-laden rumination on God, free will, predestination, and the origin of myths. He seems to ask whether, in the game of life, the creator plays dice with the world, and if so, whether the dice are loaded.

Coover's other nod to sport literature was his 1971 short story "McDuff on the Mound," which retold the poem "Casey at the Bat" from the pitcher's point of view.

—*Fred Nielsen*

See also: Literature, Sport in; Metaphor, Sport as, for Life

For further reading:

Andersen, Robert. 1981. *Robert Coover.* Boston: Twayne Publishers.

McCaffery, Larry. 1982. *The Metafictional Muse.* Pittsburgh, PA: University of Pittsburgh Press.

COSELL, HOWARD (1918–1995)

As a radio and television reporter, Howard Cosell changed the nature of sport journalism by applying the techniques of print media and introducing relevancy and depth into a field previously dominated by superficial reporting and broadcast cheerleading.

Born Howard William Cohen in Winston-Salem, North Carolina, Cosell moved to New York and became a basketball star and school newspaper sport editor in Brooklyn's Alexander Hamilton High School. After graduating Phi Beta Kappa from New York University (NYU) and receiving a law degree, Cosell enlisted in the army during World War II, rising to the rank of major.

In 1956, Cosell gave up a successful law practice to host New York's first regular show of sport reportage and commentary on radio and television. In 1959, he accepted the position of boxing commentator on ABC's *Wide World of Sports.* Controversy arose, however, when Cosell became the first sportscaster to honor Muhammad Ali's request to be called by his Muslim name, and in 1967, Cosell defended Ali's right to refuse induction into the army during the Vietnam War. Declaring the sport "sleazy," Cosell

Sportscaster Howard Cosell playfully socks former heavyweight champion Muhammad Ali, during a dinner celebrating the 20th anniversary of ABC-TV's Wide World of Sports. *The affair was held at the Waldorf-Astoria in New York City (April 13, 1981).*

(BETTMANN/CORBIS)

ended his coverage of boxing in 1982.

In 1970, the acerbic reporter began a fourteen-year tenure on ABC's *Monday Night Football*. Program ratings soared, in large part because of Cosell's ability to enrage the audience. Voters in one opinion poll voted him both the most popular and the most disliked sportscaster, at the same time. After publishing a memoir that was strongly critical of his network colleagues, Cosell was pulled off the reporting staff of *Monday Night Football*.

Other controversial episodes of Cosell's career included his sympathetic interviews with black athletes who were protesting at the 1968 Olympics in Mexico City, his reportage of the Israeli hostage crisis at the 1972 Munich Olympics and his subsequent criticism of the decision to continue the competition, his support of Curt Flood's antitrust suit against major league baseball, his advocacy of increased opportunities for African Americans in baseball management, and his criticism of the media's propensity for hiring as sport reporters ex-athletes who became shills for their sport.

Noting that sport is the "toy department of life" and taken much too seriously by all concerned, Cosell's patronizing manner and boastful "I tell it like it is!" angered his critics. In failing health following a 1991 operation for cancer, Cosell died of a heart embolism in 1995.

—*David Bernstein*

See also: Ali, Muhammad; Olympic Games; Television, Impact on Sport

For further reading:
Cosell, Howard. 1985. *I Never Played the Game*. With Peter Bonventre. New York: William Morrow.
———. 1991. *What's Wrong with Sports*. New York: Simon and Schuster.

COUBERTIN, BARON PIERRE DE
(1863–1937)

The French idealist, educator, and historian Baron Pierre de Coubertin, as the primary architect of the modern Olympic Games movement, is arguably the single most important figure in the history of modern sport; his influence on amateur sport and physical acumen is worldwide. Raised in a family whose male genealogy could be traced back five centuries to the Roman Fredi family as well as to French aristocracy of the Havre region, Coubertin was destined for a life in public service. After a brief sojourn in military officer's training and a short stint in law school, the young Coubertin committed his life to social reform.

Convinced that the humiliating defeat of France in the Franco-Prussian War was in part due to the physical inferiority of French youth, Coubertin turned his attention to national revival through physical education. To accomplish this goal, he formed the League of Physical Education and campaigned for the introduction of physical training in the *lycées* (secondary schools). Between 1883 and 1887, Coubertin traveled extensively in England, where he came into contact with the famed English public school educational curriculum, with its emphasis on classical education, athletics, and spiritual values. Driven by a desire to attach his name to great pedagogical reform, Coubertin embraced the English didactic view of character-building sport and increasingly became convinced that the quest for moral, physical, and intellectual excellence offered an educational model worthy of universal acclaim and recognition.

The marriage of mind, body, and spirit was also a classical Greek conception, and the connection was never lost on Coubertin. His admiration for Hellenic completeness or *arête*, as well as his reverence for the English sporting tradition, led him to conceive of a modern version of the ancient games at Olympia as the symbol of his own allegiance to educational sport, *la pédagogie sportive* as he called it.

In 1894, at the Congress of the Sorbonne, Coubertin established a twelve-member International Olympic Committee to oversee international sport competitions to be held every four years.

The first meeting of the International Olympic Committee, organized for the 1896 Olympic Games. They are, from left to right, Willabald Gebhardt of Germany, Baron Pierre de Coubertin of France, Jiri Guth of Bohemia, President Dimitrius Vikelas of Greece, Ferenc Kemey of Hungary, Aleksei Butovksy of Russia, and Viktor Balck of Sweden (ca. 1896). (HULTON-DEUTSCH COLLECTION/CORBIS)

The celebration of the first modern Olympic Games took place in 1896 in, appropriately, Athens, Greece. Between 1896 and 1925, Coubertin served as the second president of the self-recruiting International Olympic Committee.

In order to more fully consummate the marriage of muscle and mind, in 1906, Coubertin organized a conference of representatives of art, literature, and sport in Paris to study the ways in which the arts could be included in the Olympic celebrations. The resulting Pentathlon of the Muses was first held in conjunction with the 1912 Olympic Games in Stockholm, where, under a pseudonym, Coubertin won a gold medal in literature for his "Ode to Sport."

A consummate internationalist and visionary, Coubertin dedicated his entire life to formulating and proselytizing his Olympic philosophy, Olympism, and to nurturing and promoting the Olympic Games. Inspired by an almost-religious dedication to the principles of international peace and harmony, Coubertin envisioned and labored for a global Olympic Games that would embrace all sport, all nations, and all peoples. A prolific writer and speaker, he authored numerous tracts, articles, and books, including two informative autobiographies, *Une campagne de vingt-et-un ans, 1887–1908* (1908) and *Mémoires olympiques* (1931). Although Coubertin was not the first person to conceive of reviving the ancient Olympic

Games, he succeeded where others had failed, and in so doing, he set in motion what was to become the greatest sporting spectacle in history: the modern Olympic Games.

—*Jeffrey O. Segrave*

See also: *Arête;* International Olympic Committee; Olympic Games

For further reading:

Macaloon, John J. 1981. *This Great Symbol: Pierre de Coubertin and the Origins of the Modern Olympic Games.* Chicago: University of Chicago Press.

CURLING

Introduced to North America by the Scots, curling has evolved into an official Olympic sport and a cherished winter pastime for over a million people in Canada and the northern United States. Curling is a physically vigorous sport similar to shuffleboard or English lawn bowls but played on ice. One player of a four-person team slides a forty-pound stone made of polished granite toward a circular target, while teammates run alongside each shot trying to influence its path by sweeping clean the pebbled ice surface immediately in front of the moving stone.

Scottish immigrants introduced curling to North America in the eighteenth century as a focal point for wintertime social activity. Curling flourished in upper Canada and then spread to the prairie provinces, which became the sport's true heartland in Canada. Canada now boasts more than one million curlers, including, in most years, the world champions.

With warmer climates and fewer ties to Scotland, the United States has been less receptive to curling. Still, the country has roughly fifteen thousand registered players in more than 130 clubs, concentrated mostly in the upper Midwest and the Northeast. In addition, teams, or "rinks," from the United States won the men's world championship four times during the 1960s and 1970s, including the first victory ever by a non-Canadian rink, that of Bud Somerville's rink from Superior, Wisconsin.

The rules of curling were formalized during the nineteenth century when it became an increasingly serious competitive pursuit. It was added as a regular event to the 1998 Winter Olympics. Despite the sport's development, which included corporate sponsorship and television coverage, it has remained a mostly amateur affair, thanks largely to strict regulation by the sport's governing bodies.

—*Peter S. Morris*

See also: Olympic Games

For further reading:

Weeks, Bob. 2002. *Curling for Dummies.* St. Paul, MN: Hungry Mind Publishing.

D

DEAN, JAY HANNA "DIZZY"
(1911–1974)

With a name befitting his off-the-field antics and his disregard for the traditional rules of English grammar, former St. Louis Cardinals pitcher and longtime television broadcaster Jay Hanna "Dizzy" Dean popularized brief, attention-grabbing statements, that are now called sound bites by sportscasters, became one of the key figures in U.S. sport folklore, and inspired a new class of sport broadcasters, including Howard Cosell and Harry Caray.

The son of a poor Oklahoma sharecropper, Dean enlisted in the army at the age of sixteen after only four years of formal schooling. As he was developing his pitching skills for an army camp team, a scout for the St. Louis Cardinals noticed his potential and signed him to a minor league contract in 1929.

Overpowering minor league hitters for three years, Dean dominated National League teams and led the Cardinals to a World Series championship in 1934. His and his teammate Pepper Martin's penchant for pranks and tomfoolery led reporters to refer to the Cardinals as the "Gashouse Gang," a moniker that contributed to the team's and Dean's popularity.

While setting several pitching records and capturing the National League's Most Valuable Player Award in 1934, Dean mastered the art of public relations by delighting both reporters and the general public with his daily assassination of the English language and his stupefying array of one-liners. Never one to downplay his own accomplishments, the quintessentially immodest Dean quipped, "If ya' does what ya' sez, ya' ain't braggin'." After being knocked out by a ball while pinch-running in the 1934 World Series and being taken to a hospital, Dizzy splendidly announced, "The doctors x-rayed my head and found nothing."

Dean retired from baseball in 1941 and immediately began a career in television broadcasting. If anything, Dean's popularity increased with his new role, and he quickly came to be regarded as a spokesperson for the common man. Dean personified the iconoclastic groundswell of popular opinion that served to counterpoint the stodgy baseball establishment during the 1940s and 1950s. Dean's symbolic role in U.S. sport culture is perhaps best revealed in longtime baseball commissioner Kennesaw Mountain Landis's pronouncement that Dean's diction was "unfit for a national broadcaster" and the subsequent removal of Dean from the broadcast booth during the 1944 World Series.

The removal only served to fuel Dean's popularity, so much so that he became the logical choice to host ABC's *Game of the Week* in 1953, propelling that network to national prominence and commercial viability. When CBS bought the contract for the program in 1955, Dean jumped networks as well, catapulting baseball to an unprecedented period of popularity during the late 1950s and early 1960s. The subsequent decline of baseball's heyday in the media could be partially attributable to the nationalization of the television contract and the attendant ousting of Dizzy Dean as broadcaster of *Game of the Week* in 1965.

—A. J. Stephani

See also: Gashouse Gang; Language of Sport; Television, Impact on Sport

For further reading:

Feldmann, Doug. 2000. *Dizzy and the Gas House Gang: The 1934 St. Louis Cardinals and Depression-Era Baseball.* Jefferson, NC: McFarland.

DEMPSEY, JACK (1895–1983)

Jack Dempsey was one of the most popular athletes of the 1920s, a period when promoters first used public relations and advertising techniques to position athletes in the mass media as the era's new heroes.

The world heavyweight boxing champion from 1919–1926, Jack Dempsey is also remembered as one of the great sport heroes of the Jazz Age. Under the direction of his manager, the flamboyant Tex Rickard, Dempsey was one of the first athletes to be marketed using sophisticated promotional techniques.

Born in Manassa, Colorado, on June 24, 1895, Dempsey was small for a heavyweight boxer, weighing less than two hundred pounds. He made up for his lack of size with an aggressive boxing style that drew many fans. On July 4, 1919, Dempsey knocked out Jess Willard in the third round to earn the heavyweight championship.

Dempsey dominated boxing during the Jazz Age. Newspaper reports of his matches resulted in increased newspaper circulation. Thus, publishers were willing to look the other way as promoter Rickard garnered what amounted to free advertising in their papers.

Gene Tunney, the "Student Champion," whose disciplined style contrasted with Dempsey's aggressive brawling, defeated Dempsey on September 23, 1926. Their rematch on September 22, 1927, drew more than a hundred thousand fans and a gate of more than $2.6 million. The fight resulted in what has become known as the "long count." In the seventh round, Tunney appeared to be knocked out, but the referee refused to start the count until Dempsey moved to a neutral corner, thus giving Tunney time to recover. Tunney eventually won the match.

Dempsey retired from boxing in 1940. After serving in the Coast Guard during World War II, he became a successful restaurateur in New York City.

—John Carvalho

See also: Boxing; Marketing of Sport

For further reading:

Kahn, Roger. 1999. *A Flame of Pure Fire: Jack Dempsey and the Roaring '20s.* New York: Harcourt Brace.

Roberts, Randy. 2003. *Jack Dempsey, the Manassa Mauler.* Urbana: University of Illinois Press.

DETECTIVE STORIES AND SPORT

The number of mystery/detective stories with a sport theme or setting reflects an American interest in both sport and the mystery genre. Mystery/detective stories are among the best-selling forms of leisure reading material, and mystery/detective stories with a sport setting or theme make up a sizable subgenre of them. Regardless of the sport, the most common role for the sleuthing character is either as an active or former player or as a writer associated with the sport, and former professional athletes have written a number of mysteries.

There are mystery/detective stories about most major sports, but by far the greatest number feature baseball. One of the earliest was *Death on the Diamond* (1934) by Cortland Fitzsimmons. Since then, dozens of books have been written in this subgenre, covering a huge variety of scenarios. The novels of Troy Soos, set in the first few decades of the twentieth century, include an active player who solves murders, each in a different city to which he has been traded. Books by the pseudonymous Crabbe Evers have a retired sportswriter solving crimes for the commissioner of baseball. The fiction and baseball may be connected in any number of ways—for example: a novel written by former major league pitcher Tom Seaver with writer Herb Resnicow, *Beanball: Murder at the World's Series* (1989); a female sportswriter who solves crimes in the novels of Alison Gordon; a book, *The Fan* (1995), that was made into a Hollywood movie, by Peter Abrahams; a novel of historical fiction, *The Plot to Kill Jackie Robinson* (1995) by Donald Honig; and even amateur sleuths who are the wives of major league players, *Caught in a Rundown* (1997) by Lisa Saxton.

There are several detective series in which at least one of the books includes a baseball setting or plot connection: Robert Parker has his detective Spenser investigating the possibility that a Boston Red Sox pitcher is throwing games (*Mortal Stakes*, 1975); Christopher Newman has his detective, New York City Lt. Joe Dante, investigate the death of a pitcher (*Dead End Game*, 1994); and Lawrence Block includes the theft of a baseball card in the plot of one of the books in his series featuring professional thief Bernie Rhodenbarr (*The Burglar Who Traded Ted Williams*, 1994).

Titles and authors of other works involving sport and mystery include: about basketball, Richard Rosen's *Fadeaway* (1986), C. C. Risenhoover's *Murder at the Final Four* (1987), Kin Platt's *The Giant Kill* (1974), and Robert Parker's *Playmates* (1989); regarding football, Eliot Asinof's *The Name of the Game Is Murder* (1968), George La Fountaine's *Two-Minute Warning* (1975), and *Murder at the Super Bowl* (1986) by former pro football player Fran Tarkenton with

Herb Resnicow; representing horse racing, dozens of books about "the sport of kings" by Dick Francis, novels set in Saratoga Springs, New York, by R. Austin Healey and by Steven Dobyns, and novels in this subgenre by former jockey Willie Shoemaker; on golf, Agatha Christie's *Murder on the Links* (1951) and titles by Miles Burton; about tennis, novels by Jack Bickham and by former tennis star Martina Navratilova along with Liz Nickles; concerning soccer, *The World Cup Murder* (1988) by former soccer star Pelé with Herb Resnicow and Richard Hoyt's *Red Card* (1994).

In addition, the 1977 reference work *Murder Ink* by Dilys Winn includes an article on sport and murder mysteries, listing a number of older novels on a wide variety of sports, including British rugby football, archery, and bullfighting. At least one anthology of short stories has been published: *The Sport of Crime* (1989) collects sport mysteries by famous names in mystery fiction, such as Ellery Queen, Ed McBain, and Rex Stout. Andy McCue's *Baseball by the Books* (1991) is a complete listing of baseball fiction in general, including mysteries, and *Everything Baseball* (1991) by James Mote has lists of baseball fiction, including mysteries.

—*Peter Sisario*

See also: Sport Literature as Discipline

For further reading:
McCue, Andy. 1991. *Baseball by the Books.* Dubuque, IA: William C. Brown and Benchmark Publishers.

DEVERS, GAIL (1966–)

With four gold medals to her name, outrageous fingernails, and a heart-wrenching personal history, sprinter Gail Devers gained the title of world's fastest woman with courage and style. Born Yolanda Gail Devers in Seattle, Washington, her quest for Olympic gold was made famous in a 1996 cable movie, *Run for the Dream: The Gail Devers Story.* Starring Charlene Woodard as Dev-

World Indoor Track and Field Championships (2004) in Budapest. Gail Devers runs the women's 60-meter hurdles. (MICHAEL LECHEL/REUTERS/CORBIS)

ers and Lou Gossett Jr. as her coach Bobby Kersee, the film outlined her battle with Graves' disease, which surfaced just before the 1988 Olympic Games in Seoul, Korea. Failing to make the hur-

dles finals, Devers sought medical advice, only to be told that she was in good health. It was not until two years later, when plagued by insomnia, migraines, and vision problems in her left eye, that Devers had tests run on her thyroid and the proper diagnosis was made.

After a two and one-half year absence from athletics and a long and painful healing process, Devers began training again. She captured a national hurdles title and continued her success at the Barcelona Olympics in 1992, running the fastest 100-meter in history and participating on the gold medal 400-meter relay team. She repeated her successes at the Atlanta Olympics.

Her flashy fingernails, so long that they are curved under, are unique. Devers is unwilling to let anyone measure her fingernails, and she scrunches up her fingers while in the starting block, rather than spreading them out as her competitors do, in order to avert breakage. Spectators in Atlanta were shocked when the trademark nails were nowhere to be seen during the 400-meter relay. Not willing to cut her nails, Devers had wrapped them with tape in order to prevent cutting her teammates during the baton pass.

—*Amy Bass*

See also: Olympic Games

For further reading:

Dyer, Nicole. 2000. "Born to Run." *Science World*, September 4, 18.

Gutman, Bill. 1996. *Gail Devers*. Austin, TX : Raintree Steck-Vaughn.

DEVIANCE IN SPORT

Deviance in sport takes many forms, from cheating on the field to dishonesty in college recruitment practices, drug and alcohol abuse, sexual assault, and murder. It can be divided into two basic categories: "on-the-field cheating," including such things as norm violations that occur while preparing for or participating in sporting events; and "off-the-field deviance," including criminal activity, fights, and drug and alcohol abuse. Research and literature on the subject exist in both the academic and popular press, reflecting U.S. culture's fascination with sport and athletes. The public is drawn to the exploits of those who are labeled as deviant, such as Mike Tyson, Pete Rose, and Tonya Harding, as well as of those who live on the edge, such as Michael Jordan, Muhammad Ali, and Bobby Knight.

In addition to acts, the environment in which some sport takes place may be considered deviant. There are sporting environments where such deviant activities as hustling, cheating, gambling, or institutionalized violence occur. Because people learn deviance through directly and indirectly observing such behavior, sociologists are beginning to discuss the ramifications of association with the deviant culture of sport and its deviant environment. Within the subculture of sport, athletes often behave in deviant and even criminal ways. It is important to note that a good deal of sport behavior would be considered felony assault outside the sporting venue. For example, boxing would be considered assault and battery, and racing drivers would be arrested for speeding and reckless driving. Much of what occurs on the football field would horrify many sport fans if it occurred off the field. Even when deaths take place on the field or in the ring, criminal charges are rarely filed, nor do civil suits generally succeed.

> *U.S. culture is fascinated with sport and athletes. The public is drawn to the exploits of those who are labeled as deviant, such as Mike Tyson, Pete Rose, and Tonya Harding, as well as of those who live on the edge, such as Michael Jordan, Muhammad Ali, and Bobby Knight.*

Hate, self-destructive behavior, and other activities that are not condoned in society outside of sport are routine on the field. And within sport, there is often acceptance of violating such norms as playing by the rules, playing fair, or not seeking to injure an opponent. Commentators have put forward a number of reasons for the increase of deviance in sport. Bureaucratization and commercialization of sport, which have led to greater pressures for victory and its consequent profit, are prime suspects. And the increase in rules has led officials to enforce them selectively.

It is, of course, necessary to note that deviance in sport, as elsewhere, varies along a continuum. Thus, generally speaking, most behavior falls within limits of conformity; those extreme cases labeled as "deviant" fall outside the normal range. Finally, there is a general perception that athletes tend to get a break when they are accused of violating the law. Felony sex crimes provide an area that has been well documented and studied. Certainly, there is little doubt that in the culture of male athletes, women are often viewed as objects. The issue is whether this perception has actually caused a higher rate of violence against women than that found in the general public. The arrest rate for male athletes on these charges is higher than that of the general male population. Conviction rates, however, tend to be lower. These results lead to interesting interpretations. It is difficult to deny that at least some favoritism in treatment is present in jury trials, since juries are often swayed by fame and athletes in our society have a good deal of fame. Whether male athletes are more prone to violence against females than are other men is problematic, but that they receive some preferential treatment once in the system seems a fact.

Deviance in sport has become a major concern in U.S. society. College recruiting scandals, injuries, drug and alcohol abuse, violence on and off the field, and other acts of deviance upset the old notion that sport is a model for youth. Many reasons are presented to account for the growth in violence. Generally, the growth in sport deviance is tied to other cultural and structural changes in society.

—*Frank A. Salamone*

See also: Athletes, above the Law; Fan Behavior

For further reading:

American Association for Higher Education. 1990. "Ethics and Intercollegiate Sport." *AAHE Bulletin,* February, 3–7.

Armstrong, G., and R. Harris. 1991. "Football Hooligans: Theory and Evidence." *Sociological Review* 39, no. 3: 427–458.

Benedict, J., and A. Klein. 1997. "Arrest and Conviction Rates for Athletes Accused of Sexual Assault." *Sociology of Sport Journal* 14: 86–94.

DIMAGGIO, JOE (1914–1999)

Arguably the most famous U.S. athlete of the twentieth century, New York Yankees outfielder Joe DiMaggio combined outstanding athleticism and graceful reserve to become one of the greatest cultural heroes of the postwar United States.

Born in California to Italian immigrant parents, DiMaggio became one of the most celebrated players in the history of baseball. In a remarkable career with the New York Yankees, DiMaggio appeared in ten World Series and made the All-Star team every year of his major league career. In 1941, he set a major league record with a fifty-six-game hitting streak, which was commemorated in the hit song, "Joltin' Joe DiMaggio."

As he cemented his reputation as one of the best outfielders ever to play the game, DiMaggio also became one of the highest paid. In 1949, DiMaggio was the first baseball player ever to earn $100,000, ushering in the age of high-paid athletic superstars. His celebrity was as great off the field as it was on. After his retirement from baseball in 1951, DiMaggio stayed in the public eye, hosting a television program and appearing in numerous commercials for banks and coffeemakers. DiMaggio's brief marriage to the legendary actress Marilyn Monroe also captivated the U.S. public and contributed to the sport legend's aura.

In retirement, the "Yankee Clipper" became a modern American icon. His mythic greatness as a baseball legend made DiMaggio a central reference point in U.S. culture, and he is mentioned both in Ernest Hemingway's *Old Man and the Sea* and in Paul Simon's 1967 theme song for the film *The Graduate.* DiMaggio continues to be revered

In 1949 Joe DiMaggio was the first baseball player ever to earn $100,000, ushering in the age of high-paid athletic superstars.
(BETTMANN/CORBIS)

as an athlete and sport hero who represents a simpler, more innocent age in U.S. history.

—*Michael A. Lerner*

See also: Baseball; Italian Americans in Sport

For further reading:
Cramer, Richard. 2000. *Joe DiMaggio: The Hero's Life.* New York: Simon and Schuster.

DISC GOLF

Disc golf began humbly as an unorganized pastime in the public parks of mid-1970s California. It has become, if not a national phenomenon, then at least a well-organized source of entertainment, leisure, and exercise for a diverse group of enthusiasts. As the name implies, disc golf is much like traditional golf. There are, however, two main differences: one is in the equipment used, and the other is social. First, and most obviously, disc golf differs from traditional golf in equipment. The projectile forwarded hundreds of feet into a waiting container is not a ball but a flying disc. In its most evolved form, specially designed and weighted discs are thrown into a wire basket on a post. The most rudimentary courses are makeshift routes that require players to hit designated landmarks, typically trees, with their discs. The game is scored like traditional golf; players who make their way from each marker into each basket and around the course in the least number of throws win the round.

A simple difference between disc and traditional golf that has greater cultural impact is the fact that nearly all disc golf courses are located in public parks and are available for use without expensive green fees or membership requirements. Although disc golfers can spend hundreds of dollars on equipment, putters and specialty drivers included, and on designer disc carrying bags, the sport can be enjoyed and played well with minimal investment. Beginners can happily play with one well-chosen versatile disc, and many veterans choose to play with only two or three. In fact, Pro Disc Golf Association (PDGA)–approved disc golf discs typically cost less than ten dollars. The low equipment and course costs make the game readily available to people of all socioeconomic groups, regardless of their available time to practice the game and their levels of athletic prowess.

—*John Zavodny*

See also: Fads and Trends; Golf

For further reading:

Gregory, Michael Steven. 2003. *Disc Golf: All You Need to Know about the Game You Want to Play.* Duluth, MN: Trellis.

DISCRIMINATION, RACIAL, IN SPORT

Racial tension has been a predominant theme in U.S. history, and sport has reflected that tension, sometimes ameliorating it but at other times exacerbating it.

Minority athletes are such a prominent part of the modern sport landscape that it is difficult to believe that for much of the twentieth century, nonwhite athletes found themselves marginalized and denied access to the highest levels of competition. For most of the early to mid-twentieth century, black athletes had to deal with the effects of widespread Jim Crow policies that excluded them from participation alongside whites. On the other hand, when minority groups were allowed to participate in sport, they met with tremendous success. For example, African American athletes provided the most accomplished trainers and jockeys for professional horse racing, but by 1911, almost all black jockeys had been denied license renewals. Similar closing of doors occurred in professional baseball in the 1890s, when an informal but iron-clad agreement among owners and league officials removed black players from the national pastime until after World War II.

Discrimination in Boxing

Although most of the better-known African Americans of the early twentieth century were athletes, their marginalization from white sport limited their opportunities. Further reducing the chance for athletes of color to succeed was the lack of resources and access to facilities. Jim Crow barriers in the South made many public sporting facilities off-limits to black athletes, and the situation was not much better in the North. Although the Young Men's Christian Association, the Young Women's Christian Association, private clubs, and black schools and colleges attempted to fill the gaps, these efforts were often too little and were certainly not effective at removing the impediments that kept athletes of color from entering the mainstream of U.S. sporting society. Even when they were able to do so, more often than not athletes of color discovered that their time on stage could be fleeting. Jack Johnson became an idol for millions of African Americans when he became the first black boxer to win the world heavyweight championship and to break the color line in that sport. At the same time, Johnson was vilified by many in the white community and even by some prominent blacks, and Johnson's attitude only worsened their opinion of him. By the 1920s, there was a de facto blackballing of African Americans at the highest level of boxing, something that would not fully change until the emergence of Joe Louis in the 1930s.

Negro National League

The 1920s marked the crystallization of segregation in professional sport in the United States. Andrew "Rube" Foster founded the Negro National League, which ultimately produced some of the greatest baseball players in history. During a time when baseball was at the center of the U.S. sporting consciousness, Jackie Robinson, Larry Doby, Willie Mays, Hank Aaron, Josh Gibson, and Satchel Paige were some of the superstars from the Negro Leagues, which captured black imaginations for more than three decades until full-scale integration of the major leagues was underway in the 1950s. Prior to integration, teams of Negro League All-Stars would often barnstorm against their white counterparts. The black teams won more than 75 percent of these confrontations. In basketball, the New York Renaissance and the more famous Harlem Globetrotters were formed to give black players an opportunity to excel in a sport that white ranks would not let them play. Almost all other professional sport barred blacks from participation as well; the only exception was the National Football League (NFL), which remained open to black stars until 1934. However, from that year until 1946, football too was a segregated venue in professional play.

Heroes

Even in the midst of such widespread discrimination against black athletes, the 1930s provided black sport fans with ample exploits about which to cheer. In addition to watching the burgeoning Negro Leagues, black and white sport fans alike could escape the Great Depression long enough to admire the performances of the "Brown Bomber," Joe Louis, who reigned as heavyweight champion throughout much of the decade and who helped bring Fight Night at Madison Square Garden into

the public arena. In 1936, Jesse Owens electrified the world, winning his four gold medals in the Berlin Olympics. Even while Americans cheered Owens's unprecedented performance, few saw the irony in their celebrating Owens's disproving of Adolf Hitler's views of racial superiority while at the same time maintaining a rigorous form of sporting apartheid that would linger in the United States for more than a decade longer. During that era, African American athletes participated in what they called the "Big Five"—baseball, football, basketball, track, and boxing—but their access to other sports was limited by opportunity and money.

Jackie Robinson

The post–World War II decade opened U.S. sport to black athletes. Between 1946 and 1950, every major professional sport paved the way for integration, albeit often in piecemeal and gradual fashion. In those years, basketball, football, baseball, tennis, golf, and bowling all integrated or reintegrated at professional levels of competition. Certainly, the most famous case was that of Jackie Robinson, the former four-sport star at the University of California, Los Angeles, professional football player for the Los Angeles Bulldogs, and Negro League standout whom Branch Rickey handpicked to integrate the Brooklyn Dodgers in 1945.

In April 1946, Robinson went to the Montreal Royals, the top farm team for the Dodgers. He excelled there amid a great deal of abuse from northern fans. On April 15, 1947, Robinson made his debut at first base for the Dodgers against the Boston Braves at Ebbets Field, breaking the more than half a century of unstated official segregation in major league baseball. One of the key factors in this decision was the change in commissioners from the dictatorial Judge Kennesaw Mountain Landis to the more accepting William "Happy" Chandler.

Robinson faced tremendous pressure in that first year. He took merciless abuse from opposing fans, players, and coaches. The Philadelphia

Phillies, led by their manager Ben Chapman, were particularly ruthless. Even Robinson's own teammates were skeptical, particularly early on when several players, led by southern-born Dixie Walker, threatened to boycott if Robinson were allowed to be on the team. Leo Durocher, the Dodgers manager, quelled any talk of such a player rebellion. Robinson excelled, however, winning National League Rookie of the Year for 1947. Wherever he went, he faced racism, but he was able to keep from retaliating and in so doing, paved the way for those to follow.

In July 1947, Larry Doby joined the Cleveland Indians of the American League, thus integrating the junior circuit. Before long, black stars were taking their rightful places alongside their white counterparts. The last team to integrate was the Boston Red Sox, who held out until 1959 before signing Pumpsie Green.

Civil Rights Movement

Of course, integration did not mark the end of racial discrimination, but the civil rights movement led to an awakening in sport as well as in the rest of society. Throughout the 1960s, many black athletes grew ever more outspoken about the issues of racism in professional and college sport. As barriers fell, those that did not crumble so easily became increasing areas of contention. Muhammad Ali became a hero to many Americans at the same time that many vilified his refusal to register for the draft during the Vietnam War. Although Ali went to prison for his stance, many Americans of color viewed Vietnam as a racist war, and in such turbulent times, Ali's refusal represented a major victory. The Supreme Court finally vindicated Ali in 1971. A similar political position occurred during the 1968 Olympics when 200-meter medalists John Carlos and Tommie Smith stood on the awards platform and delivered black power salutes in protest of U.S. policies.

Coming full circle in the 1980s and 1990s, attention was focused on racially insensitive comments from sport commentators, other athletes, and sport management. Jimmy "the Greek" Snyder of CBS television and Al Campanis, an administrator for the Los Angeles Dodgers, both lost their jobs as a result of statements that many Americans, whites and people of color, saw as racial slurs. Similar examples of prominent persons in the sport world who received censure as a result of dubious comments were commonplace throughout the latter portion of the twentieth century.

The latter half of the twentieth century produced an explosion of success for black athletes. In the late 1990s, African Americans made up approximately 80 percent of all National Basketball Association (NBA) rosters and a great percentage of its stars. More than 65 percent of the athletes in the NFL were black. Major league baseball was just under 20 percent African American, but more than half of its players were members of minority groups since many of the game's premier stars were Latino, coming from such areas as the Dominican Republic and Venezuela (Center for the Study of Sport in Society, 2001).

Although racial issues were still at the forefront of U.S. sporting society, one of the chief ironies of late-twentieth-century sport was the reverse stereotyping of athletic prowess. In earlier decades, white athletes assumed they had intellectual and physical superiority over their black counterparts, whereas in the late twentieth century, phrases such as "white men can't jump" became an accepted part of sport jargon. Black athletes were assumed to be faster and to be able to jump higher and farther, superiority often attributed to genetic superiority.

Race continues to be a dilemma in the United States, and sport continues to be a testing ground for society. Nonetheless, modern sport demonstrates that the arena is open to athletes of extraordinary prowess from all groups.

—*Derek Catsam*

See also: Ali, Muhammad; Negro Baseball Leagues; Racial Superiority, Myth of; Robinson, Jack Roosevelt "Jackie"

For further reading:

Ashe, Arthur. 1993. *A Hard Road to Glory: A History of the African American Athlete.* 3 vols. New York: Amistad Press.

Center for the Study of Sport in Society. 2001. "2001 Racial and Gender Report Card." http://www .sportinsociety.org/rgrc2001.html. Accessed July 2004.

Rust, Art, and Edna Rust. 1985. *Art Rust's Illustrated History of the Black Athlete.* Garden City, NY: Doubleday.

Wiggins, David K. 1997. *Glory Bound: Black Athletes in a White America.* Syracuse, NY: Syracuse University Press.

DOUBLEDAY, ABNER (1819–1893), MYTH OF

The fanciful legend that a young Abner Doubleday "invented" the American game of baseball in 1839 was aggressively promoted by sporting goods magnate Albert G. Spalding in 1907. The tale proved to be an appealing creation myth for a sport that had actually evolved slowly from English stick-and-ball games.

Abner Doubleday was a real existing historic personage, a Civil War captain and brevet major general who served at Fredericksburg, Gettysburg, and Fort Sumter, where he ordered that Union artillery fire its first volleys of the war. In his later life, Doubleday authored histories of the major battles of the Civil War, including *Reminiscences of Forts Sumter and Moultric* (1876) and *Gettysburg Made Plain* (1888). During his lifetime, he was regarded as a minor war hero but never as the "father" or "inventor" of baseball. In fact, baseball historians have argued that Doubleday never visited Cooperstown, New York, in 1839, that his diaries and other writings do not refer to baseball, and that an 1893 obituary suggests he did not even enjoy outdoor recreation.

The sole evidence of Doubleday's "invention" of baseball was a letter written by a mining engi-

A military officer in the Mexican War and the Civil War, Abner Doubleday (1819–1893) was credited with the invention of baseball for many years.
(CORBIS)

neer named Abner Graves in 1907. In that year, a blue-ribbon commission, headed by A. G. Mills, was established to investigate the origins of U.S. baseball. Among the prominent businessmen and politicians on the Mills Commission was Albert Spalding, once a star pitcher and then a sporting goods mogul. In July 1907, Spalding produced a letter from Graves claiming that in 1839, Doubleday interrupted a marbles game behind a shop in Cooperstown, drew a diagram of a baseball field, and devised a set of rules for the game. Spalding then prevailed upon the other commissioners to accept Graves's account, and with some hesitation they agreed. The first two conclusions of the Mills Commission were that baseball had its origin in the United States and that the first scheme for playing it, according to the best evidence obtainable to date, was devised by Abner Doubleday, at Cooperstown, New York, in 1839.

The tentative wording of the second conclusion, "according to the best evidence obtainable to date," hints at the discomfort some members felt in accepting Graves's dubious tale. Spalding, however, had what he wanted: an American hero and an American origin for the game of baseball. In the succeeding years, he successfully promoted this patriotic myth in his *Official Base Ball Guide* (1905), the leading baseball guidebook of the day, and in books such as *America's National Game* (1911).

On the other hand, the not-so-glorious truth was that U.S. baseball evolved slowly from a number of English ball games, including rounders, one old cat, town ball, and cricket. In fact, some early baseball writers and managers, including Spalding's longtime editor, Henry Chadwick, frequently applied cricket terms such as "batsman" and "excellent field" to the U.S. game. In the 1840s, two versions of the game prevailed in New England: one known as the Massachusetts game, which was played on an asymmetrical four-sided field; and the other, the New York game, which was played on a diamond. Because of the popularity of the New York Knickerbocker Club, the New York game came to predominate in the 1850s, but with many rule changes and adjustments along the way.

Why then did the Doubleday myth succeed so spectacularly? It was a lie that particularly appealed to the U.S. public at the beginning of the twentieth century: to U.S. jingoists, afraid of European influences; to the growing number of European emigrants, who sought to create their own American identities; and to the great masses of city dwellers, who longed for "pastoral" recreation.

—*Jeffrey Powers-Beck*

See also: Baseball

For further reading:

Seymour, Harold, Dorothy Z. Seymour, and Dorothy Jane Mills. 1989. *Baseball: The Early Years.* New York: Oxford University Press.

DRAFT

Drafting of players by professional sport organizations has occurred since the 1890s when baseball became formalized as a sport. More recently, drafts have become media events on their own. The expansion of cable stations specializing in sport coverage has changed the way drafts are conducted and has turned the draft into a significant ceremonial event of the sport year.

Baseball has the most extensive draft. In 2000, for example, there were fifty rounds of picks, resulting in over fifteen hundred players being selected for teams. True to baseball's pastoral roots, many of these players develop through the farm systems of various teams. Football held its first draft in 1936, and hockey adopted a draft system in 1963. The draft for each of these sports is a multiday event, but neither has as many rounds as baseball does. The National Basketball Association (NBA) has been much more aggressive about tailoring their annual draft to television coverage. Their draft has been reduced to two rounds of strictly timed selections by each team, and cable coverage of the event spans about four hours. In 1985, the NBA instituted a draft lottery system to prevent teams from intentionally losing games in order to secure the top draft pick. The lottery and the revelation of which teams have secured the top picks is also a media event.

Although the advances in cable television may offer more access and on-the-spot coverage, the accessibility offered by cable alone does not explain the attraction of the draft as an annual event. One possible explanation, however, is that the drafts are contemporary rituals that operate symbolically on many levels. The draft offers rites of passage and renewal for the teams and for sport in general. The infusion of new talent invigorates the sport and sets up the classic competition between age and experience, youth and veteran, or experienced player and rookie. In addition, drafts are designed to improve parity. The worst teams are allowed to draft first; consequently, they can draft better players and have more hope for improvement in the next season. Thus, the drafts simultaneously represent the end of the old season and the beginning of the new, and fans can celebrate through them.

The draftees also go through a rite of passage. They are transformed from poor or middle-class college students or amateurs to financially secure professional athletes. Media coverage of these events often reflects these themes. They also suggest the achievement and personification of the American Dream.

The drafts are also richly metaphoric. Frequently, the color scheme for the event is heavily red, white, and blue, suggesting that the draft is of national importance. Players are referred to as "machines," "horses," "rocks," and the like, which implies that even though they are exalted and rewarded financially, they are also treated as commodities—products to solve team needs. Thus, the draft is simultaneously a celebration of human potential and a dehumanizing act—just one of the complexities that explains their popularity with fans and scholars alike.

—Richard K. Olsen

See also: Metaphor, Sport as, for Life; Television, Impact on Sport

For further reading:

Attner, Paul. 2000. "A New Perspective on the Draft." *Sporting News*, April 17, 53.

Siegfried, John J. 1995. "Sports Player Drafts and the Reserve System." *CATO Journal* 14: 443–453.

DREAM TEAM

Part honor and part National Basketball Association (NBA) marketing ploy, the phrase "Dream Team" originally referred to the All-Star 1992 U.S. men's basketball team that competed in the Olympic Games in Barcelona. The term has since become a nickname or catchphrase to refer to all subsequent U.S. men's Olympic basketball teams, as well as any other dominant conglomeration, from the 1999–2000 national women's soccer team to presidential cabinets and even to O. J. Simpson's trial lawyers. The concept also encourages Americans to revel in their global dominance, as symbolized by basketball, and reflects the post-Communist era in sport.

On April 7, 1989, the majority of members of the International Basketball Federation—the United States *not* among them—voted to allow NBA players to participate in Olympic basketball games. Prior to this decision, the United States sent only collegians to the events and won all but two basketball games over fifty-six years. The 1988 games featured an especially bitter defeat for many Americans because the U.S. squad "only," in the minds of some, placed third, losing to the Soviet Union in a close semifinal match. The U.S.S.R. team would go on to win a gold medal, and Yugoslavia won the silver. Many Americans consoled themselves after such losses with the reminder that their best players, that is, the professionals, never played in these games; thus, ironically, U.S. victories did *and* did not symbolize U.S. superiority.

Prior to 1992, NBA player Earvin "Magic" Johnson personally invited and assembled the greatest active professional players available for the Barcelona Olympics, inspiring the media to dub the squad the "Dream Team." The original Dream Team members were Charles Barkley, Larry Bird, Clyde Drexler, Patrick Ewing, Magic Johnson, Michael Jordan, Christian Laettner, Karl Malone, Chris Mullin, Scottie Pippin, David Robinson, John Stockton, and coach Chuck Daly. Laettner, a recent Duke University graduate, was the lone collegian. The Dream Team's foreign opponents were content to play against the best of the best, using the U.S. squad as a marker of their own abilities, and conceded the gold medal to the United States even before the games began.

Coming on the heels of a successful and dominant military triumph in the 1991 Persian Gulf War, the mainstream media often described U.S.

victories in martial terms: the Americans were said to "take no prisoners" in their routs over the opposition; the media likened players to the best U.S. "troops" who were out to "conquer" a gold medal. With the former Soviet team dissolved, the United States steamrolled over relatively lightweight squads from Lithuania, Angola, and Croatia, among others. In sum, the Dream Team concept helped inject hegemony into popular sport culture, as U.S. dominance appeared inevitable and justified.

The presence of the NBA megastars also highlighted the disparity among the Olympic athletes: Dream Team members resided in a hotel rather than in the Olympic Village, and the players and games received a lion's share of the network coverage, although all of their games were runaways and not the least suspenseful. Because many of the players endorsed competing products, for example, Nike and Reebok, a conflict of commercial interests arose. Many observers criticized Nike spokesman Michael Jordan when he draped a U.S. flag over the Reebok insignia on his team warm-up jacket while he stood on the victory stand. The dispute highlighted the marriage of sport commercialism and professionalism and also revealed many athletes' unquestioning loyalty to capitalism in the late twentieth century. Subsequent U.S. men's squads are still referred to as Dream Teams, although, like film sequels and franchises, they are compared unfairly to the original and are almost always considered inferior and weak imitations.

Finally, the Dream Team phenomenon, along with the Internet, helped shape and popularize the fantasy games concept in the late 1990s. Although the rules vary, in most fantasy leagues, fans can create their own Dream Teams in various sports, drawing on a roster of current players in a given professional league.

—*La'Tonya Rease Miles*

See also: Basketball; Fantasy Games; National Basketball Association; Olympic Games

For further reading:
Callahan, Tom. 1992. "The Lopsided Dream." *U.S. News and World Report,* August 10.
Daly, Chuck. 1992. *America's Dream Team: The Quest for Olympic Gold.* With Alex Sachare. Atlanta, GA: Turner.

DUELING

A duel is a prearranged contest with deadly weapons, traditionally swords or pistols, between two individuals concerned with a point of honor. Dueling may have begun originally as a trial by combat, called the "wager of battle" or "ordeal." In about the eleventh century, it was an early means of determining guilt: an accused person fought with his accuser under judicial supervision. Duels involved a fight between two persons, at an appointed time and place, to resolve a preceding quarrel. The steps involved are (1) the offended party issues a challenge; (2) the challenged party accepts the challenge or risks dishonor; (3) seconds—that is, the duelists' assistants—conduct negotiations and act as witnesses; (4) the duel is stopped after a prescribed number of shots or after blood is drawn.

Duels of honor as an institution for resolving disputes—closely linked to the chivalric code of knighthood—were condemned and forbidden over the years; nevertheless they persisted, especially among aristocrats and army officers, down to the late nineteenth century in the United States. Some authorities trace dueling from ancient times through the antagonistic struggles of Greek and Roman epic heroes, the jousts and tournaments in history and romance of the Middle Ages, and the Renaissance *code duello*, not to mention more trivial modern examples like "dueling banjos" and auto racing. Modern sporting contests, with rules, regulations, and notions of good sportsmanship, inherit this ancient practice—like a societal safety valve for aggression or violence.

—*Raymond J. Cormier*

The duel between Alexander Hamilton (left) and Vice President Aaron Burr. Duels of honor as an institution for resolving disputes persisted, especially among aristocrats and army officers, into the late nineteenth century in the United States. (MICHAEL LECKEL/REUTERS/CORBIS)

See also: Mythology of Sport

For further reading:
Truman, Ben C., and Steven R. Wood. 1993. *Duelling in America.* Classical Library of the Obscure and Remote. San Diego, CA: Joseph Tabler.

DUMB JOCKS

The stereotype of the "dumb jock" lives on even as athletes are raised to pinnacles of acclaim as superheroes and multimillionaires. Stories, true or apocryphal, abound about real or alleged lack of intelligence among athletes. For example, New Orleans Saints running back George Rogers is said to have responded to an inquiry about his goals that he wanted "to rush for 1,000 or 1,500 yards, whichever comes first." Washington Redskins quarterback Joe Theismann is reported to have said, "Nobody in football should be called a genius. A genius is a guy like Norman Einstein." There are, of course, more stories to support the dumb jock stereotype. Los Angeles Lakers star Shaquille O'Neal, for example, stated that he couldn't remember if he had seen the Parthenon on his trip to Greece because "I can't really remember the names of the clubs that we went to."

In spite of the humorous and not-so-humorous stories of stupidity on the part of athletes, the dumb jock stereotype is just a stereotype. Bill Bradley was a Rhodes scholar and U.S. senator as well as a star basketball player for Princeton and the New York Knicks. Brigham Young University (BYU) boasts that about 70 percent of its varsity athletes have a 3.2 or better average out of a possible 4.0. BYU's efforts to raise the performance and image of student-athletes are, perhaps, the most successful of many such efforts. The scandals that have hit college sport have spurred many schools to reassert that the most important part of college is academics, not athletics.

Brian Mackie, writing in *Social Psychology Quarterly,* warns all athletes that people expect a great deal of them, including peak performance and high grade-point averages as well as community service and an unblemished public image. Sometimes the public gets what it wants. Often, however, athletes can't live up to the expected ideal image. Mackie speculates that it simply makes people feel better to have someone to look down on, especially if it is someone whom it has raised so high.

Certainly, students in college who idolize star athletes but also resent the real or imagined perks they get display this attitude. For example, there are the digs that every professor hears when honor students complain that athletic facilities receive more money than the library or that star players have no-show jobs or free meals. The tutorial aid athletes receive and real or alleged pressure exerted on their behalf for grades also come in for jokes. Alternatively, there is real pride when the school team wins. As in other cases of humor, ambivalence finds an outlet in mocking the cause of confusion.

Of course, there are real cases of "dumb jocks," but not every jock is stupid. Ambivalence generates humor, and privilege calls for leveling mechanisms. Americans, collegiate and otherwise, have raised athletes to impossible heights. It is not surprising, therefore, that humor, often a form of attack, has chosen to portray all athletes as dumb jocks.

—*Frank A. Salamone*

> *The stereotype of the "dumb jock" lives on even as athletes are raised to pinnacles of acclaim as superheroes and multimillionaires. Stories, true or apocryphal, abound about real or alleged lack of intelligence among athletes.*

See also: Athletes as Symbolic Heroes

For further reading:

Mackie, B. (1983). "The Domestication of Self: Gender Comparisons of Self-Imagery and Self-Esteem." *Social Psychology Quarterly,* 46, 343–350.

McClellan, Jeff. 1997. "Athletes Aren't Dumb Jocks." *Brigham Young Magazine,* Summer, 6.

E

EATING DISORDERS AMONG ATHLETES

The sociocultural message that equates thinness with physical beauty and personal worth, combined with the demands for leanness in specific sports, makes athletes especially vulnerable to eating disorders. Anorexia nervosa and bulimia are serious eating disorders that afflict millions of people in the United States annually. Anorexia nervosa is characterized by an intense fear of becoming obese, a lack of self-esteem, and a distorted body image that results in self-induced starvation. Bulimia is an emotional disorder characterized by recurrent episodes of binge eating usually followed by a variety of practices such as self-induced vomiting, purging with laxatives and diuretics, and fasting. It is not uncommon for anorexic individuals also to demonstrate bulimic behavior.

Research indicates that females with eating disorders outnumber males by a ratio of 9 to 1. The vast majority of those with the disorders are adolescent and young adult women. Cultural messages from the media and from uninformed parents and other adults that equate physical attractiveness and personal worth with thinness may promote a preoccupation with achieving extremely low body weight. The excessive focus on body weight can ultimately contribute to the formation of irrational attitudes and distorted body images. The prevalence of eating disorders is higher in groups that stress a combination of competition, perfectionism, and self-discipline. Therefore, it has been suggested that athletes are highly susceptible to eating disorders and that sport may actually contribute to the development of such problems.

Distance runners, wrestlers, gymnasts, body-builders, swimmers, and dancers have been identified as being at high risk for developing eating disorders. One source of pressure for some athletes is the fear that excessive body weight will prevent them from making the team or from performing well. Others fear not meeting weight restrictions for performance. Research also indicates that the types of clothing required for certain sports, such as leotards, tights, swimsuits, tank-tops, and briefs, may cause athletes to become overly concerned with how they look. In addition, well-meaning parents or coaches may make uneducated and unrealistic demands on athletes to maintain a certain weight for competition.

The signs and symptoms of anorexia nervosa include weight loss not due to other illnesses, loss of 25 percent or more of standard body weight, severe reduction of food intake, denial of hunger, compulsive or excessive exercising, absence of menstrual cycles, and the wearing of baggy clothing or the layering of clothing to hide the body. Warning signs for bulimia include extreme concern about weight and food, secretive purging following binge eating, fasting following purging, and depression. The ramifications of eating disorders can be serious. Health problems include malnutrition, dehydration, cardiac irregularities, electrolyte imbalance, organ damage, and seizures. In some cases, anorexia nervosa leads to death from cardiac arrest, starvation, or suicide.

Since people with eating disorders usually deny they have a problem, treatment is frequently postponed. Coaches, family, and friends who recognize signs of an eating disorder in an individual typically refer the person to a health professional. Intervention programs involving the help of psychologists, psychiatrists, counselors, or nutritionists are successful if the problem is recognized early.

—*Sharon Huddleston*

See also: Television, Impact on Sport

For further reading:
Otis, Carol L., and Roger Goldingay. 2000. *The Athletic Woman's Survival Guide: How to Win the Battle against Eating Disorders, Amenorrhea and Osteoporosis.* Champaign, IL: Human Kinetics.

ECONOMICS OF GOLF COURSES

Golf courses influence the social fabric of society by linking pure recreation with business networking. There are three types of economic ownership structures—private, municipal, and daily fee courses—which determine the clientele of golf courses.

Member golfers own private golf courses for their exclusive use as well as for their families' and guests' use. Membership is de facto limited to those with high incomes, and in some cases membership is also limited by golf course rules restricting membership along racial, religious, or gender lines. If business networking takes place at private clubs, excluded groups may be at a disadvantage since membership is often restricted.

Municipal golf courses are open to the general public at subsidized prices. These courses are owned and operated by city governments for the benefit of the citizens. Although some municipal courses actually create a surplus of revenue over operating costs, they are still subsidized because the surplus is small compared to the market rental value of the land and the value of the property taxes that could be earned if the land were developed for more profitable business. Offsetting this loss is the fact that golf courses are often seen as an amenity that increases surrounding property values and tax revenues. Operating practices are often hammered out in city council meetings and may result in resident or senior-citizen discounts. Such courses tend to become social havens for senior citizens, especially on weekday mornings when the discounts apply.

Daily-fee courses, which also allow public access, are privately owned and operated for profit. These courses do not offer resident or senior-citizen discounts but use a variety of pricing and advertising strategies designed to increase profit. Daily-fee golf courses range from low-priced and consequently low-quality courses to some of the highest-priced facilities in the country, for example, Pebble Beach Golf Links in California.

—*Stephen Shmanske*

See also: Communities, Impact of Sport on; Golf

For further reading:
Shemano, Gary, Art Spander, and Dick Schaap. 1997. *Keeping on Course: Golf Tips on Avoiding the Sandtraps of Today's Business World.* New York: McGraw-Hill.

ECONOMICS OF SPORT

Economic analysis of sport provides interpretations that influence society's perception of athletes and of sport franchises. Issues in sport that interest economists include the economics of league sports, the economics of salaries and discrimination, the factors that influence attendance at sporting events, the economics of sport gambling, and the public financing of stadiums.

Spurred by major league baseball's exemption from antitrust legislation and legal attacks on the reserve clause in the Curt Flood case, early economic analyses focused on the somewhat peculiar characteristics of league sports. Teams compete on the playing field but seek to limit economic competition. Complicating this is the decrease in fan interest if athletic competition becomes too one-sided. Thus, many unusual practices in league sports can be explained by the leagues' desire to even up the athletic competition. These practices include limitations on labor mobility such as the reserve clause; salary caps and rules governing compensation when free agents change teams; limitations on a franchise's right to relocate, which requires a vote by the owners; limitations on competition for new talent through drafting procedures; and, perhaps most important, rules to equalize the resources available to pay for talent, known as revenue sharing.

Baseball, basketball, and football have implemented these practices with variations, thus giving economists a natural laboratory. For example, the National Football League (NFL) has been more successful than major league baseball in collectively negotiating its network television contracts, which has led to larger shared revenues in football. On the other hand, baseball's unshared, individually negotiated television contracts in large cities have left small-market teams relatively underfunded.

Once the era of limited free agency began, baseball salaries increased dramatically, turning the middle-class players into multimillionaires. Economists have addressed the worth of the players in two steps. First, they determined quantitatively how different combinations of skills, measured by abundant statistics, produced winning records. Second, they quantified how winning games and titles increased attendance and rev-

enues. Thus, adding the values for each of the independently measured skills produced a perceived "value" of any player to a team. This line of research has had mixed results, however.

Many statisticians examine the factors affecting attendance. Research has been conducted on all major sports, including baseball, football, basketball, ice hockey, soccer, and cricket, with the following influences being considered significant: prices of tickets, population of the area, per capita income in the area, winning performance of the team, team being in a pennant race, games being televised, time of day of the game, absolute and relative strength of the opposition, weather on game day, distance from team's home location to venue, turnover on the team's roster, racial characteristics of the team, the age of the stadium, indoor or outdoor stadium, and even the anticipated level of violence, particularly in ice hockey. Most of these influences show positive correlation; however, the more provocative results are that indoor stadiums reduce attendance for baseball games, violence increases attendance at ice hockey matches, and lower income increases attendance at ice hockey and soccer bouts. The last result implies that different socioeconomic groups have different experiences because they follow different sports.

No analysis of the economics of sport can neglect the effect of gambling. Most research focuses on whether point spreads and odds are efficient predictors of the outcome of competition. Betting markets are efficient even though many gamblers claim they can beat the odds. These gamblers report what their systems, applied retroactively, could have done, but information on how these systems actually work is rare. Logically, the social impact of gambling differs for bets placed casually between family and friends versus bets placed through bookmaking operations, whether legal or illegal.

Finally, an issue of growing importance is the public financing of stadiums. Although difficult to quantify, major professional sport franchises provide entertainment and civic pride while creating income and tax revenues. Cities compete by building stadiums to lure new franchises or to retain current ones. These political "hot potatoes" often require that voters approve projects granting public subsidies to wealthy owners and players. The subsidies can be direct, as in the creation of bonded indebtedness, but they are often hidden in tax breaks, free land, relaxed environmental standards, or favorable rental agreements.

—*Stephen Shmanske*

See also: Stadiums; Supreme Court Decisions

For further reading:

Downward, Paul, and Alistair Dawson. 2000. *The Economics of Professional Team Sports*. New York: Routledge.

EDWARDS, HARRY (1942–)

As leader of the Olympic boycott movement by black athletes in 1968, Harry Edwards brought racial politics directly onto the playing fields of U.S. sport. As a means of escaping an impoverished childhood in St. Louis, Missouri, Harry Edwards found the road to higher education through his athletic ability. However, he eventually tired of dealing with the racial politics of the locker rooms and classrooms at San Jose State College, focused his attention on his studies, and received his doctorate in sociology from Cornell University.

While acquiring his graduate degree, Edwards spearheaded the Olympic Project for Human Rights (OPHR). Founded on October 7, 1967, the group was created to raise awareness about racial discrimination in U.S. sport. Its platform revolved

Harry Edwards, lecturer at San Jose State University who called for a boycott of the Olympic Games in Mexico City by African Amercian athletes, talks with two African American athletes at the University (ca. 1968).
(TED STRESHINSKY/CORBIS)

around six demands: restoring the heavyweight title to Muhammad Ali, removing Avery Brundage as head of the International Olympic Committee, banning South Africa and Southern Rhodesia from the Olympics, adding two black coaches to the U.S. Olympic team, adding two black members to the U.S. Olympic Committee, and desegregating the New York Athletic Club. The group failed in its primary goal to initiate a black boycott of the Mexico City Olympic Games.

The visibility of the OPHR reached an apex on October 16, 1968, when Americans Tommie Smith and John Carlos, respectively gold and bronze Olympic medalists in the 200-meter race, raised black-gloved fists over their heads in a black power salute as part of the victory ceremony during the playing of the national anthem. Although Smith shattered the world record, the political statement overshadowed the athletic feat, and the two were forced out of Olympic Village and sent home.

Edwards, a professor of sociology at the University of California, Berkeley, has since published several books on the subject of race and sport in the United States, including *The Revolt of the Black Athlete* (1969), which outlines the creation of the OPHR.

—Amy Bass

See also: Civil Rights and Sport; Discrimination, Racial, in Sport; Mexico City Summer Olympic Games; Olympic Boycotts

For further reading:

"Harry Edwards Hints at College Sports Boycott." 1987. *Jet*, October 26, 51.

Lomax, Michael E. 2000. "Athletics vs. Education: Dilemmas of Black Youth." *Society* 37, no. 3 (March-April): 21–23.

ENDORSEMENTS

Celebrity athletes endorse everything from shoes to sandwiches, providing an interesting commentary on U.S. culture and its obsession with sport. Merchandisers with considerable money should consider an athlete as spokesperson. Sport is pervasive in U.S. society, and its appeal is universal. It is consequently no surprise that manufacturers have found athletes effective endorsers for all manner of products. Market research has shown that people are more likely to purchase merchandise endorsed by celebrities than merchandise that is not. In fact, in 1996, for example, a significant percentage of all television commercials featured an athlete as spokesperson. As the number of children involved in sport and sponsorship dollars have increased, manufacturers consider athletes worth the price.

Athletes today can make more money endorsing products or services than they can playing their sport. This is only true, however, for those who excel. Individuals like Michael Jordan make over $40 million in endorsements per year (http://www.murch-sitaker.org/beatrice/fun/5.html). And from Oscar Dixon, *USA Today*, Jordan, who earned $33 million in his last season with the Chicago Bulls in 1998, is the league's "best buy" (Dixon 2004). Others such as Shaquille O'Neal and Tiger Woods have also taken advantage of their popularity, making endorsement deals valued in the millions. These athletes are often more than worth their cost. A case in point: Nike profited by $100 million in sales from their Air Jordan line during Michael Jordan's early success with the Chicago Bulls.

In response to their marketing success, criticism has been leveled at these athletes. This criticism is focused in part on the astronomical amounts of money they make, but it also addresses the influence they exert on consumers, especially younger ones. Legally, an endorsement, as defined by the Federal Trade Commission (FTC), which regulates advertising, is a message that consumers are likely to believe reflects the opinions, beliefs, findings, or experience of a party other than the sponsoring advertiser. Because endorsements are a powerful force for

Tennis star Venus Williams holds up her signature Venus Williams Reebok tennis shoes next to Reebok International Ltd. Vice President Angel Martinez at a news conference in New York on December 21, 2000. After Williams signed a multimillion-dollar endorsement contract with Reebok, Williams, the winner of the 2000 Wimbledon, U.S. Open, and Olympic singles titles, signed what Reebok called the most sweeping product endorsement and marketing contract ever for a female athlete. The five-year deal was said to be worth close to $40 million.
(REUTERS/CORBIS)

manufacturers, the concern is understandable. Fortunately, most athletic endorsers are reflections of what is good in sport, and those like Michael Jordan and Tiger Woods are admirable role models. But there are exceptions. One problem with using such celebrity athletes is that the manufacturers cannot control them. Mike Tyson and O. J. Simpson are illustrative of this dilemma. When a celebrity generates negative publicity, the manufacturers suffer, and most are very careful whom they select to represent their product or service. An athlete who is not held in esteem and respected by the buying consumer is not going to be a credible or a successful endorser.

Apart from the marketing aspect, athlete endorsers provide a commentary on U.S. society. There was a time in the not-so-distant past when advertisers believed the perfect endorser was a blond Caucasian football quarterback. Today, African American superstar Michael Jordan is the premier salesman, a reminder that times have changed. The United States is no longer an exclusively Caucasian society. It is a pluralist population with a richer, more complex culture. Sport and its heroes have changed but they have never been as popular as now. A wonderful athlete with charisma and a winning smile is a real marketing prize. And although athletic passions differ, the smile is universal and a powerful tool.

—*Janice L. Bukovac*

See also: Jordan, Michael; Marketing of Sport; Woods, Eldrick "Tiger"

For further reading:

Dixon, Oscar. 2001. "Jordan Gives Most Bang for Buck" http://www.usatoday.com/sports/basketball/nba/ 2003-03-17-salary-report_x.htm. Accessed July 2004.

Goldberg, Karen. 1987. "If the Shoe Fits . . . Endorse It." *Insight on the News,* March 3, 38.

Hiestand, Michael. 1989. "Do Black Athletes Get a Fair Shake?" *Adweek's Marketing Week,* March 6, 73.

"Michael Jordan's Salary." 2001. http://www.murch -sitaker.org/beatrice/fun/5.html. November 10. Accessed July 2004.

ESPN

Riding the wave of cable television during the 1980s, the all-sport cable network ESPN has grown into a national leader in sport broadcasting, beaming thousands of contests into millions of homes every year. Founded in 1979 as the Entertainment and Sports Programming Network, ESPN has one of the most successful stories in the history of cable broadcasting. Based in Bristol, Connecticut, the network is 80 percent owned by ABC, which is, in turn, a subsidiary of the Walt Disney Corporation. The full name of the network was dropped in 1985 since it was universally recognized by the acronym ESPN.

Initially short of programming, ESPN aired a wide variety of sporting events, including stock car racing, surfing, beach volleyball, and billiards. As the network evolved, however, it tapped the national appetite for televised sport, an appetite that translated into multimillion-dollar contracts for the rights to broadcast sports such as major league baseball and games of the National Football League and the National Hockey League.

ESPN has played a crucial role in popularizing National Collegiate Athletic Association (NCAA) basketball by broadcasting hundreds of games every season. By airing every game of the opening two rounds of the NCAA men's basketball tournament, the network has helped make March Madness one of the most successful sporting events of the year. ESPN has also created its own sporting events, such as the Extreme Games, which give exposure to less-traditional sports such as skateboarding and snowboarding.

The network is home to the daily sport highlight and commentary show *SportsCenter,* known for its irreverent attitude and in-depth reporting. Because ESPN eventually had more programming than it could accommodate, ESPN2, nicknamed "the Deuce," was launched in September 1993. ESPN also lends its name to an all-sport radio station and to one of the most popular sites on the World Wide Web, Sportszone.

—*Michael Manning*

See also: Television, Impact on Sport

For further reading:

Freeman, Michael. 2000. *ESPN: The Uncensored History.* Dallas, TX: Taylor Publishing.

EVERT, CHRISTINE MARIE
(1954–)

Control, consistency, and class not only made Christine "Chris" Evert one of the greatest women tennis players of all time but also made her a symbol of sportsmanship on and off the court as well as a role model to a countless number of girls and young women.

Born in Fort Lauderdale, Florida, four days before Christmas in 1954, Chris Evert was the second of five children of James Evert and Colette Thompson Evert. James Evert, a teaching tennis professional, coached his young daughter in order to compensate for a lack of natural ability. She was taught to focus on the mental aspects of the sport—concentration, discipline, and poise—and to develop a baseline game that relied on steadiness, patience, and pinpoint accuracy.

That training was effective and was helped by the fact that Evert lived in Florida, where she could play tennis year-round. Turning professional on her eighteenth birthday, Evert amassed a singles record of 1,309–146, won 157 professional singles titles, captured 21 Grand Slam titles, 18 of them in singles, and secured at least one Grand Slam singles title for each of thirteen straight years.

Evert's discipline, poise, and steadiness went beyond just hitting a tennis ball. During her career, she was the personification of sportsmanship: magnanimous in victory, gracious in defeat, and always cooperative with the press. Such class was also shown in the way Evert handled her private life. Despite having romantic relationships with Jimmy Connors and Burt Reynolds and being married to and divorced from John Lloyd, Evert always exhibited discretion and never stooped to sensationalism.

Although criticized by her detractors for not playing with flair or publicly displaying her emotions, Chris Evert proved that these qualities are not necessary for success.

—*Angelo J. Louisa*

See also: "Battle of the Sexes"

For further reading:
Flink, Steve, and Chris Evert. 1999. *The Thirty Greatest Tennis Matches of the Twentieth Century.* Danbury, CT: Rutledge Books.

EXTREME SPORTS

Extreme sports, also known as alternative sports, were a growing phenomenon of the late twentieth century. Including such bizarre, adrenaline-pumping sporting pursuits as skysurfing, downhill mountain biking, snowboarding, street-luge racing, river running, river surfing, shark diving, white-water kayaking, and others, extreme sports appealed most to the 18 to 34-year-old age bracket.

This segment of the population expressed a strong desire for individuality, and extreme sports offered challenges without teams, rules, uniforms, or organizations. Instead, these competitions offered participants the ultimate opportunity to test their mettle against the elements, nature, speed, and ultimately, an ever-present threat of death. Providing insights into the minds and souls of the generation, extreme sports echoed a powerful cultural message: that the world at the end of the twentieth century had become too placid, too safe. The majority of people in the age group involved in extreme sports had never experienced a war firsthand and had been coddled with warnings about lack of exercise, poor dietary habits, and the evils of cigarettes, alcohol, and drugs. Thus, to experience risk-taking behavior became a rite of passage—a chance to prove individual worth or, as skydiver Cheryl Stearns aptly phrased it, "trusting yourself to save your own life" (Bower 1995, 3).

Including such bizarre, adrenaline-pumping sporting pursuits as skysurfing, downhill mountain biking, snowboarding, street-luge racing, river running, river surfing, shark diving, white-water kayaking, and others, extreme sports appeal most to the 18 to 34-year-old age bracket.

Although snowboarding and free-style skiing were added to the Winter Olympic Games and mountain biking was added to the Summer Olympics, no exclusively extreme games competition was held until 1995 in Providence, Rhode Island. Originally broadcast as the Extreme Games by ESPN, the name was eventually changed to the X Games after "Generation X," the nickname given to the children of baby boomers. The initial events featured four hundred athletes—many of world-class caliber—competing in nine sports for $337,900 in prize money. In the

A snowboarder makes a jump. No exclusive competition for extreme sports, such as snowboarding, free-style skiing, and mountain biking, was held until ESPN's X Games in 1995 in Providence, Rhode Island. Free-style skiing and snowboarding were added to the Winter Olympics in 1988 and 1998, respectively. Mountain biking was added to the Summer Olympics in 1996.
(PETER BARRETT/CORBIS)

same year, nineteen million amateurs were participating in in-line skating and over two million were engaged in snowboarding.

One example of extreme sports is street luge. In this sport, the athlete lies flat on his or her back on a board situated exactly one inch above the pavement and rides downhill, occasionally through traffic, at incredible speeds with nothing but specially designed footwear for a braking system. The leading organizer and exponent of the street luge, Bob Pereya, holds the world record, at eighty-seven miles per hour. He founded the Roadracers Association for International Luge (RAIL) in 1990.

Ever alert to marketing trends, companies such as the Outward Bound Wilderness School showed a 66 percent increase in business between 1992 and 1996. By 1997, more than eight thousand companies in the United States packaged tours for adventurers, netting a profit in excess of seven million dollars.

—*Joyce Duncan*

See also: ESPN; Olympic Games; X Games

For further reading:

Bower, Joe. 1995. "Going over the Top." *Women's Sports and Fitness,* 17, October, 21–24.

Genereaux, Bruce. 2002. *Beyond the Comfort Zone: Confessions of an Extreme Sports Junkie.* Hanover, NH: Class Five Press.

Olsen, Marylin. 2003. *Women Who Risk: Profiles of Women in Extreme Sports.* New York: Hatherleigh Press.

F

FADS AND TRENDS

Like other fields that have cross-cultural and cross-generational links, sport is subject to fads, which disappear and reappear, and to trends, which reflect the personal predilections of a particular period or particular group. Fads are easily identifiable—they are new and exciting and often odd or unusual. In the 1950s, a colorful piece of circular plastic began to appear in sporting goods stores. At first glance the apparatus seemed less than exciting and certainly less than athletic. It was not long, however, before the Hula-Hoop craze swept the nation and teenagers were contorting their bodies in sinuous movements to spin thirty or forty of the rings simultaneously. Later in the century, another circular plastic disc floated into retail sales, and languid summer days in the nation's parks were filled with airborne Frisbees and, subsequently, with disc golf players.

As the nation entered the complexity and passivity of the 1990s, fads turned to the bizarre and often included risk-taking behavior. A popular fad of the era, primarily among the young or the adventurous, was bungee jumping, in which a participant is attached to a device resembling a gigantic, dangling rubber band at an extreme height and jumps or is dropped to experience free fall and, during rebounding, accelerations of greater than the force of gravity. Free-fall skydiving and parasailing also took their turns as fads in the late 1980s and 1990s. Skydiving became so popular that it was added to the Extreme Games lineup of events. In addition, a few endorphin junkies even selected a skydiving venue as the perfect spot to be married with a minister in tow and the ceremony conducted between the plane and the ground. Parasailing incorporates water-skiing and parachuting and allows the participant to fly above the water while being dragged behind a fast-moving speedboat.

Trends have more staying power than fads and usually reflect lifestyle changes of a particular era. The most pervasive change in the late twentieth century was a consumer desire for individuality and uniqueness, coupled with a national interest in health and wellness. Supported by the growing disposable incomes of baby boomers, working women, and teenagers, in-line skating and home gyms acquired enough supporters to establish them as trends of the 1990s. According to the Sporting Goods Manufacturing Association, sales of in-line skates and home gyms doubled in the three years between 1992 and 1995, and at least three million adults began to participate in in-line skating or worked out on home gym equipment.

In-line skating appealed to the late-twentieth-century consumer's requirements for individuality because the sport can be enjoyed alone as well as in company. In addition, skating is a strenuous activity that does not require a particular field or court; it can be practiced on any reasonably smooth surface and at any time. Beginning as an off-season exercise for hockey players, in-line skating produces the same exercise results as running or jogging and evolved into the team sport of street hockey, which employs the same rules as ice hockey but can be played anywhere.

As team sports and professional gym affiliation declined due to the time crunch created by the twentieth-century pace, home gyms became a trend. Appealing particularly to older consumers and working women, who accounted for more than half of this growth, home gyms offer privacy, safety, and convenience. The fastest-growing trend in home gym equipment was the treadmill, which replaced stationary bikes and stepping machines (e.g., StairMasters) due to its flexible speed control.

—*Joyce Duncan*

See also: Extreme Sports; Marketing of Sport; X Games

For further reading:
Hoffmann, Frank W., and William G. Bailey. 1996. *Sports and Recreation Fads.* New York: Haworth Press.

FAN BEHAVIOR

Over 80 percent of Americans attend at least one live sporting event annually and some of the largest crowds in the United States are recorded at sporting events; thus, spectator sports and fan behavior at these events provide important insights into this integral part of the U.S. cultural landscape. According to the 1990 U.S. Census, the top ten spectator sports drew over 343 million paying sport fans. Nearly all Americans report having viewed a sport on television at least once in a previous year.

Clearly, spectator sports have permeated the U.S. cultural landscape—as have the actions and behaviors of sport spectators. No longer confined to the stadium or the arena, many behaviors have been adopted and integrated into other areas of social life in which large numbers of people gather to consume mass spectacles and entertainment, especially in the performing and visual arts. These expressive actions and behaviors include such things as "the wave" and "high fives," as well as a myriad of variations of rhythmic chanting, clapping, booing, and singing at certain intervals during the course of the event.

Insight into fan behavior may be gleaned from theories of fans' motivation for attending sporting events. These include

1. Stress and stimulation theories, which assert that fans who live an otherwise-dull existence seek stress, stimulation, arousal, and excitement;
2. Catharsis and aggression theories, which attribute fans' behavior to their desire to vent pent-up stresses and aggressions characteristic of capitalist societies;
3. Entertainment theories, which attribute fans' behavior to their desire to witness an aesthetically pleasing product that displays grace, beauty, and confirmation of societal values;
4. Achievement-seeking theories, which hold that fans desire to bask in the reflected glory of successful sporting by others and to establish an association with them so as to be perceived favorably by friends and associates;
5. Salubrious effects theories, which hold that fans seek increased physical and mental rejuvenation as a result of sport spectatorship.

Researchers have developed several theories to explain collective crowd behavior and crowd responses that, in turn, contribute to the aforementioned degree of excitement, arousal, catharsis, and enjoyment fans seek. These theories include:

1. Contagion theory, holding that fan behavior spreads among crowd members and, combined with the anonymity of the crowd, changes them from rational human beings

into an irrational and at times uncontrollable mob that accepts uncritically any suggestions presented to them;

2. Convergence theory, which sees fan behavior as a result of people with similar behavioral dispositions coming together to express themselves collectively to a commonly shared stimulus: the sporting event;

3. Emergent norm theory, which roots fan behavior in norms that arise in the sporting setting; in other words, the sport fan behaves in a particular way because he or she believes the behavior is appropriate or required.

At times, fan behavior erupts into spectator violence. This particular form of fan behavior has existed throughout the history of spectator sport—some of the earliest reports of spectator violence are of incidents occurring during the chariot races in ancient Rome—and has continued to the well-publicized riots and hooliganism that have marred soccer events in Europe and Central and South America throughout the twentieth century. In the United States, spectator violence has been prevalent in all major professional

> *Over 80 percent of Americans attend at least one live sporting event annually and some of the largest crowds in the United States are recorded at sporting events; thus, spectator sports and fan behavior at these events provide important insights into this integral part of the cultural landscape.*

men's team sports, as well as during many college and high school men's athletic contests, especially football and basketball games.

Social scientists attribute the likelihood of fan violence to social, cultural, and environmental factors surrounding the sporting event itself. In general, fan violence is related to (1) the action in the sport event itself, (2) situational crowd dynamics, and (3) the historical, social, and political context in which the contest is played. Specifically, these factors include crowd size and crowd density; crowd noise levels; standing or seating patterns; crowd composition in terms of age, gender, race, and social class; the amount of alcohol consumed by crowd members; the location of the event; the system of crowd control used at the event; the history of the relationship between the teams involved and their supporters; the importance of victory to opposing spectator supporters; and perceived injustice in officiating.

—*John R. Mitrano*

See also: Fetishes in Sport; Marketing of Sport

For further reading:
Guttmann, Allen. 1986. *Sports Spectators.* New York: Columbia University Press.
McPhail, Clark. 1991. *The Myth of the Madding Crowd.* New York: Aldine de Gruyter.
Smith, Michael. 1983. *Violence and Sport.* Toronto: Butterworths Publishing.

FANTASY GAMES

Fantasy role-playing games have become a pervasive activity in contemporary youth culture, both feeding and being fed by a public ever more avid for science fiction and fantasy. Military campaign reenactment, typically through the use of miniatures, has a long history. When, in the mid-1970s, a group of war-gaming enthusiasts melded miniatures with the rising interest in heroic fantasy, they formed Tactical Strategy Rules, Inc. (TSR) and soon published a basic version of what became known as Dungeons & Dragons (D&D). By the time the game was casually used in establishing scenes in *ET The Extra-Terrestrial* (1982), it had become well known among the teen and college set. One of the early developers, Gary Gygax, estimated that there were six million active players during the mid-1980s, and millions more have been exposed to the game or its many manifestations since then.

Initially a collaborative activity among friends, devotees form leagues and sponsor competitive tournaments, also known as conventions, or "cons." These games have influenced popular art, television, cinema, and electronic gaming, such as Nintendo games. Their more recent avatars have been less collaborative and more combative. Though generally accepted as innocent entertainment for "nerds," some observers have objected that the games are cultist, demonic, or psychologically dangerous. Even so, interest continues unabated.

—*Scott D. Vander Ploeg*

See also: Computers and Sport; Video Games

For further reading:
Bock, Philip. 1992. "A Monstrous Adventure." *Journal of Anthropological Research* 48 (Fall): 261–265.
Cardwell, Paul, Jr. 1994. "The Attacks on Role-Playing Games." *Skeptical Inquirer,* Winter, 157–166.

FAULKNER, WILLIAM
(1897–1962)

In his fiction and nonfiction writings, Nobel Prize–winning author William Faulkner celebrated qualities of individual skill and courage through woodcraft, marksmanship, and a deep connection with nature. His best-known stories, such as "The Bear," one chapter in *Go Down, Moses,* appeal to a nostalgia for a diminishing wilderness and indict the increasingly mindless complexity of modern life.

While securely rooted in his imaginary creation of Yoknapatawpha County, Mississippi, Faulkner borrowed from the traditions of the British gentleman farmer and huntsman in his passions for raising horses and foxhunting. He championed the outdoors both in his own life—ranking his hobbies as breeding and training horses first, hunting second, and sailing third—

and in his fiction, where forces of nature test the individual's maturity. Faulkner's hunting stories are considered the most advanced and sophisticated examples of the nineteenth-century tall tale and southern humor traditions, both of which celebrate cleverness, craftiness, and a predominantly male storytelling genius.

—*Petra M. Gallert*

See also: Literature, Sport in

For further reading:
Meriwether, James B., and Michael Millgate, eds. 1980. *Lion in the Garden.* Lincoln: University of Nebraska Press.

FELLOWSHIP OF CHRISTIAN ATHLETES

Founded in 1954 by Don McClanen, the Fellowship of Christian Athletes (FCA) was organized as an interdenominational group aimed at introducing athletes to Christianity. In the United States, a majority of the population participates in or watches a sporting event each week, and thus sport offers a perfect way to proselytize, to spread the word. The purpose of the organization, stated as their mission statement, is "to present to athletes and coaches, and all whom they influence, the challenge and advantage of receiving Jesus Christ as Savior and Lord, serving Him in their relationships and in the fellowship of the church" (www.fca.org). To accomplish this goal, the group focuses on junior and senior high school athletes as well as those at the collegiate level. The work is carried out by volunteers and paid staff and supported by donations from individuals and corporations. Approximately 500,000 students were involved in the FCA in 2000.

Much of the FCA's work is done in camping experiences, where students and coaches are introduced to the idea of the Huddle. Huddle captains are trained and sent back to their home schools to work with athletes, providing a safe and nurturing environment in which to introduce them to Christianity. The first camp opened in 1956 in Estes Park, Colorado, and the organization expanded from there. Over thirteen thousand people attended camps for athletes and coaches in 1995 alone. The FCA introduced a new emphasis with its "One Way 2 Play Drug Free" campaign. This project uses posters, charts, and videos to show young athletes how avoid the lure and temptation of performance-enhancing drugs.

In 1959, the magazine *Christian Athlete* was first published to help forward the organizational mission. It was replaced in 1982 by *Sharing the Victory*—which is published nine times a year and has a Web version—with stories of inspiration and courage from all athletic endeavors. In 1997, the organization expanded its focus internationally.

—*Leslie Heaphy*

See also: Religion and Sport

For further reading:

Dunn, Joseph. 1980. *Sharing the Victory: The 25 Years of the Fellowship of Christian Athletes.* New York: Quick Fox.

Fellowship of Christian Athletes. http://www.fca.org. Retrieved June, 2004.

FENWAY PARK

Opened in 1912, Fenway Park is the oldest major league baseball park in the United States, a cozy monument to the development of the national pastime that has been long considered the best major league park in which to watch a ball game. Originally known as the Fenway Park Grounds or

Fans watch from the stands of Fenway Park as the Boston Red Sox play the Toronto Blue Jays on September 24, 1995. Opened in 1912, Fenway Park is the oldest major league baseball park in the United States.
(KEVIN FLEMING/CORBIS)

Red Sox Park, Fenway Park has been home to the Boston Red Sox since opening on April 20, 1912. Boston's mayor, John Fitzgerald, grandfather to future president John F. Kennedy, threw the ceremonial first pitch on May 17. Babe Ruth, perhaps the most recognized icon in the history of baseball, began his career at Fenway, and in 1941, Ted Williams was the last player to hit .400 in the park.

Fenway Park is admired for its intimate and odd dimensions. Defining left field is the "Green Monster," a forty-foot-high wall that can turn home runs into singles and pop flies into home runs. The wall officially stands 315 feet from home plate, and Landsdowne Street runs directly behind it. Thus, because Fenway Park was shoehorned into the surrounding streets, it is not so much surrounded by the city as built into it.

Because of its rich history, "Friendly Fenway" remains one of the most popular tourist attractions in Boston, whether the home team is playing or not. It was one of the settings for *Field of Dreams* (1989), a film celebrating the mythology of the national pastime and its place in U.S. culture. No major league baseball park celebrates that mythology more than Fenway Park.

—*Donald P. Gagnon*

See also: Baseball; Baseball Films; Ruth, George Herman "Babe," Jr.

For further reading:
Shaughnessy, Dan. 1999. *Fenway: A Biography in Words and Pictures.* Boston: Houghton Mifflin.
Smith, Curt. 1999. *Our House: A Tribute to Fenway Park.* Lincolnwood, IL: Masters Press.

FETISHES IN SPORT

Fetishism stems from treating objects as if they actually embody the qualities or the person that they represent. With the increased commercialization of sport in the twentieth century, sport fetishism has taken on various forms in U.S. athletic, spectator, and consumer life. Whereas in the past such impulses would be satisfied among youths by "official" equipment endorsed by prominent athletes and among adults by trophies and scrapbooks, the growth of leisure time and disposable income has provided fertile, profitable ground for industries catering to fans. The distinction between casual clothing and athletic apparel has blurred; the market for "collectibles" has exploded; electronic simulations of sport occupy more leisure time than activity in the actual sport; and food and drink products with "official" ties to teams have been widely marketed. Fetishism appeals to those sport fans who feel they can overcome their own athletic inadequacies by owning a representation of the prowess they desire; it also appeals strongly to those who attempt to define their identities through association with athletes and teams they admire.

> On any given college football Saturday, thousands of fans demonstrate their commitment to the team by wearing the school's initials printed in the school colors or by dressing from head to toe in those colors.

Although some sport fetishism concerns the eroticization of athletes, corporations have carefully avoided overt exploitation of this impulse. Obviously, the image of healthy, vibrant, beautiful people, when associated with a product, can increase sales. However, granting the widespread reverence accorded athleticism, any suggestion of self-perceived eroticism on the part of athletes in endorsements suggests a salacious compromise of the wholesomeness of sport. In the 1990s, for example, only the most revered sport figures, like Michael Jordan, could be found in long-running national advertising campaigns for Hanes underwear, and those commercials emphasized home and family and contained only occasional flirtatiousness. On the other hand, Dennis Rodman's leering participation in a Victoria's Secret advertising campaign lasted only a few weeks. Women athletes have endorsed beauty and health products in U.S. advertising, but with limitations; for example, Cathy Rigby's endorsement of Playtex tampons in the 1980s initially stirred controversy through its mere public acknowledgment that a celebrity athlete would need such a product. Although some isolated pockets of U.S. culture celebrate athletes for their sexual allure and while major pharmaceutical companies have acquired big-name celebrity endorsements for products to relieve erectile dysfunction, the mainstream prefers to isolate its appreciation of athletic physicality from questions of sexual prowess, and the marketers have respected this preference.

In some cases, sport fetishism has gone so far beyond recognition of a person's or a team's accomplishments that the fetish has taken on iconic qualities. On one hand, the icon can represent a particular person, as demonstrated by NASCAR's success in marketing merchandise bearing only the numbers associated with specific drivers. Usually, however, merchandisers recognize that they can achieve better long-term sales by increasing consumer desire for the object itself than by relying solely on the attraction of specific athletes. The trading card industry, after suffering declining sales in the mid-1980s, began offering an increasing number of "chase" cards with limited distribution in order to sell more goods to the dwindling yet devoted card market. With that marketing strategy, consumers often become so concerned with completing a set of cards that their interest in the sport depicted is secondary.

Team logos can also stimulate a great deal of devotion, especially among fans whose teams enjoy a long tradition and are likely to change star players on a regular basis. On any given college football Saturday, thousands of fans demonstrate their commitment to the team by wearing the school's initials printed in the school colors or by dressing from head to toe in those colors. In like manner, the International Olympic Committee has established its symbol of five interlinked rings

as an icon that represents the highest ideals of athletic competition. One is left to decide whether the hypercommercialization of these icons compromises the ideals that they have come to represent.

—*Thomas Alan Holmes*

See also: Apparel, in Sport; Marketing of Sport; Olympic Games; Team Colors and Symbols

For further reading:
"eBay Launches eBay Sports as Annual Gross Merchandise Sports Sales Near One Billion Dollars." 2002. *Business Wire*, October 2, 79.
"NASCAR: How Bad Do You Want It?" 2002. *Retail Merchandiser*, July, S3–S4.

FILM AND SPORT

The importance of sport films lies in their attitudes toward winning. Early sport films typically followed narrative patterns that began with an athlete's efforts to establish himself, followed by an initial victory, a devastating defeat, and, finally, an inevitable, if miraculous, comeback. Stories often focus on the turbulent lives or careers of the characters; for example, the agitated, gifted young musician who becomes a prizefighter in *Golden Boy* (1939), or John Garfield's character in *Body and Soul* (1947), a boxer who claws his way to the top. A number of boxing movies expose corruption or ills within the game. Still other films detail an athlete's decline in the grip of a debilitating disease, such as Lou Gehrig in *The Pride of the Yankees* (1942), or they gloss over the athlete's real disabilities, such as Grover Cleveland Alexander's in *The Winning Team* (1952).

The conventional pattern of these early films was destined for revision in the 1980s, as the already-high value Americans placed on sport escalated. The merging of sport and the media formed a grand undertaking supported by the proliferation of sport franchises, the pervasiveness of sport on television, and a general displacement of scholarship by athletics on many college and

Sylvester Stallone as Rocky Balboa and Talia Shire as his girlfriend, Adrian, in the movie Rocky. Rocky *resonated with the renewed value that U.S. culture placed on the American Dream, on a positive outlook, and on success.* (JOHN SPRINGER COLLECTION/CORBIS)

high school campuses. The country's intensified economic competitiveness in the 1980s reflected the sport boom and the obsession with winning, witnessed by the advent of films that manipulate the original sport genre convention into a mere formula that tends to push all values but winning into the background.

Out of the cynicism typical of 1976 emerged a Bicentennial tribute that became the most popular film of its time. *Rocky,* a type of fairy tale created by Sylvester Stallone, maintains that with hard work and a desire to succeed, a good-natured bum like his hero, Rocky Balboa, could become a contender overnight. Beyond the appeal of winning, however, *Rocky* resonated with the renewed value that U.S. culture placed on the American Dream, on a positive outlook, and on success.

Even though the decision in the film's culminating fight went to his opponent, Balboa's personal victory is sustained through his gritty struggle to "go the distance." This quality is depreciated in the *Rocky* sequels (1979, 1982, 1985, 1990), in which hard work, family loyalty, friendship, and other traditional values are relegated to the background as mere supports for the more important business of winning. *Rocky*'s director, John Avildsen, continues these somewhat simplified patterns in *The Karate Kid* (1984) and through two sequels to that film, in 1986 and 1989.

The Natural (1984) based on Bernard Malamud's novel of the same name, capitalized on and contributed to the interest in baseball and nostalgia and reinforced the cultural value of winning. Director Barry Levinson altered the ending of Malamud's story—in which Hobbs, the protagonist, takes a bribe and throws the game—to one in which Hobbs leaves his hospital bed and, swinging his bat, "Wonderboy," in Ted Williams's fashion, hits the winning homer, thus setting off spectacular special effects. The film's overstatement of the formulaic achievement of glory rejects any real appreciation of strategy, teamwork, or the texture of real experience, and it also undermines Hobbs's depth of character. The film's happy ending further simplifies sport values by interconnecting heroic individualism, the nostalgic American Dream, and winning. Certainly, other sport than baseball lend themselves to film formulas for winning—for example, the film about Indiana basketball, *Hoosiers* (1986), which is essentially configured around the winning shot—but baseball—the All-American game—seems especially vulnerable. In the case of *Field of Dreams* (1989), an Iowa farmer, instructed by a mysterious voice, converts his cornfield to a baseball diamond, upon which Shoeless Joe Jackson and other players magically appear. The sentimental film seems less about baseball than about the fulfillment of dreams, happy endings, and winning in the final scheme of things.

More realistic views, of athletes whose conflicts

resist simplification, appear in *Chariots of Fire* (1981). One runner encounters a conflict between running and his own moral code and follows his beliefs. Similarly, in *Eight Men Out* (1988), John Sayles's account of the 1919 Chicago "Black Sox" scandal, heroic individualism disappears in the face of Sayles's emphasis on the team members, who are complex and all-too-human mixtures of good and evil.

Still other films depict athletes for whom the failure in their personal lives creates a bizarre counterpoint for their athletic success. Martin Scorsese's *Raging Bull* (1980) concerns the rise and fall of middleweight champion Jake LaMotta, whose failure is evoked through a richness of interwoven detail that negates *Rocky* and suggests the demise of the American Dream. *Everybody's All-American* (1988) follows an All-American Louisiana State tailback whose life after football is a disappointment and a failure. He attempts the proverbial comeback, which also fails. The film's nostalgia for college football and homecoming queens suggests that the director places undue emphasis on past glory and on the inability to move beyond it when the success it seemed to guarantee was not forthcoming. Winning at life is not assured by victory in sport.

Although *Bull Durham* also celebrates and satirizes sport mania, Ron Shelton's 1988 film projects an attitude toward winning that is rare in sport films. Aging catcher Crash Davis, new to the Durham Bulls, is saddled with the task of tutoring Nuke LaLoosh in the art of becoming a good pitcher. Arguing that Nuke should acquire finesse and abandon force, Davis is compelled to follow his own advice when he discovers that his major league prospects have failed and that a new career as a minor league manager awaits him. The film does not focus on sensational heroics; rather, it intricately connects sport and life, focusing on the need to adjust and to go on when the game ends. More recently, in *Tin Cup* (1996), also written and directed by Ron Shelton, a golf hustler comes to appreciate the integration of

sport and life. Thus, sport films are vital in determining the value of winning and in reincorporating it into other values.

—*Mary Hurd*

See also: Baseball Films; Gehrig, Lou

For further reading:

Mintz, Steven, and Randy Roberts, eds. 1993. *Hollywood's America: United States History through Its Films.* St. James, NY: Brandywine Press.

O'Brien, Tom. 1990. *The Screening of America: Movies and Values from "Rocky" to "Rain Man."* New York: Continuum.

FISHING, FLY AND BAIT

Originally an English import, fly-fishing in the United States traces its beginnings to the trout streams of Pennsylvania and upstate New York. Fly-fishing remained a sport of the affluent and influential well into the twentieth century. True to its English roots, gentlemen anglers joined private clubs that held exclusive rights to sections of streams. Brodhead Creek in Northeast Pennsylvania boasted one of the earliest private clubs, Henryville House. Established in 1836, Henryville welcomed such prominent Americans as Presidents Grover Cleveland and Benjamin Harrison. Other selective clubs followed, including the Brooklyn Fly Fishers and the Anglers Club of New York.

The expense of fly-fishing and the mastery it required reinforced the tradition of genteel exclusivity. However, as middle-class Americans' affluence and leisure time increased and as mass-manufactured, cheaper equipment became more available, anglers took to trout waters in the West, the Midwest, and the South. Still, fly-fishing culture retained, to a large degree, its northeastern, upper-class, Anglophilic exclusivity.

Fly-fishing has also been the subject of a literary output unparalleled by any other type of fishing: from Englishman Izaak Walton's seven-

Fly-fishing guide Robbie Hilliard teaches Kori Jo Schloemer to cast for rainbow and brown trout in Silver Creek, Idaho, near Sun Valley. Silver Creek is a top ten, blue-ribbon fly-fishing stream (2002).
(KARL WEATHERLY/CORBIS)

teenth-century classic *The Compleat Angler* to U.S. treatises on the art of fly-fishing, such as Henry Well's *Fly Rods and Reels* (1885) and Norman Maclean's literary memoir *A River Runs Through It* (1976). Although not an affluent northeasterner, Maclean reinforces the idea that fly anglers are a select and superior group: learning that Christ had been a fisherman, a young Maclean assumed that "all first class fishermen on the Sea of Galilee were fly fishermen and that John, the favorite, was a dry fly fisherman" (Maclean 1976, 1).

Bait-fishing in North America began when humans first sought sustenance from rivers and streams. In its most basic form, bait-fishing requires little investment and few skills—equipment can be as simple as a long stick, a string, and a worm impaled on a hook. Bait-fishing may form a youngster's first experience with fishing, often in a nearby stream or urban recreational lake.

Lacking the tradition of class exclusivity and regional associations, proponents of bait-fishing view it as a more egalitarian and red-blooded American activity than the snobbish fly-fishing. As one observer put it, "Unlike those fly-fishing wussies, real men aren't afraid to get down and dirty when they catch fish the old fashioned way: with bait." Fly fishers, on the other hand, often derisively refer to their bait-fishing counterparts as "gear-chuckers" and "jellybean fishermen" because they will put anything from marshmallows to corn on a hook. One is seen as an art for the initiated; the other, as recreation for all people.

Issues of conservation, catch limits, catch-and-release programs, and "artificial-only" lakes and streams (allowing only the use of artificial flies and lures) have exacerbated this cultural divide. Some bait fishers point out that restricting areas, especially on public lands, to catch-and-release or artificial flies and lures is unfair discrimination. Many fly-fishing advocates argue that unless such measures are enforced, the quality of U.S. fisheries will continue to decline. In the end—for the fish—a hook is still a hook and a thing to be scrupulously avoided.

—*Scott C. Zeman*

See also: *The Compleat Angler;* Women and Fishing

For further reading:

Atcheson, Dave. 2003. "Common Ground: When Flies Hit the Water, Rich and Poor Look the Same." *Alaska,* February, 54–60.

Carlton, Michael. 1994. "Rivers of Dreams." *Southern Living,* April, 128–136.

Maclean, Norman. 1976. *A River Runs Through It and Other Stories.* Chicago: University of Chicago Press.

Sawyer-Fay, Rebecca. 1994. "Fly Fishing Fever." *Country Living,* April, 120–124.

FITNESS MARKETING AND MAGAZINES

The fitness and health market has been a major segment of the leisure industry since the emergence of the "fitness craze" of the late 1970s. Jim Fixx, a former magazine editor, is widely credited with popularizing the trend with the publication of his *Complete Book of Running* in 1977. The book sold more than a million copies and was the most successful work on running ever published. Yet fitness marketing long predated Fixx's book. Gilded Age tycoon and health food proponent John Harvey Kellogg touted the virtues of a healthful diet based, of course, on consuming his cereal products. In 1936, bodybuilder Jack La Lanne opened the country's first modern health spa chain in California and in 1952 began the nation's first nationally televised exercise program, which ran until 1986.

However, physical fitness–related merchandising during the last decades of the twentieth century reached far beyond diet foods and health spas, encompassing exercise equipment, clothing, shoes, classes, music, videotapes, interactive media, travel, books, and magazines. Jane Fonda is considered a pioneering figure in health and fitness cross-marketing. Starting her own chain of workout centers in 1978, Fonda published her first book on fitness in 1981; she followed it with workout records, a series of workout videotapes beginning in 1982, and a line of exercise clothing. Fonda's videos were the first mass-marketed workout tapes; such tapes have since become one of the most lucrative segments of the industry. Perhaps the most distinctive aspect of the market in the 1980s and 1990s was that women emerged as the dominant consumers of health-and-fitness products in what had historically been a male-dominated field.

Another major niche in fitness marketing is magazine publishing, and health-and-fitness magazines have a long history. In 1899, Bernard McFadden began publication of *Physical Culture,* a periodical that carried the slogan "Weakness is a Crime. Don't Be a Criminal" and preached that one could live to be 125 with the proper diet and exercise. In 1950, Jeremy Irving Rodale, a publisher who lauded the virtues of vitamins, natural foods, and exercise while condemning the commercial food industry, started *Prevention* magazine. Spreading largely by word-of-mouth, by 1976 the publication's subscribers had grown to more than 1.5 million, many of them older women. Other diet and fitness magazines, notably *Weight Watchers* and *Health,* followed in the 1960s.

In 1973, tennis star Billie Jean King created a new genre, the women's sport magazine, when she created *WomenSports* three weeks after defeating Bobby Riggs in the "Battle of the Sexes." The magazine, which became *Women's Sports* in 1979, created some controversy when it spoofed the *Sports Illustrated* Swimsuit Issue with a photo layout of male athletes in bathing suits. Picking up on the fitness craze, the magazine changed its name again in 1984 to *Women's Sports and Fitness.*

Other women's fitness titles existed, most important among them *Self,* a Condé-Nast publication that began in 1979. By 1984, twenty-three women's fitness magazines were on the market, but few lasted very long. In the 1990s, there was a continued interest in the periodicals but, by then, they had integrated a total wellness approach, combining physical fitness with beauty, fashion, and mental and emotional health concerns. During the latter part of the 1990s, there was a popularization of similar publications for men, such as *Men's Health,* started in 1989.

—*Stephanie Dyer*

See also: "Battle of the Sexes"; Marketing of Sport

For further reading:
"Mixing Merchandise." 2003. *Video Business,* May 26, 38.

FOOTBALL

Emerging as the most popular spectator sport at U.S. colleges in the late nineteenth century, football has become the country's most prominent sporting spectacle, its most loved and hated sport, and a symbolic representation of cities, regions, institutions, and traditional values. If baseball is America's pastime, then football is its passion. Although other sports boast far more recreational participants, football is the country's premier spectator sport, the primary sporting focus of homecomings and holidays, and one of the most prominent faces the country presents to the world. Through widely watched events, such as college and professional bowl games, football provides a stage for Americans to celebrate geographic, ethnic, collegiate, and other identities and for U.S. corporations and universities to pro-

mote themselves and their products. Indeed, no other sport carries as much symbolic baggage as does football. A violent, rigidly hierarchical, and highly gendered sport, football has been seen as the embodiment of everything that is right—and everything that is wrong—about U.S. culture and society.

Origins of American Football

A transplant from England, early football in the United States was relatively disorganized. Different towns and schools played by their own sets of rules, but all involved two sides of a dozen or more men—on foot rather than on horseback, hence the sport's name—attempting to direct a ball toward goals at opposite ends of the field. In 1863 in England, proponents of the relatively nonviolent, no-handling version of the game created the Football Association, whose distinctive "soccer" rules have since become the world's most popular football code. But footballers in the United States, like those at Britain's Rugby school, came to prefer more "manly" versions of the sport, in which the ball could be played and carried with the hands, thus requiring a more violent style of tackling. For example, the first football club, Oneida of Boston Common, preferred the rugby-like "Boston Game," as did students at Harvard University, whose pair of well-publicized matches in 1874 with rugby-playing McGill University did much to popularize the rugged-handling versions of the sport.

It was at Yale University, however, that the distinctive American "gridiron" game would emerge. In the 1870s, Yale students such as Walter Camp, a tireless promoter of both the game and himself and the "Father of American Football," began tinkering with the rugby code and found it to be overly reliant on interpretations grounded in British schoolboy tradition. Eager to develop an unambiguous code of football for intercollegiate play, a rules committee led by Camp gradually developed a more rigid, complicated, and formalized version of football, a game of technical coordination, specialized roles, and scripted plays that resonated with the emerging corporate, industrial society those Ivy League men would soon lead. The most prominent changes made by Camp's committee occurred in 1880 and 1882, when the relatively fluid play and "scrummage" of rugby were replaced by formal play-initiating exchanges between a designated "center" and "quarterback" at a line of "scrimmage," and when ball possession was limited by a down-and-distance system, which necessitated the "gridiron" marking across the field at five-yard intervals.

Early Cultural Significance

American football served the multiple roles of holiday spectacle, promotional vehicle, and symbol of American virtue and vice from an early date. In 1876, the newly created Intercollegiate Football Association played its first championship game in New York City on Thanksgiving Day. The Thanksgiving matchup became an annual event in 1882, and by the end of the decade, it had become one of the city's leading social engagements, "more of a spectacle than an athletic contest," according to *Harper's Weekly* (December 9, 1893). Although the Thanksgiving Day football tradition remains today in the professional ranks, New Year's Day became the primary holiday for collegiate football championships, beginning in 1902, when an intersectional game was first made the centerpiece of the Tournament of Roses in Pasadena, California. The Rose Bowl football championship became an annual tradition in 1916, and it was followed by imitators in Florida, Texas, and Louisiana during the 1930s.

These holiday bowl games were outstanding vehicles to promote Sunbelt tourist destinations and real estate opportunities. The success of their football team also became a marketing opportunity for the colleges themselves, as football became a primary ceremonial event tying alumni to their alma mater. Administrators quickly recognized the potential for the sport to generate needed revenue, and in 1903, in addition to atten-

tion from prospective students and donors, Yale received $106,000 from football, equal to the combined budgets of its medical, divinity, and law schools. Thus, upon assuming the presidency of the newly endowed University of Chicago, Yale alumnus William Rainey Harper made his first order of business the hiring of Yale legend Amos Alonzo Stagg as football coach.

More than promoting the schools themselves, successful college football teams became a vehicle for communities only tangentially related to the schools to celebrate their place in U.S. society. The country's Catholic population, for example, saw the historic 1913 victory of Knute Rockne's Notre Dame over Army as a symbolic achievement against the traditional northeastern, Protestant elite. Likewise, when the University of Alabama upset the heavily favored University of Washington in the 1926 Rose Bowl, it was not just the first victory by a southern school in an intersectional football game, it was also, to fans throughout the South, both a long-awaited victory over the North and a sign that the region was not "backwards" and could indeed participate in modern, industrial U.S. society.

> *Football has become the country's most prominent sporting spectacle, its most loved and hated sport, and a symbolic representation of cities, regions, institutions, and traditional values.*

Football's ability to carry this symbolic load was aided by the very nature of the game. From the beginning, football's proponents argued that the rugged athleticism, the near-"savage" violence, and the technically demanding teamwork provided a necessary masculine tonic to postfrontier U.S. society and a valuable training ground for the future captains of modern industry. The violence and commercialism of turn-of-the-century college football, however, were also the source of great controversy. The use of mass-formation plays, most notoriously the flying wedge introduced at Harvard in 1892, led to numerous on-field fatalities.

One of these deaths was of a Union College

halfback in a game against New York University. In response to his death, as well as to concerns regarding unethical recruiting and payment of players, NYU President Henry McCracken organized a conference of college officials. The result was the founding of the Intercollegiate Athletic Association (IAA), which became the National Collegiate Athletic Association (NCAA) in 1910. Despite resistance from Walter Camp's Intercollegiate Rules Committee, the IAA introduced dramatic reforms during the next five years, such as legalization of the forward pass and other changes designed to make the game more open and offensive and less based on brute strength.

A Modern Entertainment Industry

Concerns about commercialism, professionalism, and brutality in college football persisted into the 1920s; in fact, they continue today. But NCAA-led reforms of player recruiting and eligibility standards and the continuing evolution of pass-oriented, offensive-minded rules and tactics helped college football further increase and broaden in popularity.

Equally important was the rise of legendary players and coaches during the hero-worshipping "golden age" of the 1920s. Grantland Rice and others introduced a new style of sportswriting, creating almost mythical heroes out of stars like Notre Dame's George Gipp and the "Four Horsemen," and on the West Coast, Andy Smith's "Wonder Teams" at the University of California. To house the burgeoning crowds, universities built enormous new stadiums; during the 1920s, the nationwide count of facilities able to hold more than seventy thousand spectators increased from one to seven. More important, fans who were unable to attend the games could follow their heroes' exploits through such new technologies as radio and cinema newsreels.

This process of commercialization and professionalization of college football continued after World War II with the advent of television coverage, athletic scholarships, and expanded regula-

tory powers for the NCAA, although some schools—most prominently the traditional Ivy League powers—chose not to participate in all of these developments. As a result, by the end of the twentieth century, college football had become a two-tiered system: a modern, nationwide, sports-entertainment industry for the roughly one hundred schools participating in the NCAA's Division I-A; and a more traditional spectator sport for the lower-division schools, where the nationwide attention and direct financial benefits were not as great but where the pressure to win among alumni and fans was just as strong.

The Rise of Professional Football

Coincident with the rise of college football as a modern entertainment industry was the rise of professional football. The earliest professional football player of record was Yale's William "Pudge" Heffelfinger, who, in 1892, received $500 to play for the Allegheny Athletic Association against the rival Pittsburgh Athletic Club. Until the 1920s, such semipro club competitions remained concentrated in small and medium-sized industrial cities of Ohio and Pennsylvania, and they provided an alternative source of identity and entertainment for the working classes. For some players, professional football also provided a chance at limited fame and fortune. Most notably, Jim Thorpe of the Carlisle Indian School followed his double-gold-medal performance at the 1912 Olympics by leading the Canton Bulldogs to three straight Ohio League titles for $250 per game.

Modern professional football emerged after 1920, when clubs from four midwestern states met in Canton, Ohio, to standardize rules and form the American Professional Football Association, changed in 1922 to the National Football League (NFL). In a truer sense, however, modern pro football did not arise until 1925, when George Halas's Chicago Bears signed University of Illinois star Harold "Red" Grange. Grange, the "Galloping Ghost of the Gridiron," was the most famous of

The field at Reliant Stadium in Houston is seen from overhead just before the start of Super Bowl XXXVIII, featuring the New England Patriots and the Carolina Panthers (February 1, 2004).
(RICHARD CARSON/REUTERS/CORBIS)

the 1920s college football heroes, bursting on the national scene with a four-touchdown performance against the University of Michigan. Working in tandem with promoter Charles Pyle, Grange defied the ideal of the Victorian gentleman, which frowned upon college athletes' capitalizing financially on their athletic talents. Grange endorsed everything from chocolate to clothing, and in the process, he galvanized public interest in the fledgling NFL; in fact, 73,000 fans came to see him play at New York's Polo Grounds shortly after his signing with the Bears.

The NFL struggled during the Depression years of the 1930s, resulting in the demise of all of the league's smaller-city teams but the Green Bay Packers. After World War II, however, professional football found a perfect partner in television. In addition to being relatively well suited to the new broadcast medium—that is, the action is concentrated in both time and space—football benefited from having a close-knit group of owners who willingly gave centralized control to strong league commissioners: Bert Bell and Alvin "Pete" Rozelle. Unlike in baseball, in which teams negotiated broadcast rights individually, Bell and Rozelle pioneered sport television by negotiating centralized contracts with national television networks eager for exclusive, viewer-delivering programming.

The NFL's television-driven success of the 1950s quickly drew competition, most notably from the American Football League (AFL), which used money from a $42 million television deal with NBC to lure college talent, such as the University of Alabama quarterback Joe Namath. The result was a merger agreement in 1966, which retained Rozelle as the league chairman and introduced an annual AFL-NFL championship game in 1967: the Super Bowl.

Football at the End of the Century

At the turn of the twenty-first century, football had built on passions for the game among college alumni and capitalized on the opportunities provided by the new electronic media better than any other U. S. sport. The Super Bowl became the single greatest televised sporting event in the late-twentieth-century United States. Workplace watercooler talk the following Monday is as likely to concern the new advertisements, which debut in thirty-second, million-dollar advertising slots, as the game itself. Like the Thanksgiving Day college games in New York during the 1890s, football in the late 1990s was as much a spectacle as a sporting event.

Football is not just a televised marketing and entertainment vehicle; it is also the cornerstone of extracurricular life at high schools nationwide. In some areas, passion for football is so great that the identities of entire communities are wrapped up in the local football teams—places like Stark County, Ohio, where the Massillon High School Tigers draw more than a hundred thousand spectators per year, or Midland-Odessa, Texas, where the annual Permian-Lee rivalry draws more than twenty thousand partisans.

Football's popularity helps make the sport a symbolic battlefield in U.S. "culture wars." For its proponents, football provides the ideal proving ground for young men to test and develop their manhood, instilling such values as teamwork and self-reliance. At the same time, traditional ideas of femininity are promoted in such corollary institutions as cheerleading and pep squads, and the ideas are playfully challenged, but also reinforced, by role-reversing powder-puff games. Often these traditional gender roles and "family values" are promoted in an explicitly religious setting, with clergy of Protestant, Catholic, Mormon, and other faiths being prominent partici-

pants in pre- and post-game rituals. Of course, this makes football a target for those less enamored with the social status quo. Football is thus denounced as a promoter of violence, sexism, and greed. In short, as in the 1890s, football in the 1990s remained one of the country's most loved and hated sports.

—*Peter S. Morris*

See also: Camp, Walter; College Football

For further reading:

Bissinger, H. G. 1990. *Friday Night Lights: A Town, a Team, and a Dream.* Reading, MA: Addison-Wesley.

Rader, Benjamin G. 1996. *American Sports: From the Age of Folk Games to the Age of Spectators.* 3rd ed. Englewood Cliffs, NJ: Prentice-Hall.

Riesman, David, and Reuel Denney. 1951. "Football in America: A Study in Culture Diffusion." *American Quarterly*, 309–325.

FORD, RICHARD (1944–)

One of the best contemporary U.S. novelists and winner of the 1995 Pulitzer Prize for fiction, Richard Ford has consistently drawn on the sporting images and characters in his novels to question the U.S. fascination with sport as a guide or solution to human problems. Ford's *The Sportswriter* (1986) is his creation most clearly about the world of sport, but its narrator and protagonist, Frank Bascombe, also narrates Ford's Pulitzer Prize–winning novel *Independence Day* (1995). In both novels, Bascombe sees in sport and athletes a simplicity and grace that he cannot achieve in his own life, but he also encounters athletes struck by tragedy. In *The Sportswriter*, Bascombe meets an ex–football player, now a paraplegic, who tells him that sport is "a pretty crummy preparation for life." In *Independence Day*, the narrator tries to bond with his teenage son by taking him to the basketball and baseball halls of fame, only to end up in an argument with him at the batting cage in Cooperstown. Sport holds the promise of order in the lives of Ford's characters, but that order or simplicity is never achieved.

The failed natural athlete is usually a peripheral but striking character in Ford's novels. In *A Piece of My Heart* (1976), *The Ultimate Good Luck* (1980), and *Wildlife* (1990), the natural athletes have not so much given up their games as failed to attain the kind of clarity and certainty that was within their reach. Ford has not written a novel focused specifically on one sport, but he is persistently drawn to images and characters from the sporting realm.

In a 1983 article in *Esquire* magazine, Ford wrote affectionately of the three kings of U.S. literature: Ernest Hemingway, F. Scott Fitzgerald, and William Faulkner. His own work and treatment of sport in that work can be seen as part of this U.S. tradition of literature, both stylistically and in its understanding of the integral place of sport in U.S. life.

—*Kevin Brooks*

See also: Literature, Sport in; National Baseball Hall of Fame

For further reading:

Ford, Richard. 1995. *The Sportswriter.* Reprint, New York: Vintage Books.

FOREIGN STUDENT-ATHLETES

By providing a multinational presence in college sport, foreign student-athletes reveal the world of sport as a global system. At the same time, the internationalization of collegiate sport can produce a degree of xenophobia and chauvinism. Given that foreign student-athletes account for only about 3 percent of all student-athletes in the United States, they have a disproportionate amount of visibility. Some of the greatest college athletes have been foreign, and many have been Olympic gold medalists.

Until the 1950s, native-born student-athletes dominated the world of collegiate sport in the United States. This is not to say that no foreign student-athletes were involved in U.S. intercollegiate sport before that date. A steady trickle of Canadians was participating on college squads in the 1930s, and athletes from the Caribbean were present, notably in track and field, in the 1940s. The 1950s witnessed a slight increase in the rate of immigration of student-athletes from countries such as Australia, and European student-athletes began to appear on the rosters of U.S. college teams. It was in the 1960s and 1970s, however, that the recruiting of foreign athletes became more widespread. In the 1990s, student-athletes were recruited from Africa, Asia, and the former Communist world of eastern Europe. There was a complex network of recruiting contacts, often alumni. Sport was arguably the most obvious form of global culture, and as a result, the world became the recruiter's oyster.

All the evidence suggests that the number of foreign student-athletes in U.S. universities continues to increase. The estimated number of foreign student-athletes at the National Collegiate Athletic Association (NCAA) level rose from 6,833 in 1991 to 8,851 in 1995–1996. The respective average number per institution went from 8 percent to 10 percent. Over half of those recruits are men. Canada is, not surprisingly, the prime foreign origin of such student-athletes, accounting for 28 percent of the total. Other major donors of athletes are Great Britain, Sweden, and Australia. Few recruits come from Asia. In particular sports, however, nations that appear insignificant in overall exporting terms can assume dominance. For example, Kenya has supplied many track-and-field athletes to U.S. collegiate squads. The sports that dominate foreign recruiting are, in relative terms, skiing for women and ice hockey for men. These data may reflect the proximity of Canada to the United States. In terms of absolute numbers, soccer is the major foreign recruiting sport for men, numbering 1,341; while for women, the sport is tennis, with 700.

Such internationalization has led to intercultural contacts in sport. Some evidence suggests, however, that foreign student-athletes, particularly those from Africa, tend not to integrate with other student-athletes or, indeed, with other students. In addition, some observers have considered offering athletic scholarships to overseas athletes a denial of opportunity for U.S.-born students. Given the win-at-all-costs ideology that pervades much of college sport, however, it seems unlikely that foreign recruiting will disappear.

—*John Bale*

See also: Immigrants, Community and Sport

For further reading:
Bale, John. 1991. *The Brawn Drain: Foreign Student-Athletes in American Universities.* Urbana: University of Illinois Press.

FOREMAN, GEORGE EDWARD
(1949–)

With his thunderous punches, quick wit, and voracious appetite, George Foreman won the hearts of an adoring public on his way to regaining the heavyweight boxing championship. Raised on the mean streets of Houston's Fifth Ward, George Foreman was a self-described big, shy kid who walked to school to avoid the bad crowd. Soon, though, he became the leader of his peers, with stints as a mugger, a pickpocket, and a brawler.

A Jobs Corps commercial sent him to California, and by 1968, Foreman had won the gold medal at the Olympics in Mexico City. He became heavyweight champion in 1973 by knocking out

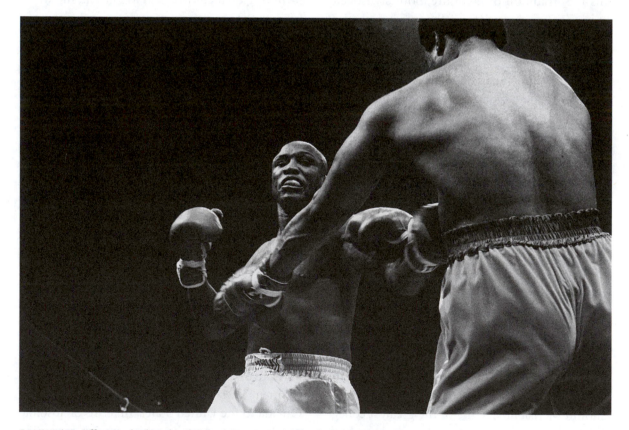

Joe Frazier suffers at the hands of George Foreman in the first round of a bout between the two former heavyweight champions at the Nassau Coliseum in Uniondale, New York. Foreman won via a fifth-round technical knockout (June 15, 1976).

(BETTMANN/CORBIS)

Joe Frazier in two rounds; however, he lost the title to Muhammad Ali the next year in the famous "Rumble in the Jungle" in Zaire. In 1977, Foreman retired from boxing to preach the gospel at his church in Houston.

Foreman returned to the ring in 1987 to support the George Foreman Youth and Community Development Center, a two-acre complex that offers children recreational activities. Although the sport press dismissed his comeback as a publicity stunt and a joke, Foreman regained the championship with a knockout of Michael Moorer in 1994.

Foreman's fun-loving personality has opened a world of endorsement possibilities to him. Among the companies with which he has contracts are Frito-Lay, the Kentucky Fried Chicken Corporation, and Meineke Discount Muffler Shops. In addition, Foreman can be seen on infomercials hawking his Lean Mean Fat Reducing Grilling Machine. The author of *By George* (1995), Foreman starred in a short-lived ABC television sitcom, also entitled *George.* Married to his fifth wife, Mary, Foreman has nine children, including four boys, all named George Edward after their father. He officially retired from boxing in 1997.

—*Scott A. Misner*

See also: Ali, Muhammad; Boxing; Endorsements

For further reading:

McCoyd, Ed. 1997. *To Live and Dream: The Incredible Story of George Foreman.* New York: New Street Publishers.

FOSTER, ANDREW "RUBE"
(1879–1930)

In 1920, Andrew "Rube" Foster, a former All-Star pitcher among African American ballplayers, challenged white control of black baseball by establishing the first Negro Baseball League, organized predominantly with African American team owners. Foster was born in Calvert, Texas, but after completing the eighth grade, he ran away to nearby Fort Worth to become a baseball player. For African American players, banned from the white major leagues since 1887, "black ball" consisted for the most part of barnstorming black teams playing each other and semipro white teams in various city leagues, mostly in the North. Entering professional baseball in 1896, Foster became a star pitcher with teams in Fort Worth, Philadelphia, and Chicago. Often playing without contracts, the black players commonly changed teams, looking for the best salary offer available. Such fluidity affected player and fan loyalty as well as team finances.

In 1906, Foster joined Frank Leland's Chicago Giants, becoming part-owner, manager, and star pitcher. Four years later, with a new white partner, saloon keeper John Schorling, Foster wrested control of the team from Leland and changed the name to the American Giants. The Giants began a ten-year period as one of black baseball's most successful teams, appearing on the West Coast, in the South, and in Cuba.

Although his playing career ended in 1916, Foster continued to direct the club's fortunes both on and off the field. In 1920, he organized the Negro National League, an eight-team alliance with one white and seven African American owners. Foster's goal was to create a stable African American ownership group in a successful Negro League to keep black money in black pockets. A secondary goal was to have a reliable structure ready when the white major leagues integrated, inevitability in Foster's view. As its creator, Foster became commissioner of the Negro National League, forcing trades when necessary to balance team strengths, helping weaker clubs financially, and adjudicating contract disputes. Rival black leagues formed in the South and East, and although some bidding wars ensued for star players, generally Negro baseball developed in a more assured manner. Salaries and team profits increased, schedules were regularized, and a Black World Series began.

In 1926, Foster's behavior suddenly became erratic, forcing his wife to have him committed to the state insane asylum at Kankakee, Illinois. After a four-year commitment, Foster died. As one of the founding fathers of Negro League baseball, Foster was elected to the Baseball Hall of Fame in 1981.

—*David Bernstein*

See also: Baseball; Discrimination, Racial, in Sport; Negro Baseball Leagues

For further reading:

Rutkoff, Peter. 2001. *Shadow Ball: A Novel of Baseball and Chicago*. Jefferson, NC: McFarland.

FRAZIER, JOE (1944–)

Renowned for his punching power and determination, Joe Frazier battled Muhammad Ali in three of boxing's most celebrated and exciting matches. When he was a small boy, Frazier and his family moved from Beaufort, South Carolina, to Philadelphia. It was there that the young and hefty Frazier began boxing as a way to lose weight. However, over the next several years, he combined his fearsome left hook with a relentless determination that earned him the nickname "Smokin'."

As a young heavyweight, the fighter's blue-collar work ethic earned him a gold medal in the 1964 Olympics, and he won the heavyweight championship of the world in 1968 with an eleventh-round knockout of Buster Mathis. Yet Frazier's fame is forever tied to Muhammad Ali, with whom he fought three epic battles between 1971 and 1975. These contests were compelling not only because they matched two great boxers but also because of the stylistic and personal contrasts represented by the two pugilists. Frazier's power-punching and aggressive style made him the ultimate adversary for Ali's unsurpassed speed and agility. Furthermore, Frazier's reserved, no-nonsense demeanor served as the perfect foil for Ali's flamboyant braggadocio. As a result, their encounters outside the ring were often as colorful as those that took place inside, including one exchange on national television (*Wide World of Sports*, January 23, 1974) that ended with the two boxers wrestling on the floor.

In 1973, Frazier lost the heavyweight championship to George Foreman; he failed in his only attempt to regain the title, stopped by Muhammad Ali in 1975. This third fight with Ali, promoted as the "Thrilla in Manila," is considered by many to be the greatest boxing match of all time.

—*Thomas C. Reynolds*

See also: Ali, Muhammad; Boxing

For further reading:

Frazier, Joe. 1996. *Smokin' Joe: The Autobiography of a Heavyweight Champion of the World*. With Phil Berger. St. Paul, MN: Hungry Mind Press.

FRISBEE

Frisbee games, or disc games, now played the world over, are quintessentially American. The centerpiece of the activity, a plastic disc with pleasing aerodynamic properties, is a product of modern U.S. technology and entrepreneurial ingenuity. Mass production, popularization, and ease of use have made the item such a fixture in U.S. life that the Smithsonian Institution, charged with conserving and celebrating the nation's cultural heritage, has held annual Frisbee celebrations in the nation's capital, and New York City's park commissioner has welcomed spring with the toss of a Frisbee in Central Park.

Meanwhile, games employing discs in capacities beyond simply throwing and catching have emerged and have acquired the familiar trappings of modern athletic competition with the development of rules; the formation of clubs, leagues, and a governing association; the regularization of contests and championships; the tracking of records; and the celebration of individual and team legends. At the same time, exhibiting another sort of tradition, that of nonconformity and independence, practitioners of disc games have remained stubbornly different from conventional organized sport, priding themselves on their "alternative" philosophy, offbeat reputation, and self-officiating ethos.

"Frisbee" is a trademarked name for the discs manufactured by the Wham-O Corporation, although many people have come to use the term "Frisbee" generically. Since the product's introduction in the late 1950s, however, what many once saw as a lightweight toy has become the central prop in a variety of challenging and increasingly popular athletic endeavors. Dozens of companies worldwide make Frisbee-type discs, including regulation-weight varieties for specific games. Wham-O alone claimed to have sold more than 300 million Frisbees by the end of the late 1990s.

Historians of disc sport find Frisbee forerunners in pie tins or cookie-tin lids that were tossed back and forth on New England college campuses in the 1940s and trace the name "Frisbee" to the Frisbie Pie Company of Bridgeport, Connecticut. But modern discs are largely a product of late-twentieth-century plastic injection-molding technology. California inventor Walter Morrison made the first plastic flying disc in 1948, improved it in 1951 into a design that would serve as the basis for what Wham-O initially called the Pluto Platter, and sold the concept to Wham-O in 1957.

Writer Gay Talese scoffed at the product in the *New York Times Magazine,* saying, "Like most other fast-selling pieces of goofy merchandise, the Frisbee is novel, portable and cheap (79 cents). Neither stamina nor brains are needed to make it work" (1957, 175). The disc outlived the disdain, becoming an enduring prop of U.S. backyards, beach parties, and picnics and spreading worldwide. The Frisbee remains eminently portable and affordable. Retail prices for new discs in various categories are around eight to twelve dollars, although among collectors, early editions, prototypes, and novelty adaptations sell for much more.

The scientific principles behind the disc are simple: the slightly curved shape provides aerodynamic lift, spinning lends stability, and the thrower can make the disc go straight, skip, hover, or boomerang by controlling such things as spin, speed, and angle of release. The aesthetic results, markedly different from the trajectories of balls, have given rise to the saying, "When a ball dreams, it dreams it's a Frisbee" (Johnson 1975).

Structured disc sports have evolved in many directions, including disc golf, free-style competition, and double-disc, a court game involving two discs in play simultaneously. Canine Frisbee brings man's best friend onto the playing field in routines involving humans and their dogs. The most widely played disc game is "ultimate," a strenuous and strategic team game that for passionate players borders on religion. Invented by New Jersey high school students in 1967 as a spoof, ultimate expanded from pickup games to local and high school leagues to college clubs and international championships. Organized play has spread to nearly forty countries, and estimates of the number of casual and competitive players range as high as 200,000.

Ultimate combines elements of numerous other sports, from the continuous action of soccer and the cutting and guarding of basketball to the kickoff and field sense of football and the patterns of hockey and lacrosse in a manic athleticism offering a unique repertoire of maneuvers (with tantalizing names, such as a catch called the "layout" and throws such as the "hammer" and the "blade"). The aerobic workout is intense, with players on teams of seven running up to three miles in a game. It is a noncontact sport, although injuries from diving, colliding, running hard, and stopping quickly are not unusual. Players may not run while holding the disc and have only ten seconds to throw it. Points are scored by catching the disc in the opponents' end zone.

Ultimate players are known not only for their pride in technique, endurance, and aesthetic fulfillment but also for their emphasis on community, integrity, and mutual respect along with a wacky sense of fun. Players officiate their own games according to a code of ethics called "the spirit of the game," emphasizing honesty and self-regulation. Disputes are settled by returning the disc to the thrower and redoing the play. Although debate over the need for outside officiating surfaces periodically and although championships now have referees of sorts, called observers, most calls are still left to players. Veteran player Jim Parinella, whose Boston team has been five-time national champions, explains the moral implications: "Ultimate doesn't build character; it reveals character. It gives individuals the opportunity to display their personalities on the field, whether they're going to be fair in their dealings with people or weasel their way out of things" (Robbins 1999).

Many teams maintain a counterculture position, displayed via irreverent names and antics, along with the determination to play in all seasons and any weather. On the other hand, the game also has associations with the young, well-educated, upwardly mobile, technocratic sectors of society. It is also viewed as nonsexist and is often played in coed teams. Although high school leagues are becoming more common, the game is most rooted at colleges, where ultimate is a minimally funded sport and students usually subsidize their own tournament trips. There is no professional circuit, and the sport's participants pride themselves on shunning all but the most sport-specific sponsorship. Ultimate was introduced as an exhibition sport in the World Student Games in West Germany in 1989 and debuted as a medal sport in the 2001 World Games in Japan.

—*Judy Polumbaum*

See also: Disc Golf; Fads and Trends; Hula-Hoops

For further reading:

Johnson, Stancil. 1975. *Frisbee: A Practitioner's Manual and Definitive Treatise.* New York: Workman's Press.

Malafronte, Victor A. 1998. *The Complete Book of Frisbee.* Alameda, CA: American Trends Publishing.

Robbins, Alexandra. 1999. "Ultimate Frisbee Test Character, Fitness." *USA Today.* http://www.ultimatehandbook.com/Webpages/Media/mediausa.html. Retrieved June 2004.

Talese, Gay. 1957. "Frisbees, Yo-Yos, Goo-Goos, Etc.: Dig Those Crazy, Grown-up Toys." *The New York Times Magazine,* 11 August, 175.

G

GAMBLING

A percentage of legalized gambling is devoted to sport books and race books, where the fans, or fanatics, can put their money where their mouth is, risking monetary gain or loss on the basis of their predictions of the outcome of an event; however, gambling—whether in a formal setting, like a casino, or casually, such as by purchasing a lottery ticket at a convenience market's drive-through window—is itself a sport. Gambling requires skill, luck, and finesse, and it can require big bucks—in other words, all the ingredients of organized sport.

At the end of the twentieth century, legalized gambling was available in almost every state in the United States, whether a state lottery, riverboat gambling, slot-machine houses on Indian reservations, bingo parlors, the casinos of Atlantic City, New Jersey, or the glitz and glitter of Nevada. Those who predict cultural trends point out that there could be a casino situated within a two-hour drive of every major U.S. city by the year 2010. Organized gambling is one sport that combines the key ingredients of late-twentieth-century choice: risk-taking behavior combined with mainstream entertainment, tourism, and shopping.

American Demographics, citing a survey conducted by Harrah's Casino and published in *U. S. Casino Gambling Entertainment*, notes that adults from half of all U.S. households have gambled in a casino at some time in their life. The majority of these persons are upper middle class, with a median age of forty-nine. Slot machines are the biggest draw, followed by such video games as poker, bingo, and blackjack. Table or pit games, blackjack, craps, and roulette, tend to appeal to those who are younger, better educated, and more affluent. The majority of casino revenue in

> *At the end of the twentieth century, legalized gambling was available in almost every state in the United States, whether a state lottery, riverboat gambling, slot-machine houses on Indian reservations, bingo parlors, the casinos of Atlantic City, New Jersey, or the glitz and glitter of Nevada. Those who predict cultural trends point out that there could be a casino situated within a two-hour drive of every major U.S. city by the year 2010. Organized gambling combines the key ingredients of late-twentieth-century choice: risk-taking behavior combined with mainstream entertainment, tourism, and shopping.*

Nevada is produced from slot and video games, which are rumored to cover all casino overhead including salaries and astronomical utility bills.

Often, gambling is viewed as a savior for state

economic woes, but although the industry does produce enormous tax and tourism revenues, there are also negative consequences. The infrastructure of gambling cities is often strained to meet the demand of an excess population, from increased traffic, crime, and noise to air pollution. In addition, gambling tends to transfer money from local businesses to the casinos without increasing jobs or area revenue. Although they are pitched as a tourist lure for an area, casinos attempt to keep their clientele in delirious captivity by offering restaurants, shows, and shopping in addition to gambling; consequently, many tourists never venture outside their hotel or casino complex. In Atlantic City, New Jersey, for example, there has been a population decrease since the legalization of gambling in 1976 due to increased rents. Furthermore, the downtown area, once scheduled for revitalization, has progressively deteriorated while available funds have been channeled to the gambling-funded bright lights of the Boardwalk.

Due to the negativity associated with the term "gambling," by the late 1990s, most professionals referred to the sport as "gaming" and to casinos as "festival gaming centers."

—*Joyce Duncan*

See also: Atlantic City, New Jersey; Las Vegas, Nevada

For further reading:

Fost, Dan. 1993. "Fear and Marketing in Las Vegas: Casino Gambling is Fast Becoming Mainstream Entertainment for Affluent Adults." *American Demographics*, October, 15, 19–22.

Isaacs, Neil D. 2001. *You Bet Your Life: The Burdens of Gambling*. Lexington: University Press of Kentucky.

GAMBLING SCANDALS

Gambling scandals in U.S. sport are not, unfortunately, a novel occurrence. Where big money is so readily available, it is not unusual to find hands willing to grasp it. Perhaps the most infamous of the scandals are the Chicago "Black Sox" scandal of 1919 and the frequent point-shaving in college basketball. The first scandal threatened to end professional major league baseball; the second led to cries for reform and promises to bring about changes.

The so-called Black Sox scandal of 1919 involved the throwing of the World Series by the Chicago White Sox, the best team in baseball and a team that might have formed the greatest dynasty in the sport. Eight members of the White Sox were eventually indicted on charges of conspiring to defraud the public because there were no laws against fixing a sporting event at the time.

The players worked for low pay, essentially in contract slavery, and the reserve clause prohibited free agency and bound a player to a team at the whim of the owner. The White Sox had the highest caliber of players in the game and close to the lowest payroll. The owner of the White Sox, Charles Comiskey, even refused to pay for cleaning the uniforms, and it was the griminess of their togs that originally gave the team the name "Black Sox." The general public knew little about the stinginess of the team's salaries because Comiskey was generous with the press, wining and dining them in return for positive publicity.

There was, however, a great deal of dissension on the team. Members almost went on strike in July, but when the strike did not materialize, some of the players mulled over the possibility of fixing the World Series. There were precedents of gambling influence in baseball, whispered stories about players feeding information to gamblers and chumming around with them. Hal Chase, for example, was known for his skill at the "blown play." Owners knew that Chase fixed games from time to time, but they elected to trade him rather than expose him. They feared that such exposure would jeopardize the integrity of the game.

Although Chicago's legal system could not or would not convict those involved in the Black Sox scandal, baseball was in danger of losing respectability and the owners decided to appoint a commissioner of baseball to monitor activity. That first commissioner, Kennesaw Mountain Landis, a no-nonsense judge, "suspended each of the players, and initially promised them reinstatement if they were found not guilty. He still banned them all for life in spite of the fact that they were cleared of criminal charges. 'Regardless of the verdict of the juries,' he said, 'no player that throws a ball game . . . will ever again play professional baseball'" (Everstine 2004). Baseball had made the firm decision that "the great American pastime" must be above reproach. No taint of a fix could ever be allowed again.

On the other hand, college basketball and other collegiate sports appear to roll on despite periodic point-shaving scandals. In 1997, two Arizona State players pled guilty to point-shaving in games dating back to 1994. In 1992, five basketball players at Bryant College owed $54,000 in gambling debts and were suspended, while a former player was arrested for bookmaking. Other college sports had offenders as well. At the University of Maine, for example, thirteen baseball players and six football players were suspended in 1992 for gambling on their games. In 1996, Boston College suspended thirteen football players, two of whom had bet against their own team.

Despite the obvious need for control of gambling in sport, there has been little effective action. The National Collegiate Athletic Association has supported congressional action against all betting on college and amateur athletics, but opposition from the gaming industry has prevented Congress from enacting effective legislation. The major legal outlet for college betting is Nevada, where gambling interests are quite strong.

The first case of an arrest for college gambling was in 1951, when Henry Poppe and John Byrnes, cocaptains of Manhattan College's basketball team, were arrested for attempting to fix the Manhattan-DePaul game. Soon after, City College players Ed Warner, Ed Roman, and Edward Gard were arrested on bribery charges. Sherman White, LeRoy Smith, and Adolph Bigos of Long Island

University were next. During the summer of 1951, five Bradley University players admitted taking bribes from gamblers to hold down scores in two games. In 1954, Jack Molinas of the professional team the Fort Wayne Pistons was accused of gambling, and in 1962 he was charged with heading a gambling ring that fixed college games. Between 1960 and 1990, over forty college basketball players were convicted of point-shaving and gambling.

Although professional sport has managed to keep gambling scandals at a reasonable distance, colleges have not. Perhaps the fact that professional athletes are paid for their efforts and college athletes are not accounts for the difference. The temptation to make money from their effort is obviously great. Gambling is prevalent throughout U.S. society, and it is only surprising that more college athletes are not involved.

—*Frank A. Salamone*

See also: Athletes, above the Law; Black Sox Scandal; College Football

For further reading:
Cardoza, Avery. 1999. *The Basics of Winning Sports Betting.* New York: Seven Stories Press.
Everstine, Eric. 2004. "1919 World Series: Black Sox Scandal." http://www.mc.cc.md.us/Departments/hpolscrv/blacksox.htm. Accessed June 2004.
Ginsberg, Daniel E. 1995. *The Fix Is In: A History of Baseball Gambling and Game Fixing Scandals.* Jefferson, NC: McFarland.
Rosen, Charles. 1999. *Barney Polan's Game: A Novel of the 1951 College Basketball Scandals.* San Diego, CA: Harcourt Brace.

GASHOUSE GANG

The "Gashouse Gang," the St. Louis Cardinals of the mid-1930s and World Series champions in 1934, is one of the most famous and colorful baseball teams in U.S. sport history. In 1934, in the midst of the Great Depression, the St. Louis Cardinals captivated the country with their hustling, aggressive play and their raucous behavior, both on and off the field. The team was filled with a cast of talented and colorful characters, including Johnny "Pepper" Martin; Jay "Dizzy" Dean and his younger brother, Paul "Daffy" Dean; Leo "the Lip" Durocher; Joseph "Ducky" Medwick; James "Ripper" Collins; and no-nonsense player-manager Frank "the Fordham Flash" Frisch. In the best tradition of the American success story, they dramatically won the National League pennant on the final day of the season and went on to defeat the Detroit Tigers in an exciting and boisterous seven-game World Series. They also took part in close pennant races in 1935 and 1936, finishing second in both years.

Although there is more than one version as to who first applied the "Gashouse Gang" appellation to the Cardinals, it was ultimately the New York media that popularized the team's famous nickname. The Gashouse district was a tough, crime-ridden slum in New York City that had spawned a notorious street gang. "Gashouse Gang" or "gashouser" had thereby entered the U.S. idiom as a reference to brawling and disorderly behavior. The Cardinals' pugnacious "gashouse" reputation was formally sealed during the 1935 season when they arrived in New York for a series with the Giants and, not having time to have their uniforms changed, were forced to take the field in their rumpled, dirt-stained uniforms.

—*Robert P. Nash*

See also: Baseball

For further reading:
Fleming, Gordon. 1984. *The Dizziest Season: The Gashouse Gang Chases the Pennant.* New York: William Morrow.

GASTON, CLARENCE "CITO" EDWIN (1944–)

Clarence "Cito" Edwin Gaston was the first black manager in major league history to win a World Series, and his Toronto Blue Jays were the first Canadian team to win baseball's championship. Gaston became the fourth black manager in major league history when he was hired by the Blue Jays in 1989. His hiring came two years after Los Angeles Dodgers executive Al Campanis had remarked that blacks "may not have some of the necessities" to manage in the major leagues (quoted Gammons 1987, 31). Campanis's remarks forced major league baseball to acknowledge that blacks were seriously underrepresented in managerial and front-office positions.

Gaston guided the Blue Jays to back-to-back World Series victories in 1992 and 1993. Although major league baseball had been in Canada since 1969, Toronto's consecutive championships reinforced the fact that the U.S. "national pastime" had become an international game.

Unfortunately, Gaston was fired in August 1997 as the Blue Jays struggled through their fourth straight losing season. However, he was a cowinner of the 1993 *Sporting News* Sportsman of the Year Award. In 1994, he became the first recipient of the Rube Foster Character Award, which is given to the coach or manager who best embodies dedication, character, and devotion to the game.

—*Daryl Baswick*

See also: Baseball; Discrimination, Racial, in Sport; Robinson, Jack Roosevelt "Jackie"

For further reading:
Gammons, Peter. 1987. "The Campanis Affair." *Sports Illustrated,* April 20, 31.

GAY GAMES

The Gay Games, launched in San Francisco in 1982, were open to all athletes regardless of age, race, gender, sexual orientation, or physical ability. In the words of event founder, Thomas Waddell, the games were "modeled on the ancient Olympics but modified, open to everyone regardless of age or race or gender or sexual orientation, or even ability" (Waddell and Schaap 1996, 146). Waddell developed the games in 1980 as the Gay Olympics. However, shortly before the opening of the event in San Francisco, a case was brought against Waddell by the U.S. Olympic Committee (USOC) to prevent him from using the word "Olympics" in the title. The case was settled in favor of the USOC, and the word "Olympics" was replaced with the word "Games." The Gay Games have been held at four-year intervals since 1982. At the first Gay Games in 1982, there were 1,700–1,800 athletes and 10,000 spectators. At the 1994 games in New York City, there were 15,000 athletes and 500,000 spectators.

—Tom Peele

See also: Homosexuality and Sport; Olympic Games

For further reading:
Waddell, Tom, and Dick Schaap. 1996. *Gay Olympian: The Life and Death of Dr. Tom Waddell.* New York: Knopf.

GEHRIG, LOU (1903–1941)

Lou Gehrig had stood as a model of the endurance, persistence, and indomitable spirit of athleticism, despite being one of the great tragic

Lou Gehrig, the "Iron Horse" of baseball, who was forced to the bench by amyotrophic lateral sclerosis after playing 2,130 consecutive games, is touched by a New York fans' demonstration; he is acclaimed in a manner unrivaled in baseball history. Nearly 75,000 fans jam Yankee Stadium to honor Gehrig. Handkerchief to his face, Gehrig is deeply moved by the fans' ovation. July 4, 1939.
(BETTMANN/CORBIS)

figures of U.S. sport. Lou Gehrig was one of baseball's greatest stars, playing with the New York Yankees of the 1920s and 1930s until his early death from amyotrophic lateral sclerosis, a disease referred to commonly as Lou Gehrig's disease. Gehrig was discovered while he was playing baseball for Columbia University and began his career with the New York Yankees in the mid-1920s, joining Yankee great Babe Ruth. Gehrig's tireless work ethic earned him the nickname of "Iron Horse" as he set a record by playing in 2,130 consecutive games, a record that lasted until broken in 1995 by Cal Ripkin Jr.

Gehrig's baseball achievements were remarkable. His lifetime batting average of .340 ranks as one of the highest in major league history. Gehrig drove in over 150 runs seven times in his career and holds the record of twenty-three career grand-slam home runs. Gehrig's amazing prowess as a baseball player made his rapid physical deterioration even more bewildering. With his body failing him, Gehrig was forced out of the game at the age of thirty-five, and he died, in 1941, at the age of thirty-eight.

In 1942, Gehrig's story was told in the film *The Pride of the Yankees,* starring Gary Cooper as the athlete. In the climactic final scene, Cooper re-creates Gehrig's emotional speech at Yankee Stadium in which the ailing baseball great told his fans, "Today I consider myself the luckiest man on the face of this earth."

—*Michael A. Lerner*

See also: Baseball; Baseball Films; Ruth, George Herman "Babe," Jr.; Yankee Stadium

For further reading:
Robinson, Ray. 1991. *Iron Horse: Lou Gehrig in His Time.* New York: HarperCollins.

GENDER TESTING

Gender testing has incited arguments over the definition of gender and the effects of gender testing on women and women's sport. Gender testing is intended to ensure that only women compete in women's athletic events, thereby guaranteeing competitive fairness. Unfortunately, this attempt at fairness presupposes that women are athletically inferior to men. Gender tests are administered to women before international competitions in tennis, basketball, track and field, swimming, the Olympic Games, and similar multisport games. These tests are motivated in part by the anxiety that women with male genetic characteristics, who are afforded physical advantages over other women, will compete to unfair advantage. In addition, they are motivated more recognizably by the concern that a man might try to compete with women, though there is no unambiguous case on record of this occurring.

Fears about nonfemale athletes competing as women were first publicly articulated in response to several incidents in the early 1960s in which competitors in women's events were suspected, on the basis of their superior athletic performances, of not being "true women." One such incident involved Russia's Irena Press and Tamara Press, who set twenty-six world records and won five gold medals in Olympic track-and-field competition between 1960 (Rome) and 1964 (Tokyo). Their superiority over the field, witnessed by a culture committed to the idea that women were athletically inferior, cast suspicion on their gender. They thus represented the possibility that a woman in appearance might not be a woman genetically or athletically.

The first gender test was administered before the 1966 European Athletics Championships in Budapest, Hungary, and involved a physical examination. Chromosomal gender testing was first instituted in the 1968 Olympics in Mexico City. However, chromosome testing has, since its inception, been criticized as inconclusive because several known genetic conditions give a male chromosomal profile to someone who is in appearance and by stated identity a woman. Most Olympic federations discontinued the chromosome test, while still testing women's gender physically. Notably, however, the International Olympic Committee retained the chromosomal gender test. Arguments over both physical and chromosomal tests left the final definition of gender unclear.

This concern over the gender of female athletes, sparked in the 1960s, produced several public gender trials. One involved the Spanish hurdler Maria Patino, who, in 1985, failed the gender test for the World Student Games in Tokyo. She withdrew from that competition but later contested the ruling, was determined to be a woman, and was reinstated on the Spanish women's Olympic team. Like most cases tried since the 1960s, Patino's involved not deliberate deceit but, rather, an unclear definition of gender. Unlike Patino, however, most accused athletes have not contested the ruling because such a confrontation involves a potentially embarrassing and defamatory public proceeding. Most have instead opted to withdraw permanently from competition. The fact that many athletes have shared this end and that the definition of gender employed in gender testing remains uncertain has been the basis for the criticism of gender testing.

—*Kris R. Cohen*

See also: Olympic Games; Steroids

For further reading:

"No Gender Testing." 2000. *New Scientist*, June 17, 166, 19.

Simpson, Joe Leigh, Arne Ljungqvist, Malcolm A. Ferguson-Smith, Albert de la Chapelle, Louis J. Elsas II, A. A. Ehrhardt, Myron Genel, Elizabeth A. Ferris, Alison Carlson. 2000. "Gender Verification in the Olympics." *JAMA* 284 (September 27): 1568.

GIBSON, ALTHEA (1927–)

Althea Gibson was a pioneer in the sports of tennis and golf both as a woman and as an African American. Her many titles and the respect she generated opened doors for others to follow in her

Darlene Hard kisses Althea Gibson after Miss Gibson defeated her 6-2, 6-3 in the finals of the women's singles tennis championship at Wimbledon, England. Althea became the first African American to win the coveted tennis title. The trophy she is holding was presented by Queen Elizabeth (July 7, 1957).
(BETTMANN/CORBIS)

path. Her victories, from the New York State singles tennis championship for African American girls to her later wins at Wimbledon and in the U.S. Open, were triumphs for all women tennis players, especially for African American women. In 1957, the Associated Press named Gibson Woman Athlete of the Year for her wins at Forest Hills and Wimbledon. She became the first African American to play in the French Open as well. During her long career, Gibson won five Grand Slam titles and approximately one hundred championships. In 1971, the athlete was selected to join the National Lawn Tennis Hall of Fame.

Gibson's career was not always smooth sailing. She experienced marked racial discrimination, ranging from not being allowed to play on certain courts to having opponents refuse to compete against her to being harassed by the fans. Despite these incidents, Gibson achieved great success and has served as a role model for other young African American women, showing them what is possible if they persist.

Following her stellar career in tennis, Gibson joined the Ladies Professional Golf Association in 1963, the first African American woman to hold a membership. Gibson's pioneering efforts in tennis and golf created opportunities for other women and other African Americans to participate more fully in these formerly exclusive sports.

—*Leslie Heaphy*

See also: Ladies Professional Golf Association

For further reading:

Davidson, Sue. 1997. *Changing the Game: The Stories of Tennis Champions Alice Marble and Althea Gibson.* Seattle, WA: Seal Press.

GOLF

A sport of individual effort played with passion by amateurs and for large prize money by professionals, golf reflects its aristocratic origins and private, country-club venues even as it seeks to be more accessible and inclusive. Golf began in Scotland in the fifteenth century, but it was briefly banned for interfering with military training for the wars against England. St. Andrews was the first golf course; Mary Queen of Scots played there in 1563, and the course is still used as one of the sites for the British Open Championship. In the 1750s, a golf club was formed at St. Andrews, where rules of the game were first adopted.

It was not until the 1880s, however, that golf took root in the United States with the founding of the first courses, St. Andrews in Yonkers, New York, and Shinnecock Hills on Long Island. Within a few years, there were more than a thousand courses on which Americans could play. In 1895, the first U.S. Open and U.S. Amateur Championships were held, sponsored by the U.S. Golf Association, the country's foremost amateur golf organization. Shortly thereafter, other tournaments began, such as the Professional Golfers' Association (PGA) Championship in 1916 and the Masters in 1934. Professional golf tours for men and women formed before World War II and grew exponentially in prize money and public visibility in the late twentieth century as a result of television and corporate sponsorships.

Golf as Sport

More than 25 million people, including men, women, and juniors, play golf, making it one of the most popular participant sports in the United States. The allure of the game can be traced to its outdoor environs and to the natural beauty of green grass, trees, water, and hills that typically define its landscape as well as to the leisurely pace of play—about four hours for an eighteen-hole round. Golf is an individual rather than a team sport, requiring neither opponents, as in tennis, nor teammates, as in football, basketball, or baseball. Though an individual challenge, golf is a sociable game, played in small groups—typically foursomes—of friends and acquaintances. Unlike bowling, golf has experienced no trend toward "golfing alone."

Never a sport requiring physical strength or stature, golf can readily be played by men and women of all ages, from juniors to the elderly. The advent of the golf cart, enabling players to ride rather than walk around the course, has facilitated this accessibility by reducing still further the athleticism necessary to participate in the game. Professional golfers are generally required to walk, though exceptions are made for seniors over age fifty and, on occasion, for the physically challenged.

Golf is also a spectator sport, attracting millions of viewers to professional tournaments in person or on television. It is commonplace to see a football stadium–sized crowd of spectators, forty thousand people or more, spread across a golf course, watching the professionals play, either by walking "outside the ropes" that separate players from spectators or by sitting behind tees and greens having especially favorable views.

Golf has been greatly popularized by television. The game's "simultaneity of action," in Marshall McLuhan's terminology (1967), is better suited to the medium of television than is the linear progression of such sports as baseball. Televised golf, perfected to an art form by CBS and its longtime golf producer, Frank Chirkinian, easily shows dozens of golfers and their shots within a few minutes of coverage. Though network television ratings for golf are well below those for football or basketball, the demographics of the viewers, predominantly wealthy and male, are appealing to advertisers. Cable television has greatly expanded the coverage of golf, and in 1995, the Golf Channel was launched, becoming the first special-interest channel devoted exclusively to one sport.

Golf and U.S. Culture

Golf is largely understood and recognized by the U.S. public as a game of individual achievement. The progression of male superstars identified with golf moves from the greatest amateur golfer, Bobby Jones in the 1920s, to the World War II generation of Ben Hogan, Sam Snead, and Byron Nelson, to the 1960s when Arnold Palmer and Jack Nicklaus dominated, to the young phenomenon Tiger Woods in the late 1990s. By the 1980s, golfers from outside the United States, such as Nick Faldo of England, Greg Norman of Australia, and Seve Ballesteros of Spain, became equally recognizable superstars in the United States and around the world, leading to an internationalization of golf that paralleled, albeit more slowly, the story of tennis. Women golfing greats, such as Babe Didrikson Zaharias in the 1950s, Mickey Wright in the 1960s, and Nancy Lopez in the 1980s, also achieved a smaller measure of fame and fortune.

Widely viewed as a sport for the wealthy and the leisure classes, golf has struggled, with limited success, to become more accessible to the masses. Golf's origins in the United States lie in the private country clubs built in the early twentieth century. These clubs were highly exclusive, actively keeping out blacks and other peoples of color, Catholics, and Jews, who eventually formed their own clubs. Women too were typically excluded, except as the spouses of members; as such they might be given limited playing privileges, for example, being allowed to play on weekdays only. These exclusions and restrictions softened only slightly, contributing to virtually all-white professional golf tours throughout the twentieth century and to *de facto* segregated golfing communities. By the 1980s, most new golf courses were being built around new housing, either gated communities for the wealthy, with private courses, or upscale communities and golf courses for retirees and resort visitors. Though there have been a few professional golfers of color, the emergence of multiracial golf superstar Tiger Woods, of Chinese, Native American, African American, and Caucasian heritages, represents the first challenge to the image of golf as a "white sport."

The limited representations of golf in popular culture reflect the game's lesser status in the pantheon of sport. Many instructional books and videos about golf have been produced, but there are few biographies of golfing greats, and even fewer novels and films using golf as a central story line. Actor Kevin Costner's irreverent portrayal of a professional golfer in the 1996 film *Tin Cup* and sport essayist John Feinstein's titling of his book about golf *A Good Walk Spoiled* (1995) reflect and reinforce a contemporary cultural view that golf is a game rather than a sport played by well-conditioned athletes.

—*John Paul Ryan*

> *More than 25 million people, including men, women, and juniors, play golf, making it one of the most popular participant sports in the Americas.*

See also: Discrimination, Racial, in Sport; Ladies Professional Golf Association; Palmer, Arnold; Woods, Eldrick "Tiger"

For further reading:
Feinstein, John. 1995. *A Good Walk Spoiled.* Boston: Little, Brown.
McLuhan, Marshall. 1967. *The Medium Is the Message.* New York: Bantam.
Peper, George, ed. 1988. *Golf in America: The First One Hundred Years.* With Robin McMillan and James A. Frank. New York: Harry N. Abrams.

GORGEOUS GEORGE
See Wagner, "Gorgeous George" Raymond

GOWDY, CURT (1919–)

Curt Gowdy was one of network television's busiest and most popular sportscasters in the 1960s and 1970s. He described nearly every major sporting event, from the World Series to the Super Bowl, for millions of fans across the country.

Born and raised in rural Wyoming, Gowdy was working for an Oklahoma radio station when, in 1949, he was made Mel Allen's partner for the New York Yankees' radio and television broadcasts. In 1951, Gowdy became the chief announcer for the Boston Red Sox games.

In 1961, as televised sport became a national passion, Gowdy was hired by NBC, and his flat, slightly nasal voice quickly became associated with the network's *Baseball Game of the Week,* World Series, and American Football League telecasts. He broadcast the first Super Bowl game for NBC in 1967. In 1964, Gowdy, an avid outdoorsman, also became the host and producer of *The American Sportsman,* a weekly show on hunting and fishing that featured celebrity guests and was broadcast by ABC.

Among the first truly national sport broadcasters, Gowdy was accepted by millions of fans as a neutral commentator rather than a partisan cheerleader. He won numerous honors, including the prestigious George Foster Peabody Award for broadcasting excellence in 1970. By the late 1970s, however, Gowdy's heavy workload led critics to charge that he was no longer adequately prepared when he stepped behind the microphone. After leaving NBC in 1979, he was elected to the broadcasters' section of the National Baseball Hall of Fame in 1984 and the Pro Football Hall of Fame in 1993.

—*Tim Ashwell*

See also: Allen, Mel; Radio Broadcasting; Television, Impact on Sport

For further reading:
Smith, Curt. 1998. *Of Mikes and Men: From Ray Scott to Curt Gowdy; Broadcast Tales from the Pro Football Booth.* South Bend, IN: Diamond Communications.

GRETZKY, WAYNE (1961–)

Wayne Gretzky's trade to the Los Angeles Kings in 1988 heightened interest in hockey throughout the United States and enhanced the celebrity status he had achieved as the most dominant player in National Hockey League (NHL) history.

The NHL's all-time leading scorer, Gretzky's combination of athleticism, attractiveness, and charisma made him a nationally known figure before his trade to Los Angeles from Edmonton, Alberta. Gretzky shattered goal-scoring records and led the Edmonton Oilers to four Stanley Cup championships. His dominance of the game earned him *Sports Illustrated*'s Sportsman of the Year Award in 1982 and a spot on the cover of *Time* magazine. Gretzky's celebrity status transcended the sporting world as he guest-starred on the soap opera *The Young and the Restless,* had his portrait painted by Andy Warhol, and married actress Janet Jones.

Edmonton Oilers team captain Wayne Gretzky lifts the Stanley Cup high over his head after the Oilers beat the New York Islanders, 5-2, to win the 1984 Stanley Cup series.
(BETTMANN/CORBIS)

The trade to Los Angeles sparked outrage in his native Canada, where Gretzky had been long established as a national hero. However, the perpetually anemic Kings were revitalized by Gretzky's presence, and interest in the team reached unprecedented levels. Hollywood stars flocked to rinkside as Kings games, like those of the National Basketball Association's Los Angeles Lakers, became social events and not just sporting contests.

This aura of excitement spread throughout the United States. The Walt Disney Corporation purchased an NHL expansion franchise for Anaheim, California, and the Mighty Ducks, named after a Disney movie of the same name, were born.

Within a decade of Gretzky's move to California, NHL franchises had taken root in Florida, Texas, Colorado, and Arizona, and the NHL had signed a deal with the Fox Television Network, which was to provide the league with the national television exposure it had long sought.

—*Daryl Baswick*

See also: National Hockey League

For further reading:
Podnieks, Andrew. 1999. *The Great One: The Life and Times of Wayne Gretzky.* Chicago: Triumph Books.

GRIFFITH JOYNER, FLORENCE
(1959–1998)

Recognized globally for her colorful and unusual attire and her six-inch fingernails, Florence Griffith Joyner was the fastest female sprinter who ever lived, breaking records in two events and becoming the first woman in forty years to win three gold medals and one silver medal in a single Olympics. Dubbed "Flo-Jo" by the media but preferring to be called "Dee Dee," a nickname given to her by her mother, Florence Joyner was as well known for her vibrancy, beauty, and uniqueness as she was for her running. Often, she would appear at competitions in multicolored, skintight running ensembles, occasionally with one leg covered and one leg bare. Eventually, she became a designer and model of her own line of sportswear.

After a rigorous training schedule—which daily included a 3.7-mile run, a thousand sit-ups, and weight training—she achieved her ultimate goal of becoming the world's fastest woman in the Seoul Olympic Games in 1988. During that competition, she broke the world record for the 200-meter race and the Olympic record in the 100-meter dash, bringing home three gold medals for the United States team. She was inducted into the U.S. Track-and-Field Hall of Fame in 1995.

As an outspoken advocate for children and a positive role model for girls and young women in

American sprinter Florence Griffith Joyner waves to the crowd after setting an Olympic record in the 100-meter dash at the 1988 Summer Olympics in Seoul, South Korea (September 24, 1988).
(BETTMANN/CORBIS)

sport, Joyner was appointed cochair of the President's Council on Physical Fitness and Sports upon her retirement from competition. She held that position, as well as running her own nail-kit firm and coaching children on behalf of the youth foundation bearing her name, until her death in 1998. Bill Hybl, president of the U.S. Olympic Committee, said her legacy includes kindness and an interest in children.

—*Joyce Duncan*

See also: Olympic Games

For further reading:

Aaseng, Nathan. 1989. *Florence Griffith Joyner: Dazzling Olympian*. Minneapolis, MN: Lerner.

Griffith Joyner, Florence and John Hanc. 1999. *Running for Dummies*. Foreword by Jackie Joyner-Kersee. Foster City, CA: IDG Books.

HAMILTON, SCOTT SCOVELL
(1958–)

"Figure skater extraordinaire" best describes the multitalented entertainer, Stars on Ice showman, and television sport commentator Scott Hamilton, who during the 1980s became one of America's best-known and best-loved athletes through both his natural talent and his personal courage in fighting adversity. Hamilton's life story is well known to most sport enthusiasts. Ernest Hamilton and Dorothy Hamilton, professors at Bowling Green University, adopted him at an early age, and at about the age of two, he contracted a mysterious illness that caused him to stop growing. After undergoing several years of treatment, Hamilton was misdiagnosed as having cystic fibrosis and was given six months to live.

Refusing to accept the medical prediction, his parents took the child to a variety of doctors and specialists, finally admitting him to Boston's Children's Hospital, where the illness began to correct itself through special diet and moderate exercise. During his recovery, Hamilton became interested in ice-skating and showed great potential and a natural ability for the sport. He took formal lessons and even joined a hockey team. Within a year, his illness had disappeared completely, and the young man began growing again, although he would remain small. His recovery was attributed to the effects of intense physical activity in the cold atmosphere of the rink.

During the late 1970s, Hamilton's skating lessons and training paid off, and he won or placed in several regional and national amateur competitions. By 1980, he was good enough to place third in national competition and secured a berth on the U.S. Olympic squad for the winter games held in Lake Placid, New York, where he placed fifth in the overall men's competition. From there, he won three more consecutive national and world titles, as well as the gold medal at the 1984 Winter Olympics in Sarajevo, Yugoslavia.

Later that year, Hamilton turned professional and began what has become one of the most lucrative careers in ice-skating. He starred in the Ice Capades of 1984–1986, the Stars on Ice tour of 1986–1987, and the Discover Stars on Ice tour from 1987–1997. He has also produced several notable television specials. In 1987, the skater was presented the Olympic Spirit Award by the U.S. Olympic Committee for best exemplifying the ideal athlete of the 1984 Winter Olympic Games, and in 1998, he became one of only four recipients of the Jacques Favart Award, the highest recognition of merit presented by the International Skating Union. Easily the most entertaining crowd-pleaser of the ice-skating stars of his generation, Hamilton has an extraordinary repertoire of skills that include fancy footwork, triple jumps, speed, and virtuoso stunts, including a back flip.

Since 1985, Hamilton has served as the CBS Sports color commentator for figure skating and was the figure skating analyst for the coverage of the Olympic Winter Games in 1992 in Albertville, France; in 1994 in Lillehammer, Norway; and in 1998 in Nagano, Japan. Knowledge of the sport and thoughtful remarks are his notable trademarks.

The sport world was saddened when Hamilton was diagnosed with testicular cancer in March 1997 but was soon able to rejoice when, following twelve weeks of successful chemotherapy treatments and surgery and six weeks of recuperation, the irrepressible Hamilton was back on the ice, rehearsing for his twelfth season of Discover Stars on Ice. Because of his personal high standards of excellence and achievement, Hamilton has outlasted many of his fellow competitors. Any viewer can tell by watching as he performs that he truly loves the sport and is willing to give his all so that the audience is ultimately the winner.

—*Stephen Allen Patrick*

See also: Olympic Games

For further reading:

Hamilton, Scott, and Lorenzo Benet. 1999. *Landing It: My Life On and Off the Ice.* New York: Kensington Publishing.

Wilner, Barry, and Scott Hamilton. 1998. *Stars on Ice: An Intimate Look at Skating's Greatest Tour.* Kansas City, MO: Andrews McMeel.

HANDBALL

Handball is an internationally popular court game played on college campuses, in athletic clubs, in health clubs, in YMCA gyms, and on playgrounds. Nurtured in the late-nineteenth-century United States by the Amateur Athletic Union (AAU), the game gained popularity in the last decades of the twentieth century.

Several games are known as handball; they are all played by hitting a small, hard rubber ball with the hand, bare or gloved, against one to four walls of an enclosed court. Competitions are held for men—both amateur and professional—women, boys, and girls, in singles or doubles. The object of the game is to hit the ball so it rebounds at an angle difficult or impossible for the opponent to return. Handball originated in ancient Rome as *expulsim ludere,* was popular in Ireland by 1200, and was known as *pelota* in fifteenth-century Spain and France. By 1700, English public school students at Eton and Rugby called the game "fives," and by 1763, fives was played in North America.

In the 1880s, handball in its modern version, wherein players wore thin leather gloves, traveled from Ireland to North America. An Irish immigrant, Philip Casey, built the first American handball court in Brooklyn, New York, in 1883 and was the U.S. champion from 1887 to 1900. New rules standardized the court dimensions at 65 feet long and 25 feet wide, with a 30-foot front wall and two 25-foot side walls. Michael Eagan, another Irish immigrant, won the first handball championship under the auspices of the AAU in Jersey City, New Jersey, in 1897. Handball thus became an entrée into sport for many immigrants who were otherwise excluded from organized competition.

When the Spalding Company published authoritative rules for the sport in 1903, firefighters, police officers, and copper miners were among the only devotees. The game was always more common in working-class urban neighborhoods than were the more-elite sports, such as squash or tennis.

By 1970, handball was somewhat overshadowed by racquetball, but the proliferation of health clubs in the 1980s increased the appeal of handball on the newly built racquetball courts. Although the U.S. Handball Association (USHA) was formed in 1952, the group did not grow significantly until the 1990s, when it included six million handball aficionados. By the end of the twentieth century, handball, played on a smaller court with four walls and using a smaller and softer rubber ball, was popular around the world.

—*Peter C. Holloran*

See also: Amateur Athletic Union; Immigrants, Community and Sport

For further reading:
Haber, Paul. 1970. *Inside Handball.* Chicago: Contemporary Books.

HARLEM GLOBETROTTERS

Presenting a mixture of slapstick comedy and finely tuned athleticism, the basketball-playing Harlem Globetrotters were a force in public entertainment for decades. Called the Houdinis of the Hardcourt, the Globetrotters amassed a winning streak that encompassed twenty-four years and 8,829 games, broken only once, in 1995, by an all-star team headed by Kareem Abdul-Jabbar.

In 1993, the team was purchased from a financially ailing International Broadcasting Company (IBC) for $6 million. The purchaser was Mannie Jackson, one of the wealthiest black executives in the country, and the acquisition of the Globetrotters made him the only African American majority owner of a professional sport franchise. Not only was IBC in financial ruin, but the franchise was also struggling. There had been some negative press surrounding some of the key team members; the Continental Basketball Association and the European professional leagues were recruiting the best of the second tier African American players.

Jackson added to the family comedy fare of established routines, like the water-bucket gag and trick ball, replaced the roster of players, updated the music, added a team mascot, Globie, and resurrected touring, thus also resurrecting the Globetrotters' reputation. One of his major changes to the roster was the addition of Lynette

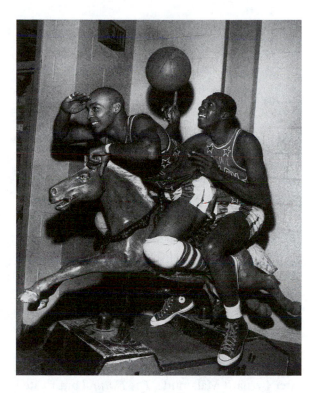

Freddie Neal and Meadowlark Lemon (behind) were off to a flying start as the Harlem Globetrotters opened their 40th season. Freddie is looking ahead for opponents while Meadowlark twirls a ball in complete relaxation. The Globetrotters entered the season with a 1,059-game winning streak against only 322 defeats (October 26, 1965).
(BETTMANN/CORBIS)

Woodard, the first woman Globetrotter, who was hired in 1985. In addition, he acquired the corporate sponsorship of major companies, such as Northwest Airlines, Sony, and Apple. Image became Jackson's primary mission, and he required his team to deal with socially relevant issues, to talk to young people about their lifestyles, and to participate in charity fund-raisers. Due to the vaudeville-type antics employed by the team, they made the sport of basketball intriguing to a wider audience.

—*Joyce Duncan*

See also: Abdul-Jabbar, Kareem; Basketball

For further reading:
Butler, Robbie. 2002. *The Harlem Globetrotters: Clown Princes of Basketball.* Mankato, MN: Capstone Press.

HARRIS, MARK (1922–)

Mark Harris's Henry Wiggen tetralogy played a significant role in shaping the modern sport novel. More specifically, the second of the four novels, *Bang the Drum Slowly* (1956), through its adaptation to the big screen, paved the way for the treatment of serious subject matter in conjunction with stories about athletes and sport. Harris wrote four novels in the voice of left-handed pitcher Henry Wiggen, tracing Wiggen's life from his first to his last professional season. The first Wiggen book, *The Southpaw* (1953), appeared one year after Bernard Malamud's *The Natural* but treated baseball in realistic and vernacular terms rather than representing the sport as America's mythology. *Bang the Drum Slowly* followed and was adapted originally for television in 1956 with Paul Newman and George Peppard in starring roles. In 1973, the story was filmed for the big screen, starring Robert De Niro and Michael Moriarty. The film preceded a cinematic interpretation of *The Natural* by eleven years and remains one of the most powerful and highly regarded sport movies.

Ticket for a Seamstitch (1957) and *It Looked Like Forever* (1979) rounded out the Wiggen books, but Harris also wrote about car racing in *Speed* (1990). His essay "Horatio at the Bat, or Why Such a Lengthy Embryonic Period for the Serious Baseball Novel?" is an important contribution to the field of sport literature and locates his own work in relation to the Horatio Alger, Ring Lardner, and vernacular traditions in U.S. literature. His work as a whole is considered innovative and a substantial contribution to the genre.

—*Kevin Brooks*

See also: Literature, Sport in; Malamud, Bernard

For further reading:
Harris, Mark. 1989. *It Looked Like Forever.* Lincoln: University of Nebraska Press.

HEALTH, POTENTIAL NEGATIVE IMPACT OF SPORT ON

Since the mid-1950s, a primary concern in the United States has been the health and well-being of its citizens, particularly its children. Studies conducted in the middle of the twentieth century concluded that the majority of the population had poor dietary habits and were not getting sufficient exercise to maintain optimum health. Following that revelation, education systems increased athletic programs and the number of mandatory classes in physical education.

The concern persisted for decades, culminating in the fitness craze of the 1980s and 1990s. Experts' recommendations trickled down from the school systems to the general population, and exercise became highly advised for all segments of the population, and urban gyms, jogging tracks, and tennis and racquetball courts flourished in every corner of the nation.

With the persistent interest in exercise, one might expect general health to have improved. However, later studies determined that not all exercise is healthy. Many took their interest in fitness to an extreme, engaging in exercise routines beyond their body's capability or becoming so wrapped up in body image that they became the victims of eating disorders or body-enhancing drugs like steroids.

Sport can be rated according to the physical demands made on muscles, lungs, and hearts, ranging from a fairly passive low end, such as pitching horseshoes or fishing, to high-impact sports such as the decathlon or marathoning. Even a seemingly physically harmless sport like golf can be damaging to health if one becomes emotionally exhausted from tension caused by not meeting one's expectations on the course. In addition, certain outdoor sports, like fishing, which exposes the participant to fresh air and sunshine, can occasionally cause either an increase in appetite or heat exhaustion and dehydration.

In formal athletic programs sponsored by educational institutions, one can expect that frequent injuries will occur. In sports, such as football, soccer, or hockey, these injuries can be serious and are occasionally fatal, especially if they involve damage to the neck or spinal cord.

—*Joyce Duncan*

See also: President's Council on Physical Fitness and Sports; Urban Gymnasiums

For further reading:
Kolata, Gina. 2003. *Ultimate Fitness: The Quest for Truth about Health and Exercise.* New York: Farrar, Straus and Giroux.

HEISMAN TROPHY

Awarded annually to the best college football player, the Heisman Trophy, though frequently the focus of controversy, has become synonymous with outstanding individual achievement. Named after player, coach, and steward of the game John W. Heisman (pronounced "Hise-man," not "Hize-man"), the Heisman Trophy was first awarded by the Downtown Athletic Club (DAC) of New York City in 1935 to the University of Chicago's Jay Berwanger. Then as now, the only guideline stipulated was that the award be presented to "the most outstanding player in college football." Ironically, Heisman, who always viewed football as the consummate team game, originally opposed such an award for individual recognition. However, he relented, to the overwhelming support of the

The Heisman Memorial Trophy is awarded annually to the outstanding college football player in the United States. (DUOMO/CORBIS)

club's membership, who subsequently commissioned perhaps the most recognizable trophy in all of amateur athletics, a leather-helmeted player, carrying the ball in his left arm and sidestepping an imaginary opponent while stiff-arming another.

Over the years, the DAC has awarded the Heisman to some of the game's greatest players, in the process making it a cultural icon for individual success. The award received perhaps its greatest exposure in a gesture that Heisman himself would have approved, when 1973 winner John Cappelletti of Penn State re-awarded the trophy to his thirteen-year-old brother, Joey, who was dying of leukemia. Cappelletti's gesture later became the subject of the movie *Something for Joey* (1977).

However, the trophy's ambiguous guidelines have left room for criticism in that it has always gone to a player from Division I-A, only one defensive player has ever received it, and only twice has it gone to a player from a losing team.

—*Kurt Edward Kemper*

See also: Football

For further reading:
Bynum, Mike. 1994. *The Best There Ever Was: The History of the Heisman Memorial Trophy and the Men Who Made It Famous.* Atlanta, GA: Gridiron Football Publishing.

> *The Heisman Trophy is annually presented to "the most outstanding player in college football." Ironically, Heisman, who always viewed football as the consummate team game, originally opposed such an award for individual recognition.*

HEMINGWAY, ERNEST
(1899–1961)

One of the most influential prose writers in U.S. literature, Ernest Hemingway related his own experiences as a record-holding deep-sea fisherman, amateur boxer, expert big-game hunter, and bullfight aficionado. Extolling the virtues of honor, dignity, courage, and endurance, Hemingway's characters *defined* the idea of "grace under pressure."

Born in Oak Park, Illinois, Hemingway had a "normal" childhood—hunting, fishing, playing high school football, and writing for the school paper. Deciding against college, in addition to indulging his abiding interest in sport, he spent time as a reporter, a volunteer ambulance driver in World War I, a war correspondent, a partisan freedom fighter, a submarine chaser, and an expatriate.

A major underlying theme of Hemingway's works addresses the notion of how the individual deals with adversity. Whether on the battlefield, in a bullfighting ring, on the Serengeti Plain, or in a small fishing dinghy in the Caribbean, his characters, both men and women, often face trials on their own. Even if they lose, if they show dignity and courage, the battle proves to be worthwhile.

Hemingway's 1952 Pulitzer Prize–winning work, *The Old Man and the Sea,* offers perhaps the best example of this ideal. In this work, an old Cuban fisherman, scoffed at because of recent bad luck, sets out in his small boat. He hooks, fights for two days and nights, and finally lands a monster marlin—a fish that will reclaim his honor. Unfortunately, sharks attack the carcass, and despite the old man's heroic efforts, it is reduced to a mere skeleton. Undaunted, the old man takes solace in the fight well fought.

Thematically similar works include his books *The Sun Also Rises* (1926) and *Death in the Afternoon* (1932) on bullfighting, *Green Hills of Africa* (1935) and "The Snows of Kilimanjaro" (1936) on hunting, and *A Farewell to Arms* (1929) and *For Whom the Bell Tolls* (1940) on war.

—*Steve Legrand*

See also: Athletes as Symbolic Heroes; Blood Sport; Bullfighting; Men's Issues; Sport Literature as Discipline

For further reading:
Hemingway, Ernest. 1998. *By-Line, Ernest Hemingway:*

Selected Articles and Dispatches of Four Decades.
Edited by William White. New York: Touchstone.
————. 1999. *Ernest Hemingway on Writing.* Edited by
Larry W. Phillips. New York: Touchstone.

HIGHLAND GAMES

Highland games are expressions of a Scottish heritage that reinforce a collective ethnic identity among participants. Highland games have their roots in local festivals that have been held each fall in the Scottish Highlands since at least the seventeenth century. When Scots immigrated to North America during the eighteenth and nineteenth centuries, they brought the highland traditions with them. Some of the festivals continued on a local level during the nineteenth century, but they became increasingly popular in the 1920s as Americans developed interest in and began to celebrate their Scottish roots. Today, these events, usually including a "Gathering of the Clans," last several days and attract thousands of participants and observers who enjoy traditional Scottish music, dance, food, and sport.

Highland games revolve around sports that test physical strength. The most famous is the caber toss, in which participants attempt to throw a twenty-two-foot-long tapered spruce pole end over end so that it lands perpendicular to the ground. The hammer throw challenges athletes to toss a sixteen-pound steel hammer as

The Grandfather Mountain games in Linville, North Carolina. Highland games usually include a "Gathering of the Clans," last several days, and attract thousands of participants and observers who enjoy traditional Scottish music, dance, food, and sport.
(COURTESY OF JOYCE D. DUNCAN)

The Grandfather Mountain games in Linville, North Carolina. This event involves throwing a fifty-six-pound weight as far as possible with one hand.
(COURTESY OF JOYCE D. DUNCAN)

far as possible while remaining somewhat stationary. Another event involves throwing a fifty-six-pound weight as far as possible with one hand.

Individual festivals have variations in events and rules. Some have recently begun to host cross-country foot races and other less-traditional forms of competition. Whatever form they take, Highland games use sport to celebrate the richness of traditional Scottish culture and to commemorate the contributions of Scots to North American society.

—*Richard D. Starnes*

See also: Immigrants, Community and Sport

For further reading:
Donaldson, Emily Ann. 1986. *The Scottish Highland Games in America.* Gretna, LA: Pelican.

HOCKEY

Although there are some who feel that hockey personifies the violence in organized sport, it is the national game in Canada and has impacted every geographical location in the U. S. Once a regional game played only in cold climates, ice hockey has spread across the continent and has gained in popularity with North American athletes and sport fans. Hockey is a game played on ice in which two teams of five skaters use curved sticks to propel a rubber disk, or puck, down the ice with the object of lobbing it into a small goal guarded by a sixth teammate. The origins of this sport are obscure, but a number of rival claims compete for the honor of having invented hockey. The game probably evolved from a similar but unstructured game called "shinney" played widely across Canada in the mid-nineteenth century. In 1875, a student at McGill University in Montreal drew up a set of rules that were quickly copied across the country with minor local variations. By the 1890s, hockey was played in virtually all parts of Canada.

By the end of the nineteenth century, U.S. sportsmen became acquainted with the game. The most commonly repeated claims for the first game in the United States cite either a match at Johns Hopkins University in 1893 or one at Yale in 1894. In December 1893, an all-star team of players from Brown, Yale, and Harvard visited Toronto to play local college teams with alternating Canadian and U.S. rules. Although the "U.S. rules" may have been for ice polo, all three schools were thus introduced to Canadian hockey at once. By 1895, organized clubs began regular play in New York, and hockey quickly spread to other northeastern communities.

Initially, hockey was embroiled in disputes between amateurism and professionalism. Early teams in both Canada and the United States were amateur clubs; however, they occasionally resorted to paying "ringers" under the table to ensure successful seasons. As early as 1900, Cana-

Calgary Flames right winger Jarome Iginla (left) scores on Tampa Bay Lightning goaltender Nikolai Khabibulin during third period action in game three of the Stanley Cup Finals in Calgary, Alberta, on May 29, 2004. The Flames defeated the Lightning 3-0, taking a 2-1 game lead in the series.
(JEFF VINNICK/POOL/REUTERS/CORBIS)

dian newspapers reported local players were being lured to the United States to play professionally. In 1907, three Canadian players on a New York amateur team were suspended for "rough play," an occasional euphemism for the professional game. Indeed, the first openly professional league, operating in northern Michigan and Pennsylvania from 1904 to 1907, tolerated violent transgressions of the official rules.

Women's hockey, on the other hand, has not been characterized by violence. Women have been playing hockey since at least 1889, and prior to World War I, women's contests were often as popular with Canadian spectators as were men's. Initially, many people felt that hockey was too vigorous an activity for the "fairer sex," but women enthusiasts pressed for ice time and, in some cases, built their own rinks. Although women's play declined in the middle decades of the twentieth century, the sport has enjoyed renewed interest among female players.

Migrating northeasterners brought hockey with them to the Sunbelt cities of the United States in the 1980s and 1990s. With accompanying advances in artificial-ice technology, first used in

> *A cult of violence surrounds hockey in both Canada and the United States, accentuated by national rivalries and collective anxieties.*

1895, ice hockey broke out of its cold-weather limitations. This expansion, coupled with international success for U.S. teams, helped raise the sport's profile in the United States.

—Alan Gordon

See also: Hockey, Mythology of; Hockey Hall of Fame; National Hockey League

For further reading:

Falla, Jack, Jack Batten, Lance Hornby, et al. 2001. *Quest for the Cup: A History of the Stanley Cup Finals, 1893–2001.* San Diego, CA: Thunder Bay Press.

Howe, Colleen, and Gordie Howe. 1995. *And—Howe!: An Authorized Autobiography.* Traverse City, MI: Power Play Publications.

Robidoux, Michael A. 2001. *Men at Play: A Working Understanding of Professional Hockey.* Montreal: McGill-Queen's University Press.

HOCKEY, MYTHOLOGY OF

A cult of mythologized violence surrounds hockey in both Canada and the United States, accentuated by national rivalries and collective anxieties. Canadians have long felt a sense of proprietorship over hockey, arguing that the game was invented in Canada and that its best players have historically been Canadians. This confidence was shaken, but not broken, by the 1972 Summit Series between Canadian professional players and the national team from the Soviet Union, which Canada just won, scoring a goal in the final minute of play in the final game. In the 1990s, however, anxiety about "losing" the game was directed against the United States as U.S. players improved and Canadian-based National Hockey League (NHL) franchises moved to U.S. cities in 1994 and 1995. In fact, the proportion of Canadian teams in the NHL dropped to 23 percent of the total in 1997–1998 from a high of 38 percent in 1987–1988.

The potential for Canadian NHL expansion is limited. These developments have been portrayed as the inevitable outcome of market economics,

but they have also been seen, in Canada, as appropriation by the United States of Canada's game. Probably the greatest shock to the Canadian hockey psyche occurred when the Edmonton Oilers' Wayne Gretzky was transferred to the Los Angeles Kings in 1988. Many Canadians considered the transfer the selling of a national treasure and a crass commercialization of the national culture. Indeed, some of the most influential nonfiction writing about hockey in Canada laments the dual Americanization and commodification of the game.

On the other hand, many Americans continue to see ice hockey as a Canadian game. As U.S. television programming penetrates Canadian markets, producers often insert "inside" jokes for the benefit of Canadian audiences. This strategy frequently takes the form of references to hockey. For instance, in the first season of *Spin City,* the character of the New York City deputy mayor, portrayed by Canadian actor Michael J. Fox, kept a hockey stick in his office. In another example from the highly successful sitcom *Cheers,* the recurring character "Eddy" was a French-Canadian hockey player plying his trade in Boston.

Such favorable or quaint images have been overshadowed, however, by the perception of hockey as a violent game. In one episode of *Cheers,* a hockey player threatens to show an unlikable character how he "got suspended from the NHL." The "humor" of the situation depends on the audience's perception of hockey as a violent game overflowing with fighting.

Canadians generally emphasize that their brand of rough play develops character and is "just part of the game," but they have been quick to accuse European players of dirty tactics. Americans, on the other hand, have long associated rough play with Canadians. As early as 1907, the *New York Sun* newspaper fretted that the Canadian style would ruin the game. This image has long persisted. Paul Newman's feature film *Slap Shot* (1977) portrayed on-ice violence for comic effect. The film, replete with references to Canada, culminates in a "championship game" between Newman's team and an all-star squad of violent criminals from Canada. In response to this image, the NHL, which sees itself as the guardian of the game, has tried to minimize fighting in order to increase its U.S. audience.

—*Alan Gordon*

See also: Gretzsky, Wayne; Hockey; National Hockey League

For further reading:

Atkinson, Jay. 2001. *Ice Time: A Tale of Fathers, Sons and Hometown Heroes.* New York: Crown.

Freeberg, Lloyd. 1998. *In the Bin: Reckless and Rude Stories from the Penalty Boxes of the NHL.* Chicago: Triumph Books.

HOCKEY HALL OF FAME

The Hockey Hall of Fame preserves for cultural memory the significant builders, broadcasters, players, and referees of the sport and signifies hockey's expanding intercorporate commercialism. The Hockey Hall of Fame grew out of a feeling of dislocation. During the dark days of World War II, Canadians sought a nostalgic return to stability, and hockey was at the nation's center. The Hall of Fame's founder J. T. Sutherland wanted to acknowledge those who made significant contributions to the game. In 1945, the first of the Hall's honored members were inducted, including U.S. player Hobey Baker.

However, there was no Hall to house these inductees, and following Sutherland's death in 1955, interest in constructing one waned. But with Canada aglow in postwar prosperity and with the help of Conn Smythe, interest was rekindled. In 1961, the Hall opened at Toronto's Canadian National Exhibition (CNE).

In 1993, under chairman Scotty Morrison, the Hall entered the corporate era. It moved from the CNE to the old Bank of Montreal building at the corner of Yonge and Front. Housed within

Canadian hockey great Wayne Gretzky (left), former NHL Director of Officiating Scotty Morrison (center), and former referee Andy Van Hellemond (right) stand with Hall of Fame sticks after their induction into the Hockey Hall of Fame in Toronto on November 22, 1999. (REUTERS/CORBIS)

Toronto's commercial core and rich shopping area, the Hall was a site surrounded by potential consumers. Unlike the National Baseball Hall of Fame in Cooperstown, New York, which has a detached, pastoral quality, the Hockey Hall of Fame is urban in its location and rhythms.

The Hockey Hall of Fame is interactive: At the Coca-Cola Rink Zone, fans become virtual goalies or forwards; at the TSN/RDS exhibit, fans can watch a simulated hockey broadcast from inside a mobile unit; and upstairs, in the Great Bell Hall, fans study National Hockey League trophies, including the Stanley Cup, which is stored in a bank vault, and tributes to the Hall's three hundred inductees. Moreover, like the hum of business in the city, corporate sponsorship—Bell Canada, Coca-Cola, TSN, and others—dominates the Hall's spectacle, suggesting the global synergies that have driven hockey's rapid growth since 1967.

—*Grant Tracey*

See also: Gretzky, Wayne; Hockey; National Hockey League; Orr, Robert Gordon "Bobby"

For further reading:
McKinley, Michael. 1996. *Legends of Hockey: The Official Book of the Hockey Hall of Fame.* Chicago: Triumph Books.

HOGAN, HULK
See Bollea, Terry Gene

HOGAN, WILLIAM BEN
(1912–1997)

American golfer Ben Hogan personified the stamina, stubbornness, and resiliency that characterizes so many American athletes. He became an icon for the work ethic by his devotion to routine, his mechanical precision, and his comeback from a near-fatal automobile accident. His message was simple: practice. Hogan began working as a caddie at the age of eleven and became a professional golfer at seventeen after he dropped out of school. Following a long and frustrating apprenticeship, he responded to his repeated failures by extending his practice to eight-hour days of hitting the ball. Due to his diligence, he was dominating the Professional Golfers' Association (PGA) tour by 1946.

In June 1948, Hogan won the first of his four U. S. Open tournaments; however, eight months later, an automobile accident shattered his legs. During his slow recovery, a movie about his life, *Follow the Sun,* starring Glenn Ford, was released in November 1949. Three months after the movie opened, a limping and gaunt Hogan returned for

the opening PGA event of 1950, the Los Angeles Open, but he lost to Sam Snead in the play-offs. Hogan emerged as an appealing underdog whose fans accepted and even admired his icy, stoic, self-absorbed, and loner ways. That summer, he won the U.S. Open again. After a prolonged putting slump in 1951–1952, he had his finest year in 1953, winning the Masters Tournament and the U.S. and British Opens; he did not enter the fourth tournament, the PGA, because its extended match-play format was too much for his legs.

Hogan's mystique rests on his devotion to practice; his book *Ben Hogan's Five Lessons: The Modern Fundamentals* (1957), the bible of the golf swing; and his white hat, impeccable wardrobe, and cold stare. Image aside, Hogan's competitive record, nine majors with sixty-three wins overall, behind only Sam Snead and Jack Nicklaus, in a career interrupted by a World War II tour in the army and a crippling auto accident, speaks for itself.

—*Patrick K. Dooley*

See also: Golf; Professional Golfers' Association

For further reading:
Sampson, Curt. 2001. *Hogan.* Nashville, TN: Rutledge Hill Press.

HOME-RUN RACE OF 1998

In 1998, Mark McGwire and Sammy Sosa shattered baseball's record for home runs hit in a single season, leading millions of fans back to the game after a disastrous player strike in the 1994–1995 season had eroded fan loyalty to the sport. Not since Babe Ruth of the New York Yankees crushed fifty-four home runs in 1920 had there been such an obliteration of the single-season home-run record, possibly the most emotionally charged record in U.S. sport. Ruth, who broke his own previous record of twenty-nine home runs by a margin of twenty-five in 1920, held the record for another forty-one years, setting new

In the first inning, St. Louis Cardinals' Mark McGwire watches his 65th home run of the year off Chicago Cubs pitcher Steve Trachsel on October 3, 1999, at Busch Stadium in St. Louis. McGwire won the home-run title, beating Cubs' Sammy Sosa by two home runs.
(REUTERS/CORBIS)

marks of fifty-nine in 1921 and sixty in 1927. Because of its association with Ruth, the home-run record came to stand for raw power and masculine excess.

When Roger Maris of the Yankees hit sixty-one home runs in 1961, many resented the displacement of Babe Ruth from the record books. Maris's record was explained away as a function of expansion in baseball before the 1961 season.

Some suggested that the record be marked with an asterisk to explain that it took Maris 162 games to achieve what Ruth had achieved in 154. Maris, a private man, was tortured by the publicity that accompanied his record chase. The prevailing ethos of 1961 prohibited him from showing emotion after his home runs. Though the mystique of his record was considerable, Maris became a marginal figure in baseball history, and as of 1998, he had not been elected to the National Baseball Hall of Fame.

By contrast, the 1998 home-run race was a lovefest. When Mark McGwire of the St. Louis Cardinals finished the 1997 season with fifty-eight home runs and Ken Griffey Jr. of the Seattle Mariners hit fifty-six to lead the American League that year, commentators predicted that Maris's record would fall in 1998. True to form, McGwire hit a home run in each of his first four games in 1998 and added three more in a game on April 14 to move five weeks ahead of Maris's 1961 pace. He never fell behind. On September 8, McGwire hit his sixty-second home run in his 144th game and finished the year with an astonishing seventy home runs. That year was, like 1961, an expansion season, but the scale of McGwire's accomplishment prevented anyone from denigrating his record.

Meanwhile, Sammy Sosa of the Chicago Cubs, after hitting just six home runs in April and seven in May, hit an unprecedented twenty home runs in June, still remaining well behind McGwire. He caught McGwire—only momentarily—later in the season, but he challenged him all the way. Sosa finished the season with a total of sixty-six home runs. Griffey, touted by many as the most likely person to break Maris's record, finished with a second consecutive year of fifty-six home runs, but McGwire and Sosa generally obscured his achievement.

Small controversies detracted from the race. McGwire was criticized for using a legal diet supplement to build muscles and overcome minor injuries. Some observers felt that McGwire, a white American, got more attention from the media than did Sosa, a black man from the Dominican Republic. Fans competed for possession of the baseballs that the pair hit, including a fistfight on the streets of Chicago over Sosa's sixty-second home-run ball.

The dominant note, however, was one of love for and a revival of interest in the sport. As the National Basketball Association succumbed to labor strife in the summer of 1998, baseball reveled in the exploits of McGwire and Sosa. The two openly supported each other. Sosa, who was playing the field when McGwire hit his sixty-second home run, ran to McGwire and hugged him. Expressions of delight from both players helped redefine an image of baseball as a children's game and stood in stark contrast to the impassivity imposed on Roger Maris as he strove to break the same record thirty-seven years earlier.

—*Timothy Morris*

See also: Baseball; "Boys of Summer"; Ruth, George Herman "Babe," Jr.

For further reading:

McNeil, William F. 1999. *Ruth, Maris, McGwire and Sosa: Baseball's Single Season Home Run Champions.* Jefferson, NC: McFarland.

Verdi, Bob. 1998. *They Went Yard: McGwire and Sosa; An Awesome Home Run Season.* Chicago: Bonus Books.

HOMO LUDENS

Homo Ludens: A Study of the Play Element in Culture by Johan Huizinga is an articulation of the concept of *homo ludens*—humans at play—and represents a theory of the place and significance of play in human culture. *Homo Ludens* is, in essence, an extended argument that play is one of the main foundations of civilization and that it is actually the ludic, or playful, aspect of human beings that sets us apart and allows us to move beyond mere survival to achieve a level of civilization. Games are one manifestation of the play element in culture but are subsumed within the sphere and definition of play.

According to Huizinga, all play occurs within a sphere marked off beforehand, either materially or ideally, either deliberately or as a matter of course. Following this line of reasoning, he sees the arena, the card table, the magic circle, the temple, the stage, the screen, the tennis court, the court of justice, and other spheres of human endeavor as forms of playgrounds, functioning as isolated and enclosed spheres with their own set of rules. These are all temporary worlds within the larger world, dedicated to specific functions, but in their entirety they also constitute the sum of human activity. Thus, all aspects of human civilization are extensions of the play element, governed by special rules and played in specific areas. The definition of play is broad enough to encompass all of human society.

—*Dale Jacobs*

See also: *Arête;* Playground Association of America

For further reading:

Caillois, Roger. 2001. *Man, Play and Games.* Urbana: University of Illinois Press.

Huizinga, Johan. 1970. *Homo Ludens: A Study of the Play Element in Culture.* London: Maurice Temple Smith Ltd.

HOMOSEXUALITY AND SPORT

Homosexuality functions in sport in the same way it functions in the culture that produced sport: It exists, but it is not discussed. Professional athletic organizations do not want to be associated with homosexuality; hence, homosexual men and women do not, by and large, reveal their sexual orientation. This lack of disclosure creates and perpetuates the idea that there are no gay people participating in professional sport. *New York Times* columnist Degen Pener writes, "To say that gay men simply aren't welcome in the world of big league sports is an enormous understatement" (quoted in *Gay Almanac* 1996).

Stereotypes of homosexual men as effeminate and noncompetitive also work to keep intact the idea that gay men do not participate in sport. On the other hand, the short but impressive list of male athletes who have come out publicly exposes the truth: David Kopay, former National Football League (NFL) running back; Bruce Hayes,

Olympic swimmer; Bob Jackson-Paris, Mr. America and Mr. Universe; Justin Fashanu, soccer player; Dave Pallone, major league umpire; and Greg Louganis, Olympic diver.

Women's sport carries the same prejudices. The stereotype of homosexual women as strong does not serve them well in women's sport. Even in professionally competitive settings, women are still not supposed to be too strong or too competitive, characteristics this culture considers to be masculine attributes. Tennis star Martina Navratilova was the first woman athlete to reveal her orientation while still active in her sport.

Homosexuality is problematic in male athletic communities because it is associated with femininity. Femininity is perceived in these communities as weak and passive, and these are not qualities thought of as desirable in male athletic competitions. In effect, because of the excessive fear about disclosing one's sexual orientation, gay men and lesbians have, in recent years, developed professional and nonprofessional sport organizations, like the Gay Games, in which they can participate without fear of ostracism or physical punishment. Ed Gallagher, a football star for the University of Pittsburgh in the 1970s, was unable to reconcile his homosexuality and his sport. He attempted suicide by throwing himself from a bridge; the fall did not kill him but rendered him paraplegic.

David Kopay was the first professional U.S. athlete to reveal his homosexuality. His book, *The David Kopay Story: An Extraordinary Revelation* (1977), remained, until 1990, the sole autobiographical representation of a gay professional athlete who made his sexual orientation public knowledge.

According to the *Gay Almanac* (1996), no openly gay men or women have ever competed in National League football, basketball, hockey, or baseball, and no openly gay athlete has ever competed in the Olympics. In the late 1990s, there was a wide array of gay athletic associations, including ones for running, rodeos, swimming, and wrestling.

—*Tom Peele*

See also: Gay Games

For further reading:
The Gay Almanac. 1996. National Museum and Archive of Lesbian and Gay History: A Program of the Lesbian and Gay Community Services Center. New York: Berkley Books.
Kopay, David, and Perry Deane Young. 1977. *The David Kopay Story: An Extraordinary Self-Revelation.* New York : Arbor House.

HOUSTON ASTRODOME

The Astrodome illuminated Houston, Texas, building civic pride and exemplifying modernization. Judge Roy Hofheinz, the original owner of the major league baseball Houston Astros, billed the Houston Astrodome as the "Eighth Wonder of the World." Opening in 1965, the facility was the world's first indoor, air-conditioned stadium with AstroTurf, an artificial plastic grass developed especially for the Astrodome. The word "Astro-Turf" entered the U.S. language and culture, and the product became widely used in stadiums and on backyard patios.

During the 1960s and early 1970s, the Astrodome was one of ten multipurpose, state-of-the-art stadiums. The Astrodome led the way, having cushioned seats, fifty-three skyboxes, and a $2 million scoreboard. At the time, these cavernous, perfectly configured stadiums contrasted starkly with the decaying ballparks built before the Depression and situated amid the blight of the inner city; thus, they were considered models of progress and order.

The Astrodome exemplified Texas-sized boosterism during the post–World War II era of affluence, particularly in the developing Sunbelt region of the U.S. South. As an example, the scoreboard not only featured numerous statistics and cartoons but also, after a home run, flashed an electronic fireworks display, including shooting cowboys, ricocheting bullets, and a snorting steer upon which a mounted cowboy twirled a lariat.

On another level, the Astrodome also reflected a U.S. culture streamlined for fast food, express checkout, television sound bites, and Disney-like packaged, predictable entertainment for a mass audience. By the 1990s, many people had come to see these stadiums as a symbol of what was wrong with baseball and felt that the nostalgic feel for a game played in open air in irregularly shaped ballparks had been lost. This paved the way for the construction of retro-antique stadiums, such as the proposed $265 million Ballpark at Union Station in downtown Houston.

—*Stephen W. Charry*

See also: Big Business, Sport as; Stadiums; Economics of Sport

For further reading:
Doherty, Craig A., Katherine M. Doherty, and Nicole Bowman. 1996. *The Houston Astrodome: Building America.* Woodbridge, CT: Blackbirch Press.

HOWE, GORDON "GORDIE" (1928–)

Gordie Howe, "Mr. Hockey," is one of professional sport's great Iron Men, playing a total of thirty-one seasons in professional hockey and, in the process, defining North American hockey as a combination of skill and toughness. Howe began his professional career with the Detroit Red Wings of the National Hockey League (NHL) in 1946, and, as part of the "Production Line" with Sid Abel and Ted Linsey, he led the Red Wings to three Stanley Cups before retiring in 1970. Howe's loyalty to Jack Adams, general manager and coach of the Red Wings, thwarted the attempts of Linsey and other players to force owners to be more generous with and accountable for pension funds. Howe represented old-time hockey, concerned with the game, trusting of management, and, until later, naive about marketing.

Howe came out of retirement in 1973 to play the game with his sons, Mark and Marty, for the

Red Wings' Gordon Howe (right) is completely relaxed in the dressing room after scoring the 545th goal of his career during the second period of the Detroit-Montreal game on November 10, 1963. Howe is the sole holder of the record for most games played during a career in the National Hockey League: 1,767. At left is team captain Alex Delveccio. (BETTMANN/CORBIS)

Houston Aeros of the World Hockey Association (WHA), initiating one of the first and longest-lasting father-son relationships in professional sport. He returned to the NHL for one season, 1979–1980, when the two leagues merged, and four teams from the WHA, including Howe's Hartford Whalers, continued play in the NHL. He retired once more at the age of fifty-two, but in 1997, at the age of sixty-nine, he made a one-game comeback with the Syracuse Crunch of the American Hockey League (AHL) and firmly established himself as the Methuselah of professional sport.

—Kevin Brooks

See also: Hockey; World Hockey Association

For further reading:

MacSkimming, Roy. 1994. *Gordie: A Hockey Legend.* Vancouver, BC: Greystone Books.

HULA-HOOPS

The standard by which all other U.S. fads are measured, the Hula-Hoop occupies a rare position as a "toy" that is widely used in international sporting events. Arthur "Spud" Melin and Richard Knerr invented the Hula-Hoop for the Wham-O Corporation in 1958. It was modeled on wooden hoops that were widely used in Australian gym classes.

> The Hula-Hoop was the largest fad to sweep the United States and one of the first to start on the West Coast and spread to the East, the direction most fads have taken since. Within five months, sales reached over $30 million.

The movement needed to keep a hoop rotating around the hips appears simple. It does, however, take practice to master the skill. This seeming contradiction gave rise to a national and international desire to perfect the hip-swaying motion. Within months of its introduction to the market, the Hula-Hoop sparked both local and national Hula-Hooping contests. Throughout the balance of the twentieth century, competitors vied for world records for continuous rotations around the waist and for the number of hoops that could be set in simultaneous motion.

The toy was the largest fad to sweep the United States and one of the first to start on the West Coast and spread to the East, the direction most fads have taken since. Within five months, sales reached over $30 million. The Wham-O Corporation was unable to patent the product, however, and many companies produced imitations. Within four months of the introduction of the imitations, it was widely estimated that 25 million Hula-Hoops had been sold. The market became saturated, and with few ways to alter the product, sales fell. The fad did, however, spread to Europe and to Asia, and within a few years, sales had topped around 100 million Hula-Hoops.

The Hula-Hoop is also widely used in rhythmic gymnastic routines, where it is employed primarily in conjunction with high throws and complex catching techniques rather than for twirling around the hips. Although many toys, such as Hot Wheels and Nerf balls, serve as playful imitations of sporting objects, the Hula-Hoop is a toy that has become fully integrated into the international sporting arena.

—David P. O'Donnell

See also: Fads and Trends; Marketing of Sport

For further reading:

Asakawa, Gil, Leland Rucker, and Martha Kaplan. 1992. *The Toy Book: A Celebration of Slinky and G.I. Joe, Tinker Toys, Hula Hoops, Barbie Dolls, Snoot Flutes, Coon-Skin Caps, Slot Cars, Frisbees, Yo-Yos.* New York: Knopf.

HULL, ROBERT "BOBBY" MARVIN (1939–)

Bobby Hull, nicknamed the Golden Jet, possessor of a booming slap shot, and the first million-dollar player in hockey, was an integral part of the

A grinning Bobby Hull, forward for the Chicago Blackhawks, holds up a puck in the locker room following a game against the New York Rangers at Madison Square Garden. The puck Hull is holding is the one he launched past Ranger goalie Lorne Worsley, at the time making Hull only the third person in NHL history to score 50 goals in a season (March 25, 1962).

(BETTMANN/CORBIS)

modernization and expansion of hockey in North America. Hull began his professional career with the Chicago Blackhawks in 1957 and led his team to a Stanley Cup in 1961. His speed, power, and blond hair earned him his nickname, but he was also an innovator, on and off the ice. The sharply curved blade of his hockey stick contributed to the power and accuracy of his shot, and players ever since have used similar sticks. Off the ice, Hull and Bobby Hull Enterprises capitalized on product endorsements, ranging from automobiles to sportswear to a Bobby Hull table-hockey game.

In 1972, Hull was signed away from the Chicago Blackhawks by the Winnipeg Jets of the World Hockey Association to be the marquee player of the new league. Along with a $1.75 million contract over ten years, he received a million-dollar signing bonus. In 1974, he was put on the "Hot Line" with two Swedish players, Ulf Nilsson and Anders Hedberg, to form a scoring trio that rivaled the best of the National Hockey League. The success of the Hot Line ensured the further integration of European players into North American professional hockey and began the transformation of the game from a hard-hitting, close-checking game into a more wide-open, high-scoring event.

—*Kevin Brooks*

See also: National Hockey League; World Hockey Association

For further reading:

MacInnis, Craig, ed. 2001. *Remembering the Golden Jet: A Celebration of Bobby Hull.* Toronto and Niagara Falls, NY: Stoddart.

HUMOR IN SPORT

Sport humor tends to fall into two major categories based on the common person's capacity to participate in the sport. Sport fandom and sports such as golf and fishing, where participants tend to compete more against themselves than against other people, provide situations for self-deprecating humor, often at the expense of the absolute devotion enthusiasts display for those sports. Team sports, however, tend to draw humor from the differences between the "regular" people and the more-capable athletes. These themes appear throughout U.S. popular culture and suggest underlying prejudices in the popular perception of athletes.

Sympathy for the common person makes the self-deprecating sport humor gentler. It is simple to recognize the amiable disapproval in the host of jokes concerning sport fanatics whose sense of priority has shifted from the norm, so that they end up offending their family by watching televised football during Thanksgiving dinner or risking eternal damnation for fishing on Sunday instead of attending church services. The sitcom cliché of the new father bringing sporting equipment to his newborn's crib addresses the familiar aspirations the U.S. public has for themselves and their children. This desire to be better is evidenced in the comic strip *Peanuts* in Charlie Brown's repeated attempts to win a baseball game or to give a football one good kick. Such humor recognizes the playfulness inherent in sport and emphasizes that sport should be fun. The audience for this type of humor tends to identify with the butt of the joke.

This quality of mutual self-deprecation plays no significant role in the other major category of sport humor, which makes the accomplished athlete the subject of derisive jokes. This antagonistic sport humor has numerous varieties. One prominent theme suggests that accomplished athletes suffer some type of deficiency in other parts of their lives. For example, jokes about the "dumb jock" permit the audience to feel intellectually superior. Other such stereotype-perpetuating humor serves to alleviate the threat perceived by an insecure audience and can often reflect various forms of bigotry, including racism and sexism. This derisive humor also occurs between fans of long-standing rivals. In recent years, when more people have become aware of the hurtful nature of ethnic humor, some jokesters have replaced the ethnic element of the joke with a school affiliation.

Another prominent theme in antagonistic sport humor places the accomplished athlete in the position of a bully who enjoys victimizing the "regular guy" who attempts to succeed in sport. This theme generally takes one of two forms. In some instances, the novice athlete's skill startles the accomplished athlete, leading the accomplished athlete to cheat, unsuccessfully, providing humor from the novice's good fortune and the implication that the star has not fairly earned past accolades. More commonly, antagonistic sport humor features a "regular guy" or a team of misfits who compete against acknowledged champions. The audience's sympathy rests squarely with these outcasts, since, after all, the audience usually has more in common with the outcasts than with the athletic elite. Usually in this theme, the accomplished athletes demonstrate petty characteristics and exploit their athletic prowess to gain unfair advantages off the field as well. The audience is thus encouraged to view the champions' defeat as a moral victory as well as a sport victory for the underdog. This humor affirms the value of the "regular guy" and expresses the idea that wit, cunning, and determination can help anyone become a winner.

—*Thomas Alan Holmes*

See also: Cartoons and Sport; Comics and Sport; Popular Culture and Sport

For further reading:

Ebert, George. 1992. *Golf Is a Good Walk Spoiled.* Foreword by C. Grant Spaeth. Dallas, TX: Taylor Publishing.

Queenan, Joe. 2003. *True Believers: The Tragic Inner Life of Sports Fans.* New York: Henry Holt.

Tosches, Rich. 2002. *Zipping My Fly: Moments in the Life of an American Sportsman.* New York: Perigee.

HUNTING

Throughout America's early history, the sight of a successful hunter returning with game was a welcome event. However, the technological changes of the twentieth century and a curious transformation in cultural attitudes during the last generation have recently changed hunting from celebrated activity to controversial societal issue. The early hunting heritage of this country was predominantly utilitarian. Pioneers simply hunted for sustenance. As the nation developed, hunters supplied the marketplace with game. The challenges for these hunters were largely in understanding the biology of their prey and the local ecosystem, coupled with effective tactics and skilled weaponry. In modern urban culture, the formidable challenges also include diminishing access to land and increasing legislation and regulation, as well as active opposition.

The problem of access to land was previously solved by hunting in the expanses of the country and by gaining permission to hunt on private land. Increasing development and the proliferation of No Trespassing signs have significantly reduced potential hunting ground. Hunters protest that available public lands are scarce of game and abundant with hunting pressures. However, recent innovative programs, such as the Master Hunter Program (sponsored by Advanced Hunter Education in Oregon and Washington), are designed to reduce land-access problems by providing incentives for landowners to grant program graduates permission to hunt.

The issue of increasing regulation of hunters is probably the result both of shameful mistakes of the past and the adamancy of antihunting groups. Pioneers clearly contributed to striking reductions in waterfowl, near extinction of the buffalo, and extinction of the passenger pigeon. Subsequent generations participated in disgraceful slaughters of deer and pheasant. Contemporary hunters, on the other hand, have clearly emerged from this dubious past and are arguably the most important force in game management. Sportsmen contribute over $1.5 billion per year to wildlife conservation efforts, and over ten thousand private groups, such as Pheasants Forever and Ducks Unlimited, commit an additional $3 million per year to conservation. Despite the moneys these groups add to the ecological coffers, proposed legislative actions to eliminate various kinds of hunting have increased at an alarming rate and clutter congressional hallways and state ballot boxes.

For the most part, animal rights groups are the most active opponents of hunting. These groups tend to be well-organized, competent lobbyists and effective manipulators of the media whose arguments read like mission statements and slogans. In essence, antihunting groups argue that humans have evolved past the point of causing unnecessary animal suffering for the purposes of attaining food and clothing. Hunting, they contend, is disrespectful to nature and an expression of mindless aggression and violence; therefore, it perpetuates barbarism.

In contrast to the well-organized antihunting special-interest groups, hunting proponents are individualistic, unorganized for the most part, inactive, and quiet. Rebuttals of antihunting arguments are found primarily in specialty magazines, such as *Field and Stream, The American Hunter,* and *Sports Afield.* Specifically, hunting advocates contend that there has not been sufficient time for modern people to make significant evolutionary changes in mind or body from their Paleolithic ancestors, an argument supported by most behavioral psychologists. Hunting, they argue, is an instinctual behavior and is consistent with human evolution's determined niche as an opportunistic omnivore. Furthermore, a quick kill by a skilled hunter is preferable to the slow and torturous fates provided by Mother Nature or a captive life of exposure to hormones and preservatives. Finally, there is no evidence that hunters are more likely to commit violent crimes. In fact, because of the cooperation necessary among early bands of humans and the fact that hunting success in not equally divided, those who argue in favor of hunting contend there is an innate impulse for sharing and cooperation, rather than for killing and cruelty, among hunters.

The future of hunting in the United States stands in precarious balance. Legislation and regulation designed to erode one aspect or another of hunting rights are currently under consideration. In opposition, programs designed to provide for hunting rights have been formulated, such as the Fish and Wildlife Diversity Funding initiative (funded by state taxes and federal grants) and the Master Hunter Program. In contention are organized groups that will never support hunting and resolute individualistic hunters. Without active resistance to the restriction of hunting activities, the U.S. hunting culture will decay to restricted private gentlemen's hunt clubs and a once-essential American tradition will be eliminated.

—*Wayne S. Quirk*

See also: Boone and Crockett Club; National Rifle Association

For further reading:
Evans, Will F. 2001. *Hunting Grizzlys, Black Bear and Lions "Big Time" on the Old Ranches.* Silver City, NM: High Lonesome Books.
Hemingway, Ernest. 2001. *Hemingway on Hunting.* Edited and with an introduction by Séan Hemingway. Guilford, CT: Lyons Press.

IMMIGRANTS, COMMUNITY AND SPORT

Historically, immigrants used participation in sport both to preserve their cultural identities and to become assimilated into U.S. culture and society. Immigrants tended to settle in communities according to their ethnic origins, and the sports and games in which various nationalities engaged depended largely upon their acceptance into U.S. sporting society, the availability of facilities for sport in the community, income levels, and ethnic characteristics.

Beginning in the mid-nineteenth century, middle- and upper-class Americans excluded certain ethnic groups from participation in athletic clubs and sporting organizations and in the more popular sports. Nativist opposition to admitting the Irish into the "sporting fraternity," for example, resulted in their decades-long dominance in boxing, a sport that reflected the Irish propensity for more-violent athletic activities. In crowded slums that afforded little space for team sports, Irish pugilists found outlets for their athletic energies in gymnasiums and through occasional street or barroom fights. For some, boxing meant upward social mobility, acceptance in U.S. sporting society, escape from poverty, and the opportunity as ethnic heroes to promote Irish nationalism.

Lack of space also contributed to immigrant participation and proficiency in basketball, a sport in which Jewish and Irish newcomers excelled after the turn of the century. Pool halls and bowling alleys provided outlets for immigrants who sought competition and camaraderie without great physical exertion, and a game of handball required little more than a suitable vacant wall. Using neighborhood streets as playgrounds, first- and second-generation immigrant children played stickball as a substitute for baseball and as an attempt to Americanize themselves, in defiance of their parents who were trying to preserve their cultural identities.

Prior to the 1920s, the more-educated and affluent immigrant groups, such as the English, Scots, and Germans, organized athletic clubs that tended to promote and maintain their culture as well as offering physical fitness. Cricket, track-and-field events, and gymnastics, respectively, were part of their efforts to alleviate alienation in their new surroundings. However, the exclusive nature of English cricket clubs drove other ethnic groups to baseball. The widespread popularity of the Scottish Caledonian games made them the first, apart from jockey clubs, to make spectator sport a business. Often, athletic clubs served other purposes. The German *turnverein*, or turner's society, not only taught gymnastics but also held political forums to improve the lot of the working class through socialism.

For immigrant sport spectators, baseball was a significant Americanization tool with a decidedly political aspect. On the field, U.S., Irish, and German players dominated until the 1920s, when Italians entered the game in significant numbers. In the stands, immigrant spectators, who could afford the price of inexpensive seats, became part of the democratic process of rooting for a team or protesting an umpire's decision even if they could not fully understand the subtleties of the game. They learned the rules that governed the conduct of the game, just as they were learning the new rules that governed their everyday lives in the United States. Although baseball helped immigrants to become Americanized, as did other sports, it did not deprive them of their culture.

—*Sue D. Taylor*

See also: Baseball; Latino Athletes

For further reading:
Barth, Gunther. 1980. *City People: The Rise of Modern City Culture in Nineteenth Century America.* New York: Oxford University Press.
Nasaw, David. 1985. *Children of the City: At Work and at Play.* New York: Oxford University Press.
Riess, Steven A. 1989. *City Games: The Evolution of American Urban Society and the Rise of Sports.* Urbana: University of Illinois Press, 1989.

INDIANAPOLIS 500

The best-known of all automobile races, the Indianapolis 500 reflects a unique merging of fascination with technology, spectator sport, and the commercialization of holidays in the United States during the twentieth century.

From 1911 to the present, the Indianapolis 500 race has been held annually on Memorial Day weekend, excluding the war years of 1917–1918 and 1942–1945. Many cities in the early part of the century, including Indianapolis, competed to become a center of the nascent and quickly growing automobile industry. Carl G. Fisher, a pioneering automobile salesman in Indianapolis, led a group of local businessmen in financing and building the Indianapolis Motor Speedway, which opened in 1909, to serve as a location to test automobile performance and design and to help position the city as a center for developing automobile technology. From the beginning, Fisher's Indianapolis Motor Speedway drew a large number of automobile enthusiasts and curious observers. Fisher, realizing the potential profitability of automobile racing, developed a one-day extravaganza in 1911, the inaugural 500-mile race.

Prior to World War I, the Indianapolis 500 encountered vehement criticism from important members of the Indianapolis community who argued that the race demeaned the spirit and true meaning of Memorial Day. The most vocal critics were the politically powerful Civil War veterans who had been part of the Grand Army of the Republic and who were responsible for creating Memorial Day in the late nineteenth century to honor the Civil War dead and bolster patriotism. However, as the Civil War veterans aged and younger veterans recognized the importance of the race to the local economy, criticism of the race as a desecration of a solemn holiday faded. By the 1920s, local civic and business leaders were arguing that attending the race and all the festivities around it was, in fact, a patriotic act that celebrated U.S. technological skill and bravery.

During the Great Depression, despite the nation's economic difficulties, the Indianapolis 500 attracted fans and its attendance grew. During World War II, however, the track was shut down completely for four years. Anton Hulman, a businessman from Terre Haute, Indiana, purchased the track in 1945 and quickly resurrected the race, which soon returned to its former prominence. The facilities were renovated under Hulman's guidance, and significant improvements—such as concrete-and-steel grandstands, new and safer pit areas, a technologically advanced control tower, private viewing suites, and improved garage facilities—were built. The prize money distributed to race participants increased steadily in the postwar years, adding to the race's prestige. These efforts led to greater

Ray Harroun, driving his Marmon Wasp, was the first winner of the Indy Race. His average speed was 74.59 miles per hour (1911).
(BETTMANN/CORBIS)

attendance, with annual estimates increasing to over 500,000.

Nicknamed "the greatest spectacle in racing," the Indianapolis 500 is integral to the shared community life of Indianapolis and the surrounding region. The entire month of May is given over to events leading up to the race and is a boon for local businesses of all types that cater to the racing fans. The race attracts fans from all levels of society and has become one of the truly unique annual sporting events in the United States.

—*Alexander Urbiel*

See also: National Association for Stock Car Auto Racing

For further reading:

Carnegie, Tom. 1989. *Indy 500: More Than a Race.* New York: McGraw-Hill.

Fox, Jack C., and Bob Mount. 1995. *The Illustrated History of the Indianapolis 500: 1911–1994.* Speedway, IN: Carl Hungess Publishing.

INTERNATIONAL OLYMPIC COMMITTEE

Originally commissioned and structured by Baron Pierre de Coubertin in the late nineteenth century to promote and nurture the fledgling Olympic Games movement, the International

Olympic Committee (IOC) is located at the heart of a complex system of interlocking sport bureaucracies and is arguably the most powerful and influential body in the world of sport.

Voted into existence at the Paris Congress on June 23, 1894, the first International Olympic Committee comprised fifteen members from twelve nations. The brainchild of Coubertin, the IOC was established to oversee the conduct of the newly revived Olympic Games, the first of which was held in Athens, Greece, in 1896. Dimitrius Vikelas served as the first president, and Coubertin served as secretary-general. With unquestionable power as guide, guardian, and arbiter, the IOC remains the umbrella organization and ultimate authority within the Olympic movement.

Structure and Aims

As described by the Olympic Charter, the IOC is a nonprofit body incorporated under international law and has juridical status and perpetual succession. It owns all rights concerning the Olympic symbol, the Olympic flag, the Olympic motto, the Olympic anthem, and the Olympic Games. Financed by lucrative television contracts, corporate sponsorship, and money accrued from the games themselves, the IOC's jurisdiction includes such areas as entry, eligibility, program, events, equipment, art exhibits, traveling expenses, housing, technical aspects, prizes, media, choice of site, time and duration, music, and sponsorship—in short, all aspects of the modern Olympic Games.

Among its many important aims, the IOC seeks to encourage the organization and development of sport and sport competition, collaborate with private and public organizations and authorities to place sport in the service of humanity, ensure the regular celebration of the games, participate in actions to promote peace, encourage the promotion of women in sport at all levels and in all structures, oppose any political or commercial abuse of the games or the athletes, lead the fight against drugs, and encourage the development of sport for all.

Instituted in 1921 by Coubertin, the affairs of the IOC are managed by the powerful Executive Board, consisting of the president, four vice presidents, and six IOC members. Among its many duties, the Executive Board ensures that the rules are observed, assumes direct responsibility for the administration and management of finances, reports to the IOC on any proposed rule change, and enacts all regulations necessary to ensure the proper implementation of the Olympic Charter and the Olympic Games themselves.

Numerous permanent and ad hoc commissions, councils, and working groups deal with matters such as medicine, finance, eligibility, and publicity. Some of the best-known commissions, such as Olympic Solidarity, Sport for the Masses, and the International Olympic Academy, focus on the educational processes that protect and reinforce the philosophy, ideals, and spirit of Olympianism. Operating as focal points and outreach mechanisms to establish local, regional, national, and global dialogues among athletes, coaches, educators, and administrators, the IOC's commissions play a significant role in the infrastructure of the Olympic movement.

Another component of the IOC, the Olympic Congress, or Tripartite, comprises the IOC membership, delegates of the International Federations, and the recognized National Olympic Committees (NOCs). Appointed by the International Olympic marketing program in 1985, the Olympic Program (TOP), in conjunction with the Swiss-based International Sports and Leisure (ISL), serves as the worldwide sponsoring agent for the IOC.

Membership

To ensure its political independence, the IOC was established as a self-recruiting body from the very beginning. Co-opted as trustees of the Olympic project and grounded in Coubertin's principle of "delegation in reverse," the members of the IOC serve as representatives of the IOC in their respective countries, not as delegates from their countries to the IOC. Selected on the basis of their knowledge of sport and their position and respect within their particular national organizations, members must reside in a nation that possesses a recognized National Olympic Committee. Membership ceases if a member resigns, becomes inactive, reaches the age of eighty if elected after 1966, changes nationality, or is deemed unworthy. Technically, only one member from any nation should sit on the IOC, except for those countries where the Olympic Games have been held. Served by almost four hundred members over the course of its lifetime, the IOC currently comprises 118 members. The General Assembly usually meets once a year but meets twice in years when games are held.

Served by eight presidents in all, the IOC's most recent leader is Juan Antonio Samaranch. Although historically the IOC has been dominated by elite, upper-class males of European patrimony, including royalty, it has more recently increased the number of members from third world countries as well as the number of women and athletes. Although women were eligible for selection to the IOC in 1973, the first woman member, Pirjo Haggman of Finland, was not elected to the IOC until 1981. In 1997, Anita DeFrantz of the United States became the first woman elected as an IOC vice president, and twelve women sat on the IOC during that decade. Sixty IOC members have participated as athletes.

Throughout the twentieth century, the IOC has been continuously enmeshed in a variety of complex, persistent, and vexing problems and issues, including the role of women in Olympic competition, drugs, the amateur/professional controversy, nationalism, commercialism, the explosion of television marketing, and a host of delicate political issues. Precipitated by allegations of bribery during the bidding for the 2002 Winter Olympic Games in Salt Lake City, Utah, the IOC most recently has found itself at the center of a swirling corruption scandal that has threatened the foundation of the Olympic movement and submitted the workings of the IOC itself to intense global scrutiny. Attacked and vilified from a multitude of quarters as variously elitist, oligarchic, capitalistic, sexist, imperialistic, and repressive, the IOC has striven to protect and honor the founding ideals of the Olympic movement, even as it has sought to adjust to the development of sport and the changing geopolitical environment.

Given life at the end of the nineteenth century, when both national and international sport were largely in their infancy and when sport was primarily celebrated for its character-building qualities, the IOC was, in the waning years of the twentieth century, at the center of a complex system of interlocking sport bureaucracies that organized and administered highly commercialized and politicized sport on national and international levels. Increasingly immersed in a world of government-supported, corporate-sponsored, elite-level international sport, the IOC has been forced to shed the cloak of apolitical sanctity and amateur athletic competition it once championed and to operate as an influential political body in the arena of international diplomacy and mass-mediated, commodified sport.

—*Jeffrey O. Segrave*

See also: *Arête;* Coubertin, Baron Pierre de; Marketing of Sport; Olympic Games

For further reading:

International Olympic Committee (IOC), ed. 1994. *The International Olympic Committee: One Hundred Years.* Lausanne, Switzerland: IOC.

Simson, Vyv, and Andrew Jennings. 1992. *The Lords of the Rings.* Toronto: Stoddart.

ITALIAN AMERICANS IN SPORT

Sport has played a significant role in the acculturation of second-generation Italian Americans into the mainstream of U.S. society.

With the exception of bocce ball, the great

majority of the more than four million Italians who immigrated to the United States between 1880 and 1920 had almost no tradition of participation in sport. However, for second-generation Italian Americans living in the ethnic enclaves of large cities in the Northeast and Midwest, organized sports such as baseball, basketball, and soccer, sponsored by local parishes and community centers, provided a means of channeling youthful energy and exuberance into disciplined activity. Involvement in sport was a source of pride and prestige, not only for the individuals involved but also for the communities of which they were a part.

At a time when most avenues of entry into mainstream U.S. society were closed to Italian Americans, sport also offered a means of acculturation. This was especially true of baseball, which for most of the first half of the twentieth century was unrivaled as the American pastime. For those few gifted with exceptional athletic ability and lacking in other skills that would promise economic advancement, professional sport offered a means of achieving financial success and some measure of social mobility.

Often, however, participation in sport was a source of tension between second-generation Italian Americans anxious to assimilate into the mainstream and their immigrant parents, who saw sport as a waste of time. Many boxers, both amateur and professional, fought under assumed names to hide their activities from disapproving parents. Italian Americans who played major league baseball in the 1940s and 1950s have frequently told of how at least one of their parents voiced strong opposition to their foolish hopes of making a living by playing a boy's game.

Following the typical pattern of ethnic succession, second-generation Italian Americans found the most success in boxing and baseball. Between 1920 and 1935, there were more boxing champions of Italian heritage than there were from any other ethnic group. Boxing promoters, anxious to exploit the ethnic rivalries prevalent in large cities,

particularly among Irish, Italians, and Jews, often recruited street fighters from low-income, heavily populated ethnic neighborhoods.

Some of those early champions fought under assumed names. Johnny Dundee, for example, was born Giuseppe Carrora. Known as "the Scottish Wop," he held the featherweight title four different times between 1921 and 1924 and is a member of the International Boxing Hall of Fame. Eight other Italian American fighters are in the Hall of Fame, although three of them, Lou Ambers, Joey Maxim, and Willie Pep, also fought under assumed names. Two of the nine, Rocky Graziano and Jake La Motta, became the subjects of major motion pictures, *Somebody up There Likes Me* (1956) and *Raging Bull* (1980), respectively. Italian American fighters have held the title in every weight class, from flyweight to heavyweight.

The most famous Italian American fighter was Rocky Marciano. Born Rocco Marchegiano, the "Brockton Rock" was the only heavyweight champion to go undefeated in his career, winning forty-three of his forty-nine fights by knockout. He retired in 1956 after defending his title six times.

In the 1920s, New York baseball franchises hoped to find ethnic stars to appeal to the large Jewish and Italian populations in the city. In 1926, the Yankees found their Italian hero in Tony Lazzeri, one of the first of many Italian American players from San Francisco who would make it to the big leagues. Italian American fans flocked to Yankee Stadium to cheer the slugging second baseman, whom they nicknamed "Poosh-'Em-Up Tony" for his ability to advance runners.

Lazzeri was the first of what would be a string of famous Yankees of Italian origin, including Hall of Famer Lawrence "Yogi" Berra, who became an icon of popular culture for his idiosyncratic use of the English language. However, it was not until the late 1930s that Italian American players made it to the majors in significant numbers. By 1941, Italian Americans constituted 8 percent of all major leaguers, more than twice their percentage in the total white population.

As was typical of the era, Italian players were portrayed in the press in stereotypical terms. Not even the great Joe DiMaggio was immune in the early years of his career. It was probably a combination of his stature as the best player in baseball and his service in World War II that brought about his transition from an ethnic hero to an American hero. Following the war, ethnic references gradually disappeared as DiMaggio was acknowledged as the great American hero of his time.

By the 1960s, Italian Americans were moving into managerial and executive positions in baseball, and in 1987, A. Bartlett Giamatti, who had been president of Yale, was named president of the National League. One year later, he became commissioner of baseball, a position he held for only five months until his death in April 1989, at the age of fifty-one. The success of Giamatti, the grandson of Italian immigrants, brought the evolution of Italian American involvement in baseball full circle.

Although less numerous than their counterparts in boxing and baseball, Italian Americans have excelled in a variety of other sports: Eddie Arcaro in horse racing, Mario Andretti in auto racing, Gene Sarazen in golf, Phil Esposito in hockey, Dan Marino and Joe Montana in football. No account of Italian American involvement in sport would be complete without mentioning Vince Lombardi, the legendary football coach who has become a symbol of the U.S. commitment to winning. Lombardi set the standard for professional football coaches as he led the Green Bay Packers to five National Football League titles between 1961 and 1967 and the first two Super Bowl titles, in 1967 and 1968.

—*Lawrence Baldassaro*

See also: Berra, Lawrence Peter "Yogi"; DiMaggio, Joe; Immigrants, Community and Sport

For further reading:

Baldassaro, Lawrence. 2002. "Before Joe D: Early Italian Americans in the Major Leagues." In *The American Game: Baseball and Ethnicity.* Carbondale, IL: Southern Illinois University Press, 92–115.

Bazzano, Carmelo. 1994. "The Italian-American Sporting Experience." In *Ethnicity and Sport in North American History and Culture,* ed. George Eisen and David K. Wiggins. Westport, CT: Greenwood Press, 103–116.

Renoff, Richard, and Joseph A. Varacalli. 1990. "Italian-Americans and Baseball." *The Nassau Review* 6, no. 1: 92–119.

IVY LEAGUE

One of the oldest athletic conferences in the United States, the Ivy League is known for combining academic and athletic excellence. The first use of the term "Ivy League" is generally credited to *New York Tribune* reporter Caswell Adams. The newsman coined the term in 1937 to refer to a league of football teams from eastern universities that was created to formalize competition among a number of similar institutions. The modern Ivy League was formed officially in 1954, when the original football-only agreement was extended to include all sports. In the fall of 1956, the agreement was implemented by all member institutions: Brown, Columbia, Cornell, Dartmouth, Harvard, Pennsylvania, Princeton, and Yale.

At the heart of the Ivy League is the dual pursuit of academic and athletic excellence, and some view it as one of the last bastions of the true "student-athlete" in college athletics. The member institutions do not offer athletic scholarships to any of their students, but they do encourage competition in a wide range of sports, including crew, squash, and fencing. A number of Ivy League schools regularly seek the national crown in crew, and Princeton has won multiple national championships in men's lacrosse. In addition, Princeton's men's basketball team gained national recognition by upsetting the defending champion, the University of California, Los Angeles (UCLA), in the first round of the 1995 National Collegiate Athletic Association tournament.

Although it is no longer an athletic power on the national scene, the Ivy League has produced a number of athletes who went on to achieve fame in other areas, including former U.S. senator Bill Bradley and former president George H. W. Bush.

—*Michael Manning*

See also: Army-Navy Rivalry

For further reading:

Bernstein, Mark F. 2001. *Football: The Ivy League Origins of an American Obsession.* Philadelphia: University of Pennsylvania.

Goldstein, Richard. 1996. *Ivy League Autumns: An Illustrated History of College Football's Grand Old Rivalries.* New York: St. Martin's Press.

J

JACKSON, REGINALD MARTINEZ "REGGIE" (1946–)

As one of the greatest baseball superstars of his day, Reginald Martinez "Reggie" Jackson symbolized the bombast and excess of professional sport and U.S. culture in the 1970s. A home-run hitter who helped win the World Series championship for the Oakland Athletics, the New York Yankees, and the California Angels, Jackson was a hard-swinging, fast-living, free-agent superstar. Though his defensive skills were subpar and he set the all-time record for career strikeouts, Jackson nonetheless excelled as a home-run hitter, especially in championship games. His multiple home runs in World Series games, including a record-setting four consecutive homers in the 1977 World Series, earned Jackson the moniker of "Mister October." Between 1971 and 1982, Jackson's teams won six pennants and five World Series titles.

Jackson was known for his difficult relationships with two of baseball's most colorful owners, Charles Finley of the Oakland Athletics and George Steinbrenner of the New York Yankees, as well as for his run-ins with baseball manager Billy Martin. His intense and often-tumultuous relationships with owners and managers characterized the high financial stakes of professional sport in the 1970s, the egos of superstar athletes, and the increasing importance of high-priced free-agent sluggers in baseball.

A dynamic personality, Jackson was also emblematic of the materialism and commercialism of the 1970s sport era as he cashed in on his fame with a "Reggie" candy bar as well as appearances in designer-jeans commercials and other advertisements with his Yankee teammates of the latter part of that decade.

—*Michael A. Lerner*

See also: Baseball; Endorsements

For further reading:

Angell, Roger. 2003. *Game Time: A Baseball Companion.* Edited by Steve Kettmann. San Diego, CA: Harcourt.

Kahn, Roger. 2003. *October Men: Reggie Jackson, George Steinbrenner, Billy Martin and the Yankees' Miraculous Finish in 1978.* Orlando, FL: Harcourt.

JAI ALAI

Representing the indigenous culture of many Spanish immigrants in the U. S., jai alai is a traditional Basque sport that was brought to many countries of the Americas, including the United States, where it is played professionally as a vehicle for betting. A traditional game of the Basque region of northern Spain, the term "jai alai" in the Basque language means "happy festival." The sport spread throughout Spain and southern France and was carried to Spanish America,

Martin Perfit, a Brooklyn-born ex-GI who was one of the few American jai alai players in the world to make the grade in the pro game, executes a ballet-like leap. "Marty", as he was called because jai alai players use only one name, learned the game in a fronton in Belgium, where he was stationed during the war (1949).
(BETTMANN/CORBIS)

where it was developed, especially in Cuba, Mexico, Argentina, Uruguay, and areas of the southern United States.

The general term for a family of closely related games that includes jai alai is *pelota vasca*, "Basque ball game." All forms of the game use a three-sided indoor or outdoor court, a fronton, consisting of front, left-side, and back walls. The fourth side is open, there is a boundary line marked on the floor and on the front and back walls, and a fence or screen is placed outside the boundary line to keep the ball within the general court area. A horizontal line on the front wall marks the lower limits of the legal hitting area.

The principle variations in *pelota vasca* are related to the hitting implement. A basket, cesta, is strapped on the right hand for jai alai; other games may use a tennis racquet, the hands, or a slender wooden paddle, *pala,* with a thin covering of leather. In jai alai, the basket is used to catch the ball and sling it forward. All forms may be played as singles or doubles. The courts vary greatly in size, the largest being the fronton for jai alai, which measures fifty by seventeen meters. The most unusual form of the game, played with *palas,* uses a four-walled court, *trinquette,* with the left side consisting of two offset vertical walls connected by an inclined surface, thus giving the effect of the sloping rooftop adjoining a medieval tennis court. The version of the game that uses a racquet is called *frontenis.* It is popular in Mexico among persons who can afford to construct courts at their homes or to belong to private clubs that have courts, such as the Chapultepec and Reál España.

During the early years of the twentieth century, Mexico City had several frontons that were also used for other events, such as boxing matches. The modern jai alai fronton in Mexico City occupies a prominent site on the northeast side of the Plaza de la Revolución. In Mexico, runners placed bets for customers, using old tennis balls, cut part way through, with inserted small pieces of paper that recorded the amount of the bet and the odds at that moment. Transactions between bettors and runners went on by means of throwing the tennis balls back and forth.

In the United States, professional jai alai has existed for many years in Florida and Connecticut, both areas with high numbers of Cuban immigrants, in part related to cigar manufacture and the cultivation of cigar tobacco. In the 1990s, the professional game was played in Miami, Tampa, and Ocala, Florida; in Milford, Connecticut; and in Newport, Rhode Island. Many of the professional players, *pelotari,* are Basques. Although the sport is an exciting spectacle of running, leaping, and hurling the lively and extremely hard ball at speeds of 150 miles an hour, betting is the attraction of the game for most spectators.

—*Richard V. McGehee*

See also: Gambling; Latino Sport

For further reading:

Barrena, Jose O. 1993. *The Jai Alai and Us.* Madrid: Olimpo Publishing House.

Codden, Hal. 1978. *Jai Alai: Walls and Balls.* Amsterdam: Gamblers' Book Club.

JENKINS, DAN (1929–)

In novels, books, and magazine articles, Dan Jenkins has written humorous accounts of the profession of sports, primarily football and golf, that depict the love of games as a metaphor for life in the United States. A native Texan, Jenkins worked as a sportswriter for newspapers in Fort Worth and Dallas prior to beginning a career as a popular football and golf writer for *Sports Illustrated* in 1962. During his twenty-two-year stint at the magazine, he contributed more than five hundred articles. In 1985, as a monthly columnist for *Playboy* magazine, Jenkins began writing on a variety of topics, including satirical attacks on the conventions of the National Football League and the hypocritical workings of the National Collegiate Athletic Association.

Jenkins's first novel, *Semi-Tough* (1972), was described by fellow writer Roy Blount as "the first raunchy sports book." Jenkins parodied the athlete's diary to tell the story of his narrator, Billy Clyde Puckett, a Texas football star playing for the New York Giants. During the week before the Super Bowl, Billy Clyde tells his story directly into a tape recorder, recounting the crude, reckless, uninhibited lives of players off the field, including drinking, chasing women, and making racist jokes. The novel brought Jenkins tremendous success and was adapted for a motion picture in 1977.

Jenkins continued the story of Billy Clyde in *Life Its Ownself* (1984). After quitting football due to an injury, Billy Clyde becomes a television announcer, and pro football eventually disintegrates as players strike for free agency and the game struggles to maintain fan interest. Jenkins's other novels include *Dead Solid Perfect* (1974), a golf comedy featuring Billy Clyde's uncle; *Limo* (1976); and *Baja Oklahoma* (1981).

—*Robert J. Cole*

See also: Football; Golf; Literature, Sport in

For further reading:

Jenkins, Dan. 1989. *You Call It Sports, but I Say It's a Jungle out There.* New York: Simon and Schuster.

———. 1994. *Fairways and Greens: The Best Golf Writing of Dan Jenkins.* New York: Doubleday.

JOGGING

With a new name for an old activity, jogging became one of the most important forms of recreation in the United States after the 1960s. Americans have always run, but jogging—recreational running at less than full speed—is a relatively recent phenomenon, emerging in the 1960s and 1970s as a result of several factors. American athletes had long dominated international track events at short distances, but only in the 1960s did U.S. runners begin to have success in longer races. In the 1964 Olympics, Americans won the 5,000- and 10,000-meter races for the first time in history. Two years later, Jim Ryan broke the world record for the one-mile run, the first American to do so in thirty-two years. Special television coverage of the Olympics and regular network programs, such as ABC's *Wide World of Sports*, popularized events that had long been dominated by foreign athletes. In 1972, Frank Shorter of the

> In the 1964 Olympics, Americans won the 5,000- and 10,000-meter races for the first time in history. Two years later, Jim Ryan broke the world record for the one-mile run, the first American to do so in thirty-two years.

United States captured the Olympic marathon at the Munich games.

Although television coverage of newly found U.S. success at distance running heightened public interest in the sport, a desire for personal fitness prompted more Americans to lace up their shoes and go jogging. Kenneth Cooper's *Aerobics* (1968) stressed the value of running to cure and prevent heart problems, as well as to promote general health. The magazine *Runner's World* was first published in 1970, and James F. Fixx's *Complete Book of Running* (1977) helped spread the gospel. As Fixx noted, jogging appealed both to Americans' desire for self-betterment and to their narcissism.

One could run alone, but there were increasing opportunities to do so in organized ways. The Road Runners Club of America began staging frequent events for joggers in 1964. In 1972 alone, 124 marathons were held in the United States. When Cooper's *Aerobics* first appeared, there were only about 100,000 Americans running or jogging; however, that number exploded to 6 million in 1977 (Fixx 1980, xiii) and to 45.9 million in 1982 (Wellner 1997, 3). By 1995, there were 52.5 million (Wellner 1997, 3) participants in the sport. Although the young were more likely to run than the old, jogging proved to be a relatively democratic form of recreation. By 1995, 38 percent of Americans with annual household incomes over $100,000 ran for exercise, as compared to 26 percent of those with incomes between $25,000 and $50,000 (Wellner, 21). Men were more likely to run than women; blacks and Hispanics were more likely to run than whites.

By the 1990s, annual spending on running apparel was increasing faster than was the number of Americans actually engaged in the sport. From 1986 to 1996, sales of running shoes declined by 25 percent, while those of walking shoes quadrupled as another ancient activity became a fad.

—*Fred Nielsen*

See also: Marketing of Sport; Sneakers

For further reading:

Costill, David L., and Scott Trappe. 2002. *Inside Running: The Athlete Within.* Traverse City, MI: Cooper Publishing.

Fixx, Jim. 1980. *Second Book of Running.* New York: Random House.

Noakes, Timothy. 2003. *Lore of Running.* Champaign, IL: Human Kinetics Publishers.

Wellner, Alison S. 1997. *Americans at Play: Demographics of Outdoor Recreation and Travel.* Ithaca, NY: New Strategist Publications.

JOHNSON, EARVIN "MAGIC," JR.
(1959–)

Earvin "Magic" Johnson Jr. has graced the basketball court, the crusade against acquired immunodeficiency syndrome (AIDS), and the African American business community since his emergence on the national scene in 1979. Magic Johnson learned the city game of basketball in Lansing, Michigan, and earned his nickname in high school, where he powered his team to a state championship in 1977. Two years later, he led Michigan State to the National Collegiate Athletic Association championship.

After his sophomore year in college, Johnson joined the Los Angeles Lakers. As a rookie, the prodigy played on his third championship team in four years. With Magic leading the fast break, the up-tempo, showy style of playing dubbed "showtime" became the toast of Los Angeles and the Lakers became the team of the 1980s in the National Basketball Association (NBA), winning five titles and finishing as runner-up three times. Epic championship series against the Boston Celtics in 1984, 1985, and 1987 pitted Magic against Celtics star Larry Bird and featured West Coast speed versus East Coast power.

The illusions of Magic were shattered in 1991 when it was discovered that he carried the HIV virus, forcing his retirement. Despite fears that he could spread the disease, Magic played in the 1992

Magic Johnson of the Los Angeles Lakers dribbles the basketball past Darrell Griffith of the Utah Jazz in an NBA game at the Forum in Inglewood, California (1987).
(BETTMANN/CORBIS)

NBA All-Star game and on the Olympic Dream Team. He even came out of retirement and rejoined the Lakers in 1996. Off the court, Johnson applied the same determination to conquering AIDS that he had to defeating NBA foes. He served on the Presidential AIDS Commission and established the Magic Johnson Foundation with the mission of furthering HIV/AIDS education, prevention, and care.

Johnson also devoted his energies to business interests. He became a minority owner of the Lakers and established the Johnson Development Corporation. The company invested in movie theaters and retail stores, often aiming to revitalize African American neighborhoods.

—*David L. Richards*

See also: Basketball; Dream Team; National Basketball Association

For further reading:

Gottfried, Ted. 2001. *Earvin "Magic" Johnson: Champion and Crusader.* New York: Franklin Watts.

Johnson, Earvin "Magic." 1992. *My Life.* With William Novack. New York: Random House.

JOHNSON, JACK (1878–1946)

An African American boxer in the early twentieth century, Jack Johnson's status as heavyweight champion and his practice of flaunting cultural mores in an era of widespread racial segregation led to both expressions of black pride and repeated attempts by white authorities to supplant his title. Raised in Galveston, Texas, Jack Johnson's ascension to the heavyweight championship in 1908 was marked by an increasing aggressiveness in the ring and a growing rejection of stereotypical notions of black behavior. Johnson openly courted white women, wore garish clothes, and drove fancy cars, infuriating many in the white public whose image of Johnson was the sexual stereotype of black male virility.

Throughout his reign as champion, Johnson was the victim of repeated attempts to unseat him and to minimize his exposure. Former champion Jim Jeffries was summoned out of retirement in 1910 to challenge Johnson, a move both white and black journalists of the era interpreted as a battle for black legitimacy. Johnson's consequent thrashing of Jeffries inspired black celebrations and white rage that resulted in numerous race riots throughout the country and led some white reformers to try to abolish boxing altogether and to ban the video of the fight from crossing state lines.

Johnson was finally defeated, not by another boxer but by the U.S. Congress. Jack Johnson received bad publicity by the press for his two marriages, both to Caucasian women. Due to the racist attitudes of the times, interracial marriages were prohibited in most of America. Johnson was convicted in 1912 of violating the Mann Act by transporting his wife across state lines before their marriage and was sentenced to a year in prison. While awaiting appeal, Johnson escaped. Posing as a member of a black baseball team, he crossed the border into Canada and later went to Europe. It was seven years before he returned to the U. S. to serve his sentence. After his release from prison, Jack Johnson's boxing career was behind him. To make ends meet, he worked in vaudeville, appearing with a trained flea act.

Johnson's lasting image is that of a rebellious black champion who resisted his prescribed social role, ultimately offending white authorities to such a point that his cultural authority was dramatically usurped. Jack Johnson wrote two memoirs, *Mes Combats* (1914) and *Jack Johnson in the Ring and Out* (1927). He died in an automobile accident in 1946.

—*Aram Goudsouzian*

See also: Boxing; Discrimination, Racial, in Sport

For further reading:

Roberts, Randy. 1985. *Papa Jack: Jack Johnson and the Era of White Hopes.* New York: Free Press.
———. 2002. *Fight of the Century: Jack Johnson, Joe Louis and the Struggle for Racial Equality.* Armonk, NY: M. E. Sharpe.
Wells, Jeff. 1999. *Boxing Day: The Fight That Changed the World.* Pymble: HarperCollins Australia.

JONES, ROBERT TYRE, JR.
(1902–1971)

Robert Tyre Jones Jr., the consummate amateur, is the only golfer to win the Grand Slam—the U.S. Open, the U.S. Amateur, the British Open, and the British Amateur—in one year. His golfing exploits thrust U.S. golfers into the limelight of world sport. His indelible imprint on the game includes the construction of the Augusta National course, the home of the Masters, where he was later named president in perpetuity.

The citizens of St. Andrews, the home of golf, adopted Jones, gave him the nickname "Bobby," and conferred Scottish citizenship upon him. In appreciation for his contributions to the game, they named the tenth hole at St. Andrews "Bobby Jones." Due to his impeccable manners and modesty on and off the course, his name is synonymous with the standards of highest integrity. For Jones, the game was more important than the player and his honesty—his willingness to call penalty strokes on himself—is still practiced by modern professional golfers.

Jones engendered enormous popularity as a golfer; whenever he played in tournaments, thousands of noisy, idolatrous golfing enthusiasts

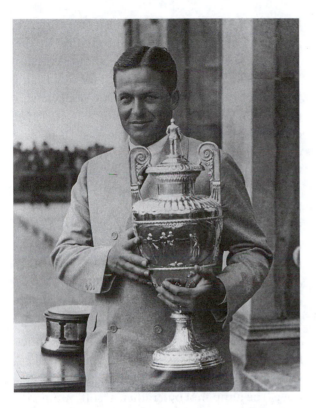

Bobby Jones holds his victory cup, emblematic of his winning the British Amateur Golf Championship at St. Andrews, Scotland, when he beat Roger Wethered, the British star, by 7 and 6 (1930).
(BETTMANN/CORBIS)

would create a tense, unmanageable gallery. Bobby Jones appealed to the common man because he was genuinely free of vanity and ego.

Although Jones played competitive golf for only fourteen years, he left a permanent mark on the game. He won thirteen national championships, wrote a nationally syndicated column, appeared on radio, and penned two books, *Down the Fairway* (1927) with O. B. Keeler and *Golf Is My Game* (1960). In 1930, he signed with Warner Brothers to make twelve reels entitled *How I Play Golf,* which introduced thousands to the game. In 1931, he designed the first set of flanged golf clubs for Spalding.

—*Mike Schoenecke*

See also: Golf

For further reading:
Jones, Robert T., and O. B. Keeler. 2001. *Down the Fairway.* 2nd ed. Atlanta, GA: Longstreet Press.
Keeler, O. B. 2003. *The Bobby Jones Story: The Authorized Biography.* Chicago: Triumph Books.

JORDAN, MICHAEL (1963–)

Called the world's foremost celebrity and the most familiar face on earth, Chicago Bulls superstar Michael Jordan is listed, along with Muhammad Ali and Babe Ruth, as an athlete whose fame transcends the sport that supplied it. According to a joint poll conducted by the *Wall Street Journal* and NBC News, 95 percent of Americans interviewed recognized Jordan, whose popularity spans age, regional, professional, ethnic, and political groups.

Throughout intense media scrutiny, criticism of the astronomical fortune he has amassed through basketball and endorsements, and the violent death of his father, who was shot while napping in his car in July 1993, Michael Jordan retained a quiet dignity. Unlike many of his contemporaries, Jordan came from a stable, middle-class background in Wilmington, North Carolina, and it is to this upbringing that he attributes many of his values, including doting on his wife and children while shielding them from the spotlight glare of his fame.

In addition to his career accomplishments, including being the National Basketball Association (NBA) Most Valuable Player five times and the league scoring leader ten times since 1984, Jordan has produced a $10 billion impact on the U.S. economy, according to *Fortune* magazine. From sales of the products he endorses, rising television ratings, gate receipts, and sales of NBA merchandise and of his own sport videos and games, Jordan has almost single-handedly improved the financial viability of basketball and sport merchandising. Jordan has contributed $5.2 billion in sales to Nike, his primary endorsement, through his Air Jordan campaign, and a combined $408 million to Wheaties, Gatorade, and others, as well as being instrumental in helping increase players' minimum salaries from the low six figures to $2.5 million. The revenue from his sport videos exceeded $80 million, and his film, *Space Jam* (1996), netted $230 million at the box office and an additional $209 million in video sales. In its yearly review of the rich and famous, *Forbes* magazine listed Michael Jordan as the most highly paid athlete in 1997, with an annual income of $78.3 million, including $31.3 million in salary and $47 million from endorsements.

After many attempts to do so, Jordan retired from basketball in 1999. Many observers speculate that he will eventually enter the political arena.

—Joyce Duncan

See also: Basketball; Endorsements; National Basketball Association; Sneakers

For further reading:
Greene, Bob. 1993. *Hang Time: Days and Dreams with Michael Jordan.* New York: St. Martin's Press.
Halberstam, David. 2000. *Playing for Keeps: Michael Jordan and the World That He Made.* New York: Broadway Books.
Smith, Sam. 1994. *The Jordan Rules.* New York: Pocket Books.

JUMP SHOT

Creating an impact on the way in which basketball is played, many African American athletes added their own innovations to the game. Although it was derided as "Negro ball" through the 1950s, the jump shot evolved with fast-break basketball to become an integral part of the game and an example of the increasingly important contributions of African American players. The fastbreak, the jump shot, and fancy ball handling were so strongly associated with African American players that they were called simply "Negro basketball" for several decades. Two African American players at white universities in the 1930s occasionally used jump shots. William "Dolly" King, who began playing for Long Island University in 1937, and Frank "Doc" Kelker, who played for Western Reserve from 1937 to 1940, contributed to a developing black style in evidence on many all-black teams at college and professional levels.

The jump shot evolved after a 1937 rule change by the National Basketball Committee eliminating the center tip-off after each score, making a full-court game possible. Faster, running-style teams immediately began using what was then called the "race horse" maneuver, today known as the fast break. African American teams specialized in this move. Stanford's All-American Angelo "Hank" Luisetti was taking unorthodox one-handed shots as early as 1936 and is often credited with inventing the play. However, Luisetti's was not a true jump shot but, rather, a "soft" jump, rising about two inches off the floor. On the other hand, "Jumping" Jim Pollard led Stanford to a National Collegiate Athletic Association championship in 1942 with a jump shot, and Wyoming's Kenny Sailors dazzled Madison Square Garden audiences in the 1943 National Invitation Tournament (NIT) championship. "Jumping" Joe Fulks, a six-foot-five self-described hillbilly who played for Murray State Teachers College in Western Kentucky, captivated crowds in 1946 with his "turnaround jumpers" for the Washington Capitols. Bud Palmer is said to have "pioneered" the jump shot in the East, playing for Princeton in the late 1940s. Paul Arizin took Villanova to the nation's lead in scoring with a "spectacular low-trajectory jump shot." Playing for all-white teams, these players were the renegades of white ball because everyone knew the jump shot was a "Negro" move.

A by-product of the fast-break style, the jump shot is integral to contemporary basketball. Coach Cal Irvin of North Carolina Agricultural and Technical State University attributes the rise of fast-break basketball to the innovations of African American players following the 1937 rule change.

—*Gena Dagel Caponi*

See also: Basketball; Discrimination, Racial, in Sport

For further reading:

Christgau, John. 1999. *The Origins of the Jump Shot: Eight Men Who Shook the World of Basketball.* Lincoln: University of Nebraska Press.

Peterson, Robert W. 1990. *Cages to Jump Shots: Pro Basketball's Early Years.* New York: Oxford University Press.

K

KAHN, ROGER (1927–)

Writing interesting, often-eloquent profiles of some of the greats in the game of baseball, Roger Kahn, a New York sport journalist, has created a lasting body of books contributing to the best of baseball literature. Kahn is probably best known for his book *The Boys of Summer* (1972), a moving recollection of the glory days of the Brooklyn Dodgers. Kahn contacted the members of the 1950s team in the 1970s and interviewed them for his book. He offers portraits of the heroes of Ebbets Field while providing present-day profiles of the players. The book is also recognized for its emotional description of Branch Rickey's selection of Jackie Robinson to be the first African American to play in major league baseball.

Good Enough to Dream (1985) is a touching, often-amusing story of Kahn's year as part owner of the Utica Blue Sox, a minor league baseball team in the New York–Pennsylvania League. The book provides colorful insight for readers who may have fantasized about professional baseball ownership and the opportunity to run their own club.

In 1986, Kahn published *Joe and Marilyn: A Memory of Love,* a retelling of the relationship between New York Yankee great Joe DiMaggio and movie star Marilyn Monroe. In 1997, Kahn followed with *Memories of Summer: When Baseball Was an Art and Writing about It a Game,* a work chronicling his developing love for baseball from his boyhood in Brooklyn to his work in sport journalism for the *New York Herald Tribune, Sports Illustrated,* and *Newsweek.*

—*Robert J. Cole*

See also: Baseball; "Boys of Summer"; Literature, Sport in

For further reading:

Kahn, Roger. 2002. *The Era 1947–1957: When the Yankees, the Giants and the Dodgers Ruled the World.* Lincoln: University of Nebraska Press.

Little, Craig. 1993. "Roger Kahn: In His New Book, the Brooklyn Dodgers' Chronicler Returns to the Diamond." *Publishers Weekly,* October 4, 49–51.

Yampolsky, Selma. 2000. "Roger Kahn." *Current Biography,* June, 39–44.

KARRAS, ALEX (1935–)

Although not the first football player to move into the entertainment industry, Alex Karras proved more versatile than most, succeeding in television, motion pictures, and books. The son of a first-generation Greek immigrant, Karras spent his early years in Gary, Indiana. After starring in football at Emerson High School, the heavily recruited Karras accepted a football scholarship at the University of Iowa. A two-time All-American, he propelled the Iowa Hawkeyes to high rankings in 1956 and 1957, one Big Ten Championship, and a Rose Bowl victory.

Karras was a first-round draft pick by the Detroit Lions in 1958 and became a premier defensive tackle in the National Football League (NFL). Along with Paul Hornung, the all-purpose backfield player for the Green Bay Packers, Karras was suspended during the 1963 season by Commissioner Pete Rozelle for betting on NFL games.

After retirement in 1971, Karras carved out a remarkable career in entertainment. He starred in *Webster,* a long-running—from 1983 to 1987—situation comedy series on ABC. He also won acclaim for his performances in movies such as *Blazing Saddles* (1974), *Victor Victoria* (1982), *Against All Odds* (1969), *Porky's* (1982), and *Babe* (1975).

George Plimpton featured Karras and John Gordy, his offensive guard teammate on the Lions, in *Mad Duck and Bears* (1973). Karras also wrote books about himself, especially noteworthy is *Even Big Guys Cry* (1977).

—*Chuck Quirk*

See also: Athletes as Actors; Football; Gambling;

For further reading:
Karras, Alex. 1977. *Even Big Guys Cry.* New York: Henry Holt.

KING, DON (1931–)

In every profession or avocation, there are always a few that stand out from the rest—some for their prowess, some for their stamina, and some for their character. Others are noted for their divergence from the mainstream, for their refusal to admit defeat, or for their unusual approach to life. Promoter Don King falls into the latter grouping.

With his trademark hair pointing toward the sky, King has led a colorful life, both personally and professionally. As a child, he was an indifferent student from an impoverished family. His father died working in a steel mill when the boy was ten years old; later, King bought the mill and burned it to the ground. He was trained in street smarts in Cleveland, Ohio, where it is alleged that

Boxing promoter Don King (left) raises the arm of Mike Tyson after Tyson beat James "Bonecrusher" Smith in a heavyweight title fight in Las Vegas, Nevada (March 7, 1987).
(BETTMANN/CORBIS)

as a young man he ran numbers for the mob. King parlayed his skill into a global sport empire.

As a promoter, King arranged matches for some of the best-known figures in championship boxing—from Mike Tyson to Muhammad Ali to Julio Cesar Chavez. Using $10 million of other people's money, he arranged the heavyweight championship bout between Ali and George Foreman in Zaire. Through consecutive battles of his own with various insurance companies, disgruntled clients, and the Internal Revenue Service and while serving a prison term for manslaughter, King has persisted in his pursuit of the American Dream, the ability to amass a fortune by whatever means necessary. Among others, Lloyd's of London took him to court for defrauding them of $350,000, and boxer Mike Tyson took him to court for cheating him out of millions over more than a decade.

In spite of entanglements, the promoter staged forty-seven world title bouts in 1994 and holds the records for promoting the events with the richest purse, the largest live gate, and the biggest pay-per-view audience. He was elected to the International Boxing Hall of Fame in 1997. Through it all, King has attributed his success to his faith in the Lord and his unquestionable patriotism. To underscore these beliefs, he helped to launch a national literacy program, donating $200,000 to teach grade school children about the Constitution. In addition, he writes a regular newspaper column entitled "Only in America," which advocates love of country.

—*Joyce Duncan*

See also: Ali, Muhammad; Tyson, Mike

For further reading:

Newfield, Jack. 2002. *The Life and Crimes of Don King: The Shame of Boxing in America.* Harbor Electronic Publishing.

Raab, Scott. 1998. "The Last Boxing Story." *Esquire* 130, 94–102.

KINSELLA, WILLIAM P. (1935–)

Although many twentieth-century U.S. fiction writers have written one or two works on baseball, only author William P. Kinsella has produced a whole body of novels and short fiction on the sport. Born in Edmonton, Alberta, Kinsella received a bachelor of arts degree from the University of Virginia in 1974 and a master of fine arts degree from the University of Iowa in 1978. He has taught creative writing at both the University of Iowa and the University of Calgary, but for several years he has been a full-time writer and lecturer.

In his best-known works, Kinsella presents a view of baseball that is romantic, nostalgic, and even sentimental. He is most widely known for his award-winning novel *Shoeless Joe* (1982), which was the basis for the film *Field of Dreams* (1989). His novels, *Shoeless Joe* and *The Iowa Baseball Confederacy* (1986), and many of his short stories contain elements of what Kinsella calls "magic," in which baseball is the medium connecting characters to a golden past. However, his less well-known but more realistic pieces depict the pain characters often feel when they realize that baseball, either as a game or as magic, cannot always help them deal successfully with other aspects of their lives.

Both the realistic and the "magical" works are grounded in U.S. geography and culture. Most are set in the Midwest and include references to actual baseball teams, players, stadiums, and events from baseball's past. The pain, pleasure, and preoccupation of U.S. adolescence and the compromises that make up so much of U.S. adulthood are featured prominently in many of the plots, usually as sharp contrasts to a vision of an idyllic life centered around baseball.

—*Judy Hakola*

See also: Baseball, Minor Leagues; Canadian Writers of Sport Literature; Film and Sport; Literature, Sport in

For further reading:

Jenkins, Clarence. 1995. "Kinsella's *Shoeless Joe.*" *The Explicator* 53 (Spring): 179–182.

Randall, Neil. 1987. "*Shoeless Joe:* Fantasy and the Humor of Fellow-Feeling." *Modern Fiction Studies* 33 (Spring): 173–183.

Schwartz, Alan. 1987. "Postmodernist Baseball." *Modern Fiction Studies* 33 (Spring): 135–150.

Slopen, Beverly. 1986. "Look North for Writers." *Publishers Weekly,* February 28, 59–64.

KNIEVEL, ROBERT CRAIG "EVEL" (1938–)

Perhaps one of the stranger cultural sport phenomena of the twentieth century was the need to go beyond the norm, to challenge unexplored sporting arenas and to push human endurance past its accustomed limits. Long before the X Games, the advent of extreme sport, and ESPN's desire to bring those games to the public, one man stepped out from the pack and entertained millions of awestruck fans by mounting a motorcycle, revving it up, and leaping over parked cars, rows of buses, fountains, and canyons.

Evel Knievel, née Robert Craig Knievel, made a career of satisfying the public's taste for outrageousness, thrill seeking, and the lure of danger in sport. In the process, he spent a total of three and one-half accumulated years in various hospitals and suffered thirty-five broken bones. Although his successes—including clearing nineteen cars parked on a racetrack and thirteen Greyhound buses on *Wide World of Sports*—outnumbered his defeats, it is his odd or aborted attempts that remain in the public awareness. On New Year's Eve 1967, Knievel attempted to clear the fountains in front of Caesar's Palace in Las Vegas, a mere fifty yards. He missed and spent the next twenty-nine days in a coma in a local hospital. His son and successor, Robbie, eventually made a jump of 223 feet on February 24, 1998, a fact that caused some dissension between the two. Evel Knievel's last and most memorable feat was an aborted attempt in 1980 to clear Idaho's Snake River canyon by attaching rockets to his motorcycle.

In the 1970s, the daredevil motorcyclist became an industry. His action figures revitalized toy sales, bicycles made by AMF with his signature were very popular, and he added his sponsorship to everything from toothbrushes to lunch boxes. He cited a $60 million profit over ten years, which he invested in boats, aircraft, race horses, Rolls Royces, homes, and, of course, motorcycles. Since his retirement, Knievel has made a comfortable living by capitalizing on his own fame. He endorsed several companies' products, including those of Choice Hotels and Little Caesar's Pizza, made public appearances for car dealers and car

shows, and claimed a $10,000 a week income from the Stimulator, a pain-relief machine he hawked on his Happy Landings Web site. In the late 1990s, Knieval was spending half of his time in his Florida home and the balance of the year in Las Vegas, where he liked to be known as the biggest gambler in town.

—*Joyce Duncan*

See also: Extreme Sports; X Games

For further reading:

Dexter, Pete. 1985. "A Portrait of Evel: Some Call His Life Foolish; Knievel Calls It Art." *Esquire,* March, 45–47.

Robertson, Anne. 2002. "Evel Knievel Takes New Role." *Business Journal,* January 25, 10.

Salholz, Eloise. 1983. "Knievel's New Career: Another Amazing Leap." *Newsweek,* June 13, 12.

KOUFAX, SANFORD "SANDY" (1935–)

The preeminent power pitcher of the early 1960s, Los Angeles Dodgers star Sandy Koufax personified the great breakthrough for U.S. Jews in the postwar period, disproving stereotypes and living the American Dream of upward mobility through sport. Never comfortable with the public's definition of him as a symbol for U.S. Jewry, Koufax nevertheless offered to many Americans living proof that Jewish ballplayers were the equals of their peers. When he passed on a World Series start in the 1965 series because the game was scheduled on Yom Kippur but won the clinching game seven, he legitimized his religion on the national stage.

Born and raised in Brooklyn, New York, Koufax was signed by the hometown Dodgers in 1955 while still an undeveloped talent. Possessing a blazing fastball but very little control, the pitcher suffered through six seasons of mediocrity before finding his poise and his way into the record books following the team's move to Los Angeles.

Baseball's premier hurler Sandy Koufax of the Los Angeles Dodgers, en route to a 3-hit shutout (2-0) against the Minnesota Twins, goes through his motions. The win gave the 1965 World Series to the National League champion Dodgers. (BETTMANN/CORBIS)

He put together a string of five seasons, beginning in 1962, as remarkable as any in the modern era of the game. He put to use his reputation for wildness to intimidate hitters, who feared that neither he nor they could predict if the next pitch would be coming straight at their heads.

In the process, Koufax helped his team to three World Series victories and became something of a sex symbol in the Hollywood of the Doris Day–Rock Hudson era. The gossip pages followed his dates with starlets, and he, along with fellow Dodger ace Don Drysdale, attempted to use their celebrity status to hold out for larger contracts. Although essentially unsuccessful, the holdout in many ways marked the beginning of players' attempts to overcome team owners' limits on their salaries and autonomy, eventually bearing fruit in the birth of player free agency in the 1970s. In 1966, Koufax retired suddenly at age thirty. Although he was at the top of his game, he was the victim of chronic debilitating pain in his pitching arm. In the following decades, he kept a low profile, wary of demands that he stand as a one-dimensional symbol of his religion. When he retired, he held numerous pitching records, notably career, single-season, and World Series marks in strikeouts. He won three Cy Young Awards and a National League Most Valuable Player Award in addition to being elected to the National Baseball Hall of Fame.

—*Mark Santangelo*

See also: Baseball

For further reading:

Gruver, Ed. 2000. *Koufax.* Dallas, TX: Taylor Publishing.

Horvitz, Peter S. 2001. *The Big Book of Jewish Baseball.* New York: SPI Books.

Leavy, Jane. 2002. *Sandy Koufax: A Lefty's Legacy.* New York: HarperCollins.

L

LACROSSE

Lacrosse is the most popular sport indigenous to North America. In amateur clubs, intercollegiate competitions, professional leagues, and international matches, thousands play, watch, and enjoy modern renditions of the traditional ball game. Lacrosse refers to a number of diverse games played by Native Americans. The object of the sport, formerly concentrated in the northeast, the southeast, and around the Great Lakes, is to score more goals than the opposing team. For indigenous participants and spectators, however, lacrosse was more than a recreational activity. The playing of lacrosse possessed important spiritual components, reinforced local kin-based social organization, and had deep associations with physical combat.

In the seventeenth century, French missionaries offered the first description of the sport. For much of the next century, largely in New France, Europeans watched and wagered on matches between Native Americans, and by the middle of the eighteenth century were engaging in competition with them. Beginning in the early nineteenth century, Euro-Canadians, particularly in the vicinity of Montreal, began playing the game themselves, systematizing it in 1867.

Although indigenous peoples outside of Canada played lacrosse, it did not capture much public attention in the United States until after the Civil War. Traveling exhibitions, initially from Canada but later featuring Native Americans from the South, toured the eastern United States, receiving an enthusiastic reception because of the novelty of the sport and also because of the popular perceptions of its Native American players as wild and uncivilized. In short order, club teams began to form throughout the Northeast, beginning with the establishment of the Mohawk Club of Troy, New York, in 1868. In the final third of the nineteenth century, Americans rapidly institutionalized the nascent sport, organizing in succession intercollegiate play, inaugurated in a contest between New York University and Manhattan College in 1877, a national amateur association in 1879, and an intercollegiate association in 1882.

Against this background, lacrosse enjoyed growing popularity and wider diffusion over the course of the twentieth century. Women began playing the sport shortly after the turn of the century and formed a national governing body in 1931. Whether played by men or women, lacrosse has spread beyond its traditional centers in the East, attracting interest throughout the United States. An important sign of its new national character was the recognition of the sport by the National Collegiate Athletic Association (NCAA) in 1971 for men and in 1981 for women. More recently, an indoor version of lacrosse, box lacrosse, has served as the basis for the professionalization of the game.

The institutionalization of lacrosse in the

A spirited scramble for the ball during a practice game between the first and second Huron teams in preparation for the national championship of the Ladies Lacrosse League of America (1926).
(UNDERWOOD & UNDERWOOD/CORBIS)

United States eclipsed but did not eradicate the indigenous forms of the sport. Throughout the twentieth century, indigenous communities continued to play local versions of the ball game and began to embrace modern lacrosse. Importantly, for many Native Americans, the game fostered the rediscovery of cultural heritage and the validation of ethnic identity. Indeed, a pivotal moment in indigenous activism and sport occurred in 1990 when the Iroquois National Team played in the Lacrosse World Cup.

At the start of the twenty-first century, lacrosse is a vital and emergent sport, reflecting the contours of U.S. culture: a cultural practice of indigenous people, modified to fit the ideals of Euro-American sport and society, fashioned to entertain a mass audience, and repossessed as a resource of ethnic identity.

—*C. Richard King*

See also: Native American Athletes

For further reading:

Blanchard, Kendall. 1981. *The Mississippi Choctaw at Play.* Urbana: University of Illinois Press.

Lipsyte, Robert. 1986. "Lacrosse: All-American Game." *New York Times Magazine,* June 15, 29–38.

Vennum, Thomas. 1994. *American Indian Lacrosse: Little Brother of War.* Washington, DC: Smithsonian Institution Press.

LADIES PROFESSIONAL GOLF ASSOCIATION

Founded in 1950, the Ladies Professional Golf Association (LPGA) merged the conflicting social norms of the feminine and the athletic to sell women professional golfers to corporate America as ideal sponsors for women's products. Since its inception, the LPGA has endeavored to develop and to maintain the mass audience appeal of professional women golfers, primarily through the marketing skills of its male administrators and the athleticism and support of its female players. By selling tournaments as events and as potential advertising venues and by presenting players as sport entertainers rather than competitors, the LPGA delivered women golfers into the living rooms of the U.S. mainstream.

Under the successive LPGA leadership and salesmanship of Fred Corcoran, Ray Volpe, and John Laupheimer, the feminine professional golfer was highlighted. Consequently, manufacturers of women's products and apparel, sporting equipment companies, and television networks became promoters of the sport and the association. The LPGA offered support for these endorsements that made sense economically, politically, and socially.

The Women's Professional Golf Association, the predecessor of the LPGA, was chartered in 1944 to organize and promote professional golf tournaments for women. However, under LPGA leadership, golf tournaments became a business, an entertainment, and an advertising vehicle. Although the LPGA never marketed tournaments as competitions, the number of golf tournaments for women professionals tripled, from seven events in pre-LPGA 1948 to twenty-one events in post-LPGA 1951.

With corporate sponsorship, annual prize money on the women's professional tour grew from $50,000 in 1952 to $200,000 by 1959. Thirty years later, annual prize money had increased to $14 million, and by 1997, it had reached $30.2 million. Until 1963, when Sears and Roebuck signed on as a sponsor, the final round of the U.S. Women's Open Championship had never been televised. Nineteen years later, all four rounds of the Nabisco Dinah Shore Tournament were aired. By 1997, thirty-one of the forty-three tour events received televised coverage.

Handmacher, the manufacturer of Weathervane sportswear for women, was among the earliest of the corporate sponsors, employing the best-known female golfer of the early 1940s and 1950s, Babe Didrikson Zaharias, as one of their player representatives. In 1972, in a move to capture the women's market that was showing increased participation and interest in sport, the Colgate-Palmolive Company became a tour sponsor. Colgate wanted to increase sales in its recreation and leisure divisions and to use women sport stars to sell household products. Noting the advertising and endorsement successes of the other firms, the Nabisco, McDonald's, and Mazda Corporations soon followed as primary tour sponsors.

Early on, the LPGA added sex appeal to the tour with the promotion of various athletes, and in the 1970s, the association highlighted its most attractive players, featuring Jan Stephenson, Laura Baugh, Cathy Reynolds, and Judy Rankin. Although Rankin and Stephenson consistently finished high in the tournaments, Baugh failed to place higher than fifteenth from 1975 to 1982.

Headquartered in Daytona Beach, Florida, the LPGA gained visibility for women professional golfers, pioneered a training program for women golfers who wanted to become professionals, established a pension plan for players—the first of its kind for individual sports—controlled the licensing of its products and logo, created a catastrophic-illness fund for players, and founded a Hall of Fame. The association is civic-minded and sponsors charities, training clinics, scholarships, and programs for junior golfers. From 1981 to 1995, the LPGA raised $78 million for charity.

—*Rebekah V. Bromley*

See also: Golf; Marketing of Sport; Television, Impact on Sport; Zaharias, Mildred "Babe" Didrikson

For further reading:
Sanson, Nanette, ed. 2002. *Champions of Women's Golf: Celebrating Fifty Years of the LPGA.* Naples, FL: QuailMark.

LANDRY, TOM (1924–2000)

With his trademark hat and taciturn grimace, Dallas Cowboys coach Tom Landry served as a benchmark for coaches throughout the U. S. during the 1970s. By bringing the Cowboys to prominence in the NFL, Landry created a national following for what became known as "America's Team." Born in Mission, Texas, Landry played college football for the University of Texas. After his freshman year, however, he was inducted into the U.S. Army Air Corps, where he served as a B-17 bomber pilot during World War II. After the war, Landry completed college and spent five seasons as a defensive back for the New York Giants. While only in his second year as a professional, he demonstrated his understanding of the game by designing a play known as the 4–3 defense, a defensive scheme used by teams throughout the 1990s.

In 1960, Landry became the head coach of the NFL's expansion team in Dallas. Although the Cowboys struggled through its initial years, Landry, through innovative coaching strategies, had led the team to the top of the Eastern Division by the middle of the decade. Although not known for his charisma, Landry continued his success in Dallas during the 1970s. Under his leadership, the Cowboys went to the Super Bowl five times, winning in 1971 and 1977 and earning the franchise of colorful players the designation "America's Team."

When the team was sold to Jerry Jones in 1989, Landry was replaced as the Cowboys' coach. However, he was inducted into the Pro Football Hall of Fame in 1990. Landry died in 2000 in Dallas, Texas, after a year-long battle with leukemia.

—*Byron Holland*

See also: Football

For further reading:
Freeman, Denne H., and Jaime Aron. 2001. *I Remember Tom Landry.* Champaign, IL: Sports Publishing.
Jensen, Brian, and Troy Aikman. 2001. *Where Have All Our Cowboys Gone?* Dallas, TX: Taylor Publishing.
St. John, Bob, and Roger Staubach. 2000. *Landry: The Legend and the Legacy.* Nashville, TN: Word Publishing.

LANGUAGE OF SPORT

The strong influence of sport on U.S. culture is evidenced by the prevalence of sport terms and metaphors in U.S. English. When someone says that an idea "came out of left field" or that a struggling company is "on the ropes," he or she is using metaphors originating in baseball and boxing, respectively. So common is the use of sport terminology in everyday speech that many speakers may not realize how influential sport has become. Some observers have theorized that because people perceive life as tough and competitive, they have turned to the world of sport to help them explain their thoughts.

Figurative Language

Baseball

Baseball is such a dominant sport in U.S. society that many baseball terms have made their way into everyday speech. When something unexpected occurs, people say that fate or someone has "thrown them a curve." "I can't get to first base" is often a way to express frustration; to have "two strikes" against one is to be in peril, and to have "three strikes" is to be beyond saving. Someone doing everything perfectly is "batting a thousand"; to make sure that something is done completely, a person "touches all the bases" or "covers all the bases." The term "rain check," originally from baseball, is now in common use in other sports as well as in the world of retail. People get help when someone "pinch hits" or "goes to bat" for them, and an odd person is often referred to as a "screwball."

Football

Football, that uses many war-oriented metaphors, has passed those metaphors on to the public to explain what happens on the battlefield of football and, by extension, in life. The quarterback is a "field general," throwing "bombs" to "riddle the defense." Games may end in "sudden death," a critical situation may bring a "two-minute warning," or one might maneuver around a problem with an "end run." A person who knows the right thing to do after the fact is a "Monday morning quarterback," and a woman who is without her husband's companionship because he is watching a game on television is a "football widow," a term that has also been applied to other sports, such as golf. An act of desperation is sometimes referred to as a "Hail Mary play."

Boxing

Boxing has contributed a significant number of metaphors to the English language. Someone may be "down for the count"; something of beauty is a "knockout"; when people give up, they "throw in the towel," although they may be "saved by the bell." A dirty tactic is a "low blow," as is hitting "below the belt"; one is candid by telling it "straight from the shoulder," and politicians "toss their hat into the ring." Among other boxing terms common in everyday speech are "bob and weave," "main event," "pull no punches," "roll with the punches," and "go the distance." Speakers of English may describe someone of importance as a "heavyweight" as opposed to a "lightweight," and an excellent location at an event is a "ringside seat." While, in life, persons may hope to have someone "in their corner."

Horse Racing and Other Sports

Because political contests are seen as "races," many horse-racing terms are used, including a "dark horse" candidate, a "dead heat" or "photo finish," a race going "down to the wire," or beating a deadline by getting in "just under the wire." Someone might win "by a nose." In addition, a person with class or distinction in any area of life is often called a "thoroughbred."

Basketball has given the language "high five," "alley-oop," and "slam dunk." Cricket has contributed "sticky wicket" and "hat trick." From various gaming sports come "crap shoot" and "sweepstakes." Golf lingo includes "handicap," "in the rough," "up to par," and "teed off," used to indicate annoyance or anger. In life, a confrontation is a "face-off," borrowed from hockey, as are "penalty box," "body check," and "power play." Track and field offers "jumping the gun" and the expression for possessing an advantage, "having the inside track." Tennis instructs one to "put the ball in the other guy's court," hunting warns against "barking up the wrong tree," and pool and billiards have one "call the shots" so as not to "get behind the eight ball."

Quotes, Nicknames, Expressions

In addition to the contributions of specific sports, many general sport terms have made their way into everyday speech. The democratic concept that all people should be subject to the same rules in the "arena" of life is displayed through several expressions. "Fair play," "being a good sport," and "cricket" imply adherence to rules, whereas "dirty pool" suggests the opposite. Leo Durocher's famous quote that "Nice guys finish last" warns that following the rules may not lead to success. Ideas that do not meet a suggested "game plan" might be "out of bounds," "off the mark," or "in the gutter," but a "bull's eye" or a "home run" are clearly "on the mark."

Many nonmetaphorical expressions, nicknames, and quotations are common in U.S. speech, often carrying beyond the association with their initial sport. The fractured English of Yogi Berra and Casey Stengel, for example, have become popularly known as "Yogi-isms" and "Stengelese," and their expressions, such as "It ain't over till it's over" and "You could look it up," have meaning in the general lexicon. The title of the 1989 movie *Field of Dreams* has entered the vocabulary to such an extent that a CNN special on sport violence was called *Field of Screams*. A phrase from that same film, "If you build it, they will come," has been modified for use in numerous advertisements. Muhammad Ali's "I am the greatest" has become part of the U.S. vocabulary, and the title of the famous Bud Abbott and Lou Costello skit "Who's on First?" is often used to describe a situation of total confusion.

> *Many baseball terms have made their way into everyday speech. When something unexpected occurs, people say that fate or someone has "thrown them a curve." In addition, "I can't get to first base" is often a way to express frustration; to have "two strikes" against one is to be in peril, and to have "three strikes" is to be beyond saving. Someone doing everything perfectly is "batting a thousand"; to make sure that something is done completely, a person "touches all the bases" or "covers all the bases."*

The vocabulary of other fields has been affected by sport. In medicine, amyotrophic lateral sclerosis is best known as Lou Gehrig's disease, named for its most famous victim. People may suffer from a charley horse, athlete's foot, or tennis elbow, and boxers have cauliflower ears. A bacterial infection known to doctors as external otitis is more commonly known as swimmer's ear. The world of fashion has not escaped the influence of sport either. Boxer shorts, rugby shirts, jerseys, ski parkas, and fanny packs, for example, all originated in the sport world.

Expressions and nicknames are embedded in the speech. Few people have not heard of the Babe, the Mick, the Fighting Irish, or, even if they do not know its roots, would fail to recognize "No pain, no gain," "Win one for the Gipper," or "We wuz robbed!" The terms "fan," perhaps short for "fanatic," "instant replay," "according to Hoyle," and "Wait till next year" are part of U.S. English. Fred Merkle's base-running error in 1908 borrowed the old term "bonehead" to popularize "bonehead play" and "boner," both commonly used without specific reference to baseball to mean any stupid action. Basketball coach Pat Riley coined the word "threepeat" to signify three consecutive championships by the Chicago Bulls.

Sport names have not escaped social controversy. The use of Native American names for team nicknames has been a sensitive issue in U.S. culture. The 1995 World Series between the Atlanta Braves, with its fans waving fake tomahawks, and the Cleveland Indians, with its grinning Indian logo, brought the issue into the national spotlight, and in the face of social pressure, many college and high school teams have either changed their nicknames or given serious consideration to doing so.

—*Peter Sisario*

See also: Berra, Lawrence Peter "Yogi"; Gehrig, Lou; Metaphor, Sport as, for Life; Sport Slang

For further reading:
Ammer, Christine. 1992. *Southpaws and Sunday Punches and Other Sporting Expressions.* New York: Plume Books.

Gray, Ryan. 2002. *The Language of Baseball: A Complete Dictionary of Slang Terms, Clichés and Expressions.* Champaign, IL: Coaches Choice Publishing.

Hendrickson, Robert. 1994. *Grand Slams, Hat Tricks and Alley-Oops: A Sports Fan's Book of Words.* Englewood Cliffs, NJ: Prentice-Hall.

Phillips, Louis, and Burnham Holmes. 1994. *Yogi, Babe, and Magic: The Complete Book of Sports Nicknames.* Englewood Cliffs, NJ: Prentice-Hall.

LAS VEGAS, NEVADA

The pinnacle of sport entertainment in the United States is a speck of real estate in the middle of the southwestern desert covered by the most flamboyant light show on earth. Las Vegas, Nevada, is unlike any other city on the planet, a surreal atmosphere where time, and often logic, is held in suspended animation. Tour-bus clientele and camping-style vacationers flood the narrow streets of the downtown area, seeking cheap steaks, drink coupons, and twenty-five-cent-minimum crap games, while the affluent and the bedecked swarm the area known as the Strip, drifting from one opulent and intriguing edifice to another, often divesting themselves of years of disposable income in the process.

From the early-1990s trend of luring the family vacationer with theme parks, circus midways, and babysitting "edutainment" facilities to the late-1990s appeal to the cultured baby-boomer set, Las Vegas has more than tripled its tourist fare as well as its resident population and has acquired a berth on the list of the best American cities in which to retire. The zenith of the building craze of the 1990s is gaming magnate Steve Wynn's $1.6 billion Bellagio Hotel and Casino, replete with a $300 million collection of museum-quality art by such masters as Picasso and Van Gogh. The nadir of the same period is that of diversion: with the glut of establishments from which to choose, tourist dollars are spread more thinly, and with the added attractions—roller coasters, battling pirate ships, and erupting volcanoes, not to mention shopping and shows—many tourists are doing more sightseeing than gambling.

Gambling was legalized in Nevada in 1931, and Las Vegas was established with funds from organized crime, a stigma it has never completely outgrown. Gangster Bugsy Siegel opened the first major casino, the Flamingo, in 1946. By 1959, corporate gambling took over when the state instituted a Gaming Commission to establish rules and regulations for casino operation and a Gaming Control Board to police those rules. The first theme hotel, Caesar's Palace, was inaugurated in 1966.

Other Nevada cities, such as Reno, Lake Tahoe, and Laughlin, also experienced the gaming boom, while the smaller towns acquired auxiliary income from one of the state's other legalized industries, prostitution.

—Joyce Duncan

See also: Atlantic City, New Jersey; Gambling

For further reading:

Basten, Fred, and Charles Phoenix. 1999. *Fabulous Las Vegas in the 50s: Glitz, Glamour and Games.* Santa Monica, CA: Angel City.

Chung, Su Kim. 2003. *Las Vegas: Then and Now.* San Diego, CA: Thunder Bay Press.

Earley, Pete. 2000. *Super Casino: Inside the "New" Las Vegas.* New York: Bantam.

LATINO ATHLETES

The Latino athletes who have most affected the culture of the United States are major league baseball players from Cuba, the Dominican Republic, Puerto Rico, Mexico, and other Hispanic countries. Hispanic American athletes have also made important contributions to other U.S. amateur and professional sports. Latino athletes are underrepresented in sport in the United States with the exception of major league baseball, where foreign-born Latinos are a conspicuous and valuable component. In 1995, the percentages of Latinos in the National Basketball Association, the National Football League, major league baseball, and the National Hockey League, respectively, were zero, less than 1 percent, 16 percent, and less than 1 percent (Leonard 1996, 294). By contrast, census data for 1990 show that Hispanics made up around 11 percent of males ages fifteen to thirty-nine in the United States. The odds of a U. S.-born Hispanic becoming a professional athlete in one of the four major sports are lower than they are for Caucasians and African Americans.

The first Latina athlete to compete on the United States winter Olympic team, Catherine Machado of Los Angeles takes time out to pose for a picture as she works out in the Appolonio Stadium at Cortina, Italy, in preparation for the Winter Olympics. (January 1956).
(BETTMANN/CORBIS)

A 1988 study of base salaries for blacks, whites, and Hispanics in major league baseball found no apparent systematic discrimination regarding salaries for Hispanic players. However, Latinos were underrepresented at all managerial levels in comparison to African Americans and whites. The few Hispanic managers hired surpassed white managers in most categories of prior performance and experience. Most Hispanic managers had been outfielders as players, whereas most non-Hispanic managers were formerly shortstops, second basemen, and catchers, ironically positions in which Hispanics are actually overrepresented.

It has been observed that Latinos occupy a larger proportion of "core" positions in baseball than would be expected if there were a completely uniform distribution in all positions, excluding pitchers. This relationship is different from that of black players, who occupy the outfield in disproportionately large numbers. Latinos are underrepresented at first and third base. Studies of Hispanic students in interscholastic sport in the United States indicate Hispanic students may find that participation in sport opens doors for them to be accepted within the majority culture of the school. However, other Latino youths use rejection of school sport as a symbol of their feelings of estrangement from that same culture. Immigrant youth may find participation in school sport especially difficult because of language problems, lack of economic resources, and unfamiliarity with traditional U.S. sports, such as football.

Latino residents and citizens of the United States are extremely varied demographically: in how many generations of their family have lived in the United States or, for recent immigrants, how long they have been in the United States; in their country of origin; in their economic and educational status; in their race; and in other cultural characteristics. As a result, their feelings of Latino identity are extremely varied. The accomplishments of many Hispanic American athletes may thus go unnoticed by the general public due to this vagueness of ethnic identity.

Hispanic Americans have contributed to U.S. Olympic efforts since 1924, when Joe Salas won a silver medal for boxing in Paris. The first Hispanic American woman to represent the United States in the Olympics was figure skater Catherine Machado in the 1956 Winter Games. Others have participated on the U.S. Olympic squads, on collegiate and national teams, and in professional sport.

—*Richard V. McGehee*

See also: Baseball; Immigrants, Community and Sport; Latino Sport

For further reading:

Leonard, Wilbert M., II. 1996. "The Odds of Transiting from One Level of Sports Participation to Another." *Sociology of Sport Journal*, 13, 288–299.

Longorio, Mario. 1997. *Athletes Remembered: Mexicano/Latino Professional Football Players, 1929–1970.* Tempe, AZ: Bilingual Press.

Menard, Valerie. 2001. *Careers in Sports: Latinos at Work.* Bear, DE: Mitchell Lane Publishing.

LATINO SPORT

Sport is an important ingredient of popular culture throughout Latin America, where professional soccer, boxing, and baseball attract most spectator interest; however, in the United States, rodeo is the sport of Latino/Mexican origin that has had the most effect on the culture. In the United States, the sports most associated in the public mind with Latinos include baseball, soccer or *futbol*, and possibly bullfighting. The sports with the longest tradition in Spain include bullfighting and various forms of *pelota vasca*, including jai alai. Both bullfighting and jai alai were brought to Latin America, and jai alai is played professionally in Florida, Connecticut, and Rhode Island. Spain has a relatively recent tradition of excellence in rhythmic gymnastics and also yields top athletes in many modern sports, including golf, tennis, and soccer. Most Latin American countries are predominantly soccer-oriented and have both professional teams and massive amateur participation. Historically, Argentina, Brazil, and Uruguay have experienced the greatest success in soccer. One of the most prominent structures in the architecture of most Latin American cities is their soccer stadium. Radio and television game broadcasts and programs of interviews, news, and commentary on soccer activity are widespread. Sport coverage is extensive in most Latin American newspapers. Mexico City has several daily newspapers devoted entirely to sport, largely soccer.

On the other hand, baseball is king in Cuba, the Dominican Republic, Puerto Rico, Nicaragua, and Panama. The national stadiums in these countries are baseball stadiums, like the shrine of Santo Domingo, Quisqueya Stadium, and El Cerro in Havana, the pinnacle of Latin American stadiums. Baseball results and stories find prominent places in the newspapers of these regions, and not only is English-language terminology widely used within the context of baseball and other sports, but metaphors using English words or mixed Spanish and English, "Spanglish," words may be encountered in political writing and speeches as well in other aspects of daily life. Latino baseball players are also prominent in major league teams in the United States.

World-class Latino professional boxers, such as Julio Cesar Chavez of Mexico, are well known in the lighter weight classes, and Cuban boxers of all weight categories have dominated amateur boxing for years. Tennis players are perhaps the next-best-known Latino professionals. Amateur sport is highly developed in most of Latin America, but except for soccer, baseball, and boxing, amateur sport is generally available only to the upper and middle social classes. Among amateur sports, women's volleyball in Cuba, Brazil, and Peru and men's volleyball in Argentina and Brazil are especially strong. Within their own countries and internationally, world champions such as marathoner Mateo Flores of Guatemala and top

professionals such as Puerto Rico's Roberto Clemente, Argentinean race-car driver Juan Manuel Fangio, and Brazil's soccer legend Pelé earn considerable prestige. In Cuba's social structure, amateur athletes are highly respected.

Both baseball and American football are popular enough among Latinos within the United States that there are Spanish-language broadcasts of the games in both these sports. Los Angeles and other heavily Hispanic cities have had Spanish-language broadcasts of major league baseball games for years. One New Orleans radio station, La Fabulosa, broadcasts the Saints' games, both at home and on the road, in Spanish. The terminology used by La Fabulosa's announcers is nearly all Spanish, but they frequently use English expressions, such as "run the ball," in their literal translations.

Bullfighting, brought to the New World by Spaniards, became an important sport in much of the Americas, especially in Peru and Mexico, where it might be considered as much an art form or a dramatic presentation as a sport. In addition to its traditional and classical forms, bullfighting in Mexico evolved into one of the activities of sporting festivals known as *jaripeo* and *charreria*. In addition, the tasks of ranch workers, such as breaking horses and managing cattle, inspired many of the activities in these festivals. In time, these activities were adopted as both work skills and entertainment in the southwestern United States and became the North American sport of rodeo. Although its origins lie in working-class men, *charreria* in the twentieth century carries the connotations that its participants are men and women of high social class and political power.

—*Richard V. McGehee*

See also: Bullfighting; Jai Alai; Latino Athletes; Rodeo

For further reading:
Breton, Marcos. 2003. *Home Is Everything: The Latino Baseball Story; From the Barrio to the Major Leagues.* El Paso, TX: Cinco Puntos Publishing.
Marvis, Barbara J., and Theresa Swanson. 1996. *Contemporary American Success Stories: Famous People of Hispanic Heritage; Pedro Jose Greer, Jr., Nancy*

Lopez, Rafael Palmeiro, Hilda Perera. Multicultural Biography Series. Childs, MD: Mitchell Lane.

Wendel, Tim. 2003. *The New Face of Baseball: The One Hundred Year Rise and Triumph of Latinos in America's Favorite Sport.* New York: Rayo Publishing.

LEWIS, CARL (1961–)

The most successful track-and-field athlete in Olympic history, Carl Lewis's sport talent and business acumen have transformed his sport, but full acceptance in his home country has eluded him. The son of two Willingboro, New Jersey, teachers, Lewis went from being an awkward teenager to winning ten Olympic gold medals before he retired in 1997, setting numerous world records along the way. Qualifying in the long jump for the first of his U.S.-record five Olympic teams in 1980, Lewis missed the Moscow games because of the U.S. boycott. He then won gold medals at the 1984 Los Angeles games in the 100-meter race, 200-meter race, 4x100-meter relay, and long jump, matching Jessie Owens's feat at Berlin in 1936. In the process, Lewis not only tied Owens's record for track-and-field gold medals in a single game but also revived popular appreciation for Owens's achievements.

Lewis continued to win gold at the 1988 Seoul games, the 1992 Barcelona games, and the 1996 Atlanta games. In winning the long jump in Atlanta, he became only the second athlete, after Al Oerter, to win gold in an event in four Olympiads. Lewis aggressively controlled his own career and marketing, using his success to professionalize track and field, which allowed runners to support themselves through athletics. He also lobbied for increased testing to end the use of performance-enhancing drugs in track. Despite Lewis's success, however, he failed to win the acclaim and endorsements in the United States that greeted him elsewhere. Media portrayals of him as aloof and rumors about his sexuality, which he has denied, have contributed to his lukewarm reception by the U.S. public.

—*John Smolenski*

See also: Marketing of Sport; Olympic Games; Owens, James "Jesse" Cleveland

For further reading:

Klots, Steve, and Nathan I. Huggins. 1995. *Carl Lewis.* New York: Chelsea House.

LITERATURE, SPORT IN

The sporting experience has played an important role in U.S. literature. For writers ranging from Nathaniel Hawthorne to Joyce Carol Oates, sport as subject, metaphor, and inspiration has contributed significantly to the development of U.S. literature. Baseball has generally been the most popular sport of fiction writers and poets, but the entire gamut of sporting activities, from ritual games to hunting and fishing to modern team sports, has always had a place in U.S. literature. The tradition of sport is as old as U.S. literature itself. They evolved on parallel and sometimes intersecting tracks that led both to acquire a distinctly American form.

Colonial Period

The colonial and revolutionary periods represented a developmental beginning for both American sport and American literature. Sport was a communal affair, and early writers were generally interested in the collective behavior of a community's inhabitants. This fictional community is often a place where values come into conflict, and sporting activities, themselves a source of controversy in the colonial period, are frequently the literary device employed to dramatize that conflict. Although stories are clearly set in colonial America, the style, prose, and subject interest of early writers, such as Hawthorne and Washington Irving, reveal European influences. In the works of these writers, sport is associated with ritual forms of play that originated in British and Continental traditions and holiday games. Sporting activities of the time, much like literature, had not fully developed a distinctly American style and remained largely European in nature.

Early National Period

By the early national period, both literature and sport had shed foreign influences and emerged to help define a distinct U.S. culture. For politicians, artists, and writers alike, the wilderness experience, absent in Europe, became a source of national and cultural identity. Sporting activities in the wilderness setting are central to such key literary figures of the time as James Fenimore Cooper and Henry David Thoreau, who were exploring the wilderness as an alternative to what they viewed as the overcivilization of urbanized and industrialized society. Thoreau and Cooper exalt sport as a symbol of the pastoral ideal, something to be captured before it is lost. Of the primary wilderness sports, hunting, fishing, canoeing, and hiking, only canoeing is native to America. Yet Thoreau and Cooper ignore European associations and link these activities to the wilderness in ways that emphasize American self-reliance and individuality while questioning modernizing society.

> *Baseball has generally been the most popular sport of fiction writers and poets, but the entire gamut of sporting activities, from ritual games to hunting and fishing to modern team sports, has always had a place in American literature.*

Postbellum to World War II

During the postbellum period, the country rapidly moved away from the pastoral ideals of Cooper and Thoreau and into a modern era of competition and commercial progress. As U.S. values shifted into closer alignment with the marketplace, the development of organized team sport both reflected and contributed to changes in the larger society. Organized sport, such as rowing, baseball, football, basketball, and track and field, emphasized the virtues of cooperation, hard work, discipline, and manly strife, lessons that prepared one for the new market economy. Writers of fiction, such as Horatio Alger Jr., whose targeted audience was American youth, were the first to incorporate these object lessons into their work, a practice that remained popular in fiction for young readers until the 1950s. As a literary source, organized sport dramatizes the virtuous efforts that bring success and the rewards that come with it. For the reader, the playing field becomes a metaphor for life.

During the same period, the sport hero emerged in both adult and youth literature. In the work of Stephen Crane, for example, the sport hero is the embodiment of traditional values, industry, civic virtue, self-reliance, and integrity, upon which America was built. Typically, he, and in some cases she, comes from modest beginnings and hurdles obstacle after obstacle to lead the team to victory. For this, the hero receives fame and sometimes fortune.

Some writers reject the mythic sport hero who succeeds on behalf of his team and himself. The sport hero of realists like Ernest Hemingway and William Faulkner, for instance, is a solitary figure, much like Cooper's protagonist, Natty Bumppo, locked in a contest usually with nature and always with himself. His sporting experience represents a personal journey that frequently leads to defeat and then, ultimately, to enlightenment, a self-realization of the individual's limited capacity.

Post–World War II Period

During the post–World War II period, all areas of the U.S. sporting experience, professional and amateur, were fully absorbed into the corporate world, and the age-old controversy over the commercialization of sport reached new heights. Writers were less likely to romanticize sport than to use it for the purpose of critiquing U.S. society and even sporting activities themselves. Many writers turned to sport to illuminate the experiences of women and of blacks and other ethnic minorities in the United States. In the works of Chaim Potok, Ralph Ellison, and others, sport contest and organizations represent the U.S. system or mainstream society against which the protagonist struggles while trying to find a respectable place in it. An excellent example of using sport to define the social experience of a cultural group can be found in Maya Angelou's poignant description in *I Know Why the Caged Bird Sings* (1970) of the 1935 heavyweight match between Joe Louis and Primo Carnero. Louis's victory translated into a collective one for African Americans in Stamps, Arkansas, who lived under the heavy burden of racial discrimination.

The post–World War II period also saw the expansion of sport literature beyond classic fiction and poetry. The sport autobiography and biography, women's sport poetry, and sport history all grew in popularity. With the first publication of *Aethlon: The Journal of Sport Literature* in 1983, the academic field of sport literature assumed a place in the very genre under its study.

—*Jack E. Davis*

See also: Faulkner, William; Hemingway, Ernest; Metaphor, Sport as, for Life; Oates, Joyce Carol; Sport Literature as Discipline

For further reading:

Messenger, Christian K. 1981. *Sport and the Spirit of Play in American Fiction: Hawthorne to Faulkner.* New York: Columbia University Press.

Umphlett, Wiley Lee, ed. 1991. *The Achievement of American Sport Literature: A Critical Appraisal.* Cranbury, NJ: Associated University Presses.

LITTLE LEAGUE

Little League changed the way children played baseball from an unguided, spontaneous approach primarily for fun to one of structure and organization focused on winning. Carl Stotz of Williamsport, Pennsylvania, created the Little League concept in 1939 when two of his nephews were denied access to local baseball fields by older boys. The concept of adult-supervised baseball for youths aged twelve and younger thus began and expanded rapidly across the United States in the 1940s and worldwide in the 1950s. Close to three million youngsters participated annually in Little League in the 1990s. In 1947, a play-off system was established between all-star teams representing each league and culminating in the Little League World Series played each August in Williamsport.

Before the popularity of Little League, children played pickup games whenever they had time, with whoever was available, and on whatever empty space they could find. There were no time limits and no adults to settle disputes or interfere with play. Children were said to gain independence and leadership from this experience, as well as proficiency in batting and fielding fundamentals through continual practice.

With the advent of Little League, adults assigned youths to a team through a talent-selection process. Teams competed in leagues under strict supervision, with formal practices and scheduled games played on community fields with diamonds two-thirds the size of major league diamonds. Players competed for awards and honors, and records and standings for the games played were maintained. Critics of Little League contend that the benefits of directed play, safety equipment, and learning the game have been more than offset by the inordinate emphasis on winning, which places a heavy physical and emotional strain on youngsters.

—*Charlie Bevis*

See also: Children in Sport: Competition and Socialization; Sandlot Baseball

For further reading:

McIntosh, Ned. 2000. *Managing Little League Baseball: Recollections of America's Favorite Pastime.* New York: McGraw-Hill.

Mitchell, Greg. 2002. *Joy in Mudville: A Little League Memoir.* New York: Washington Square Press.

LONDON, JACK (1876–1916)

One of the most widely read U.S. writers of all time, Jack London's personal and literary adventures have captured the public imagination worldwide. Born in San Francisco, California, London initially worked in a variety of jobs before earning a living from his writing after 1900. His first published piece, "Story of a Typhoon off the Coast of Japan" (1893), came after his travels aboard the *Sophia Sutherland*, which sailed between California and Japan.

After dropping out of the University of California in the spring of 1897, London headed north to take part in the Klondike gold rush. Although the trip left him with a serious case of scurvy and only five dollars, it provided him a wealth of experience that he soon turned into literary gold. When reviewers celebrated the compelling narrative of his first book, *The Son of the Wolf* (1900), London began to gain recognition. At the time, his fiction represented a fresh perspective that embodied a charismatic individualism constantly in search of new frontiers.

London initiated a series of lifelong adventures that served as material for his later books and publications. From these experiences, London created literary heroes who lived rugged, sporting lives; through these heroes, he inspired countless other global adventurers, including Ernest Hemingway. In the summer of 1902, he took up residence in London's East End. From there, he traveled to Japan and Korea in 1904, to Hawaii and the South Seas between 1907 and 1909, and around Cape Horn in 1912. In 1914, as a correspondent for *Collier's* magazine, he toured Mexico, where he developed a near-fatal case of dysentery.

London's writings concerned many important issues of the day, including race, labor, and gender relations. For a time, he was an advocate of socialism. After 1910, London increasingly devoted his attention to maintaining a ranch he purchased north of San Francisco. He died in November 1916.

—*Andrew G. Wood*

See also: Literature, Sport in

For further reading:
Acerrano, Anthony. 1983. "Jack London: Outdoor Adventurer." *Sports Afield,* December, 56–61.
"Literary Vagabond." 1991. *American Heritage,* November, 42–44.
Watson, Bruce. 1998. "Jack London Followed His Muse into the Wild." *Smithsonian,* February, 104–114.

LOPEZ, NANCY MARIE (1957–)

The first bona fide charismatic women's golfing champion of the television era, Nancy Lopez remains the biggest drawing card of the Ladies Professional Golf Association (LPGA) and its most popular golfer. Born in Torrance, California, Lopez was raised in Roswell, New Mexico. As a Latina American, she was allowed, as a young golfer, to play only on municipal courses until golf tournaments were instituted at country clubs. After winning the New Mexico Women's Amateur at the age of twelve and the U.S. Girls' Junior Championship at fifteen, she was awarded a golf scholarship to Tulsa University in Oklahoma.

When Lopez was a rookie on the LPGA tour, she earned more prize money than had any previous rookie, man or woman, by winning nine tournaments, five of them consecutively. She was the first woman to average fewer than seventy-two strokes per round, and she was inducted into the LPGA Hall of Fame in 1987.

Lopez's shot-making skills, infectious smile, unorthodox swing, and intense desire to win were partially responsible for the growth of the LPGA and increased television revenues for the sport. She transformed golf and gained acceptance for women's sport because she played with a sense of purpose previously unknown at that level and because she personified restraint. Her strong religious beliefs and her desire for professionalism as well as a home and family have endeared her to her fans, known as "Nancy's Navy."

In the 1990s, Lopez began developing her own

equipment line with the Arnold Palmer Golf Company, which features women's irons with a longer shaft.

—*Mike Schoenecke*

See also: Golf; Ladies Professional Golf Association; Palmer, Arnold; Television, Impact on Sport

For further reading:

Hahn, James. 1978. *Nancy Lopez: Golfing Pioneer.* St. Paul, MN: EMC Paradigm.

Vaughan, Roger, and Nancy Lopez. 2001. *Golf: The Woman's Game.* New York: Stewart, Tabori and Chang.

LOUIS, JOE (1914–1981)

Joe Louis, boxing's heavyweight champion from 1937 to 1949, earned the adoration and respect of all Americans, yet his career and image were constant reminders of the second-class status of blacks during that era. A man of quiet dignity in an era of powerful racial prejudice, Louis was often condescendingly referred to as "a credit to his race." Although most black Americans adored Louis as an example of black achievement, his popularity was, in large part, based on his willingness to live by a code imposed by boxing promoters, journalists, and his own handlers, a code that would not offend white sensibilities. He lived clean and fought honestly, never gloated or even smiled around a white opponent, and never posed for pictures with white women.

Two of Louis's fights illustrate his heroic status and the symbolic nature of boxing. His 1935 knockout of Italian boxer Primo Carnero was marketed as a metaphor, painting Louis as a symbol of black pride against fascist dictator Benito Mussolini's upcoming invasion of the independent black nation of Abyssinia (now Ethiopia). His 1938 title defense against German Max Schmeling, whom Adolf Hitler held as an example of Aryan supremacy, stoked the patriotic fervor of all Americans. Louis's first-round knockout of a rep-

The breeze from Joe Louis's left hook makes Welsh Tommy Farr gasp for breath during one of the fifteen hectic rounds of their battle at Yankee Stadium. "Brown Bomber" Louis took the decision, retaining his World's heavyweight title (ca. 1937).
(BETTMANN/CORBIS)

resentative of Nazi Germany helped popularize the notion of Louis as a genuine U.S. hero.

The boxer's stint in World War II, regularly featured in newsreels of the era and honored by the Legion of Merit Award in 1945, was an important part of the U.S. government's wartime propaganda. Although never the same athlete after the war, Louis held on to his title until 1949. His tragic later life, marred by irrational paranoia and tax troubles that forced him to take up professional wrestling, fails to obscure his status as a hero for not only black Americans, but for all Americans.

—*Aram Goudsouzian*

See also: Boxing; Discrimination, Racial, in Sport

For further reading:

Bak, Richard. 1998. *Joe Louis: The Great Black Hope.* New York: Da Capo.

Mead, Chris. 1995. *Champion Joe Louis: A Biography.* New York: Robson.

LUGE

One of the predecessors of the modern fascination with extreme sport, luge tobogganing is one of those "you just have to try it" sports that was not invented by some caffeine junky from a northern U.S. college, but it should have been. It is actually attributed to the Vikings and is recorded as a sport as early as AD 800 Luge was introduced into the Winter Olympics in Innsbruck, Austria, in 1964 after becoming an international sport in 1883. The U. S. participated in the first and subsequent Olympic events and U. S. doubles team, Gordy Sheer and Chris Thorpe, won silver in 1998. One does not have to be crazy to go screaming down an ice-hard plume at eighty miles per hour flat on one's back on a sled, protected only by a layer of spandex and a helmet, but it helps. Teams or singles, men or women, with no limit on size or endurance, lugers need only to be able to see between their feet to rocket successfully down the course.

A typical luger steers by slightly lifting the front tip of the inside runner, toeing in the opposite runner tip, and shifting the weight over the inside runner. It is a difficult combination to duplicate from run to run or to execute well during any run. Luges are not accident free, and falling off guarantees a long and bumpy, though not necessarily bruising, slide. Wearing knee and elbow pads is common sense. At least one death from luging has been recorded. Since luge runs lack the running start of bobsled runs, luge courses are a bit steeper in order to facilitate acceleration: gravity, ice, and sharp runners do the rest of the work. Excess weight does not make a luge faster, but a smooth, small frontal profile does. The sled weighs a maximum of 44 pounds, and is a maximum of 59 inches long and 17.5 inches wide.

In modern sport, luge has taken on a new profile: that of street luging in extreme sport or of downhill runs on concrete as a thrill ride in amusement areas.

—*Charles Moore*

See also: Olympic Games

For further reading:

Bingham, Walter. 1987. "Pathway to the Olympics: Speed." *Sports Illustrated,* December 14, 67, 51–58.

Johnson, Phil. 1988. "Luge." *WomenSports,* December, 39–43.

Walmsley, Ann. 1988. "Courting Danger." *Maclean's,* February, 154.

M

MACLEAN, NORMAN
(1902–1990)

The acclaimed author of *A River Runs Through It* (1976), Norman Maclean helped increase interest among Americans in fly-fishing as both a physical sport and a spiritual practice. Born in Clarinda, Iowa, in 1902, Maclean received a bachelor's degree from Dartmouth College in 1924 and a doctorate from the University of Chicago in 1940. He worked as a logger and forest ranger in Montana and Idaho and rose to become the William Rainey Harper Professor of English at the University of Chicago, where he taught from 1930 until his retirement in 1973.

Maclean devoted much of his retirement to writing. His first book, *A River Runs Through It and Other Stories* (1976), was the first work of fiction published by the University of Chicago Press. Considered for the Pulitzer Prize in 1977, *A River Runs Through It and Other Stories* was also a popular success. It increased interest among Americans in the sport of fly-fishing, especially after the release in 1992 of a film version of the title novella, directed by Robert Redford and starring Brad Pitt.

A semiautobiographical account of Maclean's youth spent fly-fishing on the Big Blackfoot River in western Montana, *A River Runs Through It* has often been compared to Ernest Hemingway's "Big Two-Hearted River" (1925), another classic fishing tale. Unlike Hemingway's story, however, Maclean's novella addresses the relationship between fly-fishing and religion. With his father, a Scottish-born Presbyterian minister, Maclean is forced to confront the mysteries of existence when his younger brother Paul, a remarkably talented fisherman, is senselessly killed in a gambling brawl.

Maclean's second book, published posthumously as *Young Men and Fire* (1992), concerns Montana's Mann Gulch Fire of 1949. It received the National Book Critics Circle Award in 1992.

—*Daniel J. Philippon*

See also: *The Compleat Angler;* Fishing, Fly and Bait; Literature, Sport in; Religion and Sport

For further reading:

Maclean, Norman. 1953. *The Years of Fulfilment.* London: Hodder and Stoughton.

McFarland, Ron. 1993. *Norman Maclean.* Boise, ID: Boise State University.

MADISON SQUARE GARDEN

Madison Square Garden has hosted nearly every sort of event, sporting and otherwise, in U.S. popular culture, and its location in the heart of New York City assures that the Garden and the events it holds are in the forefront of public entertainment and media coverage. Madison Square Gar-

New York City's Madison Square Garden marquee showing the last advertising of a heavyweight championship fight at the old Garden before the future bouts shift to the new Madison Square Garden later in 1967 (March 3, 1967). (BETTMANN/CORBIS)

den has undergone several incarnations in its long existence. In 1874, it was located in an old railroad terminal on Madison Square; in 1890, it was rebuilt under the auspices of society architect Stanford White; and in 1925, boxing promoter Tex Rickard developed plans for a new, uptown Madison Square Garden. It was there that the Garden entered the national consciousness as a venue for sporting events and pop-culture happenings. In 1968, Madison Square Garden reached its final and present location on the site of the old Pennsylvania Station.

Although the Garden has become famous in all areas of U.S. culture, the arena is most famous for its role as a host to major sporting events. Numerous professional sport teams have called the arena home. College basketball grew to national stature through the National Invitation Tournament, and indoor track and field became part of the sporting public's consciousness as a result of the Millrose games. By the 1930s, Fight Night at Madison Square Garden became the world's premier showcase for boxing. Joe Louis fought in the New York arena for much of his career. The Garden gained its magnetic allure by showcasing such stars as Sugar Ray Robinson as well as by presenting numerous championship fights, including the 1971 Muhammad Ali–Joe Frazier rematch in which Frazier won a bitterly fought unanimous decision. It also presented hockey and basketball games. In June 1994, the New York Rangers won the Stanley Cup on Garden ice, breaking a fifty-four year championship drought. In 1970, the New York Knicks defeated the Los Angeles Lakers in an epic series to win their first National Basketball Association championship.

—*Derek Catsam*

See also: Ali, Muhammad; Boxing; Louis, Joe

For further reading:
Durso, Joseph. 1979. *Madison Square Garden: 100 Years of History.* New York: Simon and Schuster.

MADISONS (SIX-DAY RACES)

Madisons, or six-day races, were the most grueling, popular, and lucrative urban sporting events in the United States between 1890 and 1930. Initially, bicycle riders in the Madisons literally competed for six days, twenty-four hours a day. By 1900, most U.S. and many European cities had velodromes, where six-day races drew large crowds. Good riders were well paid; in 1920, when Herman "Babe" Ruth was paid the kingly salary of $20,000 a year by the New York Yankees, some riders in the Madis-

ons were making similar or higher wages, often $700 to $1,000 for a week's competition.

The most famous six-day race in the United States was held in New York City's Madison Square Garden. Beginning in 1891, the annual activity quickly became one of the city's greatest social events, where men and women, rich and poor, black and white rubbed elbows, listened to the latest jazz bands and songwriters, and screamed encouragement to their heroes. When New York passed a law in 1898 limiting single competitors to riding twelve hours per day, Madison Square Garden's promoter brought in two-man tag teams, generating even more excitement and larger crowds. Due to the increase in the sport's popularity as a result of its association with Madison Square Garden, six-day races are known worldwide as "Madisons." In addition to promoter's prizes, Madison racers competed in midrace sprints for large cash awards offered by fans, such as Al Jolson, Douglas Fairbanks, and Bing Crosby.

In the United States, the sport declined rapidly in the 1930s with the onset of the Great Depression, the rise of automobile racing, and the deaths of key promoters. However, Madison races are still popular in Europe, offering a midwinter sporting spectacle for cycling fans.

—*Daniel R. Mandell with Scott E. Sherman*

See also: Bicycling; Madison Square Garden

For further reading:
Battista, Garth, ed. 1994. *The Runner's Literary Companion: Great Stories and Poems about Running.* New York: Breakaway Books.
McMeel, Andrews. 2002. *Looniness of Long Distance.* London: Carlton Books.

MALAMUD, BERNARD
(1914–1986)

One of the most acclaimed writers of fiction in the twentieth century, Bernard Malamud gave both impetus and artistic credibility to the sub-genre of baseball fiction with his early novel *The Natural* (1952). Bernard Malamud's impressive body of fiction includes the novels *The Assistant* (1957) and *The Fixer* (1966), winner of the National Book Award and the Pulitzer Prize for fiction in 1967, and the collection of short stories *The Magic Barrel* (1958), winner of the National Book Award in 1959. Malamud also had a long career as a teacher in New York City high schools, at Oregon State University, and at Bennington College in Vermont.

The Natural, made into a popular film starring Robert Redford and released in 1984, tells the story of Roy Hobbs, loosely based on Shoeless Joe Jackson of the 1919 White Sox, who was involved in the Black Sox scandal. Hobbs's ambition is to become the greatest baseball player ever, but his career ends before it begins when a woman shoots him in her hotel room. Later, at the age of thirty-four, Hobbs receives another chance when the struggling New York Knights sign him. His second opportunity, however, is clouded by personal failings, illness, and attempts to fix the league play-off game.

Malamud's novel rises above the realistic and comic approach of Ring Lardner's earlier baseball fiction and anticipates the later work of W. P. Kinsella by combining realism with fantasy within a moral framework. *The Natural* also includes considerable symbolism, and the story develops within the context of the Knight and Holy Grail legends. Although baseball did not remain one of Malamud's primary fictional subjects, he continued to use both realism and fantasy in many of his later works.

—*Edward J. Rielly*

See also: Black Sox Scandal; Kinsella, William P.; Literature, Sport in

For further reading:
Bloom, Harold, ed. 1986. *Bernard Malamud.* New York: Chelsea House.
Salzberg, Joel, ed. 1987. *Critical Essays on Bernard Malamud.* Boston: G. K. Hall.

MANLEY, EFFA (1900–1981)

Effa Manley successfully fought both racial and gender prejudice in the 1930s and 1940s as one of that sport era's rarest persons: a black woman involved in professional baseball. An assertive personality who strove to have her voice heard in all her endeavors, Effa Manley and her husband, Abraham, owned the Newark, New Jersey, Eagles of the Negro National League. Many of Manley's black colleagues, with whom she often argued during her campaigns for better playing conditions and a more responsibly run league, frequently resented her intrusion into their otherwise all-male domain.

Nonetheless, Manley worked from 1935 through 1948 to field and promote one of the most successful black teams, and the Eagles became the Negro World Series champions in 1946. She handled all their business and public relations duties and insisted that her team function as an important part of Newark's thriving black community. Manley was a civil rights advocate as early as 1934, when she was an organizer of a fair-employment boycott, and the success of her team and of the black population that supported it were uppermost in her considerations. She often used the Eagles as a fund-raising attraction, scheduling benefit games for such institutions as the Urban League and the Negro Hospital in Newark and selling "Stop Lynching" buttons for a dollar apiece to fans in the stands.

—*James Overmyer*

See also: Baseball; Discrimination, Racial, in Sport; Negro Baseball Leagues

For further reading:
Overmyer, James. 1998. *Queen of the Negro Leagues: Effa Manley and the Newark Eagles.* Metuchen, NJ: Scarecrow Press.

MANTLE, MICKEY CHARLES (1931–1995)

Through Herculean feats on the field, followed by personal tragedy and ultimate redemption off the field, Mickey Mantle, center fielder for the New York Yankees of the 1950s and 1960s, was the sport icon and popular hero of the baby boomer generation. Born in Spavinaw, Oklahoma, Mantle's prodigious athletic ability was evident at an early age and was his ticket off the tenant farms and out of the zinc and lead mines, which had been the fate of the men in preceding generations of his family. As a nineteen-year-old rookie for the Yankees, he was inserted into right field next to the legendary Joe DiMaggio, whom he was being groomed to replace. To avoid colliding with the aging and fragile DiMaggio while chasing a fly ball, Mantle contorted his body and incurred the first of an unprecedented score of injuries that curtailed his individual accomplishments.

Over his eighteen-year career—all played for the same team—those achievements were nonetheless the stuff of legend: Most Valuable Player three times, Triple Crown winner (for leading in home runs, runs batted in, and batting average), selected to the All-Star team sixteen times, holder of World Series records for home runs, runs batted in, runs scored, walks, extra-base hits, and total bases. He retired with 536 career home runs, at the time third only to Babe Ruth and Willie Mays, and was inducted into the Hall of Fame in 1974.

Mantle's gregarious off-field image was shattered in 1994 by his public confession to alcoholism, a battle he won following a stay at the Betty Ford Clinic. The victory was short-lived, however, because the following year it was revealed that his life would be lost to cancer unless he had a liver transplant. The apparently successful operation inspired Mantle to speak out against alcohol and drugs and, in particular, to spearhead a drive for organ and tissue donation. The culmination of this effort was the Mickey Mantle Foundation, which, even though his baseball career was glorious measured by any standard, is likely to be Mantle's most enduring cultural and societal legacy.

It is perhaps ironic that in the democracy touted as the strongest in the world, more citizens go to baseball games than vote for president. Mickey Mantle transfixed a generation, as did Chuck Berry, Elvis, the Beatles, and John Fitzgerald Kennedy. But whereas few could realistically aspire to be president of the United States or had the talent to sing or play, every kid could catch a ball. When the baby boomers were youngsters, a bad day became a good day if Mickey hit one out of the park. He retired in 1968, and by that culturally turbulent time, there was not and perhaps never could be another Mickey Mantle. For the baby boomers, Mickey Mantle was a compelling hero, and perhaps no one since has enjoyed the purity of that accolade.

—*Gerard S. Gryski*

See also: Baseball; Yankee Stadium

For further reading:

Castro, Tony. 2002. *Mickey Mantle: America's Prodigal Son.* Washington, DC: Brassey's.

Falkner, David. 1995. *The Last Hero: The Life of Mickey Mantle.* New York: Simon and Schuster.

MARATHONS

In the United States, the marathon, an extended footrace created in the late nineteenth century, has developed from a generally working-class sport, engaged in by only a small group of men, to an event in which over 300,000 men and women representing a broad social spectrum participate annually. The first marathon was held in April 1896 at the first modern Olympic Games in Athens, Greece. The race commemorated the 490 B.C. run of Pheidippides, who, according to legend, died after he raced about twenty-four miles from Marathon to Athens. There was no marathon footrace in ancient Greece, so the precise distance could only be guessed. Thus, early marathons ranged between 24.8 and 26.5 miles, with 26.2 adopted officially in 1924.

Long-distance footraces existed in the United States well before the advent of the marathon. The

American runner Joan Benoit jogs around the Los Angeles Coliseum track carrying the American flag after winning the gold medal in the first-ever Olympic marathon for women (August 5, 1984).
(BETTMANN/CORBIS)

nineteenth century, in particular, saw the rise of professional pedestrianism, a highly popular spectator sport involving walking, running, or both, sometimes for extreme distances. In the years after the U.S. Civil War, amateur races, facilitated by such groups as the New York Athletic Club, became increasingly popular.

The revival of the Olympics in 1896 helped promote widespread interest in amateur sport, including long-distance running. Inspired by the Olympic marathon, the Boston Athletic Association organized one of the first U.S. marathons on Patriots' Day, April 19, 1897. The Boston

Marathon is, aside from the Olympic marathon, the oldest continuously run marathon race in the world.

The Olympic marathons of the first decade of the twentieth century were both memorable and defining for U.S. long-distance runners. Although the 1904 Olympic marathon, held in St. Louis, Missouri, was won by an American, Thomas Hicks, his victory was undercut by the fact that another U.S. contestant, Fred Lorz, rode almost half the distance in a car, crossed the finish line first, and was offered a laurel before his "joke" was exposed and he was suspended by the Amateur Athletic Union (AAU).

In the 1908 Olympic marathon in London, Dorando Pietri, an Italian, crossed the finish line first but only after collapsing, receiving assistance, and thereby being disqualified. John Hayes, an Irish American, was declared the winner, but British and Italian sentiment favored Pietri, who received a replica of the winner's cup. This famous Olympic moment intensified U.S. interest in the marathon; indeed, it led to the "marathon craze" of the next few years in the United States, especially in New York City.

Until the 1970s, marathon runners in the United States were a relatively small group of skilled athletes, primarily working and middle class. Among the leaders in the 1920s and 1930s was Clarence DeMar, a printer from Massachusetts, who won the Boston Marathon seven times between 1911 and 1930. The New York Pioneer Club developed a significant marathon team in the late 1940s, and the Road Runners Club of America, established in 1957, actively promoted long-distance running and was important to the expansion of the marathon in the United States in the ensuing decades.

Following the growth of popular interest in physical fitness and jogging in the 1960s, the United States exploded in support of marathons in the 1970s. In Munich in 1972, for the first time since 1908, an American, Frank Shorter, won the Olympic marathon. Concurrently, there was a marked increase in the number of marathons held around the country. The highly publicized New York City Marathon, first traversing the city's five boroughs as part of the U.S. bicentennial celebration in 1976, was a primary catalyst for the marathon boom.

Since the 1970s, runners in marathons have increasingly been upper- and middle-class recreational runners. Over three hundred marathons are offered annually in the United States, some drawing over thirty thousand contestants. The social expansion has also extended to women, for whom the marathon was sanctioned by the AAU in 1972. An American, Joan Benoit, won the first women's Olympic marathon, which was instituted in 1984.

—*Anne E. McIlhaney*

See also: Amateur Athletic Union; Boston Marathon; Jogging; Olympic Games

For further reading:

Cooper, Pamela Lynne. 1995. "26.2 Miles in America: The History of the Marathon Footrace in the United States." Ph.D. diss., University of Maine.

Derderian, Tom. 1994. *Boston Marathon: The History of the World's Premier Running Event.* Champaign, IL: Human Kinetics Publishers.

Lovett, Charlie. 1997. *Olympic Marathon: A Centennial History of the Games' Most Storied Race.* London: Praeger.

MARBLES

As persons "knuckle down to business," "go for all the marbles," "play for keeps," or "lose their marbles," they seldom think of these phrases as originating in the simple children's game of marbles, which has long been a part of U.S. culture. Marbles existed before recorded history and have been uncovered in archeological digs on every continent, dating as far back as the Ice Age. In the United States, the settlers in the New World discovered Native Americans playing games with marbles. These indigenous peoples

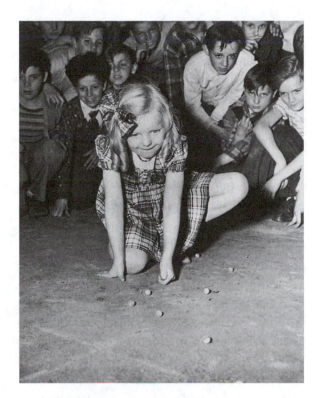

Six-year-old Nancy Raudenbush of Philadelphia is the youngest entrant in the Philadelphia Marbles Tournament. She's shown getting in some practice for the opening day of the contest on May 13, 1946.
(BETTMANN/CORBIS)

played marbles long before any European set foot on their soil.

Marbles have been played throughout U.S. history by all levels of society. George Washington, Thomas Jefferson, John Quincy Adams, and Abraham Lincoln played marbles. In more-recent history, marbles appear in the artwork of noted U.S. artist Norman Rockwell in *Marbles Champ,* in which two young boys look on as a young girl knuckles down to take a shot. Not only are marbles present in U.S. art, but they are also evident in the lyrics of a popular country music tune, "Dumas Walker," by the Kentucky Headhunters. Another window on U.S. culture is Charles Schulz's cartoon strip *Peanuts.* In one of Schulz's offerings, Linus is on all fours shooting marbles, proclaiming he has become a marble playing fanatic and announcing his entrance into the Rolley Hole competition held in Standing Stone State Park in Tennessee.

> *Marbles have been played throughout American history by all levels of society. George Washington, Thomas Jefferson, John Quincy Adams, and Abraham Lincoln played marbles.*

In the early years of the twenty-first century, the popularity of marbles waned among U.S. children, replaced in part by video and computer games. Marbles are, however, used in board games such as Chinese Checkers and Aggravation. They have also become a popular object of trade, with prices for a single marble reaching more than $5,000.

—*Chris A. Ayers*

See also: Artists of Sport; Cartoons and Sport; Language of Sport

For further reading:

Barrett, Marilyn. 1994. *Aggies, Immies, Shooters and Swirls: The Magical World of Marbles*. Boston: Bulfinch Press.

Grist, Everett. 2000. *Everett Grist's Big Book of Marbles: A Comprehensive Identification and Value Guide for Both Antique and Machine-Made Marbles*. Paducah, KY: Collector Books.

MARCHING BANDS

High school and college marching bands and high school and college football are inextricably linked and have been since both began to grow in popularity in the early part of the twentieth century. In the modern era, college football and college bands enjoy unprecedented media coverage and popularity. Large stadiums, improved instruments, and expanded competitions have significantly changed bands' programs; no longer are they the small, often inept, attempts at halftime entertainment and pageantry of the early twentieth century. Marching bands have also provided a venue for less-athletic students to participate in the glory of the contest.

Instrumental music and marching units have been in existence since ancient times. Early band music is associated with the military, royalty, religion, and athletics. In ancient Greece, trumpet contests were a part of the Olympic Games. Military bands began to develop in Europe during the Middle Ages and increased in size in the sixteenth century with the development of new and improved instruments. These bands were organized into three basic types: mounted, or cavalry; marching, or infantry; and civilian. These groupings provided functional music as well as music for public ceremonies and festivities.

In the American colonies, bands developed along European models, and several British military bands were present in North America during that time. George Washington, himself a flutist, recognized the importance of military bands and incorporated them into the Continental Army. Because of shortages, these units used only fifes and drums. However, the bands were important to the military for moving troops, providing entertainment, and performing for ceremonies and celebrations of victory. By the end of the nineteenth century, professional bands led by such visionaries as Patrick Gilmore and John Philip Sousa replaced military bands as the source of public band entertainment. Many of these groups were hired to perform during professional baseball games.

In the early part of the twentieth century, the popularity of performance bands began to decline with the advent of radio and film. However, two new phenomena—the increasing popularity of high school and college football and the U.S. school band movement—led performance bands to shift to high schools and colleges. Athletic competition and military training have long been associated; thus, the use of military-style bands at athletic competitions was logical. Bands provided stirring music to inspire fans and athletes alike as well as to entertain crowds during lulls in the action and before and after the contests.

The University of Notre Dame claims to have the oldest continuous college band; it played at the school's first football game, against the University of Michigan in 1887. The band has not missed a home game since. The Notre Dame "Victory March," composed by John Shea and Michael Shea in 1908, is probably the most famous college fight song of all time.

One of the most significant developments in college bands came in 1907 in a game between the University of Illinois and the University of Chicago. Under the leadership of director Albert Austin Harding, the Illinois marching band performed the first halftime show. Other firsts claimed by this group include the first homecoming, in October 1910; the first use of sousaphones at the collegiate level, in 1906; and the first performances at a televised football game and at the first color broadcast of a football game. Other institutions of higher education followed the trend toward establishing both football teams and marching bands. The Harvard Band, formed in 1919, has as its original stated purpose to support Harvard football and baseball. The high school band movement began in the 1920s with band competitions and the growth of instrumental music programs in schools, and marching bands became an integral part of the high school football experience.

In recent years, several trends have emerged. To be heard in the multilevel college stadiums built since the 1960s, bands need to be larger in number, and many major university bands are now over three hundred strong. Another trend is the increase in the number and importance of high school marching band contests. High school bands often prepare only one halftime show for the entire year, which they present in a number of weekend competitions throughout the fall. In many cases, these events are more important than the Friday night football game itself. In fact, for some schools, the Friday night high school football game is simply another opportunity to practice the competition show before a live audience, with the hope of being invited to perform in the Macy's Thanksgiving Parade or the Rose Bowl Parade often the driving force.

What true effect high school and college bands have on the outcome of football games is difficult to determine empirically or to quantify; however, the two remain intertwined and inseparable.

—*Joseph Borden*

See also: Football; Music and Sport

For further reading:
Holston, Kim R. 1994. *The Marching Band Handbook: Competitions, Instruments, Clinics, Fundraising, Publicity, Uniforms, Accessories, Trophies, Drum Corps, Twirling, Color.* Jefferson, NC: McFarland.

MARIS, ROGER (1934–1985)

Over the years, the public has elevated many baseball stars to cultural icons because of those players' drive to exceed standing records. New York Yankees right fielder Roger Maris's quest to break Babe Ruth's single-season home-run record sparked enormous media pressure, provided him with substantial economic benefits, and defined his career. As an all-around player on the last New York Yankee team to dominate baseball, Maris won the American League's Most Valuable Player Award in 1960 and 1961. In 1961, this man from Fargo, North Dakota, hit sixty-one home runs, eclipsing Babe Ruth's record of sixty home runs, which had held since 1927.

Before Maris broke the record, his chase prompted international coverage and a doubling of the number of U.S. newspaper reporters assigned to cover baseball. The Sports Broadcasting Act of 1961, which allowed professional sport and broadcast media to negotiate broadcast packages and included "blackout rules" to eliminate airing a live game on home turf, in addition to the expansion of AT&T's landlines and new cameras all came together to make broadcasting games more economically feasible and to widen their appeal to audiences and advertisers. In consequence, television beamed Maris's quest daily, and he endured this media barrage without the protection of an organization that could persuade media outlets to drop unflattering stories or to give them a positive perspective.

Several sportswriters viewed Maris as snarling or too dry. Some asked questions such as "How could you dare break Babe Ruth's record?" Weekly articles contrasted the equipment and the play during the two eras to find a quantifiable answer for Maris's success. On the other hand, fans generally supported Maris, sending him approximately three thousand messages weekly. Advertisers realized this support, and Maris became the highest-paid athlete off the field. He endorsed clothing and cigarette and shaving products nationally; co-wrote his autobiography, *Slugger in Right* (1963); and appeared on radio, on television, and in the Columbia Pictures film *Safe at Home* (1962).

Breaking the record defined Maris and established high home-run standards for other players, while limiting discussion of the other skills he used to win championships in New York and St. Louis. He died of cancer in 1985.

—*Brett L. Abrams*

See also: Baseball; Blackouts, Television; Marketing of Sport; Ruth, George Herman "Babe," Jr.

For further reading:

Maris, Roger, and Jim Ogle. 1963. *Slugger in Right.* New York: Argonaut Books.

Rosenfeld, Harvey. 2002. *Still a Legend: The Story of Roger Maris.* http://backinprint.com.

MARKETING OF SPORT

Sport no longer means a day at the park, enjoying a hot dog while watching a recreational event. It is big business. The game is no longer played exclusively on the field; it is also played across conference tables around the country, and the stakes are high. Sport has always been an important part of U.S. culture; U.S. fans have a powerful emotional attachment to both the teams and the athletes. Although the sport industry has gone through substantial changes during the latter half of the twentieth century and the beginning of the twenty-first, spectator attachment has only increased. The mass media brought sporting events to an ever-widening audience and helped push the price of sport contracts into the cosmos. Sport revenues skyrocketed during the last decades of the twentieth century. Revenue from broadcast rights alone was phenomenal. The National Football League (NFL), for example, enjoyed one of the most lucrative arrangements: Its agreement with the Fox Broadcasting Network guaranteed the league over $1 billion in broadcast revenue each year. The National Basketball Association (NBA) and the National Hockey League (NHL) quadrupled their revenue intake during the 1990s.

In response, athletes and their teams have adopted sophisticated marketing practices to tap into financial sources that were once subordinate to ticket sales. Marketers took advantage of fans' attachment to their sport in hopes of increasing product sales, awareness, and goodwill. With the market glutted, teams continually reinvented themselves as the competition for fan attention and dollars became a difficult and ongoing task.

Consequently, sport has become an entertainment industry of immense proportions. Although this largely market-driven phenomenon has benefited both the athletes and the fans, built successful sport franchises, and made professional sport accessible to more people, the changes have brought with them a sense of cultural loss. Ticket prices alone make a day at the ballpark out of reach for the average family. Nevertheless, there has been explosive growth of interest in sport in the United States, and much of this growth has been spurred by marketing efforts.

Athletes and products are marketed as part of a larger package. Although higher costs and excessive salaries have been criticized, the bottom line is performance. The athlete is still the most valuable commodity, and the most valuable marketing tool is, of course, a winning team. No one has control over that outcome, which makes image and ancillary products as important, perhaps more important, than the actual core product of the team itself. Outside the United States, the popularity of sport is dependent not on league expansion but on manifestation. Licensed merchandise is eagerly gobbled up worldwide, often with little relation to the failures or successes of the teams. The Anaheim Mighty Ducks hockey team, for example, was not even in the 1996 NHL play-offs, yet the team's licensed merchandise sales surpassed that of all other NHL teams. Clothing, in particular, is a major contributor to the merchandising profits of a team. What was once a fan-based desire to support a favorite team by wearing its logo has now become a fashion statement. Young children, teens, and college students—the market with seemingly the highest amount of disposable income—are particularly drawn to team apparel.

Individual athletes are also promoted for consumption. The idea of favoring an athlete over the team has been successful from a marketing perspective, for consumers tend to identify with an individual. This identification has brought the game to an intimate level and given it personality and recognition that is blended with on-court or on-field performance. Michael Jordan is the quintessential example of the athletes who have promoted the game, and themselves, through endorsement deals worth millions of dollars. Some wonder whether such personal financial windfalls, centers of power outside the control of the league, tarnish the sport and make individual athletes less inclined to perform. On the other hand, windfalls can come to all, and poor performance is rarely rewarded with commercial success.

Is the importance of sport marketing diminishing the importance of the athletic event? Is athletic competition at risk as more money and more priority are devoted to peripherals? The answer is, not necessarily. The future of professional sport lies in its packaging, since the teams that are to survive and prosper tomorrow must reach young fans with marketing efforts today. The core product is thus sold by building a larger, augmented product, a task that is only successful if sport knows its fans.

Regardless of the ever-changing tactics, success is a function of fan attachment to a sport. Judging by rising merchandise sales, attendance figures, and television ratings, interest in sport is at an all-time high, and professional sport is more popular than ever, remaining rooted in the cultural life of the United States.

—*Janice L. Bukovac*

See also: Apparel, in Sport; Endorsements; Jordan, Michael

For further reading:

Cashmore, Ellis. 1996. *Making Sense of Sports.* 2nd ed. New York: Routledge.
Schlossberg, Howard. 1996. *Sports Marketing.* Cambridge, MA: Blackwell.

MARTIAL ARTS FILMS

As a popular crossover between the action and adventure genres, martial arts films encompass the Chinese kung fu films of the 1970s as well as the karate and kickboxing films of the 1980s and 1990s. These films feature continuous high-energy, sophisticated stunts; adventurous heroes; nonstop motion, rhythm, and pacing; and plain old-fashioned fun. Martial arts films have been around for decades. Chinese filmmakers have created masterful martial arts–style fights since the *Wu Xia Pian*, the martial arts hero films, of the 1920s. The Mandarin term *wu xia pian* originally referred to the genre of martial arts films. "Wu xia" means chivalrous combat, and "pian" means film (http://www.brightlightsfilm.com/31/hk brief1.html).

In these films, the heroes could fly, fight with supernatural martial arts skills, control weapons with their minds, and shoot "death rays" out of their hands. Akira Kurosawa was one of the more notable directors to explore this genre, in *Judo Saga* (1945). Countless other directors and performers, some of them highly talented in kung fu or in acting and a few skilled in both, kept audiences on the edges of their cinema seats.

The *Gung-fu Pian*, kung fu films, of the late 1960s took on a more believable and realistic tone when the characters became more plausible and the fights began to flow more naturally. These films soared to new heights with the skill and expertise of numerous U.S., Asian, and other international actors.

There is a notable difference between U.S. and Chinese styles of martial arts films. U.S. stunt coordinators and fight choreographers have the opponents fight the hero unidirectionally and one at a time, with extended pauses between each technique. Chinese heroes move constantly, running, jumping, and throwing punches simultaneously at anyone who attacks them. U.S. and European martial arts film stars appear to have done their best fight-choreographed work in the early stages of their careers, before their personal popularity and paychecks grew. Once that happened, the number of fight scenes dwindled, the use of guns increased, and the choreography became sloppy.

The pinnacle of the genre, actor Bruce Lee, was elevated to cult status based on a string of action films made in Hong Kong and featuring karate, kung fu, and other martial arts. He worked as a karate adviser and stunt supervisor on several films before starring in the 1972 classic *The Big Boss/Fists of Fury* and in *The Chinese Connection* (1972). At the time of his death, he was publicizing his 1973 hit *Enter the Dragon,* and its sequel, *Return of the Dragon* (1973), which was released posthumously.

The action-packed *Game of Death* (1979) had been in production and was partially reshot and completed with body doubles for Lee. This film was released in 1979, some six years after the star's death, much to the delight of his fans. Although critics panned Lee's martial arts films, they were quite successful at the box office. Following the actor's sudden and mysterious death in 1973, a flurry of look-alike clones of Bruce Lee began to appear, but none were as good as the original.

The apparent successor to Bruce Lee is the popular Hong Kong actor and director Jackie Chan, who was the director of Lee's *Fists of Fury.* Since 1973, Chan has become a martial arts coordinator and film star as well as director, pleasing audiences with his hair-raising, acrobatic stunts and deftly choreographed fight scenes. Among his U.S. film releases are *Super Cop* (1992), *First Strike* (1995), and *Rumble in the Bronx* (1996). Although Chan owes his reputation to martial arts films, his acting role models are actually the great silent-era comedians Buster Keaton, Charlie Chaplin, and Harold Lloyd, who communicated through stylized movement rather than through dialogue (http://www.imdb.com/name/nm0000 329/). Chan, however, prefers to use his personalized movements, along with comedic touches, to give audiences a thrill of danger, not laughs. Like Lee, Chan, a veteran of forty-three films, performs all of his own stunts, is frequently injured in the course of filming, and shows those injury-making scenes as outtakes.

Belgian-born action-film hero Jean-Claude Van Damme has starred in several martial arts–related films. He began studying martial arts at the age of eleven and is a former European middleweight karate champion. Van Damme got his first break in a bit part opposite Chuck Norris in *Missing in Action* (1984). That role led to a contract under which he starred in a string of low-budget, action-adventure films, most notably *Bloodsport* (1988), in which he played American ninja Frank Dux. Those movies proved Van Damme's marketability as a leading cinema hero and earned him the nickname "Muscles from Brussels." Besides starring in films such as *Death Warrant* (1990) and *Double Impact* (1991), he also worked as a choreographer on *Kickboxer* (1989) and started a directing career with *The Quest* (1996).

Dolph Lungren, from Sweden, has also starred in action-adventure films in the United States in which he displayed his martial arts talents. He is a former heavyweight martial arts champion in his native country and was winner of the British Open kickboxing championships in 1980–1981 and of the Australian Open in 1982.

Among the most notable of the U.S. martial arts actors are Chuck Norris and Steven Seagal. In 1962, Norris was the owner of a karate school. He went on to win several professional world middleweight karate championships between 1968 and 1974. Among the films in which he had starring roles are *A Force of Action* (1979), *Forced Vengeance* (1982), *Missing in Action* (1984), and two sequels to *Missing in Action,* in 1985 and 1988. From 1993 to 2000, he was featured in the television series *Walker, Texas Ranger.*

Seagal, unlike his counterparts, studied martial arts under masters in Japan. He earned a black belt in numerous disciplines, including karate and aikido, and operated several martial arts academies, both in Japan and in California. He too has worked as a martial arts choreographer/coordinator on several of his films, such as *Above the Law* (1988), *Hard to Kill (1990), Out for Justice (1991),* and *Under Siege (1992).*

As in all other genres, there are both good and bad martial arts films. U.S. movie audiences apparently enjoy both and reward them well at the box office, even though film critics, with few exceptions, continue to give them thumbs down. One thing making these films likable is that many are so poorly done they fall into the category of camp. Along the way, this group of films has created a series of larger-than-life heroes and action characters, many of whom have found a niche in U.S. hearts.

—*Stephen Allan Patrick*

See also: Film and Sport

For further reading:

"Jackie Chan." http://www.imdb.com/name/nm0000 329/. Retrieved 6/15/04.

"Martial Arts Films." http://www.brightlightsfilm.com/ 31/hk_brief1.html. Retrieved 6/15/04.

Meyers, Richard. 2000. *Great Martial Arts Movies: From Bruce Lee to Jackie Chan and More.* New York: Citadel Press.

MARTIN, ALFRED MANUEL "BILLY," JR. (1928–1989)

Billy Martin was a Quixotic figure in the transition from sport conceived as U.S. leisure to sport as an outgrowth of the entertainment industry, in particular, and corporate America, in general. Born in Berkeley, California, to a dysfunctional family composed of an Italian mother and a Portuguese father who was a musician from Hawaii, Martin did not know that his real name was "Alfred" until junior high school. His grandmother had nicknamed him "Bellitz," Italian for beautiful, which his friends reduced to Billy.

As a baseball player, Martin had a rather undistinguished eleven-year career as a second-baseman with a batting average of .257, but he shone in postseason play, where he achieved a .333 average in five World Series contests, accompanied by stellar defensive play. Yet, it was as a manager that Martin made his lasting mark. He managed the Texas Rangers, Minnesota Twins, Oakland A's, and, in various stints, the New York Yankees. As manager of the Yankees, he variously won and lost and was hired and fired. His image of a baseball manager came from an earlier era, when the shop foreman was a senior worker elevated from the assembly line. That pitted him squarely against a cultural and organizational trend in which sport was becoming an entertainment industry, merely one element of a corporate superstructure. Martin was most noted for unsuccessfully contending with tempestuous

George Steinbrenner, the team's owner, and a variety of high-priced superstars, like Reggie Jackson—the quintessential case of small guy versus big guy. His playing and managerial careers were checkered at best; both were ended by a fatal car accident.

—*Gerard S. Gryski*

See also: Baseball; Big Business, Sport as

For further reading:

Golenbock, Peter. 1994. *Wild, High and Tight: The Life and Death of Billy Martin.* New York: St. Martin's Press.

Shropshire, Mike. 1999. *Seasons in Hell: With Billy Martin, Whitey Herzog and "the Worst Baseball Teams in History," the 1973–1975 Texas Rangers.* New York: Donald Fine Publishing.

MATHEWSON, CHRISTOPHER "CHRISTY" (1880–1925)

Many sport heroes become media darlings due to their quarrelsome behavior during games, their on-field charisma, or their off-field encounters with the law, but handsome, charming, and talented Christopher "Christy" Mathewson was not only a great baseball pitcher but also a real-life Frank Merriwell and the symbol of the gentleman athlete. Born in Factoryville, Pennsylvania, on August 12, Mathewson was the eldest of six children. His father was a gentleman farmer; his mother came from a wealthy, long-established family in the Factoryville area. Both parents were strong advocates of education, and Mathewson was therefore sent to Keystone Academy and later to Bucknell University.

It was at Bucknell that Mathewson began to take on the image of Frank Merriwell, the fictional all-American hero. During the three years he was at the university, before leaving in his junior year, he participated in three sports, received high grades in the classroom, was chosen president of his freshman class and class historian, played bass horn in the university band, sang in the glee club, wrote poetry, and was a member of several literary organizations, a fraternity, and an honor society. Being a touch taller than six foot one and good-looking only added to this image.

Mathewson's image increased after he entered the majors in 1900 and pitched for seventeen years in the National League, mostly for the New York Giants. On the field, he amassed 373 wins, threw 79 shutouts and 2 no-hitters, and helped lead the Giants to five pennants and one World Series championship. Off the field, he married his college sweetheart; read books; was outstanding at playing chess, checkers, and bridge; and was always courteous to his fans.

In part because of his talents but also because he was a cultured baseball star at a time when the majority of ballplayers were a rough lot, sportswriters and fans made Mathewson the symbol of the gentleman athlete. In reality, Mathewson was no saint. He smoked, drank in moderation, used profanity at times, and gambled at cards; once, in a ballpark brawl, he punched a rival team's lemonade boy. However, Mathewson's positive image has remained and was enhanced by his tragic death from tuberculosis at the age of forty-five.

—*Angelo J. Louisa*

See also: Baseball; Merriwell, Frank; National Baseball Hall of Fame

For further reading:

Robinson, Ray. 1994. *Matty: An American Hero; Christy Mathewson of the New York Giants.* New York: Oxford University Press.

Seib, Philip M. 2003. *The Player: Christy Mathewson, Baseball and the American Century.* New York: Four Walls Eight Windows Press.

MAYS, WILLIE HOWARD, JR. (1931–)

One of major league baseball's first African American superstars, Willie Mays is widely considered

Willie Mays expresses his appreciation after receiving two coveted awards from National League President Warren Giles between games of a doubleheader at Candlestick Park against the St. Louis Cardinals on July 4. The San Francisco center fielder accepted plaques for the National League's Most Valuable Player of the Year in 1965 and the Mel Ott Award for the Most Home Runs in 1965.
(BETTMANN/CORBIS)

the most exciting and perhaps the best all-around player in baseball history. Mays made his major league debut in 1951 at the age of twenty, only four years after Jackie Robinson's historic breaking of baseball's color line in 1947. Over the course of twenty-two seasons, from 1951 to 1973, with the New York and San Francisco Giants and the New York Mets, Mays thrilled baseball fans with his spectacular play and wholehearted enjoyment of the game. Although he excelled in all phases of the game, it was his amazing feats on the field that brought him his greatest fame. He is best remembered for "the Catch," his legendary over-the-shoulder grab of Vic Wertz's hard-hit fly ball in the opening game of the 1954 World Series against the Cleveland Indians.

Dubbed "the Say Hey Kid" for his favorite expression, Mays gained folk-hero status early in his career by playing stickball with children in the streets of New York City. He also became forever linked with two other baseball icons, Mickey Mantle of the New York Yankees and Duke Snyder of the Brooklyn Dodgers, in an ongoing debate over who was the best center fielder in New York during the 1950s.

Popular far beyond the baseball diamond, Mays became a permanent fixture on the U.S. cultural landscape. In 1954 alone, the Wanderers, the Nite Riders, and Johnny Long all produced songs in his honor. Mays recorded a song himself with the Treniers in 1954, entitled "Say Hey (the Willie Mays Song)."

—*Robert P. Nash*

See also: Baseball; Robinson, Jack Roosevelt "Jackie"

For further reading:

Burkhardt, Mitch. 1992. *Willie Mays: Black American Series.* Los Angeles: Holloway House.
McDonald, Thomas "Porky." 2002. *Over the Shoulder and Plant on One: An Irishman's Tribute to Willie Mays.* Bloomington, IN: First Books.

MEN'S ISSUES

By occupying a central place in the lives of many men, sport has become an inseparable part of dominant notions of male identity. Men have always competed in sport, but only recently have scholars begun to focus on the importance of sport to individual men and to men as a group. A quick glance over the broad expanse of Western literature attests to the fact that male identity, loosely referred to as "manhood" or "masculinity," has always been closely tied to games and contests. Beowulf conquers several sea monsters and proves his worth by defeating Unferth in a swimming race; and Arthurian knights, such as Sir Gawain, gain a seat at the Round Table by feats of valor. Ben-Hur wins his freedom in a chariot race. Even contemporary novels, such as Bernard Malamud's *The Natural* (1952), John Updike's *Rabbit, Run* (1960), or Don DeLillo's *End Zone* (1972), have focused on the relationship between sport and male identity.

That relationship is so strong that the development of U.S. professional sport in the early twentieth century can, in part, be traced to crises in U.S. masculinity. Football, for instance, emerged as a unique masculine preserve in which men, facing important cultural shifts that threatened traditional paths to manhood, could retain a sense of masculinity based on physical prowess and conquest. Women were altering the face of the workforce, long hours on industrial assembly lines removed men from the pride of individualized labor, and the frontier, long a place where men could prove their worth, was rapidly disappearing. But on the baseball diamond and on the gridiron, men remained heroes who won greater glory through physical exploits, while women cheered from the sidelines. Even with the advances made in women's athletics, sport today is still seen as part of a larger masculine cult of distraction, a space that is separate from modern society, one that allows men to celebrate traditional masculine traits and to escape the advances of feminism, changing gender roles, and social and economic realities that threaten their manhood.

Although there is little doubt that sport is closely tied to dominant notions of what it means to be masculine, there is great debate over whether sport has a positive or negative effect on men's lives. Historically, it has been assumed that sport teaches men sportsmanship, sacrifice, cooperation, loyalty, leadership skills, and ways to overcome adversity, all of which allegedly prepare boys for the competition of the world of work. In addition, athletic participation has been associated with toughness, conquest, and winning—elements central to U.S. notions of masculinity.

Still, feminist scholars in the last half of the twentieth century argued that sport actually has deleterious effects on men. In their view, sport reconstructs hegemonic masculinity, a brand of manhood that hurts both men and women. For instance, they see a sport like football not as teaching men life skills but instead as encouraging men to abuse their bodies by using them as weapons, to view other men as enemies who must be defeated, and to see the only women in the game, scantily clad cheerleaders, as sex objects. Football, they hold, does not teach men to toughen up and have courage; it teaches them to be violent and willful. Allegedly, the eventual results of such sporting experiences include physical disabilities, a lack of intimacy with women, a lack of close male friendships, and alienation from a society that now elevates intellectual skills over physical exploits. Part of hegemonic masculinity is machoism, a type of hypermasculinity that springs from insecurity and fears about one's own self-worth yet manifests itself either in the aggressive, gladiatorial behavior typically seen in a sport like ice hockey or in the cultic glorification of the male body. The sport of bodybuilding, for instance, is often associated with macho posturing, with its emphasis on young men with exaggerated, muscular builds posing nearly nude before audiences who gaze at their impressive muscular girth. A traditionalist might look at such displays as signs of strength and power, but contemporary scholars have pointed out that many bodybuilders sculpt their bodies to compensate for a poor self-image, often suffering in silence behind their muscles, a rippling facade for their private fears.

Interestingly, some men have used sport to fashion unique masculine styles that differ greatly from either the idealized masculinity of U.S. mythology or the bleak version of masculinity advanced by feminists. Many Christian men, for example, play to glorify God by aesthetically using the body in athletic endeavor; indeed, the maintenance of the body as a holy vessel reflects their respect for God. Former tennis great Arthur Ashe wrote extensively about how African American men have always developed distinctive styles of play meant, in part, to resist white oppression. Adopting the standards of ancient Greece, many men play for their health, defining masculinity in positive terms as something that helps men live longer because it allows them to achieve a combination of intellectual and physical excellence that represents the highest level of human achievement. Hispanic American men, particularly those who have been in the United States for less than two generations, have used soccer to maintain ties to masculine standards that prevailed in their country of origin but that enjoy less prestige in mainstream U.S. culture. This process has always been vital in the United States, where men of various races, ethnicities, and nationalities have continuously contributed to the ongoing evolution of U.S. notions of masculinity. In all likelihood, this process will continue and become more dynamic as an increasingly diverse body of American men celebrate manhood through sport. Thus, while men play for different reasons, it is clear that sport is and will continue to be central to the divergent notions of manhood to which men aspire.

—*Don L. Deardorff II*

See also: Latino Sport; Muscular Christianity

For further reading:

Messenger, Christian. 1981. *Sport and the Spirit of Play in American Fiction: Hawthorne to Faulkner.* New York: Columbia University Press.

Messner, Michael, and Donald F. Sabo. 1994. *Sex, Violence, and Power in Sports: Rethinking Masculinity.* Freedom, CA: Crossing Press.

Oriard, Michael. 1993. *Reading Football: How the Popular Press Created an American Spectacle.* Chapel Hill: University of North Carolina Press.

MERRIWELL, FRANK

The creation of writer Gilbert Patten, Frank Merriwell is an idealized fictional character whose sportsmanship and integrity made him a hero to devotees of dime novels from the end of the nineteenth century into the twentieth.

Under the pseudonym of Burt L. Standish, Gilbert Patten conceived the character of Frank Merriwell as the embodiment of athleticism, honesty, and clean living. Though he played many sports, Frank Merriwell was fondest of baseball. This preference may reflect a time when baseball could be played by virtually anyone, with no special talent required, and games would spring up on sandlots and in parks throughout the country.

The adventures of Frank Merriwell began with the 1896 publication of *Frank Merriwell's School Days* in the *Tip Top Weekly,* a dime-novel series, and continued with stories of his younger brother, Dick Merriwell, and eventually his son, Frank Merriwell Jr., until the series ended in 1915. Throughout that time, Patten was the primary author, though other writers were engaged to continue the work when Patten stopped.

One of the most prolific and popular writers of children's fiction about sport, Patten watched his stories sell by the millions. He admitted in his autobiography that the stories gave him the opportunity to impart to his young readers a sound, moral education through the example of characters such as Frank Merriwell. Earlier attempts to socialize youth into positive behaviors were generally the province of religion; thus, Frank Merriwell is an illustration of the secularization of moral education.

—*Debra A. Dagavarian-Bonar*

See also: Adolescent Sport Novels; Children in Sport, Necessity of Play; Literature, Sport in

For further reading:

Rudman, Jack, ed. 1970. *Frank Merriwell's Schooldays.* Brooklyn, NY: National Learning Corporation.

Zuckerman, George. 1973. *Farewell, Frank Merriwell.* New York: E. P. Dutton.

METAPHOR, SPORT AS, FOR LIFE

Metaphors are essential ingredients of the primordial stew of life. Humans come to understand life through metaphor, through metaphor's appearance in story and through the accumulation of metaphor and story into mythology. Consequently, it is possible to understand life through the metaphor of sport.

The argument that sport serves as a metaphor for life is hardly a difficult one to support, especially in the twentieth century. Parents screaming at officials who are refereeing their children's baseball games; hooligans engaging, in the name of civic pride, in violence against an opposing team; nations galvanizing into support for an athlete with a shot at Olympic gold—such instances and others point out all too clearly that games are more than just athletic competitions. Victories are marked by a baptismal bucket of Gatorade, a garland of roses, a medal of gold, and the lifting skyward of the victor upon mass shoulders. On the other side of the coin, consider Charles Schulz's *Peanuts* comic strip, specifically, the annual autumnal ritual of Charlie Brown's attempting to kick the football that Lucy holds. Charlie Brown runs at it with determination animating his face; a foot arcs, a hand slowly moves the football, and a desperate wannabe jock falls flat upon his back again, stars dancing above his head. Charlie Brown would be the first to affirm that the *last* thing his unsuccessful kickoff attempt is about is football.

Therefore, to a certain extent, sport is no mere metaphor for life; sport *is* life, though not in the same sense as in Vince Lombardi's terse "Winning isn't everything. It's the only thing" (George, 2). Rather, sport and life are strands of the same web, innings of the same game, and, as Yogi Berra astutely observed, "The game isn't over till it's over" (Miner and Rawson 2000, 119). Though millions and millions of years have ticked away on the game clock, the game continues.

In *The Power of Myth,* Joseph Campbell argued

that the "mythmakers of earlier days were the counterparts of our artists" (1988, 107). The notion that modern artists are mythmakers has a corollary: Modern athletes, like those throughout the past, are artists and mythmakers both. Mircea Eliade, in *Myth and Reality*, argued that myth supplies "models for human behavior and, by that very fact, gives meaning and value to life. To understand the structure and function of myths in these traditional societies not only serves to clarify a stage in the history of human thought but also helps to understand a category of our contemporaries" (1963, 2). Furthermore, Campbell identified four functions of myth: first, the "mystical function," the awareness of "what a wonder the universe is, and what a wonder you are, and experiencing awe before the mystery" (1988, 38); second, the "cosmological dimension," the scientific understanding that, far from diminishing the awe, reinforces the mystery (1988, 39); third, the "sociological function," which is "supporting and validating a certain social order" (1988, 39); and last, the "pedagogical function, how to live a human lifetime under any circumstances" (1988, 39). Sport—simultaneously both metaphor and mythology, disguised in the trappings of play—fulfills, now as throughout the past, the same four functions of myth described by Campbell and serves as those "models for human behavior" of which Eliade wrote.

As a child, one finds all manner of delight in the abilities to crawl, walk, climb, run, and jump, but as adults, many outgrow this once-held awe. Some, leaving adolescence behind, study the mechanics that allow athletic performance, leaving behind also the individual delight and awe. Sociologically, sport has shaped civic and national identities: Christians pitted against wild animals, gladiators, and instruments of torture, all in the name of "sport"; championships, such as the World Series; international competitions, such as World Cup soccer, Davis Cup tennis, and the Olympic Games—these often feature the warrior as athlete to fight battles on another kind of playing field. If the mystical function is marked by awe and the cosmological function is marked by X's and O's and velocities and resistance formulas, then the sociological function of sport is marked by box scores and obituaries. As for the pedagogical function, sport, like myth, clearly has the potential to teach as much through failures as through successes.

Mythologies that developed throughout the ages depict one incredible athletic performance after another. Creation myths mirror intense physical lives. The gods performed incredible feats, and humans aspired to similar feats: finding the Northwest Passage, scaling Mount Everest, swimming the English Channel, cycling across North America—thus aspiring to the powers of the gods. Whether a pantheon such as the Greek gods, Murderer's Row, the Gashouse Gang, the Bad News Bears, America's Olympic Dream Team or the Four Horsemen of Notre Dame, or an individual such as Zeus, Diana, Babe Ruth, Babe Didrikson, Dizzy Dean, "Golden Bear" Jack Nicklaus, or Sisyphus, who came to play day in and day out—each has left a far-reaching legacy, one that extends forward to the future, taking the world into a new millennium. The roots of sport are as complex as any mythology: archetypal roots that echo evolutionary beings; mythological roots that guide us in being human; sociological roots that often pit Us versus the Other; psychological roots that bear upon the need to excel, to succeed, to lead, to receive accolades, even adulation; physiological roots that include a release of endorphins, a chemical reaction that enhances the ability to run, to throw, to jump, or to swing from branch to branch. In the modern era, humans may have to content themselves with throwing baseballs rather than hurling thunderbolts, or they might experience, with Charlie Brown, the eternal return of defeat each autumn. But regardless of the instru-

> *The argument that sport serves as a metaphor for life is hardly a difficult one to support, especially in the twentieth century.*

ments used, the competitors faced, the venues played, humans remain enamored of sport and the metaphor inherent in it.

—*Joseph Rice*

See also: Language of Sport; Literature, Sport in

For further reading:

Campbell, Joseph. 1983. "Mythologies of the Primitive Hunters and Gatherers." Part 1 of *The Way of the Animal Powers,* vol. 1 of *Historical Atlas of World Mythology.* New York: Van der Marck, 1983. Reprint: New York: Perennial Library.

———. 1988. *The Power of Myth.* With Bill Moyers. Ed. Betty Sue Flowers. New York: Anchor Books.

Eliade, Mircea. 1963. *Myth and Reality.* Trans. Willard R. Trask. New York: Harper and Row.

George, Gary, ed. 1997. *Winning is a Habit: Vince Lombardi on Winning, Success, and the Pursuit of Excellence.* New York: HarperResource.

Leeming, David, and Margaret Leeming. 1994. *A Dictionary of Creation Myths.* New York: Oxford University Press.

Miner, Margaret, and Hugh Rawson. 2000. *The New International Dictionary of Quotations. 3rd edition.* New York: Signet.

Sagan, Carl. 1977. *The Dragons of Eden.* New York: Random House.

Strickland, Carol. 1992. *The Annotated Mona Lisa.* Kansas City, MO: Andrews McMeel.

MEXICO CITY SUMMER OLYMPIC GAMES, 1968

During the Summer Olympic Games of 1968 in Mexico City, African American athletes used international sport's most visible event as the stage for a dramatic expression of civil rights and black power sentiment, creating a controversy in the United States and raising questions about the relationship between sport and politics. Few who witnessed Tommie Smith's and John Carlos's black power salute on the medal stand on October 16, 1968, following their gold and bronze medal performances in the 200-meter race at the Mexico City Olympic Games, could remain neutral about the sentiments behind their protest. Fewer still could challenge the symbolic significance of their actions. Nor was it possible to explain their stance as the actions of isolated extremists, for although they provided the most public protest of those games, their deed articulated a political sentiment that was widespread among African American athletes competing for the United States. Smith's and Carlos's stance on the podium during the playing of the U.S. national anthem—in stocking feet, wearing black beads and a black scarf and with their black-gloved fists raised over their heads—used sport's biggest stage to air black grievances about racial injustice in the United States.

The Mexico City Olympics occurred during a transitional period in the African American civil rights movement. Although the movement had achieved important successes in gaining legal protection for African Americans, particularly in dismantling the Jim Crow laws mandating segregation in the southern states, the movement had been less successful in ameliorating economic disparity between whites and blacks. Frustrated by white America's lack of commitment to change, many younger African Americans, especially men, increasingly supported the more militant black power wing of the movement, turning away from older leaders who emphasized alliances with white liberals.

These changes were reflected within the world of sport. Led by Harry Edwards, a sociologist at San Jose State University in the late 1960s, a group of fifty to sixty African American athletes representing several sports, particularly track and field, formed the Olympic Project for Human Rights, an organization that hoped to use its visibility within the world of sport for political action. However, reflecting prejudices that existed even among the individuals fighting against bigotry, project membership was limited to men. Although the majority of members of the project rejected a suggestion that they boycott the Mex-

American sprinters Tommie Smith and John Carlos raise their fists and give the black power salute at the 1968 Olympic Games in Mexico City. The move was a symbolic protest against racism in the United States. Smith, the gold medal winner, and Carlos, the bronze medal winner, were subsequently suspended from their team for their actions. (BETTMANN/CORBIS)

ico City games in protest, some athletes resolved to take individual action. The assassination of civil rights leader Martin Luther King Jr. in April 1968 only heightened tensions in the months leading up to the games, as did attempts by the white Olympic leadership to allow South Africa to participate in the games despite that nation's policy of racial apartheid.

The 1968 Summer Olympics featured tremendous performances by African American athletes, as many resolved to make their statement through competition. African American athletes won ten gold medals and set seven world records in track and field. Several black athletes, including heavy-

weight boxer George Foreman, also won gold medals in other events.

But it was ultimately Smith's and Carlos's gesture that attracted controversy. Both men were stripped of their medals, becoming the only athletes ever denied medals by the U.S. Olympic Committee for political reasons. Their protest, however, highlighted the relationship among race, politics, and sport in their era, much as Jesse Owens's victories in the 1936 Berlin games had done for his era.

—*John Smolenski*

See also: Civil Rights and Sport; Discrimination, Racial, in Sport; Edwards, Harry; Olympic Games

For further reading:
Bass, Amy. 2002. *Not the Triumph but the Struggle: The 1968 Olympics and the Making of the Black Athlete.* Minneapolis: University of Minnesota Press.

MINNESOTA FATS
See Wanderone, Rudolf, Jr., "Minnesota Fats"

MONTANA, JOE (1956–)

Known as the Comeback Kid among his teammates, his opposition and his many fans, Joe Montana represented the true grit required to be a great football star. In the 1980s, Joe Montana was the paragon of professional athletics, an All-American football quarterback with a squeaky-clean image who epitomized humility and quiet dignity in an era when the brash, trash-talking athletes were attracting increasing attention, but he is probably best remembered for saving thirty-one of his career games in the 4th quarter (http://www.thedebster.com/magic.html).

A native of western Pennsylvania, Montana attended Notre Dame and led the Fighting Irish to a national championship in 1977. Although only

Quarterback Joe Montana throwing the football (January 22, 1989). In his third year with the San Francisco 49ers, starting quarterback Montana led the team to its first Super Bowl title.

(REUTERS/CORBIS)

a third-round draft pick in 1979, Montana was the starting quarterback for the San Francisco 49ers by 1980, and in his third year, he led the team to its first Super Bowl title. In addition, the team, under his leadership, won world championships after the 1984, 1988, and 1989 seasons, and Montana became the only three-time winner of the Super Bowl Most Valuable Player Award.

Montana is perhaps best known for leading dramatic comebacks. He led Notre Dame to a victory over Houston in the 1979 Cotton Bowl, while fighting off the flu by downing chicken soup at halftime, and overcoming a 22-point deficit in the final eight minutes. He engineered long drives in the closing minutes of the 1982 National Football Conference (NFC) championship game and during Super Bowl XXIII.

Montana's comebacks were not limited to games, however. In 1986, he underwent career-threatening back surgery but returned to the field within six weeks. In addition, he suffered a wrist injury in the 1991 NFC championship game that caused him to miss the 1991 season and most of the 1992 season. Thus, he became a role model for persistence in the face of adversity for many young players. He was traded to the Kansas City Chiefs, where he retired after the 1994 season.

Joe Montana is considered by many to be the greatest quarterback ever. In his honor, Ismay, Montana, population twenty-two, even changed its name to Joe.

—*Richard D. Loosbrock*

See also: Football

For further reading:

Hetz, Stanley. 2000. *Joe Montana: Just Another Player.* Philadelphia: Xlibris Press.
"Joe Montana." http://www.thedebster.com/magic .html. Retrieved 6/15/04.

MOUNTAINEERING

North American mountaineering is distinguished from its European roots by practices and appeals to enthusiasts that are closely related to cultural notions about personal challenge and the joy of activity in wilderness settings. People have climbed mountains for a variety of reasons unconnected to recreation. Native Americans in the West climbed peaks for hunting or religious purposes, and white explorers attempted prominent summits for the publicity associated with a first ascent. As a sport, though, mountaineering is distinguished from these pursuits and from related activities like mountain hiking in two ways: First, in practice, mountaineering is ascending peaks by routes from which a fall could have serious consequences, and the tools used by climbers, such as ropes and ice axes, are thus designed to facilitate safe passage. And second, in motivation, mountaineers achieve gratification by overcoming the challenges imposed by terrain and environment.

Mountaineering developed in Europe in the mid-nineteenth century, the result of the English leisure class's changing romantic sensibilities toward mountain landscapes and of improved transportation into the Alps. The mountaineering tradition was transplanted to the Canadian Rockies, along with the custom of building climber's huts to ease the logistics of multiday treks. In the United States, the heritage was strongest in the Northeast, where the Appalachian Mountain Club, established in 1876, built huts and taught members the latest in European climbing techniques. Similar organizations introduced many to the sport. By 1900, group ascents, including by women, of the Cascade Range's volcanoes, California's Mount Whitney, and Colorado's Front Range peaks were commonplace. Mountaineering clubs, many with university affiliations, sprang up in coastal cities and even in the heartland of Chicago and Iowa City; these continue to thrive as social and instructional centers.

A fierce strain of individualism also runs through North American mountaineering history. The sport has never approached mainstream status, and elements of risk and adversity attract iconoclasts. Even if it is not done for the sake of school, team, spectators, or material rewards, competition is still a spur for climbers to attempt new and increasingly difficult routes. Most, however, climb for the sheer joy of movement in incomparable natural settings; it is no accident that a standard instructional text on the sport, published by the Seattle Mountaineers since 1960, is titled *Mountaineering: The Freedom of the Hills.*

Some of North America's noteworthy peaks, such as Mount Rainier, Grand Teton, Mount McKinley, and Long's Peak, are symbols of public lands, especially national parks, while others, by their location, are qualified for inclusion in lands reserved as wilderness areas. North American mountaineering has a tradition of self-reliance; parties need backcountry living skills in addition to climbing skills, a hearkening back to the mythology of the frontier that is part of the cultural fabric.

A number of people associated with the philosophical notions behind wilderness appreciation and preservation were climbers—Henry David Thoreau musing from the top of Maine's Katahdin, the Sierra climbs of John Muir and Sierra Club president David Brower, and the deep affection for the Cascades held by Supreme Court Justice William O. Douglas. North American climbers have taken this heritage worldwide, becoming leading voices in promoting low-impact expeditions to environmentally fragile alpine areas.

—*Timothy M. Rawson*

See also: Outdoor Clubs; Rock Climbing

For further reading:

Graydon, Don, and Kurt Hanson, eds. 1997. *Mountaineering: The Freedom of the Hills.* Seattle, WA: Mountaineers Books.

MUSCULAR CHRISTIANITY

Muscular Christianity is a religious attitude that places health and manly vigor, especially as evidenced in sport, ahead of piety or intellectual understanding.

The phenomenon dates to the early Victorian era. Generally associated with the Christian Socialist movement of the 1840s and 1850s and with British public schools (that is, elite private schools), it was shaped largely by the Reverend Charles Kingsley, especially in his novel *Alton Locke* (1850), and by Thomas Hughes, in his novel for younger readers, *Tom Brown's School Days* (1857).

Muscular Christianity actually has roots in the classical Greek view of harmony between body and soul. During the Crusades, religious soldiers expressed religious power as physical force, meanwhile slaughtering and being slaughtered in very unreligious ways. In the nineteenth century, conflicts among doctrinal religions, dissenting Protestant sects, and the Tractarian or Oxford movement and between religion, on the one hand, and science, the geological and biological theories encapsulated by Darwin, on the other hand, fostered this movement away from intellectual concerns and toward athletics as a preparation for the "game" of life.

In that setting, the stereotypical Muscular Christian was a gentleman educated in the public schools, nominally practicing the Anglican religion, active as a youth in cricket and football and as an adult in hunting and fishing, and always healthful and vigorous. His strength was overtly dedicated to God and the betterment of England. Most important, he did not waste his time with "effeminate" activities: he was rough and active, and masculine endeavors made his life happy. Among the practical reasons for requiring so much physical activity of students was the simple fact that it kept the youngsters busy; thus, they were docile in the classroom and dormitory.

In the United States, the need to present a masculine image is culturally embedded. The stereotype of the man who goes to war or even merely to work and later returns, victorious in his endeavor, to his wife and children is only slowly disappearing. Man's work, and sometimes his play, is often excuse enough to miss church on Sunday. Even the precedence given to Sunday games over Sunday church, with the idea of honoring God through athletic success, owes much to this same ideal.

Muscular Christianity remains alive in a most visible and direct way, as many college and professional athletes actively integrate Christian signs into their sporting successes: A team may huddle in a pregame prayer, a batter may make the sign of the cross before stepping into the box, or a running back or receiver may genuflect and briefly meditate with a post-touchdown prayer. Overtly Christian sport groups abound in inner cities and on college campuses. In many ways, the Young Men's Christian Association (YMCA) and the Fellowship of Christian Athletes practice the same Muscular Christian ideals as did their Victorian predecessors.

—*Mark D. Noe*

See also: Religion and Sport

For further reading:

Ladd, Tony, and James A. Mathisen. 1999. *Muscular Christianity: Evangelical Protestants and the Development of American Sport.* Grand Rapids, MI: Baker Books.

Putney, Clifford. 2003. *Muscular Christianity: Manhood and Sports in Protestant America, 1880–1920.* Cambridge, MA: Harvard University Press.

MUSIAL, STANLEY "STAN THE MAN" (1920–)

The most dependable hitter of his era in baseball, Stan "the Man" Musial, St. Louis Cardinals outfielder and first baseman, symbolized midwestern values in the transitional era following the breaking of the game's color line. Perhaps the most decent man ever to put on a baseball uniform, Musial led the St. Louis Cardinals to four World Series titles in the 1940s, and for two more

decades, he stood as one of the greatest hitters of his time.

Before the 1950s, the Cardinals were both the southernmost and the westernmost major league baseball team. Consequently, their games were broadcast on powerful KMOX radio throughout the Midwest, and Musial became one in a series of Cardinals icons. Modest and unassuming, he simply went to work at the ballpark day in and day out, symbolizing for many fans their shared work ethic, especially since he, as did they, worked for one employer for his entire career. Musial's popularity in the St. Louis region continued at a high level for decades after he retired in 1963. After retirement, he acted as an ambassador for his sport and was considered a hero by others of Polish ancestry. His teammates considered Musial a unifying presence in the clubhouse. After Jackie Robinson broke the color line, Musial refused to allow the issue of race to hinder the team's cohesiveness.

The son of a coal miner from Donora, Pennsylvania, Musial was originally a pitcher who could hit well, but he was moved to the outfield following an injury to his pitching shoulder. In later seasons as a first baseman, his personal statistics remained extraordinary for what became an ordinary team shortly after World War II. His nickname, "the Man," came from Brooklyn Dodgers' fans lamenting as he strode to the plate: "Here comes *that man* again." Among Musial's accomplishments were three National League Most Valuable Player Awards and seven batting titles, including one set in 1957 when he was thirty-six. He retired in 1963 in the top ten all-time in almost every major hitting category and was inducted into the Baseball Hall of Fame in 1969.

—*Mark Santangelo*

See also: Baseball

For further reading:
Roberts, Robin, C. Paul Rogers, and Stan Musial. 2003. *My Life in Baseball.* Chicago: Triumph Books.

Despite the 12-5 walloping the St. Louis team took from the Brooklyn Dodgers on June 3, 1955, the Cardinals' Stan Musial happily holds a bat attesting to his 300th home run. "Stan the Man" made sure his 300th was a good one; he drove in three runs on his fifth-inning homer.

(BETTMANN/CORBIS)

MUSIC AND SPORT

The relationship between music and sport has existed since ancient times. The Greeks included trumpet-playing contests as well as musical pageantry in their Olympic Games. Marching bands, pep bands, singers, and organs have been part of U.S. athletic contests since the latter part of the nineteenth century, often offering on-field opportunities to less-athletic students. The extent to which music has affected outcomes of sporting events may be indeterminable, but that there is a relationship between music and sport is undeniable.

Professional bands began playing for professional baseball games and college bands began playing for college football and basketball contests prior to the 1900s. The Notre Dame University band played for its first football game in 1887, and the University of Michigan band played for the first time in 1898. During the early part of the twentieth century, college and high school marching bands developed along with the growth of high school and college interscholastic football competitions. In the latter half of the twentieth century, the two became inseparable.

Music figures directly into certain athletic competitions. Free-style figure skating, ice dancing, and free-style gymnastics rely heavily on the coordination of the athletes' movements to music. In addition, Gallaudet University, a school for the deaf, had difficulty winning football games because the offensive line could not hear the signals being called and could move only when they saw the football centered. This put the team at a great disadvantage until they began to use a bass drum on the sideline to pound out a rhythmic cadence for the snap count, which the linemen, though deaf, could feel. As a result, the offense was able to move with the count, and the team began to win football games.

Some teams have tried to influence games by using music in subtle ways. During home games, one baseball team played upbeat music when its team members came to bat and played slow, sad music when the visiting team was up at bat. Whether this gave an edge to the home team or not, it was a psychological attempt to incorporate music to influence competition. In football, some larger bands often try to drown out the signal calling of the opposing team's quarterback. In basketball games, however, musicians are not allowed to use their instruments during the game because of the power of even small pep bands.

Organs have been a significant part of professional baseball in the United States. Most ballparks have an organ and an organist to lead the fans in cheers with the "charge" cadence and to provide entertainment between innings and during pitching changes. In addition to performing or accompanying the singing of "The Star Spangled Banner" or "Take Me Out to the Ball Game," the organist sometimes plays specific tunes for each home-team player as he comes to bat.

Though Stephen Foster's "Camptown Races" (1850) was the first U.S. song about any sport, the most popular U.S. sport song of all time remains baseball's "Take Me Out to the Ball Game." Written in 1908 by Jack Norworth and Albert von Tilzner, it became the number-one hit record of that year. The song remains the most frequently sung tune during the seventh-inning stretch in ballparks throughout the country.

Various sports have inspired composers writing in numerous musical styles, from opera to Broadway to ballads to rock 'n' roll. Athletes have also entered the realm of the singer and musician, from vaudeville to recording to film and television, but few have made the transition successfully.

In *Diamonds in the Rough* (1989), Joel Zoss and John Bowman describe how "The Star Spangled Banner" became associated with baseball games and, hence, with most sporting events. Because of the strong patriotic feeling during World War I, bands played the unofficial national anthem, officially adopted by Congress in 1931, at major league games during 1917–1918. During the seventh-inning stretch in the first game of the 1918

World Series between the Chicago Cubs and the Boston Red Sox, the band unexpectedly began playing the anthem. The fans sang along, producing a unifying patriotic experience for all. The future anthem was played again during the next two games, and when the series moved to Boston, the song was played prior to the start of the competition. Because of its popularity during the 1918 World Series, "The Star Spangled Banner" became a feature of opening games, holiday games, and the World Series. When public-address systems became standard features of ballparks, allowing recorded songs as well as live performances, the tradition became part of all major league baseball games. In the late twentieth century, the singing or playing of the national anthem preceded almost all sporting events throughout the United States; however, Zoss and Bowman point out that baseball, as much as anything, has kept Americans singing this most difficult to sing anthem.

—*Joseph Borden*

See also: Baseball; Football; Marching Bands

For further reading:

Zoss, Joel, and John Bowman. 1989. *Diamonds in the Rough.* New York: Macmillan.

MYTHOLOGY OF SPORT

The mythic dimension is a crucial part of the origin of sport, and it persists in many of the cultural practices and subtexts associated with sport today. In the 1998 race for a single-season home-run record, U.S. baseball offered an especially rich example of the mythic dimension at play. When Mark McGwire and Sammy Sosa vied for the title, both surpassing the decades-old marks held by Roger Maris and before him Babe Ruth, they inspired an important national ritual of mythic celebration. Their unprecedented feats in baseball, like all record breaking in sport, reenacted the Promethean theme of stealing fire from the heavens and providing humankind with a further

taste of its own heroic semidivinity through yet another unique achievement.

Such a mythic interpretation may seem overblown in light of the out-of-touch greed and corporate hubris often associated with professional sport. However, one needs only to begin cataloging all the ways the home-run race found its way into popular discourse to witness, for better or worse, a mythic drama infecting a culture. It was a metaphor for overcoming obstacles and "living the dream," for human potential, discipline, aspiration, and achievement. The home-run race was even spun in the media, for example, as a welcome relief from the collective sense of distress over the political scandals that permeated that season.

The mythic origins of sport in the Olympic Games are extended to the modern era in this most explicit and deepest-rooted contemporary inflection of sport mythology. The games began in Greece in 776 B.C. as a ceremony to honor the gods and the spirits of the dead. The great choral poet Pindar wrote odes that immortalized the games as a human expression of and tribute to the divine powers. The opening of the contemporary games, a torch relay that culminates in the lighting of the Olympic flame, is a tribute to their origins in ancient Greece. The Greeks kept a flame perpetually burning at the altar of the goddess Hera throughout the era of the initial games. The Olympic Flame Relay began in 1936 and traditionally employs thousands of runners to transfer the flame from the Olympia Stadium in Greece to the site of each contemporary Olympics as a symbol of connection to the games' ancient roots. The latter-day mythic resonance of the Olympics is carried in the five linked rings of the Olympic emblem, which symbolize the nations in unity, and at least one of the five rings' colors can be found on any of the world's national flags.

Since the first Olympic Games, sporting events have been conceived in terms of the standard mythic formula, what author James Joyce calls the monomyth and mythologist Joseph Campbell calls the hero's journey (1949, xx). Campbell summarizes the journey's pattern of rites of passage as separation, initiation, and return, stating, "A legendary hero is usually the founder of something . . . In order to found something new, one has to leave the old and go in quest of the seed idea, a germinal idea that will have the potentiality of bringing forth that new thing" (Campbell 1988, 136). The sporting event's "region of supernatural wonder" is its preconceived, ritual space and time; the "boons" brought home to the fans are the elixirs of vicarious victory and achievement, which, as in the home-run race of 1998, can spill over onto fans' sense of personal and cultural identities.

The mythic journey is played out in sport culture from Peewee leagues to high school sport to sumo championships and Super Bowls. Players go through regularly scheduled rites of passage with their communities on hand to see them off and to receive them at journey's end, whether those communities consist of pathologically competitive parents and a scared, jealous kid brother or a nation and a viewing public of millions. Fans and a few lower-echelon players themselves go over the trials and tribulations of their team's road schedule or injury roster at the coffeemaker or the local tavern. A home team's championship run offers a brightening influence on the mood of the community.

Among sport heroes and villains are the mythic archetypes that reflect particular attributes that fans choose to embrace or to vilify as part of their own identities: the deeply religious gratitude of a star runner, the extensive police record of the million-dollar wide receiver, the rise from immigrant roots in poverty to home-country hero on another continent, the cross-dressing crazy-haired anarchy of a defensive basketball forward, the humility and dedication, the arrogance and lack of self-control, the holding out for more millions in free agency, the love of the game for its own sake. The mythic formula is enacted in sport with every level of subplot: every at bat, series of downs, individual match, play-off series, full season, four-year Olympiad, and story of a career trajectory. The sense in which all human stories are mythic journeys from birth to initiation in culture to death makes the deliberate planning and scheduling of ritual journeys in sport an especially viable way of marking and expressing the universally human mythic impulse.

—*Geoffrey Rubinstein*

See also: Audience Rituals; Olympic Games

For further reading:
Campbell, Joseph. 1949. *Hero with a Thousand Faces.* Princeton: Princeton University Press.
Campbell, Joseph with Bill Moyers. 1988. *The Power of Myth.* New York: Doubleday.

N

NAMATH, JOE (1943–)

Confident and flamboyant, Joe Willie "Broadway Joe" Namath flaunted his prowess with women, guaranteed his team, the New York Jets, a Super Bowl victory, and became a symbol for New York City. On wounded knees and beneath the brightest lights, the confessed womanizing signal caller always delivered when pressed to fulfill, vicariously, every man's dream. Namath was born in Beaver Falls, Pennsylvania, a region famous for producing such legendary quarterbacks as Joe Montana, Dan Marino, and Johnny Unitas. As a student at the University of Alabama, Namath led the team under legendary coach Paul "Bear" Bryant to a national title in 1964, one year after Bryant suspended Namath from the team for excessive partying. Nonetheless, Bryant said Namath was the greatest athlete he had ever coached.

The New York Jets of the American Football League (AFL) agreed with Bryant and signed Namath to a contract worth twice what the other players were receiving. Namath's glamorous career and lover-boy image captivated New Yorkers. He sported a Fu Manchu mustache and wore white cleats, but little else about his image was squeaky-clean. Broadway Joe was a partial owner of Bachelors III, a Manhattan nightclub known for its questionable clientele. Namath used the club as his own private retreat, hanging out with celebrities like Elvis Presley, Frank Sinatra, and Dean Martin. Eventually, Commissioner Pete Rozelle ordered Namath to sell his share in the establishment.

Despite his raucous private life and despite playing with badly damaged knees, Namath managed to engineer an upset over the National Football League's powerhouse, the Baltimore Colts, in Super Bowl III, even though the Jets took the field as more-than-nineteen-point underdogs. His boast that he could guarantee victory rang louder than any since Babe Ruth's home-run call.

That victory coupled with Namath's good looks and personality led to multiple endorsements, his own television show, a spot in the *Monday Night Football* booth, and his autobiography, aptly titled *I Can't Wait until Tomorrow 'Cause I Get Better Looking Every Day* (1969).

—Bradley A. Huebner

See also: Athletes, above the Law; Football

For further reading:

Berger, Phil. 1969. *Joe Namath, Maverick Quarterback.* New York: Cowles.
Ralbovsky, Marty. 1976. *The Namath Effect.* Englewood Cliffs, NJ: Prentice-Hall.

DO NASCIMENTO, EDSON ARANTESM, "PELÉ" (1940–)

Possibly the greatest soccer player ever, Pelé is a popular figure all over the world. He has won converts to the game, fans for his Brazilian team, and

Soccer superstar Pelé runs with the ball during his first game for the New York Cosmos on June 16, 1975; the Cosmos played the Dallas Tornadoes.
(Bettmann/Corbis)

celebrity even in the United States. In his birthplace of Tres Coracoes, Brazil (in Minas Gerais State), the young Edson was called Dico by his family, but his soccer friends began to call him Pelé for reasons he claims not to understand. Aided by his father, Joao Ramos do Nascimento, who played professionally, Pelé developed his athletic skills with several amateur teams before joining the soccer team Santos in 1956 and being named to the national team, Selecao, in 1957.

In Pelé's years with Santos, the team won multiple state, national, and international championships. His Brazilian Selecao won three World Cups, in 1958, 1962, and 1970, when perhaps their best team permanently retired the Jules Remet Cup. Over his career, Pelé was credited with 1,284 goals in 1,363 games. Yet he was a multifaceted player, as much a dribbler, passer, and

field leader as a scorer, and he could head as well as kick. In many ways, it was Pelé's style more than his numbers that captivated admirers.

Pelé left the national team in 1971, retired from Santos in 1974, and played for two years with the New York Cosmos of the North American Soccer League (NASL), which ultimately failed. In the process of crossing cultural boundaries, Pelé began a long campaign to raise the level of interest in soccer in the United States. Part of that campaign included his insistence that the Fédération Internationale de Football Association (FIFA), soccer's international governing body, conduct a World Cup competition in the United States, a stance he took publicly when Colombia pulled out of hosting the event in 1986. When Mexico won the bid, Pelé joined Henry Kissinger and others in successfully pushing for a U.S. site in 1994. He later served as spokesperson for Japan in an effort that eventually allowed that country and Korea the right to jointly host the 2002 World Cup competition.

Among the most recognizable athletes in the world, Pelé held a multitude of jobs in entertainment and international business, coached youth teams, and served as Brazil's minister of sport. He had difficult times as well: failed commercial ventures, an emotional divorce, affairs with various women, criticism for not being more active politically, and disagreements with Brazil's soccer leadership. But he remarried in 1994, his finances flourished, and he remains an admired hero among his countrymen: "the King," the "Black Pearl" of Brazilian *futbol*.

—*Joseph L. Arbena*

See also: Soccer; World Cup Competition

For further reading:

Harris, Harry. 2002. *Pelé: His Life and Times.* New York: Parkwest.

Pelé. 1977. *My Life and the Beautiful Game: The Autobiography of Pelé.* With Robert L. Fish. Garden City, NY: Doubleday.

NATIONAL ASSOCIATION FOR STOCK CAR AUTO RACING

The National Association for Stock Car Racing (NASCAR) is the premier automobile-racing organization in the United States; millions of fans attend the events each year while millions more watch the races via televised coverage. NASCAR, consequently, provides a vehicle for the advertisement of products ranging from gasoline to laundry soap to tobacco, a product which has created controversy affecting many other athletic events.

NASCAR began with a three-day meeting of racing promoters and racetrack owners in December 1947. Under the leadership of William "Big Bill" France, Sr., the meeting resulted in the first NASCAR-sponsored race, which was run at Daytona Beach, Florida, on February 15, 1948. By the late 1990s, the association was a multimillion-dollar organization sponsoring two national levels of stock car racing, the Winston Cup Series and the Busch Grand National, a pickup truck series, and the regional Winston West Series. NASCAR-sanctioned races are held every weekend from mid-February until early November.

From a low point in the late 1950s and early 1960s, when the sport could not even draw support from automobile manufacturers, NASCAR racing became a major outlet for the advertisement of automobile-related products and also for nonautomobile-related products ranging from laundry soap to tobacco products to cable television channels. En route to becoming a marketer's dream, the sport suffered through periods of controversy. In the middle and late 1950s, the media and politicians criticized stock car racing for encouraging high speeds and reckless driving, and fans are accused of being ghouls who attend races only to see wrecks and bloodshed. In addition, sponsorship of the Winston Cup by R. J. Reynolds Tobacco Company spearheaded controversy over sponsorship of athletic events by tobacco companies and over the effect of tobacco use on teens. Added to that, NASCAR has been criticized for involving women as decorative beauty queens but not as competitors and because very few African Americans drivers compete in the races. Wendall Scott is the only African American to win a NASCAR race.

Even though the organization did not have strictly southern origins, NASCAR began the 1960s with a definite southern orientation. The stereotype of a typical driver was a redneck moonshine-runner who raced his car on weekends, and the cars were seen as models of the modified vehicles used by those moonshiners to store their wares and to escape apprehension. However, as the second generation of drivers, such as Richard "King Richard" Petty, Glenn "Fireball" Roberts, and Ned "Gentleman Ned" Jarrett, came to dominate the racing circles, NASCAR assumed a more mainstream image.

Race action during the NASCAR Nextel Advance Auto Parts 500 at Martinsville Speedway in Martinsville, Virginia (April 18, 2004).
(GEORGE TIEDEMANN/NEWSPORT/CORBIS)

The R. J. Reynolds Tobacco Company's sponsorship of the Winston Cup, beginning in 1972, changed the image of NASCAR. The infusion of tens of millions of dollars upped the ante and allowed car owners to spend much larger sums on their automobiles. By the late 1990s, NASCAR was a big-money sport with several drivers earning prize money in excess of one million dollars each year.

—*Harry E. Carpenter III*

See also: Indianapolis 500; Television, Impact on Sport

For further reading:
Hagstrom, Robert G. 2001. *The NASCAR Way: The Business That Drives the Sport.* New York: John Wiley and Sons.
Howell, Mark D. 1997. *From Moonshine to Madison Avenue: A Cultural History of the NASCAR Winston Cup Series.* Bowling Green, OH: Bowling Green State University Popular Press.

NATIONAL BASEBALL HALL OF FAME

Membership in the National Baseball Hall of Fame, the pantheon of the "national pastime," has long been one of the most coveted honors in U.S. cultural life, the athletic equivalent of the congressional Medal of Honor. Proposed by future National League president and major league baseball commissioner Ford Frick in 1935, the National Baseball Hall of Fame became a reality a year later, when a special committee selected five former players to be the Hall's first inductees.

in the Hall is invariably accompanied by an exhaustive public discussion of comparative statistics and performance, both in the press and among fans.

Guarding the integrity and standards of the Hall has become an important element of the game's mystique, and the cultural significance of Hall of Fame status is reaffirmed each year when inductees are enshrined during a public ceremony in Cooperstown. For serious baseball fans, a pilgrimage to the National Hall of Fame is almost obligatory and reinforces and personalizes the cultural meaning of the "national pastime."

—*Raymond Arsenault*

See also: Baseball; Doubleday, Abner, Myth of; Ruth, George Herman "Babe," Jr.;

For further reading:

Silverstein, Herma. 1994. *Basketball Hall of Fame.* Mankato, MN: Crestwood.

Smiling Jackie Robinson, who broke baseball's color line in 1947, holds a plaque after he was inducted into baseball's Hall of Fame (July 23, 1962).
(BETTMANN/CORBIS)

In 1939, Cooperstown, New York, the boyhood home of alleged baseball pioneer Abner Doubleday, became the site of a Hall of Fame building and museum. The prototype for the many sport halls of fame that followed, the shrine at Cooperstown celebrates the accomplishments of professional baseball's greatest players, managers, umpires, owners, and writers as well as the general history and heritage of the game. Over the past six decades, the Hall has developed an elaborate selection process for those who will be included. To be elected to the Hall of Fame, an individual must receive an affirmative vote from 75 percent of the votes cast by the National Association of Baseball Writers. Consideration for membership

NATIONAL BASKETBALL ASSOCIATION

The National Basketball Association (NBA) is the first and only established, long-running, professional basketball league in U.S. history. Although many other leagues have come and gone, the NBA has thrived by consuming or eclipsing its competition, thus equating itself with basketball supremacy worldwide in the minds of fans, players, and the media. Furthermore, and in more recent times, it has set the standard for sport marketing and provided a forum and showcase for black masculine performances.

Early Years

It is significant that the NBA marks its origin with the founding of the Basketball Association of America (BAA) on November 1, 1946. A group of arena owners made up the BAA and entered the basketball business primarily to fill their arenas year-round. These men had extensive experience in sport promotion, albeit very little or none in basketball. Nevertheless, their marketing acumen has shaped and guided the NBA philosophy over the years.

The NBA must be credited for making basketball a national phenomenon, while simultaneously associating the sport with urban cities. When the BAA and the National Basketball League (NBL) merged in 1949, the owners renamed the new creation the National Basketball Association and sought to emphasize the "national" component of the title. Prior to this partnership, there had been several fledgling pro basketball leagues throughout the country, but those groups primarily catered to regional interests. The NBL, for example, had teams in Fort Wayne and Indianapolis, Indiana, and in Waterloo, Iowa, while the BAA teams played in major metropolitan areas, like Boston, New York, and Detroit. Under the guidance of Maurice Podoloff, the original BAA commissioner, the NBA expanded from coast to coast. By 1962, all of its teams had moved to major cities, where they could play in larger arenas.

NBA basketball development coincided with an explosion in electronic communications, including sport broadcasts on radio. The invention of television had a great impact on the league's growth and marketing. For instance, in 1954, league executives established the 24-second shot rule (in essence, forbidding a team to have possession of the ball for more than twenty-four seconds without taking a shot), not only to prevent teams from stalling when they had the lead but also to accelerate the game and to make it look more interesting on the small screen. This regulation also favored quicker men and those who grew up playing street ball in urban areas, which included many black players.

Race and the NBA

Although many people now view the league as a predominantly black institution, there was little media coverage when the NBA broke its racial barriers. In 1947, the New York Knickerbockers, then a BAA team, drafted Wat Misaka, a Japanese American, who became the league's first minority player. Three years later, the first black players entered the NBA: Nat "Sweetwater" Clifton, Chuck Cooper, and Earl Lloyd. Their arrival was less heralded but no less significant than the Brooklyn Dodgers' drafting of Jackie Robinson in 1947. The 1950 draft officially ended the "gentlemen's agreement" the NBA owners had with Abe Saperstein, the owner of the Harlem Globetrotters. Because the professional leagues did not draft blacks, Saperstein was able to keep the talented players for himself.

Once racial segregation formally ended, a number of exceptional black players became part of the league, and many of them, including Bill Russell, Elgin Baylor, and Wilt Chamberlain, significantly altered the game's style. For years, there was an unofficial quota of black players on NBA teams because owners feared that their audiences would not come to see a team play if the majority of its players were black. However, it was not until the 1970s that the league earned a reputation for being "too black."

Postintegration, the NBA symbolizes successful racial integration, as it appears to be one venue where its mostly black players have a significant amount of leverage: Michael Jordan and Kevin Garnett negotiated historic and precedent-setting contracts; the dress code relaxed to reflect urban fashions and trends; the Players Association is particularly influential; and many superstar players are loyal to the league, often returning as coaches, owners, and game commentators after they retire from playing. In fact, the league sells this image to the public and often promotes a rags-to-riches, or a ghetto-to-NBA, narrative for certain players. In this regard, the league often becomes a savior for wayward youth.

The Stern Era

Basketball historians commonly note that by the 1970s, the league had an image problem. Not only was it considered too black, but it was also thought to be drug-infested. In 1984, newly appointed commissioner David Stern began to reinvent the league, emphasizing the entertainment aspects of the game. Most important, he heavily promoted individual marquee players. Stern, who, like his BAA predecessors, established a new paradigm for sport marketing, is arguably the most powerful and influential executive in U.S. sport history. Under his leadership, central league offices micromanage the individual franchises: They coordinate advertising, oversee team Web pages, and suggest halftime acts, among other things. The NBA promotes and celebrates itself through video games, T-shirts, jerseys, and magazines. The league also has its own network and cable television shows, a retail store in New York City, and a restaurant in Orlando, Florida. In 1997, Stern established the Women's National Basketball Association (WNBA), the most financially stable professional women's league in the United States. Because its marketing strategies are so successful, the NBA has convinced the U.S. public and most of the world that it is *the* basketball establishment. There have been and are other professional leagues, but they are seen as inferior imitations or minor leagues.

One could make the case that capitalism shapes all U.S. sport, but whereas baseball actively resists such a claim and instead markets itself as an unspoiled and pure game, NBA basketball revels in its ingenuity and commercialism. On one hand, its blatant self-promotion makes the league an easy target for blame for the ills of modern professional sport: inflated players' contracts, owners' greed, and blatant excesses. But the NBA continues to thrive. U.S. culture did not feel the force of the NBA impact until the late 1980s, and by the 1990s, basketball seems to have supplanted baseball as America's pastime. This phenomenon can be attributed to the NBA.

—*La'Tonya Reese Miles*

See also: American Basketball Association; Basketball; Big Business, Sport as; Women's Basketball

For further reading:

Koppett, Leonard. 1968. *Twenty-four Seconds to Shoot: An Informal History of the NBA.* New York: Macmillan.

Salzberg. Charles. 1998. *From Set Shot to Slam Dunk: The History of Professional Basketball.* Lincoln: University of Nebraska Press.

Schoenfeld, Bruce. 1998. "David Stern's Full-Court Press." *New York Times Magazine,* October 18, 95–100.

NATIONAL HOCKEY LEAGUE

The National Hockey League (NHL) is a professional ice hockey league formed in November 1917 with four franchises in three Canadian cities: Montreal (two franchises), Ottawa, and Toronto. In 1924–1925, the league began an aggressive expansion program in the United States by adding a club in Boston and relocating the Hamilton, Ontario, team to New York. For the following season, new teams were added in New York, Detroit, Pittsburgh, and Chicago. With the collapse of rival professional leagues in Canada, the NHL emerged as the pinnacle of professional hockey, attracting the best players and paying the highest salaries. However, in subsequent years, especially during the Great Depression, the number of teams dwindled to six: Montreal, Toronto, New York, Chicago, Detroit, and Boston. These six franchises later became known as "the original six."

Between 1942 and 1966, the league was remarkably stable; the original six played as a closed circuit and there was little player mobility among them. In many ways, this stability reflected the enormous expense of owning and maintaining arenas, the tight control and high profitability of franchise owners, and the limited appeal of the game outside its traditional markets. Hockey remained a relatively minor North American sport with a regional audience confined to the northeastern states and Canada. For many fans of the league, those were the glory years of the NHL.

In 1966, the NHL doubled in size, adding six teams primarily in the U.S. West and Midwest. Faced with the double challenge of a new rival league, the World Hockey Association (WHA), and increasing revenue demands, the NHL continued to expand through the 1970s. By 1980, the league had twenty-one teams in four divisions and a play-off format that extended the season, which now lasted from October to May. Over the 1980s and 1990s, the NHL aggressively expanded its U.S. base. Expansion brought the league to a total of twenty-nine teams in the 1999–2000 season, twenty-three of them in the United States. Indicative of this expansion program was the awarding of franchises in nontraditional markets in the South and Southwest. This strategy was directed toward increasing the league's television exposure and, consequently, revenues from the broadcasting of games.

The NHL has long been viewed as the premier professional hockey league in the world and as owner of the sport's most famous trophy, the Stanley Cup. Although NHL teams competed for the cup from the league's inception, it only became the NHL's exclusively during the 1926–1927 season. This feeling of world superiority was accentuated by the defection of star eastern European players in the 1980s and, with the collapse of the Soviet Union in the mid-1990s and the subsequent opening of the former Eastern Bloc, the wholesale exodus of the world's top players to the NHL. Although Canadian players continue to make up the majority of team rosters, the infusion of talent from around the world helps the league maintain its claims of global superiority.

—*Alan Gordon*

See also: Hockey; Hockey, Mythology of; Hockey Hall of Fame; World Hockey Association

For further reading:

Pincus, Arthur, Len Hochberg, and Chris Malcolm. 1999. *The Official Illustrated NHL History: From the Original Six to a Global Game.* Chicago: Triumph Books.

Strachan, Al, and Eric Duhatschek. 2001. *One Hundred and One Years of Hockey: The Chronicle of a Century on Ice.* San Diego, CA: Thunder Bay Press.

NATIONAL RIFLE ASSOCIATION

Commonly viewed as nearly fanatical defenders of gun ownership, the National Rifle Association (NRA) is not a hunting organization, and hunters are not necessarily in agreement with the tenets of the NRA. Organized in 1871 as a group of rifle and gun enthusiasts to promote shooting, hunting, gun safety, and wildlife conservation, the NRA has since taken a different slant, touting a Second Amendment mantra and, based on the sacred language of that amendment, preaching individual gun-owning freedom as gospel against intrusion at all levels by government. With 2.5 million members affiliated with 14,000 clubs, the NRA promotes not only gun safety marksmanship but also collective resistance to government control of guns. The membership feels that to attack the NRA is to attack the Constitution and patriotism; consequently, the group has on occasion found itself on the outside of the mainstream political arena by maintaining its fierce last-bridge stands.

Functioning as a lobby based in Washington, D.C., spearheaded by matinee-idol Charlton Heston, the NRA maintains a staff of three hundred and a budget of $66 million. The organization maintains membership through five club publications, club and civic work, competition shooting, public education, and accidental death and dismemberment insurance.

—*Charles Moore*

See also: Outdoor Clubs

For further reading:

Brown, Peter, and Daniel Abel. 2002. *Outgunned: Up against the NRA—The First Complete Insider Account of the Battle over Gun Control.* New York: Free Press.

Rodengen, Jeffrey L., and Tom Clancy. 2002. *NRA: An American Legend*. Edited by Melody Maysonet. Fort Lauderdale, FL: Write Stuff.

NATIVE AMERICAN ATHLETES

The first Americans were surely the continent's first athletes as well. In each of the several hundred societies native to North America, men and women engaged in sporting activity, including running, ball games, horse races, archery, and wrestling. These events often served spiritual, social, political, and recreational functions, weaving ceremonial, communal, and competitive features into the fabric of sport. Beginning in the sixteenth century, social interactions, cultural conflicts, and governmental policies profoundly altered these patterns of play. In the wake of Euro-American colonization, marked by assimilation, dispossession, and the eradication of indigenous institutions, including sport, Native Americans have embraced athletics, enjoying, reinterpreting, and excelling at sport under often-oppressive circumstances.

Superstars

Countless great indigenous athletes have participated in sport in North America, but undoubtedly Jim Thorpe is the best-known Native American in the history of sport. He distinguished himself at the Carlisle Indian School in Pennsylvania as an All-American in football and again at the 1912 Olympics, where he won the pentathlon and the decathlon. He went on to careers in both professional football and major league baseball, served as founding president of the National Football League (NFL), and had a brief but successful stint in film. Thorpe was deemed by many to be the greatest athlete of the first half of the twentieth century.

Although often overshadowed by Thorpe's achievements, countless other Native Americans have excelled in various sports. To name only a few of the representative indigenous superstars in North American sport: Louis Tewanima and Billy Mills in running; Charles A. "Chief" Bender, Allie "Superchief" Reynolds, and Jack "Chief" Meyers in baseball; Gus Welch, John Levi, and Bemus Pierce in football; Ron "the Chief" Delorme and George Armstrong in hockey; Angelita Rosal in table tennis; Thurman Munsell Jr. and Danny "Little Red" Lopez in boxing; Rod Curl and Notah Begay in golf. It speaks to both U.S. culture and to Native American culture that the involvement in sport is so widespread, yet the stars are hardly household names.

In addition to these individuals, a number of all-Indian teams have risen to prominence. During the early years of the twentieth century, the exploits of the teams at boarding schools, particularly those at Carlisle and at the Haskell Indian School in Kansas, dazzled Americans. At the same time, barnstorming baseball teams, like Green's Nebraska Indians, formed by Lincoln businessman Guy W. Green, excelled both as athletes and as entertainers. The Oorang Indians, a short-lived professional football franchise captained by Jim Thorpe, strove to duplicate the same antics, staging stereotypical Indian dances, dressing in feathers, and putting on displays of Native American skills during halftime. Later, the Hominy Indians football team of Oklahoma briefly captured the public imagination as they bested nearly all opponents, including the Cleveland Browns and the New York Giants of the National Football League.

Social Structures

For much of U.S. history, indigenous participation in mainstream sport has mirrored prevailing intercultural relations, reflecting both public perceptions and governmental policies. A few individual Native American athletes, particularly in the northeastern United States, participated in athletic competition before the final quarter of the nineteenth century. In the 1860s, the Iroquois runner Louis "Deerfoot" Bennett was one of the few who engaged in athletics and achieved public

Billy Mills, a 26-year-old Marine lieutenant, keeps his lead in the 10,000-meter run on October 14 despite an attempt by Tunisia's M. Gammoudi to jostle his way past during the 1964 Olympic event. Mills hung on to win the race, the first time in Olympic history that an American has won the event.
(Bettmann/Corbis)

notoriety for his accomplishments. Significantly, it was not until the bulk of Native Americans were installed on reservations that they became active in Euro-American sport. In fact, the federal boarding school system established in the last quarter of the nineteenth century became an important training ground for many Native American athletes. Sport, as a means of assimilation, was an increasingly important element of such schools. In addition, many Native American athletes found sport to be an important venue through which to define themselves and to make social statements. Sport teams at Carlisle and later at Haskell achieved national prominence, earning individual athletes both media attention and career paths, while securing for Native Americans an important presence in sport. As changing federal policy de-emphasized boarding schools, however, the number of Native American athletes participating in sport declined steadily. In fact, between the start of World War II and Mills's triumph at the 1964 Olympics, few indigenous athletes attained national success. After the 1960s, another cultural shift led to an increasing emphasis on self-determination, and a broader cultural rejuvenation led to the development of local and national athletic organizations that enhanced Native American athletic participation in general and in professional sport to a lesser extent.

Although not as critical to Euro-American understanding of Indianness as spirituality, warfare, or social organization, sport increasingly promoted efforts to make sense of and correct cultural differences. Until perhaps the middle of the nineteenth century, most Euro-Americans viewed indigenous athletes and athletics, like Native American communities more broadly, in overly romantic and decidedly racist terms, stressing their primitiveness, physicality, and wildness. Sport coverage and fan comments often reflected these broader stereotypes as well. The regularity with which indigenous athletes were dubbed "Chief" brings the racial biases shaping indigenous athletic participation to the foreground.

Moreover, the development of American Indian mascots during the period, precisely at the height of Native American participation in sport, confirms the hold of such prejudice, and stereotypes continue to shape public perceptions of Native American athletes, although not as starkly as in the past.

Importantly, the history of indigenous athletes suggests comparison with that of African American athletes. Even though Native Americans never experienced outright segregation in sport, they did encounter overt discrimination, such as in the rule differences in early lacrosse, a traditional game with indigenous origins. In addition, early-twentieth-century popular commentary on the physical advantages and cultural deficiencies of Native Americans is remarkably similar to the ways African Americans are often discussed in media accounts.

Indian Country

Throughout the twentieth century, indigenous athletes had a profound significance in Native American communities. Sport in Native American communities has the common pleasures and problems of spectatorship and participation; in addition, individual players, whether nationally celebrated or locally renowned, have great social meaning. Importantly, they have long facilitated the formulation of ethnic identity, both tribal and pan-Indian. Thus, the Navajo golfer Notah Begay is a source of pride both for the Navajos and for Native Americans in general.

Athletes and athleticism have fostered efforts to improve indigenous lives and communities. For example, through his organization Running Strong, Olympic great Billy Mills endeavors to encourage character development and community outreach. More broadly, since the early 1970s, the National Indian Activities Association has organized all-Indian competitions, promoting athleticism in harmony with indigenous ethics.

Other athletes have seized upon sport as a means of ethnic revitalization. Members of the

Iroquois nation in upstate New York, for instance, established a national lacrosse team. In the process, they hoped both to enliven the rich heritage of ball play among the Iroquois and exert a claim that the Iroquois were a sovereign nation. The Iroquois National Team began participating in international competitions in the 1990s.

Despite often being forgotten and, worse, reduced to stereotypical symbols, Native Americans have had a profound impact on U.S. sport. Indeed, indigenous athletes offer a powerful reminder that the history and significance of sport in U.S. culture is incomplete without them.

—*C. Richard King*

See also: Lacrosse; Native American Mascots; Sockalexis, Louis Francis

For further reading:

Bloom, John. 2000. *To Show What an Indian Can Do: Athletics in Native American Boarding Schools.* Minneapolis: University of Minnesota Press.

Churchill, Ward, Norbert S. Hill Jr., and Mary Jo Barlow. 1979. "An Historical Overview of Twentieth Century Native American Athletics." *Indian Historian* 12: 22–32.

Oxendine, Joseph B. 1995. *American Indian Sports Heritage.* 2nd Ed. Lincoln: University of Nebraska Press.

NATIVE AMERICAN MASCOTS

Mascots offer a unique perspective on sport in U.S. culture. Although many mascots, like the Jayhawks, the Dragons, or the Leathernecks, have largely innocuous histories, the nearly ubiquitous use of Indians in association with athletics reveals the racial and political significance of sport. In fact, the invention, elaboration, and recent critique of such signs and spectacles of Indianness outlines the often-invisible role of cultural difference in U.S. athletics.

Native American mascots are a common feature of sport in the United States. Nearly 4,500 schools refer to their teams as the Warriors, the Braves, the Indians, or the Redskins. At the collegiate level, according to the National Coalition on Racism in Sports and Media, over eighty institutions have Native American mascots. In addition, dozens of professional and semiprofessional teams either employ or have employed images of Indians as part of their marketing efforts.

Educational institutions, professional franchises, and amateur clubs have seized upon Indianness for a variety of reasons. Some, like Dartmouth College, chose Native American mascots to reflect a historical link between their institution and indigenous people. Others, like the University of Illinois or the University of Utah, selected such symbols to enshrine regional history and legitimately claim territory occupied by indigenous peoples. Still other uses are largely accidental, hinging on school colors, often red, on team play described as "savage" or "wild," or on the enthusiasm of an individual—coach, band leader, student, or alumnus—for Indians and Indianness.

Whatever their specific origins, Native American mascots crystallized in a historical context that made it possible, pleasurable, and powerful for Euro-Americans to incorporate images of Indians in athletic contexts. Beginning with the Boston Tea Party, Euro-Americans have taken on those roles by "playing Indian." Simultaneously, the conquest of Native America empowered Euro-Americans to appropriate, invent, and otherwise represent Native Americans and to long for aspects of the cultures destroyed by that conquest. In addition, countless spectacles, exhibitions, and other sundry entertainments centered on Indianness proliferated during the last quarter of the nineteenth century. Native American mascots were built on these patterns and traditions.

Not surprisingly, given these sociohistorical foundations, whereas Native American mascots have afforded to many Euro-American individuals and institutions an assumed identity, many indigenous peoples see these athletic icons as perpetuating inauthentic and hurtful images. Halftime performances, fan antics, and mass merchandising transform somber and reverent artifacts and activities into trivial and lifeless forms that simultaneously reduce Native Americans to a series of well-worn clichés and efface the complexities of Native American cultures and histories.

> *Native American mascots are a common feature of sport in the United States. Nearly 4,500 schools refer to their teams as the Warriors, the Braves, the Indians, or the Redskins, in spite of protests from Native activists.*

Beginning in the early 1970s, energized by the red power movement, Native Americans criticized the tradition of "playing" Indian during halftime activities and demanded that it end. Although initially successful, forcing retirements at Dartmouth College and Stanford University and changes in halftime activities at Marquette University and the University of Oklahoma, the movement encountered strong resistance among fans, alumni, and boosters and failed to make much progress for the following two decades. In the early 1990s, activists confronted mascots with renewed energy, fostering public debates and policy changes. During the subsequent decade, the following events took place: several universities either retired (for example, St. John's University and the University of Miami) or revised (for example, Bradley University and the University of Utah) their use of Indian likenesses; a number of school districts, notably in Los Angeles and Dallas, and state boards of education encouraged or required the end of mascots; countless political, social, and professional organizations—including the National Congress of American Indians, the National Association for the Advancement of Colored People, the American Anthropological Association, and the National Education Association—condemned such symbols and spectacles; and the federal Trademark Trial and Appeals Board voided the trademark rights of the Washington Redskins of the National Football League, finding that the name and logo used by the team were disparaging and hence violated the law. Despite these trends, it is unlikely that Native American mascots will disappear from U.S. sport anytime in the near future.

Native American mascots serve as a reminder of the racial politics in U.S. sport. First, they underscore the white privilege central to the formation and elaboration of U.S. athletics. Second, they illustrate the terms through which white Euro-Americans have imagined themselves and others as they make plain the formulation of dominant American identities. Finally, they clarify the politicization of sport in the wake of the civil rights movement.

—*C. Richard King*

See also: Native American Athletes; Team Names

For further reading:

Davis, Laurel. 1993. "Protest against the Use of Native American Mascots: A Challenge to Traditional American Identity." *Journal of Sport and Social Issues* 17: 9–22.

King, C. Richard, and Charles F. Springwood, eds. 2001. *Team Spirits: The Native American Mascot Controversy.* Lincoln: University of Nebraska Press.

Spindel, Carol. 2000. *Dancing at Halftime: The Controversy over American Indian Mascots.* New York: New York University Press.

NAZI OLYMPICS

The so-called Nazi Olympics were held in Berlin in 1936, three years after Adolf Hitler and his National Socialist German Workers Party (the Nazis) came to power. These were the eleventh modern Olympic Games, and they remain an important milestone in Olympic history, more for the political environment in which the games were completed than for the actual athletics.

Although the modern Olympics had been politicized almost from the moment Pierre de Coubertin organized the competitors into national teams, the 1936 games marked a turning point in the overt politicization that had dogged the Olympic movement. The institutionalized anti-Semitism of the Nazis resulted in a series of laws, passed in July 1935, that stripped German Jews of their citizenship. These laws and the consequent removal of Jewish athletes from the German team led many groups in the United States to campaign for a U.S. boycott of the games. The attempted boycott failed when the National Olympic Committee narrowly voted to participate, on the grounds that as long as the United States had diplomatic relations with Germany, the National Olympic Committee should remain "nonpolitical."

Hitler considered the games to be a valuable showcase for German progress and an exhibition of resurgent German power in the wake of the devastating Treaty of Versailles that had been imposed on the German nation after World War I. Furthermore, the Nazis hoped that German success in the games would demonstrate to the world the alleged superiority of the Aryan "race." This hope was dashed by the electrifying performances of many African American athletes, most notably Jesse Owens, who led all U.S. athletes with four gold medals in track and field, thus dashing Hitler's hope for victory and claim to supremacy.

—*P. F. McDevitt*

See also: Coubertin, Baron Pierre de; Olympic Games; Owens, James "Jesse" Cleveland

For further reading:

Bachrach, Susan D. 2000. *The Nazi Olympics: Berlin 1936.* Boston: Little, Brown.

Cohen, Stan, and Carol Van Valkenburg. 1996. *The Games of '36: A Pictorial History of the 1936 Olympic Games in Germany.* Missoula, MT: Pictorial Histories.

NEGRO BASEBALL LEAGUES

When most avenues of U.S. culture were racially segregated, a loose association of baseball leagues and independent teams, now called the Negro Leagues, provided a high-level professional venue for thousands of African American men who were denied a chance to play in the major leagues. As such, the Negro Baseball Leagues exemplify both business and recreation in the segregated communities of the 1900s through the 1950s.

The Negro Leagues are central to the image of baseball in U.S. culture. Contemporary fans saw, in the play of the segregated stars, a vindication of the talents and energies of African Americans. Indeed, the cultural significance of these teams and their times grows larger as they pass out of living memory.

The growth of Negro League baseball parallels the development of other segregated institutions. The first organized African American team, formed in Babylon, Long Island, New York, in 1885, was made up of waiters from the Argyle Hotel. Other teams followed in urban black neighborhoods, at black colleges, and in segregated army units. A frequent pretense made by individual players, and sometimes by entire teams, was that the African American players were really Cuban. In the unsophisticated logic of prejudice in segregated America, foreign black players were more tolerated as competitors and as teammates than were black natives of the United States.

Black baseball remained informal until after World War I. Teams in the first two decades of the twentieth century flourished in the growing cities, where professional and amateur competition from both black clubs and white teams lay within easy reach. This was the age of great independent city champion teams like the Cuban X Giants in New York and Rube Foster's Chicago American Giants.

Foster's organization of the Negro National League in 1920 established the framework for subsequent African American baseball. Like many other institutions, from businesses to churches and entertainment circuits, the Negro Leagues formed a cultural universe parallel to white America; in other words, they mirrored yet were separate from the white major leagues. Negro League clubs played in the same cities as their white counterparts and often in the same stadiums. The caliber of baseball was comparable; black All-Star teams were frequently pitted against teams of the best white players. Yet, cultural habits of prejudice kept black and white baseball separate, even though equal in terms of athletic prowess.

> *The growth of Negro League baseball parallels the development of other segregated institutions. The first organized African American team, formed in Babylon, Long Island, New York, in 1885, was made up of waiters from the Argyle Hotel. Other teams followed in urban black neighborhoods, at black colleges, and in segregated army units.*

Negro League baseball developed showcases for talent, including All-Star games and championship series. Many star players became legendary for their unique talents: the wizard-like pitcher Satchel Paige; the unhittable "Bullet" Joe Rogan; "Double Duty" Ted Radcliffe, who could both pitch and catch; the awesomely powerful "Mule" Suttles and Josh Gibson; dazzling fielders like Judy Johnson and "Bingo" DeMoss; and the almost mythically fast runner "Cool Papa" Bell.

During the 1920s and 1930s, in the big cities where Negro League teams played, the fan base was largely segregated. White fans followed white clubs and black fans came out for the local Negro Leaguers. In rural areas, however, black teams frequently found white audiences on their tours. Like the House of David and other barnstorming outfits, black clubs, most notably the Kansas City Monarchs in the West and the Homestead Grays in the East, traded on the novelty of the challenge they presented to community semipro and amateur teams in the rural United States.

That novelty extended to the accouterments of the game as well as the play. The Monarchs toured the Midwest with a portable lighting system that brought night baseball to many communities for the first time. Traveling black clubs like the Indianapolis Clowns were part vaudeville act and part sport team. In fact, they were akin to the Harlem Globetrotters in mixing showmanship with talent. Thus, white Middle America became accustomed to seeing black men in the dual roles of athlete and entertainer, roles that have become linked in cultural stereotypes.

The Negro Leagues collapsed when white major league teams tapped their pool of talent and began to sign black players in the late 1940s. Already strapped by economic setbacks incurred during World War II, black teams and leagues faced financial ruin. Ironically, the success of individual black players in integrating the major leagues led to the failure of the model black-owned businesses that could not survive segregation.

It was not until the 1970s that Negro Leaguers began to be admitted to the National Baseball Hall of Fame. In the subsequent decades, baseball nostalgia became big business, and memorabilia of the Negro Leagues was popular at baseball shows, creating a brisk trade in replica uniforms, books, and film. Aging baby boomers expressed themselves ambivalently, honoring these cultural trappings of a segregated time.

—*Tim Morris*

See also: Baseball; Discrimination, Racial, in Sport; Foster, Andrew "Rube"; Manley, Effa; National Baseball Hall of Fame

For further reading:

Holway, John B. 1992. *Voices from the Great Black Baseball Leagues.* New York: Da Capo.

Peterson, Robert W. 1992. *Only the Ball Was White.* New York: Oxford University Press.

NEGRO LEAGUE TEAMS AND THEIR COMMUNITIES

The teams and players of the Negro Leagues, the product of segregation in U.S. sport through the

1950s, enhanced their significance to their followers because of the statement their success made about black equality. The Negro Leagues existed continuously for four decades and had member teams in cities throughout the East, Midwest, and South. The first of the six black major leagues, the Negro National League, was established in 1920, and the last, the Negro American League, went out of business in 1960. Since 1897, black players had been quietly banned from organized baseball including the all-white major leagues and the minor leagues that were affiliated with them. In fact, by the time former star pitcher and Chicago club owner Andrew "Rube" Foster organized the Negro National League, there had not been an African American major leaguer since 1884.

One of Foster's intentions was to stage competitions of such high quality that the best players and teams in his league would be welcomed into the majors, but the color line held firm and, instead, the blacks in urban communities who made up the faithful core of Negro League fans became the beneficiaries. Fan devotion was legendary, and Sunday doubleheaders often attracted entire families, dressed in their best clothes and provisioned with a full picnic basket.

The leagues returned the fans' admiration in two important ways. First, Negro League games often served as fund-raisers for black enterprises that had nothing to do with baseball, and the choice of the recipient of these funds sometimes spoke volumes about black society's core priorities. One of the most important venues for Negro League games was New York's Yankee Stadium, which was often rented for showpiece extravaganzas to show off well-known black teams. An early stadium doubleheader in July 1930, between the Lincoln Giants and the Baltimore Black Sox, was a benefit for the Brotherhood of Sleeping Car Porters, a black union striving for equality in railroad jobs as well as championing other civil rights causes. As World War II loomed, a burning question among black journalists and political leaders

was whether black soldiers and sailors would be allowed to fight alongside their white counterparts or would be relegated to mess-hall and ditch-digging duties. The Newark, New Jersey, Eagles made their statement on the subject on opening day in 1941, when the entire 372nd Infantry Regiment, an all-black outfit, 2,500 strong, was the team's special guest.

The players were regarded as significant members of the black neighborhoods in their teams' home cities, not only for their individual abilities but also for what they proved about the abilities of African Americans in general. That the mainstream newspapers, owned and managed by whites, ignored Negro League games was of little consequence to the black fans. Word-of-mouth news, aided by coverage in the weekly black papers, ensured that the exploits of the players and teams did not go unnoticed. Real Negro League fans also knew that the segregation of professional baseball into segments of black and white was purely arbitrary and not based on a lack of merit among black players.

Competition between the races, although proscribed by white baseball officials, was not unknown. White and black players often met in postseason exhibition games and in integrated Latin American winter leagues. Negro Leaguers won upwards of half the exhibition games against white competitors, although it should be noted that the white All-Star teams featured in these contests often did not include a full complement of major league players.

Individual triumphs by black players, however, often became the stuff of black baseball legend, as when catcher Bruce Petway reputedly threw out the great Ty Cobb for attempting to steal twice in a game in Havana in 1910.

—*James Overmyer*

See also: Civil Rights and Sport; Manley, Effa; Negro
    Baseball Leagues

For further reading:
Overmyer, James. 1998. *Queen of the Negro Leagues:*

Effa Manley and the Newark Eagles. Lanham, MD: Scarecrow Press.

Rogosin, Donn. 1987. *Invisible Men.* New York: Athenaeum.

NEIMAN, LEROY (1927–)

Flamboyant artist and painter of brilliantly colored and stunningly energetic athletic images, often seen attending major sporting events with a sketchbook and colorful pens, well known for his contributions to *Playboy* magazine and much criticized yet conspicuous, LeRoy Neiman is easily recognized by his broad handlebar mustache and trademark cigar. Born in St. Paul, Minnesota, Neiman was a street kid, always drawing pictures and showing off. As a youngster, he inscribed pen-and-ink tattoos on classmates' arms, and in his teens, he earned money from local grocers by painting sale items on store windows. After a stint in the army, where he painted sexually suggestive murals in military kitchens and dining halls, he returned to Chicago, where he entered the School of Art Institute of Chicago. In the early 1950s, Neiman met Hugh Hefner, the publisher of a new magazine called *Playboy*. Hefner liked Neiman's work and asked him to produce sketches and paintings for the magazine. Neiman gained wide recognition for his Man at His Leisure features. Over the years, Neiman's success with the magazine took him to the world's most expensive and glamorous social and sporting scenes.

Neiman hit his stride in 1953 when he came upon partially used and discarded enamel paint cans and discovered that free flowing paint and fast brushstrokes gave the impression of fast-moving action. Described as a colorist, Neiman's work appeared abstract when viewed up close but more detailed when seen from a distance. Thus, as the perspective changed, so did the art, and that is what Neiman tried to achieve.

Neiman found the best locations from which to create his art. He made his way to wherever athletes were—dugouts, benches, or dressing rooms—and observed the action with a sociologist's eye as well as an artist's. He became a fixture on television during Super Bowls and Olympics, drawing the action as it occurred and demonstrating his remarkable skills at portraiture and stop-motion drawing. He painted hundreds of famous sport figures in action, including Muhammad Ali, Bobby Hull, Tom Seaver, Reggie Jackson, and others in baseball, basketball, football, golf, tennis, boxing, and horse racing.

Even though Neiman was popularly recognized for his body of work, the critics ignored his artistic ability or dismissed it as superficial, vulgar, or overly commercial. Despite his thick skin, some remarks did hit their target. He was criticized for his work in *Playboy,* for his television art, and for the mass production of his silk screens. He was often called an illustrator rather than an artist. No amount of fame or wealth could completely insulate him from neglect or abuse, yet Neiman continued to enjoy his work and his success and served as a vehicle to popularize consumer sport art and stop-action style.

LeRoy Neiman's artwork and the world of sport have both seen tremendous increases in popularity since 1950. Although neither can lay claim to the other's success, a synergy was at work, and both have benefited greatly from the relationship.

—*Marc L. Seror*

See also: Ali, Muhammad; Artists of Sport; Jackson, Reginald Martinez "Reggie"

For further reading:

Neiman, LeRoy. 1983. *Winners: My Thirty Years in Sports.* New York: Harry N. Abrams.

———. 2003. *LeRoy Neiman.* New York: Harry N. Abrams.

NELSON, LINDSEY (1919–1995)

One of the early celebrity sportscasters of radio and television, Lindsey Nelson typified a journalistic approach to sportscasting that eschewed hyperbole and theatricality for plainspoken wit and insight. Born in Columbia, Tennessee, Nelson's involvement with sport began in the late 1930s when he was an English tutor to student-athletes at the University of Tennessee. His first professional announcing job was in 1947, broadcasting high school football for radio station WKGN in Knoxville. By the late 1950s, Nelson's exciting but never overstated play-by-play style, complete with friendly southern twang, brought him to the attention of NBC. Oddly enough, he was hired as an administrator, but he eventually became the network's principal college football announcer. Although college football remained his first love, Nelson worked at a relentless pace throughout his career as an announcer for the National Football League, the National Basketball Association, and the Professional Golfers' Association.

In 1962, Nelson became the play-by-play voice of the New York Mets, a job he held until 1981. It was during this time that he began wearing garish plaid sport coats, a sartorial affectation that would become his trademark. During his time with the Mets, the seemingly inexhaustible Nelson was also the television voice of Notre Dame football from 1967–1979 and did the play-by-play for twenty-six Cotton Bowls.

He retired from broadcasting in 1981 and returned to his beloved University of Tennessee to teach seminars in radio and television broadcasting. Nelson was a five-time National Sportscaster of the Year winner, and in 1988 he was inducted into the Writers Wing of the National Baseball Hall of Fame.

Nelson's style was engaging and direct—his high-pitched voice was immediately recognizable—and he approached sporting events with a reporter's objectivity and eye for detail. He never made himself the center of attention, always believing that the game was more important than the announcer, but he never held back his emotions when describing a thrilling moment. This enthusiastic but nonhysterical approach to sportscasting became the model for younger play-by-play announcers like Keith Jackson, Al Michaels, and ESPN's Jon Miller.

After a twelve-year bout with Parkinson's disease, Nelson died in Atlanta, Georgia, on May 10, 1995.

—*John Dougan*

See also: Sport Journalism

For further reading:
Nelson, Lindsey. 1985. *Hello Everybody, I'm Lindsey Nelson.* New York: William Morrow.

NICKLAUS, JACK (1940–)

Jack Nicklaus is one of the greatest golfers of all time, as well as being a leading golf-course architect, an entrepreneur, and a businessman.

Born in Columbus, Ohio, Nicklaus had a distinguished amateur and college golf record, winning two U.S. amateur championships while attending Ohio State University. He turned professional, quickly won the U.S. Open at the age of twenty-two, developed a rivalry with Arnold Palmer, then the game's most charismatic golfer, and eventually won more than ninety professional golf tournaments worldwide.

Nicknamed the "Golden Bear," Nicklaus won twenty major golf championships between 1962 and 1986, far more than any other golfer including the legendary Bobby Jones. Voted Golfer of the Century by sportswriters in 1988, Nicklaus was the longest driver, best putter, and mentally toughest golfer of his era and has become the standard for younger golfers, including Tiger Woods. Nicklaus also played successful senior golf, but he gives that facet of his career little significance in his autobiography, *Jack Nicklaus: My Story* (1997), written with Ken Bowden.

Unlike his golfing peers, Nicklaus made a lasting mark as a golf-course architect by designing more than one hundred courses. His best design

Jack Nicklaus raises his arms after winning the U.S. Open at Baltusrol Golf Course in Springfield, New Jersey (June 15, 1980).

(BETTMANN/CORBIS)

is widely viewed to be Muirfield Village in Dublin, Ohio, the site of an annual Professional Golfers' Association (PGA) tournament. His course design philosophy, emphasizing large target areas and greens with severe hazards, greatly influenced both modern golf architecture and the resulting televised images of golf. Amateur golfers at all levels now demand to play the most visually exotic and toughest courses—"just like the pros."

Nicklaus was one of the first athletes from any sport to use successful business ventures to amass a level of personal wealth unattainable solely by playing. Unlike many other famous athletes who earned their money primarily through celebrity marketing, Nicklaus earned his fortune through entrepreneurial skill. He not only designed courses but also created a business, employing others to implement those designs. In addition, he is listed as part owner of the MacGregor Golf Equipment Company.

The father of five children, Nicklaus remains an admired figure in U.S. sport as much for his grace and sportsmanship as for his enduring excellence in golf.

—*John Paul Ryan*

See also: Economics of Golf Courses; Professional Golfers' Association; Woods, Eldrick "Tiger"

For further reading:

Nicklaus, Jack. 2002. *Nicklaus by Design: Golf Course Strategy and Architecture.* New York: Harry N. Abrams.

———. 2003. *Jack Nicklaus.* With John Tickell. New York: St. Martin's Press.

Nicklaus, Jack with Ken Bowden. 1997. *My Story.* New York: Simon and Schuster.

NOMO, HIDEO (1968–)

The first Japanese baseball player to become a star in the North American major leagues, Hideo Nomo became a fan favorite in the United States and a national hero in Japan. His success in North America inspired other major league teams to expand their search for talent in Asia.

A native of Kobe, Japan, Nomo became one of Japan's top amateur pitchers while in his teens. He won a silver medal as a member of Japan's 1988 Olympic baseball team. Drafted by the Kintetsu Buffaloes in 1989, Nomo became a star in the Japanese major leagues, reaching a thousand career strikeouts faster than any player in Japanese baseball history. Though Japanese rules prohibited it, Nomo dreamed of going to America to compete against the best players in the world. The only way he could legally sign with an American team, however, was to retire from the Japanese league, which he did after five seasons with the Buffaloes. Intrigued by his potential, the Los Angeles Dodgers signed the six-foot-two, 210-pound pitcher on February 12, 1995.

Although expectations were muted at first, Nomo's pitching performance early in his rookie season of 1995 soon captured the imagination of the baseball public. His emergence as a star was important as baseball struggled to rebuild its fan base after the devastating strike of 1994. By June, Nomo had struck out sixteen batters in a game; by July, he was the National League's starting pitcher in the All-Star game, becoming the first rookie to start since Fernando Valenzuela in 1981.

Like Valenzuela, Nomo's nationality and ethnicity inspired a legion of fans. Both Japanese nationals and local Asian Americans trekked to Dodger Stadium to see him pitch. His games were televised live in Japan and shown on thirty-one large outdoor screens in thirteen cities. By June, Japanese travel agencies were offering special travel packages to Los Angeles specifically to see Nomo pitch. The Dodgers were soon selling special Nomo merchandise, including T-shirts, jackets, and posters. Japan's NHK television network aired a twelve-hour special on his life on New Year's Eve, 1995.

At the conclusion of the 1995 season, Nomo was named the National League's Rookie of the Year and finished fourth in the voting for the Cy

Young Award. In 1996, he continued where he left off, pitching a three-hit shutout in the Dodgers' home opener. Later in the season, he had a seventeen-strikeout game and capped the year by pitching a no-hitter against the Colorado Rockies.

By the end of the 1996 season, Nomo had appeared on the cover of at least twenty-two different magazines and publications and was the subject of twenty-three books in Japanese and two in English. The greatest legacy of his career may be the impact he had in bringing other players from Asia to the American major leagues. Before Nomo, there was only one other Asian player, but since his success, there have been at least five other Asian pitchers who have made the majors, most notably Korea's Chan Ho Park with the Dodgers and Japan's Hideki Irabu with the New York Yankees.

—*Brian Niiya*

See also: Baseball; Valenzuela, Fernando

For further reading:

Fagen, Herb. 1996. *Nomo: The Inside Story on Baseball's Hottest Sensation.* Boca Raton, FL: Demco Media.
McNeil, William F. 1997. *The King of Swat: An Analysis of Baseball's Home Run Hitters from the Major, Minor, Negro and Japanese Leagues.* Jefferson, NC: McFarland.

O

OATES, JOYCE CAROL (1938–)

Novelist, essayist, poet, playwright, and short-story writer, Joyce Carol Oates has successfully mastered nearly every genre of writing, including reportage. Her knowledge of the sport of boxing as well as her insightful comments on its participants provides a distinctive view of a fascinating sport. Raised in the town of Lockport in upstate New York, Oates became interested in boxing as a young girl while watching Golden Gloves fights with her father, a subscriber to *Ring* magazine, a boxing publication in New York City.

Oates's contributions to the literature of boxing include the book-length essay *On Boxing* (1987) and *Reading the Fights* (1988), a collection of pieces she edited with Daniel Halpern. In addition, three other essays on the sport are included in *(Woman) Writer: Occasions and Opportunities* (1988): "Mike Tyson," a portrait report on the heavyweight and his championship bout in Las Vegas, "Blood, Neon, and Failure in the Desert," and "Tyson/Biggs Postscript."

In *On Boxing,* Oates focuses on the sport from several different angles, including art and literature, history, sexuality, and politics. At the same time, she provides a feminist look at a contact sport dominated by males. With a rigorous enthusiasm for informative detail, she explores the sense of struggle and survival at the core of boxing. "In the magical space of the boxing ring," Oates writes, "there as in no other public arena does the individual as a unique physical being assert himself" (Oates 1994, 114). Oates concludes that "in the brightly lit ring, man is *in extremis,* performing an atavistic rite or *agon* for the mysterious solace of those who can participate only vicariously in such drama: the drama of life in the flesh. Boxing has become America's tragic theater" (Oates 1994, 116).

—*Robert J. Cole*

See also: Boxing; Literature, Sport in

For further reading:
Milazzo, Lee, ed. 1989. *Conversations with Joyce Carol Oates.* Jackson: University Press of Mississippi.
Oates, Joyce Carol. 1994. *On Boxing.* Hopewell, NJ: The Ecco Press.

OLYMPIC BOYCOTTS: 1976, 1980, AND 1984

By exposing the apolitical sanctity of the Olympic Games in particular and of sport in general as an ideal that had been eroding badly for decades, the successive boycotts of the Summer Olympic Games in Montreal (1976), Moscow (1980), and Los Angeles (1984) forced the world, as well as the leadership of the Olympic movement, to recognize that sport had become an indelible component of the international political landscape.

As an emergent part of late-nineteenth-century social life, sport was considered an extraneous recreational pastime. Athletes participated for their own reasons, and amateurism served as the dominant code. Purity of mind and spirit rather than material considerations guided the philosophy and practice of sport.

Born of this late-nineteenth-century conception of educational sport and an expression of Olympic revivalist Baron Pierre de Coubertin's passion for internationalism and fair play, the Olympic Games encoded the amateur perspective. In Coubertin's high idealism, sport transcended ideology and politics, and successive presidents of the International Olympic Committee (IOC) decried the intrusion of politics into sport, insisting that sport was apart from the world of diplomacy and foreign policy.

Efforts to insulate international sport from the rancor of politics failed. The production and manipulation of athletes for nationalistic purposes, the use of sport as a medium of ideological expression, the exploitation of the Olympic Games by host cities for propaganda purposes, and the efficacy of political sanction through sport served to place sport firmly in the realm of geo-global politics. As a result, throughout most of its early history, the IOC was increasingly forced to confront manifestations of the burgeoning politicization of sport, including the overt use of sport as Nazi propaganda during the 1936 Olympics in Berlin, the controversial status of East and West Germany after World War II, the student massacres and the black athletes' protests at the 1968 games in Mexico City, and the invasion of the 1972 games in Munich by Black September, a group of Palestinian terrorists.

In 1971, in what was to become known as "Ping-Pong diplomacy," a table-tennis team from the United States visited the People's Republic of China (PRC) in a pioneering effort to normalize relations between the two countries. In other words, by the 1970s, international sport in general and Olympic sport in particular had become an identifiable feature of the world of realpolitik.

Olympic Boycotts

The most blatant political use of sport was the boycott. In 1956, Spain, the Netherlands, and Switzerland withdrew from the Summer Olympic Games in Melbourne, Australia, to protest the Soviet invasion of Hungary. In the same year, the Anglo-French seizure of the Suez Canal precipitated a boycott by Iraq, Egypt, and Lebanon. Political sanctions through sport were also brought to bear against apartheid policies in South Africa and Rhodesia.

In 1976, the controversial issue of apartheid in South Africa and the status of the PRC spilled over into the Olympic forum, causing the first of three successive and injurious boycotts of the Summer Olympic Games. Angered over rugby matches played between New Zealand and South Africa, the Supreme Council of Sport in Africa called for a boycott of the games in Montreal. Although teams from the Ivory Coast and Senegal were permitted by their governments to stay and compete, twenty-six other African National Olympic Committees (NOCs) bowed to political necessity and withdrew their athletes. Nationalist Chinese athletes also withdrew from the games. Politically compromised by the official recognition of the PRC by the Canadian government as well as by the IOC, Nationalist China refused to compete under the name "Taiwan."

Four years later, the intrusion of cold war politics into the Olympics posed an even greater threat to the stability of the Olympic movement. Responding to Soviet military intervention in Afghanistan in 1979, U.S. President Jimmy Carter launched a diplomatic drive to persuade the non-Communist world to join a U.S. boycott of the 1980 games in Moscow. In all, sixty-two nations, including the United States, West Germany, Israel, Japan, and the PRC, boycotted the games.

Although cold war politics were held in abeyance during the winter games in Sarajevo, on May 8, 1984, the Russian NOC announced that Soviet athletes would not participate in the games in Los Angeles. The boycott included the Soviet Union and sixteen of its allies.

Olympic Realpolitik

Recognizing that the Olympic movement could not survive in isolation from international politics, the IOC instituted measures to counter the political turmoil that had surrounded the games for most of the century. In 1980, Juan Antonio Samaranch assumed the presidency of the IOC. An IOC member since 1966, an experienced politician, and a consummate diplomat, Samaranch projected the Olympic movement into the world of international diplomacy. Although Samaranch could not avert the Soviet boycott of the 1984 games in Los Angeles, under his leadership the IOC became an increasingly viable force in the world of international politics.

In the 1980s, Samaranch undertook an unprecedented odyssey around the world during which he met with 168 Olympic member nations, including every one of the forty-five NOCs on the African continent as well as fifty heads of state. In conjunction with the NOCs and International Federations, he succeeded in opening the games of the 1990s to most professional athletes. The Olympic Tripartite Commission, who sends out the invitations to athletes to participate, was strengthened, business transactions with international networks and corporations were consummated, and financial aid to the economically underprivileged nations was increased. Under Samaranch's auspices, Olympic leaders and games organizers attended conscientiously to the problems of security against terrorism, the high cost and political issues involved with hosting the games, and the political challenge of maintaining universal participation.

The worldwide success of the Summer Olympic Games in Seoul (1988), Barcelona (1992), and Atlanta (1996) and the Winter Olympic Games in Calgary (1988), Albertville (1992), and Lillehammer (1994) was in no small measure due to Samaranch's diplomatic efforts as well as to the IOC's

recognition that it was itself a significant actor on the stage of international relations.

—*Jeffrey O. Segrave*

See also: Coubertin, Baron Pierre de; International Olympic Committee; Olympic Games

For further reading:

Guttmann, Allen. 1992. *The Olympics: A History of the Modern Games.* Urbana: University of Illinois Press.

Lucas, John A. 1992. *Future of the Olympic Games.* Champaign, IL: Human Kinetics Publishers.

OLYMPIC GAMES

Born as humble religious ceremonies in ancient Greece and revived in the late nineteenth century by Baron Pierre de Coubertin, the modern Olympic Games represent the most profound and awe-inspiring expression of modern international sport. Standing apart from all other sporting events, the modern Olympic Games have emerged as a prodigious celebration of an ideology that places sport in the service of an enlightened humanity. Commonly construed as a distinctly twentieth-century phenomenon, the modern Olympic Games are, in fact, the derivative of an ancient Greek project that identified sport as something more than a perfunctory and transient expression of the human circumstance.

The Ancient Olympic Games

First held in 776 B.C. at Olympia, the ancient Olympic Games remained a significant component of the ancient Greek calendar until their abolition in A.D. 393 by Holy Roman Emperor Theodosius I. One of a series of Pan-Hellenic games, the games at Olympia were the oldest, most prestigious, and most famous of all the sporting festivals of antiquity. Although the precise origin of the games remains shrouded in prehistory, the Olympics began as religious ceremonies and developed into cultural celebrations whose influence was felt throughout the ancient Greek world. A classic expression of the Greek love of athletics, the games also promoted unity and solidarity among the various city-states. Held every four years in conjunction with the worship of Olympian Zeus, the games glorified the quest for excellence and perfection that became the hallmark of ancient Greek culture.

From 776 B.C. until 724 B.C., the only event in the games was the stade race. From that time on, however, the Olympic program grew, finally reaching a total of twenty-three events held over a five-day period and including a variety of footraces and field events, combat sports, equestrian events, and music contests. Increasingly trained by professionals, sponsored by city-states, and awarded lavish prizes at home, much like modern commercial endorsements, Olympic athletes attained heroic status and were immortalized in both history and verse. Despite the cultural preeminence of the games, the truly refined notion of Hellenic athleticism declined. Buffeted and compromised by civil war, military conquest, and Christian asceticism, the last of the ancient Olympic Games were held in A.D. 392.

The Modern Olympic Games

Voted into existence in 1894 at the International Congress of Paris, the first modern Olympic Games were held in 1896 in Athens, Greece. With the exception of the war years, 1916, 1940, and 1944, and the interim games of 1906, the Olympics have been held quadrennially ever since. The centennial games were held in 1996 in Atlanta, Georgia.

As the chief architect of the modern Olympic movement, Coubertin revived the ancient games as an expression of his profound belief in the enduring educational values inherent in competitive sport. Committed to the ideal of sport as a social and moral endeavor, he conceived of the Olympic movement as a broad-based humanitarian project and enlisted the services of the games in the pursuit of international harmony, peace,

and goodwill. In order to further enrich and ennoble the Olympic games, competitions in the arts were introduced at the 1912 games in Stockholm, and exhibitions in the arts are still held in conjunction with the games.

Born of a late-nineteenth-century conception of sport, with its attendant emphasis on the character-building qualities of amateurism, the Olympic Games have been transformed from a fin de siècle curiosity into a sporting performance of truly global magnitude and dimensions. In the 1896 games held in Athens, 311 athletes from thirteen countries participated; nearly 3,800 athletes from 197 countries competed in the 1996 games in Atlanta. Once the preserve of a European, male, social elite and, for the most part, free from political and commercial exploitation, the Olympic Games have increasingly become a highly politicized component of mass-mediated and commercially sponsored international sport. Buttressed by the institutionalized commercial incentives available through television marketing, the modern Olympic Games generate enormous funds that sustain and nourish the Olympic movement throughout the world. For example, NBC recently paid $705 million for 171.5 hours of televised coverage of the Summer Olympic Games in Sydney, Australia.

The Winter Olympic Games

Although the 1894 Congress of the Sorbonne listed ice-skating as one of its desired sports, it was fourteen years before skating appeared on the Olympic program at London in 1908, and it was not until 1924 that the International Olympic Committee (IOC) grudgingly allowed French organizers to arrange an "International Week of Winter Sports" in Chamonix. Attracting more than ten thousand spectators, the games were so successful that two years later, the IOC retroactively recognized Chamonix as the first official Winter Olympiad.

Criticized as being socially elitist, geographically limited, lacking in global appeal, and susceptible to the intrusion of professionalism, commercial exploitation, and inclement weather, the Winter Games have nonetheless thrived. Although only 258 athletes from sixteen countries took part in the opening ceremonies in Chamonix in 1924, almost 2,500 athletes from seventy-two countries participated in the 1998 Winter Games in Nagano, Japan, which are estimated to have cost almost ten billion dollars, which included improvements in infrastructure and new buildings.

Beginning in 1994 with the games in Lillehammer, and in order to accommodate television networks and maximize audience ratings and income, the Winter Olympics have been arranged on a staggered, rather than concurrent, yearly schedule with the Summer Games. CBS paid $50,000 for the broadcast rights to the 1960 games at Squaw Valley, California; NBC will pay $613 million for the privilege of televising the games in 2006.

Olympic Ceremonial

Recognizing the need to privilege and elevate the Olympic Games above all other sporting events and seeking to encode the lofty principles of the Olympic ideology in displays of memorable dimensions, Coubertin sought to institutionalize ceremonies that would stimulate awe, reverence, and understanding. Coubertin grounded the Olympic ceremonial in an appropriate solemnity and dignity and arranged it around three moments: the official opening of the games, the distribution of medals, and the closing of the games.

Although the proclamation of the opening of the games by the head of state of the host country was the only act of ceremonial until 1920, since then the Olympic ceremonies have burgeoned to embrace a wide variety of rituals, symbols, and logos that have captivated the imagination of an increasingly global audience. The Olympic flag, with its five interlocking rings symbolizing the five continents of the world locked in understanding and friendship, flew for the first time at Antwerp during the 1920 games; the

Olympic flame, representing the quest for perfection and the struggle for victory, was first introduced at the 1928 games in Amsterdam; the Olympic Flame Relay, which has become one of the most captivating and moving moments in all sport, was initiated during the 1936 games in Berlin; doves, the classical symbol of peace, were first released during the opening ceremonies in 1920 at Antwerp; and the Olympic oath, which Coubertin adopted from the very beginning of the modern Olympic movement, was also first pronounced in 1920. The official Olympic motto, *"Citius, Altius, Fortius"* (Faster, Higher, Stronger), made its first appearance in 1920, and the Olympic hymn, although composed in 1896, was not officially adopted until 1958.

Criticized as an overt display of excessive nationalism, the victory ceremony integrates the distribution of medals with the presentation of national anthems and national flags. Spectacular opening and closing ceremonies, which celebrate the games as well as the culture of the host country, remain among the most popular moments of the modern games. A carefully articulated protocol that includes the parade of nations, the entrance of the Olympic flag, and the presentation of speeches is followed by distinctly choreographed and orchestrated performances, all of which distinguish the Olympic Games as representing a profound and increasingly understood idealistic ideology.

The Olympic Village

Although the first collective accommodation for athletes was provided at the 1924 games in Paris, the first official Olympic Village was not built until the games of 1932 in Los Angeles. Initially introduced as a way to reduce costs, the village plan was so successful that it has remained a part of Olympic protocol ever since. Compromised by the Eastern Bloc countries' establishment of their own village in 1952, by the Palestinian terrorist attack against the Israeli Olympic team in 1972, and by the separatist tendencies of highly paid professional athletes in recent years, the Olympic Village has nonetheless endured as a powerful symbol of the modern Olympic movement. Housing athletes from around the world, the village serves as a microcosm of the global Olympic family and symbolizes the Olympic ideology of benevolent internationalism.

—*Jeffrey O. Segrave*

See also: *Arête;* Coubertin, Baron Pierre de; International Olympic Committee

For further reading:

Lucas, John A. 1980. *The Modern Olympic Games.* South Brunswick, NJ: A. S. Barnes.

Segrave, Jeffrey O., and D. Chu, eds. 1988. *The Olympic Games in Transition.* Champaign, IL: Human Kinetics Publishers.

ORR, ROBERT GORDON "BOBBY" (1948–)

Robert Gordon "Bobby" Orr, along with Gordie Howe and Wayne Gretzky, is considered one of the greatest hockey players. He entered the National Hockey League (NHL) at a crucial point in its development from a regional to a continental sport league. Orr helped establish professional hockey as a major team sport in the United States, on a par with baseball, football, and basketball.

In 1967, during Orr's second season playing defense for the Boston Bruins, the NHL expanded from the "Original Six" to twelve teams, basing teams for the first time outside the Snowbelt. Although hockey, on many levels, had long been popular in New England and some upper-midwestern states, the NHL expansion brought hockey to areas of the United States where it had had little previous exposure.

Orr was the first superstar of the new continental era of professional hockey, and he helped ensure its popularity by transforming the way the game was played. Traditionally, hockey had been largely a defensive, tight-checking game with defensemen seldom involved in scoring. Orr was the first "offensive defenseman," often rushing the puck deep into the offensive zone, creating scoring opportunities and frequently scoring himself. His remarkable skating and stick-handling ability were nearly impossible to defend against, thus making hockey a much more open, free-skating, and high-scoring game. Orr's trademark end-to-end rushes and higher-scoring games made hockey more exciting to its new fans in the United States and, not coincidentally, made hockey a much more telegenic game.

Orr accomplished feats achieved by no defenseman before him and by few since. He was the first defenseman to score more than one hundred points in a season and is the only defenseman ever to win a scoring championship, which he did twice. Despite having his career hobbled and shortened by knee injuries, he won every major trophy in professional hockey and was unanimously inducted into the Hockey Hall of Fame with the mandatory waiting period being waived as a testament to his impact on the sport.

—*Christopher Berkeley*

See also: Hockey; National Hockey League

For further reading:

MacInnis, Craig, ed. 1999. *Remembering Bobby Orr: A Celebration.* Toronto: Stoddart.

Podnieks, Andrew. 2003. *The Goal: Bobby Orr and the Most Famous Shot in Stanley Cup History.* Chicago: Triumph Books.

OUTDOOR CLUBS

Although beginning as associations of like-minded recreationists, many outdoor clubs broadened their interests and activities to become politically significant in conservation issues, especially in the preservation of lands for recreational use. Americans have long been enthusiastic in voluntary organizations, and sportsmen were early to organize. The Schuylkill Fishing Company that

Former Boston Bruins star defenseman Bobby Orr (left) watches as a banner with the number four is raised to the rafters. The Bruins retired his number in ceremonies at Boston Garden on January 9, 1979. Orr, assistant general manager with the Chicago Blackhawks, was forced into early retirement by knee injuries. He played most of his career in Boston. (BETTMANN/CORBIS)

began in 1732 was probably the first outdoor club; many hunting and angling groups followed during the nineteenth century. In 1922, the Izaak Walton League became the first national sportsmen's group to have a distinct political agenda for conservation.

As for most modern sports, the number of people participating in outdoor recreational activities, such as hiking and camping and birdwatching, expanded after the Civil War. City-based clubs helped identify those with similar interests and helped to organize activities, and "outing clubs" sprang up on many college campuses. People involved in clubs shared an appreciation for nature and were active participants, not spectators, in recreational activity, which explains why political activism emerged. From its Boston and Cambridge roots as a group of hiking enthusiasts in 1876, the Appalachian Mountain Club (AMC) became an important regional force in preserving landscapes and recreational opportunities, most notably in helping create the 2,100-mile-long Appalachian Trail. In California, the Sierra Club, formed in 1892, was modeled on the AMC, with a preservation focus on the Sierra Nevadas. After World War II, the Sierra Club expanded nationally to become the country's most influential citizen's conservation group.

Important legislation influenced by politically active outdoor clubs includes the 1964 Wilderness Act and the 1968 National Wild and Scenic Rivers Act. Despite their political clout, tensions emerged within groups between the ideals of preservation and the impact of recreationists, symbolized by the Wilderness Society's termination in 1977 of its own sponsored back-country trips.

—*Timothy M. Rawson*

See also: Mountaineering; Rock Climbing

For further reading:

Bryson, Bill. 1999. *A Walk in the Woods: Rediscovering America on the Appalachian Trail.* New York: Broadway Books.

Winnett, Thomas, and Kathy Morey. 2003. *Guide to the John Muir Trail.* Berkeley, CA: Wilderness Press.

OWENS, JAMES "JESSE" CLEVELAND (1913–1980)

Jesse Owens's record-breaking performance in the 1936 Summer Olympic Games dispelled Adolf Hitler's claims of Aryan superiority and established the African American track-and-field star as a national hero. The son of Alabama share-croppers, Owens moved to Cleveland, Ohio, as a young boy and later attended Ohio State University, where he became a champion sprinter, hurdler, and long jumper. Owens first gained fame in 1935 when he broke three world records and tied a fourth at the Big Ten Championship meet in Ann Arbor, Michigan.

Named to the U.S. Olympic team in 1936, Owens won four gold medals at the games in Berlin, breaking Olympic records in the 100-meter and 200-meter dashes, the 400-meter relay, and the long jump. Because he was snubbed by German chancellor Adolf Hitler, who refused to acknowledge the African American star's unprecedented feat, Owens emerged from the games as a symbol of opposition to Nazi theories of Aryan superiority.

Unfortunately, his eagerness to translate athletic success into monetary gain soon led to struggles with the Amateur Athletic Union (AAU) over his amateur status and with the Internal Revenue Service over unpaid taxes. During the 1936 presidential campaign, his willingness to accept money from Republican leaders, after agreeing to support Alf Landon, tarnished his image as a national hero. Owens's later efforts to regain his stature met with limited success, although frequent ceremonial appearances at athletic events and activities with the Republican Party and the Illinois Youth Commission kept him in the public eye.

Unable to adapt to the rising black activism of the civil rights era, he became a spokesperson for black conservatives and made an ill-fated effort to mediate the black power controversy at the 1968 Summer Olympic Games. Rising interest in the

American track athlete Jesse Owens makes the long jump that set an Olympic record in Berlin at the 1936 Olympic Games. His performance in several events at the games was one of the major upsets to German dictator Adolf Hitler's hopes that German athletes would prove their superiority in athletic endeavors.
(Bettmann/Corbis)

Olympics ensured Owens's continuing fame as an athletic hero, but his conservative activism and a 1966 conviction for tax evasion diminished his status as a cultural icon.

—*Raymond Arsenault*

See also: Civil Rights and Sport; Nazi Olympics; Olympic Games

For further reading:
Baker, William Joseph. 1988. *Jesse Owens: An American Life.* New York: Free Press.
McRae, Donald. 2003. *Heroes without a Country: America's Betrayal of Joe Louis and Jesse Owens.* Hopewell, NJ: Ecco Press.

P

PAIGE, LEROY "SATCHEL" (1906–1982)

Ageless, unhittable, tricksterish, and endlessly quotable, pitcher Leroy "Satchel" Paige was the greatest box-office draw in baseball during segregation times and the best-known African American ballplayer before the integration of the major leagues. Paige pitched in the minor leagues until he was in his fifties and made a major league appearance at age fifty-nine. He was basically a limber-armed fastball pitcher, but he used an assortment of trick pitches and stunts that excited fans across the United States. Paige and his Kansas City Monarchs have served as the models for touring Negro League players in fiction and film.

Paige excelled against star competition from the white majors leagues, and he was one of the first African American players to break into the integrated major leagues. Paige's brilliance was magnified by his showmanship. At times he seemed superhuman, putting on displays of throwing for distance and accuracy and calling in his fielders before striking out the batter. As famous as these tricks were, Paige may be best remembered for his often-wise sayings, such as "Don't look back; something might be gaining on you." Though he often played the clown, Paige made hundreds of thousands of dollars in baseball and was famed for his contract negotiations. He represents the athlete as sage, comedian, and magician, a unique mix of roles that helped define parts of the cultural image of the African American ballplayer.

—*Tim Morris*

See also: National Baseball Hall of Fame; Negro Baseball Leagues; Robinson, Jack Roosevelt "Jackie"

For further reading:

Paige, Leroy Satchel, and John B. Holway. 1993. *Maybe I'll Pitch Forever: A Great Baseball Player Tells the Hilarious Story behind the Legend.* Lincoln: University of Nebraska Press.

Peterson, Robert W. 1984. *Only the Ball Was White: A History of Legendary Black Players and All Black Professional Teams.* New York: McGraw-Hill.

Ribowsky, Mark. 2000. *Don't Look Back: Satchel Paige in the Shadows of Baseball.* New York: Da Capo.

PALMER, ARNOLD (1929–)

Arnold Palmer's aggressive, risk-laden golf style emerged as television was first discovering sport, and the combination pushed golf to unprecedented popularity. Palmer's emotional, photogenic face and his lunging swing appealed to millions of people who were unfamiliar with golf in the 1950s, and nongolfers were attracted to Palmer's golfing abandon in a genteel game. He is noted for his charge, his charismatic personality, his hitching up of his pants, and his exuberant walk. These traits personified traditional masculinity and Palmer was a tough, courageous, and hard man who conquered golf courses with a "can do" attitude.

His gallery of fans became known as "Arnie's Army," and Palmer is affectionately called "the King." Palmer's go-for-broke style of play, his youthful gusto and his spirit of adventure electrified fans as he risked losing a tournament while trying to make an impossible shot. In addition to renewing an interest in the sport, his successes were instrumental in causing purses to quadruple, and he became the first professional golfer to reach a million dollars in career earnings.

Palmer's career transformed the marriage between the sport and the public because his matches were televised. The athlete of their dreams mesmerized viewers as he attempted to conquer the United States via its golf courses. During his career, Palmer had sixty-one tour victories and victories in eight majors, including one U.S. Amateur, one U.S. Open, and two British Opens. He resuscitated the British Open with back-to-back victories in 1961 and 1962.

Palmer parlayed his successful career and dynamic personality into a business empire, including a line of golf equipment, golf-course designs, and advertising. He earned almost $200 million through winnings, endorsements, and merchandising. Although Palmer's golfing successes declined in the 1990s, his devoted fans did not. Whenever he played a Senior or Professional Golfers' Association (PGA) tournament, Arnie's Army cheered for the man who demonstrated how to have a rousing good time on the golf course.

—*Mike Schoenecke*

See also: Golf; Professional Golfers' Association

For further reading:

Palmer, Arnold, and James Dodson. 1999. *A Golfer's Life.* New York: Ballantine Books.

Sampson, Curt, and Dan Jenkins. 2000. *The Eternal Summer: Palmer, Nicklaus and Hogan in 1960, Golf's Golden Year.* New York: Villard Publishing.

PAN-AMERICAN GAMES

Since their inauguration in 1951, the Pan-American Games have promoted Western Hemispheric interaction and athletic improvement. At the Paris Games of 1924, the International Olympic Committee (IOC) encouraged Latin Americans to establish regional "Olympics." The first result was the Central American Games, hosted by Mexico in 1926, with three countries attending. The games were repeated irregularly until 1935 when they were renamed the Central American and Caribbean Games. In 1938, Bogatá, Colombia, was the site of the first Bolivarian Games. There were no games between 1938 and 1946 because of World War II; after that, they were held every four years, but the 1958 games were held in 1959 and the 1994 games were held in 1993. In 1973, the more-limited Central American Games were created to allow the smaller countries of the isthmus to compete without the presence of the more powerful Mexican and Cuban teams.

In the 1930s, plans were drawn to launch hemispheric Pan-American Games in Buenos Aires in 1941. But World War II delayed that event until 1951, when the host government of Juan Perón used the games to promote both Argentine nationalism and the image of its populist program. After 1951, the United States dominated virtually all facets of the games as the teams regularly took the Pan-American Games as an opportunity to prepare for the following year's summer Olympics. In the 1990s, however, U.S. superiority declined, in part because expanded international competitions reduced the importance of the games to North Americans, who sent slightly weaker teams. In addition, revolutionary Cuba continued to improve its sport program. Thus, at the games Cuba hosted in 1991, Cubans won more gold medals than did the United States and almost as many medals total. At the 1995 games in Mar del Plata, Argentina, the Cubans trailed the United States in both categories but still overwhelmed the rest of the field. Limited

Fans cheer as athletes parade during the opening ceremonies at the XIV Pan-American Games in Santo Domingo, Dominican Republic, on August 1, 2003. Over 7,000 athletes from 42 countries competed in 38 sports during the games, which ran through August 17.
(REUTERS/CORBIS)

winter Pan-American Games were added in the 1990s, but their future is much in doubt.

—*Joseph L. Arbena*

See also: Olympic Games

For further reading:

Dworshak, Bruce, and Jay Soule, eds. 1987. *Games of August: Official Commemorative Book, the Tenth Pan American Games.* Wichita, KS: Showmasters.

Olderr, Steven. 2003. *The Pan American Games: A Statistical History, 1951–1999.* Bilingual Edition. Jefferson, NC: McFarland.

PARENTAL INVOLVEMENT

If one were to ask any coach of Pop Warner football, T-ball, Little League baseball, or junior high and high school athletic teams to cite the most difficult problem in working with children, the majority answer may well be the parents of those children. Parents of young athletes, with their criticism of coaches, managers, and umpires, can put Hollywood stage parents to shame in their avidity to be involved in their children's lives. As one high school coach noted, his true test of patience came not from the teenagers but from parents with hidden agendas.

One can observe this trend in action at any public ballpark in the early spring or summer. The applause and cheers may momentarily drown out the mumbling and grumbling, but the criticism returns audibly as parents lament their child's being benched, berate the other players for making their child look bad, or accuse the umpire of nearsightedness, blindness, or stupidity. Parents of young athletes tend to keep score of more than runs, hits, or touchdowns; they also keep extremely accurate records of how many playing hours their child has had on the field and how many hours he or she has had on the bench. Often this information is noted loudly each time the coach is within earshot.

Attitude is often as important as ability in athletics. Young children and teenagers model their behavior on their parents' and play to please their parents, whose praise is so important to their development. Dangerous precedents can be set for young athletes by parents who constantly criticize the adults for whom children and young people must show respect in order to compete.

—*Joyce Duncan*

See also: Children in Sport: Competition and Socialization

For further reading:

Fish, Joel. 2003. *101 Ways to Be a Terrific Sports Parent: Making Athletics a Positive Experience for Your Child.* New York: Simon and Schuster.

PATRIOTISM AND SPORT

Sport in the United States has become an arena of great patriotic fervor and nationalism, especially during times of social crisis. In 1907, a special commission, established by professional baseball, sought the origin of the game. Their charge, although perhaps not officially, was to establish baseball as the American game without connection to English sport. Out of this commission came the Cooperstown–Abner Doubleday myth and the firm connection between baseball and America. As time progressed, baseball became known as America's pastime, and it was thought to embody all that was good about U.S. society.

> *Sport in the United States has become an arena of great patriotic fervor and nationalism, especially during times of social crises.*

This link became central to baseball's image over the years, and overseas baseball tours were founded to help spread U.S. ideals to other countries. During World War II, baseball stadiums became central locations for blood drives, recruitment drives, scrap metal collections, and other events on behalf of the war effort. Soldiers overseas were often asked to answer baseball questions as proof of U.S. citizenship. It was at this time that the national anthem, previously played only during holiday games, became an everyday part of the baseball ritual.

Other sports followed the lead established by baseball. Most sports now include the national anthem as part of their pregame ritual, and during special events, the fields become sites for patriotic tributes. The chant of "U.S.A." has become commonplace at international sporting events featuring U.S. squads. Basketball, baseball, hockey, and yachting teams drape themselves with the flag and travel the globe as representatives of the United States, their wins and losses reflecting the country's image. To play poorly or outside the rules is seen as being "un-American." In no other entertainment forum are such patriotic symbols so clearly expressed or so taken for granted.

—*Robert S. Brown*

See also: Doubleday, Abner, Myth of; Music and Sport; Olympic Games

For further reading:

Allison, Lincoln, ed. 1986. *The Politics of Sport.* Wolfeboro, NH: Manchester University Press.

Duke, Vic, and Liz Crolley. 1996. *Football, Nationality and the State.* New York: Addison Wesley Longman.

Feinstein, John. 2001. *The Last Amateurs: Playing for Glory and Honor in Division 1 College Basketball.* Boston: Back Bay.

Wilcox, Ralph C. 1994. *Sport in the Global Village.* Morgantown, WV: Fitness Information Technology.

PATTERSON, FLOYD (1935–)

Heavyweight champion Floyd Patterson was one of the prototypes for athletes who pulled their way out of poverty with their athletic prowess. At age 21, Patterson was the youngest person ever to win boxing's heavyweight title. In addition, he was the first to regain the title, and the first to turn an Olympic gold medal into a lucrative heavyweight career. The self-effacing Floyd Patterson became the symbol for all that was good in boxing. Raised in Brooklyn's Bedford-Stuyvesant section, the third of eleven children, Patterson had adolescent difficulties and attended schools for problem children before he was discovered by legendary trainer Cus D'Amato.

After winning the 1952 Olympic middleweight gold medal, Patterson began a professional career marked by his peekaboo stance, bending forward at the waist with his gloves nestled on either side of his face, considered an unorthodox and dangerous defense. On November 30, 1956, he knocked out the aging Archie Moore to win the heavyweight title vacated by Rocky Marciano.

In 1959, Patterson lost in an upset with a third-round technical knockout (TKO) by Ingemar Johansson, considered the Swedish white hope. Embarrassed by the loss and by U.S. praise of Johansson, Patterson regained the title a year later with a fifth-round knockout of Johansson. In 1961, he knocked out the Swede again in six rounds. Patterson once again lost face and the title when he suffered first-round knockouts in 1962 and 1963 by boxing's bad boy, Sonny Liston. Patterson's other embarrassing encounters were with Muhammad Ali, whom Patterson called unworthy of the title because Ali had joined the Nation of Islam. Patterson refused to call Ali by his Muslim name, and when Ali won with TKOs in 1965 and 1972, he taunted Patterson in the ring with cries of "What's my name?"

Patterson, who once retrieved an opponent's mouthpiece during a fight, has been called boxing's last gentleman. In 1995, he became chairman of the New York State Athletic Commission, which regulates professional boxing and wrestling.

—Harry Amana

See also: Ali, Muhammad; Boxing

For further reading:

Brooke-Ball, Peter. 2001. *The Great Fights: Eighty Epic Encounters from the History of Boxing.* London: Southwater Publishing.

Heinz, W. C., and Nathan, Ward, eds. 1999. *The Total Sports Illustrated Book of Boxing.* New York: Total Sports.

Patterson, Floyd, and Bert Randolph Sugar. 1974. *Inside Boxing.* Chicago: NTC/Contemporary Books.

PAYTON, WALTER (1954–1999)

Due in part as a consequence of his untimely death, Walter Payton has become an icon for personal and professional chivalry and integrity. He also served as a role model as he strove to become the first African American team owner in the league. Using a rare combination of power, speed, and control, Walter Payton rushed his way to the Hall of Fame as the all-time leading rusher (16,726 yards) in the National Football League (NFL). Payton took those abilities, combined with a dogged work ethic and keen business acumen, to the owners' playing field. Affectionately nicknamed "Sweetness" by his Chicago Bears teammates, Payton was called "the very best football player I've seen period—at any position" by his coach and fellow Hall of Famer, Mike Ditka. Payton's induction into the Hall of Fame, where he was introduced by his twelve-year-old son Jarrett, a 1986 Super Bowl ring, and numerous league records highlighted his NFL career.

The Chicago Bears hero attributed part of his success to grueling hill workouts that started on the sand hills near his hometown of Columbia, Mississippi, and continued at the levees of the Pearl River and at a place he simply referred to as "the hill" near Arlington Heights, Illinois. This work ethic clearly contributed to Payton's success on the NFL playing fields and to its transfer to the business field. Payton was part owner of several

Chicago area businesses and a race-car team, for which he also drove, as well as an investing partner of a near-successful bid for an NFL expansion franchise. His autobiography *Never Die Easy*, started before his death and completed by writer Don Yaeger, was published in 2001.

In 1999, after Payton died of cancer at only forty-five years of age, his family, former Bears players, and the entire 1999 team entered Soldier's Field carrying roses in his honor. The Reverend Jesse Jackson led Payton's fans in a last ovation. The Chicago Bears wore a football-shaped patch with Payton's number 34 over their hearts for the remainder of the season.

—*Wayne S. Quirk*

See also: Football

For further reading:

Media, H. S., ed. 1999. *Sweetness: The Courage and Heart of Walter Payton.* Chicago: Triumph Books.

Payton, Walter, and Don Yaeger. 2001. *Never Die Easy: The Autobiography of Walter Payton.* New York: Random House.

Towle, Mike. 2000. *I Remember Walter Payton: Personal Memories of Football's "Sweetest" Superstar by the People Who Knew Him Best.* Nashville, TN: Cumberland House.

PELÉ
See do Nascimento, Edson Arantesm, "Pelé"

PETTY, RICHARD (1937–)

Richard "King Richard" Petty was the most popular and best-known driver of the National Association for Stock Car Auto Racing (NASCAR) from the late 1960s into the 1980s. Born and raised in Level Cross, North Carolina, Richard Petty, the son of NASCAR champion Lee Petty, began his racing career in 1958 at the age of twenty-one. Beginning in 1959, with his first NASCAR win, Petty drove to victory in two hundred NASCAR races and is tied, at seven, for the most NASCAR championships. In response, he was given the nickname "King Richard" for his near-total domination of the sport.

After Petty's record twenty-seven wins in 1967, he became the best-known driver in NASCAR, but it was his combination of successful driving and fan accessibility that propelled him into the limelight. Petty's willingness to sign autographs and speak to fans at all the races and his annual barbecue, open to the public, at his shop in Level Cross set an example for all NASCAR drivers and earned him the Most Popular Driver Award nine times. Consequently, NASCAR became one of the most fan-friendly sports in the United States, one of the major reasons for the success of the sport.

After retiring from competitive racing, Petty became an owner of a NASCAR Winston Cup team. Petty parlayed his popularity into becoming a successful spokesman for many products, both automobile-related and nonautomobile-related, and into a political career. He served twenty years as a Randolph County commissioner, and he was the Republican Party nominee for secretary of state in North Carolina in 1996.

—*Harry E. Carpenter III*

See also: National Association for Stock Car Auto Racing

For further reading:

Chandler, Charles. 2002. *Quotable Petty: Words of Wisdom, Success and Courage by and about Richard Petty, the King of Stock-Car Racing.* Nashville, TN: TowleHouse Publishers.

Vehorn, Frank. 1992. *Farewell to the King: A Personal Look Back at the Career of Richard Petty, Stock Car Racing's Winningest and Most Popular Driver.* Asheboro, NC: Down Home Press.

PHOTOGRAPHY, SPORT IN

The familiar adage "A picture is worth a thousand words" captures the true essence of sport photography, especially when it comes to documenting the performance of a lifetime, "the thrill of victory and the agony of defeat." The still photograph and its offspring, the motion picture, also increased accessibility to sporting events for the public, thus whetting the cultural appetite for increased participation.

For centuries, humans have elevated athletes to the status of hero or icon. During the Greek and Roman eras, statues were created and erected to honor those who achieved greatness, as well as those who possessed tremendous athletic strength and physical beauty. Other artists, likewise, created paintings of such sporting events as foxhunting, horse racing, and regattas. However, it was not until the invention of photography that ordinary people could own an artistic image of their favorite sport hero.

Developing technological advances during the late nineteenth century allowed not only scientists but also painters, photographers, and enthusiasts to study the movement of persons and objects. One of the most notable of the photographers was Eadweard Muybridge (1830–1904), who is best known for his motion studies conducted between 1883 and 1887. Muybridge captured still images that detailed exact sequential patterns of movement that were normally too fast for the human eye to see. Among his images are "Eighteen Frames of Race Horse Galloping" (1883–1887) and "Baseball Throwing" (1887). This work with multiple imagery enabled him to devise the zoopraxiscope, or zoogyroscope, which projected a series of moving pictures onto a screen, thus becoming the forerunner of motion pictures.

In 1931, Harold Edgerton (1903–1990) pioneered the development of stroboscopic photography, thereby enabling photographers to capture activities that were occurring faster than the eye could perceive. Although not a sport photographer, Edgerton produced images similar to the Muybridge motion studies, including "Tennis Serve" (1952).

Until the years following World War II, many sport photographers were actually photojournalists who were employed by newspapers and magazines, from the *New York Times* to *Collier's*, *Life*, and the *Saturday Evening Post*, and assigned to cover specific sporting events. By the end of the twentieth century, photographers specialized in sport coverage and flourished as either freelancers or contract employees of such magazines as *Sports Illustrated* and *Yachting*. Notable among those photographers are Richard Clarkson, Israel Kaplan, Mark Kaufmann, Walter Loss Jr., Neil Leifer, George Silk, and John Zimmerman.

Sport photographers have been elevated to the status of celebrities and entertainers. Many of the brightest and most talented photographers are in high demand to immortalize athletic heroes and cult figures, consequently becoming celebrities themselves. Among the elite in celebrity photography is Annie Liebovitz (1949–), whose images, seen in a variety of publications, are noteworthy for their theatrical poses.

In the latter years of the twentieth century, U.S. culture was inundated by visual images of athletic events. Sport photographs and posters of athletic heroes, school and college athletic teams, and a host of other visual memorabilia adorned the bedroom walls of children, teenagers, college students, and adult sport enthusiasts. It is the action, drama, and excitement of sporting events that capture the hearts and minds of these individuals. Who can forget the magic moments of a photo finish at the Kentucky Derby, the last-second, game-winning point in a championship basketball game, the halftime spectacle of the Super Bowl, or the opening and closing festivities of the Olympics? Photographic documentation of these and thousands of other sporting events has allowed all to participate.

—*Stephen Allan Patrick*

See also: Film and Sport; Marketing of Sport; Television, Impact on Sport

For further reading:
Crisp, Steve, and Monique Villa. 2003. *The Art of Sport:*

The Best of Reuters Sports Photography. Englewood Cliffs, NJ: Prentice-Hall.

Looss, Walter. 1999. *Walter Looss: A Lifetime Shooting Sports and Beauty.* Edited by B. Martin Pederson. Cheshire, CT: Graphics Press.

Wombell, Paul. 2000. *Sportscape: The Evolution of Sports Photography.* London: Phaidon.

PLAYGROUND ASSOCIATION OF AMERICA

The Playground Association of America, founded in 1905, was responsible for the development of urban playgrounds and playground programs across the United States. Based on their successful work with the Young Men's Christian Association (YMCA), Luther Gulick and Henry S. Curtis cofounded the Playground Association in an effort to introduce organized, directed play into U.S. cities. Early support and leadership for the association came from urban reformers such as Jane Addams, and the association gained presidential approval from Theodore Roosevelt, who was named honorary president in 1906.

The primary goal of the association was to provide space and supervision for urban play areas. The association lobbied municipalities, arguing that urban youth needed directed activities for their free time. This organized play was intended to develop the youth socially, physically, and intellectually.

In the association's peak period, between 1906 and 1917, the number of municipal playgrounds increased from approximately 1,500 to 4,000. On the eve of World War I, however, Gulick and Curtis shifted their focus to public schools and the development of the Public School Athletic League, founded in 1903. During the war, the Playground Association was renamed the Playground and Recreation Association of America (PRAA), and plans were revised toward directing healthy and decent lifestyles for young U.S. soldiers. Following the war, the PRAA concentrated on lobbying for federal physical education programs for secondary schools, and by 1930, thirty-six states had adopted such programs.

Critics of the Playground Association pointed out that, at its peak, attendance at urban playgrounds never exceeded 10 percent of the youth population, yet the concept of urban playgrounds continued throughout the century.

—*Sean C. Madden*

See also: Muscular Christianity

For further reading:

Crawford, Robert W. 1985. "The Playground Movement Celebrates 100 Years." *Parks and Recreation* 20 (August): 34–35.

Eccles, Jacquelynne S. 2003. "Adolescent Participation in Structured and Unstructured Activities: A Person-Oriented Analysis." *Journal of Youth and Adolescence* 32 (August): 233–242.

Hartsoe, Charles E. 1985. "From Playgrounds to Public Policy." *Parks and Recreation* 20 (August): 46–52.

PLIMPTON, GEORGE
(1927–2003)

The consummate gentleman amateur, George Plimpton offered fans a unique perspective on sport by competing with professional athletes and then recounting his adventures in several best-selling books. Born in New York City, Plimpton was a cosmopolitan man of letters who edited the *Paris Review*, a highly regarded literary journal, from 1953 until his death and published nearly thirty books.

As experiments in participatory journalism, he practiced and played with the National Basketball Association's Boston Celtics, the Detroit Lions of the National Football League, and leading professional golf and tennis players. His most popular work, *Paper Lion* (1966), chronicles the Lions' preseason training camp and concludes with a play-by-play account of Plimpton's appearance in an exhibition game as the quarterback for the

Lions. *Paper Lion* was subsequently made into a semidocumentary film featuring several Detroit players and coaches as themselves and Alan Alda as Plimpton.

Plimpton's generally upbeat insider accounts of life among professional athletes humanized sport stars by revealing their frailties, but they also depicted athletes as skilled performers possessing physical gifts far beyond those of the average man. Plimpton's books include *Out of My League* (1961), *The Bogey Man* (1968), and *The Curious Case of Sidd Finch* (1987). The last is a novel about a devout Buddhist pitcher for the New York Mets who can throw a fastball at 168 miles per hour. The work first appeared as an elaborate April Fools' hoax in *Sports Illustrated*. Plimpton also edited *The Norton Book of Sports* (1992), an anthology of sport journalism and literature. Although Plimpton lived life on the edge, he died peacefully in his sleep at the age of 76.

—*Tim Ashwell*

See also: Literature, Sport in; Sport Journalism; *Sports Illustrated*

For further reading:

Plimpton, George. Reprint 1993. *Out of My League*. New York: Lyons and Burford.

———. Reprint 1993. *Paper Lion*. New York: Lyons and Burford.

POLITICAL CORRECTNESS

As part of an influential period of reform, political correctness has paved the way for important changes in U.S. sport; on the other hand, it has also been criticized for being oppressive in its own right. Political correctness refers to the process by which administrators, legislators, the media, and interest groups challenge language and practices that are seen as marginalizing particular groups. In sport, this has meant challenging white, male control of sport, ensuring greater participation for women and minorities. This powerful movement has fostered some impressive changes. Opportunities for women have increased dramatically since the 1980s, especially in sports such as basketball, soccer, tennis, and golf, in which women have thrilled audiences at the Olympics as well as in collegiate and professional events. In addition, racist nicknames have been replaced at some colleges. St. John's University, for example, changed its team name from "Redmen" to "Red Storm." Increased coaching and administrative opportunities for minorities is another feather in the cap of political correctness, as is the increased financial involvement of wealthy professional sport teams in poor neighborhoods of the cities in which they play.

Still, political correctness has its problems. Affirmative action has sometimes resulted in reverse discrimination. At some schools, important traditions have been sacrificed, overly restrictive limits have been placed on free speech, unnecessary financial strains have resulted in the elimination of some sports, and decisions have been made to serve special interests at the expense of the university. For instance, some have criticized schools that have tried to reach artificial gender equity quotas by eliminating men's programs, pointing out that these cuts hurt men without adding any opportunities for women.

Affirmative action, gender equity, and race issues, such as team nicknames and hiring policies, have kept political correctness in the limelight.

—*Don L. Deardorff II*

See also: Discrimination, Racial, in Sport; Men's Issues

For further reading:

Fitzgerald, Mark. 1994. "Downside of Political Correctness." *Editor and Publisher,* June 11, 9.

Jefferson, Margo. 1999. "The Presence of Race in Politically Correct Ambiguity." *New York Times,* February 8.

Laskaris, Sam. 1998. "Some Braves Will Change, Some Braves Won't." *Wind Speaker,* December, 24.

Parris, Matthew. 2000. "A Lexicon of Conservative Cant." *Spectator,* February 19, 12–14.

Seligman, Dan. 1998. "This Is Sports Coverage?" *Forbes,* January 26, 52–54.

Slovenko, Ralph. 1994. "Politically Correct Team Names." *Journal of Psychiatry and Law* 22 (Winter): 585–592.

POPULAR CULTURE AND SPORT

As U.S. sport entered the twenty-first century, the progressive reduction of athletic achievement to readily marketable products became obvious. Team logos—even those of dominant amateur powers—became little more than trademarks, hype for professional championships generated devotion once associated only with high religious holidays, and the inspiration to play was replaced by association with teams or players through accumulation of consumer products. Even the proliferation of "official," heavily regulated youth leagues risks driving spontaneous games from the playgrounds. "The thrill of victory and the agony of defeat" have been simulated, replicated, licensed, sanctioned, diluted, homogenized, mass produced, globally distributed, and discounted to such a point that those who love a game for its own sake find themselves in the minority.

> For some sports, the accumulation of accessories has supplanted the perceived need to develop skills.

Nowhere is this tendency more apparent than in U.S. material culture. The pervasive growth of consumer electronics, for example, has led to the introduction of a wide range of sport simulators, from computerized baseball to handheld deep-sea fishing games. For some sports, the accumulation of accessories has supplanted the perceived need to develop skills. By the mid-1990s, for example, so many golf videos, devices, magazines, and fashions had reached the market that they could support cable television's Golf Channel, hawking wares twenty-four hours a day. The athletic shoe industry, in particular, has enjoyed a booming business since the late 1970s, their advertisements implying, not always subtly, that owning the right shoes leads to greater athleticism. Such companies as Nike and Reebok followed their shoe lines with other athletic apparel, some so desired and expensive that by the 1980s there were news reports of youths committing murder to steal these goods from their victims. Some of these trademark logo items even became badges of identification for certain urban gangs. Memorable trademarks and the strong appeal of group identity, eagerly exploited by corporations shilling products to help assuage consumers' feeling of inadequacy, made a poor replacement for the decreasing playtime average working Americans enjoy. And as Americans found less leisure time to play, they started reading less as well, reducing sport publishing to large picture books; "inspirational" books—disguising autobiographies, often ghostwritten—by successful coaches; quickie biographies, usually unauthorized, of new sport stars; and self-aggrandizing autobiographies, again often ghostwritten, by professional athletes whose notoriety rivals their athletic ability.

Such publishing ventures play into the nurtured perception that true fandom lies in collecting memorabilia of all sorts, ranging from traditional baseball cards to special-edition die-cast toys, consumer products with the likenesses of sport figures on the package, and actual uniforms, or even replicas, and equipment used by favored players. By the mid-1990s, sport figures even appeared on cable television's home-shopping channels to sell their memorabilia or products bearing their endorsements. They also exploited their marketability by attending "sport shows" and charging fans for autographs, opting to make the first profit from something likely to be sold later.

In popular music, sport-themed songs appeared throughout the twentieth century, with "Take Me Out to the Ball Game" and "They Call Him Mr. Touchdown" becoming standards as familiar as the fight songs of dominant college teams. However, new sport songs have appeared less frequently as rock and country have become the dominant genres of U.S. music. Occasionally, novelty songs like Mel and Tim's "Backfield in Motion," which uses football terminology to describe a lover's infidelity, become one-hit wonders and earn a permanent place in pop history. Established artists usually shy away from sport songs; however, John Fogerty's "Centerfield" and its exhilarating celebration of playing baseball expresses more sincere affection than most of the conventional love songs released at the time. Possibly the two sports most celebrated in pop songs are surfing and racing, subjects dominating the era of beach music by such 1960s groups as Jan and Dean and the Beach Boys. However, as an off-shoot of increasing television exposure, Americans have become accustomed to associating specific nonsport songs, like the drum-laden "Rock and Roll Pt. 2" by Gary Glitter and the adrenaline-releasing "We Will Rock You" by Queen, with various types of sport. By the late 1990s, ESPN began marketing collections of these stadium favorites in a series of *Jock Rock* albums that merely repackaged songs readily available in other collections, and NASCAR licensed similar collections.

Although sport on television obviously offers a means for advertisers to promote their products, it has also become a curious form of competition in itself. Although traditional sport enjoys a great deal of exposure, during the late 1990s the ratings fell sharply due to the growth of cable television, the introduction of new television sport networks, and the greater range of choices available to consumer-viewers. Astronomical costs resulting from bidding wars for the rights to televise major franchises led some critics to question the prestige afforded in winning those rights. In addition, some media moguls attempted the introduction of new professional football and basketball franchises for the sole purpose of having less-expensive professional sport programming. By the 1990s, some broadcasters also affected the viewers' perception of what sport is. For example, ESPN and ESPN2 included competitions in aerobic dance, lumberjack skills, and cheerleading in

their programming. Media mogul Ted Turner established the Goodwill Games as an alternative to the Olympic Games, and the ESPN networks presented the X Games, including such high-risk street competitions as trick biking, skateboarding, and downhill street luge.

On the other hand, sport-themed television drama and comedy tends to have a limited appeal. An exception is *The White Shadow*, a critically lauded drama that follows an inner-city basketball coach as he attempts to guide his students, both on and off the court. Another fine but short-lived show, the Steven Boccho–produced *Bay City Blues*, offered a gritty look at the lives of a minor league team's members. Still, these programs are far outnumbered by such scarily bad sitcom fare as the television adaptation of the hit film *The Bad News Bears;* the mercifully short-lived (one month) adaptation of Jim Bouton's *Ball Four*, starring the author; the cliché-riddled *Coach*, portraying the life of a pigheaded, loud-mouthed university football coach; and Home Box Office's "adult" fare such as *Arli$$*, a sitcom about a sport agent, and *First & Ten*, a sitcom about pro football in which National Football League retirees, such as O. J. Simpson, could cavort with cheerleaders, who were likely to wind up topless sometime during the episode. Unfortunately, more access to broadcasting has meant that more dubious programming has wound up on television; in fact, many who once enjoyed the communal spirit of pitching "Howie bricks" (styrofoam bricks created to throw at the television during Howard Cosell's airtime) during *Monday Night Football* may now feel provoked into throwing the real things.

Sport film, however, can convey aspirations and hopes in a manner not often seen in other facets of pop culture. There are, of course, the hokey comedies that merely use sport as a backdrop, like *Major League* (1989) and *Semi Tough* (1977), and the kitschy dramas that lose all sense of proportion, for example, *Knute Rockne: All American* (1940), *Blue Chips* (1994), *Personal Best*

(1982), and *The Program* (1993). Fortunately, sport on film can embody mythic concepts so that the analogies work effectively. It is difficult not to feel stirred by such films as *The Pride of the Yankees* (1943), *Chariots of Fire* (1981), *Heart Like a Wheel* (1983), *Rocky* (1976), and *Hoop Dreams* (1994). At their best, sport films remind viewers that they have an opportunity to contend, excel, and achieve if they will only play. Films like *Raging Bull* (1980), *North Dallas Forty* (1979), *Eight Men Out* (1988), and *A League of Their Own* (1992) also humanize heroes, indicating that they too play out personal dramas, merely in ways different from the ways those in the audience play out their own.

On the other hand, film dramas have increasingly begun to express a theme of cynicism regarding corporate intrusion into sport. There is no irony in the fact that one of the most acclaimed sport movies of the late 1990s, *Jerry Maguire* (1996), featured a down-on-his-luck sport agent attempting to resurrect his personal integrity while negotiating the largest possible contract for his grandstanding client. Ironically, this movie stirred controversy and litigation because the athletic-wear company Reebok did not get the product placement it expected in the film. As movies project both human dreams and concerns, *Jerry Maguire* indicates how far sport, via pop culture, has gotten away from the sandlots.

—*Thomas Alan Holmes*

See also: Film and Sport; Marketing of Sport; Music and Sport; Sneakers; Television, Impact on Sport

For further reading:

Brooks, Tim, and Earle Marshe. 1995. *The Complete Directory to Prime Time Network and Cable TV Shows, 1946–Present.* 6th ed., rev. New York: Ballantine Books.

Romanowski, Patricia, Holly George-Warren, and Jon Pareles, eds. *The New Rolling Stone Encyclopedia of Rock and Roll.* Rev. ed. New York: Fireside.

Sage, George H. 1998. *Power and Ideology in American Sport.* 2nd ed. Champaign, IL: Human Kinetics Publishers.

PRESIDENT'S COUNCIL ON PHYSICAL FITNESS AND SPORTS

Originally established to focus on youth fitness and later evolving to encompass fitness for all ages, the President's Council on Physical Fitness and Sports was created to raise public awareness and consciousness of the need for physical activity, thus enabling citizens to maintain a healthy and improved quality of life.

On July 16, 1956, by Executive Order 10673, President Dwight D. Eisenhower established the first U.S. President's Council on Youth Fitness that was made up entirely of members of the president's cabinet. This action was prompted by a report that children in the United States were less fit than their European counterparts. In addition, Eisenhower created the President's Citizens Advisory Committee on the Fitness of American Youth.

In 1961, President John F. Kennedy expanded the focus of the council to include physical fitness for all age groups and changed the name to the President's Council on Physical Fitness. His successor, President Lyndon B. Johnson, created the Presidential Physical Fitness Award in 1966 and added "and Sports" to the council's name and mission in 1968.

During President Richard M. Nixon's administration in 1972, the council premiered the Presidential Sports Award, which can be earned by participants, age six and older, through a long-term commitment to regular participation in sport. And in 1978, President Jimmy Carter transferred the council from the jurisdiction of the Executive Office of the President to that of the U.S. Department of Health, Education, and Welfare, which became the U.S. Department of Health and Human Services in 1980.

Over the years, the council has provided millions of Americans with guidance on a variety of issues, from exercise and training to health and nutrition. It championed the role that sport and physical fitness play in the everyday lives of Amer-

President Eisenhower chats with a little girl on the White House lawn (April 2, 1956). On July 16, 1956, President Eisenhower established the first U.S. President's Council on Youth Fitness.
(JACK LARTZ/CORBIS)

icans by promoting not only the Olympics but also the Paralympics and the Special Olympics World Games, among others, as being important for all individuals in maintaining good health, both physical and mental.

During the 1990s, the council delivered its proactive message in new forums, including via public-service television announcements, work on the "Surgeon General's Report on Physical Activity and Health," and an exhibit in Washington, D.C., on the role of U.S. presidents in promoting fitness and sport. The council also published a variety of newsletters and other resource materials that are distributed to public libraries.

As a strong and vocal advocate for physical fitness and training, for good nutrition and health habits, and for active participation in individual or team sport, the council is made up of notable members from the fields of medicine, professional and amateur sport, physical education and training, and advocacy for the physically challenged, thus ensuring a balance of national concerns and interests of all citizens.

—*Stephen Allan Patrick*

See also: Fitness Marketing and Magazines

For further reading:
President's Council on Physical Fitness and Sports.

1986. *National School Population Fitness Survey, 1985.* Washington, DC: GPO.

———. 1990. *Living Fit.* Emery, CA: Parlay.

PROFESSIONAL GOLFERS' ASSOCIATION

Enhancing the visibility of golf in the United States through tournaments, corporate partnerships, and televised network coverage, the Professional Golfers' Association of America (PGA) was founded in 1916 to promote national interest in golf and to improve the status and welfare of the golf professional. The organization has grown from 82 charter members to over 23,000 golfing professionals.

The PGA conducts more than thirty annual tournaments both for "club pros," those who staff the many public and private golf clubs in the United States and give instruction to amateur golfers, and for "touring pros," those who make a full-time living by playing tournament golf. The PGA also sponsors youth and junior programs, National Golf Month in August, and awards, such as the PGA Player of the Year, won in 1997 by rookie phenomenon Tiger Woods.

The most prominent golf event sponsored by the PGA is the Ryder Cup Matches, in which twelve-man teams from the United States compete against their counterparts from Great Britain and Europe for national honors rather than prize money. Conducted biennially since 1927, the Ryder Cup now garners worldwide attention among both dedicated and casual fans, primarily because the matches are so competitive. Great Britian made a three-match comeback in 1985, 1987, and 1989, after a long period, from 1959 to 1983, dominated by the United States.

Because the PGA represents the interests of all golf professionals, the overwhelming majority of whom are club pros, tournament professionals broke away from the organization in 1968 to form a group of their own. However, they quickly agreed to a compromise solution under the umbrella of the PGA, creating a fully autonomous Tournament Players Division, renamed in 1975 as the PGA Tour.

The PGA Tour sponsors most of the tournaments in which male touring pros and senior touring pros participate. Through the efforts of a powerful and entrepreneurial commissioner, Deane Beman, who served from 1974 to 1995, as well as because of the talents of the players, the tournaments grew dramatically in network and cable television coverage; in corporate, community, and charitable involvements; and in prize money, to about $50 million for the regular men's tour in 1997. The PGA Tour is highly visible both to the general public and in the more than fifty communities hosting annual tournaments. The Ladies Professional Golf Association (LPGA) serves a parallel role for women touring golf professionals, but its efforts have been much less successful in the commercial marketplace.

The PGA's own championship, conducted annually since 1916, reflects the continuing tension between the interests of club and touring professional golfers. A large number of the approximately 150 invitational places in this tournament were at one time reserved for club pros, drawing protests from touring pros about the exclusion of more-qualified players. In the late 1990s, only twenty spots were reserved for club pros, who could not compete effectively with such golfing greats as Jack Nicklaus and Lee Trevino. The 1997 PGA champion, Davis Love III, was a particularly popular winner who momentarily bridged the gap between the two worlds of golf professionals. Love's father, Davis Love Jr., killed in an airplane crash in 1988, was one of golf's leading teaching and club professionals.

—*John Paul Ryan*

See also: Golf; Ladies Professional Golf Association; Nicklaus, Jack; Woods, Eldrick "Tiger"

For further reading:

Butler, Herbert. 1975. *The PGA: The Official History of*

the Professional Golfers' Association of America. New York: Crowell.

Gabriel, Mike. 2001. *The Professional Golfers' Association Tour: A History.* Jefferson, NC: McFarland.

"PUMPING IRON"

"Pumping iron," vernacular for lifting weights, is one of the most popular forms of exercise of the late twentieth and early twenty-first centuries, a form that has been instrumental in creating a new standard of health and physical beauty for men and women. Weight lifting was introduced in the United States as a response to industrialism and the new factory labor. Proponents of weight lifting worried that the nation's male workers would be weakened by the physically repetitive nature of factory work. These ideas, however, were then only a curiosity and found a limited audience.

On the other hand, the belief that lifting weights is healthful pervades late-twentieth-century and early twenty-first-century U.S. culture. Although the phrase "pumping iron" refers to a vigorous mode of working with weights, the popularization of weight lifting as exercise has rendered the phrase "pumping iron" more broadly connotative. "Pumping iron" is thought to benefit general health and is integral to a range of specific activities, including weight loss, professional sport training, injury rehabilitation, and combating bone disease.

Public approval of women's weight lifting has lagged far behind the popularity of the activity for men. Only in the late twentieth century were muscles thought appropriate and attractive for women. Similarly, the image of the strong man is no longer recognized as only a heterosexual image; it is also an image attractive to homosexual men, who have incorporated "pumping iron" and muscled bodies into gay culture.

Weight lifting has special importance to a culture and an economy that prioritizes mental over physical labor but that still believes in the moral value of physical work. Consequently, a multimillion-dollar industry has grown around the marketing of "pumping iron" to a public who feels morally compelled to exercise.

—*Kris R. Cohen*

See also: Fitness Marketing and Magazines; Men's Issues

For further reading:
Gaines, Charles, and George Butler. 1984. *Pumping Iron II: The Unprecedented Woman.* Hammond, IN: Horizon Publishing.

Smith, Edward W. L. 1989. *Not Just Pumping Iron: On the Psychology of Lifting Weights.* Springfield, IL: Charles C. Thomas.

R

RACIAL SUPERIORITY, MYTH OF

The myth of racial superiority is the enduring yet erroneous belief in the Western world that dark-skinned peoples have an innate physical advantage when it comes to athletics and that this advantage accounts for the statistical overrepresentation of people of African descent in the ranks of elite athletics. The continuing widespread prevalence of this notion has had several important and disturbing ramifications.

The concept or myth of racial superiority promotes the belief that there are biologically significant physical differences between the so-called races. As numerous scientists demonstrated over the course of the twentieth century, owing to the lack of physiological homogeneity within "racial groups," any theory based on the concept of biologically determined "races" must be viewed as suspect.

Furthermore, the emphasis on the "natural" superiority of black athletes over their white counterparts sustains and propagates the worst of the nineteenth-century racist stereotypes that were the product of the general acceptance of social Darwinism in the West. These stereotypes included the belief that the success of black athletes is the result of naturally endowed physical gifts, whereas, in contrast, the success of white athletes is attributed to either hard work and training or a purportedly superior intellect. One of the abiding effects of this belief is the preponderance of white athletes in "thinking positions," such as the quarterback in football and the catcher in baseball. It is likely that social factors and prejudices, rather than biological factors, account for the relative scarcity of black athletes in these positions.

Many scholars have argued that the myth of racial superiority in athletics contributes to the belief that all people of color are well suited for unskilled or menial tasks but are ill suited for endeavors that call for extended concentration and intellectual acumen. This persistent view tends to limit the range of opportunities open to all people of African descent, not only athletes, by focusing on black physicality at the expense of black intellectual capabilities.

The myth of black superiority was traditionally restricted to sports requiring speed and strength, such as boxing, basketball, football, and sprinting, as opposed to sports requiring stamina, such as marathon running, allegedly the biological strong suit of white athletes. However, the emergence of world-class distance runners from Africa, most notably from Ethiopia and Kenya, in the 1980s and 1990s made this position untenable.

The roots of this myth lie in the eighteenth and nineteenth centuries—first, in the institution of slavery, and second, in the "scientific racism" of the late nineteenth century. Despite the abolition of slavery in the British Empire in 1833 and in the United States thirty years later, many of the racist suppositions that supported the institution remained. These prejudices were bolstered by the emergence of social Darwinism, which posited that there existed a hierarchy of races, with fair-skinned Europeans on top and dark-skinned Africans at the bottom.

This self-serving ideology worked for the West as long as white imperial and industrial elites maintained political, cultural, and, by extension, athletic global superiority. However, when athletes of color gained prominence in the sport world, many white observers clung to the myth of racial superiority to explain away black sporting success without upsetting the generally inferior position of people of color in Western society, thereby, maintaining a status quo of inequality.

—*P. F. McDevitt*

See also: Discrimination, Racial, in Sport

For further reading:

Gems, Gerald R. 1998. "The Construction, Negotiation and Transformation of Racial Identity in American Football: A Study of Native and African Americans." *American Indian Culture and Research Journal* 22 (Spring): 131–133.

Harrison, L., C. K. Harrison, and L. N. Moore. 2002. "African American Racial Identity and Sport." *Sport, Education and Society* October 1, vol. 7: 121–134.

RADIO BROADCASTING

From the 1920s until the rise of network television in the 1950s, radio provided sport fans with immediate, firsthand accounts of major events and the exploits of sport heroes. Within months of the introduction of radio broadcasting in 1920, broadcasts of sporting events began to fill the air. KDKA in Pittsburgh, the nation's first commercial station, broadcast live accounts of boxing matches and baseball and football games in 1921. By the mid-1920s, virtually every major sport could be caught on radio, and networks of stations linked by telephone lines broadcast such important events as the World Series, the Rose Bowl game, and heavyweight championship boxing matches to listeners across the country.

Some sport promoters initially feared that radio broadcasts would convince fans to stay home rather than attend events, but by the mid-1930s, most professional and intercollegiate teams agreed that radio provided valuable publicity and actually increased fan interest and attendance. Radio also proved to be a source of revenue. In 1935, for example, radio networks paid $400,000 for broadcast rights to the World Series.

Radio played an important role in nationalizing sport in the 1920s and 1930s. Fans across the country could listen in on events and hear announcers such as Graham McNamee, Ted Husing, and Clem McCarthy describe the heroics of Babe Ruth, Jack Dempsey, and Joe Louis. Radio's mass audience declined as television became popular in the 1950s, but game broadcasts, sport scores, and sport interview and talk shows remain a staple of the medium and a source of publicity and revenue for sport organizations.

—*Tim Ashwell*

See also: Television, Impact on Sport

For further reading:

Bender, Gary, and Michael L. Johnson. 1994. *Call of the Game: What Really Goes On in the Broadcast Booth.* Chicago: Bonus Books.

Eisenstock, Alan. 2001. *Sports Talk: A Journey inside the World of Sports Talk Radio.* New York: Pocket Books.

Halberstam, David J. 1999. *Sports on New York Radio: A Play-by-Play History.* New York: McGraw-Hill.

RECRUITING VIOLATIONS, COLLEGE

The negative cultural impacts of college recruiting violations are numerous. One of the most significant impacts is the erosion of the integrity of college athletics, which has impacted the entire higher education system as well as professional athletics. Responding to recruiting violations by the University of Oregon football program, sports writer Alex Tam of the *Oregon Daily Emerald* speculates that because of the negativity surrounding college sports, many high school students are opting to skip college and enter the professional sports arena, even though they may not be physically or emotionally mature enough to compete at the professional level. Tam also believes this negative image dilutes the quality of both professional sports and college athletics (Tam 2004, 1).

The National College Athletic Association (NCAA) has established specific recruiting rules intended to eliminate any unfair advantages one educational institution may gain over another in the recruitment of student-athletes. These rules are intended for all persons associated with the educational institution, including coaches, staff, alumni, and booster organizations. The NCAA recruiting rules state that educational institutions and their representatives may not: offer any financial incentives to a prospective student-athlete (PSA) or any relatives or friends of the PSA; offer any reward without checking with a compliance officer; pay for or offer tickets to events; or invite a PSA to an alumni event (NCAA Compliance, 2004). Additionally, the NCAA has established rules regarding contact with or establishing relationships with the PSAs, their family, friends, or neighbors. Rules regarding transportation and lodging expenses are also very specific. In addition to providing recruiting rules for educational institutions, the NCAA also provides information to student-athletes regarding what is and what is not allowed during the recruiting process.

Despite these clearly defined NCAA rules regarding recruiting, violations continue to occur. On March 11, 2004, the House Energy and Commerce Subcommittee on Commerce, Trade, and Consumer Protection held a hearing on college recruiting practices for athletes. This subcommittee has a long history of oversight of the NCAA. The chairman of the subcommittee, Representative Clifford Stearns, pointed out that the commercial nature of college sports has eclipsed the educational mission. Sterns stated, "The most important point arising from this hearing is that university administrators must be held accountable for enforcing National College Athletic Association recruiting rules" (NCAA Recruiting 2004, 1). Stearns also stated that football coaches now earn millions of dollars in salaries per year. Coaches at public educational institutions are among the highest paid individuals working for state governments. In addition, the commercial pressures of college sports have universities jumping to different conferences looking for title games, seeking ever-larger financial payouts, and filing lawsuits over who gets the money, especially from the NCAA tournament and the bowl championship series.

The University of Colorado football program was recently involved in one of the most egregious and public recruiting scandals in recent times. Responding to allegations of misconduct by the football staff, Elizabeth Hoffman, president of the university, testified before the subcommittee regarding recruiting of football players. She stated that her institution believed in the most stringent policies regarding recruiting and outlined steps that would be taken by the University of Colorado to assure adherence to the recruiting rules.

David Berst, chairman of the NCAA Task Force on Recruiting, also testified before the house subcommittee. He told the subcommittee that the task force intended to propose changes that would allow prospective student-athletes to evaluate institutional environments on appropriate conduct and accountability. Representative Stearns encouraged the NCAA to "take strong steps and harsh penalties to curtail violations and abuse in the recruiting process" (NCAA Recruiting 2004, 2).

On May 19, 2004, the House Energy and Commerce Subcommittee on Commerce, Trade, and

Consumer Protection held a second hearing on college athletics and recruiting. Testifying before the subcommittee, C. Thomas McMillen, a former house member, professional basketball player, and member of the Knight Foundation Commission on Intercollegiate Athletics, stated, "It is kind of like the movie 'Groundhog Day'; you keep getting up every day and the same thing happens. That is basically the plight of intercollegiate athletics" (Gooden 2004, 1). Wally Renfro, senior advisor to the NCAA president also testified before the commission, addressing the treatment of prospective incoming athletes. According to Renfro, "The competition among institutions for highly skilled prospects has escalated. Expectations among prospects for transportation via private jet, five-star luxury suites, extravagant meals, and 'game-day' simulations that glorify feats of these athletes before they have ever enrolled or set foot on the field" (Gooden 2004, 2). Renfro said the NCAA recommended the practices be stopped and recruiting visits be returned to the purpose for which they were originally intended.

The commission found that thirty-one schools had been penalized for major recruiting violations since 2000. Subcommittee chair Stearns expressed his desire that universities take a preventative instead of reactionary approach to recruiting violations and that institutions move toward an academics first philosophy.

The 2004 Congressional hearings outlined some of the primary causes of NCAA recruiting violations by educational institutions and their representatives. The commercial nature of college athletics creates significant pressure to succeed and to obtain money as well as institutional prestige. Top prospective athletes expect extravagant treatment as part of the recruiting process.

Although recruiting infractions occur in every intercollegiate sport and at every collegiate level, the most serious and significant infractions tend to be in men's division 1-A football and basketball, where the most money is made and lost in college athletics. The college football Bowl Cham-

pionship Series and the college basketball NCAA Tournament offer the two most lucrative incentives to educational institutions' athletic programs. At stake are literally millions of dollars for an institution and its programs through advertising, television revenues, and booster donations.

In 2004 a random Internet search for "NCAA recruiting violations" yielded over 17,000 citations. One of the stories involved the firing of Ohio State University men's basketball coach, Jim O'Brien. According to school officials, O'Brien knowingly violated NCAA recruiting rules, including giving over $6,000 to players over a five-year period. Coach O'Brien's contract contained a clause that he could be fired for recruiting violations and his $850,000-a-year position terminated. Another example is the two-year probation of the University of Colorado football program. This case received widespread national media attention with allegations that sex was used as a recruiting tool for prospective football players. According to the NCAA Infractions Committee, "this was a serious case in which a football coaching staff, led by the former head football coach, in a calculated attempt to gain a recruiting advantage, pushed beyond the permissible bounds of legislation, resulting in a pattern of recruiting violations" (Renfro 2004, 1).

These incidents have had not only a negative impact on specific athletic programs but arguably on two of the premier public universities in the country. It is reasonable to assume that unless new strict rules, extensive oversight measures, and harsh penalties are enacted, recruiting violations will continue. The long-term impact college recruiting violations will have on college athletics remains open to debate.

—*Craig Riordan*

See also: Academic Skepticism of Sport; Academics and Sport; College Football

For further reading:
Gooden, Beverly T. 2004. "Stearns Conducts Hearing on College Recruiting Practices for Athletes."

http://gop.house.gov/item-news., March 11, 1–2. Accessed July 2004.

Mazzoni, Wayne. 1998. *The Athletic Recruiting and Scholarship Guide.* New York: Mazz Marketing, Inc.

"NCAA Compliance: Guidelines Boosters, Alumni and Friends Should Know. www. Javelinatheltics. com, 1-4. Retrieved July 2004.

"NCAA Recruiting Reforms Subject of Capitol Hill Hearing." 2004. *Scripps Howard Foundation Wire,* www.axcessnews.com/national, May 19, 1–2. Accessed July 2004.

Renfro, Wally. 2004. "Recruiting and Scholarship Limits Placed on University of Colorado Program; University Receives Two-Year Probation." www .ncaa.org/releases/infractions, 1–4. Accessed July 2004.

Tam, Alex.2004. "Clean-up College Recruiting." *Oregon Daily Emerald,* June 29, 1–2.

RELIGION AND SPORT

In U.S. history, the relationship between religion and sport has evolved from one of conflict, as sport was at first thought to be sinful, to one in which religion conscripted sport for evangelistic purposes, most recently, to one in which sport and religion converge, as sport has assumed a quasi-religious character in contemporary U.S. culture.

Conflict between Religion and Sport

Since the earliest days of Puritan settlement in New England, Americans have remarked on conflicts between sport and religion. On Christmas Day in 1621, Governor William Bradford of the Plymouth Colony reprimanded young boys and men whom he found "in ye streets at play openly; some pitching ye ball and some at stooleball, and such sport" (Morrison, 1952, 97). At that time, leisure was often considered an opportunity for the devil, and playing sports on Sundays or religious holidays, like Christmas, was regarded as particularly sinful.

Before 1850, most U.S. religious groups condemned some sports, such as horse racing, because of their association with gambling and others, such as football, prizefighting, cockfighting, and baseball, because of their basic brutality. Even recreational boating and fishing were thought to lead to vice, and the "sport pages" of newspapers were thought to generate unhealthy appetites for nonspiritual concerns. Toward the end of the nineteenth century, the popularity of baseball expanded throughout the country, and thousands of amateur teams and leagues were formed to accommodate the burgeoning interest. Yet, throughout the nineteenth century, Victorian Christians who believed that sport deflected attention away from possible service to God or the study of God's word often held sport and leisure in suspicion.

With the rise of baseball's popularity and the emergence of football in the United States, especially in Christian colleges, religious opposition to enthusiasm for sport and to professionalism in sport gradually decreased in intensity, except for the prohibition that remained against competition and recreation on the Sabbath. Some Christian institutions began to blend sport into religion in an effort to provide a strong, male-oriented paradigm for Christian faith. These foundations for a "Muscular Christianity" gained strength as two Springfield College graduates—Amos Alonzo Stagg and James Naismith—combined sport competition and Christian discipline. Stagg was the pioneer coach in collegiate football. Naismith invented basketball to provide missionaries with a game involving few players, minimal equipment, and simple rules, which were initially issued as Ten Commandments and one of which reflected the Victorian value that physical contact would constitute a foul.

Conscription of Sport by Religion

The twentieth century, however, witnessed significant changes in attitudes toward sport by religious groups, ranging from the sponsorship of sport teams by religiously affiliated colleges and the coordination of church leagues for basketball and softball to the acceptance of professional competition on Sundays and the validation—if not consecration—of sporting events with invocations. Less than a century following the ban against Sunday baseball, a more violent sport, football, whose professional games are usually played on Sunday, became so celebrated that its championship event even changed the name of the day on which it is played to "Super Sunday."

The process of acceptance and accommodation accelerated in the early decades of the twentieth century. Following World War I, church-sponsored sport leagues—especially for baseball, softball, and basketball—began to organize in order to capture the attention of the unchurched and to provide social outlets for men of faith. Especially among religiously sponsored colleges and universities, sport provided opportunities for engaging in fair competition, for developing discipline, and for providing a forum through which players might express their talents and their faith. On the eve of the Depression, Methodist leaders were advised to capture athletic opportunities for their summer youth programs. And in Paducah, Kentucky, a group of ministers formed a Preachers Bowling League.

> *The modern convergence of secularized sport and traditional religious devotion suggests that sport continues to fill a religious need for many of the players and fans who are devoted to the games.*

Not only, as in these examples, did religious groups incorporate sport into their purview, but religious rituals have also occasionally transformed sport fields and arenas from their competitive orientations to specifically sacramental and spiritual functions. The use of the baseball diamond as a wedding chapel provides one of the vivid scenes in the film *Bull Durham* (1988), as Jimmy marries Millie at the pitcher's mound. More significant, however, than the cinematic scene of a wedding at a ballpark is the convergence of prayer and sport facilities found in Baltimore, Maryland. During the late 1990s, at the new Oriole Park at Camden Yards, Orthodox Jew-ish fans gathered after the fifth inning of every home game—except the ones on Sabbaths—in a small, cluttered pantry near major league baseball's first kosher food stand. Often, thirty men, some wearing baseball caps over their yarmulkes, swayed back and forth and chanted prayers in Hebrew in the tiny room. The occasion was the afternoon Orthodox prayer time known as *mincha*. Although the men praying were avid Oriole fans, their ten-minute prayer session was only coincidentally at the ballpark and not particularly a petition for the Orioles. Yet the performance of such spiritual rituals in a ballpark resonates with W. P. Kinsella's assertion in *Shoeless Joe* (1982) that "a ballpark at night is more like a church than a church" (Kinsella 1982, 135).

Throughout the middle decades of the twentieth century, prayers were frequently offered as part of the pregame ceremonies for many sporting events, and they continued to provide a point of focus for contests hosted by religious institutions. Not only did ministers sanction sport contests with invocations, but the athletes themselves also often displayed a prayerful demeanor as they prepared to play or as they celebrated success. As an act of prayer, Roberto Clemente, Hall of Fame outfielder for the Pittsburgh Pirates, crossed himself before each plate appearance, and Evander Holyfield's entire staff bowed heads and held hands in a sign of unity as the champion boxer prepared for his final title defense against Mike Tyson. At century's end, public displays of thanksgiving were fairly common: Dallas Cowboys superstar Emmitt Smith knelt in the end zone following his touchdown scampers; several Green Bay Packers, led by All-Pro defensive end Reggie White, began their interviews after their 1997 Super Bowl victory by saying they wanted to "thank God first"; and the entire Chicago Bulls team, following a National Basketball Association (NBA) championship, retreated to the inner sanctum of the locker room, as Coach Phil Jackson put it, for a postchampionship-game recitation of the Lord's Prayer before they turned to the celebration of their NBA conquest with the ritual champagne baptism.

Convergence of Sport and Religion

Because of increasing confusion about the place of sport and religion in U.S. culture—about the kinds and degrees of allegiance directed to both—religious institutions face distinct challenges as they embrace sport as vehicles for outreach. Players also confront similar issues as they attribute their athletic prowess and success to God. One of the primary challenges is to maintain the playful and creative character of sport as the athletic activities provide opportunities for evangelism. For other players and fans, a contrasting challenge is the one posed by their devotion to a game or team. Sport can co-opt the allegiance usually elicited by a religious tradition and can become, in effect, a religion in its own right. *Sports Illustrated* journalist Frank Deford was among the first to identify the kind of religious power that sport exerts on many modern Americans. Adopting Karl Marx's concept, Deford suggested that for many Americans at the end of the twentieth century, sport is the opiate of the people, anesthetizing them to the struggles of the classes and focusing their hopes on events that provide fulfillment through vicarious participation and through an often-delayed form of gratification.

As an implicit form of faith, sport dramatizes the cultural creeds and codes of a community. In this regard, a historian of U.S. religion notes that both sport and religion utilize ritual to establish a sense of order by creating an "other world" characterized by its own boundaries and rules, by its own successes and vicissitudes. "By setting up boundaries and defining the space of the game," Catherine Albanese contends in *America: Religions and Religion* (1981) "sports have helped Americans fit a grid to their own experience in order to define it and give it structure" (322). In this way, sport has reinforced a code of conduct for daily life that suggests that life itself is a struggle between winning and losing forces, that winning depends on teamwork, and that loyalty to teammates and fair play in competition are virtues.

The fusion of sport and religion in the modern United States perhaps represents a restoration of metaphysical and mystical impulses that generated or characterized early forms of play. Activities now classified as sport often first claimed the attention and participation of humans to effect religious transitions or to express stories of spiritual significance. Originally, the activities fulfilled some sort of ritual function, whether pleasing the gods, as in the ancient Olympic Games in Athens; supplicating their intervention, as with the Oglala Sioux's rite of throwing the ball; or rehearsing their roles in creating and continuation of the world, as with the Mayan game of ball. Like the early integration of sport and religion, the modern convergence of secularized sport and traditional religious devotion suggests that sport continues to fill a religious need for many of the players and fans who are devoted to the games.

—*Joseph L. Price*

See also: Muscular Christianity; Mythology of Sport

For further reading:

Albanese, Catherine. 1981. *America: Religions and Religion.* Belmont, CA: Wadsworth.

Higgs, Robert J. 1995. *God in the Stadium: Sports and Religion in America.* Lexington: University Press of Kentucky.

Jackson, Phil, and Hugh Delehanty. 1995. *Sacred Hoops: Spiritual Lessons of a Hardwood Warrior.* New York: Hyperion Books.

Kinsella, W. P. 1982. *Shoeless Joe.* Boston: Houghton Mifflin.

Morrison, Samuel Eliot, ed. 1952. *William Bradford, Of Plimouth Plantation.* New York: Alfred A. Knopf.

Price, Joseph L. 1984. "The Super Bowl as a Religious Festival." *The Christian Century* 101, no. 6 (February 22): 190–191.

RICE, GRANTLAND (1880–1954)

Newspaperman Grantland Rice helped popularize sport as entertainment and sport figures as heroes in the early decades of the twentieth century. Known as the "Dean of Sportswriters," Rice worked for more than fifty years as a newspaper reporter. His syndicated *New York Herald Tribune* column, The Sportlight, appeared six days a week in more than one hundred newspapers, reaching ten million readers at the height of its popularity in the late 1920s.

Rice gained popularity among readers by writing in a florid, sentimental style that often described the events he witnessed with unfailingly upbeat assessments. He also delved beyond what happened on the field to provide readers with insight into the sport. In addition, Rice helped make heroes of Babe Ruth, Knute Rockne, Jack Dempsey, and Bobby Jones as well as the college football players he selected to be on his All-American team for *Collier's* magazine.

Glorifying the sport hero was part of Rice's style, best evidenced by his famous depiction of the 1924 Notre Dame football backfield: "Outlined against a blue-gray October sky, the Four Horsemen rode again. In dramatic lore they are known as Famine, Pestilence, Destruction and Death. These are only aliases. Their real names are Stuhldreher, Miller, Crowley and Layden" (*New York Herald Tribune*).

Verse distinguished Rice's work. His most famous rhyme became one of sport's most enduring clichés. In 1911, he wrote:

> *For when the one Great Scorer comes to write against your name*
> *He marks—not that you won or lost—but how you played the Game. (Fountain 1993, 93–96)*

Many have said the 1920s were called the golden age of sport in large part because Rice saw them as golden and conveyed this vision to millions of readers daily.

—*Charlie Bevis*

See also: Sport Journalism

For further reading:
Fountain, Charles. 1993. *Sportswriter: The Life and Times of Grantland Rice.* New York: Oxford University Press.

RIOTS

Excessive competition arouses violence, and sport tends to reflect the violence inherent in U.S. society. Riots and confrontations erupt during and after sporting events on a fairly regular basis—some between on-field competitors and some among displeased or overzealous fans. Even the language of sport reflects a tendency to violent action: competitors slash, bash, crash, stomp, demolish, or mutilate their opposition.

Some riots have received more attention than others, and a few have been associated with sports that one might not expect to have violent overtones. In 1963, at Roosevelt Raceway on Long Island, fans disagreed with a call made by the judges on a winning horse. Over twenty thousand spectators, caught in the frenzy of the moment, set fire to a sulky, demolished concession stands, destroyed track signs, and overturned cars in the parking lot. In 1974, in Cleveland, Ohio, disgruntled baseball fans bombarded the opposing team with firecrackers and beer cans.

Football and hockey are considered the most potentially violent of organized sport, and riots associated with them occur so frequently that they have become a matter of course and are not always documented. For whatever reason, football is susceptible to racially motivated postgame rioting, whereas hockey persists in inciting action during the game. During hockey games, fistfights between fans in the stands and shoving and punching among players on the ice are par for the course, and many athletes believe if the violence were abated that the fans would stop attending the games. After a Big Ten college football game between Minnesota and Ohio erupted in rioting, a governor in Ohio called the event a public mugging and gang warfare in an athletic arena. This kind of behavior has become so commonplace that in 2003, college officials, athletic directors, and the media convened under the auspices of the National Collegiate Athletic Association (NCAA) to discuss means of averting postgame violence on university campuses.

One of the worst instances of sport riots occurred in 1964 in Lima, Peru, when three hundred spectators were killed following a disputed call by the referee of a soccer match. Even typically passive sports, like golf, can engender disputes that can end with attacks by golf club–wielding opponents and with antagonists being run down by golf carts. During riots, it is often the peacekeepers, those who intercede to restore order, who inadvertently escalate the melee.

—*Joyce Duncan*

See also: Football; Hockey

For further reading:
Russell, Gordon. 1998. "Anatomy of a Riot." *Psychology Today,* November-December, 18.
"Students Suspended for Role in Riot." 1999. *New York Times,* March 31.
Suggs, Welch. 2003. "College Officials Discuss How to Stop Mayhem after Big Games." *Chronicle of Higher Education,* March 7, A43.
Tyson, Ann Scott. 1996. "Urban Lessons on Violence-Free Victories." *Christian Science Monitor,* June 18, 4.

ROBINSON, JACK ROOSEVELT "JACKIE" (1919–1972)

In 1947, Jackie Robinson broke the color barrier in U.S. baseball, becoming the first African American to play in the previously all-white major leagues. Robinson participated in sport in both high school and college and in the Negro Leagues before he joined the Montreal Royals in 1946 at the request of Branch Rickey, the owner of the Brooklyn Dodgers. In fact, it was Robinson's past that prompted Rickey's interest. Rickey was searching for just the right player to break the color line in major league baseball, and Robinson was his choice.

Rickey knew that Robinson, playing alongside white teammates, had been a standout player at UCLA. In addition, Robinson had served in the army and played shortstop for the Kansas City Monarchs in 1945, hitting .387 in forty-seven games and playing in the All-Star game. Although many in the Negro Leagues agreed that Robinson was not their best player and although Robinson admitted that baseball was not even his best sport, Rickey thought Robinson had other attributes, such as character and self-control, that would help him desegregate the majors. Rickey knew what was in store for Robinson, admonishing him to turn the other cheek and suffer the inevitable animosity and abuse in order to validate his claim to equality and recognition.

Robinson's first season with the Dodgers was spent with their Triple-A minor league farm club, the Montreal Royals. Rickey thought Robinson would have an easier time in Canada than in the United States, facing less outright discrimination. After a successful season in Montreal, Robinson joined the Brooklyn club in 1947 and experienced trouble from the beginning. Problems ranged from strike threats by other players to hate letters and death threats from fans to constant badgering and insults on the field. Through it all, Robinson remained calm and kept his attention on the game.

Eventually, Robinson proved Rickey right, capturing Rookie of the Year honors in 1947. He followed that with the Most Valuable Player Award in 1949 and six straight All-Star appearances (1949–1954). The honors continued to accrue as Robinson won the National League batting title and led the league in stolen bases in 1949 as well as participating in six National League pennants and one World Series. In 1962, he received the ultimate honor when he was elected to the National Baseball Hall of Fame.

The esteem fans had for Robinson was shown in a number of ways. A 1947 national poll selected Robinson as the second-most-popular American, behind Bing Crosby. He later became the first baseball player to appear on a U.S. postage stamp. In 1981, writer Maury Allen listed Robinson as the eleventh-best player of all time in *Baseball's 100*, and baseball researcher Bill James ranked him as the eighth-best second baseman ever to play the game.

Once the experiment was labeled a success and other black players began to trickle onto the major league diamonds, Robinson spoke out on issues of race, campaigning in his later years for hiring African American third basemen and managers. But playing and activist honors aside, it was Robinson's courage to be the first African American to walk onto a major league field that secured his place in U.S. cultural history.

—*Leslie Heaphy*

See also: Baseball; Discrimination, Racial, in Sport; Negro Baseball Leagues

For further reading:

Allen, Maury. 1981. *Baseball's 100 : A Personal Ranking of the Best Players in Baseball History.* New York: A&W Visual Library.

Robinson, Sharon. 2002. *Jackie's Nine: Jackie Robinson's Values to Live By: Courage, Determination, Teamwork, Persistence, Integrity, Citizenship, Justice, Commitment, Excellence.* New York: Scholastic Books.

Simon, Scott. 2002. *Jackie Robinson and the Integration of Baseball.* New York: John Wiley and Sons.

Tygiel, Jules. 1988. *Baseball's Great Experiment: Jackie Robinson and His Legacy.* New York: Oxford University Press.

ROBINSON, SUGAR RAY
(1920–1989)

Boxer Sugar Ray Robinson, who held the welterweight championship of the world from 1946 to 1951 and the middleweight championship five times between 1951 and 1958, personified a version of African American masculinity that signified pride, self-worth, and strength. Robinson embodied racial empowerment without representing a serious threat to the social order.

Sugar Ray Robinson was born Walker Smith, Jr. in Detroit, Michigan. Like the majority of prizefighters of the era, he was born into an impoverished family and community. In 1936, he borrowed the amateur fight card of a boxer named Ray Robinson for his first official bout, and he kept the name. Soon after, a sportswriter told Robinson's manager George Gainford that he had a sweet fighter, to which Gainford replied, "Sweet as sugar." The description stuck and became a permanent prefix to his assumed name. After a remarkable amateur career of 85 wins and no losses and after winning the New York City Golden Gloves title as a featherweight in 1939 and as a lightweight in 1940, Robinson turned professional in 1940.

In his twenty-five-year professional career, Robinson fought 201 times, won 174 bouts with 109 by knockout, and was a world champion six times. He lost only nineteen decisions, five of them in 1965, when he was forty-four years old. Conventional wisdom holds that Robinson was the greatest combination of brains, brawn, and boxing skill in the twentieth century. But the man was more than the sum of his boxing accomplishments. According to Richard Lacayo, Robinson "was a hero to a generation of young black men, who adopted his pomaded hairstyle and admired his trademark pink Cadillac. Muhammad Ali called him 'my idol' and borrowed his dancing style. Sugar Ray Leonard borrowed his name" (1989, 89). In an era when African Americans were supposed to be humble, docile, and restrained, Robinson embodied black pride and power.

—*Daniel Nathan*

See also: Ali, Muhammad; Boxing

For further reading:

Lacayo, Richard. 1989. "Pound for Pound, the Best Ever." *Time*, April 24, 89.

Robinson, Sugar Ray, and Dave Anderson. 1994. *Sugar*

Striking with the fury of a tiger and the cunning of a fox, Sugar Ray Robinson presses his attack to the head of Jake LaMotta in the last round of their battle for the middleweight championship (Chicago, Illinois; February 15, 1951). (BETTMANN/CORBIS)

Ray. New York: Da Capo Press.

Silverman, Jeff. 2002. *The Greatest Boxing Stories Ever Told: Thirty-Six Incredible Tales from the Ring.* Guilford, CT: Lyons Press.

ROCK CLIMBING

A predecessor of the extreme sports, which would dominate the last decade, a late-developing offshoot of mountaineering, rock climbing moved from obscurity to popularity in the twentieth century, following a developmental pattern similar to that of other mainstream sports. Formerly justified as preparation for the challenges encountered during mountain ascents, rock climbing became a specialty sport in its own right in the 1930s. Europeans first developed the equipment and techniques that allowed climbers to suffer only minimal consequences from falls and other mistakes. Harvard professor Robert Underhill brought these innovations back from trips abroad, and northeastern outing clubs began climbing local crags. In 1931, Underhill visited California and taught safety techniques to Sierra Club members, who developed them to enable ascents of the walls in Yosemite Valley, the best-known rock crucible in the United States.

A rock climber reaches for footing. A late-developing offshoot of mountaineering, rock climbing moved from obscurity to popularity in the twentieth century.
(ANNE-MARIE WEBER/CORBIS)

Nonparticipants failed to understand rock climbing and viewed it as little more than a daredevil activity, but climbers reveled in the athleticism and mental strength required by the challenges of climbing sheer rock. As an extra incentive, numerous climbable crags existed across the United States, offering accessible and reasonably inexpensive recreation. After World War II, there appeared groups of "climbing bums." Disdainful of social mores and dedicated to their activity, the groups produced countercultural resonance throughout the 1960s and 1970s.

Eventually, climbing evolved to resemble more-conventional sport. Competitiveness had always been present, but when standardized climbing competitions on artificial walls migrated from Europe, the activity led to scheduled events, rankings, and rewards, with outstanding climbers turning professional. Indoor climbing gyms proliferated, allowing the year-round training necessary for top performances and risk-free venues for newcomers. In addition, women climbers became commonplace and accepted, and they demonstrated achievement at the highest levels.

Whether engaged in gymnastics on constructed "sport" climbs or in the field, solving the problems of "traditional" climbing, participants shared the pleasures of individual expression in the vertical realm.

—*Timothy M. Rawson*

See also: Mountaineering; Outdoor Clubs

For further reading:

Creasey, Malcolm, Nick Banks, and Ray Wood. 2001. *Complete Guide to Rock Climbing*. London: Lorenz Books.

Graydon, Don, ed. 1992. *Mountaineering: The Freedom of the Hills*. Seattle, WA: Mountaineers Books.

ROCKNE, KNUTE (1888–1931)

The architect of the Notre Dame football legend, Knute Rockne coached the Fighting Irish during the 1920s, becoming a key figure in the rise of big-time college football and providing Catholics with a source of pride in a decade of strong anti-Catholicism. Born in Norway, Knute Rockne arrived in the United States as a young boy and came to represent the ideal immigrant. He retained little of his native culture, instead embracing U.S. values, as he rose to the top of his profession. At Notre Dame, he compiled a record of 105 wins, 12 losses, and 5 ties as coach from 1918 to 1930 and had five undefeated seasons.

Rockne was an innovator, both on and off the field. He is credited with expanding the use of the forward pass, and his open offensive style was designed, in part, to allow spectators to follow the action more easily. He played a crucial role in converting college football into a mass-consumption spectacle by developing intersectional rivalries and varied uniform colors and by coaching such athletes as the famed "Four Horsemen" backfield.

In addition, it was Rockne who contributed the phrase "Win one for the Gipper!" to the U.S. lexicon. George Gipp, Rockne's greatest player, died of pneumonia at the end of the 1920 season. In 1928, Rockne, known for his inspirational halftime pep talks, cited the phrase as a deathbed request, possibly apocryphal, from Gipp as motivation for the team against the Army charge, a game the Irish came back to win.

Rockne died in 1931 at the peak of his popularity, one of the first notable Americans to be killed in an airplane crash.

—*Richard D. Loosbrock*

See also: Football

For further reading:

Heisler, John. 2001. *Quotable Rockne: Words of Wit, Wisdom and Motivation by and about Knute Rockne, Legendary Notre Dame Football Coach.* Nashville, TN: TowleHouse Publishers.

Robinson, Ray. 1999. *Rockne of Notre Dame: The Making of a Football Legend.* New York: Oxford University Press.

ROCKWELL, NORMAN (1894–1978)

U.S. painter and illustrator Norman Rockwell is best known for his realistic paintings of life in small towns, of humorous images, of memorable moments from childhood to old age, and of athletes in baseball, football, basketball, and horse racing. Many of his images graced the covers of the *Saturday Evening Post, Look,* and *Ladies Home Journal*. Rockwell grew up in New York and began illustrating for *Boys Life* at the age of eighteen. In addition, his illustrations appeared early on in magazines such as *Country Gentleman* and *Literary Digest.* His first cover for the *Saturday Evening Post* appeared on May 20, 1916. During a forty-seven-year period, he created over three hundred covers for the *Post,* the most popular magazine of its day.

Rockwell's popularity can be attributed to his subject matter. He painted America and Americans with themes rooted in American values and pride in those values. He portrayed a remarkable history of everyday life and ordinary people. His illustrations told stories about life as he dreamed it could be.

Rockwell created his covers in a narrative form; each image was complete, self-contained, and self-explanatory, not having to rely on text to describe the main idea, characters, or setting. For example, the April 23, 1949, *Saturday Evening Post* cover, titled "Game Called Because of Rain," reveals an incredible amount of detail along with hints of Rockwell's humor. The painting has three umpires deciding whether to stop a baseball game because of approaching rain. The background has the old Ebbets Field scoreboard displaying the facts of the game and members of both teams, each side hoping the impending decision goes their way. The outcome is left for viewers to interpret, depending on their preference in the winning of the game.

As a boy, Rockwell was clumsy, skinny, pigeon-toed, and not at all athletic, but he always appreciated sport and athleticism. He painted many sport scenes with such incredible detail and realism that they often looked like photographs. The models who posed for Rockwell were usually people in his community, and they helped him achieve the realism that was his trademark. He sometimes included well-known people in his work, such as Ted Williams of the Boston Red Sox in "The Locker Room" (*Saturday Evening Post,* March 2, 1957) and jockey Eddie Arcaro as the model in "Jockey Weighing In" (*Saturday Evening Post,* June 28, 1958).

Rockwell's autobiography, *My Adventures as an Illustrator,* published in 1959, provided wonderful insight into the artist's makeup. He continued to paint through the 1970s and was honored during the U.S. Bicentennial in 1976 with the Presidential Medal of Freedom. He died the next year on November 8, 1978, at the age of eighty-four.

During the early twentieth century, illustrations played a major role in both shaping and portraying America's self-image. As the premier illustrator of the twentieth century, Norman Rockwell brought art into every U.S. home.

—*Marc L. Seror*

See also: Artists of Sport

For further reading:

Finch, Charles S., and Christopher Robin Finch. 1995. *Norman Rockwell: 332 Magazine Covers.* New York: Artabras Publishing.

Finch, Christopher Robin. 1975. *Norman Rockwell's America.* New York: Harry Abrams Publishing.

RODEO

Originally an informal pastime in which working cowboys tested their courage and skill, rodeo has become a multimillion-dollar professional sport and a celebration of the myth of the masculine American frontier, even as it remains an important element of rural and ethnic culture for a surprising variety of people. Modern rodeo emerged around the turn of the twentieth century from two nineteenth-century roots. One was the informal contests staged by working cowboys at their semiannual roundups; the first such "cowboy tournament" on record occurred near Deer Trail, Colorado, in 1869. The other was the famous "Wild West" exhibitions that were popular during the 1870s and 1880s. Cheyenne, Wyoming, newspaperman Colonel E. A. Slack brought the two traditions together in 1897 via his highly successful Frontier Days celebration and rodeo. A number of other towns in the West staged imitations of Cheyenne's Frontier Days—for example, the

Pendleton, Oregon, Round-Up and the Calgary, Alberta, Stampede—and the modern sport of rodeo was born.

As the events grew in number, promoters organized the Rodeo Association of America in 1929 to coordinate schedules, standardize rules, and create an annual point system to determine world champions in the various events. In 1936, to promote their own interests, including standards for judging, rodeo cowboys formed the Cowboys' Turtle Association. The origin of the name is a mystery, but it was probably a response to criticism that the cowboys had been slow to organize. By 1947, the Turtles had become the Rodeo Cowboys Association and served as the sport's official governing body, a role it continued as the Professional Rodeo Cowboys Association (PRCA).

After World War II, the sport expanded rapidly, and by the 1990s, over five thousand PRCA-member cowboys entered sanctioned events each year. Only about one-third of those cowboys, however, could be described as full-time professional athletes. Although an elite few made a highly lucrative career out of rodeo through their prize money and endorsement income, fewer than five hundred PRCA cowboys grossed more than $10,000 in arena winnings in any given year.

Rodeo derives much of its appeal from its celebration of historic, rural, western America—a celebration laden with the mythology of the frontier and the rugged cowboys who tamed it. Closer inspection, however, reveals that a surprising variety of groups foster their own sense of identity through rodeo. For example, not only do women compete in the sport's second-most popular event, barrel racing, at PRCA-sanctioned rodeos, but a number of women also compete in traditionally male roughstock events—bull riding and bronco riding among them—at all-women rodeos sanctioned by the Professional Women's Rodeo Association. Other examples, whose wide range demonstrate the cultural flexibility of the sport, include the popular Mexican American

charreadas in southern California; the All-Indian Rodeo Cowboys Association, which sponsors Indian rodeos throughout the western United States and Canada; and the International Gay Rodeo Association, founded in Reno, Nevada, in 1975, and boasting more than 750 gay and lesbian contestants each year. For all of these groups, rodeo provides a way to recognize and celebrate their rural, western heritage—living proof that the mythical cowboy frontier actually was populated by a diverse mixture of peoples.

—*Peter S. Morris*

See also: Bullfighting; Latino Sport

For further reading:

Campion, Lynn. 2002. *Rodeo: Behind the Scenes at America's Most Exciting Sport.* Guilford, CT: Lyons Press.

Murray, Ty, and Kendra Santos. 2001. *Roughstock: The Mud, the Blood and the Beer.* Austin, TX: Equimedia Publishing.

Wooden, Wayne S., and Gavin Ehringer. 1996. *Rodeo in America: Wranglers, Roughstock and Paydirt.* Lawrence: University Press of Kansas.

RODEO CLOWNS

Although not traditionally considered a sport, the antics of rodeo clowns incorporate as much athleticism as does gymnastics. In addition, they serve the function of comic relief in a sport that can often be bloody and bruising. Rodeo clowns, frequently former rodeo contestants who are no longer able to ride professionally due to injury, perform an important social function, serving as intermediaries between the audience, the animals, and the contestants and melding all three into the single body of rodeo. Clowns have a long history in public entertainment, dating to early Greece, where their comic performance allowed uncomfortable subjects to be displayed and addressed in public. Likewise, in rodeo, the clowns' grease-painted faces and sartorial caricature of the Professional Rodeo Cowboy Association's prescribed

A rodeo clown performs in the ring. The clowns protect the bull rider, diverting the bull's attention from a fallen contestant with their antic movements and often putting themselves between a bull and a downed rider to save the rodeo contestant from injury or death.
(DOUGLAS KENT HALL/ZUMA/CORBIS)

cowboy costume provide a sense of the ironic during the most dangerous of rodeo's events, bull riding, and divert the audience's attention from the very real life-threatening aspect of the event. Rodeo clowns work primarily in one of three jobs: as novelty entertainment acts, as barrellmen, or as bullfighters.

Beginning as comic relief in Wild West shows, clowns made their way into the rodeo, where they helped haze the bull to make it buck in order to increase a contestant's score. At the end of the ride, the clowns protect the bull rider, diverting the bull's attention from a fallen contestant with their antic movements and often putting themselves between a bull and a downed rider to save the rodeo contestant from injury or death. Clowns also come to the aid of bull riders who find themselves entangled in their ropes and help free the contestants from belligerent, bucking animals.

Some of the legendary rodeo clowns who have made it to the National Finals Rodeo competition include barrellman Jimmy Schumacher in the 1960s, Frank Rhoades in the 1970s, Quail Dobbs from the 1970s and 1980s, and Leon Coffee in the 1980s and 1990s.

—*J. C. Mutchler*

See also: Rodeo; Rodeo versus Animal Rights Activists

For further reading:
Hartnagle-Taylor, Jeanne Joy. 1992. *Greasepaint Matadors: The Unsung Heroes of Rodeo.* Loveland, CO: Alpine Publishers.

Woerner, Gail Hughbanks, and Gail Gandolfi. 1993. *Fearless Funnymen: The History of the Rodeo Clown.* Austin, TX: Eakin Press.

RODEO VERSUS ANIMAL RIGHTS ACTIVISTS

Animal rights activists' protests against cruelty to animals during rodeo events has caused rodeo to examine more closely the care and treatment of the animal contestants within the sport. Animal rights activists, especially from the Humane Society of the United States (HSUS) and the American Society for the Prevention of Cruelty to Animals (ASPCA), have been active since the 1970s in protesting the treatment of animals in the sport of rodeo, asserting that rodeo animals are the victims of cruel and inhumane treatment in virtually every aspect of rodeo performance. Both groups claim that horses and bulls only buck in order to escape the pain of a "flank strap," a belt that is tightened around the animal's groin area, which they also assert rubs open wounds. Both the HSUS and the ASPCA avow that calf roping, in which a running calf is roped from horseback, thrown to the ground, and hog-tied by three of its legs by a dismounted cowboy, causes permanent damage to the necks and throats of young animals. In addition, the activists protest steer roping, in which a running steer is roped around the neck or horns and tripped onto its back to be tied. They also claim that the spurring of animals in bareback riding, saddle bronc riding, and bull riding is injurious to the animals. Furthermore, the HSUS and ASPCA contend that the transportation of rodeo animals in stock trailers from event to event is cruel.

Largely as a result of these complaints, the Professional Rodeo Cowboys Association (PRCA) has established more than sixty rules, covering virtually every aspect of rodeo animals' care, treatment, travel conditions, and use during competition, which they affirm protects the animals from harm. The PRCA has also started an active countercampaign to educate the public about rodeo and to publicize what they claim is the humane treatment of animals.

The PRCA makes counterclaims for each and every one of the charges leveled by the HSUS and the ASPCA. They avow that the flank strap does nothing to harm horses or bulls and that the animals are selectively bred to buck. They assert further that the blunt rowels of rodeo competition spurs do little or no harm to rodeo animals. In response to the activist attacks on calf roping, the PRCA has established new rules that authorize a rodeo judge to fine or disqualify any cowboy who treats calves too roughly.

The HSUS and the ASPCA point out that the treatment of rodeo animals at PRCA-sanctioned events is better than the treatment at approximately 70 percent of rodeos not sanctioned by that group's governing body. A 1993–1994 survey of nearly thirty PRCA-sanctioned rodeos found the injury rate for the almost forty thousand animals inspected to be less than 0.05 percent. In addition, the PRCA's rules for the treatment of rodeo animals have been cited by the American Veterinary Medical Association as a model for the treatment of all animals at spectator events.

Although the attempts of the HSUS and ASPCA to shut down rodeos across the country have had little effect, they have raised several larger social questions for discussion, including the domination of animals by humans and the more general alienation of all humans from the natural and animal worlds.

—*J. C. Mutchler*

See also: Blood Sport; Rodeo; Rodeo Clowns

For further reading:
Campion, Lynn. 2002. *Rodeo: Behind the Scenes at America's Most Exciting Sport.* Guilford, CT: Lyons Press.
Fox, Michael W. 1991. *Animals Have Rights, Too.* New York: Continuum.

Because of his tattoos, body piercings, dressing in women's clothing, and dyeing his hair in extraordinary colors, basketball player Dennis Rodman has become a national icon for the "bad boys" of sport, as well as a popular culture phenomenon.

(GREGORY PACE/CORBIS SYGMA)

RODMAN, DENNIS (1962–)

Because of his outrageous commentary and reactionary behavior, his tattoos and body piercing, and his dressing in women's clothing and dyeing his hair in extraordinary colors, basketball player Dennis Rodman, a forward for the Chicago Bulls, has become a national icon for the "bad boys" of sport, as well as a popular culture phenomenon. Raised in a Dallas ghetto, Rodman's first occupation was as a custodian. Eventually, he was signed by the San Antonio Spurs, and he spent several seasons as a nonstellar performer, while accumulating over $1 million in debts.

In 1993, Rodman met rare-coin expert Dwight Manley in a Las Vegas casino. Shortly after, Manley became Rodman's agent, and the two formed the Rodman Group to manage the player's off-court endeavors. In October 1995, Rodman was traded to the Chicago Bulls, and that move, coupled with Manley's entrepreneurial skills, made the once insolvent basketball player a multimillionaire.

The media loved to condemn Rodman's perennial disregard for the rules. He was fined $5,000 for fighting with Alonzo Mourning, received an eleven-game suspension and a $25,000 fine for kicking a courtside camera man, and was penalized for making disparaging remarks about the Mormon community in Utah.

Although constantly in trouble with the National Basketball Association and blasted by the media, Rodman garnered a fortune in prod-

uct endorsements, including acting as the spokesperson for Kodak. He performed on MTV, was featured as a guest on a variety of television situation comedies, and costarred with Jean-Claude Van Damme in the action feature *Double Team.* He authored two books, *Bad as I Wanna Be* (1996), an autobiography that sold more than 800,000 copies, and *Walk on the Wild Side* (1997).
—*Joyce Duncan*

See also: Athletes, above the Law; Basketball; Television, Impact on Sport

For further reading:
Bickley, Dan. 1997. *No Bull: The Unauthorized Biography of Dennis Rodman.* New York: St. Martin's Press.
Feinberg, Leslie. 1997. *Transgender Warriors: Making History from Joan of Arc to Dennis Rodman.* Boston: Beacon Press.

ROOSEVELT, THEODORE "TEDDY"
(1858–1919)

The twenty-sixth president of the United States, Theodore "Teddy" Roosevelt, was a leading advocate of outdoor activities, and his involvement in college football led to the creation of the National Collegiate Athletic Association (NCAA). As a young man growing up in New York, Roosevelt suffered from asthma and poor eyesight. He overcame these ailments as he consciously and vigorously participated in an active lifestyle, which included boxing at Harvard and leading cattle drives in the Dakota Territory. As he worked his way up the political ladder, Roosevelt became known as a promoter of physical fitness. In his famous "Strenuous Life" speech of 1899, Roosevelt expressed his disdain for the "over civilized" urban lifestyle he saw and preached that the only way to defend the United States and her ideals was through "hard and dangerous endeavor." He would continue to represent these ideals throughout his life, participating in numerous physical activities. Roosevelt was also a prolific author on the subject, writing many books on hunting, fishing, and other outdoor activities.

Perhaps Roosevelt's most direct involvement in organized sport came during the 1905 football season. After a series of reports on the injuries and deaths caused by college football, most notably by *McClure's* magazine, Roosevelt invited a number of faculty members, coaches, and alumni to the White House for a conference on football brutality. Although the meeting had little immediate impact, Roosevelt continued to be involved in cleaning up college football. Under his urging, in 1905 the Intercollegiate Athletic Association (IAA) was created, which in 1910 became the NCAA.
—*Robert S. Brown*

See also: Patriotism and Sport

For further reading:
Fritz, Jean, and Mike Wimmer. 1991. *Bully for You, Teddy Roosevelt!* New York: Putnam.
Morris, Edmund. 2002. *Theodore Rex.* New York: Random House.

ROSE, PETE (1941–)

Pete Rose's banishment from baseball in 1989 generated national controversy over whether a player's induction into the National Baseball Hall of Fame should be based only on his performance on the field or also on events from his personal life. Born in 1941, Peter Edward Rose became a star player for his hometown Cincinnati Reds, setting numerous records, including for most career hits and most games played. Rose was nicknamed "Charlie Hustle" for his aggressive playing style, headfirst slides, and intensity on the field.

Off the baseball field, Rose, long a compulsive gambler, had been attracted to dog and horse racing for much of his life. So pervasive was his gambling habit that, to cover bets and losses, he sold some of his cherished baseball memorabilia, such as the bat he used when he broke Ty Cobb's record. In early 1989, major league baseball began

Reds manager Pete Rose has some uncomplimentary words for a group of photographers prior to a Reds game against the Pirates. Rose, under investigation by the commissioner's office for gambling, attracted a large press corps to the Reds' facility. Plant City, Florida (March 25, 1989).
(BETTMANN/CORBIS)

investigating Rose's gambling activities. Commissioner Peter Ueberroth named special investigator John Dowd to look into the specific possibility that Rose bet on baseball games, possibly even against his own team. Both actions were strictly forbidden by the major leagues and called for severe punishment, including permanent dismissal for betting against one's own team.

After several months of intense press coverage and legal maneuvering, the baseball commissioner, A. Bartlett Giamatti, announced on August 23, 1989, that Pete Rose was permanently banished from baseball. Seven days after the historic announcement, Giamatti died of a heart attack.

Despite his outstanding career, Rose was denied acceptance in the National Baseball Hall of Fame in Cooperstown, New York, because of his lifetime banishment from the game. Not since the dark days of the so-called Black Sox scandal of the 1919 World Series was baseball so shaken by the actions of one of its heroes and premier players, nor was the national opinion so divided.

In a final effort to be inducted into the Hall of Fame and hoping admission would lead to forgiveness, Rose acknowledged his gambling in his autobiography, *My Prison Without Bars* (2004), written with Rick Hill. For the first time publicly, Rose stated that he placed bets with bookies on Cincinnati Reds games as often as five times a week while managing the team in 1987 but denied that he ever bet against his team.

—*Peter Sisario*

See also: Baseball; Gambling

For further reading:

Ginsburg, Daniel E. 1995. *The Fix Is In: A History of Baseball Gambling and Game Fixing Scandals.* Jefferson, NC: McFarland.

Gutman, Dan. 1992. *Baseball Babylon: From the Black Sox to Pete Rose; The Real Stories behind the Scandals That Rocked the Game.* New York: Penguin Books.

Rose, Pete with Rick Hill. 2004. *My Prison Without Bars.* Emmaus, PA: Rodale Books.

Towle, Mike. 2003. *Pete Rose: Baseball's Charlie Hustle.* Nashville, TN: Cumberland House Publishing.

ROTH, PHILIP (1933–)

With the publication of *The Great American Novel* (1973), a zany comic novel that creatively uses baseball as a metaphor for the mythologizing and demythologizing of the United States, Jewish American fiction writer Philip Roth inaugurated a proliferation of serious literature centered on the national pastime.

"Call me Smitty," begins narrator and ex–newspaper writer Word Smith in a novel that parodies the lore, characters, and history of baseball as well as the McCarthy hearings, cold war paranoia, and even the pretensions and conventions of the literary canon. In a prologue reminiscent of Nathaniel Hawthorne's *Scarlet Letter*—with reference to many great authors and novels—Smith explains the occasion of his attempt to write the great American novel: the deletion from the historical record of the Patriot League, a major league that flourished from 1880 to 1946. Smith, meaning to set history straight, reveals a Communist conspiracy devised to destroy the United States and the free-enterprise system by infiltrating and making a mockery of the national game. Communists in the War Department allegedly ousted the league's Port Ruppert Mundys from their home ballpark in order to camp Europe-bound U.S. soldiers there. The consequences for the colorful and grotesque Rupperts are homelessness and suffering, and they are so inept that they lose 120 games during the 1943 season, becoming the laughing-stock of baseball. Ex–Patriot Leaguer Gil Gamesh—expelled from the league for trying to kill the umpire in 1933 and since at the Russian school for Subversion, Hatred, Infiltration, and Terror—convinces league president General Oakhart that he is a double agent and should manage the Rupperts to expose the team's Russian spies and Communist Party members. The league's demise, the conspiracy of silence, and the hilarious culmination of the novel follow, yet whether the league's destruction is due to a Communist plot or nationalistic paranoia is debatable.

—*Timothy C. Lord*

See also: Literature, Sport in; Metaphor, Sport as, for Life; Patriotism and Sport; Sport Literature as Discipline

For further reading:

Bloom, Harold, ed. 1986. *Philip Roth.* New York: Chelsea House.

Pughe, Thomas. 1994. *Comic Sense: Reading Robert Coover, Stanley Elkin, Philip Roth.* Basel, Switzerland, and Boston: Birkhäuser Verlag.

ROWING

Rowing is an amateur water sport associated with an elite upper-class tradition. Whether pursued singly in sculls or in two-, four-, or eight-person boats, competitive rowing is the domain of a limited number of colleges and universities, a small number of secondary schools, and a select group of independent athletes of whom Olympians figure most prominently. Regattas in Boston and Philadelphia and long-standing competitions, such as the Yale-Harvard boat race patterned after the race between Oxford and Cambridge, perpetuate the sport's Anglo-American identity.

A poor spectator sport without commercial appeal, rowing has embraced its very lack of pop-

Two women's eight-person crews compete in the annual Head of the Charles Regatta in Cambridge, Massachusetts (October 24, 1993).
(JOSEPH SOHM/CHROMOSOHM INC./CORBIS)

ularity. Within rowing circles, idealized amateur values are highly prized, and an ethos of hard work and sacrifice is celebrated. The primary organizational body for the sport is the U.S. Rowing Association.

Rowing's origins stem from informal races between working watermen, and its leisure potential was first recognized during the early eighteenth century. Following the development of collegiate rowing teams in British universities, collegiate rowing began in the 1850s. Enthusiasm for rowing, as both a professional and an amateur sport, increased dramatically after the Civil War. Match races were major events, and it was considered a healthful and appropriate activity for young men and women. Limiting the appeal, though, were the sport's inherent costs and logis-

tical barriers. By the early 1900s, rowing was relegated to Anglophile schools and clubs located mostly in the Northeast and the Pacific Northwest.

Due to the implementation of Title IX, the numbers of collegiate women rowers swelled. An ancillary aspect of year-round training, ergometers or rowing machines have proven popular for a wide range of athletes. Indoor ergo competitions attract hundreds of participants. Rowing's visibility has also benefited from environmental concerns. When public protest arose over newer water vehicles, faster speed boats, and ear-splitting jet skis, rowing reflected the quiet solitude of days gone by.

—*David Potash*

See also: Olympic Games; Outdoor Clubs

For further reading:

Boyne, Daniel J. 2000. *The Red Rose Crew: A True Story of Women, Winning and the Water*. New York: Hyperion Books.

Churbuck, David. 1988. *The Book of Rowing*. Woodstock, NY: Overlook Press.

Lambert, Craig. 1998. *Mind over Water: Lessons on Life from the Art of Rowing*. Boston: Houghton Mifflin.

RUDOLPH, WILMA (1940–1994)

A reflection of and a spokesperson for the Olympic ideal, Wilma Rudolph overcame racial, social, physical, and economic barriers to achieve greatness. In 1960, an international television audience watched as twenty-year-old Wilma Rudolph became the first woman to win three Olympic gold medals in track and field in one Olympic competition, an achievement that forever cast this quiet, unassuming Tennessean as an inspirational Olympian role model for women athletes.

Rudolph, the twentieth of twenty-two children, knew hard times growing up in Clarksville, Tennessee. At four, she was stricken with scarlet fever and double pneumonia, the combination of which caused paralysis in her left leg. Consequently, Rudolph was eleven before she could walk without a special brace or shoe. However, at

American Wilma Rudolph springs from the starting blocks in a qualifying heat for the women's 200-meter dash at the 1960 Summer Olympics in Rome. She would go on to set an Olympic record in the heat and win the gold medal in the 200-meter final (September 3, 1960).

(BETTMANN/CORBIS)

age sixteen, through sheer determination and desire, she captured a bronze medal in the 1956 Olympics in Melbourne, Australia. Four years later, at the 1960 Olympics in Rome, Rudolph won three gold medals and set three world records, in the 100-meter and 200-meter sprints and as a member of the 4x400-meter relay team, which she anchored. A graceful six-footer, Rudolph's charisma, beauty, and heroic life story captured the attention of a world audience that included kings and queens, presidents, and prime ministers.

A member of the talented Tigerbelles, the famed track-and-field team at Tennessee State University, a historic black college in Nashville, Rudolph became known as the greatest female U.S. athlete since Babe Didrikson Zaharias. In 1961, she received the Sullivan Award, the emblem of the nation's top amateur athlete.

As a U.S. Olympic Hall of Fame member and the only woman selected among the five all-time greatest athletes by the National Sports Council, Rudolph was an international symbol of courage and determination. Her achievements are recounted in her autobiography, *Wilma* (1977), and in a made-for-television movie based on her book.

—*Rebekah V. Bromley*

See also: Discrimination, Racial, in Sport; Olympic Games

For further reading:

Flanagan, Alice K. 2000. *Wilma Rudolph: Athlete and Educator.* Chicago: Ferguson Publishing.

Ruth, Amy. 2000. *Wilma Rudolph.* Minneapolis, MN: Lerner Books.

RUGBY

Rugby, a game of tackling, scrimmaging, and kicking and carrying an egg-shaped ball, is the direct ancestor of popular U.S. and Canadian professional football. Though played extensively throughout the Americas, rugby remains a relatively obscure sport in this hemisphere. It does not enjoy the popularity of soccer or the huge commercial appeal of U.S. and Canadian football, although it has been played continuously since the mid-1800s. In the late 1990s, several million men, women, and children in over one hundred countries played the game.

Rugby became organized as a game in the early 1800s. Legend credits a student at Rugby College in England with creating the game. A monument there reads, "This stone commemorates the exploit of William Webb Ellis who with a fine disregard for the rules of football, as played in his time, first took the ball in his arms and ran with it, thus originating the distinctive features of the Rugby game. AD 1823." Actually, games involving running with a ball had existed for many centuries, at least since the days of the Roman Empire, but it was the version of the game popularized at Rugby College that grew into the modern game.

Rugby spread throughout the British Empire and also became popular in France. The original version of the game became known as Rugby Union and was strictly amateur until 1995. In Rugby Union, two fifteen-player teams carry or kick a ball forward on a field with goalposts that is wider and longer than the fields used for American football. The ball may be passed laterally; it may not be knocked or thrown forward. The teams vigorously oppose each other's progress through tackling. Play is designed to be continuous, and complicated rules define the action. There is one referee and two line judges. When the ball is physically placed on the ground in the goal area or end zone, a "try" is scored. Points can also be gained by kicking the ball through the goalposts. The game is played in cleats, long socks, sturdy shorts, heavyweight jerseys, and mouth guards. No pads or other protective gear is allowed.

In 1895, rugby split into two codes. Rugby Union continued its amateur status. Meanwhile, rugby league, a thirteen-player variation of the game, began to pay top-level players. Rugby league became very popular with working-class players, who risked lost wages from injuries. Rugby league is popular in Australia, England, New Zealand, and France.

Rugby in Canada dates back to 1861, and the United States formed a Rugby Union in 1871. Rugby enjoyed great popularity throughout North America, especially on the Pacific Coast, where the game caught on at the University of California and at Stanford University. Theodore Roosevelt was a rugby fan and promoted it over the more dangerous Harvard football that became the U.S. professional game. The United States won Olympic gold medals in rugby in 1920 and 1924; however, rugby is no longer an Olympic sport. Its popularity declined with the rise of soccer and American football; however, in South America, the game has deep roots in Argentina, Uruguay, and Paraguay, where it originated in English-style private schools.

—*Paul Chambers*

See also: Canadian Football League; Football; Olympic Games

For further reading:

Cain, Nick. 2003. *Rugby Union for Dummies.* New York: John Wiley and Sons.

Greenwood, Jim. 1998. *Total Rugby.* London: A & C Black.

RUNNING

Running, whether as competition or as recreation, has long reflected and shaped U.S. attitudes toward professionalism, class, gender, health, and consumerism. Humans have run for as long as they have had legs, yet running as a recognized sport and cultural phenomenon developed in the United States as human locomotion became less necessary. Regular professional footraces, often sponsored by horse-racing tracks, flourished in the wake of the transportation revolution of the early nineteenth century. Able to tour the country for the first time, local champions competed in so-called pedestrian contests. Athletes ran to win money, and spectators often came to gamble for it. The runners were typically among the poorest of citizens and included immigrants, African Americans, and Native Americans. Although competitive running began as a working-class activity and was considered to be below the dignity of a gentleman, its character began to change in the late nineteenth century with the increasing emphasis on nonprofessional intercollegiate competition, exemplified by the founding of the Intercollegiate Association of Amateur Athletes of America in 1875 and the Amateur Athletic Union (AAU) in 1888. Among the races sponsored by the latter organization was a marathon in Boston, first held in 1897.

With a few exceptions over the next sixty years, most U.S. runners' competitive successes came in shorter races, especially sprints. Their failure in longer events led some observers to speculate that Americans were too soft and undisciplined. According to this view, the dominance of Eastern Bloc distance runners in the 1950s and 1960s was cause for national concern. When Gerry Lindgren (1946–) won the 10,000-meter race during the U.S.-U.S.S.R. dual track meet in 1964, it was the first victory by an American in an international long-distance event in decades.

Running as a popular form of noncompetitive exercise emerged in the 1960s and 1970s, at a time when Americans were more reliant on automobiles for daily travel than ever before. In fact, in 1994–1995, the highest level of participation in running was by people who lived in households that owned three or more automobiles. After a century of emphasis on amateurism, money and running were openly joined again. The popularity of running created a substantial market for shoes and clothing. In the 1970s and 1980s, runners like Bill Rodgers (1947–) were as noteworthy for their professional status and business interests as for their athletic successes.

Claiming that women's bodies were too fragile to stand the stress of running, the AAU long forbade them from participating in long-distance races. Another rule proscribing "mixed competition" kept them from racing with men. In 1966, Roberta Gibb (1943–), finishing unofficially, became the first woman to challenge the ban on female competitors in the Boston Marathon, by then the preeminent distance race in the United States. Not until 1972, however, did the AAU allow women to compete openly in Boston and elsewhere. Norway's Grete Waitz (1953–) elevated women's distance running by winning the New York City Marathon nine times between 1978 and 1988. America's Joan Benoit (1957–) won the inaugural women's Olympic marathon in Los Angeles in 1984. Participation by women runners grew dramatically at all levels. Only 309 women participated in National Collegiate Athletic Association (NCAA) track-and-field events in 1966–1967. Thirty years later, there were over 28,000, a rate of increase dwarfing that in basketball and most other collegiate sports. Participation rates among high school girls in cross-country running and outdoor track almost matched that of boys.

Because there were no running shoes made specifically for women when Roberta Gibb was training for her first Boston Marathon, she was forced to find other footwear, including nurses' shoes and boys' size 6 athletic shoes, proof of both women's subordinate athletic status in the 1960s and the potential for enormous market growth. By 1996, Americans would spend over a billion dollars on running shoes.

—*Fred Nielsen*

See also: Amateur Athletic Union; Boston Marathon; Jogging; Sneakers

For further reading:

Bingham, John. 2002. *No Need for Speed: A Beginner's Guide to the Joy of Running.* Emmaus, PA: Rodale Press.

Bingham, John, and Jenny Hadfield. 2003. *Marathoning for Mortals.* Emmaus, PA: Rodale Press.

Kowalchik, Claire. 1999. *The Complete Book of Running for Women.* New York: Pocket Books.

RUNYON, DAMON (1884–1946)

Damon Runyon is best known as the creator of *Guys and Dolls,* a humorous, quirky collection of stories about a subculture of bumbling gangsters, two-time hustlers, and their dames that he created while covering news stories about sport. Many of the fictional characters he created were likely based, in part, on the real characters he met in the sporting venues he frequented.

Born in Manhattan, Kansas, Alfred Damon Runyon became one of the most popular sportswriters in the United States in the decades on either side of the Depression as he moved from the country to New York City and the Hearst papers. He created the so-called Runyonese style—first-person, unnamed narrator—for newspaper columns set on Broadway during the gangster era, and he populated his writing with the lower levels of comical, barely functioning gunsels and misfit railbirds. His regular newspaper pieces on sport and society became short stories, eventually collected as *Guys and Dolls* (1931), *Blue Plate Special* (1934), and other books, featuring such self-descriptive characters as Harry the Horse, Little Isadore, Spanish John, Dark Delores, Dave the Dude, and Bookie Bob. In 1950, the satirical *Guys and Dolls* was made into a Broadway musical that focuses on relationships between various human characters, including gamblers (in general, not restricted to horse racing) who are looking for a place to hold a craps game, which is to be funded by the winnings from a personal bet.

As for many columnists of his era, in the heyday of the big-city newspapers, writing came easily to Runyon, who estimated that he had written over 80 million words, including poetry, columns, stories, fiction, and nonfiction, all filled with detail, wit, and sharply defined, lovable characters stumbling their way through the topsy-turvy world of lower Manhattan in the "roaring forties." He is credited with inventing the terms "hotsy totsy" and "monkey business."

—*Charles Moore*

See also: Literature, Sport in

For further reading:

Runyon, Damon. 1979. *Slow Horses and Fast Women.* Mattituck, NY: Amereon Books.

Schwarz, Daniel R. 2003. *Broadway Boogie Woogie: Damon Runyon and the Making of New York City Culture.* New York: Palgrave Macmillan

RUSSELL, WILLIAM "BILL" FELTON (1934–)

The first African American superstar of the National Basketball Association (NBA), William "Bill" Russell accelerated the desegregation of professional sport by demonstrating that black athletes could combine athletic excellence with superior intelligence and strength of character. Born in Monroe, Louisiana, and raised in Oakland, California, Russell led the University of San Francisco to fifty-five consecutive victories and back-to-back National Collegiate Athletic Association championships in 1955 and 1956.

After helping the U.S. basketball team win a gold medal at the 1956 Olympic Games, the six-foot-nine-inch center became a key element of the Boston Celtics dynasty. Between 1957 and 1969, the Celtics won ten NBA championships, the last two with Russell as player-coach. When he succeeded Red Auerbach as the Celtics' coach in 1966, he became the NBA's first African American head coach.

During his thirteen-year career, Russell was named the league's Most Valuable Player five times, primarily because of his defensive and rebounding prowess. Aided by the Celtics' aura of invincibility and by his epic struggles with the taller but less popular Wilt "the Stilt" Chamberlain, Russell enjoyed an unrivaled reputation as a clutch performer. In a 1980 poll of the Professional Basketball Writers Association, he was judged the "Greatest Player in the History of the NBA."

Following his retirement as a player, Russell remained in the public eye as the coach and general manager of the Seattle Supersonics from 1973 to 1977, the coach of the Sacramento Kings from 1987 to 1988, a popular television commentator, a frequent lecturer on college campuses, and the coauthor of *Second Wind: Memoirs of an Opinionated Man* (1980). As the subtitle of his memoirs suggests, he cultivated a public image of unblinking honesty. Known for his forthright advocacy of civil rights and racial equality, Russell became an important role model for independent-minded and socially conscious athletes and coaches.

—*Raymond Arsenault*

See also: Basketball; Civil Rights and Sport

For further reading:

Russell, Bill, and Taylor Branch. 1980. *Second Wind: The Memoirs of an Opinionated Man.* New York: Ballantine Books.

Russell, Bill, Alan Hilburg, and David Falkner. 2002. *Russell Rules: Eleven Lessons on Leadership from the Twentieth Century's Greatest Winner.* New York: E. P. Dutton.

RUTH, GEORGE HERMAN "BABE," JR. (1895–1948)

George "Babe" Ruth Jr., baseball's best-known player, transformed both his sport and the contours of professional athletics at the dawn of U.S. mass culture. "I was a bad kid," Ruth once remarked of his childhood in Baltimore, Maryland (Ruth 1948, 1). Ruth, born to working-class parents of German origin in 1895, spent much of his early childhood in his father's Baltimore saloon. The impish youngster was also frequently found wandering about the city's streets and piers in search of mischief. Thus, when he turned seven, his parents, unable to keep him in school, had him labeled as "incorrigible" by city authorities, and he was sent to the nearby St. Mary's Industrial School.

Although Ruth briefly considered the priesthood and although the teachers at St. Mary's tried to train him as a shirt maker, his obvious talent for baseball altered those plans. As a teenager, the left-hander emerged as something of a local sensation. In 1914, his amateur pitching exploits attracted the attention of Jack Dunn, a scout for the Independent League's Baltimore Orioles. In fact, only sixteen days after Dunn's visit to St. Mary's, Ruth was on a train to Fayetteville, North Carolina, the site of the Orioles' training camp.

One of the youngest recruits at Fayetteville, Ruth earned the nickname "Babe" and a reputation for off-field misbehavior. Both the nickname and the reputation lasted, but his playing days for the financially unstable Orioles did not. In July 1914, he was sold to the powerful Boston Red Sox, for whom he amassed an impressive pitching record, throwing nearly thirty consecutive scoreless innings in the World Series of 1916 and 1918.

> As a young man, Babe Ruth briefly considered becoming a priest.

By 1919, however, Ruth's hitting prowess was earning even greater praise than his work on the pitching mound, and Red Sox manager Ed Barrow moved his young star permanently to the outfield. But it was Ruth's home-run hitting that eventually secured his privileged place in sport lore. Standing four inches taller than the average major leaguer, he shocked the baseball world by smashing twenty-nine home runs during the 1919 season. The next year, after the New York Yankees had purchased his contract for a total amount in excess of $400,000, he hit fifty-four home runs, nearly three times as many as his closest competitor.

His rank as the most sensational sport attraction in the United States was assured, and the "Sultan of Swat," with his corkscrew swing, went on to hit 714 career homers, including an astounding sixty in 1927. His reputation drew so many fans that the Yankees could finally build a stadium in 1923; in fact, Yankee Stadium has long been known as "the House That Ruth Built." Ruth eventually played in ten World Series, claimed more than seventy batting and pitching records, and was among the first five inductees into the National Baseball Hall of Fame in 1936.

During World War II, after his retirement from the diamond, the Babe gave radio talks and made public appearances in hospitals and orphanages as well as serving as a spokesperson for U.S. war bonds. In 1946, he was found to have throat cancer, but two years later, he attended the twenty-fifth anniversary of the opening of Yankee Stadium. He died in 1948.

Statistics and biography fail to convey the full measure of Ruth's impact. Baseball before Ruth was a pitcher's game. The 1880s and 1890s celebrated home-run baseball, but the new century emphasized a more deliberate strategy of play. Teams used a heavy, "dead" ball that was difficult to hit, no less because pitchers were permitted to doctor it. The well-placed single, mastered by stars like Ty Cobb, was extremely valuable, and managers were lauded for their ability to elaborate on complex game plans. In this contest of wits, one-handed grabs were considered unnecessary and spectacular.

So too were home runs: The league leader in home runs in 1915 swatted only seven—mostly by accident. Ruth's "tremendous wallops" thus augured a new, sensational style of play. To the delight of fans—and with the help of a livelier ball—batters followed the Babe's example and aimed for the bleachers. "Baseball, the past few seasons," wrote a popular magazine in 1924, "has been transformed from a scientific pastime to a contest of brute strength" (Smelser 1975, 299).

Furthermore, in this age of cultural heroes, baseball established itself as a professional, profitable industry. Owners, viewing their franchises as commodities, invented a salable tradition for

Babe Ruth is shown about to swing at the world's largest baseball (ca. 1920).
(UNDERWOOD & UNDERWOOD/CORBIS)

the game, while prominent players like Ruth began to hire agents to market their "personalities." Technical innovations like the newsreel and the radio, as well as increased newspaper coverage, were prerequisites for these developments. Those who objected to baseball's reorientation blamed the Babe's slugging revolution. Progressives and purists, who viewed sport as a means for self-improvement and an agent of moral rectitude, lamented that the home run burdened the game with empty showmanship.

Nonetheless, the public approved. The advent of mass transit and growing leisure time for urban workers—along with Ruth's thrilling performances—led to skyrocketing attendance figures. Although episodes like the 1919 "Black Sox" scandal threatened the game's newfound cultural authority, Ruth's iconic status helped make the 1920s the golden age of baseball in the United States.

—*John H. Summers*

See also: Baseball; Black Sox Scandal; Yankee Stadium

For further reading:
Creamer, Robert. 1974. *Babe: The Legend Comes to Life.* New York: Simon and Schuster.

Ritter, Lawrence. 1966. *The Glory of Their Times: The Story of the Early Days of Baseball Told by the Men Who Played It.* New York: Macmillan.

Ruth, Babe. 1948. *The Babe Ruth Story.* New York: E. P. Dutton.

Smelser, Marshall. 1975. *The Life That Ruth Built: A Biography.* Lincoln: University of Nebraska Press.

RYAN, LYNN NOLAN (1946–)

By excelling at an age when most athletes are retired and by being unpretentious in a sport notorious for large egos, Nolan Ryan, major league baseball pitcher, became a role model for an aging population.

When the name "Nolan Ryan" is mentioned, it is usually followed by numbers. Among those numbers are seven no-hitters, the most in major league history, and 5,714 strikeouts, the most by any professional pitcher in any league. Ryan was the first pitcher to be clocked throwing over one hundred miles per hour during the twenty-seven years he spent in the major leagues. Yet Ryan represents more than just numbers.

Born and raised in rural Texas, Ryan was the stereotypical all-American boy. A star athlete from a young age, he became known for his hard work, honesty, and devotion to his family. His career took him to New York and California and then back to Texas. However, he never developed the notorious big-league ego that many of his contemporaries did.

Unlike many older stars, Ryan's popularity grew with his age. The Texas Rangers were guaranteed a sellout when the over-forty Ryan pitched. Baby boomers identified with the man who endorsed pain relievers rather than running shoes. He became the role model for what an aging society could accomplish if it took proper care of itself. At age forty-four, Ryan pitched a no-hitter and still threw a ball at speeds of over ninety miles per hour. He credited his success to a rigorous conditioning program.

—*Kenneth Phillips*

See also: Baseball; Paige, Leroy "Satchel"

For further reading:

Anderson, Ken, and Melissa Roberts. 1999. *Nolan Ryan: Texas Fastball to Cooperstown.* Austin, TX: Eakin Press.

Ryan, Nolan, Mickey Herskowitz, and T. R. Sullivan. 1999. *Nolan Ryan: The Road to Cooperstown.* Lenexa, KS: Addax Press.

S

SAILING

Since humans first discovered bodies of water, they have gone down to the sea—and lakes and rivers and streams—in ships. The sea, in particular, has always been viewed as potentially dangerous; thus, it has become a frontier to be conquered by the adventurer and the sport enthusiast.

The U.S. love of sailing is as old as the history of the country. From the arrival of the first Europeans in Virginia to Henry Hudson's explorations in 1609, the history of Americans' love affair with bodies of water is well documented. Although the first ships were primarily used in commerce or to transport persons and belongings, pleasure boating in New York Harbor has been recorded as early as 1717.

In addition to navigating boats, Americans are reputed as shipbuilders, creating craft known for efficiency and speed. By the end of the seventeenth century, shipyards stretched from Maine to the Delaware River, and one-third of the ships in England were constructed in the United States. Shipyards served as the town center and were ringed with shops and taverns. The latter provided rest from the work and the weather and were quite popular with the yard hands. It has been estimated that for every ton of water a ship displaced, its builders consumed a gallon of rum.

Boating for pleasure was the sport of million-aires in the 1800s, and competition was inevitable. Racing under sail developed into a popular means of spending a weekend afternoon. Many of the competitions were classed—in other words, the ships were grouped by design and build—and the races were conducted in protected waters near local boating clubs. Other races were handicap affairs, matching boats of different sizes and designs but handicapping the smaller crafts by allowing them more time.

In 1844, John Cox Stephens, the son of a wealthy merchant, founded the New York Yacht Club and became its first commodore. Stephens and the club sponsored the *America*, the vessel for which the famous America's Cup was named. The craft defeated seventeen British vessels off the Isle of Wight in 1851 and initiated decades of U.S. superiority in sail racing.

In the modern era, with a surplus of leisure time and the ready availability of disposable income, sailing has gained a larger foothold in the middle class. Sailing craft are often preferred over motor boats or jet skis because of their old-world charm and the soothing slap of the waves against the hull in addition to requiring more skill, con-

> *In 1844, John Cox Stephens, the son of a wealthy merchant, founded the New York Yacht Club and became its first commodore. Stephens and the club sponsored the* America, *the vessel for which the famous America's Cup was named.*

trol, and finesse than do their flashier counterparts. In addition to claiming a berth in the sporting and recreational world, sailing has affected literature and the arts for centuries, including carving, woodworking, and scrimshaw as well as the creation of lyrical sea chanteys.

—*Jerry W. Nave*

See also: America's Cup

For further reading:

Anderson, Romola. 2003. *A Short History of the Sailing Ship.* New York: Dover.

Conner, Dennis, and Michael Levitt. 1998. *The America's Cup: The History of Sailing's Greatest Competition in the Twentieth Century.* New York: St. Martin's Press.

SANDLOT BASEBALL

A popular term for unorganized amateur baseball, "sandlot" entered baseball mythology and the U.S. lexicon as a place of the past that was typified by an innocent love of the game. Ford Frick, the longtime National League president and commissioner of major league baseball, was fond of saying that "baseball is the kid on the sandlot" (Dickson 1989). The use of the word "sandlot" to mean unorganized baseball games played by amateurs arose in the late nineteenth century. Folklorist Peter Tamony traced the term to a sandy tract of land in San Francisco, where the city built its town hall in 1870. Newspaper accounts of the "Sand Lot" project popularized the phrase throughout the United States, and it soon became a useful moniker for dusty baseball fields and the games played on them. Before the ascendance of Little League and recreational league baseball, many teens and young adults participated in sandlot games, often supported by local merchants or by the passing of a hat. In the book *Sandlot Seasons* (1987), Rob Ruck illustrated the immense popularity of sandlot ball in the Pittsburgh area of the 1920s and 1930s. From those sandlot games

emerged great Negro League players like Josh Gibson and great teams like the Pittsburgh Crawfords. By 1939, the term "sandlot" had also come to be popularly identified with youngsters' untarnished love of the game. In that year, baseball's Hall of Fame dedicated the statue of a barefoot boy, entitled "The Sand Lot Kid," outside Abner Doubleday Field in Cooperstown, New York. The sentimental use of the phrase has persisted in U.S. culture, as in David Evans's 1993 film *The Sandlot,* which looks nostalgically back at kids' summer ball games of the late 1950s.

—*Jeffrey Powers-Beck*

See also: Baseball; Children in Sport: Necessity of Play

For further reading:

Dickson, Paul. 1989. *The Dickson Baseball Dictionary.* New York: Facts on File.

Ruck, Rob. 1987. *Sandlot Seasons: Sport in Black Pittsburgh.* Urbana: University of Illinois Press.

SCHOTT, MARGE (1928–)

The outspoken owner of baseball's Cincinnati Reds, Marge Unnewehr Schott is one of the most visible and colorful team owners in sports, but also one who has stirred controversy and outrage with her well-publicized racially and ethnically offensive remarks. A native of Cincinnati, Ohio, Margaret Unnewehr was born into an upper-class German American family and, in 1952, married Charles J. Schott, the wealthy son of another prominent Cincinnati family. When her husband died at forty-two in 1968, Marge Schott took over his business interests and became a successful multimillionaire businesswoman. In 1981, she acquired a minority share in the Cincinnati Reds, professional baseball's oldest franchise. By December 1984, she had purchased a controlling interest in the team, ultimately taking the titles of president and chief executive officer. In becoming the principal owner of the Reds, Schott was one of the few women to own a professional sport

Marge Schott, owner of the Cincinnati Reds, hugs her star player-manager Pete Rose after he hit his record-breaking hit—number 4,192 against the Padres (September 11, 1985).
(BETTMANN/CORBIS)

franchise and only the second woman actually to purchase a major league baseball team instead of obtaining it through inheritance.

The plain-talking, chain-smoking, and hard-drinking Schott became a local and national celebrity along with her beloved and ever-present Saint Bernards, "Schottzie" and later "Schottzie 02." Dedicated to keeping ticket and concession prices down, she was a favorite of hometown fans and a fixture in her seat near the Reds' dugout at Cincinnati's Riverfront Stadium, where she enjoyed signing autographs and interacting with the fans.

Behind the scenes, however, Schott's relations with employees and business partners were often tumultuous and unpleasant. Although she generally fielded competitive teams, including the 1990 World Series champions, her penurious, hands-on management style and often mean-spirited, personal style alienated and frustrated many of her employees.

Many of her more-public actions have also cast her in a negative light. In 1993, popular former Reds star Tony Perez was fired as manager of the team only forty-four games into his first season. When the on-the-field death of veteran umpire John McSherry caused the cancellation of the Reds' opening-day game in 1996, Schott vociferously complained. Schott received her greatest notoriety, however, for her frequent racial and ethnic slurs and use of other intolerant language. She has also received much bad publicity for praising Adolf Hitler and for possessing a Nazi armband. Many of her gaffes have occurred in the national television spotlight on such venues as ESPN, *Late Night with David Letterman*, *Primetime Live*, and *60 Minutes*.

A public-relations nightmare, Schott's embarrassing and offensive behavior finally forced her fellow owners into action, and in February 1993, baseball's Executive Council reprimanded and censured Schott, fined her $25,000, required her to undergo multicultural training, and suspended her from baseball operations for one year—a

penalty that was later reduced to eight months. The punishment, which critics considered insufficient, did not, however, have the desired salutary effect, for Schott's outrageous behavior continued. In June 1996, she received another, longer suspension that barred her from the day-to-day operations of the Reds for two and a half years, that is, through the end of the 1998 season.

—*Robert P. Nash*

See also: Baseball; Discrimination, Racial, in Sport; Political Correctness

For further reading:
Bass, Mike. 1993. *Marge Schott: Unleashed.* Champaign, IL: Sagamore Publishing.
Elder, Larry. 2001. *The Ten Things You Can't Say in America.* Irvine, CA: Griffin Publishing.

SCUBA DIVING

The history of humanity's passion for undersea exploration begins with the *Epic of Gilgamesh,* the story of a Sumerian king who tied stones to his feet and fashioned a long breathing tube out of seaweed so he could walk along the seafloor and seek the seed of eternal life. The Assyrians, Greeks, and Romans also left tales of men marching and working underwater with the aid of fanciful devices. Between A.D. 1000 and 1800, imaginative designs for such devices surfaced periodically, but few had a lasting impact on the evolution of scuba diving. Leonardo da Vinci, for example, produced sketches of diving lungs. Elizabethan artisans designed "leathern suits" for underwater swimming. Edmund Halley, for whom the comet is named, invented a diving bell but did not know how to sink it or how to get fresh air down to it. Benjamin Franklin, one of the few early inventors to make a lasting contribution to the sport, designed flippers.

The early 1800s saw modest gains for the sport, such as an air compressor that would pump fresh air down to a diver, who was imagined as wearing an open-dress helmet, an open-bottomed helmet resting on the diver's shoulders, that would allow "bad air" to escape. In 1825, an "air-belt" was designed. This was the first scuba (an acronym for "self-contained underwater breathing apparatus"), a device that allowed a diver to carry air. In 1837, a practical helmet diving suit was invented in England, and seven years later, in 1844, Henri Milne-Edwards of the Sorbonne University in Paris made the first modern undersea dive. To observe marine plant and animal life in its natural element, he wore a bucket helmet that had air pumped into it from a ship floating above him.

In the second half of the nineteenth century, diving science and technology advanced in response to modernizing and industrializing society in Europe and the United States. The Industrial Revolution and urbanization increased the need for bridges, quays, and lighthouses, all of which required underwater foundations. In the 1880s, "sandhogs" building the Brooklyn Bridge worked in pressurized shafts that prevented "the bends," severe joint pain and fatigue. In 1907, Scotsman John Scott Haldane articulated an equation that explained the bends in terms of excess nitrogen absorption into the blood and surrounding tissues. His "stage decompression system" remains the most effective method of avoiding what divers now call decompression sickness. Until the 1940s, however, scuba diving technology advanced slowly. Although high-pressure cylinders for safely containing regular air and shallow-depth rebreathers were developed for military use, scuba diving did not become a sport until Jacques-Yves Cousteau, explorer, inventor, and filmmaker, lent his passion and expertise to the cause.

Jacques-Yves Cousteau

Cousteau's passion for undersea exploration influenced the development of undersea archeology, oceanography, marine biology, fishing, underwater technology and engineering, underwater photography and cinematography, and sport diving. He contributed significantly to the construction of undersea research stations and small subs, discovered petroleum in the Persian Gulf, and founded major environmental organizations in the United States, Canada, and France. Born in Bordeaux, France, in 1907, Cousteau's most significant technological contribution to the sport of diving was the Aqua-Lung, or demand-regulator system. Codeveloped with Emile Gagnan in 1943, the Aqua-Lung became standard equipment for the U.S. Navy, and because it conserved air, increased bottom time, and was inexpensive to make, companies in the United States and France manufactured it for sport enthusiasts and aquatic adventurers.

By 1950, Cousteau's accounts of undersea exploration were extremely popular in the United States. The U.S. publication *Skin Diver Magazine* began circulating in 1951 and drew much of its material from Cousteau's adventures. *Life* magazine published his first major article in 1950, "Underwater Wonders: A French Diver Explores the Haunts of Sea Monsters." In 1953, Cousteau's most famous book, *The Silent World,* was published in English. The book became a major motion picture in 1956. In 1960, three years after he resigned from the French navy, an article in *Time* proclaimed Cousteau the "patron saint" of diving. In 1961, Cousteau received the National Geographic Society's Gold Medal. The inscription read, "To earthbound man he gave the key to the silent world."

Upon retirement, Cousteau turned his attention to film and television, and by 1967, he had received three Oscars from the Motion Picture Academy in Hollywood. *The Undersea World of Jacques Cousteau* aired on ABC-TV in 1968. In an era of increasing environmental awareness, Cousteau founded a nonprofit membership society, the Cousteau Society, dedicated to the protection and improvement of the quality of all life on earth. It conducts investigations and scientific research that would not usually be funded by government or industry. The society celebrated its twenty-fifth anniversary in 1999, and it continues its work because, as Cousteau believed, "the fate of humankind is linked to the proper management of our planet's water system."

—*Laura Thomas*

See also: Swimming; Synchronized Swimming

For further reading:

Bailer, Darice. 2002. *Extreme Sports: Dive!* Washington, DC: National Geographic.

Cousteau, Jacques-Yves. 1985. *Jacques Cousteau: The Ocean World.* New York: Harry Abrams.

SCULPTURE, SPORT IN

Sculptural figures or objects relating to sport have been dated from the Mesoamerican or pre-Columbian period; however, in more recent times, sport-related sculptures tend to be commemorative. Sculpture has been used for centuries to represent athletic and military heroes; the most notable pieces date from the Greek and Roman Empires. Most admirers of works of art are familiar with the *Discus Thrower* and the *Charioteer.* These statues have been critically acclaimed for generations for their modeling detail and beauty. Other civilizations have created similar objects to depict their cultural involvement with sport.

Monumental stone sculptures from the Zapotec tribe of the middle pre-Classic Mesoamerican period (circa 900–circa 300 B.C.) in the valley of Oaxaca feature masked and jaguar-headed human figures. The masked figures represent ballplayers. A typical ball court of the Mayan culture was often decorated with narrative relief panels along the walls telling of various victories, defeats, or sacrifices of a ballplayer and of his journey to the underworld in search of *palque,* a ritual beverage. Many of the other sculptural pieces of the period featured hunter-warriors and their conquests.

During the pre-Classic period (circa 1200–circa 300 B.C.), the Olmecs of the Gulf Coast region created Mesoamerica's first great art style that included smaller sculptures of both solid and hollow clay figures. Among the artifacts archeologists have found from this tribe were also figures of ballplayers. Craftspeople of the Early Classic period (circa A.D. 250–circa 600) from the Colima region of western Mexico modeled acrobats and dancers among their figurines. Typical clay compositions from the Nayarit region show active figures in a variety of environmental settings, including village festivals, games, and dances. Similar pieces featuring ballplayers and warriors were found among the Late Classic (circa A.D. 600–circa 900) ruins in the island necropolis of Jaina, located off the coast of the Yucatan Peninsula. It is clear that many different cultures have commemorated athletic events in art forms.

In the modern era, the tradition of honoring athletes and athletic events in sculptural form continues. The Olympic Games is the largest art festival in the world, commissioning artists and artisans to create designs for the official medals as well as for ornamental and decorative sculpture. Each individual sport honors its own athletes in art, occasionally commemorating them in bronze or mixed media. Many fine examples of sport-related sculpture, from busts to life-size figures, can be found in museums and fine art galleries, private collections, sport complexes, sport halls of fame, and college campuses. A cadre of primarily local artists is commissioned to create these statues to honor one of their own.

—*Stephen Allan Patrick*

See also: Artists of Sport; Olympic Games; Popular Culture and Sport

For further reading:

Baigell, Matthew. 1996. *A Concise History of American Painting and Sculpture.* Boulder, CO: Westview Press.

Langland, Tuck. 2000. *From Clay to Bronze: A Studio Guide to Figurative Sculpture.* New York: Watson-Guptill.

Pedley, John G. 2002. *Greek Art and Archaeology.* 3rd ed. Englewood Cliffs, NJ: Prentice-Hall.

SIMPSON, ORENTHAL JAMES "O. J." (1947–)

As one of the nation's greatest football players, O. J. Simpson exemplified the heroic qualities that transform superb athletes into cultural icons. However, as the principal suspect in one of the most celebrated double murders of the century, he achieved far greater fame and challenged a nation to rethink how its heroes are made.

Orenthal James Simpson was born in San Francisco in 1947 and grew up in the city's Potrero Hill housing project. He was forced to wear a pair of leg braces fashioned by his mother, Eunice, until he was five years old in order to correct a bowed condition caused by rickets.

As a child, Simpson spent his idle hours at the Petrero Hills Recreation Center. He was a football star at Galileo High School, where his jersey still hangs in the trophy case. During his teen years, he briefly became involved with the Persian Warriors gang, and at fifteen, he spent a weekend in jail. He was rescued by baseball legend Willie Mays, who befriended the young Simpson, hoping to help him avoid future trouble with the law.

Simpson parlayed his athletic talents into a college scholarship, attending San Francisco City College before beginning his remarkable career at the University of Southern California (USC). Selected as an All-American in 1967 and 1968, he also won the Heisman Trophy in 1968. Between November 1967 and August 1969, Simpson appeared on the cover of *Sports Illustrated* four times.

In 1969, Simpson signed with the Buffalo Bills, the first player selected in that year's professional football draft, and by 1972, he was the rushing leader in the National Football League (NFL), with 1,251 yards gained. He became the first player in the NFL to rush for more than 2,000 yards in a single season, finishing with 2,003 in 1973. In 1975, he set a record, since surpassed, for the most touchdowns in a season, twenty-three. As a professional, Simpson appeared on two more *Sports Illustrated* covers, in 1973 and 1974.

Simpson made five Pro Bowl appearances; however, after his team's continued failure to reach the Super Bowl, he asked to be traded to a West Coast team, and in 1978, he joined the San Francisco 49ers. Due to injuries, he retired from football in 1979 to become a television broadcaster, actor, and celebrity spokesperson. In 1985, he was inducted into the National Football League Hall of Fame.

In 1967, while still at USC, Simpson married Marguerite Whitley. The couple had three children, one of whom, Aaren, died in a swimming pool accident at their estate on Rockingham Avenue in the Brentwood section of Los Angeles. The marriage ended in divorce in 1979. In 1985, he married Nicole Brown, whom he had met in 1977 at a restaurant where she was working as a waitress. The couple had two children, Sydney and Justin.

In the early morning hours of New Year's Day in 1989, Nicole Brown Simpson made a frantic 911 call to report that Simpson had threatened to kill her. Simpson was convicted of spousal abuse and placed on two years' probation, fined, and ordered to perform 120 hours of community service. He also had to attend battery-counseling sessions. His reputation tarnished, Simpson appeared again on the cover of *Sports Illustrated* in October 1990 as a troubled former athlete.

The couple's marriage ended in 1992, but their conflicted relationship did not. Simpson reportedly had hoped for reconciliation, but on October 25, 1993, Nicole made another 911 call, reporting that Simpson was assaulting her. On June 12, 1994, Nicole Brown Simpson and a friend, Ronald Goldman, were found brutally murdered in her townhouse on Bundy Drive, not far from Simpson's estate.

On June 27, 1994, Simpson, by then a fallen hero, appeared for the last time on the cover of *Sports Illustrated*. The lead story, entitled "Fatal Attraction," chronicled Simpson's tormented—and hitherto largely unreported—personal life. He had been arrested and charged with murder ten days before the article appeared.

Simpson's trial, which began on January 24, 1995, was broadcast live, turned into a media feeding frenzy, and captivated the U.S. viewing audience for weeks of tedious testimony. The proceedings ended in Simpson's acquittal on October 3, 1995. On October 23, 1996, he returned to court, again in televised proceedings, to face wrongful death charges in a civil suit filed by the family of Ronald Goldman. On February 4, 1997, Simpson was found liable in the slayings and ordered to pay $33.5 million. Consequently, he was forced to sell his estate and liquidate many of his assets, including his Heisman Trophy, but he remained a free man and retained custody of his and Nicole's two minor children.

In 1973, when Simpson was at the height of his professional career, *Sports Illustrated* characterized him as a "relentlessly congenial" yet "genuinely humble" sport hero. His true character and the role he played in U.S. culture have turned out to be considerably more complex.

—*Dan R. Jones*

See also: Athletes, above the Law; Football; *Sports Illustrated*

For further reading:

Cerasini, Mark. 1994. *O. J. Simpson: American Hero, American Tragedy.* New York: Pinnacle Books.

Dershowitz, Alan M. 1997. *Reasonable Doubts: The Criminal Justice System and the O. J. Simpson Case.* New York: Touchstone.

Morse, Ann. 1976. *Football's Great Running Back, O. J. Simpson.* Mankato, MN: Creative Education.

SKATEBOARDING

Permutations of skateboarding over the past four decades have ranged from cruising down asphalt to swooping around empty swimming pools to doing flips and handstands on the upswing of huge wooden or cement scoops. The common denominator is the mode of transport, a board on four wheels. Beginning literally as a street sport and evolving into daring acrobatics, skateboarding today may be seen as a pastime, performance art, cultural expression, high-level sport, or highly commercialized endeavor with associations ranging from rebelliousness and vandalism to freedom and squeaky-clean athleticism. It has spawned lawsuits and city ordinances, modernist cement parks, fashion statements, movies, and video games and has attained a type of antiestablishment legitimacy as one of the major events in the X Games as well as in ESPN's B3 Games, devoted to bikes, boards, and blades.

Skateboarding has emerged and receded several times on the U.S. scene, having had several distinct waves of popularity. Scooter-like forerunners of the skateboard date back to the early 1900s, when children fixed metal roller-skate wheels to wooden planks. However, definable communities of skateboarding practitioners emerged only in the 1960s, when sidewalk cruising became a fad among surfers in southern California. A surfing entrepreneur developed the first manufactured skateboard in 1963, along with a skating team to promote the product. Soon, rough-riding metal wheels were replaced with clay ones that rolled somewhat more smoothly. The country's first skateboard magazine was launched, and general-interest periodicals, such as *Time* and *Life,* also acknowledged the sport. In addition, the First International Championships held in Anaheim, California, in 1965 gained exposure on ABC's *Wide World of Sports.* The phenomenon also appeared in Canada, Japan, Europe, Australia, New Zealand, and South Africa.

Although the initial boom was short-lived, in the early 1970s, with the development of urethane rubber wheels, skateboarding saw a resurgence, leading to much more versatility and creativity in use of the board. The first outdoor skate park was constructed in Florida in 1976, and the sport shifted from horizontal movement along streets and sidewalks to more vertical antics on specially constructed ramps and pipes. The equipment underwent additional technical improvement,

A skateboarder competes in a half-pipe competition at the 2002 ESPN Invitational.
(DUOMO/CORBIS)

including the incorporation of precision bearings, as well as design and aesthetic changes, with wider boards and wild graphics added to the underside. Skateboarders created new styles and moves involving jumping, spinning, and feats of aerial daring.

Concern over liability at skate facilities and over safety and decorum on city streets produced another slump in the business in the early 1980s. Nevertheless, contingents of die-hard skaters kept at it, building backyard half-pipes and ramps as skate parks closed, and dodging authorities in public places where skateboarding was considered a nuisance and a threat to property. Skateboarding was viewed as an outlet for teenage alienation and was associated with punk rock and ska music.

A handful of companies producing high-end boards fueled another upswing in the mid-1980s,

as mass production overseas put cheaper skateboards into discount stores across the country. A related shoe and apparel industry grew up around the prepubescent skating uniform of oversized T-shirts, absurdly baggy pants worn low to expose boxer shorts, and backward baseball caps. During this period, the best skaters, some organized into company-sponsored teams, built reputations through local competitions, specialized media, and word-of-mouth. Two new skateboarding magazines, *Thrasher* and *Transworld Skateboarding,* appeared.

The 1990s brought much broader commercialization of the sport along with increased legitimacy. Retailers like the Gap and Old Navy as well as MTV artists appropriated skateboard fashion statements, and ESPN brought skateboarding and other "alternative sports" to a global television audience with the first Extreme Games ("X Games") in 1995. Professional skateboarders now tour the world and are successful in endorsement deals and in their own businesses.

The notion of skateboarders as vandals and juvenile delinquents has faded, and in many communities disdain has given way to condoned construction of public skate parks, which usually require that skaters wear pads and helmets. Skate-park excursions became acceptable family entertainment. By the end of the decade, the skateboard industry estimated there were nearly ten million participants in the United States alone.

Traditionally a male preserve and still predominantly male, skateboarding promotions and competitions have begun to feature more women stars and teams. The most committed skateboarders view their sport as a creative quest; its rules are constantly being redefined and new possibilities are continually being discovered. The culture of skateboarding devotes considerable energy to documenting achievements in magazines, books, videos, films, and Web sites with global distribution, so that skateboarders from Canada to Europe to Brazil are seen as part of a worldwide community. Skate parks continue to be built worldwide, and the world's largest, a 63,000-square-foot concrete complex, is in Calgary, Alberta.

—*Judy Polumbaum*

See also: ESPN; Television, Impact on Sport; X Games

For further reading:

Brooke, Michael. 1999. *The Concrete Wave: The History of Skateboarding.* Toronto: Warwick.

Davis, James, and Skin Phillips. 1999. *Skateboard Roadmap.* London: Carlton.

Hawk, Tony. 2000. *Hawk: Occupation Skateboarder.* With Sean Mortimer. New York: ReganBooks.

SNEAKERS

Of all the sport figures, sporting events, and sporting incidentals that contribute to the mind-set of a group, one item stands out as having had a greater impact on U.S. culture than any other: athletic apparel, specifically sneakers. Although sneakers are variously called running shoes, athletic shoes, tennis shoes, tennies, gym shoes, sport shoes, aerobic shoes, and other names, the definition remains essentially the same: a sneaker is a shoe featuring an upper portion made of canvas, leather, vinyl, or other synthetic material and a lower portion made of rubber. In fact, the terminology associated with athletic footwear is so broad that there exists a rather extensive Internet Web page, manned in an obviously tongue-in-cheek mode by a person known only as "Charlie," devoted exclusively to the myriad definitions and divisions. Originally designed for participation in athletics, the sneaker can now be found everywhere, from the classroom to the boardroom.

John Boyd Dunlop of Liverpool, England, developed the earliest known form of the athletic shoe in the 1830s. First called "sand shoes" because they were worn on the beach by the Victorian middle class, the athletic shoe has evolved into a mega-billion-dollar international industry. In the late 1990s, the revenues from the sale of all athletic shoes exceeded $132 billion, $13 billion in the United States alone. Due to relaxed dress codes in workplaces and a national trend toward comfortable attire, the number of adults wearing sneakers every day increased by 40 percent in the 1990s; in addition, the teenage and youth population consider sneakers a fashion statement.

The sneaker industry is such a significant phenomenon that statistical studies on buying habits are conducted annually not only to determine the amount of money spent but also to break down purchasers' demographics by age groups, educational levels, and ethnicity.

Teenagers and young adults spend about $40 per pair for new sneakers, and families with children aged 13–17 spend the most per purchase, on average. The group spending the second-highest amount per pair on average is childless couples under the age of 35. Teenagers buy an average of two pairs of sneakers per year, and families with younger children tend to spend less but to buy more frequently. Ironically, high-income households are more likely to use coupons, discounts, and other incentives than are their lower-income counterparts, and over half of those using the discounts are college educated as compared to the one third who have only high school diplomas.

Asian Americans spend more than the average on running shoes but are more likely than any other ethnic group to look for purchasing incentives. Hispanics tend to buy more pairs but to spend less, whereas African Americans spend less than Asians but more than average and purchase new shoes frequently. Caucasians spend an average amount and purchase an average quantity. Basketball shoes are the most popular type of sneakers, with cross-trainers running a tight second. So-called athleisure shoes, made from canvas or suede and designed for nonperformance, rose to fourth on the list as the nonathletic athletic market continued to escalate.

With this much money at stake in an almost recession-proof industry, it is inevitable that competition is fierce. In the 1990s, the sneaker wars were launched with key competitors, Nike and Reebok, fielding advertisements offering better, faster performance and the ability to achieve "more air" in athletic shoes. Nike emerged as and has remained the champion in this competition largely due to the visibility of their advertising, such as the "Just Do It" campaign, consumer recognition of the trademark swoosh, and the credibility of their major endorser, Michael Jordan of the Chicago Bulls. His signature sneaker, Air Jordan, retails for over $100, and for many in the industry, Nike is Jordan. Jordan may also be Nike, since the basketball superstar balked at wearing a Reebok winners' circle jacket during the Atlanta Olympic Games.

At the Atlanta Olympic Games, the global sneaker wars heated up. Initially, it seemed that Reebok would have an edge, since the company had exclusive television advertising rights for the event; however, Nike countered by outfitting many of the athletes, including the U.S. track-and-field competitors; putting up sixteen billboards surrounding the downtown event location; painting ten buses with the famous Nike logo; and hanging posters throughout Atlanta's rapid transit system. In addition, the shoe magnate manned Nike Park, a retail outlet adjacent to the Olympic site.

Although Adidas is taking a share of the urban ethnic market, Fila is catering to the young professional not involved in athletic endeavor, and Reebok is still number two and trying harder, Nike is the undisputed leader in the athletic footwear battle. According to *Fortune* magazine, when Phil Knight, founder and CEO of Nike, entered the market in 1972, he stated that if he could get "five cool guys" to wear his footwear, the rest of the world would follow suit. Evidently, Knight's comment was visionary, for by 1998, Nike controlled 47 percent of the U.S. market and Nike's overall share of the athletic shoe market was $9.6 billion dollars (Lefton 1998, 9). The famous Nike swoosh, which Knight paid a graduate student $35 to design, is evident in every corner of the globe. Whether one is a professional or amateur athlete, a teenager or a business person seeking comfort, sneakers are an indispensable part of everyone's wardrobe. As the fads and trends of "more air," flashing lights, glow-in-the-dark soles, and celebrity endorsements continue, the price of an individual pair of shoes and the profits of the manufacturers will continue to soar.

—*Joyce Duncan*

See also: Endorsements; Jordan, Michael; Marketing of Sport; Olympic Games

For further reading:

Lefton, Terry. 1996. "Nike über Alles." *Brandweek,* December 9, 25–32.

———. 1998. "Nike Set to Take Jordan Beyond Hoop." *Brandweek,* October 19, 8–9.

Mogelonsky, Marcia. 1996. "Best Foot Forward: The Majority of Men and Women Wear Running or

Other Athletic Shoes Every Day." *American Demographics* 18, no. 1 (March): 10.

Sellers, Patricia. 1998. "Four Reasons Nike's Not Cool." *Fortune*, March 30, 26–28.

SOCCER

The world's favorite spectator sport, soccer has long had only a limited following in the United States, primarily among recent immigrants and ethnic minorities, despite its emergence as a popular participation sport among U.S. youth at the end of the twentieth century. Association football, as soccer was called, emerged as the most popular code of football among British schoolboys in the mid-nineteenth century. Relatively disorganized variants of football were exported to the United States before soccer's rules were formalized in 1863. The rugby-like "Boston game" was adopted by Harvard and other northeastern universities, and by the end of the century, it had further evolved into Walter Camp's distinctive "gridiron" brand of football. Subsequently, soccer quickly assumed the secondary, minority status it would hold throughout the twentieth century.

> *The rest of the world's favorite spectator sport, soccer has long had only a limited following in the United States, primarily among recent immigrants and ethnic minorities.*

Through the 1950s, soccer persisted in scattered pockets, primarily in working-class immigrant communities of the northeast such as Fall River, Massachusetts. Attempts to establish soccer as a commercial spectator sport were largely unsuccessful, but during the 1920s, early soccer clubs produced some noteworthy players. Aging stadiums and economic depression took their toll during the 1930s; by 1941, the number of registered soccer clubs in the United States had fallen from over two hundred to eight. Rather than making soccer a widely followed spectator sport, these early leagues cemented soccer's reputation as a "foreign" game played by immigrants and prone to outbreaks of working-class violence.

In 1968, two floundering year-old leagues merged to form the North American Soccer League (NASL). The NASL blossomed with the landmark signing in 1975 by the New York Cosmos of the world's greatest player, Brazil's Pelé. Other aging foreign stars soon followed him, and by the time Pelé retired in 1977, the NASL had expanded to twenty-four teams. This proved to be overexpansion, however, and the 1984 season, with only nine teams competing, was the NASL's last.

However, the seed planted by the NASL finally bore fruit on November 19, 1989. Paul Caligiuri's late-minutes goal against Trinidad and Tobago sent the United States to the 1990 World Cup in Italy, placing the U.S. national team on the world's premier soccer stage for the first time in forty years. That feat would be repeated in 1994, thanks to a guaranteed spot as the host country, and in 1998. Caligiuri's goal helped establish the national team as soccer's primary vehicle for publicity in the United States, enabling the sport to partially shed its foreign image.

Caligiuri's goal represented another, more important dimension in the development of soccer in the United States. Unlike his predecessors early in the century, Caligiuri learned the game in a suburban, middle-class southern California community. He thus represented soccer's rise after 1970 as a popular participation sport among middle-class youth in the United States. Fueled by the fitness craze, the momentary popularity of the NASL, and the rapid rise of girls' and women's sport, soccer became a favorite alternative to traditional U.S. games. Parents liked soccer because it was less violent and cheaper to equip than American football; children liked it because it was more active and more welcoming to those shut out of other sports by their size or gender. By 1995, nearly eight million children under age twelve were playing organized soccer, second only to basketball.

The long-term impact of soccer's popularity as

By 1995, nearly eight million children under age twelve were playing organized soccer, second only to basketball.
(HUGHES MARTIN/CORBIS)

a youth sport and the successes of the men's and women's national teams during the 1990s has not been established, although the women's national team won the first women's World Cup in 1991. In 1996, yet another attempt at a national professional league, Major League Soccer, debuted with ten teams and enough television and advertising support to carry it safely into the twenty-first century. Likewise, soccer continued to grow as a participation sport, especially among adults. But soccer has yet to be established as a major spectator sport in the United States. For most Americans, it remains a mystery, a strange activity for kids and "foreigners."

—*Peter S. Morris*

See also: Latino Sport; do Nascimento Edson Arantesm "Pelé"

For further reading:
Fortanasce, Vincent, Lawrence Robinson, and John Ouellette. 2001. *The Official American Youth Soccer Organization Handbook: Rules, Regulations, Skills and Everything Else Kids, Parents and Coaches Need to Participate in Youth Soccer.* New York: Fireside.
Gambetta, Vern. 1998. *Soccer Speed.* Sarasota, FL: Gambetta Sports.
Luxbacher, Joe. 1999. *Attacking Soccer.* Champaign, IL: Human Kinetics Publishers.

SOCKALEXIS, LOUIS FRANCIS
(1871–1913)

One of the first Native Americans to play major league baseball, Louis Sockalexis embodied the ambivalence inherent in the Noble Savage stereotype and inspired the name of Cleveland's entrée into the American League: the Indians.

Born on the Indian Island reservation in Old Town, Maine, Sockalexis was a member of the Bear clan of the Penobscots. Educated in Catholic schools, he excelled on the track, the gridiron, and the diamond. His talent for baseball eventually made Sockalexis a regular on semiprofessional teams throughout the state. While playing in the Knox County League, Sockalexis so impressed one of the coaches, Gilbert Patten, that Patten later used him as a model for the character Joe Crowfoot in his popular Frank Merriwell series.

Athletic ability earned Sockalexis entry to Holy Cross College in 1895 and to the University of Notre Dame in 1897. He soon came to the attention of the Cleveland Spiders of the National League, who signed him to a contract. Despite a fleeting career spanning only ninety-four contests over three seasons, Sockalexis impressed many experts as one of the potential greats of the game. At his noblest, Sockalexis was thought of as possessing almost supernatural powers. Admirers likened his speed to that of the wind, an eagle, or a deer and dubbed him the "Deerfoot of the Diamond." The strength and accuracy of his arm drew comparisons to lightning bolts. However, for all his native nobility and natural talent, Sockalexis could not escape the alternate characterization of the Native American as a savage. A contemporary poem portrayed him in war paint ready to scalp the umpire. Spectators routinely greeted Sockalexis with war whoops and began to deride his team as the Indians. Sockalexis was no match for the taunts of fans and the temptations of society. Alcohol was his downfall, and as his fondness for liquor waxed, his fitness to perform waned. Neither entreaties nor enticements prevented the self-destructive behavior that brought about his release from baseball in 1899.

Sockalexis headed back to New England and played in the minor leagues for a few years. He finally returned to Indian Island, where he operated the local ferry in the summer and worked as a woodcutter in the winter. In his spare time, Sockalexis continued to play, coach, and umpire the game he loved. His life came to a tragic end at a lumber camp in Burlington, Maine, on Christmas Eve, 1913, when he succumbed to heart failure. In the pocket of his coat were found worn clippings of his exploits as the original Cleveland Indian.

Sockalexis's enduring legacy as the inspiration behind the team name began in 1915. In response to a contest to rename the Cleveland Naps of the American League, a fan who recalled the battle cry often heard during Sockalexis's playing days suggested "Indians." What began as a tribute to a fallen legend has evolved over time into a redfaced, toothily grinning caricature known as Chief Wahoo, to whom latter-day fanatics pay homage with face paint, rhythmic chants, drum beats, and tomahawk chops.

—*David L. Richards*

See also: Baseball; Merriwell, Frank; Native American Athletes; Native American Mascots; Political Correctness; Team Names

For further reading:

McDonald, Brian. 2003. *Indian Summer: The Tragic Story of Louis Francis Sockalexis, the First Native American in Major League Baseball.* Emmaus, PA: Rodale Books.

Rice, Ed. 2003. *Baseball's First Indian, Louis Sockalexis: Penobscot Legend, Cleveland Indian.* Windsor, CT: Tidemark Press.

SOFTBALL

Softball is one of the most popular team sports in the United States, with over forty million people of all ages participating on a sustained basis. Softball has been played in the United States for more than one hundred years. The game was originally a variation of baseball meant to be played indoors. To facilitate playing the game indoors, the legs of the diamond were made shorter and the ball used was larger and softer. By the beginning of the twentieth century, however, Americans began playing the game outdoors. Originally called by a variety of names, such as "indoor baseball" and "kitten ball," the name "softball" did not become commonly used until the mid-1920s, at which time the rules also became standardized.

Primarily an outdoor summertime sport, softball is played by people of all ages and all levels of skill. Softball can by played as slow pitch or fast pitch, and the size of the softball can vary between twelve inches and sixteen inches in circumference. Because of these variations, softball is accessible to a greater number of people than some other team sports. Persons can participate in single-gender or coed leagues. The game is played at all levels of competition, from casual recreational and church league events to highly competitive national tournaments, such as the Amateur Softball Association's national championships in slow pitch and fast pitch. However, despite attempts to organize, no professional softball leagues exist. Although millions of people play softball, it is not a spectator sport. Media coverage is scarce, and only a few books on softball have been published, the vast majority of which are merely instructional. Furthermore, softball has had few nationally renowned players.

Softball was one of the few team sports available to women in the 1930s, 1940s, and 1950s. Prior to the 1930s, more women played baseball than softball; however, by the mid-1930s, most women's baseball teams had been disbanded, and new softball leagues and teams were formed across the country. Since most colleges did not have intercollegiate sport for women, most women athletes competed only in industrial or recreational leagues.

During the 1930s, softball proved popular around the nation. In 1933, the newly formed Amateur Softball Association sponsored its first national fast-pitch tournament for women, coinciding with the World's Fair in Chicago. Only sixteen teams competed the first year, but the tournament fielded thirty-seven teams for the world title in 1941. Teams were represented from cities as diverse as Cleveland, Phoenix, New Orleans, and Chicago.

Women's participation in softball increased significantly during World War II as more women worked in war industries and played on company-sponsored softball teams. A similar trend was occurring in U.S. colleges. By 1943, softball had replaced baseball on the list of the ten most popular collegiate women's intramural sports.

During the middle decades of the twentieth century, softball, like other athletic endeavors, was not considered ladylike. Therefore, teams attempted to feminize the game by having players

> *Softball is one of the most popular team sports in the United States, with over forty million people of all ages participating on a sustained basis. Softball has been played in the United States for more than one hundred years.*

sport attractive uniforms, including satin skirts or shorts. Similarly, most women's softball teams sported names that suggested femininity, such as the "Maids" or the "Cuties."

Joan Joyce dominated women's softball during the 1960s and 1970s. She was recorded as having the world's fastest pitch, clocked at 118 miles per hour and compared to the men's record of 108. While attending college in California during the early 1960s, Joyce played for the local team, the Orange Lionettes, leading her team to the national title. Additionally, with the Raybestos Brakettes, she brought home eleven national championships. In her twenty-two seasons of pitching, Joyce lost only 33 games and won 509, including 105 no-hitters. Her dominance in softball helped prove that women could perform athletically as well as men.

Beginning in the 1960s, U.S. colleges added more women's intercollegiate sport programs, which gave the best women athletes the opportunity to break out of the recreational and industrial leagues. Since the passage of Title IX, many Division I colleges have awarded athletic scholarships in softball to women.

Softball is no longer just a substitute for baseball. The sport is becoming recognized as an independent game. In 1996, the Olympics added softball as an official sport for women, and the first Olympic gold medal in softball was won by the U.S. team led by Dot Richardson. The Olympic acceptance of the sport has given young softball players new heights to which to aspire.

—*Laura A. Purcell*

See also: All-American Girls Professional Baseball League; Baseball; Olympic Games; Title IX

For further reading:

Dickson, Paul. 1994. *The Worth Book of Softball: A Celebration of America's True National Pastime.* New York: Facts on File.

Woolum, Janet. 1988. *Outstanding Women Athletes: Who They Are and How They Influenced Sports in America.* Phoenix, AZ: Oryx Press.

SPECIAL OLYMPICS

Founded in 1968 by Eunice Kennedy Shriver, the sister of John F. and Robert Kennedy, the Special Olympics countered the experts of the era who felt that the mentally and physically challenged should not compete in sport because losing would be psychologically harmful. By the end of the twentieth century, the Special Olympics had over one million participants from fifty-two countries. The events, open to anyone eight years old and older with an IQ of 75 or below, were modeled on the international Olympic Games, featuring many of the same events but considering all participants to be winners. In this sixteen-sport competition, every entrant receives a ribbon

A competitor at the starting line in a race at the Special Olympics held at the University of California, Los Angeles (ca. 1990).

(JOSEPH SOHM/CHROMOSOHM INC./CORBIS)

or a medal, in addition to an embrace from his or her assigned "hugger," volunteers who encourage the athletes from the sidelines or finish line.

Asked by President John F. Kennedy in 1961 to write a report on recreation and physical education for a presidential panel on the mentally retarded, Shriver discovered how little research had been done in the field. The next summer, she converted the family's estate in Maryland to a day camp for one hundred challenged youngsters. Within days, under her tutelage and with the help of high school volunteers, she had the campers swimming, climbing trees, and using bows and arrows.

A tireless campaigner, Shriver procured corporate sponsorship from the Civitans, McDonald's, Coca-Cola, and other companies, eventually setting up a worldwide foundation with revenues in excess of $40 million. There is no federal subsidy for the program; each state or foreign country finances its own athletes, customarily through fund-raising or corporate sponsorship. Parents of the athletes pay only for transportation to and from the events.

According to a study conducted by Texas Technological University, participants in the Special Olympics improve significantly in physical movement and in self-esteem.

—*Joyce Duncan*

See also: Olympic Games

For further reading:

Bueno, Ana, and Rafer Johnson. 1994. *Special Olympics: The First 25 Years.* Petaluma, CA: Foghorn Press.

Dinn, Sheila, Eunice Kennedy Shriver, and Nicole Bowman. 1996. *Hearts of Gold: A Celebration of Special Olympics and Its Heroes.* Woodbridge, CT: Blackbirch Press.

SPORT CARDS

By providing a means for connecting with athletes, sport cards have mirrored the changing perceptions of professional sport and have grown from a childhood hobby to a multibillion-dollar industry. The first sport cards were produced in the late 1880s as inserts for cigarette packs. These cigarette cards became popular collectibles among smokers over the next thirty years as a number of brands competed for the smokers' business. By the early 1910s, the cigarette card market had all but disappeared, whereas cards issued with candy became increasingly popular, especially among U.S. youth.

Sport cards were first packaged with gum in the early 1930s, and this type of card dominated the industry for the next fifty years, as sport cards became an important part of youth culture. The cards not only provided a connection with athletes, especially in the pretelevision era, but also were used as a form of currency: they were bought, traded, and used in gambling games, such as card flipping.

> *By providing a means for connecting with athletes, sport cards have mirrored the changing perceptions of professional sport and have grown from a childhood hobby to a multibillion-dollar industry.*

From the mid-1950s until 1980, the Brooklyn-based Topps Gum Company dominated the sport card industry. This period coincided with a slow but steady growth in the number of adult card collectors. In 1981, Topps's monopoly came to an end as a number of new sport card producers entered the market. In the following years, the sport card market experienced incredible growth in popularity, and the rapid increase in card values made collecting less of a childhood hobby and more of an adult-oriented industry. This transition culminated in the sale at auction of a T206 tobacco card featuring baseball player Honus Wagner for a record price of $451,000 in 1991.

—*Jeffrey S. Obermeyer*

See also: Fads and Trends; Marketing of Sport; Popular Culture and Sport

For further reading:

Larson, Mark K., ed. 1993. *The Sports Card Explosion: "Sports Collectors Digest," 1973–1993: Two Decades* of America's Hottest Hobby as Seen through the Pages of "Sports Collectors Digest." Iola, WI: Krause.

SPORT IN WARS

Sport and war have long been associated in the minds of Americans, with many considering sport a perfect preparation for the battlefield. The relationship between sport and war is hardly a phenomenon original to the United States—the connection goes back to Homeric legend and the original Olympic Games and continued through the Middle Ages and the Renaissance—but Americans have emphasized the pairing. From the Civil War on, no history of the United States at war is complete without some description of the role of sport in training the citizen-soldier or as a diversion for both soldiers and citizens.

For personnel on active duty, sport has been at least partly an element of training. Indeed, U.S. military leaders have long advocated sport as the best preparation for war, noting a rough similarity between the tactics and physical efforts involved in both games and battle. Individual combat sport like boxing and wrestling are essentially part of basic military training. The service academies stress team sports, and Army and Navy teams often made it to the top of college football rankings.

> Sport and war have long been associated in the minds of Americans, with many considering sport a perfect preparation for the battlefield.

Sport has also served as an important diversion for Americans, both citizen-soldiers and the general population, during wartime. Baseball's initial popularity owes much to Civil War troops, who frequently played a primitive form of the game along with others both in garrisons and in prisoner of war camps. Twentieth-century U.S. troops likewise carried their sport equipment into combat zones. During World War II, the U.S. government sent touring teams of professional and talented amateur players to entertain troops in remote locations overseas. During the slow return to peacetime characterizing the end of major wars, sport often became a key element in occupying the occupiers, allowing troops to burn off steam while awaiting demobilization. Though professional leagues frequently altered their seasons during wartime, ostensibly to put all able-bodied men into uniform and to conserve fuel, those leagues generally continued to operate with minimal interruption. Maintenance of the status quo and the need to keep up the illusion of normalcy have inevitably won out in policy decisions; pennant races are too important to the morale of both the troops and the citizenry to stop play altogether. Sport has provided a means of forgetting, at least briefly, the horrors of war.

Sport has played an important role in U.S. political diplomacy outside of wartime. From Moe Berg's all-star spying in 1930s Japan and Jesse Owens's upsetting of Hitler's dreams in the 1936 Olympics to cold war battles centering on Olympic Games in Helsinki (1952), Moscow (1980), and Los Angeles (1984), sport has been prominent on the world political stage. In addition, the 1980 U.S. hockey team's victory over the Soviet team was laden with cold war military-political significance. Ironically, the original Olympic Games were intended partly to celebrate a truce from war.

War has entered the U.S. idiom via metaphors transferred from the military to sport and from there to other realms, certainly including politics. Tactical terms such as "game plan," "offense," "defense," "platoon player," "blitz," and "pick off" as well as such terms as "shelling" and "bombing" and even organizational titles like "the Big Red Machine" all derive from war.

—*Mark D. Noe*

See also: Army-Navy Rivalry; Language of Sport; Olympic Games

For further reading:

Ambrose, Stephen. 1996. *Duty, Honor, Country: A History of West Point.* Baltimore, MD: Johns Hopkins University Press.

Anderson, Dave. 1996. *The Story of the Olympics.* Southbury, CT: Birch Tree.

Atyeo, Don. 1979. *Blood and Guts: Violence in Sports.* London: Paddington.

Dawidoff, Nicholas. 1994. *The Catcher Was a Spy.* New York: Pantheon.

SPORT JOURNALISM

Sport journalism developed alongside sport. During a century and a half of growing cultural interest in sport, the mass media, first newspapers and then radio and television, have interpreted sport for their audiences, to the profit of both the teams and the media outlets. Professional sport first gained popularity during the nineteenth century, and sport journalism was both a catalyst for and a beneficiary of that popularity. That symbiotic relationship remains, as the mass media find sport reporting a prime attraction for audiences, while sport organizations recognize the promotional value and income potential of media coverage.

Sport journalism began in Great Britain in 1824 with the publication of the first sport journal, *Pierce Egan's Life in London and Sporting Guide.* Like most of the sport journals that followed, both in Great Britain and the United States, the publication reported on pastimes that interested the privileged class: horse racing, yachting, and hunting.

Sport journalism made its first strong impact in the United States later in that century. As distinctly U.S. sports like football and baseball began to grow in popularity, urban newspapers began to report on these sports as a way to increase circulation. Nineteenth-century sport reporting featured loquacious, overwritten prose that, in the absence of other media, allowed readers to experience the sporting event by reading about it. Leaders in the trend to promote sport journalism were the so-called yellow journalism newspapers. The *New York World,* published by Joseph Pulitzer, established the first separate department of sportswriters in 1883, and William Randolph Hearst's *New York Journal* was credited with developing the first separate sport section in 1895. However, the pejorative association with yellow journalism lowered sport journalists' professional reputation among their peers.

Sport journalism flourished during the period following World War I, when such heroes as Babe Ruth, Red Grange, and Jack Dempsey captivated fans. During that decade, radio also grew in popularity as a sport-broadcasting medium because of its ability to transmit events live, as they happened, to listeners. Much like the prose on the sport pages of the nineteenth century, sport broadcasters described the game using vocal techniques and verbal descriptions that were as entertaining as the game itself. Newspaper sport sections had to change their focus from descriptions of the event to statistical analyses and features about athletes.

The Depression and World War II diverted the nation's attention from sport. During the postwar baby boom era, however, television emerged as the new medium, and it brought immediacy and diversity to sport journalism. Although team owners first feared that television coverage might have a negative impact on attendance, they soon appreciated its income potential. During the 1960s and 1970s, the relationship between television and sport expanded. Television networks paid millions of dollars to sport organizations, both professional and amateur, for the rights to broadcast their events. Income from these arrangements also contributed to the rise in player salaries that began in the 1970s.

In the 1990s, sport journalism comprised a variety of media and styles: from daily newspaper sport pages and sport magazines, both spectator and participant, to call-in radio programs and cable-television networks. The financial relationship between sport and the media remained as strong as ever; broadcast rights to events cost networks hundreds of millions of dollars but media companies easily recouped their costs by charging high rates for commercial time.

—*John Carvalho*

See also: Marketing of Sport; *Sports Illustrated;* Television, Impact on Sport

For further reading:

Bender, Gary, and Michael L. Johnson. 1994. *Call of the Game: What Really Goes On in the Broadcast Booth.* Chicago: Bonus Books.

Eisenstock, Alan. 2001. *Sports Talk: A Journey inside the World of Sports Talk Radio.* New York: Pocket Books.

Schultz, Brad, and Mike King. 2001. *Sports Broadcasting.* Boston: Focal Press.

SPORT LAW

Law permeates nearly all aspects of sport, affecting relationships among leagues, teams, athletes, agents, officials, and spectators. "Sport law," however, refers only to the application of law to amateur and professional sport. Rather than being a separate area of the law, sport law spans such traditional legal fields as contracts, torts, labor relations, agency, trademarks, copyrights, constitutional law, and regulatory law.

Professional sport is regulated primarily by contracts, the most important of which is the collective bargaining agreement. In each of the four major professional sports (baseball, football, basketball, and hockey), a players' association, or union, represents the players and negotiates with the league to reach a collective bargaining agreement that establishes a standard contract. The standard contract may address such important issues as benefits, physical conditioning and examinations, player participation in other dangerous activities, standards of behavior and team discipline, injuries and medical care, assignment or trading of the contract to another team, severance pay, and free agency. Within the standard contract, the player, often assisted by an agent, and the team negotiate such specifics as salary,

performance incentives, and duration of the contract. The professional league's constitution and bylaws also regulate the sport, particularly relations between the league and its teams.

Amateur sport is regulated by many organizations, such as state high school athletic associations and the National Collegiate Athletic Association (NCAA). Schools voluntarily join these associations, agreeing to follow their "laws." These organizations establish rules of eligibility for athletes—such as limitations on age, years of eligibility, scholastic standing, recruitment, transfer to other schools, financial aid and gifts, and contacts with professional agents—and are authorized to impose penalties on violators, whether athletes or programs. Leagues and coaches may also impose rules on amateur athletes; such rules are valid if they reasonably relate to a legitimate sport's purpose. The International Olympic Committee (IOC) and the U.S. Olympic Committee (USOC) govern Olympic athletes.

Other laws limit the authority of governing organizations, schools, and coaches to regulate amateur and professional sport. For example, Title IX of the federal Education Amendments of 1972 prohibits gender discrimination in any program receiving federal educational funds. Antitrust statutes, enacted to prevent monopolies, have also affected sport, except professional baseball, which is exempt from antitrust law. Antitrust issues have arisen in several contexts, such as "reserve clauses" (which grant a team the right to renew a player's contract indefinitely, thus preventing that player from ever playing for another team) and league rules prohibiting a team owner from owning part of another major sport team. Constitutional issues may also arise when a public high school or state college enacts rules that limit athletes' freedoms, for example, to speak on public issues or to marry.

Tort laws allow a person whose injuries were caused by the wrongful intentional or negligent conduct of another to be compensated by the wrongdoer. Possible "sports torts" include athletes suing other athletes for injuries inflicted beyond the scope of the game; athletes suing coaches or schools for injuries from inadequate supervision, instruction, or equipment; spectators suing facility owners for injuries incurred from dangerous conditions at the stadium; and spectators suing other spectators or athletes for violence inflicted on them at sporting events.

—*David E. Fitzkee*

See also: Discrimination, Racial, in Sport; Supreme Court Decisions; Title IX

For further reading:

Appenzeller, Herb, ed. 1998. *Risk Management in Sport: Issues and Strategies.* Durham, NC: Carolina Academic Press.

Greenfield, Steve, and Guy Osborn, eds. 2000. *Law and Sport in Contemporary Society.* Portland, OR: Frank Cass.

SPORT LITERATURE AS DISCIPLINE

During the 1980s and 1990s, the literature of sport became an important subdiscipline within the field of English studies, one supported by a broad range of high-quality courses, academic research, and scholarly criticism. Sport literature's rise to respectability involved several factors. The emergence of such other subdisciplines in English departments as popular culture studies and multicultural studies made room for sport literature by expanding both the literary canon and the parameters of scholarly research. In addition, the importance of sport in the United States, signaled by a dramatic rise in participation in sport and in public interest in spectator sport, made sport an area of inquiry that academe could not ignore. Most important has been the quality of literature and film about sport created since World War II, works whose insightful portrayals of U.S. life demanded scholarly attention. Influential literary works include Bernard Malamud's *The Natural*

(1952), John Updike's *Rabbit, Run* (1960), Jason Miller's *That Championship Season* (1984), and significant films include *Chariots of Fire* (1981), *Personal Best* (1982), and *Field of Dreams* (1989).

Scholarly works such as Wiley Umphlett's *The Achievement of Sports Literature* (1983) and Christian Messenger's *Sport and the Spirit of Play in American Fiction* (1981) signaled the arrival of the new subdiscipline. Currently, researchers are producing scholarship in which sport literature is a lens through which to examine gender and race relations; the relationship between sport and identity; pressing ethical dilemmas; classism; religion; politics; our use of traditions, myths, and language; and several other important topics. Some of this scholarship is found in *Aethlon*, the only academic journal devoted exclusively to sport literature.

—*Don L. Deardorff II*

See also: Film and Sport; Literature, Sport in

For further reading:

Higgs, Robert J. 1981. *Laurel and Thorn: The Athlete in American Literature.* Lexington: University Press of Kentucky.

Johnson, Don, ed. 1996. *Aethlon: The Journal of Sport Literature* 14, no. 1.

SPORT SLANG

Sport has contributed many slang terms, particularly those related to sex and violence, to the U.S. lexicon. Many of these terms are reflected in metaphors that are used outside the sport world in such fields as business, law, and politics; other terms reflect the desire for sexual conquest or have other scatological connotations.

According to Cheris Kramarae, in *Women and Men Speaking* (1981), sport metaphors are used for two main reasons: to express the strategic and competitive nature of a situation and to accomplish male bonding and thus the exclusion of females. In many formerly exclusive professions, such as law, sport terms are used primarily by men, out of context and for a variety of meanings. Men tend to bond through sport rhetoric, even if their only athletic pursuit is watching a game, and this conversational style, whether employed consciously or unconsciously, occasionally creates exclusionary discourse for their distaff counterparts. Males tend to view women who infiltrate this male bonding domain of sport metaphor as unfeminine, and this disdain is often reflected in reverse as the last bastion of male dominance, particularly in the language of football, when coaches refer to weak players as "girls" or "ladies." On the other hand, athletic women are called "tomboys," "jocks," or "lesbians," and their athletic competitions are traditionally referred to as "women's games" rather than simply "games." Some of the sport terms frequently used in the world of work are "cheap shot," "pulling one's punches," "playing hardball," "leveling the playing field," "Monday morning quarterback," and "balls."

Another area in which metaphors abound is sport reporting, which traditionally lends itself to images of violent competition. The winning team may have stuffed, battled, blasted, murdered, stomped, mutilated, gunned down, or destroyed its competitor. It appears to be a U.S. tendency to glorify violence as our athletic heroes slaughter, pummel, clobber, and assault each other in the name of good, clean fun.

Another area in which out-of-context sport language is used is in describing sexual activity. Young men, in particular, are socialized to use sport euphemisms for sexual prowess and conquest. From the initial "getting to first base" to "scoring" to "hitting a home run," sport terms are intertwined with and inseparable from sexual acquisition.

—*Joyce Duncan*

See also: Language of Sport; Metaphor, Sport as, for Life

For further reading:
Kramarae, Cheris. 1981. *Women and Men Speaking.* Rowley, MA: Newbury House.

SPORTS ILLUSTRATED

Long considered the most important magazine in sport publishing, *Sports Illustrated* is viewed as a pioneer in high-quality sport journalism and as having been instrumental in developing a national sport audience. *Sports Illustrated* was created by the founder of Time, Incorporated, Henry Luce, in 1954. Initially, advertisers were reluctant to buy space in a publication covering spectator sports that were viewed as appealing only to boys and working-class men. This attitude propelled Luce and Sid James, the magazine's first managing editor, to target an audience of wealthy men of leisure, devoting as much space to boating, hunting, fashions, and travel as to baseball. Luce failed to recognize and capitalize on the growing leisured middle classes of the postwar period; consequently, periodical sales lagged below one million from 1945 to 1955, and the magazine failed to turn a profit.

It was only when Andre LaGuerre took over as managing editor in 1960 that *Sports Illustrated* developed the coherent focus on spectator sports that defines the current writing; this new focus had an immediate impact on circulation. LaGuerre's concern with high-quality sportswriting made the magazine a showcase for such sport journalists as Dan Jenkins and Jack Olsen, whose 1968 series "The Black Athlete," detailing the exploitation felt by African American athletes, sent shock waves through the ranks of collegiate and professional sport recruiting. In 1972, Olsen followed up this series with one on women and sport, a series that earned the periodical its first National Magazine Award for journalism. Investigative pieces on corruption in sport and colorful essays from high-profile authors such as George Plimpton characterized the magazine throughout the 1960s and 1970s. Through the 1980s and into the 1990s, the periodical became a big business, with more than three million subscribers, and diversified into a wide range of media, including a cable-television network, videos, books, and spin-off magazines for women and children. *Sports Illustrated* has also licensed its familiar logo for numerous products.

Swimsuit Issue

Undoubtedly, *Sports Illustrated*'s most famous—or infamous—creation is the Swimsuit Issue. First published in 1965 as a filler for the slow postfootball period of late January and February, the Swimsuit Issue was the brainchild of Jule Campbell, the magazine's fashion editor. Campbell selected healthy "girl-next-door" types, going against the Twiggy-thin fashion trend of the decade, and photographed them in exotic locales with a travelogue premise. The issue proved to be the best-selling one of the year, guaranteeing its return as a regular feature.

The issue also generated more reader complaints and subscription cancellations than any other feature of the periodical. In 1978, the Swimsuit Issue created a new round of controversy when it displayed a photograph of popular model Cheryl Tiegs in a wet, transparent mesh bathing suit. Although it created an initial uproar, this type of shot has since become a standard feature of the issue. In 1996, the Swimsuit Issue featured the periodical's first African American cover model, pairing Tyra Banks with a white model.

Complaints from many quarters about the issue's representation of women grew increasingly vocal in the 1980s and 1990s, forcing the magazine to publish the Swimsuit Issue as a separate publication from the regular editorial and feature content of the magazine. *Sports Illustrated* obviously has no plans for ending the issue, which remains the most lucrative feature of the magazine and spawns a variety of merchandising spin-offs, including calendars and videos.

—*Stephanie Dyer*

See also: Photography, Sport in; Plimpton, George

For further reading:

Davis, Laurel. 1997. *The Swimsuit Issue and Sport: Hegemonic Masculinity in "Sports Illustrated."* Albany: State University of New York Press.

Hoffman, Steven. 2001. *"Sports Illustrated" Knockouts: Five Decades of "Sports Illustrated" Swimsuit Photography.* New York: Time-Warner.

Sports Illustrated: Fifty Years of Great Writing. 2003. New York: Time-Warner.

SPRING TRAINING

Major league baseball's spring training has been described as both an annual ritual unique to North American culture and an industry typical of U.S. big business. Spring training is the preseason period during which ballplayers prepare for the regular season and team managers select their major league squads. Actually older than the two major leagues that form the National Commission of Baseball, the practice of spring training dates to the late nineteenth century. By the twentieth century, it had evolved into a major business enterprise in Florida and Arizona and a cultural symbol of the beginning of spring.

Some observers credit the saloon keepers of the North with the creation of spring training. Beer drinking was a favorite pastime of the professional ballplayers, and many saloon keepers contributed to the ballplayers' indulgences by providing them free beer in the hope that their patronage would draw baseball fans as paying customers. This became a problem in the off-season, when players were growing fat in local taverns, prompting some managers to proclaim a need for preseason conditioning for their players.

Whatever his motivation, William "Boss" Tweed of Tammany Hall sent his New York Mutuals to New Orleans, Louisiana, in 1869 for what may have been the first spring training of a professional team. Over the next fifty years, major league teams traveled regularly to the South in the spring for some type of preseason training. On their way back north from training camps in places like New Orleans; Washington, D.C.; Charleston, South Carolina; Jacksonville, Florida; and Hot Springs,

Yogi Berra makes a play at home plate during a Yankees' spring training game (1953).
(BETTMANN/CORBIS)

Arkansas, they often barnstormed with local teams. In 1908, the first permanent spring training site was established in Marlin Springs, Texas, by the New York Giants, who returned to Marlin Springs every year until World War I.

Florida did not develop into the center for spring training until after World War I. From the beginning, Floridians recognized the economic benefit that would accrue from luring a major league baseball team to spend the spring in their towns. Both the teams and baseball fans would spend money and boost local business. Civic and business leaders in St. Petersburg played a major role in turning spring training into an organized event. In the 1910s, local boosters began actively

recruiting teams to train in their city, which at the time was a little fishing hamlet. Early attempts to keep a team returning each spring failed until the city, under the leadership of Mayor Al Lang, a baseball fan and astute businessman, built a waterfront park in 1922. The new stadium brought the Boston Braves to St. Petersburg, and they returned until 1937, when the New York Mets replaced them. The Braves brought a 300 percent increase in the number of New England tourists to Florida each year. In 1925, Lang lured the New York Yankees to St. Petersburg. He was also instrumental in settling teams in Tampa, Sarasota, and Clearwater. By 1929, ten of sixteen major league teams were training in Florida and competing with one another in what became known as the Grapefruit League.

By midcentury, the month-long spring training season had developed into a major business enterprise in Florida and Arizona. In the early 1960s, fifteen of the twenty-four teams training in Florida pumped $30 million into the economy. Three decades later, with twenty teams, that figure had increased more than tenfold. Between 1983 and 1993, attendance at demonstration games more than doubled, to 1.6 million ticket buyers. Nearly three-fourths of all tickets were sold to revenue-generating tourists coming from outside the state. By that time, spring training had triggered high-stakes bidding between Florida communities wanting a major league team. Cities without baseball built multimillion-dollar sport complexes and offered attractive revenue packages to seduce teams away from Arizona, Texas, and other Florida cities. In return, the major league teams netted millions of dollars each spring.

Another side of spring training is reminiscent of the ritual holiday games of early America. To baseball fans of both North and South, more than nature signals a change in seasons. Sport pages throughout the country announce the coming of the vernal season with the opening of training camps, and thousands of northern fans follow their teams south for an early spring. For nearly twelve years, from 1980 to 1992, Red Barber, a sportscasting pioneer, helped popularize that spring ritual. Every Friday morning on the National Public Radio program *Morning Edition,* he reinforced the connection between sport and spring by mixing discussions of the latest events in baseball with reports on spring blossoms.

—*Jack E. Davis*

See also: Baseball; Big Business, Sport as

For further reading:
Arsenault, Raymond. 1988. *St. Petersburg and the Florida Dream.* Norfolk, VA: Donning.
Edwards, Bob. 1993. *Fridays with Red: A Radio Friendship.* New York: Simon and Schuster.

STADIUMS

Beyond serving as arenas for sporting events, modern stadiums often reflect a city's personality to a national audience, provide a colorful and spirited gathering place for fans, and establish an atmosphere advantageous for the home team. Originating with Greek and Roman amphitheaters and coliseums in ancient times, modern U.S. stadiums host mainly college and professional football, baseball, and soccer. These facilities take many forms, from sprawling, open-air arenas to domes with artificial turf, air conditioning, and retractable roofs.

On fall weekends, football stadiums become the focal point of mass migrations. Fans flock to these facilities each year to picnic, or "tailgate," around the stadiums until time for kickoff. During the games, fans take pride in the home-field advantage created by their cheering and boisterous behavior, which they hope will disrupt the other team's efforts. The noise inside many stadiums has been found to approximate the sound level of a jet aircraft at takeoff.

Over time, college football stadiums grew dramatically, to the point that many major college teams claim on-campus facilities larger than any professional arena. In the Southeastern Conference, for example, over half of the teams play in stadiums seating more than 80,000 fans. The University of Tennessee's Neyland Stadium, the largest in college football, seats over 100,000, while Auburn's stadium regularly welcomes 85,000, a crowd three times larger than the city's population.

Frequently, stadiums are the subject of sharp debate between the owners of professional football and baseball teams and their host cities. A number of owners, occasionally citing loss of potential revenue, have threatened to relocate their franchises if they are not provided, by their city's taxpayers, with a new stadium or more favorable terms for the existing one, and a few owners have actually carried through with the threat. Two such moves in the 1990s reflected the range of public sentiment over team relocations. The Oilers' move from the

Astrodome in Houston to a residence in Tennessee was greeted with general apathy by both areas, whereas the Browns' abandonment of Cleveland created a firestorm of controversy between the owner and the fans. However, in an age of player strikes and lockouts, for many fans, such disputes generally served to erode much of the existing sense of loyalty toward their local professional teams.

Dual-purpose stadiums, built mostly by professional teams in the 1960s and 1970s to host both baseball and football, tended to hold little appeal for fans and ultimately served neither sport very well. Thus, numerous U.S. cities replaced them with more traditionally designed baseball or football facilities, carefully created to furnish excellent sight lines for spectators and television cameras, to provide a more exciting and entertaining experience for the fans, and to evoke the feeling of the grand ballparks of an earlier era. These new stadiums, such as Camden Yards in Baltimore, Maryland; Turner Field in Atlanta, Georgia; and The Ballpark in Arlington, Texas, have been met with an overwhelmingly positive response from the fans, the players, and the communities.

At their best, stadiums reflect the grand old traditions and memories of sport, as well as the promise of the best of modern technology and architecture. From the century-old ballparks to the state-of-the-art complexes, stadiums span the history of modern sport and connect the games and the players with the fans on a personal level, year after year and generation after generation.

—*Van Plexico*

See also: Houston Astrodome; Yankee Stadium

For further reading:
Jewell, Don. 1978. *Public Assembly Facilities: Planning and Management.* New York: Wiley.

STATISTICS OF SPORT

Even those who are mathematically challenged can often rattle off box scores, runs batted in, point spreads, and yardages without being aware that they are engaged in statistical computation. Statistics, from the simplest scoring of the game to the most complex analysis of prediction, is an integral part of sport and of U.S. culture. Numbers and formulas thus generate terminology and enter the language of daily conversation about sport favorites and winning teams.

In sport, statistics are viewed as the tabulation of data, leaving the layman the joy of its interpretation. In fact, much of spectator involvement with sporting events has to do with statistical interpretation of data ranging from baseball, football, and basketball statistics to the track record of a favored filly at a horse race. Batting averages, runs batted in, earned run averages, yards per carry, pass yard distances, free-throw percentages, and other numbered accolades are often considered more a measure of achievement than the actual winning or losing of a game. Consequently, for example, often the final score in a baseball game is less important than the number of hits achieved by an individual player, as witnessed by the home-run race between Mark McGwire and Sammy Sosa in the summer of 1998.

Statistics generate revenue for teams and players, aid the inveterate or novice gambler in selecting likely winners, offer legal sport books and illegal bookies odds for increasing their coffers, and give the layman an understanding of statistical reasoning. Even those who are antimathematics become involved with the statistics of sport, often memorizing statistics and formulas that are integrated into everyday speech.

—*Joyce Duncan*

See also: Gambling; Home-Run Race of 1998

For further reading:
Bennett, Jay. 1998. *Statistics in Sport.* New York: Arnold.
Richards, Jack, and Danny Hill. 1974. *Complete Handbook of Sports Scoring and Record Keeping.* West Nyack, NY: Parker Publishing.

STENGEL, CASEY (1890–1975)

During a career in baseball that spanned over forty years, Casey Stengel captured the imagination of the U.S. public through his success as well as his wit and amusing quotes. Stengel began his career in professional baseball in 1910. Even early in his career, he had a reputation for an unusual sense of humor. During one game in 1919, he approached home plate to the jeering of the fans, and as he tipped his hat to them, a small bird that he had hidden flew from underneath. In 1949, Stengel was hired as the manager of the New York Yankees, and it was there that he had his greatest

Baseball's "grand ole man" New York Mets manager Casey Stengel, in spite of his team's many losses, had quite a few fans. Youths scramble for his autograph before a Mets-Cardinals game at the Polo Grounds (August 8, 1963).
(BETTMANN/CORBIS)

professional success. He led the Yankees to seven World Series titles during his twelve-year tenure.

Stengel is best remembered for what he said rather than what he did as a player and a manager. In public he spoke his own unique language, dubbed "Stengelese" by sportswriters. Stengelese quotes are famous for being witty, as well as for being long-winded and often nonsensical. Stengelese reached its zenith when Stengel was asked to testify on behalf of baseball in front of the Senate Subcommittee on Antitrust and Monopoly in 1958. He delivered an hour-long rambling dissertation during which he said little of substance and made almost no sense.

In 1962, Stengel became the manager of the New York Mets expansion team. He was a beloved leader of this team of lovable losers, and the New York media and fans hung on his every word. Stengel retired from managing in 1965 and was elected to the National Baseball Hall of Fame in 1966.

—*Jeffrey S. Obermeyer*

See also: Baseball; Language of Sport

For further reading:

Berkow, Ira, and Jim Kaplan. 1992. *The Gospel according to Casey: Casey Stengel's Inimitable, Instructional, Historical Baseball Book.* New York: St. Martin's Press.

Cataneo, David. 2003. *Casey Stengel: Baseball's "Old Professor."* Nashville, TN: Cumberland House.

Creamer, Robert W. 1996. *Stengel: His Life and Times.* Lincoln: University of Nebraska Press.

STEROIDS

Difficult to detect and seemingly impossible to eliminate from sport, anabolic steroids have increasingly become the drug of choice for both elite athletes seeking to enhance athletic performance and adolescents seeking to enhance their body image. Synthetic derivatives of the male hormone testosterone, steroids emphasize the hormone's muscle-building effect and its masculinizing, or androgenic, effect. Legally used in the medical community to treat certain conditions and illnesses, such as breast cancer, osteoporosis, endometriosis, and anemia, steroids increase lean body mass and strength and decrease body fat. Although the use of steroids to improve athletic performance is difficult to prove scientifically, athletes have experimented with massive doses of the drug in order to increase muscle mass and to intensify training regimens. For the past twenty-five years, the practice has been officially proscribed, yet it is maintained by an estimated $1 billion black market.

> *Of the estimated one million steroid users in the United States, many take these drugs for noncompetitive, cosmetic bodybuilding purposes.*

First synthesized in 1935, testosterone and its primary derivatives, the anabolic-androgenic steroids, were first used by West Coast body builders in the 1940s. News of the efficacy of steroid use in international sport came to the United States through the work of John Zeigler, the team physician at the World Weight Lifting Championships held in Vienna, Austria, in 1954. Russian doctors later confirmed Zeigler's suspicion that the Soviet team was experimenting with steroids. The Ciba Company introduced the first U.S. anabolic steroid, Dianabol (methandrostenolone), in 1958, and the steroid epidemic was born.

Generally restricted in the 1950s to athletes in strength-intensive sports, such as the field events in track and field and weight lifting, steroid use throughout the 1960s quickly entered other sports, including swimming, cycling, skiing, volleyball, wrestling, handball, bobsledding, and soccer. Although banning steroids was considered necessary as early as 1967, it was not until 1975 that the Medical Commission of the International

Olympic Committee (IOC) officially added steroids to the list of banned doping agents.

Despite being designed to suppress steroid use in sport, drug-testing programs have been seriously flawed since they were first implemented at the 1976 Innsbruck and Montreal Olympic Games. Procedures typically lacked the sensitivity needed to detect steroid use, and many elite athletes and corrupt officials learned to avoid detection through illegal practices, including the application of blocking agents.

Regardless of the prohibition of performance-enhancing drugs by national and international sports and government agencies, the use of steroids continued unabated. The political pressure on athletes to achieve success at all costs as well as the considerable financial and personal rewards to be gained from athletic prowess contributed to the escalation in the use and production of the drug. Bolstered by an increasingly sophisticated pharmaceutical industry as well as by the widespread cultural rationalization of everyday drug use, steroids have infiltrated competitive sport at all levels. Numerous high-profile athletes have been tainted by steroid use, most notably Canadian sprinter Ben Johnson and Irish swimmer Michelle Smith. Systematic and federally orchestrated programs of steroid use in East Germany and more recently in China, as well as the scandal associated with the 1998 Tour de France, demonstrated the ubiquity of steroid use.

In addition to being for many people a denigration of the ethics of sport, steroids in large doses also pose considerable danger to athletes. Their negative side effects include liver damage, gastric ulcers, personality changes, fluid retention, and cancer. Among the many highly publicized athletes whose deaths have been linked to steroid use are bodybuilder Norman Rausch, high school football player Benji Ramirez, and Oakland Raiders defensive lineman Lyle Alzado.

Steroid use is also well documented among male athletes in colleges and high schools and, more recently, among even younger populations. Of the estimated one million steroid users in the United States, many take these drugs for noncompetitive, cosmetic, bodybuilding purposes. Many athletes and nonathletes alike continue to experiment with performance-enhancing drugs, including human growth hormones, insulin derivatives, and creatine.

—*Jeffrey O. Segrave and Patricia C. Fehling*

See also: Olympic Games

For further reading:

Yesalis, Charles E., ed. 1993. *Anabolic Steroids in Sport.* Champaign, IL: Human Kinetics Publishers.

SULLIVAN, JOHN L. (1858–1918)

The athletic career of John L. Sullivan parallels the transformation of boxing from the domain of local, urban, ethnic, working-class leisure into popular entertainment for a national consumer market. An Irish American from Boston, Sullivan began his career as a bare-knuckles boxer. He subsequently reigned over the sport during its early development under the Queensbury rules, which allowed for gloves, shorter rounds, and a more consumer-oriented style.

Sullivan's engaging public personality and dominance of professional boxing in the late nineteenth century have earned him a place among the first major U.S. heroes of popular culture. Sullivan was legendary for his loud manner, generosity, and honesty in an age of modernization and increasing corporate regimentation. His personality flaws and drinking exploits were as essential to his public image as were his toughness and bravery in the boxing ring. His crude, aggressive boxing style won him admirers nationwide, though those admirers were chiefly male.

Although a remarkable eight-month national tour in 1883 and 1884 established Sullivan as a public figure in the national consciousness, his most legendary exploit was his 1889 knockout of Jake Kilrain in Richburg, Michigan. The long, brutal fight occurred in the twilight of Sullivan's career and was the last bare-knuckles match on a national stage. The fight's ambiguous position illustrated the transitional nature of boxing during the era: the fight was held illegally, since most states did not sanction the sport, yet Sullivan's knockout received national press coverage and solidified his legend among men of every class and region in the United States.

Sullivan was more than a sport figure: the rise of public information and transportation networks in the Gilded Age helped transform him into a hero for popular consumption on a national scale.

—Aram Goudsouzian

See also: Athletes as Symbolic Heroes; Boxing

For further reading:

Isenberg, Michael T. 1988. *John L. Sullivan and His America.* Urbana: University of Illinois Press.

SUMO WRESTLING

Practiced by Japanese immigrants and their descendants in the United States since the late 1800s, sumo was an important part of Japanese American culture prior to World War II. In recent years, the success of Hawaiian-born sumo

Hawaiian-born sumo wrestler Akebono, Japan's first foreign-born yokozuna *or sumo grand champion, seen performing a sacred ring-entering ritual at Tokyo's Meiji Shrine.*
(REUTERS/CORBIS)

wrestlers in Japan has led to a resurgence of popularity for the sport in the United States. A deceptively simple sport, sumo wrestling involves two men competing to push each other out of a small ring. Known as the national sport of Japan, sumo has roots in Japanese Shinto ritual and retains much of its religious connection.

Japanese immigrants, who began to arrive in Hawaii and on the U.S. mainland in 1885, brought sumo to the United States. Visits by Japanese professional sumo wrestlers to the immigrant communities in Hawaii and on the West Coast in the 1910s inspired great interest in the sport. In fact, until the outbreak of World War II, sumo was a major activity in the Japanese American community, particularly in Hawaii and in central California. Tournaments pitting leading contenders from various communities against one another or featuring visiting Japanese teams wrestling against local Japanese American teams drew crowds in the thousands. Because of sumo's association with Japanese culture and nationalism, the outbreak of war with Japan temporarily ended sumo activity in the United States.

However, by 1965, Hawaiin-born wrestler Jesse Kahaulua, given the sumo name Takamiyama in Japan, began a long and illustrious professional sumo career in Japan, opening the doors for other Americans to follow. In 1993, another Hawaiian wrestler, Akebono, née Chad Rowan, attained the pinnacle of the sport, *Yokozuna*, or grand-champion status. He and other Americans have led to sumo's increased popularity in Hawaii and throughout the United States.

—*Brian Niiya*

See also: Immigrants, Community and Sport; Martial Arts Films

For further reading:
Cuyler, P. L. 1979. *Sumo: From Rite to Sport.* New York: Weatherhill.
Hall, Mina. 1997. *The Big Book of Sumo: History, Practice, Ritual, Fight.* Berkeley, CA: Stone Bridge Press.

SUPREME COURT DECISIONS

Public opinion often holds that the Supreme Court of the United States has given professional sports special legal status, even though it never has. However, baseball, boxing, and football have all been involved in antitrust suits in the Supreme Court. Antitrust laws protect trade and commerce from unfair practices or monopolies. Baseball was first sued in 1920, and it is the only professional sport to escape the antitrust laws. Justice Oliver Wendell Holmes Jr. created this anomaly in *Federal Club v. National League* (259 U.S. 200 [1922]). The case arose when the existing major leagues wrecked the new Federal League. The Baltimore Club, the Federal Baseball Club of Baltimore, sued, claiming that the interference was illegal. Justice Holmes ruled that baseball was not interstate commerce and, thus, was not subject to antitrust laws. The leagues obviously operated across state lines, but Holmes insisted that their business was giving exhibitions in various states and that the rest was incidental.

Baseball was established as "the national pastime" in the twentieth century, attracting new audiences, first on radio and then on television. It also became more and more profitable. Players wanted to share in those profits, but the "reserve clause" in the standard contract bound a player to his original club for life and meant that no club could offer him more money. Team owners defended this as absolutely necessary to preserve the stability of the game, which they argued was different from any other business. They appealed to the fans who valued baseball as a traditional game, and many fans, indeed, feared that a free market would allow the richest clubs to sign all the stars.

Twice, the Supreme Court reluctantly refused to overturn Holmes's 1922 ruling. George Toolson, a minor league pitcher with the New York Yankees, wanted to move to another club in order to play in the majors. He hoped that the Court would see baseball as a national business and subject it to the antitrust laws. A majority of the judges answered that Congress, not the Supreme

Court, should eliminate the baseball exemption.

The Court made a similar ruling two decades later when it decided in *Flood v. Kuhn* (407 U.S. 258 [1972]). The St. Louis Cardinals had unceremoniously sent Curt Flood to the Philadelphia Phillies, but he refused to go. He asked the federal court to stop the trade and to allow other clubs to make him offers. Again, the Supreme Court decided that the original decision exempting the reserve clause should stand until Congress reversed this legal anomaly. In both cases, the press and much of public opinion applauded the decision as the only sensible means to preserve baseball.

Holmes is often misquoted as saying that baseball was a game and not a business. Another court used similar words, but the Supreme Court has never doubted that baseball and other professional sports are businesses. The mistake came to be widely believed, however, because Holmes's decision was a complete victory for the owners over the players. It must have seemed as if the Court had accepted the owners' claim that they were merely organizing games. Despite Flood's loss in the Supreme Court, the players knew that they worked in a business, and they organized the Major League Baseball Players' Association. Within a few years, the union had eliminated the reserve clause.

—*Ian Mylchreest*

See also: Baseball; Sport Law; Title IX

For further reading:

Freedman, Warren. 1987. *Professional Sports and Antitrust.* New York: Quorum Books.

Sullivan, Lawrence, and Warren S. Grimes. 2000. *The Law of Antitrust: An Integrated Handbook.* St. Paul, MN: West Wadsworth.

White, G. Edward. 1995. *Justice Oliver Wendell Holmes: Law and the Inner Self.* New York: Oxford University Press.

SWIMMING

Swimming, a popular recreational activity and amateur sport, has provided many opportunities for both female and male athletes. Recreational swimming first became common in the mid-nineteenth century, when swimming schools began teaching the breast stroke, the side stroke, and later the crawl stroke. The first national competitive swim meet was held in 1883, and the sport was included in the first modern Olympic Games in 1896.

By the twentieth century, swimming had become a widespread hobby. The Young Men's Christian Association (YMCA) made lessons widely available when it began teaching swimming in 1910. In addition, magazine articles encouraged women to learn to swim because it promoted grace and endurance, and in 1912, swimming became one of the first Olympic events for women. Swimming produced many women stars. Annette Kellerman, for example, became famous in the second decade of the twentieth century as a diver and long-distance swimmer. She introduced a one-piece swimsuit to replace the cumbersome bathing dresses that had previously limited women's mobility in the water. In 1926, Gertrude Ederle gained fame as the first woman to swim the English Channel.

The Billy Rose Aquacade, a water show presented on Broadway and at the 1939 World's Fair, featured performances by such amateur swimming champions as Esther Williams, who went on to star in a series of water-ballet musicals for Metro-Goldwyn-Mayer (MGM) in the 1940s and 1950s. Commercial water shows declined in popularity, but synchronized swimming became an Olympic event in 1984. Professional competitive swimming never became popular; however, swimming remains common as a recreational activity and amateur sport.

—*Debbie Ann Doyle*

See also: Film and Sport; Olympic Games

For further reading:

Colwin, Cecil M. 1992. *Swimming into the 21st Century.* Champaign, IL: Leisure Press.

Whitten, Phillip. 1994. *The Complete Book of Swimming.* New York: Random House.

SYNCHRONIZED SWIMMING

Synchronized swimming, or "synchro," grew out of the increasing popularity of swimming and aquatic displays in western Europe in the late nineteenth century. As a growing number of pleasure seekers spent their leisure time on the beaches of England and Germany, the number of drowning incidents increased dramatically, creating a need for trained lifeguards. In North America, the growth of seaside culture, competitive swimming clubs, lifeguard training, basic aquatics education, and a desire to be entertained by exotic, scantily clad aquatic bodies provided a rich context for the emergence of the sport and art of synchronized swimming.

In 1907, Australian swimmer Annette Kellerman was paid $5,000 per week to perform skills akin to modern synchronized swimming in a glass tank at the New York Hippodrome. Seven years later, the same year that the Amateur Athletic Union (AAU) entered women in competitive swimming races for the first time, Kellerman starred in Fox Film's *A Daughter of the Gods*. Other swimming stars such as Johnny Weissmuller, Eleanor Holms, and Esther Williams became aquatic actors, performing breath-holding feats, dives, endurance swims, and tricks in staged events or on Hollywood film sets. In 1916, the modern Olympic Games opened a handful of events to women, setting the stage for the United States to send its first women's swimming team to Antwerp in 1920. Synchro, however, remained in the realm of art and entertainment until the 1940s.

Prior to 1940, U.S. interest in water ballet, floating formations, and rhythmic and ornamental swimming was localized in colleges. Coeducational synchro programs arose primarily in schools that offered lifeguard training. The swimmers in these early programs trained for exhibitions and water shows rather than for competition. In 1934, for example, Katherine Whitney Curtis of the University of Chicago coached sixty female swimmers, the Modern Mermaids Club, to perform in the lagoon at the Century of Progress at the Chicago World's Fair. Eventually, the publicity surrounding aquatic entertainment created an increasing demand for training and competition.

On May 29, 1939, as part of the Annual Teachers' Day program, Chicago Teacher's College competed against Wright Junior College in coeducational group stunt swimming. In the wake of this event, the Central Association of the Amateur Athletic Union (CAAAU) held competitions in water ballet and duet. The AAU accepted duet and team synchronized swimming as a competitive sport in 1941 and as a national sport in 1945. However, the same decade that saw synchro become "officially" competitive also found a culture ripe to consume it as a feminine and heterosexual visual entertainment. Esther Williams, for example, denied her opportunity to swim at the 1940 Olympics because of World War II, became Hollywood's sexy modern mermaid and starred in such films as *Bathing Beauty* (1944), *Neptune's Daughter* (1949), and *Million Dollar Mermaid* (1952). Though often cited as the first or "ideal" synchro swimmer, Williams is not singularly representative of the artistic strand of synchro history. In the early 1950s, some athletes began to move away from the monotony of training for competition toward developing synchro as a high art akin to modern dance, emphasizing choreography and performance. The leader of the Aquatic Art movement was ex–national solo champion Beulah Gundling, who established the International Academy of Aquatic Art in 1955.

The same historic moment that saw Gundling and Williams succeed also saw the rise of elite, competitive synchronized swimming. In the early 1950s, Canada and the United States successfully lobbied the Fédération Internationale de Natation Amateur (FINA) to sanction synchronized swimming as an official aquatic sport for women. Both countries sent synchro swimmers and officials to demonstrate and promote the new sport at the Pan-American Games and the Olympics. In the

1960s and 1970s, second-wave feminism drove open the gates of the sporting world to girls and women, and synchro became a staple event at the Pan-American Games, the World Aquatics Championships, the Pan-Pacific Games, and the Olympics after 1984.

The legacy of synchronized swimming in U.S. sport and culture situates it uncomfortably between "competitive sport" and "entertainment." Even Title IX legislation did not lead to the typical increase in participation seen in other women's scholarship sports, such as women's basketball, soccer, or volleyball. Today, girls, boys, men, and women can compete in sanctioned U.S. Synchronized Swimming Novice, Age Group, Junior Olympic, College, and Masters competitions. Only girls and women, however, can compete officially on the international stage, and their status as athletes is often questioned. Although actual aquatic art performances are rare today, the concept of "modern mermaids" remains problematically intertwined with the status of synchronized swimmers and synchronized swimming in a male-dominated competitive sporting culture.

—*Laura Thomas*

See also: Film and Sport; Olympic Games; Swimming; Title IX

For further reading:

Rackham, George. 1979. *Synchronized Swimming.* Philadelphia, PA: Transatlantic Arts.

Williams, Esther. 2000. *The Million Dollar Mermaid: An Autobiography.* With Digby Diehl. San Diego, CA: Harvest Books

T

TEAM COLORS AND SYMBOLS

Occasionally sport teams change their colors or symbols to increase their credibility as a violent competitor or to increase marketing revenues, which produces a subsequent economic impact on the culture. Sport teams alter uniform colors and logos in search of increased merchandising sales, their chunk of the $10-billion-a-year retail market, garnered through the licensing, or granting of permission, to use an image to stimulate sales. If sales are lagging due to poor fan support, teams often change their image or their uniforms and encourage fans to identify with particular colors and symbols to net their fair share of the marketing pie. That this identity exists is evident in the ballpark or field clamor, which may include shouts such as "Come on, Blue" or "Way to go, Big Red."

In addition, teams change colors and logos to increase their professional viability. Studies, such as one conducted in 1988 by the American Psychological Association, have conclusively proved that color affects not only merchandising but also a team's professional image as tough competitors. It is no accident that black is one of the most popular team colors in both the National Football League (NFL) and the National Hockey League (NHL); black is the embodiment of the dark side, of evil, and of vicious contenders. There are no pastel uniforms in these sports. Black uniforms connote aggression and formidable intimidation, and nearly one-third of the teams in the NHL and 20 percent of those in the NFL wear black. The color does more than psychologically intimidate competitors, however; players wearing black appear to "play dirtier," and referees often deliver more penalties to those players and teams.

Even those teams who wear lighter colors have no doubt studied the psychological effects of color: there are no yellows, but there is gold, the color of the aristocracy; blues are royal or navy, probably reflecting the tie of professional sport to the rigor of the military; and orange is the tradiional color of the hunter who seeks out and slaughters his prey. In addition, the symbols, names, and logos selected by teams indicate violence and aggression: lions, tigers, bears, panthers, lightning bolts, and pirates to name a few.

Color selection not only draws on the psychology of frightening the enemy but is reflected in merchandising as well, with black and silver, the colors of the Los Angeles Raiders and other teams, netting the largest profit. Although ticket sales, television, and advertising create enormous revenue for sport teams and franchises, merchandising and the psychology behind it pull in astronomical profits for the athletic community. From the first baseball cards in packs of chewing gum in 1887 to the explosion of sport-themed paraphernalia, from bowling balls to birdhouses, in

361

the mid-twentieth century to the million-dollar sales collected through the reproduction of old uniforms in the 1980s to the familiar sight of emblems and logos on everything in the 1990s, sport and the moneys it generates are everywhere.

—*Joyce Duncan*

See also: Apparel, in Sport; Marketing of Sport; Team Names

For further reading:
Tannsjo, Torbjorn, and Claudio Tamburrini, eds. 2000. *Values in Sport.* New York: Routledge Press.

TEAM NAMES

Sport teams play a unifying role within a community. Consequently, the name and mascot chosen for the team, whether at the beginning level of sport or in the professional ranks, create an identifiable relationship between the team and its community.

During the early 1900s, common nicknames used by sport teams on all competitive levels were fierce animals, such as the Tigers, the Lions, the Wildcats, or the Bears. Also among the more popular team names at the turn of the century were simple ones, such as the Red Stockings, the White Sox, and the Athletics. Those gave way to industry-related nicknames like the Pistons and the Packers in the mid-1900s.

Representations of Native Americans, such as the Indians, the Redskins, the Braves, and the Redmen, were originally popular sport team names and mascots. Unfortunately, they were generally stereotypical misrepresentations of Native American heritage and culture. The National Congress of American Indians and the American Indian Movement have set about to educate the public on the way a name and caricature like "Redskins" can offend persons and be tied to racism. However, many Native Americans have been open to the use of specific tribal names, such as the Seminoles.

In 1992, the Portland *Oregonian* announced that it would no longer use sport team names that readers might find offensive and banned all sport references to Indian people. The paper was joined two years later by the *Minneapolis Star-Tribune*, which eliminated all but tribal references.

Consequent name changes by Miami University of Ohio, from Redskins to Redhawks, and Saint John's University, from Redmen to Red Storm, show the influence associated with this educational movement. In addition, a number of Big Ten Conference institutions have banned mascots that depict American Indians from athletic events. The tilt toward political correctness has produced sport tags like the Heat, the Magic, the Ravens, the Wiz, and the Metrostars—all names that lack a potentially offensive double meaning. Often, industry consultants are hired to create original, exciting names.

The explosion of sport in the 1990s, in addition to the popularity of team sport apparel, increased the creativity of nicknames. The Twisters, the Diamondbacks, the Timberwolves, the Blue Jackets, the Warthogs, and the Banana Slugs are some monikers created by naming consultants or via community write-in polls. Communities in the market for new sport franchises sometimes hold name-the-team lotteries in which anyone with an idea has input.

On the other hand, there was public dissatisfaction with the Tampa Bay Devil Rays' choice of a name associated with evil spirits, and the Washington, D.C., basketball team altered its original name from the Bullets due to a public outcry about its glorification of violence associated with guns.

—*Scott A. Misner*

See also: Marketing of Sport; Native American Mascots; Team Colors and Symbols

For further reading:
Donovan, Michael Leo. 2001. *From Yankees to Fighting Irish: What's behind Your Favorite Team's Nickname?* Lenexa, KS: Addax.

Lessiter, Mike. 1987. *Name That Team! The Who, What, Where, and Why behind How Ninety-Eight Professional Sport Teams Obtained Their Nicknames.* Brookfield, WI: Lessiter.

TELEVISION, IMPACT ON SPORT

The impact of television on sport has profoundly influenced both the way the games are played and the competitiveness of the teams that play them. As a result, professional sport has changed in ways that are often in conflict with the interests of fans. In the early years of broadcasting, some of the more popular sports, such as baseball and football, were less than enthusiastic about having games broadcast on television. The new medium would be welcome, but only insofar as it did not interfere with the game or the gate receipts. It soon became apparent, however, that there was a great deal of money to be made by selling broadcast rights to television networks. As professional sport received increasing amounts of broadcasting revenue, the "games" became a business, and the character of the ownership of professional teams began to change. Sport ownership was no longer a trifling thing or an expensive hobby; it had become an excellent investment opportunity.

Investment in sport teams not only promised high economic returns but also provided an excellent opportunity to generate favorable public relations and to reap valuable publicity. Many investors were attracted by the security and complexity of the tax structure that often allowed them to apply team or seasonal losses as a deduction against taxes on other sources of income. Thus, a positive cash flow was usually generated from the sport enterprise. Not surprisingly, many corporations, such as the Walt Disney Company and the Chicago Tribune Newspapers, Inc., began to diversify into ownership of professional sport clubs.

With the lure of generous financial support as the incentive, organized professional sport began "marketing" itself for television. Tradition was often abandoned, as rules, styles, and attitudes were changed to make organized sport more attractive to the camera angles. These changes and adaptations of rules, styles, and traditions were at times reluctant, gradual, solicited, or unsolicited, but they were almost always inevitable.

The lifeblood of the functional relationship between sport and television is money. The financial support that television offers organized sport is essential to sport's profitability and competitiveness. However, in major league baseball, the huge television contract the New York Yankees receive gives them a competitive advantage, allowing them to spend more money on free agents than any other team in baseball. Without the lucrative broadcast rights fees that many professional teams receive from television, the financial structure of these clubs would collapse, and it is likely that a team would not be competitive. In the early 1960s, the national broadcasting rights for major league baseball (MLB), the National Basketball Association (NBA), and the National Football League (NFL) could be measured in hundreds of thousands of dollars, gradually moving into millions of dollars toward the end of the decade. By the late 1990s, however, the NFL had a television rights deal for $18 billion over eight years, the NBA had a $2.64 billion contract covering four years, and MLB had a $1.7 billion deal for five years.

Ostensibly, in exchange for financial considerations, organized sport simply sells their broadcast rights. It is commonly accepted, however, that these sports frequently will do more than that: they will change their schedules, playing locations, rules, and sometimes the very game itself—all for the express purpose of making themselves more marketable for television.

It can be said that television's first priority is to the advertising business of which they are a part. Television executives are constantly restructuring and repackaging their product offerings so their programs become better vehicles for a sales message. Top priority is given to developing programs that reach not only large numbers of people but also viewers with desirable demographic characteristics. Sport telecasts are desirable because of their ability to deliver predominantly adult male audiences, unlike the typical prime-time program, which attracts significantly more women than men viewers. This difference in gender demographic allows the networks to package advertising for sport that have more appeal to the male viewers.

Prior to the early 1960s, most changes in sport were implemented with the idea of either improving the game per se or making it more interesting for live spectators. However, as sport figures became increasingly aware of the opportunities to earn substantial amounts of money through the medium, they altered their thinking to be more in line with the desires of the television industry. When the resulting changes took place, sports received a good deal of criticism from fans who saw their favorite teams change into businesses, unaware of the fact that sport had for many years made decisions solely for business motives.

Not surprisingly, the realities of commerce do not coincide with the necessities of sport. College football teams routinely change both the time and the date of their games at the request of television networks, seemingly giving scant regard to ticket holders who may be inconvenienced by changes in schedules. Major league baseball now schedules all its World Series games at night to attract a larger television audience, despite the fact that a night game in some northern cities, especially in Canada, can be fairly chilly during October.

In addition, professional golf changed from match to medal, or stroke, play in order to guarantee prospective television sponsors attractive celebrity golfers for their telecasts in the final stages of an event. Television networks like sport packages that fit into a neat time slot to increase a program's salability to prospective sponsors. In response, organized sport has aided television by altering dates, times, venues, and rules. For example, the NFL cut the halftime intermission from

twenty minutes to fifteen minutes so the program could fit more comfortably into a two-and-a-half-hour segment. Tennis introduced a tiebreaker to end the drawn-out deuce games. In golf, the National Open Championship's thirty-six-hole ordeal on the final day was spread over two days to get more mileage out of the event for television. The National Hockey League (NHL) changed its centerline to a broken line so it would be more visible to a television audience. Major league baseball designated Friday, the least watched night on television, a travel date no matter how close together the teams were.

Sport purists tend to think of athletic events as "sport" or as "games"; networks and independent stations, however, view sport as a product, something to be bought, packaged, and sold to advertisers. Many critics and fans feel organized sport makes too many concessions to television, all for the sake of increased revenue. Nonetheless, owners, administrators, and players' associations seem more than willing to make these changes, which they undoubtedly feel are to their advantage, at least monetarily. In the 1967 Super Bowl, for example, the Green Bay Packers went through a second kickoff to the Kansas City Chiefs because officials called time-out *during* the first kickoff because the network was in midcommercial.

Television has also had a strong influence on the competitive structure of professional team sport. It has long been argued that the more money a team can spend on such things as players, scouting, facilities, and administrative personnel, the more likely the team is to produce a championship-contending team on a perennial basis. This seems to be the case for major league baseball and the National Basketball Association but it seems less the case for the National Football League. Local broadcasting rights are an important source of revenue in professional baseball and basketball but a minor one in professional football, where over 90 percent of the broadcasting revenue comes from a league contract with the networks, shared equally by all members of the NFL. Consequently, teams in smaller television markets are less likely to succeed in baseball and basketball than in football. Compounding this problem for small-market teams is the lure of major media markets for superstars as they become free agents. Many athletes are well aware of the potential for lucrative endorsements and other entertainment options in major media centers and are eager to test their marketability. These media opportunities were probably the major reason why Shaquille O'Neal left the championship-contender Orlando Magic for the Los Angeles Lakers.

The marriage between television and sport is one that has drawn each into a situation of increasing interdependence. Although it is undoubtedly true that television could exist without sport programming, the web of financial commitments has become so involved that any attempt to disentangle the relationship would cause sport to completely reorganize the way it operates, leave television with a deep void to fill, and force millions of fans fundamentally to alter the way they spend their leisure time.

—*Donald E. Parente*

See also: Blackouts, Television; Economics of Sport

For further reading:

Barney, Robert K., Stephen R. Wenn, and Scott G. Martyn. 2002. *Selling the Five Rings: The International Olympic Committee and the Rise of Olympic Commercialism.* Salt Lake City: University of Utah Press.

Goldlust, John. 1987. *Playing for Keeps: Sport, the Media and Society.* Melbourne, Australia: Longman Cheshire.

Johnson, William O., Jr. 1971. *Super Spectator and the Electric Lilliputians.* Boston: Little, Brown.

Sandvoss, Cornel. 2003. *A Game of Two Halves: Football, Television and Globalisation.* New York: Routledge.

THORPE, JAMES "JIM" FRANCIS
(1887–1953)

The most celebrated Native American athlete in U.S. history and perhaps the best all-round male athlete of his day, Jim Thorpe became an international sport hero, a symbol of Native American athletic prowess, and an unwilling pawn in the early-twentieth-century struggle over the definition and proper role of amateurism. The son of "mixed-blood" parents, Thorpe, also known as Wa-tho-huck, "Bright Path," was born and raised in Indian Territory. As an adolescent, he attended the Haskell Indian School in Kansas and later the Carlisle Indian School in Pennsylvania, where he excelled in track and field, baseball, and football. At Carlisle, his coach was the legendary Glenn "Pop" Warner, who brought national attention to the school's football program. During the 1911 season, Warner's publicity staff dubbed Thorpe the "greatest all-around athlete in the world," and after Thorpe's running exploits led Carlisle to a shocking upset victory over a powerhouse Harvard team, the national press began to echo the claim.

At the 1912 Summer Olympics in Stockholm, Sweden, Thorpe lived up to his advance billing, winning both the pentathlon and the decathlon by a wide margin. This remarkable feat captured the imagination of the international press, which soon turned an unassuming Native American athlete into the world's first global sport hero. A ticker-tape parade through the streets of New York City and countless offers from professional sport teams and vaudeville promoters confirmed his celebrity status. That standing was jeopardized, however, when in January 1913 an American Athletic Union (AAU) investigative committee ruled that Thorpe had forfeited his amateur status by playing semiprofessional baseball prior to the Olympics. Although many observers argued that he was being held to an archaic and unreasonable standard of amateurism, Thorpe was forced to return his gold medals, and his name was expunged from the Olympic record book. Following the scandal, Thorpe played six years of major league baseball and later helped found the American Professional Football Association, the precursor of the National Football

Native American Jim Thorpe, regarded as one of the greatest athletes of all time, was given a role in RKO-Radio's She, a picture version of the famous H. Rider Haggard novel of the same name. Thorpe made football history when he played at Carlisle Indian School. As an Olympic athlete, he won the decathlon and set marks that astounded the athletic world. He stood 6' 2" and weighed 215 pounds (June 26, 1935).

League. As player-coach and owner of the Canton Bulldogs in the 1920s, he enlisted the talents of several former Carlisle Indian School players and became one of professional football's first stars.

In the 1930s, burdened by alcoholism and disillusionment with the white sport establishment, he faded into relative obscurity. During Thorpe's lifetime, several attempts to clear his name and restore his Olympic medals proved unsuccessful, but in 1982, the International Olympic Committee belatedly reawarded the medals to his heirs. He won an additional measure of redemption in 1950 when the Associated Press named him the "Male Athlete of the Half-Century," and in 1953, the year of his death, he was the subject of a popular Hollywood film, *Jim Thorpe–All-American.* Characteristically, neither Thorpe nor his struggling family received a share of the film's profits.

For Native Americans, Thorpe's life was a bittersweet saga. Although his remarkable athletic achievements were a source of ethnic pride, the widespread suspicion that the white world had cheated him out of his Olympic medals deepened Native Americans' sense of grievance and victimization. The popular depiction of Thorpe as an animalistic natural athlete reinforced notions of romantic racism, of the Noble Savage, and his unwarranted expulsion from the world of amateur sport prevented him from enjoying the full benefits of his unprecedented fame. Even so, he became a powerful symbol of Native American accomplishment and perseverance.

—*Raymond Arsenault*

See also: Football; Olympic Games; Racial Superiority, Myth of

For further reading:

Newcombe, Jack. 1975. *The Best of the Athletic Boys: The White Man's Impact on Jim Thorpe.* New York: Doubleday.

Wheeler, Robert W. 2003. *Jim Thorpe: World's Greatest Athlete.* Norman: University of Oklahoma Press.

TITLE IX

Women are continually forced to challenge historical notions and cultural biases regarding their social status, but Title IX provided them with the potential to achieve equality on the playing fields of sport. Title IX was implemented to prevent discrimination on the basis of gender at any educational institution that receives federal moneys. The act allows federal agencies to withdraw funding from such institutions if there is discrimination in any area on the basis of sex. Prior to Title IX, one in twenty-seven women played in high school sport, but since passage of the act, one in three participates. Although Title IX did not intend to target athletics specifically, that has become its legacy.

Sport programs, referred to in only 4 percent of the total text of Title IX, have created the most controversy and litigation. Traditionally, athletics were more male-dominated and less scrutinized than any other program or activity in the educational setting.

> *Title IX was implemented to prevent discrimination on the basis of gender at any educational institution that receives federal moneys.*

Although women participated in athletic programs long before the advent of Title IX, the act promoted public awareness about women's sport and changed social attitudes regarding women. The regulations forbid gender-based discrimination in any scholastic, intercollegiate, club, or intramural athletic program offered at any educational institution covered under Title IX. To comply, educational institutions must demonstrate participation by women proportionate to their respective enrollments, must document a history and continuing practice of program expansion responsive to the developing interests and abilities of the underrepresented gender, and must demonstrate that the athletic interests and abilities of students of either gender are equivalently and effectively accommodated.

When Title IX became law, the National Collegiate Athletic Association (NCAA), which had governed only men's intercollegiate athletics since 1906, began to show concern. The association felt that the call for equity would undermine and destroy men's intercollegiate sport; therefore, it vigorously challenged the legislation. Initially, the association tried through judicial and legislative systems to exclude athletics from Title IX, but that move failed. Next, it launched a strong campaign to support the Tower Amendment, which sought to exclude revenue-producing sport from Title IX jurisdiction, but that amendment died in committee. Finally, the NCAA focused on the scope of Title IX's jurisdiction. The association questioned whether Title IX extended to any program in an educational institution that received federal funds, the "institutional" approach, or whether it included only the specific programs that directly received the moneys, the "programmatic" approach. Under the programmatic approach, the athletic programs would not be required to comply with the statute, whereas under the institutional approach, the programs would fall within Title IX's scope. The programmatic approach became important to the NCAA because most schools that received federal money did not apply it directly to their athletic programs. However, the NCAA lost its bid when Congress passed the Javits Amendment, which did not exempt revenue-producing sport from Title IX coverage.

As a final effort, the NCAA began to take control of women's programs, thereby limiting the effect those programs had on men's athletics. This control eventually forced women's athletics to abandon the Association of Intercollegiate Athletics for Women (AIAW), founded in 1971 as an advocate for women's sport, and forced that association to close its doors in June 1982.

On the other hand, women's programs suffered another setback when the U.S. Supreme Court rendered a decision on the issue of "institutional" or "programmatic" approaches in *Grove City College v. Bell* (465 U.S. 555 [1984]). The justices ruled that only programs receiving direct federal assistance fell under the jurisdiction of Title IX.

Few, if any, athletic programs received direct federal aid. However, Congress enacted, over presidential veto, the Civil Rights Restoration Act of 1988, which redefined the terms "program or activity" to mean "any part of college, university, or post secondary institution . . . which is extended Federal financial assistance" (quoted in Villalobos 1990, 162).

Ironically, the Supreme Court provided a stronger impact for women's quest for equality in sport with their decision on February 26, 1992, in *Franklin v. Gwinnett County Public Schools* (503 U.S. 60). The Court's unanimous ruling allows students to sue for damages for sexual harassment and other forms of sexual discrimination. This remedy provided an enormous push for equity in schools and colleges because athletic departments are required to comply with Title IX. If they do not, the institution can face economic loss. In addition, on April 22, 1997, the Supreme Court let stand a lower court ruling that schools must ensure the proportion of female athletes mirrors the proportion of women in the student body. This ruling forces educational institutions to move quickly toward full parity.

Thanks to Title IX, sport participation by women in athletic programs increased dramatically. The law forced athletic programs to provide reasonable outlets for the athleticism and physical competitiveness of their women students. The fact that more women are now active in sport than in any other period in U.S. history suggests that, at long last, women are achieving equal opportunity on the playing field.

—*Scott P. Davis*

See also: Supreme Court Decisions

For further reading:

Heckman, D. 1992. "Women and Athletics: A Twenty Year Retrospective on Title IX." *University of Miami Entertainment and Sports Law Review* 9, no. 1: 1–64.

Kadzielski, M. 1977. "Title IX of the Education Amendments of 1972: Change or Continuity?" *Journal of Law and Education* 6, no. 2: 183–203.

Olson, Wendy. 1990. "Beyond Title IX: Toward an Agenda for Women and Sports in the 1990s." *Yale Journal of Law and Feminism* 3, no. 1: 105–151.

Villalobos, P. M. 1990. "The Civil Rights Restoration Act of 1987: Revitalization of Title IX." *Marquette Sports Law Journal* 1, no. 1 (Fall): 149–169.

TOUCH FOOTBALL

In contrast to the form of contact football played by school leagues and professional teams, touch football makes the game more accessible for people of all ages to enjoy the teamwork and cooperation of American football without the extreme physical contact employed in the traditional version of the game. Since no tackling or roughhousing is permitted in the touch version of the game, the sport can be played for sheer enjoyment without concern about physical safety. Touch football is played like American football with two noticeable differences: each team is composed of only six players, and to stop an opponent, a defender has to touch, rather than tackle, a ball carrier.

The sport was developed during World War II when the U.S. Army decided to use football as a means of conditioning soldiers, raising morale, and teaching teamwork. Because of the scarcity of available materials and the huge numbers of troops being trained, the use of traditional football gear was impractical, and the military decided to play the game without contact. Touch football, as it became known, was extremely popular among the soldiers, and after the war they brought the game home with them.

Since World War II, touch football as a sport has become increasingly popular. Hundreds of leagues thrive in the United States, Japan, China, Australia, and Israel. In addition to recreational leagues, touch football is a popular intramural sport among colleges, and high school girls are allowed to compete in powder-puff leagues. Families and friends also enjoy the sport informally. President John F. Kennedy and his family often played touch football at their family retreat in Hyannisport.

The success of touch football can be attributed to three factors: it can be played by almost anyone, it does not require any special equipment, and it inspires feelings of camaraderie and teamwork.

—*Byron Holland*

See also: Football; Sport in Wars

For further reading:

Little, Mildred J., Linus J. Dowell, and James M. Jeter. 1980. *Recreational Football: Flag, Touch and Flicker.* Dubuque, IA: W. C. Brown.

Stanbury, Dean, and Frank De Santis. 1961. *Touch Football.* New York: Sterling Publishing.

TOURISM, IMPACT OF SPORT ON

Since the late nineteenth century, the relationship between tourism and sport has changed the nature of leisure in U.S. society. Sport has played a tremendous role in the development of the tourism industry in the United States. Since the early nineteenth century, resort developers and government officials have recognized the desire of American tourists to make sport part of their leisure time. Today, sport-related tourism is a multibillion-dollar industry, encompassing activities as diverse as fishing, bungee jumping, and professional football. More important, the relationship between sport and tourism has shaped the nature of leisure in the United States.

The U.S. tourism industry is almost as old as the nation itself. By the late eighteenth century, wealthy aristocrats were frequenting seaside resorts, mountain springs, and other scenic spots, often staying for several months. At these early resorts, hunting, fishing, golf, and tennis were popular pastimes, but they were considered more diversions than true tourist attractions. Climate and scenery attracted the wealthy elite to resort villages, and sport kept them entertained while they were there.

Following the Civil War, however, improved transportation networks, more disposable income, and the emerging consumer culture changed the nature of tourism. As new resort areas opened to more Americans, sport took on increasing importance in leisure pursuits. As a result, resorts across the United States began to use sport to market themselves to potential vacationers. The sports used by these entrepreneurs fell into two broad categories. Formal sports, such as golf and tennis, previously limited to the wealthy elite, were advertised as sports for middle-class Americans. Until the Great Depression, resorts that capitalized on these types of activities saw a demographic shift in their clientele, retaining many of their wealthy visitors while attracting increasing numbers of the middle class. As a result, such sports gained wider followings in U.S. society and achieved mass-market appeal.

Other resorts used outdoor sports to attract visitors. Towns in the West and the Appalachian South capitalized on rising interest in hiking, camping, automobile touring, hunting, and fishing to attract tourists who wanted to enjoy majestic scenery and outdoor recreation. To cater to this new group of outdoor sport enthusiasts, local residents became guides and outfitters and turned property into campgrounds. President Theodore Roosevelt, himself a lover of outdoor sport, helped popularize hunting, fishing, and adventure travel as acceptable and enjoyable ways to spend leisure time. He also helped protect and perpetuate some aspects of outdoor recreation by allotting land to the national park system. In the first three decades of the twentieth century, the states followed suit, creating state parks that provided campgrounds, improved trails, and other types of recreational facilities. New Deal programs, such as the Civilian Conservation Corps and the Works Progress Administration, and state and federal agencies continued the development of outdoor-recreation facilities during the Great Depression, an investment that paid great dividends after World War II.

After 1945, tourism became an activity unrestricted by class lines, a fact that facilitated the further democratization of many sports in the United States. Boating became popular, as did diving and other water sports. In the 1950s, travel agents began to book tours centered on sport themes. Golf tours, in which visitors visited a number of famous or challenging courses, became popular among a growing, highly mobile population. Snow skiing was increasingly considered a vacation sport for the masses as well. Professional sport became more important, and any large city that hoped to attract visitors sought a baseball team and later football and basketball teams. Such professional sport franchises enhanced municipal reputations and brought in larger tourist revenues. By the late twentieth century, Americans, to a large degree, planned their vacations around sport activities, a fact that had a wide range of social, cultural, and economic ramifications.

Sport and tourism in the United States have become more intertwined and interdependent throughout the course of U.S. history. U.S. tourists place a high value on sport-related recreation, a fact that has led to the development of various types of goods and services. Moreover, this relationship has had a profound effect on the nature of leisure in U.S. culture, demonstrating the increasing importance of sport in the United States and reflecting important changes in the socioeconomic organizations of U.S. society.

—*Richard D. Starnes*

See also: Economics of Sport; Fishing, Fly and Bait; Golf; Marketing of Sport; Mountaineering; Outdoor Clubs; Roosevelt, Theodore "Teddy"

For further reading:

Brown, Dona. 1995. *Inventing New England: Regional Tourism in the Nineteenth Century.* Washington, DC: Smithsonian Institution Press.

Spivey, David, ed. 1985. *Sport in America: New Historical Perspectives.* Westport, CT: Greenwood Press.

TREVINO, LEE BUCK (1939–)

Lee Trevino's successes on both the regular and Senior Professional Golfers' Association (PGA) tours have inspired persons of humble origins, provided a hero for his fellow Mexican Americans, and contributed to an improvement of relations among peoples of different ethnic origins. Born in Dallas but a longtime resident of El Paso, Texas, Trevino overcame youthful poverty, limited education, and prejudice against people of Mexican lineage to achieve success on the links and popularity among golf fans. As a youth, he caddied at local clubs and worked at a driving range, picking up skills that served him well during his tenure in the Marines from 1956 to 1960, where he played on the Corps golf team.

Once out of the Marines, Trevino turned professional, qualifying for the PGA tour in 1967. While on that tour, he won twenty-seven PGA events, including six major titles, played in five World Cups and six Ryder Cups, and five times won the Vardon Trophy for the lowest scoring average. In 1989, he joined the PGA senior tour, and in eight years he won almost thirty tournaments. Over time, his personal fan gallery, known as "Lee's Fleas," watched as he became the first golfer to win three national titles—U.S., British, and Canadian—the second to reach $2 million in earnings in 1979, and the first senior to net $1 million in a single season by winning seven tournaments. In recognition of his accomplishments, "Super Mex," as he is called, was elected to the PGA and World Golf Halls of Fame in 1981. Based on his knowledge and personal appeal, he was hired by NBC as a television commentator on golf and by advertising agencies for commercials.

There were problems along the way, however. He was struck by lightning during the Western Open in 1975 and endured several years of serious back pain. Later he tore a ligament in his left thumb and suffered some economic setbacks. But Trevino maintained his composure, his sense of humor, and his work ethic. Though perhaps a bit more subdued and emotionally balanced than before, he moved toward the next century still competitive and popular.

—Joseph L. Arbena

See also: Golf; Professional Golfers' Association

For further reading:

Jackson, Robert B. 1973. *Supermex: The Lee Trevino Story.* New York: Hill and Wang.

Trevino, Lee, and Sam Blair. 1983. *Super Mex: An Autobiography.* London: Arrow Books.

TRIATHLON

Combining swimming, biking, and running into a single athletic event, triathlon has pioneered the multisport craze that includes duathlons, triathlons, off-road triathlons, and adventure racing. The roots of triathlon can be traced to the California coast during the early 1970s. The sport grew out of that decade's running boom when many runners looked for new challenges, while others turned to cross-training for greater cardiovascular fitness. The sport has become synonymous with the Ironman Triathlon held annually in Hawaii since 1978. Through the 1980s and into the 1990s, Americans dominated the sport, led by triathlon's Big Four: Dave Scott, Mark Allen, Scott Molina, and Scott Tinley. By the mid-1990s, however, triathlon acquired a more international look, with German competitors such as Jugen Zack and Lothar Leder and Australians like Greg Welch leading the way. New Zealander Paula Newby-Fraser dominated the women's division for much of the 1980s and 1990s.

Triathlons vary in distance, ranging from sprint triathlons—often a 1-kilometer swim, 25-kilometer bike, and 5-kilometer run—to Olympic-distance triathlons consisting of a 1.5-kilometer swim, 40-kilometer bike, and 10-kilometer run. The longest of triathlons, the Ironman, features a 2.4-mile swim, a 112-mile bike, and a 26.2-mile run and has become a worldwide icon

Participants in the 1983 Ironman Triathlon stand in shallow water waiting to begin the swimming leg of the competition. Kona, Hawaii Island, Hawaii.
(DOUGLAS PEEBLES/CORBIS)

through the marketing efforts of Timex and its Ironman Triathlon watch. Like many other sports, triathlon has had its share of problems: suspicion of drug-enhanced performances, strife between triathletes and the governing bodies, competition from other multisports, and the expense of the sport, including tri-equipment (the gear and clothing used to compete in each of the three events) and travel to competitions. In spite of these problems, triathlon grew as a sport after its addition to the roster of Olympic Games in 2000 in Sydney, Australia, and it continues to appeal to those seeking to benefit from cross-training.

—*Joseph Rice*

See also: Bicycling; Running; Swimming

For further reading:

Cook, Jeff. 1992. *The Triathletes: A Season in the Life of Four Women in the Toughest Sport of All.* New York: St. Martin's Press.

Kearns, Brad. 1996. *Can You Make A Living Doing That?: The True-Life Adventures of a Professional Triathlete.* Palo Alto, CA: Trimarket.

Plant, Mike. 1987. *Iron Will: The Heart and Soul of the Triathlon's Ultimate Challenge.* Chicago: Contemporary Books.

TUNNEY, GENE (1898–1978)

As opposed to the majority of boxers of his era, Gene Tunney was a gentleman of the working class but highly literate. Rather than engage in the violent beating of his opponents, popular at the time, Tunney studied their moves, looked for weaknesses, and used disciplined control to outbox them. Heavyweight-boxing champion in the late 1920s, he is primarily remembered for his fighting style and his pseudo-aristocratic demeanor as a foil to Jack Dempsey in their two classic bouts. At first glance, Gene Tunney seems to have lived the life of the classic American hero: well educated, a war veteran, honest, handsome, and determined. Tunney emerged from humble origins to capture the heavyweight championship

from the legendary Jack Dempsey. Yet, ironically, although Tunney won both of his much-publicized fights with Dempsey in 1926 and 1927, the bouts solidified Dempsey's reputation as an American hero and cast Tunney as his opposite in style and temperament.

In the rambunctious, consumption-oriented 1920s, Tunney failed to capture the public's imagination. A skilled defensive fighter, Tunney chose to outbox his opponents rather than to punish them, a contrast to the aggressive Dempsey. Perhaps more important, Tunney was no man of the people. He frequently carried heavy volumes of English literature with him to impress the sporting press. He spoke in an affected, pseudo-poetic manner, as if he were a character in a Shakespearean play. He further shunned the company of the boxing world in favor of intellectuals and the social elite.

Largely as a result of Tunney's uninspiring style and priggish personality, Dempsey emerged from their two bouts as a celebrity for democratic consumption, a combination of Hollywood glamour and down-to-earth nobility. Tunney, on the other hand, abruptly retired from boxing while still champion in 1928, undefeated in the ring and unpopular outside of it.

—*Aram Goudsouzian*

See also: Boxing; Dempsey, Jack

For further reading:

Evensen, Bruce J. 1996. *When Dempsey Fought Tunney: Heroes, Hokum, and Storytelling in the Jazz Age.* Knoxville: University of Tennessee Press.

Green, Benny. 1978. *Shaw's Champions: The Noble Art from Cashel Byron to Gene Tunney.* London: David and Charles Publishing.

TYSON, MIKE (1966–)

One of professional sport's perennial "bad boys," former heavyweight champion Mike Tyson made headlines throughout the 1990s more for his personal behavior than for his boxing style. Known in the ring as a heavy hitter and a knockout artist, Tyson's name gained household familiarity and public outrage in 1992 when he was convicted of sexually assaulting beauty queen Desiree Washington in his Indianapolis hotel room. Perhaps illustrating a lack of social justice in organized sport in the United States, Tyson spent three years in an Indiana prison and, following his release, returned to the ring and earned between $150 million and $300 million in six subsequent bouts.

Citing his jail-cell conversion to Islam, Tyson assured an eager media and curious fans that he would focus his pugilistic temperament on the ring. Following that promise, Tyson was fined $3 million and had his license revoked for one year by the Nevada State Gaming Commission for biting the ear of boxer Evander Holyfield during a

1997 championship fight. In 1998, he succumbed to road rage when his Mercedes was involved in a minor three-car accident. According to the others involved in the accident, Tyson struck one driver in the face and kicked the other in the groin. He made national headlines again in 1998 by filing suit against his longtime promoter Don King, stating that King had cheated him out of $100 million.

—*Joyce Duncan*

See also: Athletes, above the Law; King, Don

For further reading:

Heller, Peter Niels. 1995. *Bad Intentions: The Mike Tyson Story.* New York: Da Capo.

Illingworth, Montieth. 1991. *Mike Tyson: Money, Myth and Betrayal.* Secaucus, NJ: Birch Lane.

Torres, Jose. 1990. *Fire and Fear: The Inside Story of Mike Tyson.* New York: Popular Library.

U

UMPIRES

By maintaining the integrity of baseball for over a century, professional umpires have kept the great American pastime unsullied in the face of changing social mores. After the 1919 Chicago "Black Sox" scandal, umpires took the lead in upholding the integrity of baseball. Umpires have ever since been major league baseball's sole representatives on the field. No umpire has ever lost his job or been criminally charged for any illegal activity involving baseball. Never has an arbiter's much-maligned integrity on the field been questioned to any extent off the field.

The game of baseball continued to change throughout the twentieth century; by the end of the century, it had acquired big-money players, television deals worth millions of dollars, new marketing gimmicks, and scoreboards that tell the fans when to cheer. The essence of umpiring, however, remains unchanged. A fourth man was added to all umpiring crews in 1952, but the role of a field arbiter is the same as it was when the game began. The men in blue make the calls, enforce the rules, and supervise playing conditions. The umpire has total authority; no one can overrule his decision on the field, and only the league president can later overturn an umpire's decision, and then only after a formal and costly protest is filed and won. Not since 1983 has a league president upheld a protest. In 1983, George Brett hit a home run to put the Royals ahead of the Yankees, but Yankees' manager Billy Martin protested that Brett had too much pine tar on his bat. The umpires concurred and ruled Brett out based on the rules. Brett went into a tirade and charged the umpires. American League President Lee MacPhail later overruled the umpires. MacPhail believed the umpires' technically correct ruling went against the spirit of the game. This occurrence demonstrated the integral and professional role of an umpire. Umpires are not to translate rules at whim, but to uphold the rule book and honor the national game.

Many feel that umpires have grown more aggressive since the late 1980s. The level of aggression considered acceptable in society has increased, and this change has filtered down from the sixties generation, who rebelled against authority figures of any kind. Thus, since the umpire maintains total authority on the field, society wants to fight the power. Players too, from the Little Leagues to the major leagues, have grown more aggressive. At most Little League parks, the thought that an umpire might cost a child his chance for glory and that a parent might have no recourse can lead to expressions of antagonism and sometimes violence. In the major leagues, the same displeasure is often expressed, and societal norms are reflected in the

375

George Brett argues with the umpires who ruled out his two-run homer after an examination of the pine tar on his bat showed that the tar had exceeded the allowable area (July 24, 1983).
(BETTMANN/CORBIS)

behavior players direct at the umpires. The umpires are required to maintain their composure by not physically coming in contact or assaulting those confronting, contacting, and, at times, assaulting them.

But Americans can still differentiate between right and wrong. The 1996 incident in which Roberto Alomar spat on American League umpire John Hirshbeck is a case in point. Alomar's action brought an overwhelming outcry from the fans in support of the umpire. They denounced the weak five-game suspension that Alomar received, especially since it was to occur during the first five games of the following season, allowing him to participate in the upcoming play-offs. The league president, bowing to pressure by team owners, stated, incorrectly, that there was no precedent for suspending someone during post-season play; however, in the early 1900s, Commissioner Byron Bancroft "Ban" Johnson had suspended a player for the rest of the season for spitting on an umpire. The fan support of the umpire in the Alomar case championed the idea that cultural norms of behavior should apply to overpaid, often immature players. This support helped sustain the role and integrity of the umpire on the field.

—*Scott L. Stabler*

See also: Baseball

For further reading:
Gutkind, Lee. 1975. *The Best Seat in Baseball, but You Have to Stand: The Game as Umpires See It.* New York: Doubleday.

Kaiser, Ken, and David Fisher. 2003. *Planet of the Umps: A Baseball Life from Behind the Plate.* New York: Thomas Dunne.

UPDIKE, JOHN (1932–)

The work of John Updike, including novels, short stories, essays, and poems, provides a convincing commentary on life in the United States after World War II. His writing on golf and other sports seeks to relate the individual to sport culture in a society often obsessed with games and heroes.

Updike began writing about golf after he started to play the game at the age of twenty-five. His collection *Golf Dreams* (1996) is a selection of short stories, essays, and golf program notes published over the preceding forty years in *The New Yorker, Golf Digest,* and other publications. In his own lyrical manner, Updike divides his golf writing into learning, playing, and loving the game. He writes of relating to caddies, of the strange aspects of bad golf, and of the "bliss" of golf. In "Tips on a Trip," first published in 1973, he acknowledges that golf is neither work nor play, but a "trip." For Updike, being on the golf course is "as nowhere else, the tyranny of casualty is suspended, and life is like a dream" (Updike 1996, 17). In his address to the hundredth-anniversary celebration of the U.S. Golf Association (USGA) in 1994, included as "U.S. Golf," he states that he is "curiously, disproportionately, undeservedly happy on a golf course, and perhaps we are all here for the same reason" (Updike 1996, 169).

Apart from golf, Updike made a significant contribution to baseball literature with the publication of "Hub Fans Bid Kid Adieu," his classic essay on Ted Williams's final game at Fenway Park on September 28, 1960. In pure, artful prose, Updike offers a fan's view from the stands of Williams's last home run. In addition to his work on specific sports, Updike is known for references to sport in his fiction, particularly throughout the series of books beginning with *Rabbit, Run* (1960).

—*Robert J. Cole*

See also: Golf; Literature, Sport in

For further reading:

Broer, Lawrence R., ed. 2000. *Rabbit Tales: Poetry and Politics in John Updike's Rabbit Novels.* Tuscaloosa: University of Alabama Press.

Updike, John. 1989. *Self-Consciousness: Memoirs.* New York: Knopf.

———. 1994. *Conversations with John Updike.* Edited by James Plath. Jackson: University Press of Mississippi.

———. 1996. *Golf Dreams.* New York: Alfred A. Knopf.

UPWARD MOBILITY, SPORT AS

Young persons rarely consider doctors, lawyers, or businessmen as role models. In fact, with the possible exception of Bill Gates, it is doubtful that a teenager could name ten Pulitzer Prize winners, theorists, or innovators. On the other hand, few teenagers cannot name a sport figure, and most would list at least one sport star when asked to list their heroes. Although some sport personalities are larger than life and serve as positive influences on young persons, many are not, and for every one person who makes it to stardom, hundreds fall by the wayside.

> *Few teenagers cannot name a sport figure, and most would record at least one sport star when asked to list their heroes.*

Impoverished youth, particularly those from minority neighborhoods, frequently view sport as a way out of their circumstances or at least as a free ride into higher education. Due in part to the meteoric rise of certain minority athletes, such as Michael Jordan, Tiger Woods, Magic Johnson, and others, many minority youths consider sport the ultimate salvation and stairway to upward mobility. In a *Sports Illustrated* poll of middle schoolers, "professional athlete" was the preferred career choice of 57 percent of male African American students. Critics charge that this focus on athletics emphasizes expectations that are unrealistic for the majority of these young people. Colleges and universities have only so many athletic scholarships to award, and professional sport teams offer limited openings.

Immigrants and minorities who achieve sport star status often become media darlings and use their celebrity as a platform from which to serve as spokespersons for their ethnicity. Although the acclaim and the politicizing are not necessarily negative, the spotlight does frequently reaffirm the improbable expectations of the young.

—*Jerry W. Nave*

See also: Discrimination, Racial, in Sport; Latino Athletes

For further reading:

Jarvie, Grant. 1991. *Sport, Racism and Ethnicity.* New York: Routledge Falmer.

Newberger, Eli H. 2000. *The Men They Will Become: The Nature and Nurture of Male Character.* Cambridge, MA: Perseus Books.

Suskind, Ron. 1999. *A Hope in the Unseen: An American Odyssey from the Inner City to the Ivy League.* New York: Broadway Books.

URBAN GYMNASIUMS

Organized for the purpose of promoting physical fitness and developing public interest in the benefits of personal health and hygiene, urban gymnasiums proliferated in the mid-nineteenth century and heightened interest in physical education and amateur athletics. Beginning in the 1820s, U.S. society grew increasingly concerned with personal fitness and hygiene. Haunted by fears of unfulfilled national promise, many social critics identified connections between physical fitness, mental health, and societal success. Consequently, the willingness of individuals to pursue physical improvement became associated with the general spirit of national reform and regeneration that characterized the era.

Advocates of "physical culture" soon proliferated and called for the establishment of organizations to assist citizens in the quest for physical improvement. The concept of physical culture asserted that Americans could forestall the personal and societal evils that accompanied sedentary lifestyles, a disturbing trend especially apparent in the growing commercial and professional classes inhabiting the nation's larger cities.

Reformers advocated the establishment of "temples of health" throughout the nation; these facilities generally had large open spaces for calisthenic routines and gymnastic apparatus, such as balance beams, parallel bars, weights and pulleys, and chin-up bars. In urban centers throughout the country, organizations established gymnasiums that offered these attractions as well as regular exercise classes tailored to the urban businessman. Although the commercial class represented the major market for these gymnasiums, many opened their doors to disadvantaged urban youth in the hope that exposure to exercise regimens would impart moral character and provide a haven from the temptations of the city.

Gymnastic exercise also became associated with the development of a "positive sports creed," which was devised by reformers to curb the degenerative and corrupting influence of the city and its sporting fraternity, a hedonistic male subculture whose members patronized commercial "professional" sports, such as cockfighting, dogfighting, prizefighting, and billiards. Organized to provide opportunities for wagering, these sports drew the ire of reformers who decried the association of sport and money as immoral. Thus, urban gymnastic organizations influenced the way Americans thought about amateur and professional sport and became consistent boosters and protectors of amateur athletics.

Gymnastic advocates also maintained that in addition to developing muscles and coordination, a regular regimen provided an excellent method to introduce habits of order and exactness—desirable traits in a society becoming more routine and bureaucratic. The popularity of urban gymnasiums served an important social function as well. As more Americans moved to the city, traditional family and community systems of support either became fragmented or disappeared. The urban milieu altered norms of behavior and forms of organization, forcing citizens to seek out new opportunities for social interaction. Gymnasiums became an ideal gathering place where people with similar interests could make new acquaintances as well as combat the ill effects of modern urban life.

—*Douglas G. Knerr*

See also: Communities, Impact of Sport on; Marketing of Sport; "Pumping Iron"

For further reading:

Goodbody, John. 1983. *The Illustrated History of Gymnastics.* New York: Beaufort Books.

Simons, Minot, II. 1995. *Women's Gymnastics, A History: 1966 to 1974.* Photography by Albrecht Gaebele. Carmel, CA: Welwyn Publishing.

VALENZUELA, FERNANDO
(1960–)

The most famous Mexican-born major league baseball player, Fernando Valenzuela touched off years of "Fernandomania" that united Mexican American fans and fans from other ethnic groups in appreciation of his talents. As a twenty-year-old starting pitcher for the 1981 Los Angeles Dodgers, Valenzuela was instantly the best pitcher in the majors, winning the Rookie of the Year and Cy Young Awards and leading the Dodgers to the World Series championship. As impressive as the quality of his play was his pitching style, a wind-milling screwball delivery with his eyes raised to heaven.

Yet Valenzuela's national origin was his most marketable feature. Mexican Americans in the Los Angeles area flocked to see him pitch. In major league baseball, most Latin players were of Puerto Rican or Dominican origin. As a great Mexican star player, Valenzuela was unique. As much as his talent, what made him a popular icon was his athletic image. Short, nearly fat, with long arms, Valenzuela was the opposite of the wiry types who typically star as pitchers. Average fans of all ethnic groups could identify with his unathletic style.

By the late 1980s, Valenzuela's talents had dwindled. The Dodgers released him in 1991, and he began a wandering existence across baseball.

Los Angeles Dodgers' champion player Fernando Valenzuela sits in his locker room and autographs baseballs (May 1981).
(Bettmann/Corbis)

His annual comebacks were the stuff of headlines and brought sellout crowds. Rarely, however, did Valenzuela come up to the anticipation and achieve on-field success. But the faith that teams showed in his box-office appeal throughout the 1990s testified to the persistent image of Valenzuela as the great Mexican drawing card.

—*Tim Morris*

See also: Clemente, Roberto; Latino Athletes

For further reading:

Burchard, S. H. 1982. *Sports Star, Fernando Valenzuela.* San Diego, CA: Harcourt Brace Jovanovich
Gloeckner, Carolyn. 1985. *Fernando Valenzuela.* Mankato, MN: Crestwood House, 1985.

VENTURA, JESSE (1951–)

It is not unusual for sport figures to change professional direction upon retirement from their athletic pursuits. Although some have assumed the expected roles of coaches or sport commentators, others have opted for careers in film or in television situation comedies, in publicity and marketing, or in business and industry. Although many of those professions seem oddly compatible with professional athletics, one career change made by an athlete in 1998 rocked the U.S. cultural conception. Former professional wrestler, actor, and sport-radio talk-show host Jesse "The Body" Ventura ran for and was elected to the office of governor of the state of Minnesota.

Born James George Janos, Ventura toured on the professional wrestling circuit throughout the 1970s and 1980s as one of the sport's infamous "bad" guys. Decked out in sequins, cartoonishly oversized sunglasses, and feather boa, Ventura once wrestled before a sold-out house at Madison Square Garden before retiring from the ring in 1986. He became a notoriously outspoken sport-radio talk-show host for KFAN radio, did color commentary for the Minnesota Vikings, had a role in the film *The Predator* (1987) with Arnold Schwarzenegger, and openly opposed using Minnesota tax dollars to fund a new ballpark for the Minnesota Twins.

In 1998, running as a Reform Party candidate, Ventura combined the swift-footedness of his wrestling career with the articulate acumen of his talk-show career to win the governorship of Minnesota, beating two rather conservative and well-known competitors by receiving 37 percent of the vote. The former Navy Seal became the first Reform Party candidate to win statewide office and became only the second independent governor in the nation.

Following his election and inauguration, Ventura requested that in the future he be known as "The Mind," and with an agenda that included areas as divergent as keeping school class size small to legalizing prostitution as a means of adding revenue to state coffers, the new governor was getting "ready to rumble." When Ventura exited the political arena, he served as a commentator for MSNBC, hosting *Jesse Ventura's America,* taped before a live audience in Saint Paul, Minnesota.

—*Joyce Duncan*

See also: Athletes as Actors

For further reading:

Hauser, Tom. 2002. *Inside the Ropes with Jesse Ventura.* Minneapolis: University of Minnesota Press.
Hunter, Matt. 2000. *Jesse Ventura: The Story of the Wrestler They Call "The Body."* Philadelphia: Chelsea House.

VIDEO ARCADES

Since the late 1970s, sport games have been a major attraction in video arcades, turning restaurants and shops into social gathering places. In the course of U.S. history, different locations in towns and cities have served as places for children, for teens, and for families to meet. After the invention of the microprocessor, personal computers, and video games in the period from 1968 to 1978, arcade games became that kind of magnet, drawing people together on evenings, weekends, and long boring summer days when there was nothing to do. Adding a row of video-game units to one wall turned thousands of pizza palaces, diners, and bars into neighborhood social centers. The video-game craze peaked between 1978 and 1983, suffered an industry crash in 1984, and slowly recovered, reaching 1983 levels again in the mid-1990s.

Arcade games must be easy to learn, since most players, especially children, will not waste quarters in a machine unless they believe they can play the game successfully on the first try. Sport games have always been ideal arcade subjects because the user already knows and understands the game, be it baseball, football, or car racing, and thus the instructions need only explain how to make the joystick and buttons carry out the steps.

Unlike many games that appeal to only one age segment, sport games are enjoyed by people from all age groups—children, teens, and adults. As the technology improved during the 1990s, the faces of individual star athletes became recognizable in the cartoon likenesses featured in the games, improving the games' realism and making them more attractive.

—*Don L. Daglow*

See also: Computers and Sport; Video Games

For further reading:

Baker, Mark. 1982. *I Hate Videots: Today the Arcade, Tomorrow the World.* New York: Simon and Schuster.

Beamer, Charles. 1982. *Video Fever.* Nashville, TN: T. Nelson.

VIDEO GAMES

Starting in 1977, video games became one of the largest components of the U.S. toy market, taking playtime that once was spent in sport outside and replacing it with less-active, indoor fantasy play. Children playing in their schools, backyards, and playgrounds have always imagined themselves to be their favorite sport stars, narrating their games with, "OK, here's Willie Mays stepping up to the plate!" as they prepare to face a neighbor pitching a tennis ball. Video games transfer that fantasy to the living-room television.

The first games, released in 1977–1982 for U.S.-made machines like the Atari 2600, Mattel's Intellivision, and Coleco's Colecovision were graphically simple and relied upon the user's imagination. Like arcade games, these cartridges peaked in popularity in 1983 and then virtually disappeared in 1984, shortly after the appearance of the first sport game that imitated television-style camera angles with more realistic graphics, Intellivision World Series Baseball (1983) from Mattel.

In the late 1980s, a new generation of games was created on machines made by Nintendo and Sega, both Japanese manufacturers. Soon, U.S. companies, such as Electronic Arts and Accolade, produced games that featured recognizable player likenesses and television-style graphics. The tremendous success of Electronic Arts John Madden Football in the 1990s signified the rebirth of the big-time video-game market, and sales surpassed those of the early systems.

How well a child played video games became a matter of social status in the 1990s. Magazines, often aimed at youth aged 8–13 or 13–18, flourished by offering game hints, secret codes, and reviews to feed this process.

—*Don L. Daglow*

See also: Computers and Sport; Video Arcades

For further reading:

Bensley, Lillian, and Juliet Van Eenwyk. 2000. *Video Games and Real-Life Aggression: A Review of the Literature.* Olympia: Washington State Department of Health.

King, Lucien, ed. 2002. *Game On: The History and Culture of Videogames.* London: Laurence King.

W

WAGNER, "GORGEOUS GEORGE" RAYMOND (1915–1963)

With flamboyance unparalleled in the post–World War II United States, professional wrestler Gorgeous George became one of the most recognizable sport figures of his generation and a staple of 1950s culture. Born George Raymond Wagner, Gorgeous George spent the early part of his career as a journeyman wrestler who worked odd jobs to make a living. Since he weighed only 195 pounds and stood only five foot nine, Wagner was too small to be a superstar in a big man's sport. But in the late 1940s, Wagner had an idea for a persona that made him a U.S. icon.

Unlike his relatively colorless counterparts, Wagner made every aspect of his wrestling character unique. His appearance and ring entrance stunned all who witnessed them. He wore brightly colored robes to the ring and had his blond hair done in the latest fashion. George refused to enter the ring until it had been sprayed with perfume. His effeminate appearance and mannerisms quickly made George an enemy of the fans, who came to seem him defeated.

Gorgeous George became an immediate hit thanks to television. Although he never held the world title, he was wrestling's biggest star in the 1950s. He was named "Mr. Television" for 1949 and was often the subject of conversation on

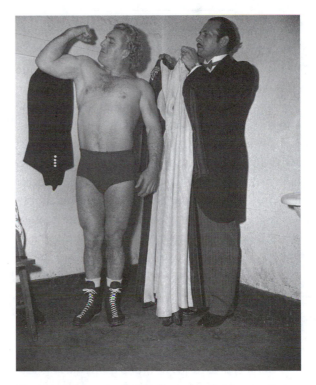

Gorgeous George in the stadium dressing room. George displays his bulging bicep while his valet holds the wrestler's velvet robe (March 19, 1948). (BETTMANN/CORBIS)

other television shows. To an entire generation, Gorgeous George, the "Human Orchid," personified professional wrestling.

Gorgeous George died following a heart attack in 1963. His influence continued, however, and wrestlers in the 1990s copied many of his characteristics.

—*Kenneth Phillips*

See also: Television, Impact on Sport; World Wrestling Federation

For further reading:
Frank, Joseph. 1974. *Whatever Happened to Gorgeous George?* Englewood Cliffs, NJ: Prentice-Hall.

WANDERONE, RUDOLF, JR., "MINNESOTA FATS" (CA. 1900/1913–1996)

Minnesota Fats was a fictional character given life through Jackie Gleason's portrayal of a pool shark in the 1961 film *The Hustler*. Rudolf Wanderone Jr. was a real person and pool hustler who, citing the film as his autobiography, adopted the name and the fame attached to it.

Wanderone was a native New Yorker of poor Swiss immigrant stock. His father, a merchant mariner, let the boy tag along when he was on leave, and the two often frequented the neighborhood pub. Wanderone learned the game of pool at the age of five, and by the time he reached puberty, he had discovered his true vocation. He dropped out of school at thirteen, and, calling himself New York Fats, he traveled the country in search of his next "pigeon."

Often, sport influences literature and film, leading to the creation of memorable characters and stereotypes. In the case of Minnesota Fats, the reverse was true: film created him, and he played the role to a sold-out house. Claiming he had been around the world six times and had beaten Adolf Hitler at pool, Minnesota Fats was the consummate con man and hustler. He died in Nashville, Tennessee, in 1996.

—*Joyce Duncan*

See also: Billiards and Pool; Film and Sport

For further reading:
Dyer, R. A. 2003. *Hustler Days: Minnesota Fats, Wimpy Lassiter, Jersey Red and America's Great Age of Pool.* Guilford, CT: Lyons Press.

WHEATIES

Since 1933, the General Mills cereal Wheaties and its slogan, "Wheaties—The Breakfast of Champions," have been synonymous with championship athletes. An appearance on the Wheaties box is one of the most prestigious rewards in sport advertising. The easily recognized slogan was created nine years after the wheat-bran-flake cereal Wheaties was introduced and just after Wheaties began its association with sport by sponsoring the broadcast of baseball games in Minneapolis, Minnesota. The broadcasts spread to nearly a hundred stations, and athlete testimonials, including comments from such baseball notables as Babe Ruth and Lou Gehrig, became a part of the programming. Later endorsers included track-and-field Olympian Babe Didrikson, ice-skater Sonja Henie, swimmer Johnny Weissmuller, and Jack Dempsey, the only boxer to be featured on the box in sixty-four years.

In the early 1950s, Wheaties left the sport market, but it returned in 1956 with two-time Olympic champion pole-vaulter the Reverend Bob Richards, who became the cereal's first long-term spokesperson. By the end of the Richards era, the Wheaties slogan had become a part of the U.S. lexicon, and an athlete's appearance on the box was an assurance of pop-culture immortality. The secret selection process at General Mills made its choices even more provocative. Wheaties also broke into television sport sponsorship.

Expansion in the 1970s resulted in many amateur, Olympic, and professional sports being represented on the boxes, and Olympic-year selections became a national guessing game. Marketing diversity continued into the 1990s as General Mills created special boxes for displays of individuals, teams, and events. These included regional, heritage, anniversary-edition, commemorative, and Special Olympics boxes. The Special Olympics regional boxes featured midwestern medal winners. Regional boxes focused on teams and individuals identified with various sections of the country, and heritage boxes featured baseball greats and the Harlem Globetrotters basketball team.

Anniversary-edition boxes celebrated events such as the seventy-fifth anniversary of the National Football League, the seventy-fifth anniversary of baseball's Negro Leagues, and the hundredth running of the Boston Marathon. Commemorative boxes celebrated team champions of such events as the World Series and the Super Bowl. The most celebrated commemorative box, issued in 1997, marked the fiftieth anniversary of Jackie Robinson's entry as the first African American in major league baseball. This national commemoration was placed on two new Wheaties cereals introduced in 1996.

> *An appearance on the Wheaties box is one of the most prestigious rewards in sport advertising.*

Wheaties also secured its second long-term spokesperson during the 1990s, contracting professional basketball superstar Michael Jordan, who appeared on boxes more times than had any other athlete before him. In addition, a new phrase, "Better eat your Wheaties," became synonymous with a desire to do what was nutritionally correct to excel in sport.

Wheaties has over one hundred featured boxes but has been carefully marketing its most prestigious honor: being displayed on a nationally distributed box. This honor has been given to only a handful of athletes. By 1997, an appearance on the box guaranteed an athlete long-time financial prospects in advertising endorsements, and many athletes lobbied for selection. Meanwhile, Wheaties officials cited the criteria for selection— outstanding athletic achievement and capturing the hearts of America—but kept its selection process secret. Many of the boxes are listed as expensive collectibles. A 1994 World Cup soccer regional box with two different backs was valued at $75 on a 1997 list.

—*Harry Amana*

See also: Jordan, Michael; Marketing of Sport; Olympic Games; Robinson, Jack Roosevelt "Jackie"

For further reading:
Steel, Jon. 1998. *Truth, Lies and Advertising: The Art of Account Planning.* New York: John Wiley and Sons.
Upshaw, Lynn B. 1995. *Building Brand Identity: A Strategy for Success in a Hostile Marketplace.* New York: John Wiley and Sons.

"WHITE HOPE"

Beginning with boxing, but also in many other modern sports, white athletes have often been referred to as "white hopes," indicating that they embody a Caucasian challenge in a sport perceived as dominated by black athletes. White athletes, especially the Irish, dominated the early days of professional boxing. There was an unwritten rule that the white champions of boxing would not put their titles on the line against black opponents. Tommy Burns, when promised the then enormous purse of $30,000, win or lose, broke that rule and accepted the challenge of black heavyweight Jack Johnson. In their 1908 bout held in Sydney, Australia, Johnson easily defeated Burns to become the first black to hold the title of world's greatest fighter.

In a time of great racial insecurity in the United States, Johnson did little to alleviate white fear. He was brash and flaunted his financial success as well as his enjoyment of white female companionship. The cry quickly went up for a white challenger who would win back the title and reaffirm white racial superiority. Johnson, however, dismissed a few lesser white opponents, while the nation waited for a true "great white hope," former champion Jim Jeffries. The challenge between the black and white races dominated conversation at the time. It was reported that Jeffries was actually sickened by the responsibility he felt as the white savior. Johnson's eventual victory in the match held on July 4, 1910, set off black celebrations throughout the country as well as scattered race riots, which cost many lives.

Even in the modern era, in arguably more racially enlightened times, the appearance of a great white athlete in a sport dominated by black athletes often brings about the nickname of "white hope." Modern examples include Gerry Cooney of boxing fame and basketball star Larry Bird.

—*Robert S. Brown*

See also: Racial Superiority, Myth of

For further reading:

Johnson, Jack. 1993. *Jack Johnson in the Ring and Out.* Mattituck, NY: Amereon Limited.

Roberts, Randy. 1985. *Papa Jack: Jack Johnson and the Era of White Hopes.* New York: Free Press.

WHITWORTH, KATHY (1939–)

In 1958, Kathy Whitworth joined the Ladies Professional Golf Association (LPGA). She eventually won eighty-eight professional tournaments, more than any other person, woman or man. She helped generate interest in women's golf by winning at least one tournament each year for seventeen consecutive years, from 1962 to 1978, thereby setting an LPGA record.

Whitworth was born in Monahans, Texas, but grew up in Jal, New Mexico, a small town along the Texas border where the main industry was the production of natural gas. She began playing golf at fifteen and won the New Mexico State Amateur tournament in 1957. Although she did not win a tournament during her first year as a professional, she was the LPGA's leading money winner eight times, Player of the Year seven times, and Vare

Trophy winner seven times. She also won five majors: the 1965–1966 Titleholders Championships, the 1967 LPGA Championship and Western Open, and the 1971 LPGA Championship. She was the first woman to win $1 million in career prize money.

Whitworth personified the persistence of the Horatio Alger–style athlete; her vision included overcoming every financial, gender, and social obstacle that prevented many young women from playing professional sport. Her style of play exuded restraint and fearlessness, and she became the perfect 1960s golfing heroine because she created action and enthusiasm by means of her grinding, concentrating style of play.

Her success on the LPGA tour helped attract larger purses for the players and also generated interest in golf among young women. She promoted women's golf by conducting clinics across the country. Whitworth was inducted into the LPGA Hall of Fame and the World Golf Hall of Fame and remains one of the most popular heroines in women's golf.

—*Mike Schoenecke*

See also: Golf

For further reading:

Eldred, Patricia Mulrooney. 1975. *Kathy Whitworth.* Mankato, MN: Creative Education.

Whitworth, Kathy, Rhonda Glenn, and Patty Berg. 1990. *Golf for Women.* New York: St. Martin's Press.

WIDE WORLD OF SPORTS

Long before there was ESPN, in fact, long before many persons had even heard of cable television, ABC penetrated the living rooms of most of the United States with an innovative sport program. Beginning in 1961, *Wide World of Sports* reported from fifty-four countries and visited forty-eight states. The brainchild of producer Roone Arledge, *Wide World of Sports* presented to an eager public a smorgasbord of often-unrelated and occasionally obscure sporting events. The program was initiated as a sport-variety show, rather like the highly successful *Ed Sullivan Show* but with rodeo performers and daredevils instead of opera divas and European jugglers. It legitimatized figure skating as television fare, introduced the world to Evel Knievel, and popularized the Harlem Globetrotters and the Acapulco cliff-diving championship. Introduced into the lineup as a summer replacement and begging for sponsors, the show secured a second season and a permanent berth largely due to its coverage of the U.S. and Soviet track meet held in Moscow during that summer.

> *Started in 1961,* Wide World of Sports *reported from fifty-four countries and visited forty-eight states. It legitimatized figure skating as television fare, introduced the world to Evel Knievel, and popularized the Harlem Globetrotters and the Acapulco cliff-diving championship.*

Diversity was the key to the program's success. By offering different events from the sporting world, the producers were successful in drawing a wider audience. On any given weekend, *Wide World of Sports* might air figure skating, a demolition derby, and a prizefight, or lumberjack competitions, chess tournaments, and the International Bikini Sports competition; its programming drew its audience both from the elite and from the man in the street, both from the passive and from the passionate.

The program ran two and one-half hours, a mammoth undertaking in a television era accustomed to resolving all conflicts in thirty minutes, and it made household names of its two cohosts, Jim McKay and Bill Flemming. The best-known and most likely to be remembered feature of *Wide World of Sports,* however, is the opening that aired consistently from 1970: skier Vienko Bogatej inadvertently became the living symbol of the program, for it was he who came crashing down the ski chute to the refrain, "the thrill of victory and the agony of defeat."

—*Joyce Duncan*

See also: Harlem Globetrotters; Knievel, Robert Craig "Evel"; Television, Impact on Sport

For further reading:

Leitner, Irving A. 1975. *ABC's "Wide World of Sports": A Panorama of Championship Sport.* New York: Golden Press.

McKay, Jim. 1999. *The Real McKay: My Wide World of Sports.* With a foreword by Peter Jennings. New York: E. P. Dutton.

WILD WEST SHOWS

For nearly half a century, Wild West shows offered dramatic accounts of historical events, cultural encounters, and athletic events to the delight of millions of viewers in the United States and Europe. These spectacles focused on the uniqueness of the West and its centrality to the U.S. character. Indeed, combining historical reenactment, melodrama, elements of indigenous cultures, and proto-rodeo forms, these performances offered popular interpretations of the American West, of relations between Native Americans and whites, and of U.S. history. From their beginnings in 1883 through their disappearance in the early 1930s, these entertainments both reflected and extended prevailing understandings of the frontier, race, nature, cultural evolution, and U.S. exceptionalism.

Wild West shows emerged at a pivotal moment in U.S. history: at the end of the military campaign against indigenous peoples and a decade before the close of the frontier. In this context, captivity narratives, dime novels, minstrel shows, and popular drama as well as political ideologies and government policies informed the interpretation of culture, history, and nation presented in the spectacles. Consequently, although promoters lauded Wild West shows for combining amuse-

Buffalo Bill Cody's Wild West Troupe (1800s). Wild West shows had a profound impact on U.S. culture. They provided the symbols and associations through which most Americans interpreted the West.
(BETTMANN/CORBIS)

ment and education, a number of scholars have underscored the fact that these popular entertainments offered important occasions to assemble public accounts of the nation, of its unique identity, and of its formation. Indeed, they fostered ambivalent and collective recollections, theorizing racial stratification and cultural evolution while prompting nostalgic yearnings for nature, tradition, and indigenous communities destroyed by progress and Manifest Destiny.

Wild West shows had a profound impact on U.S. culture. They provided the symbols and associations through which most Americans have interpreted the West. They cemented popular conceptions of regionalism, connecting the West with guns, conflict, the frontier, and the cowboy. Wild West shows, moreover, set the terms in which many Americans would come to know Native Americans. This image stressed wildness and bellicosity, suggesting that indigenous peoples were best understood as historical artifacts, bypassed by progress. At the same time, they presented a picture of the relations between Native Americans and whites that underscored not merely a violent clash of cultures but also the "just conquest" and subjugation of the indigenous nations of North America.

In many respects, Wild West shows shaped twentieth-century popular U.S. culture. Most notably, they formed the content of the film industry, influencing the characters and narratives of the Western for much of the century. Furthermore, they fostered the development of rodeo as a distinct sport subculture. Finally, Wild West shows influenced other popular elaborations of Indianness, particularly mascots and the woodcraft movement.

Wild West shows peaked in popularity and significance in the final decade of the nineteenth century and the initial decade of the twentieth. Following the death of Buffalo Bill Cody in 1917, they began to decline rapidly. Even the celebrity of film star Tom Mix could not prevent their fading from popular culture in the early 1930s. Significantly, the social and ideological themes animating Wild West shows did not lose their importance. Rather, they were increasingly supplanted by emergent cultural forms—particularly film and, to a lesser extent, rodeo—which offered more-meaningful and convenient ways for popular audiences to engage the sentimental and ideological themes that had energized Wild West shows.

—*C. Richard King*

See also: Native American Athletes; Native American Mascots

For further reading:
Kasson, Joy S. 2000. *Buffalo Bill's Wild West: Celebrity, Memory and Popular History.* New York: Hill and Wang.
Moses, L. G. 1996. *Wild West Shows and the Images of American Indians, 1883–1933.* Albuquerque: University of New Mexico Press.
Reddin, Paul. 1999. *Wild West Shows.* Urbana: University of Illinois Press.

WILLIAMS, TED (1918–2002)

Baseball legend, fighter pilot in two wars, and benefactor of children stricken with cancer, Ted Williams was a genuine U.S. hero whose rare combination of talent and personality made him one of the major sport celebrities of the twentieth century.

Boston has had its share of sport legends, but none ever attracted the attention of fans and journalists as did Ted Williams, who was throughout his career one of the most closely scrutinized figures in public life, in and out of sport.

Best remembered as one of the .400 hitters, Williams is acknowledged by many as the greatest hitter in the history of baseball, even though his career with the Boston Red Sox (1939–1960) was interrupted twice when he served his country as a fighter pilot in World War II and in the Korean War. A native of San Diego, California, Williams was a Hollywood-handsome leading man who provided journalists with plenty of drama off the field. His three divorces, his occasional temper tantrums directed at both the media and the fans, and his outspoken views on politics made him a favorite subject, and often target, of sportswriters. During his playing days in Boston, Williams made frequent unpublicized visits to children in hospitals and helped raise millions of dollars for the Jimmy Fund, which supported childhood cancer research at the Dana Farber Cancer Institute.

A man of unusual intelligence, Williams approached any subject with boyish enthusiasm and relentless curiosity. He became one of the most avid students of hitting that baseball has known and published his theories in *The Science of Hitting* (1971). His dedication to his other passion, fishing, made him one of the world's leading sport fishermen.

In his Hall of Fame induction speech into the National Baseball Hall of Fame in 1966, Williams's commitment to fairness led him to make what was probably the first public appeal for the induction of the great stars of the Negro Leagues, "who are not here only because they weren't given the chance."

—*Lawrence Baldassaro*

See also: Baseball

For further reading:
Baldassaro, Lawrence, ed. 1991. *The Ted Williams Reader.* New York: Simon and Schuster.
———, ed. 2003. *Ted Williams: Reflections on a Splendid Life.* Boston: Northeastern University Press.
Johnson, Dick, ed. 1991. *Ted Williams: A Portrait in Words and Pictures.* New York: Walker.
Prime, Jim, and Bill Nowlin. 1997. *Ted Williams: A Tribute.* Indianapolis, IN: Masters Press.

Ted Williams, Boston Red Sox slugger, is shown during batting action (1951).
(BETTMANN/CORBIS)

WILSON, AUGUST (1945–)

August Wilson, one of the most prominent play-wrights in the United States, chronicles the history of black Americans within the social and political movements of the twentieth century. Such plays as *Ma Rainey's Black Bottom,* first produced in 1984 and published in 1985, *Fences* (1986), and *The Piano Lesson* (1990) firmly established Wilson's popularity and importance as a chronicler of the black experience in the United States.

One of the many important manifestations of black culture throughout the nineteenth and twentieth centuries was baseball, especially within the immensely popular Negro Leagues. The Pulitzer Prize–winning *Fences,* set in 1957, a decade after Jackie Robinson integrated the major leagues, is the story of Troy Maxson, fifty-three years old and still proud of his achievement as a player in the Negro Leagues but resentful of the ban that kept him out of the majors and unable to acknowledge the changing times within the world of sport. Convinced that professional sport remains a white man's enterprise, Troy refuses to permit his son Cory to accept a scholarship to play college football.

The play is a perceptive reaction to the complex characteristics of integration in major professional sport. Often, in subtle ways, Wilson presents a changing world still rooted in a racist past, an ironic inversion of the common father-son theme of bonding through sport, baseball metaphors that convey the character's views of death and of his own unfulfilled life, and a picture of the new opportunities for African Americans in baseball that, at the same time, robbed the black community of an important part of its culture: the Negro Leagues.

—*Edward J. Rielly*

See also: Negro Baseball Leagues; Robinson, Jack Roosevelt "Jackie"; Upward Mobility, Sport as

For further reading:

Bloom, Harold, ed. 2002. *August Wilson*. Broomall, PA: Chelsea House.

Bogumil, Mary L. 1999. *Understanding August Wilson*. Columbia: University of South Carolina Press.

Elam, Harry J., Jr. 2004. *The Past as Present in the Drama of August Wilson*. Ann Arbor: University of Michigan Press.

WOMEN AND FISHING

Because they have excelled in fishing for centuries—a sport in which they continue to participate actively through professional competition and amateur enjoyment—British and subsequently U.S. women have demonstrated their ability to enter with relative ease into what some might consider a primarily male activity. According to Renaissance legend and beyond, the nun or noblewoman Dame Juliana Berners wrote the first angling treatise printed in English (1496). Her thesis, which provides a list of artificial flies as well as instructions on bait fishing, influenced most subsequent English angling literature. In seventeenth-century England, several women anglers appear in poetry and prose written by men; Izaak Walton, for example, mentions women anglers in his *Compleat Angler* (1653). These women of early modern England served as the literary and practical forebears of generations of British and U.S. women anglers.

Eighteenth-century U.S. letters and diaries reveal that women were angling in those years, but accounts are much more frequent beginning in the late nineteenth century. Among key women fly-fishing figures in the nineteenth century was Cornelia "Fly Rod" Crosby, a prominent sport celebrity and Maine's first registered guide, who introduced the use of the lightweight fly rod and artificial lure for women and authored a widely published newspaper column on the outdoors. Also significant in this era were a number of women who made important contributions to fly tying through invention, production, and cataloguing.

The twentieth century boasts of many women who have contributed to fly-fishing. Julia Freeman Fairchild and Frank Hovey-Roof Connell founded the Woman Flyfishers Club, the first women's fishing organization in the world, in 1932. Fly fisher Joan Wulff pioneered in a number of areas: she won one international and many national casting titles, became the first woman to win the Fisherman's Distance Event against all-male competition, was perhaps the first woman offered a salaried contract by a tackle manufacturer, toured in casting exhibitions, wrote two important books and monthly casting columns for sport magazines, and started a fly-fishing school with her husband. Other women have introduced lines of clothing for women anglers, pioneered all-women angling schools, served as consultants for tackle companies, led destination fly-fishing services for women, written books and articles on fishing, and hosted television programs.

Since the 1930s, women have been involved in big-game saltwater angling. Among the most significant pioneers in the sport were Chisie Farrington, who set eleven world records (ten women's and one men's) for the size of different species and classes of fish caught, and Helen Lerner, who was the first to catch giant tuna on rod and reel off the coast of Brittany, a feat for which she was awarded a gold medal from France's Academie des Sports. The founding of the International Women's Fishing Association (IWFA) in 1955 led to an explosion of interest in big-game fishing by women. In 1977, saltwater angler Marsha Bierman became the first woman to win the Bahamas Billfish Championship; she pioneered a short-rod stand-up technique that brings in the fish more quickly, thereby improving its chances for survival. Women have influenced saltwater angling in a number of ways: they have taken strong conservationist positions as advocates of catch-and-release fishing, have been elected to the board of trustees of the International Game Fish Association, and have achieved an array of world records and tournament wins.

Women have entered the male-dominated world of bass fishing as well. Bass'n Gal, one of the largest angling organizations in the world, created by Sugar Ferris in 1976, has become a dominant force for women in the sport. Although the Bass Anglers Sportsman Society (BASS) was opened to women in 1991, they have not joined in large numbers. Chris Houston is a legend in the Bass'n Gal circuit and has won a number of Angler of the Year Awards, Classic Star World championships and national titles. Many other women, including Linda England, Fredda Lee, and Penny Berryman, have influenced the sport through tournament championships, radio and television appearances, speaking engagements, and magazine articles.

The five-hundred-year anniversary of Dame Juliana Berners's treatise in 1996 led to a renewed interest in women and fishing in the 1990s; in fact, the subject has been discussed in articles in the *New York Times* and in popular women's magazines, such as *Victoria*. Fishing schools and organizations for women abound; one, Casting Forward, was designed specifically to help women who are recovering from breast cancer. Women have also written and edited books and anthologies about their own and others' fishing experiences and expertise.

—*Anne E. McIlhaney*

See also: *The Compleat Angler;* Fishing, Fly and Bait; Women's Issues

For further reading:

Foggia, Lyla. 1995. *Reel Women: The World of Women Who Fish.* Hillsboro, OR: Beyond Words.

Morris, Holly, ed. 1991. *Uncommon Waters: Women Write about Fishing.* Seattle, WA: Seal Press.

———, ed. 1995. *A Different Angle: Fly Fishing Stories by Women.* Seattle, WA: Seal Press.

WOMEN BICYCLISTS

The first popular bicycles, with large front and small rear wheels, appeared in the 1860s. Initially, only a few daring women rode them, but many more began to enjoy cycling after 1880 when an adult tricycle greatly expanded cycling opportunities. A safety bicycle that featured a dropped bar, allowing women to ride while remaining decently covered, followed the tricycle. As women learned of bicycling's excitement and healthy exercise and became familiar with its swiftness, convenience, and ease of travel, they quickly joined the wheeling ranks. By the mid-1890s, women made up one-third of the bicycle market.

During the 1880s and 1890s, whether women should ride bicycles remained a hotly debated issue. The Woman's Rescue League concluded that 30 percent of "fallen women" were bicyclists, but others thought cycling the greatest blessing given to modern women. Not only did women expand their horizons and learn more of their surroundings by pedaling out into the country, but they also found freedom from both prying eyes and chaperones. As a corollary feature, the bicycle aided the rational dress movement, since women found it cumbersome to ride draped in the yards of material that fashion and decency required. Among many pioneering cyclists, Margaret LeLong, Hattie McIlrath, Elizabeth Robins Pennell, and Fanny Bullock Workman served as role models, proving that women could stretch themselves and their horizons through travel and exercise.

Margaret LeLong was a woman of significant personal courage and independence. In 1897, ignoring the objections of friends and family, she rode alone from Chicago to San Francisco for no other reason other than that she had lived there and wanted to visit. Throughout her approximately seventy days on the road, she received kind and courteous treatment from those she met. She traveled in all kinds of weather and survived hunger, thirst, and numerous minor accidents.

At age twenty-two, Hattie Boyer McIlrath joined her husband on a round-the-world bicycle adventure, becoming the first woman to "circumcycle" the globe. Elizabeth Robins Pennell's bicycling career spanned two decades. In her memoir, *Over the Alps on a Bicycle* (1898), she recounts her adventures as the first woman to bicycle over the mountain range. Like her cycling sisters, Fanny Bullock Workman paid strict attention to the dress conventions of the era. Even riding in the sweltering heat of Africa and India, she dressed in an appropriate Victorian style.

Women shared similar bicycling experiences with men. It gave them the same opportunities for travel, exercise, and pleasure, and despite the terrible predictions of the Woman's Rescue League, it did not result in their destruction. It did offer them tremendous freedom, which undoubtedly aided in their campaign for equal rights. Frances Willard, president of the Women's Christian Temperance Union, wrote in a small volume explaining that she learned to ride a bicycle at fifty-three "to help women to a wider world" (Willard 1991, 74). Women proved to be as capable and as adept on wheels as were their male counterparts.

—*Duncan R. Jamieson*

See also: Bicycling; Women's Issues

For further reading:

LeLong, Margaret Valentine. 1898. "From Chicago to San Francisco Awheel." *Outing* 31 (February/March), 592–596.

Pennell, Elizabeth Robins. 1898. *Over the Alps on a Bicycle*. London: T. Fisher Unwin.

Willard, Frances E. 1991. *How I Learned to Ride the Bicycle: Reflections of an Influential 19th Century Woman*. Reprint. Sunnyvale, CA: Fair Oaks.

Workman, Fanny Bullock. 1897. *Sketches Awheel in Modern Iberia*. New York: G. P. Putnam's Sons.

WOMEN SPORTSCASTERS

By confronting the dominance of men in sportscasting as well as in the institution of sport itself, women sportscasters have increasingly become familiar to and accepted by audiences and have legitimized the voice of women in sport. Following on the heels of the commercial success of radio broadcasting, Judith Cary Waller pioneered women's radio journalism in the 1920s. Credited with producing the first play-by-play coverage of a college football game—University of Chicago versus Brown University in 1924—Waller subsequently convinced Chicago Cubs owner William Wrigley Jr. to grant her permission to broadcast the team's home games in 1925. By the Depression, two-thirds of all U.S. homes had radios, and Mrs. Harry Johnson, nicknamed the "First Lady Baseball Reporter" in radio, continued the tradition by broadcasting baseball for KFAB radio in Lincoln, Nebraska.

In 1948, Sarah Palfrey Cooke pioneered women's television broadcasting by hosting NBC's fifteen-minute show *Sportswoman of the Week*. Despite the success of televised sport, women's on-camera roles as sportscasters were extremely limited until the 1970s, when stations striving to maintain their licenses actively sought to hire women and minorities. In 1973, ABC hired tennis great Rosemary Casals to broadcast the "Battle of the Sexes" tennis match between Billie

Jean King and Bobby Riggs, and in 1975, skier Suzy Chaffee announced the ten-week "Battle of the Sexes" for CBS, a program that pitted professional male and female athletes in head-to-head competition. Often considered the true pioneer among women sportscasters, Jane Chastain, hired by CBS Sports in 1974, served as a sideline reporter and color commentator on several National Football League (NFL) broadcasts, including the 1975 Super Bowl.

Continuing to address the paucity of women sportscasters, CBS created "hostess" roles, and in 1975, former Miss America Phyllis George was hired to cohost *NFL Today*. In 1977, former *Playboy* cover girl Jayne Kennedy became the first African American woman network sportscaster. Opting to hire recognized athletes rather than models, ABC's Roone Arledge signed skater Peggy Fleming, tennis great Billie Jean King, gymnast Cathy Rigby Mason, track star Wyomia Tyus, and swimmer Donna De Verona. Hired for journalism and sportswriting talent rather than for beauty or athletic status, Lesley Visser joined CBS's *NFL Today* in 1988 after working fourteen years as a reporter with the *Boston Globe*. Riding the success of ESPN, the first all-sport cable station, Gayle Gardner, dubbed "the dean of women sportscasters," was hired by ESPN to anchor its *SportsCenter* program in 1983. In 1991, Gardner signed a multiyear contract with NBC for $300,000, making her the country's highest-paid woman sportscaster.

Although women are less visible at the network-affiliate level, several have had the opportunity to pioneer as sport anchors or reporters for local stations, and most market stations across the country can identify a first woman broadcaster, from Barbara Borin, WNAC in Boston, to Jackie Lapping, KTTV, Los Angeles. Several women have also achieved success in producing network sport programming, including Eleanor Sanger, who in 1993 became the first woman to produce sport programming for network television; Libby King, who headed ESPN's program-acquisitions depart-

ment in 1991; and Lydia Stephens, who in 1991 became ABC's first director of sport programming. To assist in recruiting and retaining women in sport journalism and broadcasting, the Association for Women in the Sports Media was formed in 1987. Despite the increase in the presence of women in the sport media, only 3 percent of the nation's ten thousand print and broadcast sport journalists are women.

—*Jeffrey O. Segrave*

See also: "Battle of the Sexes"; Sport Journalism

For further reading:

Creedon, Pamela J., ed. 1994. *Women, Media and Sport: Challenging Gender Values.* Thousand Oaks, CA: Sage.

WOMEN'S BASKETBALL

For nearly eighty years, women's basketball has been regulated, perceived, and often practiced as a sport distinct from the male version. In an effort to suppress any traces of aggression or masculinity among women, male and female coaches, administrators, and the wider public often sought to make the sport compatible with a narrow definition of womanhood, one that stressed cooperation, grace, and beauty. In this manner, women's basketball has generally paralleled the surrounding discourse about the overall place of women in U.S. society. By the 1990s, however, this traditional image had changed somewhat, due in part to the advent and relative success of professional women's basketball. The sport contributed to an overall social climate more accepting of women athletes.

Separate Spheres

At the time of basketball's invention in the United States (1891), the notion of "separate spheres" guided the public perception of appropriate male and female behavior. Men, many believed, should be leaders and risk takers and should work in the public, away from home; women, on the other hand, were to be modest, restrained, and supportive and were limited to domestic responsibilities, including housework and child rearing.

The rules of women's basketball embodied the separate-spheres concept. In 1892, Senda Berenson, the first director of physical education at Smith College, an all-women's institution, adapted the rules that James Naismith of nearby Springfield College in Massachusetts had developed for men the previous year. Attempting to downplay the roughhouse and other presumably more-masculine components of the game, Berenson divided the court into three equal sections and prohibited players from leaving their assigned areas. Centers, for example, could not leave the middle third of the court. The rules, first published in 1901, also minimized body contact, physical exertion, and any wild or rough moves among players. With some variation and modifications, the regulations remained in place until as late as 1971, creating gendered patterns in the culture of the sport and hindering the overall growth of the game, since players literally were unable to move freely.

According to sport historian Susan K. Cahn, early observers considered basketball appropriate for women because it was played indoors in a seemingly private space with limited physical contact and on a relatively small playing surface. These concerns about the appropriateness of space and audience influenced female physical educators when they called for major reform in the sport almost thirty years later. In 1923, the women's division of the National Amateur Athletic Federation mounted a campaign to curtail competition. The group fought against interscholastic contests between women's teams in mostly white high schools and colleges, and by 1930, the number of women's college teams had been drastically reduced.

Not all communities followed these gender guidelines, however. Generally, Caucasian working-class women and women of color, regardless of economic station, had fewer restrictions on their sporting experiences. For instance, the all-black *Philadelphia Tribune* squad dominated all women's teams, both black and white, throughout the 1930s and played primarily according to the men's rules of the game. Full-court basketball also flourished in racially segregated locales, such as among Japanese American internees during World War II and among Native Americans on reservations. For these marginalized groups, basketball games were communal events shared by women and men, and the teams symbolized their particular ethnic or racial heritage.

Women's basketball thrived in terms of fan popularity and participation in several midwestern cities and towns in Iowa, Indiana, and Kentucky, where supporters considered their local teams a source of pride. The fact that not all women adhered to the strict official rules reveals that some societies were more comfortable with aggressive women and unconventional femininity, at least in sport.

The Feminist Movement

The modern, national feminist movement of the late 1960s and early 1970s also had an impact on the growth of women's basketball. In 1971, a five-player, full-court game with a 30-second shot clock became official, allowing for a more athletic and fast-paced version of the game. Women's basketball made its debut at the Olympic Games in 1976, and in 1984, the U.S. team won its first gold medal in the event. Title IX regulations, which require colleges to provide equal funding and opportunities to women's sport, greatly increased the number of women players on scholarship. The ruling also had a significant impact on several National Collegiate Athletic Association (NCAA) powerhouse schools, leading to dynasties at the University of Tennessee, Louisiana Tech University, and the University of Connecticut, among others, and draining talent and support away from the historically black colleges and smaller schools that had traditionally supported women's

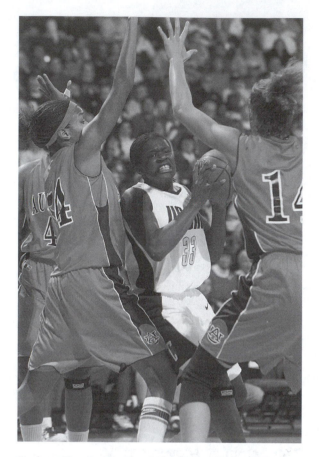

Barbara Turner (number 33), a center for the University of Connecticut, rebounds during second round NCAA Women's Basketball Tournament action against Auburn at Harbor Yards in Bridgeport. The Huskies defeated the Auburn Tigers 79-53 in the NCAA East Regional second-round game to advance (March 2004).
(DAVID BERGMAN/CORBIS)

(ABL) and the Women's National Basketball Association (WNBA) were formed in 1996 and 1997, respectively. By that time, basketball as a whole had become a more popular sport across the country, and team owners, corporate sponsors, and the general public had become increasingly receptive of women professional athletes.

Unlike their male counterparts, women basketball players cannot escape their ties to domesticity and the home. The media often focus on their spouses and children, and the WNBA actively promotes their activities as family oriented. Still, the visible presence of women as coaches, players, officials, and administrators has helped advance the cause of gender equity in sport and has influenced a significant number of young women to play. The games have proven to be a safe space for all women.

—*La'Tonya Reease Miles*

See also: Basketball; Title IX; Women's Basketball Hall of Fame

For further reading:
Cahn, Susan K. 1994. *Coming on Strong: Gender and Sexuality in Twentieth-Century Women's Sport.* New York: Free Press.
Hult, Joan S., and Marianna Trekell, eds. 1991. *A Century of Women's Basketball: From Frailty to Final Four.* Reston, VA: National Association for Girls and Women in Sport.

athletics. Standout players of the period included Nancy Lieberman Cline, Anne Myers, and Cheryl Miller.

Beginning in the 1970s, a number of professional leagues were established, including the Women's Professional Basketball Association in 1975, the Women's Professional Basketball League in 1978, and the Ladies Professional Basketball Association in 1980. All of them were short-lived, lasting only a season or two. Women's basketball gained unprecedented mainstream notoriety and acceptance when the American Basketball League

WOMEN'S BASKETBALL HALL OF FAME

Located in Knoxville, Tennessee, adjacent to the campus of the University of Tennessee and within a day's drive of sixty percent of the U. S. population, the Women's Basketball Hall of Fame opened in 1999, and forty-nine members had been inducted by 2001. Selected by the Hall's board of directors, inductees include players, coaches, and referees who meet the criteria of years of service as well as years away from the game. The location was chosen because committed funding was available from the City of Knoxville and Knox County as well as from many corporations and individuals and because of the University of Tennessee's association with women's basketball. As an additional source of revenue, the facility often serves as a unique venue for wedding receptions, banquets, birthday parties, and conferences.

At one end of the building rests a giant basketball, standing thirty feet tall and weighing ten tons. A sculpture by Elizabeth MacQueen featuring three figures, each representing an era in women's basketball, graces the entryway. The artwork depicts the mission statement of the Hall: honor the past, celebrate the present, promote the future. The film *Hoopful of Home* follows the history of the game from 1892 to the present and the "Ring of Honor," a display holding the jerseys of one hundred high school and collegiate All-American players. Like its counterpart, the Basketball Hall of Fame in Springfield, Massachusetts, the Hall features an activities area where visitors can test their dribbling and passing skills, their vertical leaps, and their jump shots.

The Women's Basketball Hall of Fame acknowledges a long history of women in sport, and the stories it depicts provide excellent role models for young women visiting it. The collection illustrates the import of basketball in the lives of women, both historically and currently.

—*Leslie Heaphy*

See also: Basketball; Women's Basketball

For further reading:

Miller, Ernestine, and Carole Oglesby. 2002. *Making Her Mark: Firsts and Milestones in Women's Sports.* New York: McGraw-Hill.

WOMEN'S ISSUES

By the end of the twentieth century, issues of inequality and lack of acceptance were beginning to have less impact on women's athletic programs than in earlier periods. This trend was evident in increased availability of athletic scholarships for women, in the increase of nonathlete positions in sport, in higher commercial targeting of women's sport, and in decreased gender stereotyping, particularly by the media.

More than twenty-five years after the passage of Title IX—a law enacted, in part, to assure equal access for women to such athletic resources as scholarship funds, facilities, equipment, and travel budgets—colleges and universities began to comply in offering equal sport opportunities to women. During those two decades preceding compliance, fewer than 20 percent of institutions of higher education obeyed the law because to do so would necessitate shifting funds from or reducing the number of men's athletic teams. The U.S. Department of Education became the force driving compliance, and women's teams made up 227 of the 248 teams added by colleges and universities during 1996–1997, with soccer dominating the additions. In 1996, male athletes received $184 million more in scholarships than women did. By 1998, of the more than 99,000 athletic scholarships offered by National Collegiate Athletic Association colleges, approximately 38,000 were awarded to women. Before Title IX, fewer than 300,000 women participated in interscholastic athletics nationwide, but by the late 1990s, there were approximately 2.25 million women involved in soccer, basketball, track and field, and softball, and additional women were involved in other sports, including water polo, fencing, golf, and rowing.

In addition to opportunities created by universities' compliance with Title IX, other openings for women in noncompetitive positions burgeoned. Women gained positions as coaches, trainers, agents, promoters, and journalists, pushed forward by a new force toward commercialism in women's sport. In the late 1990s, women made up 46 percent of the workforce in the United States and thus exerted a powerful influence on the economy, including the sport industry. As the fitness trend took hold, accompanied by a more relaxed attitude regarding daily street and office wear, that economic impact could be particularly noted in the increased marketing of women's athletic apparel. Corporate sponsorship of women's athletic events and of women athletes more than doubled, to over $600 million in a five-year period.

Consequently, television coverage of women's sports began to grow, and messages of improved health and self-esteem, featuring women athletes as role models, were commercially packaged. In a national survey, 91 percent of respondents, both men and women, said that fitness was important to them and that physical attractiveness meant "being in shape" and "having a healthy lifestyle." Responding to the national image, the media's depiction of women athletes also began to change, from the traditional mannish likeness of years past to a softer, more feminized view, implying that being athletic was not only acceptable but encouraged. To create awareness of and promote involvement in athletics by girls and women, a National Girls and Women in Sports Day was instituted by the U.S. Congress in 1986 with full media coverage.

Despite improvements, problems persist in women's athletics. There is still an overemphasis among some on body image, which can lead to eating disorders or drug use; there is still evidence of gender stereotyping and barriers to overcome; and there is still resistance to accepting women athletes as equal to male athletes. But overall, women's athletics have "come a long way, baby."

—*Joyce Duncan*

See also: Apparel, in Sport; Eating Disorders among Athletes; Television, Impact on Sport; Title IX

For further reading:

Cahn, Susan K. 1994. *Coming on Strong: Gender and Sexuality in Twentieth-Century Women's Sport.* New York: Free Press.

Dowling, Colette, and Tiffeny Milbrett. 2001. *The Frailty Myth: Redefining the Physical Potential of Women and Girls.* New York: Random House.

Duncan, Joyce. 2001. *Ahead of Their Time: A Biographical Dictionary of Risk-Taking Women.* Westport, CT: Greenwood Press.

Sandoz, Joli, and Joby Winans, eds. 1999. *Whatever It Takes: Women on Women's Sport.* New York: Farrar, Straus and Giroux.

Smith, Lissa, Lucy Danziger, and Mariah B. Nelson. 1999. *Nike Is a Goddess: The History of Women in Sports.* New York: Atlantic Monthly Press.

Zimmerman, Jean. 1998. *Raising Our Athletic Daughters: How Sports Can Build Self-Esteem and Save Girls' Lives.* New York: Doubleday.

WOODEN, JOHN (1910–)

John Wooden, who coaches the art of introspection and has reduced his teachings to the absolute basics, remains one of the most important figures in college basketball history. Born on a farm in Indiana, Wooden learned early on from his parents that gentleness, patience, and a work ethic were the most important attributes of life. Although he was a three-time All-American in basketball at Purdue University, his greatest gift to society is his love of helping others.

After a successful college playing career, Wooden was hired as coach at the University of California, Los Angeles (UCLA). During his first fifteen years in that position, his team won no National Collegiate Athletic Association (NCAA) titles, but in the last twelve years of his tenure there, the university team took home ten national championships. He did not believe in scouting the competition or looking for the weaknesses in other teams; he taught his team to be the best it could be.

In the 1930s, Wooden created his "pyramid of success" and shared it in his teachings. The Wizard of Westwood, as he is known, defines success as the satisfaction of knowing one has performed to one's optimum capability. He is a cherished public speaker and is sought not only by other coaches but also by corporate America. Wooden is the only person to be inducted into the Basketball Hall of Fame

UCLA coach John Wooden, who is referred to in basketball circles as the "Wizard of Westwood," shouts directions to his players from the bench during an NCAA championship game. Wooden won his last game as UCLA's head coach with a 92-85 victory (March 31, 1975). (BETTMANN/CORBIS)

twice, as a player and as a coach. He has authored several books, including *They Call Me Coach* (1972) and *Coach Wooden: One-on-One* (2003).

—*Scott A. Misner*

See also: Basketball

For further reading:

Biro, Brian D. 2001. *Beyond Success: The Fifteen Secrets to Effective Leadership and Life Based on Legendary Coach John Wooden's Pyramid of Success.* New York: Berkley.

Chapin, Dwight, and Jeff Prugh. 1973. *The Wizard of Westwood: Coach John Wooden and His UCLA Bruins.* Boston: Houghton Mifflin.

WOODS, ELDRICK "TIGER"
(1975–)

After winning three consecutive U.S. Golf Association Amateur Championships in 1994–1996, Tiger Woods turned professional. He won seven tournaments within twelve months, to become one of sport's most recognizable figures, a role model for a variety of ethnic groups, and a popular culture phenomenon. Raised in Cypress, California, Woods appeared, at the age of five, on *The Tonight Show with Johnny Carson* and other television programs to demonstrate his golfing skill. After enjoying unprecedented success as a junior golfer, he attended Stanford University.

Not only was Woods lauded for his youth and early success, he was the first non-Caucasian to win a major tournament. As a mixture of Chinese, Native American, African American, and Caucasian, Woods became a popular role model for a culturally mixed audience. At the age of twenty-one, he became the youngest golfer to win the Masters Golf Tournament and established a new record, shooting 270. In addition, his twelve-stroke victory was the largest winning margin in a major championship. By winning four tournaments and better than $2 million in his first year on tour, he set a new record for winnings for the game.

Within one year, Woods is credited with unleashing a tidal wave of over $650 million for the sport in increased ticket prices, concessions and souvenir sales, merchandise sales, and television contracts. His endorsement deals alone exceed $100 million, including a $40 million contract with Nike and a $20 million arrangement with Titleist.

His youthful enthusiasm, his flashing trademark smile, his tremendous golfing power, his immediate success, and his ethnic background in a sport dominated by white professionals helped move golf from the back pages of the sport section into the spotlight. Woods has established a foundation for and offers golfing clinics to inner-city minorities who wish to learn the game.

—*Mike Schoenecke*

See also: Discrimination, Racial, in Sport; Golf

For further reading:
Gutman, Bill. 1997. *Tiger Woods: A Biography.* New York: Pocket Books.

Owen, David. 2001. *The Chosen One: Tiger Woods and the Dilemma of Greatness.* New York: Simon and Schuster.

Rosaforte, Tim. 2000. *Raising the Bar: The Championship Years of Tiger Woods.* New York: Thomas Dunne.

Tiger Woods watches his tee shot on the fourth hole during the second round of the Tour Championship at the Champions Golf Club in Houston, Texas, on November 7, 2003. Woods started the round tied for 13th place.
(JEFF MITCHELL/REUTERS/CORBIS)

Brazilian team player Zito (number 19) leaps for joy after scoring the second goal for Brazil in their 3-1 defeat of Czechoslovakia in the 1962 World Cup Final at Santiago, Chile. It was Brazil's second consecutive win of the coveted Jules Rimet trophy.
(HULTON-DEUTSCH COLLECTION/CORBIS)

WORLD CUP COMPETITION

Aided by increased television coverage and by the U.S. hosting of the 1994 event, soccer's World Cup has produced heightened awareness of the world sport community, raised the level of U.S. soccer, and stimulated both participant and spectator interest in the sport. Although soccer—known throughout most of the world as football—was not codified until 1863 in England, it had spread so extensively by the early 1900s that the sport's leaders in various countries felt the need for an organization to standardize rules and to facilitate international competition. Founded in Paris in 1904, the Fédération Internationale de Football Association (FIFA) remains soccer's international governing body.

From early in its existence, FIFA considered a tournament to determine a world champion, but until the late 1920s, it was content to use the Olympic Games for that purpose. Finally, as soccer became more professional, FIFA authorized Uruguay, home of Olympic gold medalist teams in 1924 and 1928, to serve as host of the first World Cup in 1930. Thirteen countries participated in the competition, which Uruguay won. The U.S. team lost in the semifinals in Uruguay, was eliminated in the first round in Italy in 1934, and then shocked powerful England—the only U.S. victory—in Brazil in 1950. The team failed to qualify for the championships again until 1990 in Italy because U.S. national teams were composed mainly of amateurs, often first- or second-generation immigrants, and attempts to build professional soccer in the 1970s and 1980s failed except for a modified indoor game. But the sport gradually spread in the United States as a middle-class, suburban sport, and as hosts of the 1994 World Cup, the Americans advanced to the second round, losing to eventual champion Brazil. In 1996, Major League Soccer revived the outdoor professional game. As more U.S. players pursued careers at home and in Europe, the increasingly competitive national team qualified for the thirty-two-team World Cup field in France in 1998 and made a strong showing in the 2002 event held in Japan and South Korea. Following the 1928 Olympics, it was decided that the World Cup finals would be staged every four years between the Olympics. The choice of venues generally alternated between Europe and Latin America. Aside from the United States in 1994, the 2002 tournament was the first held outside those areas, in Japan and South Korea.

—*Joseph L. Arbena*

See also: Immigrants, Community and Sport; do Nascimento, Edson Arantesm "Pelé"; Soccer

For further reading:

Davidson, Gary. 1974. *Breaking the Game Wide Open.* With Bill Libby. New York: Atheneum.

Davies, Pete. 1994. *Twenty-Two Foreigners in Funny Shorts: The Intelligent Fan's Guide to Soccer and World Cup '94.* New York: Random House.

Jose, Colin. 1994. *The United States and World Cup Soccer Competition.* Metuchen, NJ: Scarecrow Press.

Ronberg, Gary. 1984. *The Illustrated Hockey Encyclopedia.* New York: Balsam Press.

Stewart, Mark. 2003. *The World Cup.* New York: Franklin Watts.

WORLD FOOTBALL LEAGUE

In 1974, the World Football League (WFL) became the first challenger to the newly minted monopoly of the National Football League (NFL) since its 1970 merger with the American Football League (AFL). Gary Davidson, an entrepreneur who had founded the American Basketball Association in 1967 and the World Hockey Association in 1972, saw the same potential for the WFL as he had for the other rival leagues he had initiated. Beginning in the late 1960s, there was an increased awareness that sport was more than just a game, that it was a source of civic pride and economic development and that it was another way to feed an ever-increasing need for television programming. The WFL, like Davidson's other "alternative" leagues, provided the first opportunities for cities like San Antonio, Texas; Charlotte, North Carolina; and Jacksonville, Florida, to belong to the major league sport landscape. The league also gave options to players in the days before free agency created the unfettered movement of players so familiar today.

Amid an economy in recession, the league was introduced at a Los Angeles press conference in January 1973, with teams proposed for New York, Philadelphia, Washington, Boston, Orlando, Chicago, Detroit, Southern California, Memphis, Birmingham, Hawaii, and Toronto. Houston replaced Toronto when legislators threatened to ban both the WFL and the NFL from Canada. Portland and Jacksonville were later added to the original lineup, and play began in the fall of 1974. The teams were stocked with a mixture of untested rookies and retreads from the NFL, with most of the recognizable names being players past their prime. The first season played out before limited-attendance audiences and against a backdrop of mismanagement and outright fraud. For example, the Portland Storm played for six weeks without a payday and depended on the booster club to pick up the check for pregame meals. Several teams played under the threat of Internal Revenue Service liens, and the Detroit Wheels filed for bankruptcy and then folded. The owner of the Southern California Sun was indicted by a grand jury on charges of making false statements to obtain bank loans for his team. And the Charlotte Hornets, which had started the season as the New York Stars, declined to participate in the play-offs in order for their owner to find new investors for the team. The Birmingham Americans defeated the Orlando Florida Blazers in the league's only championship game, but the Americans' uniforms were repossessed after the season ended.

A revamped version of the league readied for the 1975 season with a new president, all but two teams under new ownership, and a few significant additions of NFL stars to the roster. But most efforts to recruit the NFL's superstars failed. Unable to attract network coverage due to the NFL's dominance in major markets and citing $30 million in losses, the league disbanded in October 1975. Another challenger to the monopoly of the NFL would not emerge until the founding of the U.S. Football League in 1983.

—*Keith Cannon*

See also: Football

For further reading:

Davidson, Gary. 1974. *Breaking the Game Wide Open.* With Bill Libby. New York: Atheneum.

Gluck, Herb. 1975. *While the Gettin's Good: Inside the World Football League.* Indianapolis, IN: Bobbs-Merrill.

"World Football League Suspends Operation after Losses of $30 Million." 1975. *New York Times,* October 30.

WORLD HOCKEY ASSOCIATION

For seven seasons, the World Hockey Association (WHA) challenged the dominance of the National Hockey League (NHL) in professional hockey in North America. In the process, it increased salaries for professional players in both leagues, introduced hockey to new markets, initiated the flow of European players to North America, and began or revived the careers of some of hockey's all-time great players. The WHA gained credibility in its first year when the Winnipeg Jets signed Bobby Hull from the Chicago Blackhawks, largely on the basis of a million-dollar signing bonus drawn from the league's collective fund. Other high-quality NHL players followed Hull to the new league, anchoring teams in new markets, including Cleveland, Ottawa, Quebec, Houston, and Edmonton. The league also went head-to-head with NHL franchises in Boston, Philadelphia, New York, Los Angeles, Minneapolis-St. Paul, and Chicago.

In the WHA's second year, the Houston Aeros revived the career of "Mr. Hockey," Gordie Howe, bringing him out of retirement and signing his teenage sons, Mark and Marty, out of junior hockey. The signing was not simply a publicity stunt—Gordie Howe led the team in scoring, was the league's Most Valuable Player, and led the Aeros to the AVCO (Aviation Corporation of America) Cup, the WHA equivalent of the Stanley Cup.

In 1974–1975, the Winnipeg Jets signed three Swedish players: Ulf Nilsson, a center; Anders Hedberg, a right-winger; and Lars-Erik Sjoberg, a defenseman. Nilsson and Hedberg teamed with Hull to form the Hot Line, amassing 362 points in seventy-eight games. Sjoberg was one of the top defensemen in the league and earned sixty points. Collectively, the Swedes and some of the other European players signed by the WHA proved that European hockey stars could play professionally in North America.

Throughout its remaining four years, the WHA continued to attract high-quality players, but it had trouble building solid franchises. Teams came and went in Indianapolis, Cincinnati, Birmingham, Phoenix, San Diego, Baltimore, Denver, Toronto, Vancouver, and Calgary. Wayne Gretzky began his professional career with the Indianapolis team, a franchise that played only twenty-five games in the 1978–1979 season before folding. Gretzky went to the Edmonton Oilers and then into the NHL with the Oilers the next year. The WHA's four solid franchises—Edmonton, Winnipeg, Quebec, and Hartford, née New England—merged with the NHL at the start of the 1979–1980 season. The Winnipeg franchise moved to Phoenix; the Quebec, to Denver; and Hartford to Raleigh, North Carolina.

—*Kevin Brooks*

See also: Howe, Gordon "Gordie"; Hull, Robert "Bobby" Marvin; National Hockey League

For further reading:

Lautier, Jack, and Frank Polnaszek. 1996. *Same Game, Different Name: The History of the World Hockey Association.* Great Falls, MT: Glacier Publishing.

McKay, Jim, David Rowe, Geoffrey A. Lawrence, and Toby Miller. 2001. *Globalization and Sport: Playing the World.* London: Sage.

WORLD WRESTLING FEDERATION

With an aggressive business strategy and the ability to appeal to nonwrestling fans, the World Wrestling Federation (WWF) redefined an entire industry. When Vincent K. McMahon Jr. gained control of a company founded by his father in the early 1980s, he began to change the way wrestling was promoted. Rather than staying within the northeastern United States as his father had since 1963, McMahon expanded across the United States and Canada.

With a cast of characters that included Hulk Hogan (Terry Gene Bollea), Randy "Macho Man" Savage, and the Ultimate Warrior (Jim Hellwig), the WWF drove most of its competitors out of business. Whereas professional wrestlers come in all shapes and sizes, WWF grapplers looked more like comic-book superheroes come to life: charismatic, tanned, and muscular. McMahon cleaned up the image of professional wrestling by gearing his marketing toward children. The children brought their parents out to the matches, encouraging them to purchase a wide array of souvenirs. WWF merchandise, ranging from action figures to lunch boxes, was soon found in stores across North America.

The WWF was a pioneer in the pay-per-view industry, broadcasting its first program in 1985.

Events such as "Wrestlemania" became a staple of the young industry. Thanks to pay-per-view and a network television show, *Saturday Night's Main Event,* the WWF became synonymous with professional wrestling throughout the world. However, when the promotion was rocked by two steroid scandals in the early 1990s, the WWF shifted its focus away from musclemen to smaller, more athletic wrestlers.

—*Kenneth Phillips*

See also: Bollea, Terry Gene "Hulk Hogan"; Television, Impact on Sport; Wagner, "Gorgeous George" Raymond

For further reading:

Assael, Shaun, and Mike Mooneyham. 2002. *Sex, Lies and Headlocks: The Real Story of Vince McMahon and the World Wrestling Federation.* New York: Crown.

Ross, Jim. 2000. *Can You Take the Heat? The WWF Is Cooking!* New York: ReganBooks.

WRESTLING, PROFESSIONAL

In Woody Allen's *Hannah and Her Sisters* (1986), the filmmaker asks, "Can you imagine the level of the mind that watches professional wrestling?" Professional wrestling is a cultural punch line. If a stand-up comedian or a writer wants to describe an event as an over-the-top spectacle, chances are good a comparison is made to professional wrestling or, more specifically, to Vince McMahon's World Wrestling Federation (WWF). Professional wrestling gets an easy laugh because it seems so absurd: grown men in their underwear pretending to hurt each other. However, to the millions of Americans who call themselves fans, it is anything but a joke.

Wrestling is one of the oldest sports; tales of wrestling contests fill ancient literature. Wrestling matches for show began in England in the 1600s and immigrated to the United States in the 1830s. Most matches took place at carnivals; thus, carnival tradition is the backbone of pro wrestling. Wrestlers call audience members by the same name carnival workers use for attendees: "marks," that is, those who get taken by a con game.

Frank Gotch from Iowa was considered the last "real" pro wrestling champion, participating in honest contests involving holds rather than pulled punches. With Gotch being nearly invincible and with matches often lasting for hours, those marketing the sport in the early 1900s knew something had to change. Enter the promoters, the masked marvels, and the spectacle that turned wrestling from pure sport to perverse entertainment.

This new form of professional wrestling soared in popularity in the 1920s and 1930s. The fix was in, but the audiences did not care, since they thoroughly enjoyed the sight of forthright brutality, and they shelled out well over $5 million a year to watch professional wrestlers. According to a 1937 article in *Life* magazine, the more the combatants scream, snort, grunt, growl, pant, bawl, and blubber, the louder the audience shrieks its approval. Even if, as some suspect, everything in the sport, down to the howls of anguish, is rehearsed in advance, the average fan is nevertheless satisfied to come back again to see an act combining the best features of a vaudeville show and a Roman gladiatorial combat. Some scholars, including the influential French critic Roland Barthes, have taken wrestling seriously and attempted to explain its appeal. But the dominant view is that wrestling is a joke; it is the epitome of low-brow entertainment.

Easy and inexpensive to televise, professional wrestling became a staple of early programming in the late 1940s and early 1950s. Although stars emerged, none were more famous than Gorgeous George (Raymond Wagner). George was a full-blown bad guy whom fans loved to hate. In the 1960s and 1970s, wrestling became localized, having "territories" based in large cities with local television coverage, normally on infant UHF stations. Although wrestling still appeared on the national landscape—a long profile on Dick "the Bruiser," William Richard Afflis, in *Sport* magazine in the 1960s, an occasional television cameo such as one by "Classy" Freddie Blassie on *The Dick Van Dyke Show,* the movie *The Wrestler* in 1973—the sport became regionalized. The coming of cable television and, more importantly, of Vincent K. McMahon, Jr., changed all that.

McMahon's father started the WWF in 1963. Madison Square Garden was his home base, from which he ran shows all along the East Coast. In the early 1980s, with his father's health failing, Vince took over the promotion. He changed the company's name to Titan Sports and began revolutionizing wrestling. McMahon broke all the rules: he "stole" other promoters' talent, bought out their television time, signed exclusive agreements with their arenas, and put most of them out of business. McMahon's new company, headlined by Hulk Hogan (Terry Gene Bollea) as lead baby-face or good guy, used the emerging cable industry to market his events across the country. He set up syndicated shows that were number one in most markets. On the first "superstation," WTBS, Ted Turner's *Georgia Championship Wrestling* was the most watched program on basic cable. The WWF attracted the attention of the mainstream press—including a cover story in *Sports Illustrated* and a match televised on MTV—and was thrust into the national consciousness. After presenting the 1985 show Wrestlemania I, McMahon expanded the empire through licensing agreements to create products from lunch boxes to trading cards, featuring the likenesses of WWF wrestlers. The WWF landed a monthly spot on NBC in 1986 with *Saturday Night's Main Event* and appeared in prime-time specials beginning in 1988. Success followed success as the WWF dominated prime-time with events like the 1987 Wrestlemania III, which drew over ninety thousand fans to the Pon-

> *If a stand-up comedian or a writer wants to describe an event as an over-the-top spectacle, chances are good a comparison is made to professional wrestling.*

Professional wrestler Hulk Hogan, also known as Hollywood Hogan, in the ring during the 1997 World Championship Wrestling Starcade.
(Duomo/Corbis)

tiac Silverdome, and wrestling became the cash cow of the early pay-per-view (PPV) industry.

Although the success of the WWF was built on many factors, one main selling point was the physique of its wrestlers. The bubble burst, however, with the arrest of a doctor affiliated with the WWF for trafficking in steroids. McMahon was tried in 1994 for distributing illegal steroids but was found not guilty. After the steroid scandal, the WWF business hit a downturn. It soon faced serious competition in 1995 from Ted Turner's World Championship Wrestling (WCW). Losing talent, advertisers, and viewers, the WWF adopted a hard edge and built its promotions around trash-talking Steve Austin. The emergence of Austin, the hiring of Mike Tyson for PPV, and innovative match making led to the WWF's regaining its popularity with mainstream fans, and the WWF was back on top by 1998. With the company going public through a stock offering in 2000, and with a new television contract with Viacom, WWF locked itself into the leadership position for the foreseeable future.

Professional wrestling has influenced "real sport" across the board. Muhammad Ali borrowed his "act" of taunting opponents from Gorgeous George. Baseball players now have theme music—another wrestling-inspired innovation. It is hard to imagine basketball player Dennis Rodman's "character" without the pro wrestling model. Rodman even made several appearances on wrestling shows. The most profound impact of wrestling on sport culture, however, is in the making. In the summer of 2000, McMahon announced plans for the Extreme Football League (XFL) to bring the WWF influence to professional football.

Wrestling has influenced popular culture as well. Roller Derby, Roller Game, and later Roller Jam were simply wrestling on skates. Syndicated television shows like *American Gladiators, Grudge Match*, and *Battledome* were also variations on the wrestling theme. Some television talk shows, in particular Jerry Springer's, are built around outrageous characters, feuds, and drawing "heat" from the audience. Although professional wrestling's influence on movies has been less profound, the documentary *Beyond the Mat* (2000) was well received, as was *Hitman Hart: Wrestling with Shadows* (1998) about former WWF champion Bret Hart. Wrestlers have made cameo appearances in movies for years, but the few centered around wrestling—from the 1989 Hulk Hogan opus *No Holds Barred* to the 1999 *Ready to Rumble*—have not fared well at the box office.

In addition, stand-up comedian Andy Kaufman's act borrowed heavily from wrestling. A lifelong wrestling fan, Kaufman became involved in a pro wrestling feud in the Memphis promotion with Jerry "the King" Lawler. In 1992, the duo appeared on *The David Letterman Show,* where Lawler slapped Kaufman hard across the face. All of this was treated as front-page news; it was, of course, just another pro wrestling stunt. Real hand-to-hand combat, in the form of "ultimate fighting," briefly captured the public imagination as a PPV attraction based heavily on the pro wrestling model.

Wrestling's popularity and influence increased dramatically in the late 1990s. During the summer of 1997, it seemed that every teenage boy was wearing a Steve Austin "3:16" T-shirt (a shirt with a skull dripping blood and 3:16, a reference to the Bible passage John 3:16, carved into its forehead). Wrestlers Mick "Mankind" Foley and Dwayne "the Rock" Johnson wrote best-selling books, and issues of *Playboy* featuring WWF women performers Sable and later Chyna became best sellers. WWF-produced videos dominated the recreational video charts, WWF-produced music featuring wrestling theme songs shot up the recording industry charts, and WWF video games were hot sellers. When a wrestler appeared on a television show, as, for example, Steve Austin did on *Nash Bridges,* ratings went up. Wrestlers made the rounds of the late-night talk shows, and *The Tonight Show*'s Jay Leno even competed in a WCW/PPV against then bad guy Hollywood Hulk Hogan. WWF wrestlers, in particular the

Rock, made guest appearances on many shows, including *Saturday Night Live*. But the most interesting guest appearance was the Rock speaking at the 2000 Republican National Convention.

Perhaps wrestling's cultural influence is most evident in politics. The most obvious example is the success of former wrestler Jesse "The Body" Ventura and his winning the governorship of Minnesota. One of the most telling examples was the influence that wrestling produced during the 2000 Democratic National Convention. For years, the WWF used a camera shot of the champion walking by himself in the backstage area before his match. The camera would follow the wrestler as he walked toward the entrance; the music would begin; the wrestler would emerge from the backstage area; and the crowd would go wild. This scenario, almost shot for shot, is how President Bill Clinton entered to speak at the convention. Another example is George H. W. Bush's comparison, in a documentary on presidential debates, of the debates to a wrestling match where the contestants trade barbs, pretend to dislike each other, and create an over-the-top "sham" spectacle.

The consequences of that spectacle are, however, the subject of much debate. With studies linking televised violence with violent behavior among children, with a slew of sensational news stories about children being crippled while trying wrestling moves, and with kids using wrestling catchphrases at their schools, the influence of wrestling on youth is controversial. These events, plus the increased violence and sexual content in wrestling, have led to a backlash decrying wrestling as a negative cultural influence. The WWF counters that their content reflects the culture rather than creating it.

The history of wrestling demonstrates its impact, in particular in the areas of new technology. Wrestling was the mainstay of early network television, a sure ratings success for UHF stations in their infancy, the dominant programming of early cable, the one sure thing in the pay-per-view industry, and one of the most visited and profitable Web sites (the WWF's Web site). Vince McMahon's impact is documented by his high standing in the "rankings" of influential people offered in magazines covering both sport (*Sporting News*) and entertainment (*Entertainment Weekly*). Combining the best or worst of sport and entertainment, professional wrestling ended the twentieth century still pulling punches and still the object of obvious comic punch lines, but also a pressing influence on U.S. culture.

—*Patrick Jones*

See also: *American Gladiators;* Television, Impact on Sport; Ventura, Jesse; Wagner, "Gorgeous George" Raymond; World Wrestling Federation

For further reading:

Archer, Jeff. 1999. *Theater in a Squared Circle: The Mystique of Professional Wrestling.* Lafayette, CO: White-Boucke.

Barthes, Roland. 1972. *Mythologies.* New York: Hill and Wang.

Campbell, John W. 1996. "Professional Wrestling: Why the Bad Guy Wins." *Journal of American Culture* 19 (Summer): 127–132.

"Cruel Crowds Demand Mat Torture." 1937. *Life,* January 25, 61–64.

Greenberg, Keith Elliot. 2000. *Pro Wrestling: From Pro Carnivals to Cable TV.* Minneapolis, MN: Lerner.

Mazer, Sharon. 1998. *Professional Wrestling: Sport and Spectacle.* Jackson: University Press of Mississippi.

WRIGLEY FIELD

With distinctive ivy-covered walls, numerous ballpark traditions, and a national cable-television audience, Wrigley Field stands as a baseball icon, a symbol of the game's history and color. Wrigley Field was originally Weeghman Field, built by Charles Weeghman as a home for his Federal League Chicago Whales. The Federal League was an "outlaw" league that challenged the major leagues. When the Federal League folded after the 1916 season, Weeghman was given the Cubs franchise. In 1920, Weeghman sold the Cubs to

William Wrigley Jr. and the ballpark was renamed Cubs Park. In 1926, the park was renamed Wrigley Field.

The only existing Federal League ballpark, Wrigley Field carries on numerous unique traditions. Its outfield walls were covered with ivy in 1935 at the suggestion of Bill Veeck, later recognized as one of baseball's great innovators. In 1969, as the Cubs fought for the National League East title through much of the season, a group of self-named "Bleacher Bums" took up residence in the outfield bleachers. The Bleacher Bums continued several Wrigley traditions, including throwing opposing teams' home-run baseballs back onto the field. Night games are only occasionally held at Wrigley Field and only came to the park on August 8, 1988.

In 1981, Tribune Broadcasting bought the Cubs and hired legendary announcer Harry Caray to call games. Caray brought another tradition to Wrigley, leading the singing of "Take Me Out to the Ball Game" during the seventh-inning stretch. Wrigley has been featured in numerous books and films, including Troy Soos's period mystery *Murder at Wrigley Field* (1997) and the films *While You Were Sleeping* (1995) and *V. I. Warshawski* (1991).

—*Daniel T. Durbin*

See also: Baseball; Stadiums

For further reading:

Golenbock, Peter. 1999. *Wrigleyville: A Magical History Tour of the Chicago Cubs.* New York: St. Martin's Press.

Hartel, William. 1994. *A Day in the Park: In Celebration of Wrigley Field.* Champaign, IL: Sagamore Publishing.

Jacob, Mark. 2003. *Wrigley Field: A Celebration of the Friendly Confines.* Chicago: Contemporary Books.

Wheeler, Lonnie. 1989. *Bleachers: A Summer in Wrigley Field.* Chicago: Contemporary Books.

X GAMES

Featuring new sports such as in-line skating and snowboarding, which offer an exciting blend of speed and danger, the X Games evolved into an alternative Olympics for the group of teens and twenty-somethings known as Generation X.

Created in 1995 by ESPN, the X Games boast an array of high-energy sports that reflect the athletic tastes of young America. Originally dubbed the Extreme Games, the name of the annual alternative Olympics was changed to better identify with Generation X, the fifteen-to-twenty-four-year-old age group that produces nearly all of the athletes and most of the audience for the games. Summer events include such water sports as barefoot water-ski jumping and wakeboard riding, bungee jumping, skateboarding, downhill in-line skating, aggressive in-line skating, bicycle stunt riding, street-luge racing, sport climbing, skysurfing, and team endurance racing. The winter X Games include snowboarding, ice climbing, snow mountain-bike racing, and super-modified shovel racing. The popularity of the games hinges on the dangerous and unpredictable nature of the sports, which is revealed for television audiences by innovative camera work that captures the intensity of the athletes at the height of competition. The avant-garde camera work has combined with the intensity, unpre-

BMX cyclist Stephan Cerra performs tricks during the finals of the Bike Stunt Flatland Competition at the ESPN X Games skate park.
(Duomo/Corbis)

dictability, and excitement of the sports to attract several large sponsors, including Miller Brewing Company, Taco Bell, Mountain Dew, Nike, Chevrolet, and Pontiac. Two of the sports, mountain biking and snowboarding, have been adopted as medal sports in the Olympic Games. The first two X Game competitions were held in Rhode Island, featuring over 350 athletes and nearly $380,000 in prize money. In 1997, the summer and winter versions were held in California. Because both areas enjoyed significant economic benefits from the games, future games will probably be the subject of serious bidding by cities across the United States.

—*Don L. Deardorff II*

See also: ESPN; Fads and Trends; Television, Impact on Sport

For further reading:

Genereaux, Bruce, and Peter C. Allen. 2002. *Beyond the Comfort Zone: Confessions of an Extreme Sports Junkie*. Hanover, NH: Class Five Press.

Rinehart, Robert E., and Synthia Sydnor. 2003. *To the Extreme: Alternative Sports, Inside and Out*. Albany: State University of New York Press.

Y

YANKEE STADIUM

A world-renowned sporting location, Yankee Stadium in the Bronx, New York, has hosted numerous baseball, football, and boxing championships and has served as a venue for significant religious, cultural, and political events over the past seventy-five years. Yankee Stadium is the home field of the New York Yankees, one of the most dominating franchises in the history of professional sport. Although other professional baseball teams moved to modern stadiums built on urban peripheries during the 1970s, the Yankees remained in the Bronx. The stadium underwent a refurbishing in 1975 that reduced the playing field's dimensions and created Monument Park, a memorial to the team's stars.

Yankee Stadium opened for the 1923 season. Its nickname, "the House that [Babe] Ruth Built," reflects owner Jacob Ruppert's understanding that he had to promote public fascination with a star in order to sell his product to mass culture. He followed the model initiated by motion-picture corporations that showed off stars, such as Douglas Fairbanks and Mary Pickford, to bring audiences to motion-picture palaces across the country.

In addition, Yankee Stadium has provided the space for many religious and cultural rallies and milestone events in sport. Rallies have included the annual assemblies of the Jehovah's Witnesses,

A world-renowned sporting location, Yankee Stadium in the Bronx, New York, has hosted numerous baseball, football, and boxing championships and has served as a venue for significant religious, cultural, and political events over the past seventy-five years (1948).
(Bettmann/Corbis)

415

political party gatherings, and the 1994 Gay Games closing ceremony. Yankee Stadium hosted the 1958 New York Giants–Baltimore Colts championship game, which ushered in the era of professional football as the most watched televised sport. Twenty years earlier, Joe Louis had struck a blow against racism with a first-round knockout of Nazi Germany's Max Schmeling in boxing's heavyweight championship.

—*Brett L. Abrams*

See also: Baseball; Gay Games; Ruth, George Herman "Babe," Jr.

For further reading:

Durso, Joseph. 1972. *Yankee Stadium: Fifty Years of Drama.* Boston: Houghton Mifflin.

Robinson, Ray, and Christopher Jennison. 1998. *Yankee Stadium: Seventy-Five Years of Drama, Glamour and Glory.* New York: Penguin Studio.

Sullivan, Neil. 2001. *The Diamond in the Bronx: Yankee Stadium and the Politics of New York.* New York: Oxford University Press.

YASTRZEMSKI, CARL (1939–)

The Boston Red Sox fans are among some of the most avid and loyal in the U.S.; thus, when Carl Yastrzemski replaced the perennially popular Ted Williams, he was forced to excel to appease the fans. A twenty-three-year veteran of the Boston Red Sox, Carl Yastrzemski was among the last of baseball's old guard, a workhorse whose loyalty to one team earned him both cheers and jeers from hometown fans. Yastrzemski stands in baseball lore as a symbol of team loyalty. He took over left field from Ted Williams in 1961 and retired in 1983, having won seven Gold Gloves, the Most Valuable Player Award, and the Triple Crown (for leading in home runs, runs batted in, and batting average); consequently, he was inducted into the National Baseball Hall of Fame in 1989.

Often booed throughout his career by the hometown crowd for failing to live up to the legacy of Williams or his own Triple Crown feats,

his numbers were nonetheless impressive. At his retirement, he was the only American League player with more than three thousand hits and four hundred home runs. Loyalty to team owner Tom Yawkey kept "Yaz," as he was called, at Fenway Park despite occasional conflicts, one of which occurred in 1966 when other players and manager Billy Herman accused him of laziness. The end of the season saw Herman depart, while Yaz stayed on, leading the Red Sox to their "Impossible Dream" World Series.

After stints at first base as designated hitter, Yastrzemski resumed playing left field in 1975 when Jim Rice injured his hand shortly before the World Series. The following year, the ballplayer bore the taunts again when his team dropped to third place. While the fans occasionally gave up on Yaz, he never gave up on them, his team, or its owner. Having joined Ty Cobb, Stan Musial, and Hank Aaron as the only major leaguers to have played in over 3000 games, Yastrzemski retired in 1983 with the legacy of one man's devotion to his team.

—*Donald P. Gagnon*

See also: Baseball; Fenway Park

For further reading:

Bryant, Howard. 2002. *Shut Out: A Story of Race and Baseball in Boston.* New York: Routledge.

Osborn, Kevin, ed. 1995. *Take Me out to the Ballgame: A Book of History, Hits and Heroes.* Kansas City, MO: Andrews McMeel Publishing.

YOUNG, DENTON TRUE "CY" (1867–1955)

As a young man, Denton Young earned his nickname, "Cyclone," shortened to Cy, for his blinding fastball, and after his death, he was honored by having the most coveted pitching award in major league baseball named for him. In 1956, the Baseball Writers' Association of America established the Cy Young Memorial Award to honor the major leagues' outstanding pitcher of the year. Since 1967, the award has been given annually to the best pitcher in each major league.

Holding major league records for the most games started, the most games completed, the most innings pitched, and the most games won made Denton "Cy" Young a symbol of durability and dependability, and the first great pitching idol of the American League. Born on March 29 in Gilmore, Ohio, and growing up on his parents' farm, Young continued to work as a farmer until the last few years of his life. That seasonal labor, coupled with the fact that Young ran during the off-season, gave him the strength and endurance that he needed to accomplish his feats. Beginning his major league career in 1890, Young started in 815 games, completed 749 of them, pitched 7,356 innings, and amassed 511 wins, while leading the league in shutouts for seven seasons. Just as remarkably, Young threw a perfect game at the age of thirty-seven, missed by one pitch a second one at the age of forty-one, and claimed that he never had a sore arm, even though he usually pitched on only two days' rest.

Such durability and consistency made Young a pitching legend who was admired by friend and foe alike. However, Young's impact on baseball was not limited to his combination of excellence and longevity. When the American League declared itself a major league in 1901, Young, already an established star in the National League, jumped to the fledgling circuit and by doing so helped give it talent and respectability. Young's popularity in 1908 caused the *Boston Post* to create Cy Young Day, which featured an exhibition

Newcomerstown, Ohio. Baseball legend Cy Young celebrates his 80th birthday (March 31, 1947). (BETTMANN/CORBIS)

game. Over 20,000 fans poured into the stadium and another 10,000 had to be turned away.

—*Angelo J. Louisa*

See also: Baseball; National Baseball Hall of Fame

For further reading:

Browning, Reed. 2000. *Cy Young: A Baseball Life.* Amherst: University of Massachusetts Press.

Macht, Norman L. 1992. *Cy Young.* New York: Chelsea House.

Z

ZAHARIAS, MILDRED "BABE" DIDRIKSON (1914–1956)

When most women were still in the traditional role of homemaker, Mildred "Babe" Didrikson Zaharias was excelling in a variety of sports. At the end of 1932, she was voted Woman Athlete of the Year by the Associated Press, an award which she won five additional times, in 1945, 1946, 1947, 1950, and 1954 (http://www.theglassceiling.com/biographies/bio38.htm). By 1949, she had claimed every title then available in golf, although she had begun that sport only fifteen years earlier. Decades before football and baseball player Bo Jackson became the commercial and cultural symbol for the "multisport athlete," "Babe" Didrikson had a worldwide following because of her domination of every sport in which she participated, destroying the myth that women were too weak to be true athletes. In fact, she earned her nickname as a child in sandlot baseball because the boys in the neighborhood thought she batted like Babe Ruth.

But Texas-born Babe Zaharias gained international fame in 1932 when, in one year, she single-handedly won the women's team championship trophy in the national Amateur Athletic Union (AAU) track-and-field competition and then set three world records in track-and-field events in the 1932 Olympics in Los Angeles. However, she did not officially acquire her nickname "Babe," taken from baseball great Babe Ruth, until after she hit five home runs in a single baseball game.

A household name in the middle decades of the twentieth century, Babe's sense of humor, athletic achievements, and promotional exhibitions—staged by her husband George Zaharias, a wrestling promoter, and her manager Fred Corcoran—made her a media darling with an international following. In addition to being inducted into the U.S. Olympic Hall of Fame and the Ladies Professional Golf Association (LPGA) Hall of Fame, she also excelled at softball, swimming, diving, ice-skating, tennis, and basketball. She pitched an exhibition game for the St. Louis Cardinals, toured with golf legend Gene Sarazen, and gave billiards exhibitions. A natural entertainer, Zaharias also took delight in demonstrating her skill as a ballroom dancer, a harmonica player, a typist (at eighty-six words a minute), a gin rummy player, and a seamstress.

After graduating from high school, she worked as a secretary for the Employers Casualty Insurance Company in Dallas, Texas, to earn enough money to compete as an amateur athlete. She was hired not so much for her secretarial skill but for her athletic ability, playing on the company's semi-professional basketball team, the Golden Cyclones. Didrikson kept busy with softball, diving, tennis, and track-and-field workouts during the team's

The American sports world has never known a more versatile, natural athlete than Mildred "Babe" Didrikson Zaharias. The slim, wiry amazon from Beaumont, Texas, steadfastly held the women's sports spotlight for eighteen years, during which time she excelled in basketball, tennis, shot putting, javelin and baseball throwing, high and broad jumps, swimming, diving, and golf (June 1, 1947).

(BETTMANN/CORBIS)

off-season. Between 1930 and 1932 she led the team to two finals and a national championship and she was voted All-American each season.

As an amateur track-and-field competitor, she qualified for five of the six 1932 Olympic events for women but was restricted to participating in only three. She won gold medals in both the javelin throw and the 80-meter hurdles, and only a technicality kept her from receiving a gold medal in the high jump: The judges ruled that her head cleared the bar before her feet did. The judges allowed her to keep her world-record jump, however, and she was awarded the silver medal.

While still an amateur golfer, Zaharias was the first American to win the British Women's Open. After turning professional, she won seventeen consecutive tournaments, held thirty-one official LPGA titles, and was a three-time U.S. Women's Open champion. Babe won her third U.S. Open title in 1954, less than a year after cancer surgery, by a record-setting twelve strokes.

Her life achievements are chronicled in a feature film and detailed by her own hand in *This Life I've Led: My Autobiography* (1955).

—*Rebekah V. Bromley*

See also: Amateur Athletic Union; Basketball; Ladies Professional Golf Association; Olympic Games

For further reading:

Cayleff, Susan E. 1996. *Babe: The Life and Legend of Babe Didrikson Zaharias.* Urbana: University of Illinois Press.

Cayleff, Susan E., and Susan Stamburg. 2000. *Babe Didrikson: The Greatest All-Sport Athlete of All Time.* Berkeley, CA: Conari Press.

"The Glass Ceiling Biographies: Babe Didrikson Zaharias." http://www.theglassceiling.com/biographies/bio38.htm. Accessed July 2004.

Bibliography

Aaseng, Nathan. *Florence Griffith Joyner: Dazzling Olympian.* Minneapolis, MN: Lerner, 1989.

Abdul-Jabbar, Kareem. *Kareem.* New York: Warner Books, 1990.

———. *A Season on the Reservation: My Sojourn with the White Mountain Apache.* New York: William Morrow, 2000.

Abdul-Jabbar, Kareem, and Peter Knobler. *Giant Steps: The Autobiography of Kareem Abdul-Jabbar.* New York: Bantam, 1993.

Acerrano, Anthony. "Jack London: Outdoor Adventurer." *Sports Afield,* December 1983, 56–61.

Adams, Natalie Guice, and Pamela Jean Bettis. *Cheerleader! An American Icon.* New York: Palgrave Macmillan, 2003.

Albanese, Catherine. *America: Religions and Religion.* Belmont, CA: Wadsworth, 1981.

Alexander, Charles. *Our Game: An American Baseball History.* New York: Henry Holt, 1991.

Allen, Maury. *Baseball's 100: A Personal Ranking of the Best Players in Baseball History.* New York: A&W Visual Library, 1981.

Allison, Lincoln. *Amateurism in Sport: An Analysis and a Defence.* Portland, OR: Frank Cass, 2001.

———, ed. *The Politics of Sport.* Wolfeboro, NH: Manchester University Press, 1986.

Ambrose, Stephen. *Duty, Honor, Country: A History of West Point.* Baltimore, MD: Johns Hopkins University Press, 1966.

American Association for Higher Education. "Ethics and Intercollegiate Sport." *AAHE Bulletin,* February 1990, 3–7.

Ammer, Christine. *Southpaws and Sunday Punches and Other Sporting Expressions.* New York: Plume Books, 1992.

Andersen, Robert. *Robert Coover.* Boston: Twayne Publishers, 1981.

Anderson, Dave. *The Story of the Olympics.* Southbury, CT: Birch Tree, 1996.

Anderson, Ken, and Melissa Roberts. *Nolan Ryan: Texas Fastball to Cooperstown.* Austin, TX: Eakin Press, 1999.

Anderson, Romola. *A Short History of the Sailing Ship.* New York: Dover, 2003.

Andersonn, Christopher, and Barbara Andersonn. *Will You Still Love Me If I Don't Win? A Guide for Parents of Young Athletes.* Dallas, TX: Taylor Publishing, 2000.

Angell, Roger. *Game Time: A Baseball Companion.* Edited by Steve Kettmann. San Diego, CA: Harcourt, 2003.

Appenzeller, Herb, ed. *Risk Management in Sport: Issues and Strategies.* Durham, NC: Carolina Academic Press, 1998.

Archer, Jeff. *Theater in a Squared Circle: The Mystique of Professional Wrestling.* Lafayette, CO: White-Boucke, 1999.

Armstrong, G., and R. Harris. "Football Hooligans: Theory and Evidence." *Sociological Review* 39, no. 3 (1991): 427–458.

Armstrong, Lance with Sally Jenkins. *It's Not About the Bike: My Journey Back to Life.* New York: Berkley Books, 2001.

Armstrong, Stephen. "The Olympics: Who'll Win Sponsors' Gold?" *Campaign,* July 12, 1996, 26–29.

Arsenault, Raymond. *St. Petersburg and the Florida Dream.* Norfolk, VA: Donning, 1988.

Asakawa, Gil, Leland Rucker, and Martha Kaplan. *The Toy Book: A Celebration of Slinky and G.I. Joe, Tinker Toys, Hula Hoops, Barbie Dolls, Snoot Flutes, Coon-Skin Caps, Slot Cars, Frisbees, Yo-Yos.* New York: Knopf, 1992.

Ashe, Arthur. *A Hard Road to Glory: A History of the African American Athlete.* 3 vols. New York: Amistad Press, 1993.

Asinof, Eliot. *Eight Men Out: The Black Sox and the 1919 World Series.* New York: Henry Holt, 1963.

Assael, Shaun, and Mike Mooneyham. *Sex, Lies and Headlocks: The Real Story of Vince McMahon and the World Wrestling Federation.* New York: Crown, 2002.

Atcheson, Dave. "Common Ground: When Flies Hit the Water, Rich and Poor Look the Same." *Alaska,* February 2003, 54–60.

"Athletes, Agents and Image." *The Grantsmanship Center (TGCI) Magazine,* Winter, 1998. www.tgci.com (retrieved July 12, 2003).

Atkinson, Jay. *Ice Time: A Tale of Fathers, Sons and Hometown Heroes.* New York: Crown, 2001.

Attner, Paul. "A New Perspective on the Draft." *Sporting News,* April 17, 2000, 53.

Atyeo, Don. *Blood and Guts: Violence in Sports.* London: Paddington, 1979.

Bachrach, Susan D. *The Nazi Olympics: Berlin 1936.* Boston: Little, Brown, 2000.

Baigell, Matthew. *A Concise History of American Painting and Sculpture.* Boulder, CO: Westview Press, 1996.

Bailer, Darice. *Extreme Sports: Dive!* Washington, DC: National Geographic, 2002.

Bak, Richard. *Joe Louis: The Great Black Hope.* New York: Da Capo, 1998.

Baker, Mark. *I Hate Videots: Today the Arcade, Tomorrow the World.* New York: Simon and Schuster, 1982.

Baker, William Joseph. *Jesse Owens: An American Life.* New York: Free Press, 1988.

Baldassaro, Lawrence. "Before Joe D: Early Italian Americans in the Major Leagues." In *The American Game: Baseball and Ethnicity,* 92–115. Carbondale, IL: Southern Illinois University Press, 2002.

Baldassaro, Lawrence, ed. *The Ted Williams Reader.* New York: Simon and Schuster, 1991.

———. *Ted Williams: Reflections on a Splendid Life.* Boston: Northeastern University Press, 2003.

Bale, John. *The Brawn Drain: Foreign Student-Athletes in American Universities.* Urbana: University of Illinois Press, 1991.

Barney, Robert K., Stephen R. Wenn, and Scott G. Martyn. *Selling the Five Rings: The International Olympic Committee and the Rise of Olympic Commercialism.* Salt Lake City: University of Utah Press, 2002.

Barrena, Jose O. *The Jai Alai and Us.* Madrid: Olimpo Publishing House, 1993.

Barrett, Marilyn. *Aggies, Immies, Shooters and Swirls: The Magical World of Marbles.* Boston: Bulfinch Press, 1994.

Barth, Gunther. *City People: The Rise of Modern City Culture in Nineteenth Century America.* New York: Oxford University Press, 1980.

Barthes, Roland. *Mythologies.* New York: Hill and Wang, 1972.

Bass, Amy. *Not the Triumph but the Struggle: The 1968 Olympics and the Making of the Black Athlete.* Minneapolis: University of Minnesota Press, 2002.

Bass, Mike. *Marge Schott: Unleashed.* Champaign, IL: Sagamore Publishing, 1993.

Basten, Fred, and Charles Phoenix. *Fabulous Las Vegas in the 50s: Glitz, Glamour and Games.* Santa Monica, CA: Angel City, 1999.

Batson, Larry. *Jimmy Connors.* Mankato, MN: Creative Education, 1975.

Battista, Garth, ed. *The Runner's Literary Companion: Great Stories and Poems about Running.* New York: Breakaway Books, 1994.

Bazzano, Carmelo. "The Italian-American Sporting Experience." In *Ethnicity and Sport in North American History and Culture,* eds. George Eisen and David K. Wiggins, 103–116. Westport, CT: Greenwood Press, 1994.

Beamer, Charles. *Video Fever.* Nashville, TN: T. Nelson, 1982.

Beardsley, Doug, ed. *The Rocket, the Flower, the Hammer and Me: A Hockey Fiction Reader.* Vancouver, BC: Polestar, 1989.

Bender, Gary, and Michael L. Johnson. *Call of the Game: What Really Goes On in the Broadcast Booth.* Chicago: Bonus Books, 1994.

Benedict, J., and A. Klein. "Arrest and Conviction Rates for Athletes Accused of Sexual Assault." *Sociology of Sport Journal* 14 (1997): 86–94.

Benedict, Jeff. *Public Heroes, Private Felons.* Boston: Northeastern University Press, 1997.

Benner, Bill. "Big-Time Sports: Big Business, Small Minds." *Indianapolis Business Journal,* July 15, 2002, 18.

Bennett, Jay. *Statistics in Sport.* New York: Arnold, 1998.

Bensley, Lillian, and Juliet Van Eenwyk. *Video Games and Real-Life Aggression: A Review of the Literature.* Olympia: Washington State Department of Health, 2000.

Berger, Phil. *Joe Namath, Maverick Quarterback.* New York: Cowles, 1969.

Berkow, Ira, and Jim Kaplan. *The Gospel according to Casey: Casey Stengel's Inimitable, Instructional, Historical Baseball Book.* New York: St. Martin's Press, 1992.

Berlage, Gai. *Women in Baseball.* Westport, CT: Praeger, 1994.

Bernstein, Mark F. *Football: The Ivy League Origins of an American Obsession.* Philadelphia: University of Pennsylvania Press, 2001.

Bevan, Jonquil. *Izaak Walton's "The Compleat Angler": The Art of Recreation.* New York: St. Martin's Press, 1988.

Bickley, Dan. *No Bull: The Unauthorized Biography of Dennis Rodman.* New York: St. Martin's Press, 1997.

Bigelow, Bob, Tom Moroney, and Linda Hall. *Just Let the Kids Play: How to Stop Other Adults from Ruining Your Child's Fun and Success in Youth Sports.* Deerfield Beach, FL: Health Communications, 2001.

Bingham, John. *No Need for Speed: A Beginner's Guide to the Joy of Running.* Emmaus, PA: Rodale Press, 2002.

Bingham, John, and Jenny Hadfield. *Marathoning for Mortals.* Emmaus, PA: Rodale Press, 2003.

Bingham, Walter. "Pathway to the Olympics: Speed." *Sports Illustrated,* December 14, 1987, 51–58.

Bird, Larry, Pat Riley, and Jackie Macmullan. *Bird Watching: On Playing and Coaching the Game I Love.* New York: Warner Books, 2000.

Biro, Brian D. *Beyond Success: The Fifteen Secrets to Effective Leadership and Life Based on Legendary Coach John Wooden's Pyramid of Success.* New York: Berkley Books, 2001.

Bissinger, H. G. *Friday Night Lights: A Town, a Team, and a Dream.* Reading, MA: Addison-Wesley, 1990.

Black Sox. http://www.mc.cc.md.us/Departments/hpolscrv/blacksox.htm.

Blanchard, Kendall. *The Mississippi Choctaw at Play.* Urbana: University of Illinois Press, 1981.

Bloom, Harold, ed. *August Wilson.* Broomall, PA: Chelsea House, 2002.

———, ed. *Bernard Malamud.* New York: Chelsea House, 1986.

———, ed. *Philip Roth.* New York: Chelsea House, 1986.

Bloom, John. *To Show What an Indian Can Do: Athletics in Native American Boarding Schools.* Minneapolis: University of Minnesota Press, 2000.

Bock, Philip. "A Monstrous Adventure." *Journal of Anthropological Research* 48 (Fall 1992): 261–265.

Bogumil, Mary L. *Understanding August Wilson.* Columbia: University of South Carolina Press, 1999.

Boorstin, Daniel J. *The Discoverers.* New York: Random House, 1983.

Bouton, Jim. *Foul Ball: My Life and Hard Times Trying to Save an Old Ballpark.* North Egremont, MA: Bulldog Publishing, 2003.

Bower, Joe. "Going over the Top." *Women's Sports and Fitness,* October 1995, 21–24.

Boyne, Daniel J. *The Red Rose Crew: A True Story of Women, Winning and the Water.* New York: Hyperion Books, 2000.

Breton, Marcos. *Home Is Everything: The Latino Baseball Story; From the Barrio to the Major Leagues.* El Paso, TX: Cinco Puntos, 2003.

Broer, Lawrence R., ed. *Rabbit Tales: Poetry and Politics in John Updike's Rabbit Novels.* Tuscaloosa: University of Alabama Press, 2000.

Brooke, Michael. *The Concrete Wave: The History of Skateboarding.* Toronto: Warwick, 1999.

Brooke-Ball, Peter. *The Great Fights: Eighty Epic Encounters from the History of Boxing.* London: Southwater Publishing, 2001.

Brooks, Bruce. *Boys Will Be.* New York: Henry Holt, 1993.

———. *Moves Make the Man: A Novel.* New York: Harper and Row, 1984.

Brooks, Kevin, and Sean Brooks, eds. *Thru the Smoky End Boards: Canadian Poetry about Sports and Games.* Vancouver, BC: Polestar, 1996.

Brooks, Tim, and Earle Marshe. *The Complete Directory to Prime Time Network and Cable TV Shows,*

1946–Present. 6th ed., rev. New York: Ballantine Books, 1995.

Brown, Dona. *Inventing New England: Regional Tourism in the Nineteenth Century.* Washington, DC: Smithsonian Institution Press, 1995.

Brown, Peter, and Daniel Abel. *Outgunned: Up against the NRA—The First Complete Insider Account of the Battle over Gun Control.* New York: Free Press, 2002.

Browne, Lois. *Girls of Summer: The Real Story of the All-American Girls Professional Baseball League.* New York: HarperCollins, 1993.

Browning, Mark. *Haunted by Waters: Fly Fishing in North American Literature.* Athens: Ohio University Press, 1988.

Browning, Reed. *Cy Young: A Baseball Life.* Amherst: University of Massachusetts Press, 2000.

Brummett, Barry. *Rhetoric in Popular Culture.* New York: St. Martin's Press, 1994.

Bryant, Howard. *Shut Out: A Story of Race and Baseball in Boston.* New York: Routledge, 2002.

Bryson, Bill. *A Walk in the Woods: Rediscovering America on the Appalachian Trail.* New York: Broadway Books, 1999.

Bueno, Ana, and Rafer Johnson. *Special Olympics: The First 25 Years.* Petaluma, CA: Foghorn Press, 1994.

Bulger, Margery A. "American Sportswomen in the 19th Century." *Journal of Popular Culture* 16 (1982): 190–191.

Burchard, S. H. *Sports Star, Fernando Valenzuela.* San Diego, CA: Harcourt Brace Jovanovich, 1982.

Burkhardt, Mitch. *Willie Mays.* Black American Series. Los Angeles: Holloway House, 1992.

Burnett, Darrell J. *It's Just a Game! Youth, Sports and Self-Esteem: A Guide for Parents.* iUniverse.com, 2001.

Butler, Herbert. *The PGA: The Official History of the Professional Golfers' Association of America.* New York: Crowell, 1975.

Butler, Robbie. *The Harlem Globetrotters: Clown Princes of Basketball.* Mankato, MN: Capstone Press, 2002.

Bynum, Mike. *The Best There Ever Was: The History of the Heisman Memorial Trophy and the Men Who Made It Famous.* New York: Gridiron Football Publishing, 1994.

Byrne, Robert. *Byrne's Standard Book of Pool and Billiards.* San Diego, CA: Harcourt Brace Jovanovich, 1987.

Cahn, Susan K. *Coming on Strong: Gender and Sexuality in Twentieth-Century Women's Sport.* Cambridge, MA: Harvard University Press, 1995.

Caillois, Roger. *Man, Play and Games.* Urbana: University of Illinois Press, 2001.

Cain, Nick. *Rugby Union for Dummies.* New York: John Wiley and Sons, 2003.

Callahan, Tom. "The Lopsided Dream." *U.S. News and World Report,* August 10, 1992.

Campanella, Roy, and Jules Tygiel. *It's Good to Be Alive.* Lincoln: University of Nebraska Press, 1995.

Campbell, John W. "Professional Wrestling: Why the Bad Guy Wins." *Journal of American Culture* 19 (Summer 1996): 127–132.

Campbell, Joseph. *Hero with a Thousand Faces.* Princeton: Princeton University Press, 1949.

———"Mythologies of the Primitive Hunters and Gatherers." Part 1 of *The Way of the Animal Powers,* vol. 1 of *Historical Atlas of World Mythology.* New York: Van der Marck, 1983. Reprint New York: Perennial Library, 1988.

———. *The Power of Myth.* With Bill Moyers. Ed. Betty Sue Flowers. New York: Doubleday, 1988.

Campion, Lynn. *Rodeo: Behind the Scenes at America's Most Exciting Sport.* Guilford, CT: Lyons Press, 2002.

Candelaria, Cordelia. *Seeking the Perfect Game: Baseball in American Literature.* Westport, CT: Greenwood Press, 1989.

"Candlestick Reborn." *Multinational Monitor,* September 2002, 4.

Cardoza, Avery. *The Basics of Winning Sports Betting.* New York: Seven Stories Press, 1999.

Cardwell, Paul, Jr. "The Attacks on Role-Playing Games." *Skeptical Inquirer,* Winter 1994, 157–166.

Carlton, Michael. "Rivers of Dreams." *Southern Living,* April 1994, 128–136.

Carnegie, Tom. *Indy 500: More Than a Race.* New York: McGraw-Hill, 1989.

Cashmore, Ellis. *Making Sense of Sports.* 2nd ed. New York: Routledge, 1996.

Castro, Tony. *Mickey Mantle: America's Prodigal Son.*

Washington, DC: Brassey's, 2002.

Cataneo, David. *Casey Stengel: Baseball's "Old Professor."* Nashville, TN: Cumberland House, 2003.

Cayleff, Susan E. *Babe: The Life and Legend of Babe Didrikson Zaharias.* Urbana: University of Illinois Press, 1996.

Cayleff, Susan E., and Susan Stamburg. *Babe Didrikson: The Greatest All-Sport Athlete of All Time.* Berkeley, CA: Conari Press, 2000.

Cerasini, Mark. *O. J. Simpson: American Hero, American Tragedy.* New York: Pinnacle Books, 1994.

Chandler, Charles. *Quotable Petty: Words of Wisdom, Success and Courage by and about Richard Petty, the King of Stock-Car Racing.* Nashville, TN: TowleHouse Publishers, 2002.

Chapin, Dwight, and Jeff Prugh. *The Wizard of Westwood: Coach John Wooden and His UCLA Bruins.* Boston: Houghton Mifflin, 1973.

Christgau, John. *The Origins of the Jump Shot: Eight Men Who Shook the World of Basketball.* Lincoln: University of Nebraska Press, 1999.

Chung, Su Kim. *Las Vegas: Then and Now.* San Diego, CA: Thunder Bay Press, 2003.

Churbuck, David. *The Book of Rowing.* Woodstock, NY: Overlook Press, 1988.

Churchill, Ward, Norbert S. Hill Jr., and Mary Jo Barlow. "An Historical Overview of Twentieth Century Native American Athletics." *Indian Historian* 12 (1979): 22–32.

Coakley, Jay. *Sport in Society: Issues and Controversies.* 6th ed. New York: McGraw-Hill, 1998.

Codden, Hal. *Jai Alai: Walls and Balls.* Amsterdam: Gamblers' Book Club, 1978.

Cohen, Stan, and Carol Van Valkenburg. *The Games of '36: A Pictorial History of the 1936 Olympic Games in Germany.* Missoula, MT: Pictorial Histories, 1996.

Colwin, Cecil M. *Swimming into the 21st Century.* Champaign, IL: Leisure Press, 1992.

Connellan, Tom. *Inside the Magic Kingdom: Seven Keys to Disney's Success.* Austin, TX: Bard Press, 1997.

Conner, Dennis, and Michael Levitt. *The America's Cup: The History of Sailing's Greatest Competition in the Twentieth Century.* New York: St. Martin's Press, 1998.

Cook, Jeff. *The Triathletes: A Season in the Life of Four Women in the Toughest Sport of All.* New York: St. Martin's Press, 1992.

Coombs, Karen Mueller. *Jackie Robinson: Baseball's Civil Rights Legend.* Springfield, NJ: Enslow, 1997.

Cooper, John R. *The Art of "The Compleat Angler."* Durham, NC: Duke University Press, 1968.

Cooper, Kenneth H. *The Aerobics Program for Total Well-Being.* New York: Bantam, 1985.

Cooper, Pamela Lynne. "26.2 Miles in America: The History of the Marathon Footrace in the United States." Ph.D. diss., University of Maine, 1995.

Cosell, Howard. *I Never Played the Game.* With Peter Bonventre. New York: William Morrow, 1985.

———. *What's Wrong with Sports.* New York: Simon and Schuster, 1991.

Costill, David L., and Scott Trappe. *Inside Running: The Athlete Within.* Traverse City, MI: Cooper Publishing, 2002.

Cousteau, Jacques-Yves. *Jacques Cousteau: The Ocean World.* New York: Harry N. Abrams, 1985.

Cramer, Richard. *Joe DiMaggio: The Hero's Life.* New York: Simon and Schuster, 2000.

Crawford, Robert W. "The Playground Movement Celebrates 100 Years." *Parks and Recreation* 20 (August 1985): 34–35.

Creamer, Robert. *Babe: The Legend Comes to Life.* New York: Simon and Schuster, 1974.

———. *Stengel: His Life and Times.* Lincoln: University of Nebraska Press, 1996.

Creasey, Malcolm, Nick Banks, and Ray Wood. *Complete Guide to Rock Climbing.* London: Lorenz Books, 2001.

Creedon, Pamela J., ed. *Women, Media and Sport: Challenging Gender Values.* Thousand Oaks, CA: Sage, 1994.

Crisp, Steve, and Monique Villa. *The Art of Sport: The Best of Reuters Sports Photography.* Englewood Cliffs, NJ: Prentice-Hall, 2003.

"Cruel Crowds Demand Mat Torture." *Life,* January 25, 1937, 61–64.

Crutcher, Chris. *Ironman: A Novel.* New York: Greenwillow Books, 1995.

Cuyler, P. L. *Sumo: From Rite to Sport.* New York: Weatherhill, 1979.

Daly, Chuck. *America's Dream Team: The Quest for Olympic Gold.* With Alex Sachare. Atlanta, GA: Turner, 1992.

Davidson, Gary. *Breaking the Game Wide Open.* With Bill Libby. New York: Atheneum, 1974.

Davidson, Sue. *Changing the Game: The Stories of Tennis Champions Alice Marble and Althea Gibson.* Seattle, WA: Seal Press. 1997.

Davies, Pete. *Twenty-Two Foreigners in Funny Shorts: The Intelligent Fan's Guide to Soccer and World Cup '94.* New York: Random House, 1994.

Davis, Hank. *Small-Town Heroes: Images of Minor League Baseball.* Iowa City: University of Iowa Press, 1997.

Davis, James, and Skin Phillips. *Skateboard Roadmap.* London: Carlton, 1999.

Davis, Laurel. "Protest against the Use of Native American Mascots: A Challenge to Traditional American Identity." *Journal of Sport and Social Issues* 17 (1993): 9–22.

———. *The Swimsuit Issue and Sport: Hegemonic Masculinity in "Sports Illustrated."* Albany: State University of New York Press, 1997.

Davis, Ron. "Olympics Gallery." *Runner's World,* October 1988, 46–51.

Dawidoff, Nicholas. *The Catcher Was a Spy.* New York: Pantheon, 1994.

Deford, Frank. *The Heart of a Champion: Celebrating the Spirit and Character of America's Sports Heroes.* Chanhassen, MN: NorthWord Books, 2002.

Dent, Jim. *The Junction Boys: How Ten Days in Hell with Bear Bryant Forged a Championship Team.* Irvine, CA: Griffin Publishing, 2000.

Derderian, Tom. *Boston Marathon: The History of the World's Premier Running Event.* Champaign, IL: Human Kinetics Publishers, 1994.

Dershowitz, Alan M. *Reasonable Doubts: The Criminal Justice System and the O. J. Simpson Case.* New York: Touchstone, 1997.

Dexter, Pete. "A Portrait of Evel: Some Call His Life Foolish; Knievel Calls It Art." *Esquire,* March 1985, 45–47.

Dickson, Paul. *The Dickson Baseball Dictionary.* New York: Facts on File, 1989.

———. *The Worth Book of Softball: A Celebration of America's True National Pastime.* New York: Facts on File, 1994.

Dinn, Sheila, Eunice Kennedy Shriver, and Nicole Bowman. *Hearts of Gold: A Celebration of Special Olympics and Its Heroes.* Woodbridge, CT: Blackbirch Press, 1996.

DiPiero, Thomas. "Angels in the (Out)Field of Vision." *Camera Obscura* 40–41 (May 1997): 200–225.

Doherty, Craig A., Katherine M. Doherty, and Nicole Bowman. *The Houston Astrodome: Building America.* Woodbridge, CT: Blackbirch Press, 1996.

Donaldson, Emily Ann. *The Scottish Highland Games in America.* Gretna, LA: Pelican, 1986.

Donovan, Michael Leo. *From Yankees to Fighting Irish: What's behind Your Favorite Team's Nickname?* Lenexa, KS: Addax, 2001.

Dowling, Colette, and Tiffeny Milbrett. *The Frailty Myth: Redefining the Physical Potential of Women and Girls.* New York: Random House, 2001.

Downward, Paul, and Alistair Dawson. *The Economics of Professional Team Sports.* New York: Routledge, 2000.

Duke, Vic, and Liz Crolley. *Football, Nationality and the State.* New York: Addison Wesley Longman, 1996.

Duncan, Joyce. *Ahead of Their Time: A Biographical Dictionary of Risk-Taking Women.* Westport, CT: Greenwood Press, 2001.

Dundes, Alan. *The Cockfight: A Casebook.* Madison: University of Wisconsin Press, 1994.

Dunn, Joseph. *Sharing the Victory: The 25 Year History of the Fellowship of Christian Athletes.* New York: Putnam. 1980.

Durso, Joseph. *Madison Square Garden: 100 Years of History.* New York: Simon and Schuster, 1979.

———. *Yankee Stadium: Fifty Years of Drama.* Boston: Houghton Mifflin, 1972.

Dworshak, Bruce, and Jay Soule, eds. *Games of August: Official Commemorative Book, the Tenth Pan American Games.* Wichita, KS: Showmasters, 1987.

Dyer, Nicole. "Born to Run." *Science World,* September 4, 2000, 18.

Dyer, R. A. *Hustler Days: Minnesota Fats, Wimpy Lassiter, Jersey Red and America's Great Age of Pool.* Guilford, CT: Lyons Press, 2003.

Earley, Pete. *Super Casino: Inside the "New" Las Vegas.* New York: Bantam, 2000.

"eBay Launches eBay Sports as Annual Gross Merchandise Sports Sales Near One Billion Dollars." *Business Wire,* October 2, 2002, 79.

Ebert, George. *Golf Is a Good Walk Spoiled.* Foreword by C. Grant Spaeth. Dallas, TX: Taylor Publishing, 1992.

Eccles, Jacquelynne S. "Adolescent Participation in Structured and Unstructured Activities: A Person-Oriented Analysis." *Journal of Youth and Adolescence* 32 (August 2003): 233–242.

Edwards, Bob. *Fridays with Red: A Radio Friendship.* New York: Simon and Schuster, 1993.

Eisenstock, Alan. *Sports Talk: A Journey inside the World of Sports Talk Radio.* New York: Pocket Books, 2001.

Elam, Harry J., Jr. *The Past as Present in the Drama of August Wilson.* Ann Arbor: University of Michigan Press, 2004.

Elder, Larry. *The Ten Things You Can't Say in America.* Irvine, CA: Griffin Publishing, 2001.

Eldred, Patricia Mulrooney. *Kathy Whitworth.* Mankato, MN: Creative Education, 1975.

Eliade, Mircea. *Myth and Reality.* Trans. Willard R. Trask. New York: Harper and Row, 1963.

Erardi, John. "Jobs-for-Athletes Decision Draws Skepticism." *Cincinnati Enquirer,* April 23, 1998.

Evans, Will F. *Hunting Grizzlys, Black Bear and Lions "Big Time" on the Old Ranches.* Silver City, NM: High Lonesome Books, 2001.

Evensen, Bruce J. *When Dempsey Fought Tunney: Heroes, Hokum, and Storytelling in the Jazz Age.* Knoxville: University of Tennessee Press, 1996.

Fagen, Herb. *Nomo: The Inside Story on Baseball's Hottest Sensation.* Boca Raton, FL: Demco Media, 1996.

Falkner, David. *The Last Hero: The Life of Mickey Mantle.* New York: Simon and Schuster, 1995.

Falla, Jack, Jack Batten, Lance Hornby, et al. *Quest for the Cup: A History of the Stanley Cup Finals, 1893–2001.* San Diego, CA: Thunder Bay Press, 2001.

Feinberg, Leslie. *Transgender Warriors: Making History from Joan of Arc to Dennis Rodman.* Boston: Beacon Press, 1997.

Feinstein, John. *A Civil War, Army vs. Navy: A Year inside College Football's Purest Rivalry.* Boston: Little, Brown, 1997.

———. *A Good Walk Spoiled.* Boston: Little, Brown, 1995.

———. *The Last Amateurs: Playing for Glory and Honor in Division 1 College Basketball.* Boston: Back Bay, 2001.

Feldmann, Doug. *Dizzy and the Gas House Gang: The 1934 St. Louis Cardinals and Depression-Era Baseball.* Jefferson City, NC: McFarland, 2000.

Fellowship of Christian Athletes. http://www.fca.org.

Fimrite, Ron. "Good Riddance: Few Will Mourn When the Last Baseball Game Is Played at Candlestick Park." *Sports Illustrated,* October 4, 1999, R4+.

Finch, Charles S., and Christopher Robin Finch. *Norman Rockwell: 332 Magazine Covers.* New York: Artabras Publishing, 1995.

Finch, Christopher Robin. *Norman Rockwell's America.* New York: Harry N. Abrams, 1975.

Fish, Joel. *101 Ways to Be a Terrific Sports Parent: Making Athletics a Positive Experience for Your Child.* New York: Simon and Schuster, 2003.

Fitzgerald, Mark. "Downside of Political Correctness." *Editor and Publisher,* June 11, 1994, 9.

Fixx, Jim. *Second Book of Running.* New York: Random House, 1980.

Flanagan, Alice K. *Wilma Rudolph: Athlete and Educator.* Chicago: Ferguson, 2000.

Flath, Arnold William. *A History of Relations between the National Collegiate Athletic Association and the Amateur Athletic Union of the United States (1905–1963).* Champaign, IL: Stipes, 1964.

Fleming, Gordon. *The Dizziest Season: The Gashouse Gang Chases the Pennant.* New York: William Morrow, 1984.

Flink, Steve, and Chris Evert. *The Greatest Tennis Matches of the Twentieth Century.* Danbury, CT: Rutledge Books, 1999.

Foggia, Lyla. *Reel Women: The World of Women Who Fish.* Hillsboro, OR: Beyond Words, 1995.

Ford, Richard. *The Sportswriter.* Reprint, New York: Vintage Books, 1995.

Fortanasce, Vincent, Lawrence Robinson, and John Ouellette. *The Official American Youth Soccer Organization Handbook: Rules, Regulations, Skills and Everything Else Kids, Parents and Coaches Need to Participate in Youth Soccer.* New York: Fireside, 2001.

Fost, Dan. "Fear and Marketing in Las Vegas: Casino Gambling Is Fast Becoming Mainstream Entertainment for Affluent Adults." *American Demographics,* October, 15, 1993, 19–22.

Fountain, Charles. *Sportswriter: The Life and Times of Grantland Rice.* New York: Oxford University Press, 1993.

Fox, Jack C., and Bob Mount. *The Illustrated History of the Indianapolis 500: 1911–1994.* Speedway, IN: Carl Hungess Publishing, 1995.

Fox, Michael W. *Animals Have Rights, Too.* New York: Continuum, 1991.

Frank, Joseph. *Whatever Happened to Gorgeous George?* Englewood Cliffs, NJ: Prentice-Hall, 1974.

Frazier, Joe. *Smokin' Joe: The Autobiography of a Heavyweight Champion of the World.* With Phil Berger. St. Paul, MN: Hungry Minds, 1996.

Freeberg, Lloyd. *In the Bin: Reckless and Rude Stories from the Penalty Boxes of the NHL.* Chicago: Triumph Books, 1998.

Freedman, Warren. *Professional Sports and Antitrust.* New York: Quorum Books, 1987.

Freeman, Denne H., and Jaime Aron. *I Remember Tom Landry.* Champaign, IL: Sports Publishing, 2001.

Freeman, Michael. *ESPN: The Uncensored History.* Taylor Publishing, 2002.

Fritz, Jean, and Mike Wimmer. *Bully for You, Teddy Roosevelt!* New York: Putnam, 1991.

Frommer, Harvey. *Shoeless Joe and Ragtime Baseball.* Dallas, TX: Taylor Publishing, 1992.

Funk, Gary D. *Major Violation: The Unbalanced Priorities in Athletics and Academics.* Champaign, IL: Leisure Press, 1991.

Funnell, Charles E. *By the Beautiful Sea: The Rise and High Times of That Great American Resort, Atlantic City.* New Brunswick, NJ: Rutgers University Press, 1975.

Gabriel, Mike. *The Professional Golfers' Association Tour: A History.* Jefferson, NC: McFarland, 2001.

Gaines, Charles, and George Butler. *Pumping Iron II: The Unprecedented Woman.* Hammond, IN: Horizon Publishing, 1984.

Gambetta, Vern. *Soccer Speed.* Sarasota, FL: Gambetta Sports, 1998.

Gammons, Peter. "The Campanis Affair." *Sports Illustrated,* April 20, 1987, 31.

Gardner, Martin, ed. *The Annotated "Casey at the Bat": A Collection of Ballads about the Mighty Casey.* New York: Dover, 1995.

The Gay Almanac. National Museum and Archive of Lesbian and Gay History: A Program of the Lesbian and Gay Community Services Center. New York: Berkley Books, 1996.

Gems, Gerald R. "The Construction, Negotiation and Transformation of Racial Identity in American Football: A Study of Native and African Americans." *American Indian Culture and Research Journal* 22 (Spring 1998): 131–133.

Genereaux, Bruce. *Beyond the Comfort Zone: Confessions of an Extreme Sports Junkie.* Hanover, NH: Class Five Press, 2002.

George, Gary, ed. *Winning Is a Habit: Vince Lombardi on Winning, Success, and the Pursuit of Excellence.* New York: HarperResource, 1997.

George, Nelson. *Elevating the Game: Black Men and Basketball.* New York: HarperCollins, 1992.

Gill, Wesley F. *Uncommon Valor: The Army-Navy Football Rivalry.* Champaign, IL: Human Kinetics Publishers, 1985.

Ginsberg, Daniel E. *The Fix Is In: A History of Baseball Gambling and Game Fixing Scandals.* Jefferson, NC: McFarland, 1995.

Gloeckner, Carolyn. *Fernando Valenzuela.* Mankato, MN: Crestwood House, 1985.

Gluck, Herb. *While the Gettin's Good: Inside the World Football League.* Indianapolis, IN: Bobbs-Merrill, 1975.

Goldberg, Karen. "If the Shoe Fits . . . Endorse It." *Insight on the News,* March 3, 1987, 38.

Goldlust, John. *Playing for Keeps: Sport, the Media and Society.* Melbourne, Australia: Longman Cheshire, 1987.

Goldstein, Alan. *Muhammad Ali: The Eyewitness Story of a Boxing Legend.* Toronto: Metro Books, 2001.

Goldstein, Richard. *Ivy League Autumns: An Illustrated History of College Football's Grand Old Rivalries.* New York: St. Martin's Press, 1996.

Goldstein, Warren. *Playing for Keeps: A History of Early Baseball.* Ithaca, NY: Cornell University Press, 1989.

Golenbock, Peter. *Wild, High and Tight: The Life and Death of Billy Martin.* New York: St. Martin's Press, 1994.

———. *Wrigleyville: A Magical History Tour of the*

Chicago Cubs. New York: St. Martin's Press, 1999.

Goodbody, John. *The Illustrated History of Gymnastics.* New York: Beaufort Books, 1983.

Gooden, Beverly T. "Stearns Conducts Hearing on College Recruiting Practices for Athletes." http://gop.house.gov/item-news, March 11, 2004, 1–2.

Goodman, Jeffrey. *Huddling Up: The Inside Story of the Canadian Football League.* Don Mills, ON: Fitzhenry and Whiteside, 1982.

Gottfried, Ted. *Earvin "Magic" Johnson: Champion and Crusader.* New York: Franklin Watts, 2001.

Gratton, Chris, and Ian Henry, eds. *Sport in the City.* New York: Routledge, 2001.

Gray, Gary. *Running with the Bulls: Fiestas, Corridas, Toreros, and an American's Adventure in Pamplona.* Guilford, CT: Lyons Press, 2001.

Gray, Ryan. *The Language of Baseball: A Complete Dictionary of Slang Terms, Clichés and Expressions.* Champaign, IL: Coaches Choice Publishing, 2002.

Graydon, Don, ed. *Mountaineering: The Freedom of the Hills.* Seattle, WA: Mountaineers Books, 1992.

Graydon, Don, and Kurt Hanson, eds. *Mountaineering: The Freedom of the Hills.* Seattle, WA: Mountaineers Books, 1997.

Green, Benny. *Shaw's Champions: The Noble Art from Cashel Byron to Gene Tunney.* London: David and Charles Publishing, 1978.

Greenberg, Keith Elliot. *Pro Wrestling: From Pro Carnivals to Cable TV.* Minneapolis, MN: Lerner, 2000.

Greene, Bob. *Hang Time: Days and Dreams with Michael Jordan.* New York: St. Martin's Press, 1993.

Greenfield, Steve, and Guy Osborn, eds. *Law and Sport in Contemporary Society.* Portland, OR: Frank Cass, 2000.

Greenwood, Jim. *Total Rugby.* London: A & C Black, 1998.

Gregorich, Barbara. *Women at Play.* New York: Harcourt Brace, 1993.

Gregory, Michael Steven. *Disc Golf: All You Need to Know about the Game You Want to Play.* Duluth, MN: Trellis, 2003.

Grella, George. "Baseball and the American Dream." *Massachusetts Review* 16, no. 3 (Summer 1975): 550–567.

———. "The Baseball Moment in American Film." *Aethlon* 14, no. 2 (Spring 1997): 7–16.

Grist, Everett. *Everett Grist's Big Book of Marbles: A Comprehensive Identification and Value Guide for Both Antique and Machine-Made Marbles.* Paducah, KY: Collector Books, 2000.

Gruver, Ed. *Koufax.* Dallas, TX: Taylor Publishing, 2000.

Gutkind, Lee. *The Best Seat in Baseball, but You Have to Stand: The Game as Umpires See It.* New York: Doubleday, 1975.

Gutman, Bill. *Gail Devers.* Austin, TX: Raintree Steck-Vaughn, 1996.

———. *Lance Armstrong: A Biography.* New York: Simon Spotlight Entertainment, 2003.

———. *Tiger Woods: A Biography.* New York: Pocket Books, 1997.

Gutman, Dan. *Baseball Babylon: From the Black Sox to Pete Rose; The Real Stories behind the Scandals That Rocked the Game.* New York: Penguin Books, 1992.

Guttmann, Allen. *From Ritual to Record: The Nature of Modern Sports.* New York: Columbia University Press, 1978.

———. *The Olympics: A History of the Modern Games.* Urbana: University of Illinois Press, 1992.

———. *Sports Spectators.* New York: Columbia University Press, 1986.

Haber, Paul. *Inside Handball.* Chicago: Contemporary Books, 1970.

Hagstrom, Robert G. *The NASCAR Way: The Business That Drives the Sport.* New York: John Wiley and Sons, 2001.

Hahn, James. *Nancy Lopez: Golfing Pioneer.* St. Paul, MN: EMC Paradigm, 1978.

Halberstam, David. *The Breaks of the Game.* New York: Knopf, 1981.

———. *Playing for Keeps: Michael Jordan and the World That He Made.* New York: Broadway Books, 2000.

———. *Sports on New York Radio: A Play-by-Play History.* New York: McGraw-Hill, 1999.

Hall, Mina. *The Big Book of Sumo: History, Practice, Ritual, Fight.* Berkeley, CA: Stone Bridge Press, 1997.

Hamilton, Scott, and Lorenzo Benet. *Landing It: My Life On and Off the Ice.* New York: Kensington Publishing, 1999.

Hargrave, Catherine Perry. *A History of Playing Cards and a Bibliography of Cards and Gaming.* New York: Dover, 1966.

Harris, Harry. *Pelé: His Life and Times.* New York: Parkwest, 2002.

Harris, Mark. *It Looked Like Forever.* Lincoln: University of Nebraska Press, 1989.

Harrison, L., C. K. Harrison, and L. N. Moore. "African American Racial Identity and Sport." *Sport, Education and Society,* October 1, 2002, 121–134.

"Harry Edwards Hints at College Sports Boycott." *Jet,* October 26, 1987, 51.

Hartel, William. *A Day at the Park: In Celebration of Wrigley Field.* Champaign, IL: Sagamore Publishing, 1994.

Hartnagle-Taylor, Jeanne Joy. *Greasepaint Matadors: The Unsung Heroes of Rodeo.* Loveland, CO: Alpine Publications, 1992.

Hartsoe, Charles E. "From Playgrounds to Public Policy." *Parks and Recreation* 20 (August 1985): 46–52.

Hauser, Tom. *Inside the Ropes with Jesse Ventura.* Minneapolis: University of Minnesota Press, 2002.

Hawk, Tony. *Hawk: Occupation Skateboarder.* With Sean Mortimer. New York: ReganBooks, 2000.

Hayes, Matt. "The Heat Is On—and Off." *Sporting News,* June 30, 2003, 56–58.

Heckman, D. "Women and Athletics: A Twenty Year Retrospective on Title IX." *University of Miami Entertainment and Sports Law Review* 9, no. 1 (1992): 1–64.

Heinz, W. C., and Nathan Ward, eds. *The Total Sports Illustrated Book of Boxing.* New York: Total Sports, 1999.

Heisler, John. *Quotable Rockne: Words of Wit, Wisdom and Motivation by and about Knute Rockne, Legendary Notre Dame Football Coach.* Nashville, TN: TowleHouse Publishers, 2001.

Heller, Peter Niels. *Bad Intentions: The Mike Tyson Story.* New York: Da Capo, 1995.

Helyar, John. *Lords of the Realm: The Real History of Baseball.* New York: Villard, 1994.

Hemingway, Ernest. *By-Line, Ernest Hemingway: Selected Articles and Dispatches of Four Decades.* Ed. William White. New York: Touchstone, 1998.

———. *Ernest Hemingway on Writing.* Ed. by Larry W. Phillips. New York: Touchstone, 1999.

———. *Hemingway on Hunting.* Edited and with an introduction by Séan Hemingway. Guilford CT: Lyons Press, 2001.

Hendrickson, Robert. *Grand Slams, Hat Tricks and Alley-Oops: A Sports Fan's Book of Words.* Englewood Cliffs, NJ: Prentice-Hall, 1994.

Hetz, Stanley. *Joe Montana: Just Another Player.* Philadelphia: Xlibris Press, 2000.

Hiestand, Michael. "Do Black Athletes Get a Fair Shake?" *Adweek's Marketing Week,* March 6, 1989, 73.

Higgs, Robert J. *God in the Stadium: Sports and Religion in America.* Lexington: University Press of Kentucky, 1995.

———. *Laurel and Thorn: The Athlete in American Literature.* Lexington: University Press of Kentucky, 1981.

———. *Sports: A Reference Guide.* Westport, CT: Greenwood Press, 1982.

Hill, Raymond. *O.J. Simpson.* New York: Random House, 1975.

Hoffman, Steven. *"Sports Illustrated" Knockouts: Five Decades of "Sports Illustrated" Swimsuit Photography.* New York: Time, 2001.

Hoffmann, Frank W., and William G. Bailey. *Sports and Recreation Fads.* New York: Haworth Press, 1996.

Hogan, Hulk. *Hollywood Hulk Hogan.* New York: Pocket Star, 2002.

Holston, Kim R. *The Marching Band Handbook: Competitions, Instruments, Clinics, Fundraising, Publicity, Uniforms, Accessories, Trophies, Drum Corps, Twirling, Color.* Jefferson, NC: McFarland, 1994.

Holway, John B. *Voices from the Great Black Baseball Leagues.* New York: Da Capo, 1992.

Hoops Heroes: The Basketball Hall of Fame. London: Checkerbee Publishing, 2001.

Horvitz, Peter S. *The Big Book of Jewish Baseball.* New York: SPI Books, 2001.

Howe, Colleen, and Gordie Howe. *And—Howe!: An Authorized Autobiography.* Traverse City, MI: Power Play Publications, 1995.

Howell, Mark D. *From Moonshine to Madison Avenue: A Cultural History of the NASCAR Win-*

ston Cup Series. Bowling Green, OH: Bowling Green State University Popular Press, 1997.

Huizinga, Johan. *Homo Ludens: A Study of the Play Element in Culture.* London: Maurice Temple Smith Ltd.,1970.

Hult, Joan S., and Marianna Trekell, eds. *A Century of Women's Basketball: From Frailty to Final Four.* Reston, VA: National Association for Girls and Women in Sport, 1991.

Humber, William, and John St. James, eds. *All I Thought about Was Baseball: Writings on a Canadian Pastime.* Toronto: University of Toronto Press, 1996.

Hunter, Matt. *Jesse Ventura: The Story of the Wrestler They Call "The Body."* Philadelphia: Chelsea House, 2000.

———. *The Story of the Wrestler They Call "Hollywood" Hulk Hogan.* Philadelphia: Chelsea House, 2000.

Illingworth, Montieth. *Mike Tyson: Money, Myth and Betrayal.* Secaucus, NJ: Birch Lane, 1991.

International Olympic Committee (IOC), ed. *The International Olympic Committee: One Hundred Years.* Lausanne, Switzerland: IOC, 1994.

Ireland, Mary, and Aurelia Nattiv, eds. *The Female Athlete.* Philadelphia: W. B. Saunders, 2003.

Isaacs, Neil D. *You Bet Your Life: The Burdens of Gambling.* Lexington: University Press of Kentucky, 2001.

Isenberg, Michael T. *John L. Sullivan and His America.* Urbana: University of Illinois Press, 1988.

Issacs, Stan. *Jim Brown: The Golden Year, 1964.* Englewood Cliffs, NJ: Prentice-Hall, 1970.

"Jackie Chan." http://www.imdb.com/name/nm0000329/ (retrieved June 15, 2004).

Jackson, Phil, and Hugh Delehanty. *Sacred Hoops: Spiritual Lessons of a Hardwood Warrior.* New York: Hyperion Books, 1995.

Jackson, Robert B. *Supermex: The Lee Trevino Story.* New York: Hill and Wang, 1973.

Jacob, Mark. *Wrigley Field: A Celebration of the Friendly Confines.* Chicago: Contemporary Books, 2003.

Jacobs, A. J. "Battle of the Flexes." *Entertainment Weekly,* February 17, 1995, 47.

Jares, Joseph. *Basketball: The American Game.* Chicago: Follett, 1971.

Jarvie, Grant. *Sport, Racism and Ethnicity.* New York: Routledge Falmer, 1991.

Jasper, James. *More Basic Betting: Programming to Win.* New York: St. Martin's Press, 1985.

Jefferson, Margo. "The Presence of Race in Politically Correct Ambiguity." *New York Times,* February 8, 1999.

Jenkins, Clarence. "Kinsella's *Shoeless Joe.*" *The Explicator* 53 (Spring, 1995): 179–182.

Jenkins, Dan. *Fairways and Greens: The Best Golf Writing of Dan Jenkins.* New York: Doubleday, 1994.

———. *You Call It Sports, but I Say It's a Jungle out There.* New York: Simon and Schuster, 1989.

Jensen, Brian, and Troy Aikman. *Where Have All Our Cowboys Gone?* Dallas, TX: Taylor Publishing, 2001.

Jewell, Don. *Public Assembly Facilities: Planning and Management.* New York: Wiley, 1978.

"Joe Montana." http://www.thedebster.com/magic.html (retrieved June 15, 2004).

Johnson, Dick, ed. *Ted Williams: A Portrait in Words and Pictures.* New York: Walker, 1991.

Johnson, Don, ed. *Aethlon: The Journal of Sport Literature* 14, no. 1 (1996).

Johnson, Earvin "Magic." *My Life.* With William Novack. New York: Random House, 1992.

Johnson, Jack. *Jack Johnson in the Ring and Out.* Mattituck, NY: Amereon, 1993.

Johnson, Phil. "Luge." *WomenSports,* December 1983, 39–43.

Johnson, Stancil. *Frisbee: A Practitioner's Manual and Definitive Treatise.* New York: Workman's Press, 1975.

Johnson, William O., Jr. *Super Spectator and the Electric Lilliputians.* Boston: Little, Brown, 1971.

Jones, Charlie, and Frank Deford, eds. *What Makes Winners Win: Thoughts and Reflections from Successful Athletes.* Secaucus, NJ: Birch Lane Press, 1997.

Jones, Robert T., and O. B. Keeler. *Down the Fairway,* 2nd ed. Atlanta, GA: Longstreet Press, 2001.

Jose, Colin. *The United States and World Cup Soccer Competition.* Metuchen, NJ: Scarecrow Press, 1994.

Joyner, Florence Griffith, and John Hanc. *Running for Dummies.* Foreword by Jackie Joyner-Kersee. Foster City, CA: IDG Books, 1999.

Judson, Arthur. *Riding High: The Story of the Bicycle.* New York: E. P. Dutton, 1956.

Kadzielski, M. "Title IX of the Education Amendments of 1972: Change or Continuity?" *Journal of Law and Education* 6, no. 2 (1977): 183–203.

Kahn, Roger. *The Era 1947–1957: When the Yankees, the Giants and the Dodgers Ruled the World.* Lincoln: University of Nebraska Press, 2002.

———. *A Flame of Pure Fire: Jack Dempsey and the Roaring '20s.* New York: Harcourt Brace, 1999.

———. *October Men: Reggie Jackson, George Steinbrenner, Billy Martin and the Yankees' Miraculous Finish in 1978.* Orlando, FL: Harcourt, 2003.

Kaiser, Ken, and David Fisher. *Planet of the Umps: A Baseball Life from behind the Plate.* New York: Thomas Dunne, 2003.

Karras, Alex. *Even Big Guys Cry.* New York: Henry Holt, 1977.

Kasson, Joy S. *Buffalo Bill's Wild West: Celebrity, Memory and Popular History.* New York: Hill and Wang, 2000.

Kearns, Brad. *Can You Make a Living Doing That? The True-Life Adventures of a Professional Triathlete.* Palo Alto, CA: Trimarket, 1996.

Keeler, O. B. *The Bobby Jones Story: The Authorized Biography.* Chicago: Triumph Books, 2003.

Kettmann, Steve, ed. *Game Time: A Baseball Companion.* New York: Harcourt, 2003.

Keyser, Michael, and Brian Redman. *The Speed Merchants: The Drivers, the Cars, the Tracks; A Journey through the World of Motor Racing, 1969–1972.* Cambridge, MA: Bentley Publishing, 1999.

King, Kelley. "Inside College Football." *Sports Illustrated,* March 31, 2003, 46.

King, Lucien, ed. *Game On: The History and Culture of Videogames.* London: Laurence King, 2002.

King, Richard, and Charles F. Springwood, eds. *Team Spirits: The Native American Mascot Controversy.* Lincoln: University of Nebraska Press, 2001.

Kinsella, W. P. *Shoeless Joe.* Boston: Houghton Mifflin, 1982.

Klots, Steve, and Nathan I. Huggins. *Carl Lewis.* New York: Chelsea House, 1995.

Kolata, Gina. *Ultimate Fitness: The Quest for Truth about Health and Exercise.* New York: Farrar, Straus and Giroux, 2003.

Kopay, David, and Perry Deane Young. *The David Kopay Story: An Extraordinary Self-Revelation.* New York: Arbor House, 1977.

Koppett, Leonard. *Twenty-four Seconds to Shoot: An Informal History of the NBA.* New York: Macmillan, 1968.

Kowalchik, Claire. *The Complete Book of Running for Women.* New York: Pocket Books, 1999.

Krakowka, Lisa. "Bowling Throws a Strike." *American Demographics* (July 1998).

———. "Pool Parties." *American Demographics,* 1998, 20: 59.

Kramarae, Cheris. *Women and Men Speaking.* Rowley, MA: Newbury House, 1981.

Krauss, Rebecca S. *Minor League Baseball: Community Building through Hometown Sports.* New York: Haworth Press, 2003.

Krebs, Paula M. "I Bowl, Therefore I Am." *Chronicle of Higher Education,* June 22, 2001, B21.

Kriegel, Mark. *Namath: A Biography.* New York: Viking, 2004.

Krupa, Greg. "Fund Helps Athletes Win at the Game of Charity." *Boston Globe,* August 9, 1998.

Lacayo, Richard. "Pound for Pound, the Best Ever." *Time,* April 24, 1989, 89.

Ladd, Tony, and James A. Mathisen. *Muscular Christianity: Evangelical Protestants and the Development of American Sport.* Grand Rapids, MI: Baker Books, 1999.

Lambert, Craig. *Mind over Water: Lessons on Life from the Art of Rowing.* Boston: Houghton Mifflin, 1998.

Langland, Tuck. *From Clay to Bronze: A Studio Guide to Figurative Sculpture.* New York: Watson-Guptill, 2000.

Lapchick, Richard E. *On the Mark: Putting the Student Back in Student-Athlete.* Lexington, MA: Lexington Books, 1987.

Larson, Mark K., ed. *The Sports Card Explosion: "Sports Collectors Digest," 1973–1993: Two Decades of America's Hottest Hobby as Seen through the Pages of "Sports Collectors Digest."* Iola, WI: Krause, 1993.

Laskaris, Sam. "Some Braves Will Change, Some Braves Won't." *Wind Speaker,* December 1998, 24.

Lautier, Jack, and Frank Polnaszek. *Same Game, Dif-*

ferent Name: The History of the World Hockey Association. Great Falls, MT: Glacier Publishing, 1996.

Leavy, Jane. *Sandy Koufax: A Lefty's Legacy.* New York: HarperCollins, 2002.

LeCompte, Tom. *The Last Sure Thing: The Life and Times of Bobby Riggs.* Skunkworks Publishing, 2003.

Lederman, Douglas. "College Football Association, at Annual Meeting, Rejects Some Reforms Proposed by NCAA and Attacks the NFL for Interfering with Students." *Chronicle of Higher Education,* June 13, 1990, 44.

Leeming, David, and Margaret Leeming. *A Dictionary of Creation Myths.* New York: Oxford University Press, 1994.

Lefton, Terry. "Nike Set to Take Jordan Beyond Hoop." *Brandweek,* October 19, 1998, 8–9.

———. "Nike über Alles." *Brandweek,* December 9, 1996, 25–32.

Leitner, Irving A. *ABC's "Wide World of Sports": A Panorama of Championship Sport.* New York: Golden Press, 1975.

LeLong, Margaret Valentine. "From Chicago to San Francisco Awheel." *Outing* 31 (February/March 1898), 592–596.

Leonard, Wilbert M., II. "The Odds of Transiting from One Level of Sports Participation to Another." *Sociology of Sport Journal,* 13, 1996, 288–299.

Lessiter, Mike. *Name That Team! The Who, What, Where, and Why behind How Ninety-Eight Professional Sport Teams Obtained Their Nicknames.* Brookfield, WI: Lessiter, 1987.

Lipsyte, Robert. *The Contender.* New York: HarperCollins, 2003.

———. "Lacrosse: All-American Game." *New York Times Magazine,* June 15, 1986, 29–38.

"Literary Vagabond." *American Heritage,* November, 1991, 42–44.

Little, Craig. "Roger Kahn: In His New Book, the Brooklyn Dodgers Chronicler Returns to the Diamond." *Publishers Weekly,* October 4, 1993, 49–51.

Little, Mildred J., Linus J. Dowell, and James M. Jeter. *Recreational Football: Flag, Touch and Flicker.* Dubuque, IA: W. C. Brown, 1980.

Locke, Michelle. "Coach Benches Winning Basketball Team for Poor Grades." *Associated Press,* January 9, 1999, np.

Lomax, Michael E. "Athletics vs. Education: Dilemmas of Black Youth." *Society* 37, no. 3 (March-April 2000), 21–23.

Longorio, Mario. *Athletes Remembered: Mexicano/Latino Professional Football Players, 1929–1970.* Tempe, AZ: Bilingual Press, 1997.

Looss, Walter. *Walter Looss: A Lifetime Shooting Sports and Beauty.* Edited by B. Martin Pederson. Cheshire, CT: Graphics Press, 1999.

Lovesey, Peter. *The Official Centenary History of the Amateur Athletic Association.* Enfield, England: Guinness Superlatives, 1979.

Lovett, Charlie. *Olympic Marathon: A Centennial History of the Games' Most Storied Race.* London: Praeger, 1997.

Lucas, John A. *Future of the Olympic Games.* Champaign, IL: Human Kinetics Publishers, 1992.

———. *The Modern Olympic Games.* South Brunswick, NJ: A. S. Barnes, 1980.

Luxbacher, Joe. *Attacking Soccer.* Champaign, IL: Human Kinetics Publishers, 1999.

Macaloon, John J. *This Great Symbol: Pierre de Coubertin and the Origins of the Modern Olympic Games.* Chicago: University of Chicago Press, 1984.

Macht, Norman L. *Cy Young.* New York: Chelsea House, 1992.

MacInnis, Craig, ed. *Remembering Bobby Orr: A Celebration.* Toronto: Stoddart, 1999.

———, ed. *Remembering the Golden Jet: A Celebration of Bobby Hull.* Toronto and Niagara Falls, NY: Stoddart, 2001.

MacInnes, I. "Mastiffs and Spaniels: Gender and Nation in the English Dog." *Textual Practice* 17 (March 2003): 21–41.

Mackie, M. "The Domestication of Self: Gender Comparisons of Self-Imagery and Self-Esteem." *Social Psychology Quarterly,* 1983, 46: 343–350.

Maclean, Norman. *The Years of Fulfilment.* London: Hodder and Stoughton, 1953.

———. *A River Runs Through It and Other Stories.* Chicago: University of Chicago Press, 1976.

MacSkimming, Roy. *Gordie: A Hockey Legend.* Vancouver, BC: Greystone Books, 1994.

Macy, Sue. *A Whole New Ball Game: The Story of the All-American Girls Professional Baseball League.* New York: Puffin, 1995.

Maisel, Ivan. "The CFA Is Having a Devil of a Time." *Sporting News,* June 14, 1993, 44.

Malafronte, Victor A. *The Complete Book of Frisbee.* Alameda, CA: American Trends Publishing, 1998.

Mankoff, Robert, and Michael Crawford. *The New Yorker Book of Baseball Cartoons.* Princeton, NJ: Bloomberg Press, 2003.

Maris, Roger, and Jim Ogle. *Slugger in Right.* New York: Argonaut Books, 1963.

MarketResearch.com. *MarketLooks: The Women's Athletic Apparel Market.* Ebooks, 2001. http://marketresearch.com.

"Martial Arts Films." http://www.brightlightsfilm .com/31/hk_brief1.html (retrieved June 15, 2004).

Marvis, Barbara J., and Theresa Swanson. *Contemporary American Success Stories: Famous People of Hispanic Heritage; Pedro Jose Greer, Jr., Nancy Lopez, Rafael Palmeiro, Hilda Perera.* Multicultural Biography Series. Childs, MD: Mitchell Lane, 1996.

May, Julian. *Ernie Banks, Home Run Slugger.* Mankato, MN: Crestwood House, 1973.

Mazer, Sharon. *Professional Wrestling: Sport and Spectacle.* Jackson: University Press of Mississippi, 1998.

Mazzoni, Wayne. *The Athletic Recruiting and Scholarship Guide.* New York: Mazz Marketing, 1998.

McCaffery, Larry. *The Metafictional Muse.* Pittsburgh, PA: University of Pittsburgh Press, 1982.

McClellan, Jeff. "Athletes Aren't Dumb Jocks." *Brigham Young Magazine,* Summer 1997, 6.

McCue, Andy. *Baseball by the Books.* Dubuque, IA: William C. Brown and Benchmark Publishers, 1991.

McDonald, Brian. *Indian Summer: The Tragic Story of Louis Francis Sockalexis, the First Native American in Major League Baseball.* Emmaus, PA: Rodale Books, 2003.

McDonald, Thomas "Porky." *Over the Shoulder and Plant on One: An Irishman's Tribute to Willie Mays.* Bloomington, IN: First Books, 2002.

McFarland, Ron. *Norman Maclean.* Boise, ID: Boise State University, 1993.

McGimpsey, David. *Imagining Baseball: America's Pastime and Popular Culture.* Bloomington: Indiana University Press, 2000.

McIntosh, Ned. *Managing Little League Baseball: Recollections of America's Favorite Pastime.* New York: McGraw-Hill, 2000.

McKay, Jim. *The Real McKay: My Wide World of Sports.* With a foreword by Peter Jennings. New York: E. P. Dutton, 1999.

McKay, Jim, David Rowe, Geoffrey A. Lawrence, and Toby Miller. *Globalization and Sport: Playing the World.* London: Sage, 2001.

McKinley, Michael. *Legends of Hockey: The Official Book of the Hockey Hall of Fame.* Chicago: Triumph Books, 1996.

McLuhan, Marshall. *The Medium Is the Message.* New York: Bantam, 1967.

McMeel, Andrews. *Looniness of Long Distance.* London: Carlton Books, 2002.

McNeil, William F. *The King of Swat: An Analysis of Baseball's Home Run Hitters from the Major, Minor, Negro and Japanese Leagues.* Jefferson, NC: McFarland, 1997.

———. *Ruth, Maris, McGwire and Sosa: Baseball's Single Season Home Run Champions.* Jefferson, NC: McFarland, 1999.

McPhail, Clark. *The Myth of the Madding Crowd.* New York: Aldine de Gruyter, 1991.

McRae, Donald. *Heroes without a Country: America's Betrayal of Joe Louis and Jesse Owens.* Hopewell, NJ: Ecco, 2003.

Mead, Chris. *Champion Joe Louis: A Biography.* New York: Robson, 1995.

Media, H. S., ed. *Sweetness: The Courage and Heart of Walter Payton.* Chicago: Triumph Books, 1999.

Menard, Valerie. *Careers in Sports: Latinos at Work.* Bear, DE: Mitchell Lane, 2001.

Menz, Paul G. "The Physics of Bungee Jumping." *The Physics Teacher* 31, November 1993, 483–488.

Meriwether, James B., and Michael Millgate, eds. *Lion in the Garden.* Lincoln: University of Nebraska Press, 1980.

Messenger, Christian. "Expansion Draft: Baseball Fiction of the 1980s." In *The Achievement of American Sport Literature: A Critical Appraisal,* edited by Wiley Umphlett. Cranbury, NJ: Associated University Presses, 1991.

———. *Sport and the Spirit of Play in American Fiction: Hawthorne to Faulkner.* New York: Columbia University Press, 1981.

Messner, Michael, and Donald F. Sabo. *Sex, Violence, and Power in Sports: Rethinking Masculinity.* Freedom, CA: Crossing Press, 1994.

Meyers, Richard. *Great Martial Arts Movies: From Bruce Lee to Jackie Chan and More.* New York: Citadel Press, 2000.

Milazzo, Lee, ed. *Conversations with Joyce Carol Oates.* Jackson: University Press of Mississippi, 1989.

Miller, Ernestine, and Carole Oglesby. *Making Her Mark: Firsts and Milestones in Women's Sports.* New York: McGraw-Hill, 2002.

Miller, Marvin. *A Whole Different Ball Game: The Inside Story of Baseball's New Deal.* New York: Simon and Schuster, 1992.

Miller, Stephen G. *Arete: Greek Sports from Ancient Sources.* Berkeley and Los Angeles: University of California Press, 1991.

Miner, Margaret, and Hugh Rawson. *The New International Dictionary of Quotations,* 3rd ed. New York: Signet, 2000.

Mintz, Steven, and Randy Roberts, eds. *Hollywood's America: United States History through Its Films.* St. James, NY: Brandywine Press, 1993.

Mitchell, Greg. *Joy in Mudville: A Little League Memoir.* New York: Washington Square Press, 2002.

"Mixing Merchandise." *Video Business,* May 26, 2003, 38.

Mogelonsky, Marcia. "Best Foot Forward: The Majority of Men and Women Wear Running or Other Athletic Shoes Every Day." *American Demographics* 18, no. 1 (March 1996): 10.

Morris, Edmund. *Theodore Rex.* New York: Random House, 2002.

Morris, Holly, ed. *A Different Angle: Fly Fishing Stories by Women.* Seattle, WA: Seal Press, 1995.

———, ed. *Uncommon Waters: Women Write about Fishing.* Seattle, WA: Seal Press, 1991.

Morrison, Samuel Eliot, ed. *William Bradford, Of Plimouth Plantation.* New York: Alfred A. Knopf, 1952.

Morse, Ann. *Football's Great Running Back, O. J. Simpson.* Mankato, MN: Creative Education, 1976.

Moses, L. G. *Wild West Shows and the Images of American Indians, 1883–1933.* Albuquerque: University of New Mexico Press, 1996.

Murray, Ty, and Kendra Santos. *Roughstock: The Mud, the Blood and the Beer.* Austin, TX: Equimedia Publishing, 2001.

Nasaw, David. *Children of the City: At Work and at Play.* New York: Oxford University Press, 1985.

"NASCAR: How Bad Do You Want It?" *Retail Merchandiser,* July 2002, S3–S4.

National Collegiate Athletic Association. "Division I Legislation Summary by Category: Amateurism." http://www.ncaa.org/databases/legislation/1999/99summarya.html (retrieved May 2004).

"NCAA Group to Vote on Cutting Summer Recruiting and Scholarship Limits." Associated Press, April 9, 2000, np.

"NCAA Recruiting Reforms Subject of Capitol Hill Hearing." *Scripps Howard Foundation Wire,* www.axcessnews.com/national, May 19, 1–2.

Neiman, Leroy. *Leroy Neiman.* New York: Harry N. Abrams, 2003.

———. *Winners: My Thirty Years in Sports.* New York: Harry N. Abrams, 1983.

Nelson, Lindsey. *Hello Everybody, I'm Lindsey Nelson.* New York: William Morrow, 1985.

Newberger, Eli H. *The Men They Will Become: The Nature and Nurture of Male Character.* Cambridge, MA: Perseus Books, 2000.

Newcombe, Jack. *The Best of the Athletic Boys: The White Man's Impact on Jim Thorpe.* New York: Doubleday, 1975.

Newfield, Jack. *The Life and Crimes of Don King: The Shame of Boxing in America.* Harbor Electronic Publishing, 2002. http://www.hepdigital.com/books.html.

Nicklaus, Jack. *Jack Nicklaus.* With John Tickell. New York: St. Martin's Press, 2003.

———. *My Story.* With Ken Bowden. New York: Simon and Schuster, 1997.

———. *Nicklaus by Design: Golf Course Strategy and Architecture.* New York: Harry N. Abrams, 2002.

"No Gender Testing." *New Scientist,* June 17, 2000, 19.

Noakes, Timothy. *Lore of Running.* Champaign, IL: Human Kinetics Publishers, 2003.

Novak, Michael. "American Sports, American Virtues." In *American Sport Culture,* edited by

Wiley L. Umphlett, 34–49. Cranbury, NJ: Associated University Presses, 1985.

Oates, Joyce Carol. *On Boxing.* Hopewell, NJ: Ecco Press, 1994.

O'Brien, Tom. *The Screening of America: Movies and Values from "Rocky" to "Rain Man."* New York: Continuum, 1990.

Olderr, Steven. *The Pan-American Games: A Statistical History, 1951–1999.* Jefferson, NC: McFarland, 2003.

Olsen, Marilyn. *Women Who Risk: Profiles of Women in Extreme Sports.* New York: Hatherleigh Press, 2003.

Olson, Wendy. "Beyond Title IX: Toward an Agenda for Women and Sports in the 1990s." *Yale Journal of Law and Feminism* 3, no. 1 (1990): 105–151.

Oriard, Michael. *Reading Football: How the Popular Press Created an American Spectacle.* Chapel Hill: University of North Carolina Press, 1993.

Osborn, Kevin, ed. *Take Me out to the Ballgame: A Book of History, Hits and Heroes.* Kansas City, MO: Andrews McMeel Publishing, 1995.

Otis, Carol L., and Roger Goldingay. *The Athletic Woman's Survival Guide: How to Win the Battle against Eating Disorders, Amenorrhea and Osteoporosis.* Champaign, IL: Human Kinetics Publishers, 2000.

Overmyer, James. *Queen of the Negro Leagues: Effa Manley and the Newark Eagles.* Lanham, MD: Scarecrow Press, 1998.

Owen, David. *The Chosen One: Tiger Woods and the Dilemma of Greatness.* New York: Simon and Schuster, 2001.

Oxendine, Joseph B. *American Indian Sports Heritage.* 2nd ed. Lincoln: University of Nebraska Press, 1995.

Padwe, Sandy. *Basketball's Hall of Fame.* Englewood Cliffs, NJ: Prentice-Hall, 1970.

Paige, Leroy Satchel, and John B. Holway. *Maybe I'll Pitch Forever: A Great Baseball Player Tells the Hilarious Story behind the Legend.* Lincoln: University of Nebraska Press, 1993.

Palmer, Arnold, and James Dodson. *A Golfer's Life.* New York: Ballantine Books, 1999.

Parris, Matthew. "A Lexicon of Conservative Cant." *Spectator,* February 19, 2000, 12–14.

Partlett, David. *The Oxford Guide to Card Games.* New York: Oxford University Press, 1990.

Patterson, Floyd, and Bert Randolph Sugar. *Inside Boxing.* Chicago: NTC/Contemporary Books, 1974.

"The Paymasters." *The Economist,* June 6, 1998, 14–18.

Payton, Walter, and Don Yaeger. *Never Die Easy: The Autobiography of Walter Payton.* New York: Random House, 2001.

Pedley, John G. *Greek Art and Archaeology.* 3rd ed. Englewood Cliffs, NJ: Prentice-Hall, 2002.

Pelé. *My Life and the Beautiful Game: The Autobiography of Pelé.* With Robert L. Fish. Garden City, NY: Doubleday, 1977.

Pennell, Elizabeth Robins. *Over the Alps on a Bicycle.* London: T. Fisher Unwin, 1898.

Pepe, Phil. *The Wit and Wisdom of Yogi Berra.* New York: Hawthorne Books, 1974.

Peper, George. *Golf in America: The First One Hundred Years.* With Robin McMillan and James A. Frank. New York: Harry N. Abrams, 1988.

Perskie, Joe. "Shaky Foundations." *Sport,* November, 1998, 98–103.

Peterson, Robert W. *Cages to Jump Shots: Pro Basketball's Early Years.* New York: Oxford University Press, 1990.

———. *Only the Ball Was White: A History of Legendary Black Players and All-Black Professional Teams.* New York: McGraw-Hill, 1984.

Phillips, Louis, and Burnham Holmes. *Yogi, Babe, and Magic: The Complete Book of Sports Nicknames.* Englewood Cliffs, NJ: Prentice-Hall, 1994.

Pincus, Arthur, Len Hochberg, and Chris Malcolm. *The Official Illustrated NHL History: From the Original Six to a Global Game.* Chicago: Triumph Books, 1999.

Plant, Mike. *Iron Will: The Heart and Soul of the Triathlon's Ultimate Challenge.* Chicago: Contemporary Books, 1987.

"Playful Paintings." *The Economist,* April 30, 1994, 76–78.

Plimpton, George. *Out of My League.* New York: Lyons and Burford, 1993.

———. *Paper Lion.* New York: Lyons and Burford, 1993.

Pluto, Terry. *Loose Balls: The Short, Wild Life of the American Basketball Association.* New York:

Simon and Schuster, 1990.

Podnieks, Andrew. *The Goal: Bobby Orr and the Most Famous Shot in Stanley Cup History.* Chicago: Triumph Books, 2003.

———. *The Great One: The Life and Times of Wayne Gretzky.* Chicago: Triumph Books, 1999.

Powell, Harford Willing Hare. *Walter Camp, The Father of American Football.* 1929. Reprint, Freeport, NY: Books for Libraries Press, 1970.

Powell, Tom. "Midways on Road Most of Year." *Amusement Business,* June 30, 2003, 15.

President's Council on Physical Fitness and Sports. *Living Fit.* Emeryville, CA: Parlay, 1990.

———. *National School Population Fitness Survey, 1985.* Washington, DC: GPO, 1986.

Price, Joseph L. "The Super Bowl as a Religious Festival." *The Christian Century* 101, no. 6 (February 22, 1984): 190–191.

Prime, Jim, and Bill Nowlin. *Ted Williams: A Tribute.* Indianapolis, IN: Masters Press, 1997.

Prince, Carl E. *Brooklyn's Dodgers: The Bums, the Borough and the Best of Baseball, 1947–1957.* New York: Oxford University Press, 1996.

Pughe, Thomas. *Comic Sense: Reading Robert Coover, Stanley Elkin, Philip Roth.* Basel, Switzerland, and Boston: Birkhäuser Verlag, 1994.

Putney, Clifford. *Muscular Christianity: Manhood and Sports in Protestant America, 1880–1920.* Cambridge, MA: Harvard University Press, 2003.

Quackenbush, Robert M. *Arthur Ashe and His Match with History.* New York: Simon and Schuster, 1994.

Queenan, Joe. *True Believers: The Tragic Inner Life of Sports Fans.* New York: Henry Holt, 2003.

Raab, Scott. "The Last Boxing Story." *Esquire,* 1998, vol. 130, 94–102.

Rackham, George. *Synchronized Swimming.* London: Transatlantic Arts, 1979.

Rader, Benjamin G. *American Sports: From the Age of Folk Games to the Age of Spectators.* 3rd ed. Englewood Cliffs, NJ: Prentice-Hall, 1996.

Ralbovsky, Marty. *The Namath Effect.* Englewood Cliffs, NJ: Prentice-Hall, 1976.

Randall, Neil. "*Shoeless Joe:* Fantasy and the Humor of Fellow-Feeling." *Modern Fiction Studies* 33 (Spring, 1987): 173–183.

Real, Michael. "Superbowl: Mythic Spectacle." *Journal of Communication* 25 (1975): 31–43.

Reddin, Paul. *Wild West Shows.* Urbana: University of Illinois Press, 1999.

Remnick, David. *King of the World: Muhammad Ali and the Rise of an American Hero.* New York: Random House, 1998.

Renfro, Wally. "Recruiting and Scholarship Limits Placed on University of Colorado Program; University Receives Two-Year Probation." http://www.ncaa.org/releases/infractions, pp. 1–4 (retrieved June 2004).

Rennert, Richard Scott. *Baseball Great Henry Aaron.* Philadelphia: Chelsea House, 1993.

Renoff, Richard, and Joseph A. Varacalli. "Italian-Americans and Baseball." *The Nassua Review* 6, no. 1 (1990): 92–119.

Ribowsky, Mark. *Don't Look Back: Satchel Paige in the Shadows of Baseball.* New York: Da Capo, 2000.

Rice, Ed. *Baseball's First Indian, Louis Sockalexis: Penobscot Legend, Cleveland Indian.* Windsor, CT: Tide-mark Press, 2003.

Richards, Jack, and Danny Hill. *Complete Handbook of Sports Scoring and Record Keeping.* West Nyack, NY: Parker Publishing, 1974.

Riesman, David, and Reuel Denney. "Football in America: A Study in Culture Diffusion." *American Quarterly,* 1951, 309–325.

Riess, Steven A. *City Games: The Evolution of American Urban Society and the Rise of Sports.* Urbana: University of Illinois Press, 1989.

Rinehart, Robert. "Sport as Kitsch: A Case Study of *The American Gladiators.*" *Journal of Popular Culture* 28 (1994): 25–34.

Rinehart, Robert E., and Synthia Sydnor. *To the Extreme: Alternative Sports, Inside and Out.* Albany: State University of New York Press, 2003.

Ritter, Lawrence. *The Glory of Their Times: The Story of the Early Days of Baseball Told by the Men Who Played It.* New York: Macmillan, 1966.

Robbins, Alexandra. 1999. "Ultimate Frisbee Test Character, Fitness." *USA Today.* http://www.ultimatehandbook.com/Webpages/Media/mediausa.html (retrieved June 15, 2004).

Roberts, Randy. *Fight of the Century: Jack Johnson, Joe Louis and the Struggle for Racial Equality.* Armonk, NY: M. E. Sharpe, 2002.

———. *Jack Dempsey, the Manassa Mauler.* Urbana:

University of Illinois Press, 2003.

———. *Papa Jack: Jack Johnson and the Era of White Hopes.* New York: Free Press, 1985.

Roberts, Robin, C. Paul Rogers, and Stan Musial. *My Life in Baseball.* Chicago: Triumph Books, 2003.

Robertson, Anne. "Evel Knievel Takes New Role." *Business Journal,* January 25, 2002, 10.

Robidoux, Michael A. *Men at Play: A Working Understanding of Professional Hockey.* Montreal: McGill-Queen's University Press, 2001.

Robinson, Ray. *Iron Horse: Lou Gehrig in His Time.* New York: HarperCollins, 1991.

———. *Matty: An American Hero; Christy Mathewson of the New York Giants.* New York: Oxford University Press, 1994.

———. *Rockne of Notre Dame: The Making of a Football Legend.* New York: Oxford University Press, 1999.

Robinson, Ray, and Christopher Jennison. *Yankee Stadium: Seventy-five Years of Drama, Glamour and Glory.* New York: Penguin Studio, 1998.

Robinson, Sharon. *Jackie's Nine: Jackie Robinson's Values to Live By; Courage, Determination, Teamwork, Persistence, Integrity, Citizenship, Justice, Commitment, Excellence.* New York: Scholastic Books, 2002.

Robinson, Sugar Ray, and Dave Anderson. *Sugar Ray.* New York: Da Capo Press, 1994.

Rodengen, Jeffrey L., and Tom Clancy. *NRA: An American Legend.* Edited by Melody Maysonet. Fort Lauderdale, FL: Write Stuff, 2002.

Rodgers, Bill, and Tom Derderian. *The Boston Marathon: A Century of Blood, Sweat and Cheers.* Chicago: Triumph Books, 2003.

Rogosin, Donn. *Invisible Men.* New York: Atheneum, 1987.

Romanowski, Patricia, Holly George-Warren, and Jon Pareles, eds. *The New Rolling Stone Encyclopedia of Rock and Roll.* Rev. ed. New York: Fireside, 1995.

Ronberg, Gary. *The Illustrated Hockey Encyclopedia.* New York: Balsam Press, 1984.

Roosevelt, Theodore, and George Bird Grinnell, eds. *Trail and Camp-Fire: The Book of the Boone and Crockett Club.* New York: Forest and Stream Publishing Company, 1897. Reprint, Missoula, MT: Boone and Crockett Club, 1988.

Rosaforte, Tim. *Raising the Bar: The Championship Years of Tiger Woods.* New York: Thomas Dunne, 2000.

Rose, Pete. *My Prison Without Bars.* With Rick Hill. Emmaus, PA: Rodale Books, 2004.

Rosen, Charles. *Barney Polan's Game: A Novel of the 1951 College Basketball Scandals.* San Diego, CA: Harcourt Brace, 1999.

Rosenfeld, Harvey. 2002. *Still a Legend: The Story of Roger Maris.* http://backinprint.com.

Ross, Jim. *Can You Take the Heat? The WWF Is Cooking!* New York: ReganBooks, 2000.

Ruck, Rob. *Sandlot Seasons: Sport in Black Pittsburgh.* Urbana: University of Illinois Press, 1987.

Rudman, Jack, ed. *Frank Merriwell's Schooldays.* Brooklyn, NY: National Learning Corporation, 1970.

Rushin, Steve. "Willie Mosconi." *Sports Illustrated,* September 27, 1993, 44.

Russell, Bill, and Taylor Branch. *Second Wind: The Memoirs of an Opinionated Man.* New York: Ballantine Books, 1980.

Russell, Bill, Alan Hilburg, and David Falkner. *Russell Rules: Eleven Lessons on Leadership from the Twentieth Century's Greatest Winner.* New York: E. P. Dutton, 2002.

Russell, Gordon. "Anatomy of a Riot." *Psychology Today* 31 (November-December 1998): 18.

Rust, Art, and Edna Rust. *Art Rust's Illustrated History of the Black Athlete.* Garden City, NY: Doubleday, 1985.

Ruth, Amy. *Wilma Rudolph.* Minneapolis, MN: Lerner, 2000.

Ruth, Babe. *The Babe Ruth Story.* New York: E. P. Dutton, 1948.

Rutkoff, Peter. *Shadow Ball: A Novel of Baseball and Chicago.* Jefferson, NC: McFarland, 2001.

Ryan, Nolan, Mickey Herskowitz, and T. R. Sullivan. *Nolan Ryan: The Road to Cooperstown.* Lenexa, KS: Addax Press, 1999.

Sack, Allen L., and Ellen J. Staurowsky. *College Athletes for Hire: The Evolution and Legacy of the NCAA's Amateur Myth.* Westport, CT: Praeger, 1998.

Sagan, Carl. *The Dragons of Eden.* New York: Random House, 1977.

Sage, George H. *Power and Ideology in American*

Sport. 2nd ed. Champaign, IL: Human Kinetics Publishers, 1998.

Salholz, Eloise. "Knievel's New Career: Another Amazing Leap." *Newsweek,* June 13, 1983, 12.

Salter, David. *Crashing the Old Boy's Network: The Tragedies and Triumphs of Girls and Women in Sports.* Westport, CT: Praeger, 1996.

Salzberg, Charles. *From Set Shot to Slam Dunk: The History of Professional Basketball.* Lincoln: University of Nebraska Press, 1998.

Salzberg, Joel, ed. *Critical Essays on Bernard Malamud.* Boston: G. K. Hall, 1987.

Sammons, Jeffrey T. *Beyond the Ring: The Role of Boxing in American Society.* Urbana: University of Illinois Press, 1990.

Sampson, Curt. *Hogan.* Nashville, TN: Rutledge Hill Press, 2001.

Sampson, Curt, and Dan Jenkins. *The Eternal Summer: Palmer, Nicklaus and Hogan in 1960, Golf's Golden Year.* New York: Villard, 2000.

Sandoz, Joli, and Joby Winans, eds. *Whatever It Takes: Women on Women's Sport.* New York: Farrar, Straus and Giroux, 1999.

Sandvoss, Cornel. *A Game of Two Halves: Football, Television and Globalisation.* New York: Routledge, 2003.

Sanson, Nanette, ed. *Champions of Women's Golf: Celebrating Fifty Years of the LPGA.* Naples, FL: QuailMark, 2002.

Sawyer-Fay, Rebecca. "Fly Fishing Fever." *Country Living,* April 1994, 120–124.

Schlossberg, Howard. *Sports Marketing.* Cambridge, MA: Blackwell, 1996.

Schoenfeld, Bruce. "David Stern's Full-Court Press." *New York Times Magazine,* October 18, 1998, 95–100.

Schultz, Brad, and Mike King. *Sports Broadcasting.* Boston: Focal Press, 2001.

Schwartz, Alan. "Postmodernist Baseball." *Modern Fiction Studies* 33 (Spring 1987): 135–150.

Schwarz, Daniel R. *Broadway Boogie Woogie: Damon Runyon and the Making of New York City Culture.* New York: Palgrave Macmillan, 2003.

Segrave, Jeffrey O., and D. Chu, eds. *The Olympic Games in Transition.* Champaign, IL: Human Kinetics Publishers, 1988.

Seib, Philip M. *The Player: Christy Mathewson, Baseball and the American Century.* New York: Four Walls Eight Windows Press, 2003.

Seligman, Dan. "This Is Sports Coverage?" *Forbes,* January 26, 1998, 52–54.

Sellers, Patricia. "Four Reasons Nike's Not Cool." *Fortune,* March 30, 1998, 26–28.

Sennett, Ted. *Art of Hanna-Barbera: Fifty Years of Creativity.* New York: Viking Press, 1989.

Seymour, Harold. *Baseball: The People's Game.* New York: Oxford University Press, 1990.

Seymour, Harold, Dorothy Z. Seymour, and Dorothy Jane Mills. *Baseball: The Early Years.* New York: Oxford University Press, 1989.

Shaughnessy, Dan. *Fenway: A Biography in Words and Pictures.* Boston: Houghton Mifflin, 1999.

Shaw, David. *America's Victory: The Heroic Story of a Team of Ordinary Americans, and How They Won the Greatest Yacht Race Ever.* New York: Free Press, 2002.

Sheehy, Harry, Danny Peary, and Joe Torre. *Raising a Team Player: Teaching Kids Lasting Values on the Field, on the Court and on the Bench.* North Adams, MA: Storey Books, 2002.

Shemano, Gary, Art Spander, and Dick Schaap. *Keeping on Course: Golf Tips on Avoiding the Sandtraps of Today's Business World.* New York: McGraw-Hill, 1997.

Sherwood, Lyn A., and Barnaby Conrad. *Yankees in the Afternoon: An Illustrated History of American Bullfighting.* Jefferson, NC: McFarland, 2001.

Shropshire, Mike. *Seasons in Hell: With Billy Martin, Whitey Herzog and "the Worst Baseball Teams in History," the 1973–1975 Texas Rangers.* New York: Donald Fine Publishing, 1999.

Siegfried, John J. "Sports Player Drafts and the Reserve System." *CATO Journal* 14 (1995): 443–453.

Silverman, Jeff. *The Greatest Boxing Stories Ever Told: Thirty-Six Incredible Tales from the Ring.* Guilford, CT: Lyons Press, 2002.

Silverstein, Herma. *Basketball Hall of Fame.* Mankato, MN: Crestwood House, 1994.

Simon, Scott. *Jackie Robinson and the Integration of Baseball.* New York: John Wiley and Sons, 2002.

Simons, Minot, Minot Simons III, and Albrecht Gaebele. *Women's Gymnastics, A History: 1966 to 1974.* Carmel, CA: Welwyn Publishing, 1996.

Simpson, J. C. "Real-Life Davids vs. Goliaths." *Time,* October 21, 1991, 102–104.

Simpson, Joe Leigh, Arne Ljungqvist, Malcolm A. Ferguson-Smith, Albert de la Chapelle, Louis J. Elsas II, A. A. Ehrhardt, Myron Genel, Elizabeth A. Ferris, Alison Carlson. "Gender Verification in the Olympics." *JAMA* 284 (September 27, 2000): 1568.

Simson, Vyv, and Andrew Jennings. *The Lords of the Rings.* Toronto: Stoddart, 1992.

Slopen, Beverly. "Look North for Writers." *Publishers Weekly,* February 28, 1986, 59–64.

Slovenko, Ralph. "Politically Correct Team Names." *Journal of Psychiatry and Law* 22 (Winter 1994): 585–592.

Smelser, Marshall. *The Life That Ruth Built: A Biography.* Lincoln: University of Nebraska Press, 1975.

Smith, Curt. *Of Mikes and Men: From Ray Scott to Curt Gowdy; Broadcast Tales from the Pro Football Booth.* South Bend, IN: Diamond Communications, 1998.

———. *The Storytellers: From Mel Allen to Bob Costas; Sixty Years of Baseball Tales from the Broadcast Booth.* New York: Macmillan, 1995.

Smith, Curt. *Our House: A Tribute to Fenway Park.* Lincolnwood, IL: Masters Press, 1999.

Smith, Edward W. L. *Not Just Pumping Iron: On the Psychology of Lifting Weights.* Springfield IL: Charles C. Thomas, 1989.

Smith, Lissa, Lucy Danziger, and Mariah B. Nelson. *Nike Is a Goddess: The History of Women in Sports.* New York: Atlantic Monthly Press, 1999.

Smith, Michael. *Violence and Sport.* Toronto: Butterworths Publishing, 1983.

Smith, Sam. *The Jordan Rules.* New York: Pocket Books, 1994.

Specter, Michael. "The Long Ride." *The New Yorker Magazine,* July 15, 2002, 48–58.

Spindel, Carol. *Dancing at Halftime: The Controversy over American Indian Mascots.* New York: New York University Press, 2000.

Spivey, David, ed. *Sport in America: New Historical Perspectives.* Westport, CT: Greenwood Press, 1985.

"Sports Blackouts Sought." *Television Digest,* September 10, 1990, 8.

Sports Illustrated: Fifty Years of Great Writing. New York: Time-Warner, 2003.

St. John, Bob, and Roger Staubach. *Landry: The Legend and the Legacy.* Nashville, TN: Word Publishing, 2000.

Stanbury, Dean, and Frank DeSantis. *Touch Football.* New York: Sterling Publishing, 1961.

Steel, Jon. *Truth, Lies and Advertising: The Art of Account Planning.* New York: John Wiley and Sons, 1998.

Stewart, Mark. *The World Cup.* New York: Franklin Watts, 2003.

Strachan, Al, and Eric Duhatschek. *One Hundred and One Years of Hockey: The Chronicle of a Century on Ice.* San Diego, CA: Thunder Bay Press, 2001.

Stratton, Richard F. *The World of the American Pit Bull Terrier.* Neptune City, NJ: TFH, 1983.

Strickland, Carol. *The Annotated Mona Lisa.* Kansas City, MO: Andrews McMeel, 1992.

"Students Suspended for Role in Riot." *New York Times,* March 31, 1999.

Suggs, Welch. "College Officials Discuss How to Stop Mayhem after Big Games." *Chronicle of Higher Education,* March 7, 2003, A43.

Sullivan, Donald. *Winning by Computer.* Hollywood, CA: Gambling Times, 1984.

Sullivan, Lawrence, and Warren S. Grimes. *The Law of Antitrust: An Integrated Handbook.* St. Paul, MN: West Wadsworth, 2000.

Sullivan, Neil. *The Diamond in the Bronx: Yankee Stadium and the Politics of New York.* New York: Oxford University Press, 2001.

Suskind, Ron. *A Hope in the Unseen: An American Odyssey from the Inner City to the Ivy League.* New York: Broadway Books, 1999.

Talese, Gay. "Frisbees, Yo-Yos, Goo-Goos, Etc.: Dig those Crazy, Grown-up Toys." *The New York Times Magazine,* August 11, 1957, 175.

Tannsjo, Torbjorn, and Claudio Tamburrini, eds. *Values in Sport.* New York: Routledge, 2000.

Thigpen, David E. "Bungee Jumping Comes of Age." *Time,* April 15, 1991.

Torres, Jose. *Fire and Fear: The Inside Story of Mike Tyson.* New York: Popular Library, 1990.

Tosches, Rich. *Zipping My Fly: Moments in the Life of an American Sportsman.* New York: Perigee, 2002.

Towle, Mike. *I Remember Walter Payton: Personal Memories of Football's "Sweetest" Superstar by the People Who Knew Him Best.* Nashville, TN: Cumberland House, 2000.

———. *Pete Rose: Baseball's Charlie Hustle.* Nashville, TN: Cumberland House, 2003.

Trevino, Lee, and Sam Blair. *Super Mex: An Autobiography.* London: Arrow Books, 1983.

Truman, Ben C., and Steven R. Wood. *Duelling in America.* Classical Library of the Obscure and Remote. San Diego, CA: Joseph Tabler Books, 1993.

Tygiel, Jules. *Baseball's Great Experiment: Jackie Robinson and His Legacy.* New York: Oxford University Press, 1988.

Tyson, Ann Scott. "Urban Lessons on Violence-Free Victories." *Christian Science Monitor,* June 18, 1996.

Umphlett, Wiley Lee, ed. *The Achievement of American Sport Literature: A Critical Appraisal.* Cranbury, NJ: Associated University Presses, 1991.

Updike, John. *Conversations with John Updike.* Edited by James Plath. Jackson: University Press of Mississippi, 1994.

———. *Golf Dreams.* New York: Alfred A. Knopf, 1996.

———. *Self-Consciousness: Memoirs.* New York: Knopf, 1989.

Upshaw, Lynn B. *Building Brand Identity: A Strategy for Success in a Hostile Marketplace.* New York: John Wiley and Sons, 1995.

U.S. Olympic Committee. *A Basic Guide to Archery* (An Official U.S. Olympic Committee Sports Series). Irvine, CA: Griffin Publishing, 1997.

Vanderwerken, David L., and Spencer K. Wertz. *Sport Inside Out.* Fort Worth: Texas Christian University Press, 1985.

Vaughan, Roger, and Nancy Lopez. *Golf: The Woman's Game.* New York: Stewart, Tabori and Chang, 2001.

Vehorn, Frank. *Farewell to the King: A Personal Look Back at the Career of Richard Petty, Stock Car Racing's Winningest and Most Popular Driver.* Asheboro, NC: Down Home Press, 1992.

Vennum, Thomas. *American Indian Lacrosse: Little Brother of War.* Washington, DC: Smithsonian Institution Press, 1994.

Verdi, Bob. *They Went Yard: McGwire and Sosa; An Awesome Home Run Season.* Chicago: Bonus Books, 1998.

Villalobos, P. M. "The Civil Rights Restoration Act of 1987: Revitalization of Title IX." *Marquette Sports Law Journal* 1, no. 1 (Fall 1990): 149–169.

Voigt, David Q. "The Chicago Black Sox and the Myth of Baseball's Single Sin." In *America through Baseball,* 65–76. Chicago: Nelson-Hall, 1976.

Waddell, Tom, and Dick Schaap. *Gay Olympian: The Life and Death of Dr. Tom Waddell.* New York: Knopf, 1996.

Wagenheim, Kal. *Clemente!* Foreword by Wilfrid Sheed. Chicago: Olmstead Press, 2001.

Walker, Sam. "The People vs. NFL." *Wall Street Journal,* October 5, 2001.

Wallace, Joseph, ed. *The Baseball Anthology: 125 Years of Stories, Poems, Articles, Photographs, Drawings, Interviews, Cartoons and Other Memorabilia.* Foreword by Sparky Anderson. New York: Harry N. Abrams, 1994.

Walmsley, Ann. "Courting Danger." *Maclean's,* February 1988, 154.

Watson, Bruce. "Jack London Followed His Muse into the Wild." *Smithsonian,* February 1998, 104–114.

Watterson, John Sayle. *College Football: History, Spectacle, Controversy.* Baltimore, MD: John Hopkins University Press, 2000.

Weeks, Bob. *Curling for Dummies.* St. Paul, MN: Hungry Mind Publishing, 2002.

Wellner, Alison S. *Americans at Play: Demographics of Outdoor Recreation and Travel.* Ithaca, NY: New Strategist Publications, 1997.

Wells, Jeff. *Boxing Day: The Fight That Changed the World.* Pymble: HarperCollins Australia, 1999.

Wendel, Tim. *The New Face of Baseball: The One Hundred Year Rise and Triumph of Latinos in America's Favorite Sport.* New York: Rayo Publishing, 2003.

Wheeler, Lonnie. *Bleachers: A Summer in Wrigley Field.* Chicago: Contemporary Books, 1989.

Wheeler, Robert W. *Jim Thorpe: World's Greatest Athlete.* Norman: University of Oklahoma Press, 2003.

White, G. Edward. *Justice Oliver Wendell Holmes: Law and the Inner Self.* New York: Oxford University Press, 1995.

Whitten, Phillip. *The Complete Book of Swimming.* New York: Random House, 1994.

Whitworth, Kathy, Rhonda Glenn, and Patty Berg. *Golf for Women.* New York: St. Martin's Press, 1990.

Wiggins, David K. *Glory Bound: Black Athletes in a White America.* Syracuse, NY: Syracuse University Press, 1997.

Wilcox, Ralph C. *Sport in the Global Village.* Morgantown, WV: Fitness Information Technology, 1994.

Willard, Frances E. *How I Learned to Ride the Bicycle: Reflections of an Influential 19th Century Woman.* Reprint. Sunnyvale, CA: Fair Oaks, 1991.

Williams, Esther. *The Million Dollar Mermaid: An Autobiography.* With Digby Diehl. San Diego, CA: Harvest Books, 2000.

Wilner, Barry, and Scott Hamilton. *Stars on Ice: An Intimate Look at Skating's Greatest Tour.* Kansas City, MO: Andrews McMeel, 1998.

Winnett, Thomas, and Kathy Morey. *Guide to the John Muir Trail.* Berkeley, CA: Wilderness Press, 2003.

Winnicott, Donald. *The Child and the Outside World.* London: Tavistock Publications, 1957.

Woerner, Gail Hughbanks, and Gail Gandolfi. *Fearless Funnymen: The History of the Rodeo Clown.* Austin, TX: Eakin Press, 1993.

Wombell, Paul. *Sportscape: The Evolution of Sports Photography.* London: Phaidon, 2000.

Wood, Robin. "Sports Merchandise Big Business for Small Teams." *Capital District Business Review,* June 5, 2000, 1.

Wooden, Wayne S., and Gavin Ehringer. *Rodeo in America: Wranglers, Roughstock and Paydirt.* Lawrence: University Press of Kansas, 1996.

Woolum, Janet. *Outstanding Women Athletes: Who They Are and How They Influenced Sports in America.* Phoenix, AZ: Oryx Press, 1988.

Workman, Fanny Bullock. *Sketches Awheel in Modern Iberia.* New York: G. P. Putnam's Sons, 1897.

"World Football League Suspends Operation after Losses of $30 Million." *New York Times,* October 30, 1975.

Yampolsky, Selma. "Roger Kahn." *Current Biography* 61 (June 2000): 39–44.

Yesalis, Charles E., ed. *Anabolic Steroids in Sport.* Champaign, IL: Human Kinetics Publishers, 1993.

Zimblast, Andrew W. *Unpaid Professionals: Commercialism and Conflict in Big-Time College Sports.* Princeton: Princeton University Press, 1999.

Zimmerman, Jean. *Raising Our Athletic Daughters: How Sports Can Build Self-Esteem and Save Girls' Lives.* New York: Doubleday, 1998.

Zingg, Paul J. *Harry Hooper: An American Baseball Life.* Urbana: University of Illinois Press, 1993.

Zoss, Joel, and John Bowman. *Diamonds in the Rough.* New York: Macmillan, 1989.

Zuckerman, George. *Farewell, Frank Merriwell.* New York: E. P. Dutton, 1973.

List of Contributors and Advisors

Abrams, Brett
American University
Washington, DC

Amana, Harry
University of North Carolina
Chapel Hill, NC

Arbena, Joseph
Clemson University
Clemson, SC

Arsenault, Raymond
University of South Florida
St. Petersburg, FL

Ashwell, Tim
University of New Hampshire
Durham, NH

Ayers, Chris
East Tennessee State University
Johnson City, TN

Baldassaro, Lawrence
University of Wisconsin
Milwaukee, WI

Bale, John
Keele University
Keele Staffordshire, UK

Bass, Amy
State University of New York
Richmond, MA

Baswick, Daryl
McMaster University
Dundas, ON

Berkeley, Christopher
Independent Scholar
Somerville, MA

Bernstein, David
California State University
Long Beach, CA

Bevis, Charlie
Independent Scholar
Chelmsford, MA

Borden, Joseph
East Tennessee State University
Johnson City, TN

Bowers, Marvin "Trip"
Medical Doctor
Johnson City, TN

Bromley, Rebekah
University of Tennessee
Chattanooga, TN

Brooks, Kevin
University of North Dakota
Fargo, ND

Brown, Robert
Ashland University
Ashland, OH

Bukovac, Janice
Michigan State University
Okemos, MI

Cannon, Keith
Wingate University
Wingate, NC

Caponi, Gena
University of Texas
San Antonio, TX

Carpenter, Harry
Auburn University
Conover, NC

Carvalho, John
Campbell College
Buies Creek, NC

Catsam, Derek
University of Texas of the
  Permian Basin
Odessa, TX

Chambers, Paul
University of South Florida
Tampa, FL

Charry, Stephen
Central Washington University
Ellensburg, WA

Cohen, Kris
University of Chicago
Chicago, IL

Cole, Robert
Kansas City Business Journal
Independence, MO

Cormier, Raymond
Longwood College
Farmville, VA

Crepeau, Richard
Central Florida University
Orlando, FL

Crowe, Chris
Brigham Young University
Provo, UT

Dagavarian-Bonar, Debra
Thomas Edison State College
Trenton, NJ

Daglow, Don
Independent Scholar
San Rafael, CA

Davis, Jack
University of Alabama
Birmingham, AL

Davis, Scott
St. Joseph's University
West Chester, PA

Deardorff, Donald
Cedarville College
Cedarville, OH

Dooley, Patrick
U.S. Air Force Academy
Colorado Springs, CO

Dougan, John
Independent Scholar
Richmond, VA

Doyle, Debbie Ann
American University
Washington, DC

Durbin, Daniel
University of Southern California
Canyon Country, CA

Dyer, Stephanie
University of Pennsylvania
Philadelphia, PA

Evans, Mark
U.S. Air Force Academy
Colorado Springs, CO

Fea, John
State University of New York
Stony Brook, NY

Fitzkee, David
U.S. Air Force Academy
Colorado Springs, CO

Gagnon, Donald
University of South Florida
Tampa, FL

Gallert, Petra
U.S. Air Force Academy
Montgomery, AL

Gordon, Alan
Queen's University
Toronto, ON

Goudsouzian, Aram
Purdue University
Winchester, MA

Gryski, Gerard
Auburn University
Auburn, AL

Hakola, Judy
University of Maine
Orono, ME

Heaphy, Leslie
Kent State University
Canton, OH

Higgs, Jack, Emeritus
East Tennessee State University
Johnson City, TN

Holland, Byron
Independent Scholar

Holloran, Peter
Northeast Historic Association
Cambridge, MA

Holmes, Thomas Alan
East Tennessee State University
Johnson City, TN

Huddleston, Sharon
University of Northern Iowa
Cedar Falls, IA

Huebner, Brad
Independent Scholar
Columbia, SC

Hurd, Mary
East Tennessee State University
Johnson City, TN

Jacobs, Dale
East Carolina University
Greenville, NC

Jamieson, Duncan
Ashland University
Ashland, OH

Jones, Dan
Texas A&M International
  University
Laredo, TX

Jones, Patrick
Independent Scholar
Richfield, MN

Kemper, Kurt
University of South Dakota
Sioux Falls, SD

King, Richard
Drake University
Des Moines, IA

Knerr, Douglas
Roosevelt University
Glen Ellyn, IL

Kortum, Richard
East Tennessee State University
Johnson City, TN

Legrand, Steve
U.S. Air Force Academy
Colorado Springs, CO

Lerner, Michael
New York University
New York, NY

Loosbrock, Richard
University of New Mexico
Chadron, NE

Lord, Timothy
Heartland Community College
Bloomington, IL

Louisa, Angelo
University of Nebraska
Omaha, NE

Madden, Sean
California University of
  Pennsylvania
California, PA

Mandell, Daniel
Elgin Academy
Carpentersville, IL

Manning, Michael
Independent Scholar
Amherst, MA

Maslow, David
Independent Scholar
Pittsburgh, PA

McCrillis, Neal
Columbus State University
Columbus, GA

McDevitt, Patrick
Rutgers University
New Brunswick, NJ

McGehee, Richard
University of Texas
Austin, TX

McIlhaney, Anne
Webster University
St. Louis, MO

Miles, La'Tonya Rease
University of California
Los Angeles, CA

Misner, Scott
University of North Carolina
Chapel Hill, NC

Mitrano, John
Central Connecticut State
University
New Britain, CT

Moore, Charles
East Tennessee State University
Johnson City, TN

Morris, Peter
Independent Scholar
Chandler, AZ

Morris, Tim
University of Texas
Arlington, TX

Morrow, Don
University of Western Ontario
London, ON

Mutchler, J. C.
Yale University
New Haven, CT

Mylchreest, Ian
Monash University
Victoria, AUS

Nash, Robert
University of Nebraska
Omaha, NE

Nathan, Daniel
Skidmore College
Saratoga Springs, NY

Nave, Jerry
East Tennessee State University
Johnson City, TN

Nielsen, Fred
University of Omaha
Omaha, NE

Niiya, Brian
Independent Scholar
Honolulu, HI

Noe, Mark
Pennsylvania College of Technology
Williamsport, PA

Obermeyer, Jeffrey
Independent Scholar
Kirkland, WA

O'Donnell, David Patrick
Independent Scholar
Chicago, IL

Olsen, Richard
University of North Carolina
Wilmington, NC

Overmyer, James
Independent Scholar
Lenox, MA

Parente, Donald
Middle Tennessee State University
Murfreesboro, TN

Patrick, Stephen
East Tennessee State University
Johnson City, TN

Peele, Thomas
Independent Scholar
Tampa, FL

Philippon, Daniel
University of Minnesota
St. Paul, MN

Phillips, Kenneth
McMaster University
Binbrook, ON

Plexico, Van
Emory University
Norcross, GA

Polumbaum, Judy
University of Iowa
Iowa City, IA

Potash, David
Baruch College
New York, NY

Powers-Beck, Jeff
East Tennessee State University
Johnson City, TN

Price, Joseph
Whittier College
Whittier, CA

Purcell, Laura
Independent Scholar
Scottsdale, AZ

Quirk, Chuck
University of Northern Iowa
Cedar Falls, IA

Quirk, Wayne
Mankato State University
Mankato, MN

Rawson, Timothy
Alaska Pacific University
Anchorage, AK

Reynolds, Thomas
University of Maryland
College Park, MD

Rice, Joe
East Tennessee State University
Johnson City, TN

Richards, David
Northwood University
Skowhegan, ME

Rielly, Edward
St. Joseph's College
Standish, ME

Riordan, Craig
Humboldt State University
Humboldt, CA

Rubinstein, Geoffrey
Jones Media
Englewood, CO

Ryan, John
American Bar Assoc
Bannockburn, IL

Salamone, Frank
Iona College
New Rochelle, NY

Santangelo, Mark
George Washington University
Washington, DC

Schoenecke, Michael
Texas Tech University
Lubbock, TX

Schoepflin, Todd
Niagara University
Niagara Falls, NY

Segrave, Jeffrey
Skidmore College
Saratoga Springs, NY

Seror, Marc
Independent Scholar
West Hills, CA

Shmanske, Stephen
Cal State University
Hayward, CA

Sisario, Peter
Independent Scholar
Scotia, NY

Slack, John
Florida Memorial College
Miami, FL

Smolenski, John
University of Pennsylvania
Philadelphia, PA

Stabler, Scott
University of Houston
Houston, TX

Starnes, Richard
Western Carolina University
Cullowhee, NC

Stephani, A. J.
University of Cincinnati
Cincinnati, OH

Stewart, Daniel
Independent Scholar
Cincinnati, OH

Sullivan Porter, Kathleen
University of Texas
Arlington, TX

Summers, John
Independent Scholar
Gettysburg, PA

Taylor, Sue
Independent Scholar
Carrboro, NC

Thomas, Laura
University of Rochester
Gettysburg, PA

Tracey, Grant
University of Northern Iowa
Cedar Falls, IA

Turrini, Joseph
Wayne State University
Detroit, MI

Urbiel, Alexander
Ramapo College
Mahwah, NJ

Vander Ploeg, Scott
Madisonville Community College
Madisonville, KY

Wood, Andrew
University of Calif, Davis
Riverside, CA

Zavodny, John
Unity College
Unity, ME

Zeman, Scott
Idaho State University
Pocatello, ID

Index

About the Author

Joyce Duncan is a faculty member at East Tennessee State University where she teaches Service-Learning. Miss Duncan holds a masters degree in English and is completing requirements for a doctorate in education. In addition to contributing to several national periodicals and reference collections, she is the author of *Ahead of Their Time* (2002) and *Heirs to Misfortune* (1987). She is managing editor of the Sport Literature Association and founding editor of *Arête,* an online sport discussion group.